Understanding Networked Applications

A First Course

The Morgan Kaufmann Series in Networking
Series Editor, David Clark

Understanding Networked Applications

A First Course

David G. Messerschmitt

University of California, Berkeley

MORGAN KAUFMANN PUBLISHERS

An Imprint of Elsevier

SAN FRANCISCO   SAN DIEGO   NEW YORK   BOSTON
LONDON   SYDNEY   TOKYO

Senior Editor	Jennifer Mann
Director of Production and Manufacturing	Yonie Overton
Production Editors	Julie Pabst, Elisabeth Beller
Copyeditor	Judith Brown
Proofreader	Jennifer McClain
Illustration	Lineworks, Inc.
Composition	Nancy Logan
Text and Cover Design	Ross Carron Design
Cover Photo	Erich Lessing/Art Resource, NY
Indexer	Steve Rath
Printer	Courier Corporation

Designations used by companies to distinguish their products are often claimed as trademarks or registered trademarks. In all instances where Morgan Kaufmann Publishers is aware of a claim, the product names appear in initial capital or all capital letters. Readers, however, should contact the appropriate companies for more complete information regarding trademarks and registration.

ACADEMIC PRESS
An Imprint of Elsevier
525 B Street, Suite 1900, San Diego, CA 92101-4495, USA
http://www.academicpress.com

Academic Press
An Imprint of Elsevier
Harcourt Place, 32 Jamestown Road, London NW1 7BY, United Kingdom
http://www.academicpress.com

Morgan Kaufmann Publishers
An Imprint of Elsevier
340 Pine Street, Sixth Floor, San Francisco, CA 94104-3205, USA
http://www.mkp.com

09 08 07 06   5 4

Permissions may be sought directly from Elsevier's Science and Technology Rights Department in Oxford, UK. Phone: (44) 1865 843830, Fax: (44) 1865 853333, e-mail: permissions@elsevier.co.uk. You may also complete your request on-line via the Elsevier homepage: http://www.elsevier.com by selecting "Customer Support" and then "Obtaining Permissions".

Library of Congress Cataloging-in-Publication Data
Messerschmitt, David G.
        Understanding networked applications : a first course /
    David G. Messerschmitt.
                p. cm.—(The Morgan Kaufmann series in networking)
        Includes bibliographical references.
        ISBN-13: 978-1-55860-537-4
        ISBN-10: 1-55860-537-1
        1. Computer networks—Design.   I. Title.   II. Series.
    TK5105.5.M46   2000   99-44481
    658'.0546—dc21   CIP

This book is printed on acid-free paper.

To Dody and Laura

Contents at a Glance

Contents

Preface

Computing and communications technologies are becoming pervasive in our personal and professional lives, and are developing into an important factor in the performance of organizations (companies, schools and universities, and government). I believe that a broad spectrum of people from many disciplines and professions should become fluent in the application of networked computing technologies in order to meet professional and organizational challenges. Unfortunately, in the past this has required the major commitment to a suite of narrowly focused technical courses. I wrote this book to help you understand networked applications, the possibilities and limitations of the computing and networking infrastructure supporting them, and related economic, industry, and policy considerations—all in a single course. I trust that this book will empower you to invent and realize new applications that create opportunity and value in your own endeavors, and also empower you to work closely and effectively with information technology professionals to realize your ideas.

This book is an outgrowth of an undergraduate and graduate course in networked applications that I developed at the University of California at Berkeley. I have been teaching this material to both undergraduate and graduate students—from the general campus population to students specializing in business and information management—for two years. Most of the students in these courses lacked specific backgrounds in information technology, computer science, or engineering. They came from a variety of disciplines, including humanities and social sciences, information sciences, and business, as well as engineering. I believe these students have taken away sufficient understanding and fluency in networked computing and its applications to position them for fruitful exploitation in their professional careers. It has not only been a joy to strip away the mysteries of networked computing for these highly motivated students, but also has been rewarding to see them come away with a newfound appreciation of and enthusiasm for networked computing and its potential.

A shorter, less detailed version of this version of this book, *Networked Applications: A Guide to the New Computing Infrastructure*, was published in January 1999 and is targeted at information technology professionals. Details about this book are available at *http://www.mkp.com/netapps*. In this textbook version I have added considerable additional breadth and detail, as well as instructional aids like discussion questions, reviews, lists of concepts, and exercises.

What This Book Is About

This book covers three major topics. The first is the *applications* of network computing, the second is the *industry* that supplies computing, networking, and software products and services, and the third is the basic concepts and terminology that underly the *infrastructure* and *technology* of networked computing that support those applications. These topics are covered in roughly this order, although the goal is to emphasize their mutual influences. What are the major categories of applications, and how do they relate to specific and distinctive needs? How are these applications acquired? How does the technological infrastructure affect and limit application possibilities? How do economic, legal, and policy issues impact the nature of the supplier industry and the infrastructure? What are the characteristics of the technology that are ripest for exploitation in innovative new ways? How are the needed performance characteristics obtained?

A Unique Approach

This book establishes a new genre of textbook in computing and communications. No other book of which I am aware conveys a broad coverage of the applications and underlying concepts and terminologies of networked computing, nor does another book convey this broad understanding to a predominantly nontechnical audience. In fact, the book has a number of unique features:

- *Broad coverage.* This book, and a course based on it, should by itself give you sufficient knowledge and understanding to use these technologies effectively in new ways and work closely with information technology professionals to realize your ideas. If this is the only book you read or course you ever take on computing, you should gain a broad and lasting perspective on the breadth of capabilities and related industry, economics, and policy issues. If you are motivated to take more courses on computing, you will be positioned to choose wisely.

- *Application perspective.* Rather than treating applications as an afterthought or ignoring them altogether (as is typical of books on computing) this book treats applications as its *central* focus. All other topics, such as technology, infrastructure, industry, economics, and so forth, are chosen with their direct relevance to applications in mind.

- *Emphasizing basic concepts.* Everything changes rapidly in computing and communications, so my goal is to leave you with a basic understanding of concepts and understanding that will be long-lasting, avoiding an "alphabet soup" of acronyms and topical knowledge that will quickly become obsolete.

- *Forward-looking approach.* Most applied treatises on computing incorporate a retrospective look at technology. Here, the nascent or prospective

technologies are emphasized, while not ignoring or minimizing the importance of those existing and legacy approaches.

- *Top-down, general to specific.* Rather than start with "bits and bytes" and
  arriving eventually at applications, this book *starts* with detailed coverage of
  the applications and an overview of the technology before delving into individual technologies in more depth. You can safely stop reading at any stage
  and leave with a coherent and useful perspective.

- *Helpful analogies.* Illuminating analogies from everyday life are used occasionally where they relate concepts to everyday experience. These analogies
  are clearly marked so you can easily skip them should you not find them
  helpful.

- *Industrial and policy context.* When you are faced with using networked
  computing technologies, you need to be an informed customer of various
  vendors and service providers. You also need to appreciate some major societal and policy issues that will likely constrain your use of the technology. For
  these reasons, the industry and some relevant economics and policy considerations are integrated throughout the book.

- *No programming.* Perhaps you are already familiar or experienced with programming, but this isn't necessary to effectively conceptualize new applications and bring them to fruition working with the aid of professional
  programmers. This book thus assumes only a basic literacy in the use of computers. It avoids programming, except to discuss some broad issues in
  implementation that you will want to know before working closely with information technology professionals.

To the Instructor

This book is specifically designed for students outside technical computing and
communications fields, and it has been extensively classroom tested. At Berkeley, I taught an undergraduate service course with engineering, business,
humanities and social science majors, twice as a required masters level course in
the School of Information Management and Systems, and as an elective MBA
course in the Haas School of Business. It has also been taught twice at the
School of Information at the University of Michigan as an elective masters level
course. These trials with diverse audiences have resulted in refinement and
improvement, particularly addressing the pedagogical challenges of relating to
these diverse and non-technical audiences. The book does presume a working
familiarity with personal computers and their applications (which today is almost
universal with the target audience) but presumes no prior programming and
technology expertise.

This book can be used as the basis of a service course for the campus population at large. I have found that many students across a wide range of disciplines appreciate the importance of networked computing and its applications to their future careers, and are highly motivated to learn more about it. The book can also be used as a more specialized course within fields with a particular need for fluency in networked computing, such as information and library sciences, communications, engineering, medical informatics, business, and others.

The book is specifically designed to be flexible in the breadth and depth of topics covered. It can be used in a one- or two-quarter or one-semester university course, or in industrial training or continuing-education courses. Primarily, this is enabled by the top-down approach, which permits coverage at various depths while retaining breadth and coherence. In particular, some chapters and "starred" sections with more advanced material can easily be skipped. The book includes coverage of organizational computing for business-oriented students, and more technical detail for students more interested in the underlying technologies—either or both can be emphasized. See the home page (*http://www.mkp.com/netappc*) for a detailed roadmap of different approaches to using the book. In addition, a set of supplementary sections are posted on the homepage that provide more detailed coverage of some technical topics for more technically oriented courses or motivated individual students.

Teaching Aids and Accompanying Resources

This book includes aids that make it easy to develop and execute courses. Discussion questions at the end of many sections stimulate personal reflection and classroom discourse, and can be assigned as term papers or projects. Exercises at the end of each chapter ask more closed-ended and objective questions, and can be assigned as homework. A manual with solutions to exercises is available to instructors.

The book is also Web-enhanced. The home page at: *http://www.mkp.com/netappc* includes suggestions for the instructor, roadmaps to the book and suggestions for different ways it can be used, and links to the home pages of courses using the book. Supplemental sections with more in-depth and supplementary topics (for example, object-oriented programming, encryption, and digital communication) are also available—they can be printed and distributed to students or assigned as on-line reading. There are also chapter-by-chapter Web links that lead students to more detailed, topical examples, and the home pages of all products and companies mentioned. A complete set of PowerPoint slides from my own teaching are also posted.

Acknowledgments

The origins of this book can be traced to Hal Varian, Dean of the University of California at Berkeley School of Information Management and Systems, who not only suggested that I develop a course in the applications of networked computing for the new SIMS curriculum, but also helped me develop and teach it the first time.

My editor at Morgan Kaufmann, Jennifer Mann, and the consulting editor David Clark of the Massachusetts Institute of Technology Laboratory for Computer Science, have been enormously helpful in keeping my attention focused on accuracy, excellence, and the market. Karyn Johnson conscientiously sought excellent reviewers helped in many other ways. Sarah Burgundy has done an excellent job on the production of the book.

The reviewers of the original proposal for this book provided numerous excellent suggestions for retargeting and reorganization. They include Thomas Badgett of Synergy South, Michael Borrus of the Berkeley Roundtable on International Economics, Chris Dellarocas of the Massachusetts Institute of Technology Sloan School of Management, Gordy Dhatt of Goodale & Barbieri Companies, Paul Resnick of the University of Michigan School of Information, Thomas Uslaender of Fraunhofer Institute for Information and Data Processing (Germany), Michael Vitale of the University of Melbourne (Australia) Department of Information Systems, James Ware of the Berkeley Haas School of Business, Robert Wilensky of the Berkeley Computer Science Division, and Janet Wilson of the Mutual Insurance Corporation of Arizona. Reviewers of the several stages of manuscript include Al Erisman of the Boeing Company, Brian Jaffe of *PC Week*, Pamela Samuelson of Berkeley, Bart Stuck of Business Strategies LLC, Matt Tavis of Sapient Corporation, Hal Varian, Michael Vitale, Janet Wilson of the Mutual Insurance Corporation of Arizona, and Dietmar Wolfram of the University of Wisconsin-Madison. The chapters on security and electronic payments were reviewed by Marcus Ranum of Network Flight Recorder. Overall, these reviewers provided invaluable insights from a number of perspectives, and especially the industrial application of information technologies. My student William Li, my wife Dorothy and daughter Laura, and Marti Hearst of Berkeley and Chung-Sheng Li of the IBM Watson Research Laboratory provided helpful suggestions.

Special thanks go to Hal Varian, Paul Resnick, and Arie Segev of the Berkeley Haas School of Business. In co-teaching parts of this material with Hal, I learned much about the economics and policy issues, and he greatly influenced this aspect of the book. Paul twice taught a course based on manuscript drafts and provided detailed and influential comments from himself and his students. His thoughtful suggestions especially impacted the organization and content of Chapter 2. Teaching this material to business students with Arie enlightened me to many issues in e-commerce and strongly influenced Chapter 3.

I am indebted to the students in the Fall 1997 Berkeley Information Systems 206 class who endured, with enthusiasm and good humor, an early attempt to convey this material, and whose suggestions, questions, and innocent misconceptions influenced my approach in many substantive ways. Later groups of students who influenced the book include IS 206 and BA 296 in the fall of 1998, IS 106 in the spring of 1999, and SI 540 at the University of Michigan in the fall of 1998 and winter of 1999.

Finally, I appreciate the support and patience of my wife Dorothy during the lengthy process of preparing these materials and writing this book.

Introduction

1

The networking of computers—a technology more than twenty years old—is substantially impacting individuals and organizations, including government, business, and education. The global public Internet now interconnects a substantial portion of the world's computers, allowing them to communicate freely to realize shared applications. No longer is computing confined to serving isolated individuals or organizations. Networked computing supports interaction and collaboration among groups of users, commerce among enterprises, and access to information or entertainment or participation in the political process by the public at large. This is a watershed in the history of computing.

Two previous technologies profoundly affected social and cultural institutions: mass transportation and telecommunications. Modern transportation transformed the urban landscape, leading to suburban growth, often at the expense of central cities. The telephone and television irrevocably affected politics and government; the free flow of ideas and a direct window into other societies have impacted political thought. Together, transportation and telecommunications led to a globalization of many communities, organizations, and institutions. They enabled and empowered the multinational corporation and the global superpower nation.

Networked computing is a seminal addition to this technical infrastructure. Like its predecessors, it will have a substantial and lasting impact not only on individual lives but also on business, social, and cultural institutions. It will facilitate the dissemination of information and knowledge, collaboration among individuals, business processes spanning geographically dispersed organizations, and commerce (among businesses and with consumers). Unlike telecommunications (which has emphasized voice and facsimile media), networked computing supports virtually all forms of information, such as data, images, video, and even money, and allows them to be integrated in innovative ways. Beyond information transport, networked computing supports software-defined storage and manipulation of information, and automates many knowledge-intensive tasks.

We have entered an information age, for which the key technological enablers are the network, the computer, and its software applications. This book is a guide to the possibilities of this information age and to the technologies and supporting industry. It will position you to make best use of these far-reaching new technologies in your own area of expertise. The book will give you an appreciation of the possibilities of networked computing, as well as the limitations. It will also position you to work effectively with professional programmers to implement your ideas and equip you with enough understanding of the industry to be an informed customer. Armed with this knowledge, go out and change the world!

1.1 The Evolution of Computing

Computing has evolved in remarkable ways over the decades since the first commercial computers appeared in the 1950s. The networked computing covered in this book is the modern view of the technology, but several other phases preceded it. And the current networked computing era won't be the last phase. Before immersing yourself in networked computing and its applications, it is helpful to gain some perspective about both what has happened in the past and what is likely to happen in the future.

1.1.1 Previous Phases of Computing

Computing technology has changed and expanded over the years, resulting in an expanding range of applications. As originally conceived in the 1930s, the computer performed massive calculations. Due to electronics advances, its computational capability continues to expand rapidly. Later, mass storage media (such as magnetic disks) extended applications to encompass the storage, retrieval, and manipulation of massive quantities of information. The relatively recent addition of networking allows computers to communicate and interact.

Technology View

When running an organization, your first impulse—to become more flexible and responsive—is to decentralize. Then you discover there isn't enough coordination, so you establish hierarchical management structures, hold meetings, and generate memos and reports to improve internal communications. In consonance with technological advances, computer technologies have undergone precisely the same transitions, resulting in the major phases of computing technology shown in Table 1.1.

Table 1.1 Four major phases of computing

Phase	Characteristics	Typical applications
Centralized computing (a few computers for a whole organization)	Relatively few "mainframe" computers were physically large and expensive, affordable only to large organizations.	Automate major business functions such as payroll and accounting, and manage enterprise information resources such as customer lists or inventories.
Time-shared computing (a few computers shared by many users)	Terminals were added to allow a large number of workers to directly access applications on a centralized computer.	Workers could directly interact with the centralized applications to input data, initiate transactions, and extract information. Users could participate in shared applications.
Decentralized computing (a computer for every department and every user)	Less expensive centralized computers could be deployed at the departmental level. Inexpensive personal computers could be dedicated to a single user, supplementing the centralized computers.	Personal productivity was enhanced by word processing, spreadsheets, and small data management applications. Home users and students could benefit from similar applications, as well as others dedicated to personal finances, education, or entertainment.
Networked computing (computers can communicate and interact with one another)	All computers are connected by networks, allowing them to participate in geographically distributed applications on a global basis. Desktop computers provide access to information in centralized computers. Networked computing is distinct from the "network computer (NC)" discussed in Chapter 5.	Networked applications benefit from more sophisticated user interfaces (graphics, pointing devices, etc.) supported by the personal computers, and they also access the processing power and massive data residing on servers and mainframes. Groups of users can participate in applications that enable collective communication and collaboration.

These phases are not mutually exclusive. Centralized mainframes still flourish—as the repository of mission-critical corporate information—and are integrated into networked computing applications. Time-sharing still exists, in the sense that departmental-level computers support multiple users at their desktop computers. The isolated computer *is* a thing of the past; virtually all computers are networked today.

The most important enabling technology for networked computing is the network itself, which builds on data communications media (especially fiber optics) and the advances in electronics (which also made much faster and cheaper computers possible). Networked computing results in the convergence of two industries—computing and communications—irrevocably changing each.

User and Organization View

Each phase of computing brought expanded opportunities and challenges. Until the early 1990s, mainframes formed the information core of major organizations' work processes. However—in part because applications were provided by a centralized information technology (IT) organization—centralized and time-shared computing were comparatively unresponsive to the needs of departments and workers. Decentralized computing empowered users by allowing them to add their own applications and process data in personalized ways, but downsides included the organizational chaos resulting from inconsistent solutions and the higher administrative expenses.

While desktop computing had widespread ramifications, the impact of networking is even greater. In the mid-1990s, networked computing founded on networked microprocessor-based computers made significant inroads into applications previously the domain of mainframes as it became sufficiently reliable and offered a path to new and reorganized work processes and greater customer satisfaction. Some of the implications of networked computing include the following:

- The transition from centralized applications that performed hidden "back-office" functions to the expectation that most computing applications will intimately involve users is complete.
- Networked applications empower computer-mediated interaction and collaboration.
- Applications can span organizational boundaries, opening up many opportunities in commerce (the buying and selling of goods and services, and their coordination).
- Networked computing is a basic infrastructure for the society. As evident from the increasing attention from legislative, regulatory, and judicial authorities, networked computing has substantive impact on society and its citizens.

From an individual's perspective, computing has followed a trajectory from an invisible back-office function (centralized computing), to a tool for enhancing personal productivity and entertainment (decentralized computing), to an expanded role in accessing vast global information resources and in interacting and collaborating with others.

Legacy Applications

Progress in the underlying technologies of computing (processing, storage, data communications) has been dramatic and unrelenting for several decades. Likewise, driven by the rapidly decreasing costs of these technologies and better ideas on how to exploit them, the applications of computing have seen similar expansion and change. The computing industry is distinctly different from most others in this dramatic rate of change.

Applications implemented in the technology of yesterday are called *legacy applications*. One result of rapid change in the industry is an expanding set of legacy applications. Unfortunately, any application using today's most modern technology will be tomorrow's legacy application. History has seen—and this is likely to remain so for the foreseeable future—a continual evolution from today's to tomorrow's technology, while having to maintain and integrate legacy applications. One implication of this is the importance of a forward-looking rather than retrospective view of technology when conceptualizing applications—a view aided, I hope, by the understanding imparted in this book.

1.1.2   The Future

The history of computing (and technology more generally) illustrates that progress is far from steady. Technology makes big leaps—from centralized to decentralized, from decentralized to networked—that take a while to be assimilated within the industry and the applications. Can future leaps be anticipated? Probably some can—those listed in Table 1.2—because they are well under way. A summary of the table is that computing will be *anywhere*, *everywhere*, and *within*. If you find this alarming, take heart in the observation that computing will put on a much different face. Replacing the big boxes that clutter our homes and offices will be smaller, less obvious, and less obtrusive computers [Wei93].

Computing is not the first technology to follow a similar evolution. A century ago, electrification (analogous to networking) had as its major applications light and mechanical power. Both light and power followed a clear evolution to mobility (battery-operated flashlights and power tools), ubiquity (virtually every room has electric outlets and appliances), and embeddedness (small electric motors within many products). The greatest lesson from electrification—and also one evident in computing—is that the first step is retrofitting a new technology into the existing ways of doing things. Eventually, however, people figure out new ways to use the unique capabilities of the technology, and only then substantial gains become evident (see the sidebar "Electrification: Lessons from an Earlier Technological Advance" for a historical observation).

The same will be true with computing. You can tell that the technology and its applications have matured when computing is incorporated in everyday life in natural and unobtrusive ways; when computing makes things easier, more efficient, and more pleasurable; and when computing doesn't get in the way. This isn't quite true today, but it is forthcoming.

Electrification: Lessons from an Earlier Technological Advance

Electrification had its greatest impact on productivity and standards of living only after ways were found to exploit its unique characteristics. Computing will follow the same course.

In part, the industrial revolution substituted machinery and water or steam power for human labor. For a single factory, water or steam power from a central source (analogous to centralized computing) was distributed throughout a factory using cumbersome drive belts. The factory was organized around the distribution of power, with compact, multistory factories. Electric power initially had little impact because large electric motors were simply substituted for water or steam sources—nothing else was changed. It took decades to recognize that smaller electric motors powering individual machines (analogous to decentralized computing) enabled the reorganization of the factory around the needs of the work process (linear assembly lines) rather than power distribution, with dramatic improvements in efficiency and quality.

The electric motor also has a parallel to embedded computing. Today, the electric motor isn't a separate consumer product, but is embedded in many products. Like computing, electric motors passed through a "personal motor with accessories" phase, until they became small and inexpensive.

Table 1.2 Future trends in computing beyond networked computing

Trend	Description	Comments
Mobility (computing anywhere)	Networked computers can be taken anywhere and still benefit from full network services.	Laptop computers and personal digital assistants are the precursors. Mobility requires ubiquitous networking access analogous to the cellular telephone.
Ubiquity (computing everywhere)	Networked computers are unobtrusively sprinkled throughout the physical environment.	Information kiosks, mobile phones with Web browsers, and personal digital assistants are steps in this direction. In the future, as computers gain a similar size and resolution to paper, magazines, and books, computers should become as ubiquitous as the printed word is today.
Embedding (computing within)	Computers are embedded in most everyday products. In the future, many embedded computers will be networked as well.	This is already common, as many high-technology products such as automobiles, consumer electronics, toys, and appliances have computing within. In the future, many more products—even as mundane as light switches and doorknobs—may have computing within as well as network connections.

Discussion

D1.1 As far back as you can remember, describe briefly the changes in the way you have used computing. Has it become more valuable to you over time? Has it caused more problems for you over time?

D1.2 How has an organization (company, university, or other) you are familiar with been visibly impacted by networked computing? How has it impacted the nature of work or study?

D1.3 Do you have firsthand experience with centralized or time-shared computers? What was it like to use them, and how are today's networked computers easier or harder to use?

D1.4 Are you familiar with any legacy computer applications? When were they first deployed? Why are they still in operation? Would replacing them be beneficial?

D1.5 What are some examples of today's products with embedded computers? What functionality or capability does the computer add? How would these products be changed without computing?

D1.6 Do you believe that computers will become virtually ubiquitous? Discuss some of the benefits and problems of this concept.

D1.7 What are some products that allow mobile access to a network and have embedded computers? What are their limitations that you would like to see fixed?

1.2   Overview of the Book

Networked computing includes a collection of related technologies supporting a broad range of geographically distributed computer applications. (It is distinct from a similar term in current vogue—the *network computer*, or NC—which describes one specific computing technology.) The *computing* portion of networked computing enables the storage, retrieval, and processing of tremendous amounts of information, and it also serves as an interface to users. A *network* enables computers to interact and share information, much like the telephone allows people to talk. A computing *application* is a software program that provides direct and specific value to a user or an organization, and a *networked application* distributes programs across two or more computers, which then collaborate in realizing the application. *Users* are the people leveraging the application to do their jobs, to interact or collaborate with other users, or to have fun. Together, these elements define the scope of this book.

This book proceeds top-down, beginning with applications and then peeling away the layers of technology, business, and economic issues that impact and support these applications. The book is divided into six parts covering the major pieces that must come together in a successful networked computing application. These elements are the application, the architecture of both the application and the infrastructure that supports it, the supplier industry and government, the acquisition of the application and how it fits in its context, the computing and networking infrastructure that supports the application, and proper attention to performance and quality. Each of these six parts builds on the earlier parts. Each is described in more detail in the following subsections so that you first gain an appreciation of the totality of the journey on which you are about to embark.

1.2.1   Applications

A networked application uses information technology to provide capability and functionality for the benefit of users, groups of users, organizations, and commerce. In spite of the fact that networked computing is a relatively new technology, and new ideas for networked applications continue to arise almost daily, it is not an exaggeration to say that they are already changing the world in substantive ways.

Social applications—those that serve groups of users in some shared activity like socialization, collaboration, or discourse—extend the capabilities of the telephone to introduce many new capabilities. The network provides greatly enhanced information publication and access, making information stored in computers around the world accessible over the network to any user. Given the rapid advances in human knowledge, education and training lasting a lifetime are an increasing need—one served well by educational materials available over the network. These opportunities are discussed in Chapter 2.

Networked applications also serve organizations, as described in Chapter 3. Starting in the centralized computing age with on-line transaction processing applications—where volumes of information about customers, inventories, and finances were stored, accessed, and manipulated—the advent of networked computing has caused organizational applications to permeate virtually every aspect of operations. Enterprise applications serve to coordinate the acquisition and deployment of resources from suppliers to the production of a finished product or service. The commerce conducted among organizations and between organizations and individual consumers is increasingly conducted over the network—this called *electronic commerce* (or *e-commerce*).

In a sense, e-commerce applications are the most general of all networked applications, because they combine elements of social applications, information access, enterprise, and inter-enterprise applications. For this reason, Chapter 3 starts with four specific organizational and e-commerce application examples, including customer service, an on-line bookseller and stock trader, and a floral delivery service. These applications illustrate how the various application elements described earlier are combined, and they are revisited in most of the remaining chapters to illustrate concrete uses of the various methodologies and technologies.

1.2.2 Architecture

This book considers networked computing and applications primarily at an architectural level. The architecture of a networked computing system includes the specification of the pieces, what they do, and how they interact. The book does not delve deeply into detailed implementation issues, except to the extent that they directly impact what is possible or precluded at the application level.

Technology puts scientific principles to use. The term *information technology* describes the suite of technologies that manage the storage, communication, and manipulation of information. At the architectural level, information technology comprises computers, the network, storage and other peripherals, and large amounts of software. The most popular network technology is the global

Internet, which comes in some special flavors—*intranets*, which support proprietary and protected enclaves within organizations, and *extranets*, which extend
intranets over the public Internet. Computers connected to the Internet, called
hosts, manage all aspects of information processing, storage, and communication. An overview of these information technologies is the subject of Chapter 4.

The most popular architecture for networked applications today is the client-
server architecture, in which desktop computers (including those in the hands of
consumers) act as clients to various servers over the network. Clients make
requests of servers for information or computation, where servers manage large
volumes of information to realize the logic of networked applications. Client-
server computing is the topic of Chapter 5.

The *infrastructure* is that part of information technology that is shared by many
applications. The infrastructure includes not only equipment, such as hosts and
the network, but also large measures of software, including the operating system and *middleware* (software falling between the operating system and application). The infrastructure architecture consists of layers, where each layer
exploits the layers below and adds more functionality or specialization. These
ideas are discussed in Chapter 6 and are used as an opportunity to consider further what distinguishes good architectures from bad.

1.2.3   Industry and Government Context

The computing and communications industries supporting networked infrastructure and applications are large and diverse, and are described in Chapter 7.
To design and deploy a networked application, you will be forced to deal with
them. Understanding the roles of the participants is important to being an
informed customer. The structure of the industry is changing as the technologies and application needs advance rapidly, and understanding these changes
helps to anticipate future technology developments, which are determined as
much by the industry structure as by underlying scientific principle. An important enabler for industry cooperation is standardization, which determines how
the architectural pieces fit together. The standardization process itself is changing in order to enable a faster evolution of information technology.

Computing and communications technologies are subject to some unusual economic effects. More so than most other goods, many networking and software
products have the characteristic that their value to the user or consumer
depends on the number of other adopters. This is called *network effects*, and it
not only presents an obstacle to establishing a new product but also leads to
the *winner-take-all effect*, in which a single vendor or solution becomes dominant in the marketplace. The integration of products and services from different

vendors sometimes presents an obstacle to customers considering a new product. This is called *lock-in,* which presents another obstacle to innovation and should be considered by customers in their technology acquisitions. The technical properties of information and software—in particular, the ability to replicate them at low cost—result in large economies of scale and challenges for suppliers, particularly with respect to issues of pricing and competition.

As networked computing permeates every institution of society, governments have an increasing role. They create property rights for information and ideas, which is particularly important in light of their easy appropriation and replication. Government is an important source of innovation through sponsored basic research. The Internet creates increasing pressure for government intervention in issues of privacy and content regulation, but its global nature simultaneously marginalizes the traditional geographically based governmental institutions. National security and law enforcement concerns cause governments to place limits on the use of encryption technologies, which are simultaneously essential for e-commerce.

Economics and government issues are discussed in Chapter 8, and insights arising there are referenced to particular technologies throughout the remainder of the book.

1.2.4   Making It Happen

Acquiring new networked applications in an organizational context is an important but complicated process. There are many decisions to be made, including whether to start from scratch or buy an off-the-shelf solution. These are not merely decisions about technology, but greatly impact the human aspects of organizations as well. If an application is to be newly constructed, the lifecycle includes conceptualization of features and benefits, the detailed analysis of requirements, the design of the architecture defined earlier, and the implementation. Whether an application is purchased or constructed, it must be evaluated and tested in the organizational context and then deployed, often with substantial organizational impact. Finally, it is operated, maintained, and upgraded over time. These issues are discussed in Chapter 9.

The internal architecture of an application is considered in Chapter 10. Architecture design methodologies range from top-down design from scratch to the assembling of existing components. One major issue is the partitioning of application functionality, the partitioning of information gathered, manipulated, and disseminated by the application, and the relationship between the two. Two popular approaches to programming applications based on objects and components are described, especially as to how they relate to application context and functionality.

If you are interested in a more detailed view into how applications are programmed, which is advisable if you will be interacting with technologists to realize your application ideas, then read Chapter 11 where programming is discussed.

1.2.5 Infrastructure

The infrastructure of networked computing enables networked applications, but also imposes limitations. As you pursue your application ideas, it is helpful to appreciate what the infrastructure can and cannot do for you. Many application efforts are based on a view of how information technology used to be, rather than taking full advantage of its possibilities for the future. Providing you with this forward-looking view into the capabilities of the infrastructure is the purpose of this part of the book.

The basic purpose of the network and some middleware technologies is to provide a useful suite of communication services for the benefit of applications. The generic classes of these services, together with specific examples from the Internet, are described in Chapter 12.

One major issue for applications is trustworthiness. Is the application available to do the job for which it was intended, correctly, and when it is needed? There are many opportunities for the answer to this question to be no, based on design flaws, operational breakdowns, or even deliberate theft or vandalism. Applications utilizing the global Internet especially need to take careful heed of various security threats. These problems, and technologies available to address them, come under the general heading of trustworthiness and are discussed in Chapter 13. One special problem related to e-commerce is electronic payments, and the options are described in Chapter 14.

Middleware, which is software sitting between the operating system and application, is the area of greatest innovation in the infrastructure. It is important therefore to appreciate some of the core capabilities of the middleware, because innovations there provide a direct view into the future of the networked computing infrastructure. There are many middleware solutions for many purposes. They generally divide into storage middleware (covered in Chapter 15) and communications middleware (Chapter 16). These include fairly mature but still evolving technologies such as database management and many exciting new developments such as XML (extensible standards for document representation), Java (portable and mobile software), and CORBA (hiding the heterogeneity of networked computing platforms).

1.2.6   Performance

Careful consideration must be paid to achieving adequate performance attributes for an application, such as number of users served and the speed of response to them. This is becoming particularly challenging as applications expand to serve whole enterprises and commerce, where the expectations for these performance attributes can become monstrous. For such applications, a key objective is *scalability*—the ability of the application and the infrastructure that supports it to grow as necessary without major replacements or redesigns. One of the tools for scalability is *concurrency*—which means making many things happen at the same time on multiple hosts—where the operating system plays an important role. These ideas are discussed in Chapter 17.

The network is an important factor in performance, but it is also a shared resource not dedicated to a single application. Therefore, the network must manage often contradictory demands from different users and applications. Chapter 18 discusses these collective issues in network design, such as how it adjudicates competing needs during times of overuse. One basic issue for the future is whether the network should provide guarantees on performance attributes and, if so, how the associated pricing structures might work. Further, if you are interested in how the network works internally—with the Internet as the major example—then read Chapter 19.

Chapter 20 discusses the industry and technologies that provide the point-to-point communication links within the network. More so than the computer industry, this communications industry is subject to government regulation. One disappointing aspect of networked computing to date is the limited availability of high-capability network connections to residential users, which potentially puts a crimp on consumer e-commerce. This chapter discusses opportunities to redress this and also opportunities to provide telephone service over the Internet and mobile and nomadic access to the network.

The underlying technologies of communications are also described in Chapter 20. While the capabilities of all the underlying major technologies of computing and communications—electronics, fiber optics, and storage—are advancing at remarkable rates, there is one major exception: the speed of light is fixed, and hence the delay incurred in propagating information from one location to another is not subject to technological advance. This "ultimate speed limit" looms as the most important future limitation to networked computing performance and scalability.

Review

Networked computing enables applications serving *groups* of users—for example, by enhancing their collaboration or community. The network provides users with access to vast repositories of information. Networking (and especially the public Internet) also enables applications spanning organizational boundaries—for example, commerce. Networked computing supports critical infrastructures, such as electric power, transportation, and financial markets.

Computing technology has experienced four overlapping technological phases: centralized, time-shared, decentralized, and networked. Future computers will always be networked; they will be ubiquitous and embedded within many common products; and they will support user mobility.

To make most effective use of networked computing, business and social processes need to be rethought and reworked, arriving at a marriage of people and technology that best exploits the unique capabilities of each.

Key Concepts

Evolution of the computer:

- Centralized, time-shared, decentralized, networked
- Mobile, ubiquitous, embedded

Further Reading

Books that cover general areas of technology and social issues encompassed within this book are recommended at the end of each chapter. There are several other general classes of books that can be recommended. The first conveys "computer literacy," of which [Bee99] and [Oak96] are representative. The second conveys the basic ideas of computer science, where [Bir96] is the premier example. The third discusses the societal and business impact of networking and computing, including [Cai97], [Haw96], [Mit96], and [Ros97].

Exercises

E1.1 Name one networked computing application with which you are already familiar in each of the following categories (no fair looking forward to Chapter 2 or Chapter 3!):

  a. Social application

  b. Information access and management

  c. Education

    d. Business

    e. Critical societal infrastructure

E1.2   Describe briefly the general capabilities and features you would like to see in each of the following networked computing applications:

    a. Manage your bank account from home

    b. Play your favorite board game (chess, Monopoly, etc.) with friends over the network

    c. Trade stocks from home

    d. Visit with your brother, who lives in another country

E1.3   Discuss how and by whom the following computer applications were invented. If you don't know the history, just speculate.

    a. Word processing

    b. Email

    c. World Wide Web

    d. Networked game Doom

    e. America Online

E1.4   For each of the applications listed in Exercise 1.3: At what phase in the history of computing did it become possible, and why was it not possible earlier?

E1.5   Think about the process of taking a university course, and come up with some networked applications that you think would make your learning more effective, or the course more pleasurable.

E1.6   List five new things that might be possible if every car had embedded computing (which new cars already do) and was networked (which they are not), so that embedded network applications could interact with the rest of the highway system (traffic lights, metering lights, police, etc.).

E1.7   List three new applications that capture the spirit of ubiquitous computing, and describe them briefly.

The
Applications

The applications of
networked computing
provide useful features,
functionality, and services
to individual users, to
groups of users, and to
organizations.

PART

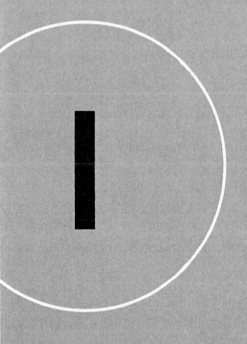

Applications Supporting Individuals and Groups

2

The global Internet liberates many activities from geographical constraints. It joins mass transportation and telecommunications in giving people and organizations considerably more freedom in geographical location while continuing their essential functions. While only a century ago the essence of an organization was centralization—to enhance internal communication—today, organizations are largely freed from this constraint [Cai97]. An enterprise can be global in extent, a university need not be confined to a campus, a library no longer needs a building, and a community no longer presumes a geographical boundary. All this presumes appropriate applications supporting the necessary activities.

The objective of this chapter and the next is to appreciate the major types of applications supported by networked computing (for a careful definition of what *application* means, see the sidebar "What's an Application?"). A *networked* application is partitioned across two or more computers, leveraging the network for communication among application elements. There are three different types of networked applications—individual, social, and organizational—listed in Table 2.1. This chapter covers individual and social applications, and Chapter 3 concentrates on organizational applications. There is of course commonality—individual users or groups of users may support an organizational mission.

2.1   Three Ingredients

A networked application has three important ingredients: the information technology that provides the processing and communications, the information content that is processed and communicated, and most importantly, the users (including groups of users) and the objectives they pursue.

What's an Application?

The term application is used for different purposes, which can and does lead to confusion. In this book, a networked application performs some function on behalf of a person or organization involving computation, manipulation of information, and/or communication. It helps us do our work, enlightens us, entertains us, or connects us with other users.

The term application is sometimes used to refer to the computer software package that implements this functionality. More generally, an application is the use to which something is put, which makes it a relative term. For example, "a computer is an application of electronics" and "a word processor is an application of a computer" are both reasonable statements, at the same time. This chapter and the next deal with the level where technology meets people, as in "capabilities aiding users and organizations that are an application of computing and networking."

Confusion also arises because telecommunications is usually associated with a service provider, and computing usually isn't. Thus, what computing people call applications are often called services by telecommunications people. For example, voice telephony is called a service by telephone companies; in this book, it is called an application.

Table 2.1 Types of networked computing applications

Type	Description		Examples
Individual	Support and empower users—people engaged in personal or professional activities—by improving productivity or extending capability.	Focused on individual users.	Access information, author a document, perform a calculation, play a game, take a course.
Social		Focused on the activity of groups of users engaged in impromptu and opportunistic interaction or collaboration.	Collaborate on a group project, socialize with friends, schedule a meeting, discuss politics with other citizens, participate in a virtual classroom discussion.
Organizational	Support and empower one or more organizations—enterprises, government, educational institutions—improving their productivity or extending capability.		Provide travel reservations, support users of a new computer application, procure parts from a supplier and control a manufacturing process, sell books to individual consumers.

2.1.1 Information Technology

Technology is the application of scientific knowledge to human needs. Information technology has the specific role of capturing, storing, communicating, and manipulating information for the benefit of users and organizations. Information will be defined more carefully later, in both technical and application terms, but for the time being you can think in terms of documents, pictures, voice, animation, and video—things that are not physical objects but nevertheless affect you or your behavior in some way. Information technology combines some important capabilities:

- *Input devices*, including keyboards, cameras, microphones, barcode and magnetic stripe readers, scanners, and optical character readers, to capture information from users.
- *Memory and storage* to make permanent records of information.
- *Computers* to manipulate information.
- The *network* to communicate information from one computer to another (and often one location to another).
- *Output devices*, including displays, loudspeakers, and printers, to display information to users.

Chapter 4 provides an overview of information technology, and Chapter 5 discusses how that technology is applied to networked applications.

2.1.2   Information Content

Information content is the basic commodity of networked applications. Computers and networks are able to store, manipulate, and communicate that content. Contrary to earlier technologies such as printing—which supports only text and pictures—in networked computing, information in many media can be captured, stored, communicated, and manipulated. These media include

- *Numerical values* and *text*.
- *Images:* Pictures captured by photographic cameras and their three-dimensional counterpart, *virtual reality*.
- *Graphics:* An artificially generated image created by a computer program.
- *Audio:* Sound captured by a microphone.
- *Synthesized audio:* Artificially generated by a computer program.
- *Video:* A sequence of images representing time as well as space.
- *Animation:* Video artificially created by a computer program.

Even more exciting, information technology can combine these media in various ways. A premier example is the *document*—often used to archive or communicate human knowledge—which can combine text, images, and graphics. Computer-mediated documents can be *multimedia*, meaning they combine the usual features of paper documents with audio, video, and animations. All these forms of information can be communicated over the network.

2.1.3   Users and Applications

The final ingredient that binds the information technology and information content to the users is the application. An application is the use to which something is put. It is important to recognize that the terms application and technology are relative, not absolute.

EXAMPLE: *The most basic information technology is electronics. A microprocessor—the unit of processing that forms the basis of most computers—is an application of electronics. The computer is an application of the microprocessor, together with other components, and information processing is an application of the computer.*

This chapter concerns the application of information technology to the needs of the user and groups of users. Before the prominence of the network, and especially the global Internet, centralized, time-share, and decentralized phases of computing emphasized *solitary* user-oriented applications. These *personal productivity* applications enhance the speed or effectiveness of users.

EXAMPLE: *The word processor helps author documents; the spreadsheet auto-mates otherwise tedious computations, allowing many what-if scenarios. Drawing editors turn users into draftspersons (although probably not graphic artists). Speech recognition automates dictation, previously available only to professionals with support staffs.*

Networked computing shifts the emphasis from personal productivity toward social applications serving a group of users with a shared mission in some collaborative or communicative activity. In addition, networked computing provides similar capabilities to users at any location, including those who are traveling (called *nomadic* users). The network supports communication among these users, and networked applications also serve to coordinate their activities.

Networked computing is also ideal for accessing and manipulating information on behalf of individuals. In *information management* applications, the network enables a single user to globally access vast information resources and enables information updated in one place to become immediately available everywhere. *Educational* applications mix the social aspect (teacher and students) with information access.

To some extent, individual and social applications predated networked computing. A time-shared computer can support individual users as well as social applications, as the users sharing that computer can communicate and coordinate. The possibilities are, however, quite limited—particularly for social applications. In contrast, the global Internet supports communication among *all* users (as well as all organizations). This removes the computing capacity and administrative boundary limitations of previous phases of computing, enabling social applications and information access across organizational, geographical, and political boundaries. Scholarship has been particularly affected, creating closer day-to-day global collaboration that wasn't possible with the telephone and the international conference, and creating global interest groups around narrowly focused or interdisciplinary topics. The global Internet allows any individual or organization to publish information, which is immediately accessible to all citizens with network access. Educational resources can be accessed by all, with fewer geographic limitations.

EXAMPLE: *Active interest groups have coalesced around issues of great interest to the Internet, such as the trade-offs between free expression and control of children's access to objectionable material, or the trade-off between unfettered electronic commerce and individual privacy. These groups have access to discussion forums and Web pages that link to one another, as well as other assets that enhance their interest group. The American Physical Society e-Print*

*archive allows physics researchers to publish paper manuscripts quickly, stimu-
lating immediate discussion and follow-on work by other researchers.*

The remainder of this chapter discusses three types of networked applications:
social, information management, and education and training.

Discussion

D2.1 Most documents you are familiar with likely do not include audio and
video. Discuss how such media might add value to a memorandum, textbook, or invoice. Also, discuss the possibilities of including programs—such
as a simulation—within a document, and what that might be useful for.

D2.2 Based on personal experience, compare the impact of a disconnected
personal computer with a networked personal computer. How does networking change the way you use the computer? Does it change the ways a
computer influences your work or pleasure?

D2.3 If you have had experience with an organization or scholarly interest
group or business, discuss the impact of networked computing on that
activity.

2.2   Social Applications

Social applications focus on supporting activities of a *group* of users, whether or
not that group is associated with an organization or enterprise. They are sometimes called "collaborative applications," although collaboration is only one of
numerous activities supported. You are no doubt familiar with many of these
applications, including telephony (two users holding a voice conversation),
email (sending written messages to someone) and voicemail (sending voice
messages to someone), newsgroups, and chatrooms. The possibilities are much
richer than suggested by these early successful examples.

Social applications can be categorized according to the characteristics of the
group of users participating and also by what the group is attempting to accomplish. Categories of groups and their characteristics will be discussed first, followed by numerous examples of applications that serve these categories. The
appreciation of the relationship between what a group is trying to accomplish
and the attributes of the applications serving it is a helpful backdrop for invent-
ing new applications for new circumstances.

2.2.1   Characteristics of User Groups

Before considering many representative networked applications, it is helpful to classify groups of users according to their characteristics. The most pertinent group attributes include

- *Number of users:* A group served by a social application can range from two users to the entire population of users with network access.
- *Narrowness of purpose:* Some groups form for the purpose of accomplishing a specific task (such as scheduling a meeting), while other groups are very unfocused (such as those coalescing around a discussion on some topic).
- *Duration:* Some groups exist for a short period of time (two users participating in a telephone call), while others can be very long lasting (the coauthors of a book).
- *Social relationships:* In some groups—particularly small ones—all the users know who the other users are and may well know them personally. In very large groups, each user will typically not even be aware of who the other users are, let alone know them. In the latter case, members of subgroups may be mutually familiar or friendly, or social relationships may be more diffuse.

With these group characteristics in mind, a classification of the types of groups supported by social applications is shown in Table 2.2. The terminology defined in this table will be used in the remainder of this chapter.

As implied in this table, these types of groups actually have a structural relationship like that of Figure 2.1. Interest groups are drawn from subsets of the citizenry. The number and composition of these interest groups change with time, but on a timescale of weeks or months. Similarly, interest groups break off to form sporadic work groups to pursue particular projects (such as the design of a product or the organization of an international conference). In turn, a work group may require sporadic task groups that interact on short-term tasks, interspersed with the individual effort of members of the task group.

EXAMPLE: *All users connected to the Internet is a citizenry, and an interest group within is the employees of General Motors (GM). When GM designs a new car, it forms a team (work group) that collaborates on the design project. That collaboration consists, in part, of numerous short-term tasks that are addressed through interaction in a meeting or conference call. A typical project is to develop a marketing plan—involving marketing, sales, development, manufacturing and distribution—with a detailed planning document as the outcome. This may take several months, during which task groups form to interact on particular issues (such as developing a schedule and coordination plan for the next month).*

Table 2.2 Classification of groups using a social application

Category of user group	Description	Examples
Individual	A solitary user working to accomplish some goal. This is the limiting case of no group; computer applications are designed to enhance quality and productivity.	A user writes a single-author memorandum; a user adds an appointment to his or her personal calendar; a user accesses stock prices using the Web.
Task group	A *task* is a short-term effort directed at an immediate goal; members of a task group interact with one another to complete a task. This interaction may require the undivided attention of all users.	One user telephones another to make a lunch date; a group of workers holds a meeting to evaluate a competitive bid or plan the next step in a project.
Work group	A *project* is a longer-term effort directed at a challenging goal. Members of a work group collaborate to complete the project. A project may spin off short-duration tasks addressed by constituent task groups.	Employees from the marketing, sales, engineering, and finance departments develop a product plan; scientists write a joint-authored paper; members and staff of a legislative committee work on a new computer security bill.
Interest group	An *interest* is a topic, profession, hobby, or goal that is ongoing and open ended. An interest group (occasionally called a *community*) pursues an interest through common discussion, study, or collective action. Interest groups typically form constituent work groups to collaborate on projects related to the group interest.	Historians share a common interest in World War II; world's coin collectors pursue an interest in coin sale and valuation; employees of General Motors Corporation pursue an interest in building and marketing automobiles; users concerned about network privacy pursue an interest in policies and laws.
Citizenry	A large group of users without a specific organized purpose who share a common network and can thus interact using networked computing applications. Typically subsets of the citizenry form ongoing interest groups around topical issues.	All the users with access to the Internet; all users with telephones.

Some typical characteristics of these categories of groups are listed (for the three largest groups) in Table 2.3. Although each user likely participates in at most one task group at a time and gives it her undivided attention, she may participate in multiple work groups and interest groups, and split her time and attention among them.

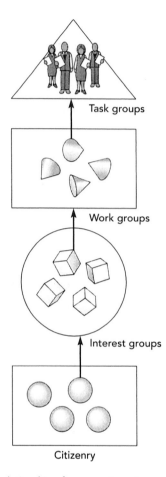

Figure 2.1 The inclusive relationship of group categories

2.2.2 Styles of Social Applications

Having categorized the groups participating in social applications, the next step is to appreciate the characteristics of the applications themselves. Examining current and emerging applications, there are two major styles (which will subsequently be broken down further):

* *Communication:* Any group effort requires the communication of information among group members. This may take the form of a discussion or the circulation of draft documents.
* *Coordination:* To accomplish its goals efficiently and effectively, a group must coordinate the different activities. Often, certain tasks or projects depend on the outcome of other tasks or projects or individual efforts, so

Table 2.3 Typical characteristics for different categories of groups

Group category	Work group	Interest group	Citizenry
Number of users	Small, typically from two to ten or twenty.	Large, typically from hundreds to tens of thousands.	Everybody sharing a common network.
Narrowness of purpose	Typically pursues a specific near-term project goal with a defined outcome.	Although constituent interactions and collaborations focus on the mutual interest, they may take the group in many different directions (even simultaneously).	No specific shared purpose or interest among all citizens.
Duration	Typically days to months.	Indeterminate, as there is no predefined goal.	Indefinite.
Social relationships	Each user typically knows who the other group members are and may personally know many of them.	Each user typically knows only a small subset of the other group members.	Each user knows a tiny fraction of the other citizens personally.

the proper ordering must be coordinated. The group may require common resources requiring coordination, such as preventing conflicts in the joint editing of a document. In addition, communication opportunities must also be coordinated, for example, scheduling the time of a meeting.

Together, communication and coordination are what distinguish social and isolated activities, and the objective of social applications is to improve and enhance both dimensions—even for a group that is geographically or administratively dispersed. Both styles are now examined further.

Communication Style

The communication style of social applications can be further divided into four substyles, as shown (with example applications) in Table 2.4. These substyles have two dimensions. One dimension accommodates the degree of knowledge that one user has of other users:

- *Direct style:* In the task group and work group, users typically know the other users in the group. This admits a direct style in which users communicate directly with other users.
- *Publication style:* In the interest group and citizenry, direct communication may not be possible because the users don't know one another, except when the group forms smaller work groups or task groups. In spite of these loose or nonexistent social relationships, communication within the group is valuable, for example, to disseminate ideas or form work groups. In the

Table 2.4 Communication applications in four substyles; examples in each row are immediate and deferred variations on the same application

Social application styles	Immediate (users participate simultaneously)	Deferred (users need not participate simultaneously)
Direct (users know precisely which other users are participating)	Telephony and video conferencing simulate face-to-face interactions of users (a meeting).	Email, voicemail, and facsimile allow one user to originate a communication and another user to access it later.
Publication (users do not know other participating users)	Broadcast video (analogous to broadcast television) allows one user to simultaneously address many other users for seminar viewing or distance learning.	Video on demand (analogous to the video rental store) allows one user to publish a video presentation and other users to view that video at a time of their choosing.
	Information push (analogous to a newspaper) allows one user to publish volatile information (such as stock quotes) to be viewed immediately by other users.	World Wide Web (an example of a more general category information pull) allows any user to publish information to be viewed later by other users.

publication style, one user (or smaller group) makes information available in a form that can be accessed by any other user. By its nature, a publication benefits the group as a whole, not specific users. Each user makes his or her own decision to access the information, and typically some do and many do not. The user publishing the information cannot anticipate who will eventually access it.

E X A M P L E : *The direct style is how the telephone network is used, or a memorandum in business with a specific distribution list (an important tool for work groups). Scholarly journals (an important tool for scholarly interest groups) and newspapers (an important tool for the citizenry) illustrate the publication style.*

The direct style of communication distributes information to a known set of recipients (possibly a single recipient), while the publication style distributes it to an unknown set of recipients. The direct style is most appropriate for task groups and work groups, while publication serves interest groups and the citizenry.

The second style dimension for communication applications makes a distinction based on whether users participate simultaneously or not:

● *Immediate style* (*sometimes called* synchronous): In this style, users participate in the application at the same time. This is practical for a task group, in which the number of users is small and they know one another. It is not practical for the citizenry, because it would be impossible to schedule them to interact at the same time, and there would be too many participants to be effective.

- *Deferred style* (*sometimes called* asynchronous): This style removes the constraint that users participate simultaneously. This eases scheduling difficulties, reduces the invasiveness of the communication to the individual user, and increases the size of the group for which communication is feasible.

A N A L O G Y :   *A mother phoning her daughter to wish her happy birthday is the immediate style, while sending a birthday card in the mail is deferred.*

Coordination Style

Group activities create dependencies among users and other resources. For example, the very viability of immediate applications makes the users dependent: They have to schedule participation at the same time. Often, deferred communication applications create similar dependencies. For example, users collaboratively editing a document have to work on it in a particular order, they have to avoid making conflicting changes, and so on. Coordination-style applications manage these dependencies, expediting the completion of a task or project. This style of application can be further broken down into two substyles, as listed in Table 2.5. Coordination applications particularly aid work group project management, as well as allow workers to minimize disruptions to work caused by conflicts or waiting for necessary resources.

Table 2.5 Two styles of coordination application

Style	Description	Examples
Resource allocation and scheduling	Members of a group share resources, which must be managed for efficiency and to avoid conflicts. One aspect of resource allocation is the scheduling of a shared resource so that it can be used by different users or groups at different times.	A meeting room must be scheduled so that only one meeting occurs at a time. In the collaborative authoring of a document, the additions or changes of different users must not conflict. Members of a task group participating in an immediate application must be scheduled. Auctions or other economic mechanisms can be used to allocate consumable resources (see Chapter 3).
Monitoring and notification	Monitoring (sometimes called *awareness*) applications allow group members to benefit from information about some remote resource or user. Notification provides an alert that some condition has occurred.	One user can monitor the availability of another worker for a direct-immediate interaction (such as a telephone call). A work group member can request notification when a conference room becomes free. The productivity of workers can be monitored (this raises privacy concerns; see [Gar89]).

Collaborative Authoring

The collaborative authoring application facilitates group authoring of a document. Its most basic function is allowing any user to view and edit the document. Because of possible conflicts when two or more users edit the same document, the application has features for coordinating the users, for example:

- *Access control* and *locking* limit who can edit and who can read documents. Access can be restricted to particular users or temporarily precluded while a document is edited.
- *Version control* keeps track of current and past versions of the document. For example, anyone can see who made what changes, see what those changes were, undo them, etc.
- *Annotation* of the document allows one user to pass comments to another user (without editing the document itself). Comments can be attached to the precise location where they apply and can be multimedia (for example, voice rather than text).
- *Replication* and *reconciliation* combine to provide a sophisticated capability. Normally, editing a given document would be restricted to one user at a time, slowing the authoring process. Replication creates two or more replicas of the document that can be independently edited. The problem, of course, is merging the changes back into a single version, which is reconciliation. Reconciliation is relatively simple

How do these application styles relate specifically to the needs of groups? In the following sections (and in sidebars) a number of social applications are described in relation to the group categories and application styles. Collectively, these applications illustrate the wealth of valuable networked applications. I hope you will also get the sense that the space of potential applications is very rich, with many unexplored possibilities.

2.2.3   Remote Conferencing with Shared Workspace

Without networked computing, a task group or work group might find a conference room in which to conduct their collaboration. In that conference room, they would hold a meeting—with face-to-face discussions—and also locate any work items (such as documents being collaboratively edited) to be examined and modified. The team would likely also use a visual aid such as a whiteboard to share ideas.

Such an interaction or collaboration can also be conducted over a large geographical area by using a social application called remote conferencing with shared workspace. This direct application serves task groups or work groups. The direct-immediate form of this application attempts to reproduce all the facets of a physical conference room, including

- *Telephony:* Speech is the most basic form of human communication, and thus telephony (holding a conversation at a distance using speech) is the most successful communications application. Telephony is provided by the telephone network, but it can be provided in a networked computing infrastructure as well.
- *Video:* Humans also communicate through facial expressions and gestures, and thus a video presentation of remote users can lend a feeling of presence, proximity, and trust that contributes to the quality of the interaction. Video conferencing is a combination of telephony and video and can be enhanced by other media, such as those listed next. (However, many feel that video is the least important element of a conference.)
- *Presentation graphics:* It is common in meetings to use visual aids such as slides and transparencies. Since they are prepared in electronic form, they can be projected to remote users.
- *Collaborative authoring of a shared document:* A document that is being collaboratively authored can be stored somewhere, and group members can view and edit it (see the sidebar "Collaborative Authoring").
- *Hand drawings and doodles:* Participants in a meeting frequently communicate ideas or designs through hand drawings on a whiteboard or blackboard. These drawings can be captured and communicated to remote users,

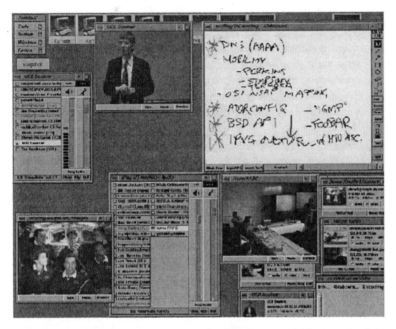

if changes are made in independent places and more complicated if common sections are
modified.

As can be seen, this application mixes
communication and coordination.
The users communicate through the
document itself as well as annota-
tions, but the application also coordinates the shared access to the
document.

Figure 2.2 Example of collaborative tools for the Mbone: vic (video), vat (audio), and wb (whiteboard) [McC95]

as they are drawn, using a *liveboard*. Alternatively, a shared whiteboard application uses a mouse or tablet to draw, with the result displayed remotely.

E X A M P L E :   *The screen capture shown in Figure 2.2 shows the visual aspect of a remote conference. Shown are standard applications developed for the multi-cast backbone (Mbone), which is an Internet capability for sending audio and video media from one source to many destinations (see Chapter 12).*

2.2.4   Groupware

Remote conferencing is primarily intended as a direct-immediate application serving a task group, where users work directly together, at the same time, and the collaboration may have their undivided attention. Unfortunately, this style becomes ineffective when a group gets too large. For example, this makes it difficult to capture and display video of everyone, along with whiteboards, on a small screen. Too many participants also reduce the quality of the interaction (as is starting to happen in Figure 2.2 as the screen gets cluttered).

EXAMPLE: *Consider the quality of the interaction when a dozen, a hundred, and a thousand people meet face-to-face. A dozen people can have an effective meeting, allowing everyone to participate and interact effectively. On the other hand, a hundred or a thousand people cannot effectively hold an interactive meeting. It takes too long to hear from everyone on any particular point— the number of inputs is beyond the point of diminishing returns—and it becomes difficult to allocate talking time fairly without hearing the same points over and over.*

These problems can be avoided by a deferred version of the remote conferencing application, called groupware. Because it is deferred—allowing group members to participate when they choose—and because it can aid larger groups, groupware is appropriate for work groups.

EXAMPLE: *The major suppliers of groupware are Lotus (a division of IBM), Microsoft, and Novell, which provide groupware products Lotus Notes and Domino, Microsoft Outlook and Exchange, Novell WebAccess and GroupWise. These products began with deferred work group and document management, but increasingly incorporate immediate conferencing capabilities as well. An example is real-time messaging, in which a message appears immediately on the screens of group members.*

Collaborative authoring, discussed earlier, is a pillar of groupware. The joint editing and coordination functions associated with document authoring don't depend on the users participating simultaneously—the functions can easily be deferred as well as immediate.

Groupware has to reproduce—in a deferred style—the communication facilities afforded by remote conferencing (see "Remote Conferencing with Shared Workspace" on page 28). It also has added coordination challenges, since the users themselves perform many needed coordination functions when they are interacting directly and immediately.

The most basic capability in groupware is messaging. Users are able to send one another a message—a package of information that one user wants to pass to one or more other users.

ANALOGY: *When one person is unable to telephone another, he might use a postal letter, which is a form of message. The letter encloses in an envelope whatever information the sender wishes to convey to the recipient. The letter could include not only text but also pictures or audio or video (stored on magnetic tape).*

Like the postal letter, a groupware message can include multimedia information, such as text, an audio recording for playback, pictures, graphics, etc. A message can even include an entire formatted document. The recipient can read the text, play back the audio or video, look at the pictures, and read the document. A message is a form of direct-deferred communication between users—the recipient need not participate at the same time as the sender, but can look at the message at the time of his choosing. The message replaces the direct interaction via audio, video, or images in remote conferencing.

EXAMPLE: *The most basic messaging service is email. A sender of an email message can designate one or more recipients for that message. Each user has an inbox where messages arrive and await access by that user. Although only text messages were supported originally, increasingly, email applications allow multimedia messages. Email is an almost direct analogy to the postal service, including notification of a nonexistent recipient or notification of delivery and access by the recipient.*

As illustrated by email, a message can be designated for a single recipient or multiple designated recipients. Since a given user can receive messages from many senders, a message system must merge these messages. Message applications can add a number of other features, such as

- *Priority:* Senders can attach priorities to messages, so that recipients can access high-priority messages first.
- *Filtering:* A fundamental issue with message systems is that recipients have no control over who can send them a message. This may result in wasted time sifting through many uninteresting messages. A message filter can discard messages that don't meet criteria specified by the user (negative filtering), or only allow messages that do meet specified criteria (positive filtering). These criteria might include the sender's identity or might be somehow related to the subject or content of the message.
- *Authentication:* It might be possible for someone to send a message under a false identity. Authentication is a verification of the identity of the sender.
- *Integrity:* A message might be modified somewhere between the time it is sent and it is read, either accidently or for some nefarious purpose. A message with integrity is guaranteed to be exactly as composed by the sender.
- *Confidentiality:* Some messages contain sensitive information that should be available only to the recipient. Confidentiality insures that only the recipient can read the message.

Priority and filtering add coordination functions, and the last three features enhance the utility of the communication (and can just as easily be incorporated in remote conferencing as well).

Calendar and Scheduling

Calendar and scheduling applications manage the personal calendar of each user and also schedule users for task groups (meetings, remote conferencing, telephone calls, etc.). They can schedule auxiliary resources (such as meeting rooms or video conference facilities). Users must publish their personal calendars for the application—minimally, times available for task group interactions or more information if automatic rescheduling is desired. The more willing the user is to relinquish personal control, the more automated and effective scheduling can be.

Calendar and scheduling illustrates the tension between automation and privacy. Without the personal involvement of the user, it may become too easy to schedule interactions of marginal value. For the future, ways are needed for users to describe priorities and automate interaction possibilities. Otherwise, users may be reluctant to cede total control to a faceless application.

Aside from collaborative authoring and messaging, groupware also includes coordination capabilities. Even in a work group, messaging is rarely sufficient for communications. Sporadic remote conferences and face-to-face meetings are valued—especially for establishing mutual trust and dealing with complex issues or negotiations. Since remote conferencing is an immediate application, it has to be scheduled at a time mutually suitable to members of the task group, and they may even have to rearrange schedules to make an immediate interaction feasible.

EXAMPLE: *You have encountered the endless round of voicemail messages often required to talk to someone (called "telephone tag"), or the time consumed in coordinating and juggling everybody's schedule for a meeting (accentuated in the global economy, where time zones reduce the feasible times). These problems reduce the viability of direct-immediate applications, in spite of their compelling advantages for task groups.*

Calendar and scheduling is a groupware application that eases the logistics of getting people together by making the calendars of individual users available to a scheduling application, which can access and manipulate them to coordinate schedules (see the sidebar "Calendar and Scheduling"). It illustrates a publication-deferred application, since each user in the group publishes his or her calendar for the benefit of anybody in the group.

2.2.5 Discussion Forums

Typically, task group interactions are scheduled with forethought to a specific purpose and agenda. This is fine for well-defined outcomes with clear steps to get there. On the other hand, discussion and creative brainstorming have no predefined outcome or stopping point. They can be performed by a task group, but often are more effective in a deferred style. Brainstorming over a longer period of time—interspersed with other activities—is often less intimidating to participants and more thoughtful and conducive to new ideas. Brainstorming is supported by the discussion forum, where any group member can propose ideas or comment on ideas previously proposed.

The remote conference is a direct-immediate style of discussion forum—one that serves task groups. The discussion forum is an even more important tool for interest groups. Direct applications such as the remote conference are not feasible for interest groups because users often don't know which other users are in the group, as they are typically realized in a publication style. That is, a discussion forum works by one user publishing an idea in the forum (by sending a message to the forum application, rather than directly to other users) where it becomes available for any user in the group to access or not access at his or her option. Thus, the discussion forum illustrates that a messaging application need not be direct—a message can be sent to an unknown set of recipients. It is also possible for discussion forums to be anonymous—the sender's identity is not revealed. There are typically many simultaneous discussion forums on different topics, serving different interest groups.

Like most social applications, the discussion forum comes in deferred and immediate styles. A deferred style of discussion forum is the *newsgroup* (see the sidebar "Newsgroup"). A discussion is started by one user sending a message (a *posting*) to a common repository of messages (a newsgroup) that is published for the benefit of the group.

Chatroom

Since a newsgroup is deferred, the immediacy of a face-to-face interaction is lost. A remote conference—being a direct style of application—is not a suitable replacement for a newsgroup. This motivates the *chatroom*—a publication-immediate style of discussion forum.

A N A L O G Y :   *The chatroom is analogous to a continuously running town meeting. Any member of the interest group can join the discussion in a town meeting at any time. Unlike a remote conference, the other participants are not known in advance.*

Any user can join an ongoing discussion, reading and posting messages to other users who happen to be simultaneously participating. It works like a remote conference associated with a named topic. Users participate by "entering" the chatroom, after which they see all postings immediately as they occur. Anybody with something to say on the topic can post a message that other participants see immediately. A posting may engender an immediate response from others—hence the spontaneity and immediacy—leading to a "conversation" that can be viewed by all.

E X A M P L E :   *The group of customers (and potential customers) of a company is an interest group. Chatrooms are used for customer service, allowing customers to communicate with service agents and one another. Acuity Corporation and Business Solutions are two providers of chatroom applications.*

The chatroom can be viewed as either an immediate variation on a newsgroup or as a publication variation on a remote conference. Like other messaging applications, messages in both newsgroups and chatrooms can be multimedia, incorporating audio, video, whiteboard, etc.

Newsgroup

As a publication-deferred application, the newsgroup associates a topic of discussion with a specific subject heading and is particularly targeted at interest groups. Any user can post a message relevant to that topic, and any other interested user can read previous postings and post responses. Typically, each message posted on a given subject stimulates responses from other group members. Those responses are posted under the same subject heading, and that group of messages forms a *thread*. The users joining a thread are a working group that collaborates on that specific subject. Note that the thread forms opportunistically about the subject—the user initiating the thread does not have to anticipate which other users may be interested in participating.

The newsgroup has mechanisms for hiding unwanted messages. For example, previously read messages can be hidden, and threads are collapsed under a single heading, with the individual messages visible only if desired. A newsgroup may also have a moderator—a user with special authority to determine which postings are allowed, to change the subject heading of a thread to make it more transparent, etc. The purpose of the moderator is to insure order and organization (rather than anarchy and chaos) and keep the discussion on track. A newsgroup may also have searching capability, to look for threads whose subjects contain specific keywords.

Listserver

With a newsgroup, each user must make a conscious effort to periodically check postings, and a chatroom requires a user's undivided attention to derive full benefit. This does not work well for extremely busy people or for interest groups with infrequent postings. A variation called a *listserver* is a publication-deferred variation on the discussion forum that eliminates the published repository of messages and follows a subscription model, in which the user doesn't ask for specific information, but rather all available information on a specific subject or topic. Subscription is an important mechanism for information access and will be discussed in that context later in this chapter.

ANALOGY: *A special-interest magazine serves an interest group. Each group member subscribes to the magazine, and each issue thereafter appears in that member's mailbox.*

A user wishing to join a topic subscribes by providing his or her email address to the listserver application. Any user can post a message to that topic, and each posting is automatically emailed to all subscribers, who therefore do not have to consciously access the postings. A user can also cancel the subscription and leave the interest group.

The email messaging system incorporated into the listserver application merges the messages coming from everywhere—other users and other listservers. A disadvantage is that a subscriber's mailbox may be inundated with messages—especially as the interest group grows large. Because some users might want to "listen in" without posting, or avoid a large number of messages, a listserver can also maintain an archive of past postings.

2.2.6 Cyberspace Applications

Societies have always had public places, such as the town square or public park. The Internet has created a new virtual public place, popularly called cyberspace. Citizens can go there to interact with others, share ideas and criticize government, or just "hang out." As in a public park, crimes can be committed there, or privacy violated, or misleading or inflammatory information distributed. Cyberspace is global—communication and interaction are independent of distance—and hence not subject to the ordinary geographically based jurisdiction of governments.

Cyberspace citizens form short-term task groups (for example, to find a suitable date for dinner); form work groups to collaborate on a project (for example, to organize a neighborhood crime watch committee); and form interest groups (for example, to run a Boy Scout troop or to rally around some cause). Thus the social applications described earlier apply to the citizenry as well. As in an interest group—but even more so—communication frequently occurs among citizens who may not know each other in advance.

What applications specifically support the citizenry? Thus far, they mostly mirror the physical world.

Broadcasting

The information content communicated through the network can be multimedia—including and mixing text, documents, audio, video, pictures, etc. Cyberspace broadcasting—similar to radio and television broadcasting—similarly sends audio and video through the network to any citizen wishing to listen or watch. The radio spectrum limits the number of different radio and television stations; for example, broadcasters using the radio spectrum must be coordinated (by government licensing) to avoid mutual interference, and the number of licensees is severely limited. On the Internet, no government license is required (at least in most countries), and the restrictions are few (although there are issues such as protecting children, as will be discussed in Chapter 8). You can imagine, for example, all the broadcasts occurring anywhere in the world being available to any citizen in cyberspace. As the Internet advances, it will accommodate many more broadcasters and many more specialized options.

Mass Publication

In the physical world, citizens are informed about current events by the mass media, including newspapers and magazines. The publication-deferred application supporting mass publication in cyberspace is the Web (see the sidebar "World Wide Web"). Many of the same publications available in the physical world are also published on the Web. Web publication can be multimedia—including audio and video—in an application called audio on demand or video on demand that is analogous to the video rental store. Broadcasting is a publication-immediate application, and mass publication is a deferred variation. Variations that mix these styles—called information push—are discussed later in the context of information management.

In cyberspace, publication and broadcasting are inexpensive and are even feasible for ordinary citizens. Publishing a Web page for the worldwide citizenry requires only Internet access and a computer with Web server software. While cyberspace is increasingly populated by large corporations and commercial activity, this in no way precludes individuals from using the medium to express their views. Also, while conventional publishing and broadcasting is predominantly a one-way medium, cyberspace is more democratically two-way. It allows various forms of interactive publishing and broadcasting.

World Wide Web

The Web is a publication-deferred application offering rich possibilities for the publication of multimedia information (that has become almost synonymous with the Internet). A user accesses the Web using a Web *browser* and sees various text, image, audio, and video pages pulled from many sources (see a typical page in Figure 2.3). Initiated by a user, the browser requests a page of information, which it displays. Each page can include *hyperlinks*, which allow immediate access to a related page (by clicking on the highlighted hyperlink).

The Web allows any user to publish information in cyberspace and any other user to access it.

Figure 2.3 A window from a Web browser, showing a typical page with hyperlinks

Information Retrieval

An overriding issue of cyberspace is, since citizens don't know one another and the volume of information available is huge, how do citizens find useful information or narrow down information to that which is useful? Similarly, how do citizens find and join interest groups?

There are a number of possibilities. The Web supports a *hypertext* model, which allows users to interactively navigate through large volumes of information by following links from one document to another. There are also *search engines* that look for information on particular topics. Like libraries and bookstores in the physical world, the Web contains information indexes. In the commercial realm, advertising is an important mechanism for alerting consumers. These and many other possibilities are described later in the context of information management.

Consumer Electronic Commerce

In the physical world, citizens go to a merchant's store to buy goods. Similarly, goods can be purchased in cyberspace from merchants who set up "storefronts" there. The Web has evolved into an application that supports consumer electronic commerce as well as information retrieval. If information goods are purchased, they can be delivered in cyberspace as well; otherwise, they may be delivered by the transportation system. Electronic commerce will be discussed in Chapter 3.

Recommendation Sharing

One way of identifying useful information, products, or interest groups is recommendation sharing. A *recommender system* is a communication publication-deferred style of application that collects recommendations from many users and makes them available to any interested user. This will be discussed later in the context of information management.

2.2.7   Back to the Big Picture

Specific social applications are listed in Table 2.6 by category of group they serve. Also listed are some analogous mechanisms in the physical world.

Discussion

D2.4 Do you think remote conferencing is a complete replacement for a face-to-face meeting? Are there ways it might be superior? What aspects of a meeting could never be re-created remotely?

D2.5 What are some of the advantages and disadvantages accruing from the geographic dispersal of user groups that has been enabled by networked applications?

D2.6 The most evident difference between the work group and interest group is the nature of the social relationships among group members. What are some other, more subtle differences?

Table 2.6 Social applications organized by target group category

Group category	Social applications	Physical-world analogy
Individual	Word processing, spreadsheet	Pencil and paper, electronic calculator
Task group	Email and voicemail, telephony and video conferencing, whiteboard	Postal letters, telephone, facsimile
Work group	Remote conferencing with shared workspace, calendar and scheduling, collaborative authoring, monitoring and notification	Face-to-face meeting, administrative assistant
Interest group	Discussion forum: newsgroup, listserver, chatroom	Town meeting, special-interest magazine
Citizenry	Publication: broadcast, Web; consumer electronic commerce; recommendation sharing	Television and radio, newspaper, newsmagazine, catalog shopping

D2.7 Discuss the relative merits, in terms of efficacy or invasiveness, of using immediate- and deferred-style variations of similar social applications. Repeat for direct and publication styles.

D2.8 What are some possible privacy implications of monitoring applications? What restrictions do you believe should be placed on them? Who should place those restrictions? How might they be enforced?

D2.9 Get together with a small group of colleagues or students, and plan how you will collaboratively author a hypothetical document using a collaborative authoring application. In the course of planning your collaboration, construct a wish list of application capabilities and features that would improve both quality and group productivity.

D2.10 What are some of your frustrations with using email? Discuss what filtering criteria you would like to see in a messaging application—without worrying too much about practicality. What are the dimensions on which you would like to filter?

D2.11 If you have actually participated in on-line discussion forums, describe the quality of the experience. What were the application's strengths and shortfalls, what could stand improvement? How would you characterize the behavior of the other participants?

D2.12 Some would say that modern telecommunications and transportation have had substantial impact on the spread of democracy by making it more difficult to maintain closed societies. Discuss this thought and other possible impacts on the citizenry. Do you believe that cyberspace will cause even more substantial impact? If so, what and how?

2.3 Information Management

One major category of networked applications is the storage, manipulation, and retrieval of information. In the physical world, this is the domain of libraries and bookstores, which store vast information resources and offer ways to identify useful or targeted information. However, as the volume of information grows, libraries exhaust their physical space. The physical shelves of the library can be replaced by information repositories (residing in computer storage) accessed using the network. The manipulation and searching of information can be performed by networked computers, often guided interactively by users or librarians.

Compared to the physical alternative, networked computing has some compelling advantages in its ability to store and manage information:

- It is especially effective in accessing volatile information—that which changes frequently (such as stock prices). Those changes—entered in one place—can be reflected immediately on the network, in contrast to the relatively slow dissemination in the physical world.
- One user can modify stored information, and other users on the network immediately see those modifications. For example, this can enhance the value of information as a tool for collaboration among users or organizations.
- The total information stored in the millions of computers on the Internet vastly exceeds what could fit in a personal computer's limited affordable storage capacity.
- Computers can process information in intensive ways, for example, to seek out more targeted or useful information.
- Computer-mediated information broadens the media from the printed page to include multimedia: audio, images, and video. The desktop computer's high-resolution screen is suitable for presentation, the computer can capture, store, and play back audio and video, and these media can be transported through the network. For example, the RealAudio and RealVideo media players allow audio and video content to be transported through the network and displayed on a desktop computer screen. A video media player is shown in Figure 2.4.

Like social applications, information management applications can be categorized according to the purpose they serve, and understanding the relationship of purpose to application attributes is a key to applying information management to new circumstances. Before doing that, however, information (and related terms) should be more carefully defined.

2.3.1   What Is Information?

In networked computing, information has several specific meanings, including technical definitions deferred to Chapter 4 and Chapter 6. In this chapter, which takes an application and user perspective, information can be defined as some recognizable pattern or meaning that influences a user in some way—such as changing the user's perspective, understanding, or behavior.

E X A M P L E :   *A document (such as this book) contains text and images. However, what makes a document useful is that it organizes these elements into sentences, paragraphs, sections, etc. These elements have an internal lexicon and grammar. Beyond this structure, the sentences have meaning to the user.*

The term *data* is used in networked computing to describe the numbers, character strings, etc. that represent information (this definition is expanded and

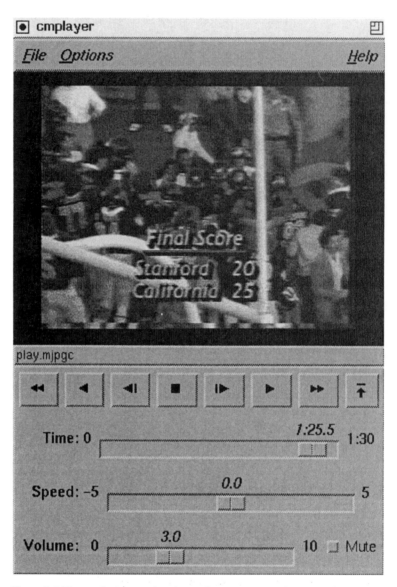

Figure 2.4 The continuous-media player allows viewing and control of a video/ audio playback [Row92]

elaborated in Chapter 4). Data and information are actually a part of a four-level hierarchy that includes knowledge and wisdom. *Knowledge* can be considered as concepts, relationships, truth, or principles derived from a large body of information. *Wisdom* is insight or judgement acquired from extensive knowledge.

E X A M P L E :   *"My bank account has $47 in it" would be information, represented in the computer by data (the number 47). The observation that "my net worth, including my bank account and subtracting my debts, is $67,986" is a simple example of knowledge, while "at the rate my net worth is increasing, and given my age and expectations for retirement income, I can't retire until age 134" is an example of wisdom.*

Networked computing applications are exquisitely successful at managing data and information. Knowledge and wisdom are almost exclusively the domains of people, not computers. Networked computing applications can assist people to acquire, represent, and manage knowledge through the organization and presentation of massive amounts of information [Ole98]. Wisdom is not a characteristic of computers, nor something generally acquired directly through computer applications.

2.3.2   Finding Useful Information

Just capturing and storing large repositories of information doesn't directly meet a user's or organization's needs. Typically, an information repository is too large to be of value *as a whole*, but rather users are interested in a targeted subset of the available information. Narrowing down information to a useful subset is a major function of information management, which the physical library addresses with information classification schemes, card catalogs, and reference librarians. Networked computing will eventually be much more effective at this, leveraging a computer's ability to process vast amounts of data.

User-Directed Access

The most straightforward way for a user to narrow down to useful information is to question or interact with an application with access to a large repository of information. There are three basic tactics listed in Table 2.7. The *search* exploits the computer's ability to systematically examine large volumes of data, if only the user can pose the right question. *Browsing* and *navigating*, on the other hand, allow the user to *interactively* guide the examination of the information, with the goal of honing in on useful information. The search is most useful in answering a specific question, whereas browsing and navigation are most useful when the user is curious or unsure of precisely what she or he seeks.

A N A L O G Y :   *An item search is like inquiring at the library about the availability of a specific book (title, author, and edition), and a topic search is like inquiring about the availability of any book on a specific topic (such as cooking Mexican cuisine). Browsing is similar to wandering around a new town, at each corner heading in the direction that looks more interesting and promising. Navigating*

Paying for Information

When a user accesses information over the network, typically someone else has to pay to create and maintain that information. There are a number of ways this happens in practice. Many organizations publish information on the network at their own expense, to aid the work functions of their workers or to publicize their products and services. Alternatively, a fee from the user for information accessed, either per view or on a longer-term subscription, may be required. This raises many issues of security and electronic payments, addressed in Chapter 13 and Chapter 14. It is increasingly common to get third parties to pay through advertising. These and other options are discussed from an economic perspective in Chapter 8.

Table 2.7 Tactics for finding useful information

Tactic	Definition	Example
Search	Pose a question, and information relevant to answering that question is returned. There are two types: • An *item search* poses a narrow question with a precise answer. • A *topic search* poses a broader question about information on a broader topic.	Find articles in the medical literature containing the words "Parkinson's disease"; the Web has search engines such as AltaVista that return pages containing specified keywords.
Browse	Examine a variety of repositories, hoping to opportunistically uncover interesting or useful information.	Follow a set of interesting Web hyperlinks; the Web hyperlink directly supports browsing.
Navigate	Follow a map or similar navigational aid to arrive directly at the desired information and possibly related information. May lead user directly to information, or may be an additional aid for browsing.	Many Web sites have a "site map" that shows a complete tree of hyperlinks and subject headings.

is like choosing a destination on the town map and working out an exact route to get there, perhaps noting alternative routes in case of traffic congestion.

EXAMPLE: *You may be familiar with some specific capabilities of Web browsers supporting each of these four tactics:*
- *Many Web sites specialize in answering queries, such as the latest selling price of a stock.*
- *The Web has a number of search engines that return Web content containing supplied keywords. Examples include AltaVista, HotBot, and Lycos.*
- *The Web hyperlink supports browsing. By adding hyperlinks, authors are helping users to find useful related information. The Web consists of a vast number of pages with hyperlinks among them.*
- *Web browsers make a history of past pages accessed available on a menu, thus supporting a primitive form of navigation by allowing the user to backtrack to previously accessed pages.*

There is wide recognition that more sophisticated searching, browsing, and navigation mechanisms are needed, and this is a focus of research. Some techniques being explored include the following:

- Searching will be based on an understanding of context of the information. Keyword searches may uncover information from distinct domains that can only be distinguished from the context (for example, "china" may apply to porcelain or a country).

- In the future, applications should automatically broaden a search to take account of variations in terminology across organizations, fields, or nationalities, and may also perform automatic language translation. Simple keyword searches are complicated by different terminology used for the same concept (for example, a car "bonnet" in England is the same as a car "hood" in the United States).
- Browsing and navigation aids based on three-dimensional representations—exploiting the user's ability to visualize information in three dimensions—will become commonplace.

Assistance from Others

A user can benefit from the assistance of others—including the author, publisher, or other parties—in finding useful information, including several aids shown in Table 2.8. As the world moves toward multimedia information, finding useful information is even more challenging. Indexing and metadata attached to audio, images, and video are particularly important, because inferring the content is difficult to automate (although this is being researched).

EXAMPLE: *The user may want a picture of a brown Chihuahua from a database with images of dogs. With current technology, automatically distinguishing a picture of a Chihuahua from an Australian Kelpie is impractical (although it is more feasible to automatically recognize pictures of dogs). An index or metadata allows the dog's breed to be included in a search.*

Metadata is particularly useful for conveying other information about a document that requires human judgement and cannot easily be inferred from the document content.

EXAMPLE: *The World Wide Web Consortium is standardizing a Platform for Internet Content Selection (PICS), which adds a form of metadata known as "labels" to Web pages [Res97b]. Unlike keyword searches, these labels can convey other attributes requiring human judgement, such as whether content is humorous, or offensive, or suitable for viewing by children.*

Third-Party or Collective Recommendations

While assistance from an author or publisher of information is quite helpful, it does presume a relationship of confidence and trust between the publisher and user. It is useless in determining the authenticity or authority of information, or conveying possibly unstated motives of the author or publisher (such as commercial gain, for example). Often, the judgement of other users or third-party authorities can overcome this difficulty.

Table 2.8 Several ways others can help the user find information

Navigation aid	Description	Examples
Hyperlink	Link or reference from one document to a related document to assist in browsing and navigation.	Web hyperlinks lead browser to related pages, references in this book lead you to related articles and books.
Index	A list of terms or subjects with hyperlinks or references to information about them.	Table of contents and index of this book, organized index to the Web, such as Yahoo!.
Metadata	Roughly translates to "data about data." In the context of a document or unit of information, metadata is a description of the content (or possibily other attributes, such as quality, date of generation, etc.).	A short cover description of this book summarizing content, subject headings, paper abstract, the title of a figure or table, textual descriptors of image content, document annotation, index.

EXAMPLE: *Consumers often depend on independent reviews of books, music CDs, and movies in a newspaper or magazine. They may rely on the collective judgement of other consumers, as represented for example by the appearance of a book or movie on a best-seller list. Or they may rely on informal word-of-mouth judgements from their friends, or the advice of others in a newsgroup or chatroom.*

Information access over the network offers many opportunities to formalize and extend these mechanisms for identifying valued information. Computer-mediated systems that assist and augment the natural social process of exploiting a collective judgement are called recommender systems (or sometimes *collaborative filtering*) [Res97a]. In a sense, they are a hybrid of information access and social applications (and were mentioned in "Recommendation Sharing" on page 37).

EXAMPLE: *The on-line bookseller Amazon.com provides recommendations on other books customers might consider buying (of course, in the interest of selling more books). One technique they use is to examine a database of books purchased by other customers. When the customer orders one book, Amazon.com examines all the purchases of other customers who have purchased that same book. Written reviews submitted by other customers are also available.*

Recommender systems are an area of research and commercial activity, and they will become increasingly common and sophisticated.

Third-Party Organization and Indexing: Digital Libraries

In the information economy, organizations of all types find that human knowledge—often acquired by the education, training, and experience of workers empowered by large, well-organized, and well-indexed repositories of information—displaces physical resources (such as real estate and machinery) as their most important asset.

EXAMPLE: *A software producer requires relatively few physical resources, compared to industrial companies, but its competitive advantage resides in the knowledge of its workers, its intellectual property (software copyrights and patents, as described in Chapter 8), and information assets such as its customer list.*

The acquisition and dissemination of knowledge throughout an organization can be assisted by the management and dissemination of huge repositories of information made possible by networked computing.

Networked computing can help in the acquisition and management of knowledge by providing large repositories of information. However, to make them most useful, these repositories must be organized and indexed (see the sidebar "Searching and Indexing"). The Web meets the criterion of being large, but fails the "well-organized" criterion. It is chaotic and disorganized. It allows anybody to publish information that can be easily accessed by others, but its weaknesses include lack of control over what is published and the proliferation of many uncoordinated publishers. The Web supports browsing well, but search engines are of limited value because there is no structured representation of the data or organized indexing or metadata. Similar problems are addressed in a physical library by adding organization and indexing to a large body of published work emanating from many (otherwise uncoordinated) publishers. This is done by a third-party librarian, largely independent of the publication process.

If the structure and organization of a library are combined with representation and access in a networked computing infrastructure, the result is called a *digital library* [Les97a, Les97b]. A digital library provides many features of a physical library—selection of information to include, archiving of volatile information, classification and organization of information, extensive indexing—with other capabilities such as searching and navigation features that make use of unique networked computing capabilities.

EXAMPLE: *Subsets of the Web can be turned into rudimentary digital libraries by adding indexing and navigation features. Yahoo! indexes a subset of the Web by subject. Many scholars maintain an organized index to the most important papers in their field and publish them for other scholars.*

Searching and Indexing

An *index* is an organized and classified list of topics within a body of information, together with pointers to one or more places those topics can be found (see Table 2.8). In a sense, an index is a concise summary of what is to be found in a body of information, but also organized (such as alphabetically or according to a classification) to make it easier to find relevant topics. It is useful in allowing users to quickly find what they need without examining all of the information.

Searching and indexing are complementary. A search can be performed on a whole body of information, or it can be limited to an index. The latter will typically result in a more concise summary of one or more locations for a topic.

e-Print: Scholarly Publication in Cyberspace

The traditional print publication of scholarly papers has many advantages, but most important is the selection of quality papers and their systematic improvement through a referee process maintained by the publisher. A disadvantage is the long delay, which slows progress in rapidly moving fields like the sciences and engineering. The Web allows each author to self-publish and make his or her work available to the community immediately, but there is no quality control, and the published archives are fragmented and chaotic. It is natural to combine the best of both worlds. e-Print is a digital library that allows individual authors in physics, mathematics, and computer science to post their own papers to an indexed central archive that offers searching facilities. Publication in e-Print does not forestall submission to a standard print journal. In the future, it is easy to imagine print journals disappearing, replaced by a limited digital library of papers that have successfully passed through a referee process.

While some say that a vast collection of digital libraries will replace traditional paper-based libraries, this will take a very long time (if it happens at all). Many materials exist only on paper and would be time consuming and expensive to digitize. There is also the question of access—only users fortunate enough to have PCs and the Internet can access a digital library. However, the digital library as a supplement to traditional libraries, particularly for newly minted information, is an idea whose time has come. For newly authored and published information, the digital library offers considerable cost savings by avoiding printing and physical distribution, and the duplication of library materials at separate geographic locations. A digital library can also represent volatile and multimedia information and can be highly interactive.

Table 2.9 lists the steps between author and information consumer. None of these important functions evaporates with digital libraries—they all continue to add value. In digital form, they assume a different form, use a different medium, and may be more automated.

EXAMPLE: *Various personal productivity applications assist in authoring, such as the word processor, draw and paint programs, and music composition programs. Many print publishers are expanding to the Web as a publication medium. Yahoo! and others index the content of the Web. Many Web sites have site maps and search engines that provide navigational aids similar to (but far less capable than) the services of a reference librarian.*

While technology can automate some of the steps between author and user, people will continue to add great value. Keyword searches can identify pages relevant to a particular topic, but there is the difficult problem of information authenticity and reliability that requires human judgement. A publisher also requires judgement to check an author's credentials, review information for accuracy, and invoke other quality-control measures. There is no complete substitute for a reference librarian, even for a digital library. The librarian can formulate more sophisticated searches after discussing user objectives and can often formulate better strategies for finding useful information.

2.3.3 Autonomous Information Sources

The user can determine what information is accessed, and when it is accessed, as discussed in the previous section. The broadcast described in "Broadcasting" on page 35 is an extreme example of a diametrically opposite approach, in which the publisher determines not only what information is provided to the user but also when it is provided. The broadcast illustrates the extreme of an *autonomous* information source. In practice, many information access applica-

Table 2.9 Steps from creation to consumption of information [Sch95]

Actor	Role	Examples
Author or performer	Creates information content.	Writes a book, performs a symphony, makes a music video.
Publisher	Verifies and improves quality, makes the work available for access or sale, controls use of its trademark.	Book publisher, record company, or movie studio.
Indexer	Classifies information and works.	Publisher of thesaurus, telephone yellow pages, library card catalog.
Librarian	Assists and guides user to appropriate content.	Reference librarian at the local library.

Table 2.10 Characteristics of information pull and push

Characteristic	Pull extreme	Push extreme
Control	The user requests specific, targeted information.	The user subscribes to information on general topics.
Notification	The user submits a specific standing question, which the publisher answers as appropriate.	The publisher provides appropriate notifications of useful information it thinks the user may want. The user can choose whether to access that information.
Timing	Information is provided at a time directed by the user (either immediately or at a scheduled time).	The publisher provides information at a time of its choosing. The user may look at information as it is provided (direct style) or later (deferred style).

tions fall somewhere between user directed (sometimes called information pull) and autonomous source (sometimes called information push). The different approaches are based primarily on three attributes of the application, as listed in Table 2.10. Most applications choose a mixture of these attributes and thus mix the pull and push models.

User Control: Subscriptions

The information-on-demand model is illustrated by the Web, where the user determines what pages are accessed and displayed. In the opposite subscription model, the publisher partitions information into what it believes to be natural categories or topics, each of which is called a *channel*. What information is actually delivered to each channel is under the control of the publisher. The user determines what channel(s) he or she wishes to receive and then makes a request (a subscription) for the subsequent delivery of those channels.

> **A N A L O G Y :** *Broadcast radio and television, newspapers, and magazines—each representing a channel—are obtained by subscription. Each publisher differentiates the information content of its channels to attract the most subscribers.*

> **E X A M P L E :** *PointCast is a push application that provides a standard set of channels on topics such as the stock price for a particular company, business news, and sports news. The user subscribes to the channels of interest, and thereafter they are presented on the screen as a screen saver. A screen of PointCast, illustrated in Figure 2.5, shows (A) where the user chooses a channel, (B) a menu of articles for that channel, (C) an advertising window (which supports this free service), and (D) the article. The presentation is similar to a Web browser, except the provider chooses the content of each channel on behalf of the subscriber.*

Subscriptions are particularly useful with volatile information, such as news reports or stock prices, since they remove the burden from the user of consciously requesting delivery. Further, if there is nothing interesting to report, the user is not bothered.

> **E X A M P L E :** *If a user subscribed to a channel carrying weather bulletins, information would be provided only when the weather bureau issued a bulletin, saving the user from having to check periodically for bulletins. This is a coordination-monitoring application.*

User Awareness: Notifications

Rather than provide a stream of information, an alternative is to make users aware of what content is available and leave it up to them to determine what they wish to access. This approach is based on indexing the information in a channel and periodically pushing only the index—but not the indexed information—to the subscriber.

> **E X A M P L E :** *Many publishers of volatile information on the Web encourage users to subscribe to notifications of new content by email. These notifications alert users to new content, attracting the user's attention and giving him or her the option of accessing the notified content (using a Web browser, through a hyperlink embedded within the email message).*

> *PointCast uses primarily a notification approach. The user is provided an index of stories available on each channel and chooses which to look at.*

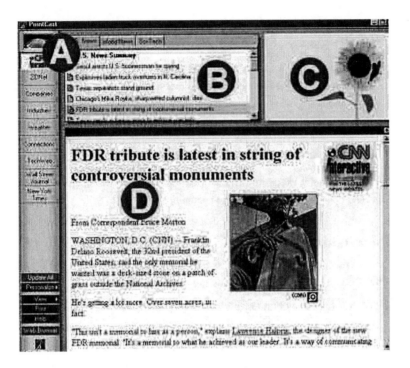

Figure 2.5 Screen from PointCast, a push application

Timing

Users may or may not have control over the timing of subscribed information or notifications. If they do not have control, the information or notifications may still be stored for access at a time of the user's choosing.

EXAMPLE: *PointCast controls when its information is provided to the user's screen, but the user chooses when to look at the stories.*

An immediate form of information pull is appropriate for timely, volatile information, such as notification of a stock market crash or extreme weather event.

Push and Pull in Social Applications

The push/pull distinction arises in social as well as information access applications, where the distinction is between one user initiating or responding to a request for interaction (or work group).

EXAMPLE: *Email is a push application, because one user "pushes" a message at another. A newsgroup is a pull application, since a user must consciously go to the newsgroup to "pull" a message from another user. In fact, the email and newsgroup applications can be viewed as push and pull variations of messaging.*

Role of Push and Pull in Work Groups

Combining push and pull in a work group can minimize the burden on users while insuring their appropriate involvement. Generally it can be said that

- Email (push) should be avoided for discussions and brainstorming, because it forces every group member to deal with every topic. Also, discussions are mixed with more time-critical interactions in the user's mailbox. The newsgroup allows each user to better control which topics to join, as well as when to participate.
- Newsgroups and the Web (pull) cannot be relied on exclusively, because users can easily forget or ignore them. Users may be unaware that a topic of interest is being discussed, and feel disenfranchised when they discover they didn't participate in decisions.

The best modality for collaboration mixes the pull and push models:

- Any documents in a work group should be posted on the Web rather than sent in an email message (proprietary information can be protected using restricted access). This pull model allows users to control which documents to read at what time, and they always access the latest version.
- Brainstorming and discussions should also use pull, that is, a discussion forum application.

In the context of social applications, each model has its strengths and weaknesses:

- Push is invasive, since users never have total control over what is "pushed" at them. Excessive reliance on push can make a user's life unnecessarily cluttered and stressful.
- Pull requires users to consciously initiate the interaction with another user or an information source. It does not alert users to the need for an interaction and thus requires more attention and conscious activity on their part.

In most contexts it is best to combine push and pull (see the sidebar "Role of Push and Pull in Work Groups" for an example).

Discussion

D2.13 Which searching services on the Web do you find most useful, and why? Do you have any ideas on how they can be improved?

D2.14 It is fair to say that any digital libraries available today are quite rudimentary. How do you think useful digital libraries will arise? How will they be paid for? Will duplication of libraries be avoided, and if so, how?

D2.15 Many university staffs are distressed at the increasing cost of acquisition of periodicals for their libraries and actively discussing publishing their own scholarly works in digital libraries as a way to bypass publishers and reduce costs. Discuss the merits of this approach. What value is the scholarly periodical publisher adding, and will universities be able to replace its functions?

D2.16 Expanding on D2.15, the Internet is often said to "eliminate the middleman." For information dissemination and management, who are the middlemen, and what is their role? Can they in fact be eliminated? If they were, would anything be lost?

D2.17 Human knowledge is known to grow exponentially with time, which raises the question of how individuals keep up with it. Some possible answers include increasing specialization coupled with collaboration among domain experts, or a cadre of generalists collaborating with domain experts, or increasing reliance on networked computing applications to help users opportunistically acquire knowledge. Discuss the merits of these and any other options you can think of.

2.4 Education and Training

One promising networked application is education and training. Several areas where networked applications offer obvious value are listed in Table 2.11. No doubt, radically new models of education and training will arise using combinations of immediate and deferred, and pull and push, applications. Education combines, in part, knowledge acquisition at the student's initiative, with a teacher to offer assistance, explanation, and guidance. Networked computing lends itself not only to access to multimedia course materials—an expanded notion of the textbook—but also to the interaction and collaboration between teacher and students and among students that would otherwise occur in the classroom.

Schools and universities are organizations, so they benefit from the type of networked applications that are covered in Chapter 3. Many other possibilities have an indirect impact on education, such as using networked computing to enhance the community of teachers and involve parents.

It is unlikely that networked computing will ever displace entirely the physical school or campus, as face-to-face interaction and socialization are important, particularly for younger students. It does offer considerable value as a supplement to the classroom and may partially replace it in some contexts—such as college education for older students, corporate training, and lifelong learning—where the traditional campus or classroom is impractical. It may also significantly shift instructional techniques in traditional institutions.

- The attention of users in the work group can be solicited by push, such as email. Typically, users should be informed by email when a new discussion topic is initiated or a new document is posted on the Web. Ideally, such "informational" messages should be sent only occasionally, aggregating discussions and documents.

As the number of people using social applications increases, using them properly becomes ever more critical. This is largely a matter of proper education of the users.

Discussion

D2.18 What are the typical roles of "pull" and "push" in education? Is the balance shifting?

D2.19 Discuss the advantages of full-time on-campus study relative to exclusively remote learning. Can the latter ever fully replace the former? If not, where might it fall short?

D2.20 What advantages might a multimedia textbook offer over a paper version (like this one)?

D2.21 What are some possible implications of computer-mediated learning to the education profession?

hyperlink, index, and metadata), third-party or collective recommendations, and third-party organization and indexing in digital libraries.

Autonomous information sources provide the user a stream of information—with the content and/or scheduling determined by the source. This includes information provided by subscription or notifications as to available content. In both information access and social applications, a useful distinction is between push and pull.

Education can make use of remote conferencing to approximate the classroom, groupware to enhance the interaction among teacher and students, and multimedia information materials to enhance the textbook and reference materials. Indirect applications can accommodate students not able to adhere to a schedule, due to travel or scheduling constraints.

Key Concepts

Social applications:

- Group characteristics: task, work, and interest groups, citizenry
- Communication versus coordination styles of social application
- Immediate versus deferred and direct versus publication social applications
- Scheduling
- Documents: annotation, replication, and reconciliation
- Message: one, multiple, or indeterminate recipients

Information and knowledge:

- Finding useful information: user directed, author or publisher assistance, third-party recommendation, third-party organization and indexing
- Autonomous information sources: push versus pull, content versus scheduling, subscription, notification

Further Reading

There are not yet books devoted to social applications of networked computing that can be recommended. General introductions to information management include [Buc91] and [Tag95]. [Les97b] is a good treatment of digital libraries; [Ole98] is a concise and readable introduction to knowledge management.

Exercises

E2.1   A "dumb terminal," the user-interface appliance from the time-shared computing era (described in "The Evolution of Computing" on page 2), displays only text (no graphics) and has only a keyboard for input (no mouse or other pointing device). If users today had only a dumb terminal, briefly describe the impact on each of the following applications. (The purpose, of course, is to appreciate the impact of graphics and pointing devices on user interfaces.)

    a. Authoring a text document

    b. Authoring a drawing to include as a figure in a document

    c. Browsing the Web

E2.2   Repeat Exercise 2.1 for a user-interface appliance that has graphics (like today's personal computers), but no pointing device (like the mouse).

E2.3   For each of the following groups, indicate what group category they would best fit in (this may be more than one), and why:

    a. A group of students completing a project assignment for a class

    b. Alcoholics in a self-help group

    c. A homeowners association

    d. Representatives from different countries to an international trade organization

    e. All the professors on a campus

E2.4   For each of the following group categories, give two examples, drawn from your personal experience and not mentioned in the chapter, of groups you feel match the category well:

    a. Task group

    b. Work group

    c. Interest group

    d. Citizenry

E2.5   Name one social application that incorporates both direct and publication styles. Describe the features that use the direct style and the features that use the publication style.

E2.6   List all the existing direct-immediate social applications you can think of. Include applications that utilize electronic communications, whether or not they utilize desktop computers.

E2.7 By definition, direct-immediate applications are intolerant of delay. However, they must all tolerate a *small* delay, since there is always some delay through the network, as discussed in Chapter 20.

  a. Based on your own experience, what interactive delays (tenth of a second, a second, tens of seconds?) might be tolerable in a direct-immediate style of social application? Do you believe there is a wide variation in the small delay that can be tolerated among applications, or fair consistency?

  b. Repeat a for information access applications.

E2.8 For each of the following, indicate whether you believe they are best classified as information, knowledge, or wisdom, and indicate briefly your reasoning:

  a. 3.14159

  b. $\pi = 3.14159$

  c. $\pi = 3.14159$ is the ratio of the area to the diameter of a circle.

  d. The ratio of the area to the diameter of a circle cannot be specified by a finite number of digits.

  e. The ratio of the area to the diameter of a circle can be represented by a finite number of digits for any practical purpose.

E2.9 For each of the following tasks, decide which method of finding useful information (user directed, author assisted, third-party recommendation, or third-party indexing) is superior, and give your reasons. If you think two or more methods are fine, list them and say why.

  a. Identifying a good Mexican restaurant for your anniversary dinner

  b. Finding the Web home page of the Grateful Dead

  c. Finding a new radiator to replace the rusted one in your 1989 Honda

  d. Finding an audio recording of Martin Luther King's "I Have a Dream" speech.

  e. Determining the population of Cleveland in the most recent U.S. Census.

  f. Finding all available painting contractors in Sydney, Australia so you can request competitive bids

  g. Determining which painting contractors in Sydney have the proper state license

   h. Determining which painting contractors in Sydney do the highest-quality work

E2.10   Give two examples different from those given in this chapter, drawn from your personal experience, of each of the following methods of finding useful information. These examples do not have to involve networked computing.

   a. Searching

   b. Browsing

   c. Navigation

   d. Hyperlink

   e. Index

   f. Metadata

   g. Third-party recommendation

   h. Library or librarian

E2.11   List at least three specific awareness applications, and describe their features and value to the user. Again, they do not have to involve networked computing.

E2.12   Repeat Exercise 2.11 for recommender systems.

E2.13   Choose a specific messaging application that will help two users accomplish some task from your personal experience.

   a. Describe briefly the value of messaging in the application.

   b. List all possibilities for the timing of the sending and receiving of the message—including immediate and deferred alternatives—from the perspective of each user. For example, one of those alternatives is user 1 originating a message at his convenience, and user 2 being interrupted by that message immediately.

   c. Describe the relative merits of these options for the application you chose.

E2.14   For each of the following publication-style social applications, decide whether they are best realized by a pull model, a push model, or both. Give a brief rationale.

   a. A user obtaining stock quotes, with the goal of finding a good time to sell ten shares of HWP

b. A local government giving notification of an approaching tornado to its citizenry

c. A user reading a weekly gossip column

d. A group of users carrying on a discussion about a topic of mutual interest

e. A user looking up facts in a reference work

E2.15 Can hyperlinks in a Web page be used for request, response, publish, or subscribe? Specifically which?

Applications Supporting Organizations

3

Individual applications described in Chapter 2 serve users in computation and authoring and access to information. Social applications support groups of users in impromptu interaction or collaboration. Another class of applications discussed in this chapter supports organizational missions. Networked computing is a natural in this role, as organizations are often geographically dispersed and have many requirements for coordination and control of the internal flow of materials, finished goods, services, and money. Any organization also has commercial and other dealings with other organizations, typically to purchase materials, goods, or services, which are supported by networked applications.

An important class of organization is the *enterprise*—an organization with a commercial mission—but others include government, educational institutions, and nonprofit institutions such as foundations and political action committees. Applications supporting individual organizations are usually called *enterprise applications*, because enterprises were the earliest and remain the largest opportunity for application software vendors. Enterprise applications serve to coordinate the myriad resources and activities required to support organizational goals, such as producing and selling a product or service. *Commerce applications* support organizations engaging in commercial relationships with one another, because most relations among organizations—including even governmental, educational, and nonprofit—are commercial in nature and involve buying and selling goods and services. In this chapter, when enterprise and commerce applications are discussed, all types of organizations (including governmental, educational, and nonprofit) are included.

Applications supporting organizations sometimes serve an enterprise as a whole and sometimes serve smaller units within the organizations. Departmental applications support the mission of compartmentalized, hierarchical departments with narrower missions—for example, inventory or payroll or purchasing. Early

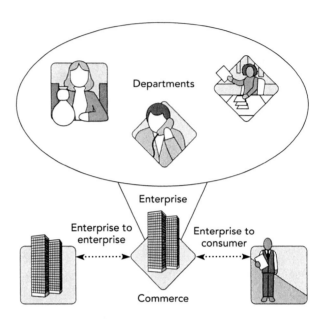

Figure 3.1 Organizational applications serve departments, enterprises, and commerce

applications were usually retrofitted into the existing departmental structure, serving to extend the capability and improve the productivity, quality, or functionality—much as a personal productivity application empowers an individual user. Individual workers are also supported by information management applications, and groups of workers engaging in impromptu interactions or collaboration are aided by social applications.

In summary, there are three types of organizational applications—departmental, enterprise, and commerce—illustrated in Figure 3.1 and summarized in Table 3.1. Commerce applications break into three distinct categories: applications among enterprises, those between enterprises and individual consumers, and those allowing individual consumers to buy and sell among themselves. Each type has distinct characteristics discussed in this chapter.

Organizational applications can be classified as shown in Table 3.2; together, these encompass most of the activities and processes that make up an enterprise and its commercial relationships.

Managing any organization is largely an issue of coordination and communication. Networked applications can dramatically lower costs and improve the quantity and quality of both coordination and communication within an organization and among organizations, so it is not an exaggeration to say that net-

Table 3.1 Three types of organizational applications

Type	Description		Examples
Departmental	Increase the productivity and capability of a functional department.		A customer service department using information management and remote conferencing, a training department serving students using remote collaboration, an accounting and finance department managing accounts payable and receivable.
Enterprise	Support activities and acquire and manage resources required to produce a product or service.		Coordinate the manufacture of a product, including managing purchasing and inventory of parts, scheduling workers and equipment, forecasting sales and controlling production; support sales, including access to product and inventory information, ordering and invoices, scheduling delivery, and managing accounts receivable.
Commerce	Support the purchase and delivery of goods and services.	Inter-enterprise commerce	An automobile manufacturer finding and procuring parts from its suppliers; an oil refiner purchasing crude oil; an office manager purchasing paper clips and pencils.
		Consumer commerce	A consumer buying *War and Peace* from an on-line book merchant.
		Interconsumer commerce	One consumer buying a used computer or antique from another.

Problems and Obstacles

Like all technologies, networked computing can be put to good purposes, but there is also the possibility of misuse and abuse. (For example, automobiles speed people to their destination but also speed bank robbers from the scene of the crime.) Networked computing as a means of cost cutting can make worker and business relationships more impersonal and anonymous. It can automate the tedious and repetitive, but it can also eliminate low-skilled jobs and reduce worker autonomy. There are serious concerns about privacy, since the technology makes it easy to track a consumer's and worker's every move. Reliance on networked computing also introduces troubling vulnerabilities to theft and sabotage, as discussed in Chapter 13.

It is up to users and organizations to make the best use of networked applications, but it is also their responsibility to avoid abuses and problems. In some cases, this means the government has to step in and set policies and limits (see Chapter 8 for examples).

worked computing is transforming the very nature of organizations. The result is major improvements in efficiency and quality, and streamlining of management and worker job functions. Of course, there are problems too (see the sidebar "Problems and Obstacles").

Organizational applications have expanded their scope in four distinct stages listed in Table 3.3. Because of the geographic dispersion of enterprises and consumers, one impact of networking has been the expansion of applications from the department to the enterprise, and from the enterprise to groups of enterprises and individual consumers. While the supporting information technology has been available for some time, the Internet has suddenly enabled enterprise and commerce applications to come to the forefront almost simultaneously. This is an outstanding example of positive feedback in network effects, which is discussed in Chapter 8.

The Internet even allows smaller firms to band together to form virtual enterprises to develop and market new products. The virtual enterprise offers many advantages previously afforded large vertically integrated firms, while benefiting from the specialization, flexibility, and innovation of small firms.

Classification of organizational applications

Function	Description
Worker collaboration	Social applications, including work groups, directly assist workers and managers in their jobs. They relax geographical constraints, allow greater interaction with workers in the field, and flatten the organizational hierarchy by increasing the number of reports to each manager.
Operations and logistics	Coordinate and control the ongoing movement of goods, information, and money throughout the enterprise. Networked applications replace paper and transportation in the flow of information and money; contribute to better coordination; and reduce delay, administrative overhead, and errors. Similarly, commerce applications coordinate and control the flow of goods, services, and money among enterprises.
Decision support	Managers and workers must make tactical and strategic decisions daily—on how to adjust to problems, what products to design and market, which suppliers to use, when and where to invest capital, etc. Networked applications can enhance the quantity and quality of information influencing those decisions.
Information and knowledge management	An increasingly important asset of organizations of all types is information and knowledge they accumulate. Information and knowledge management applications aid workers in acquiring and systematically organizing information and knowledge, and widely distributing it internally and externally.
Customer outreach	The network offers new ways of reaching out to consumers with information and advertising, selling goods and services, and providing customer support. By coupling inter-enterprise commerce with consumer commerce, enterprises are able to customize products and services to individual consumers.

3.1 Examples of Organizational Applications

Four applications—a customer-care organization, an on-line book merchant, a stock trading system, and a floral delivery service—will illustrate organizational applications throughout this chapter, as well as illustrate the applicability of concepts and technologies as they arise in the remainder of the book. In fact, the choice of these applications is driven in part by how well they illustrate various technological challenges that will be addressed in later chapters. Further, since organizations are composed of collections of individual users with a common mission, the social and information access applications covered in Chapter 2 are directly useful and can be illustrated in these organizational contexts. Thus, you are urged to read this section, even if you are not primarily interested in organizational applications and plan to skip the remainder of this chapter.

Table 3.3 The increasing scope of organizational applications in four distinct stages

Scope	Descriptive terms	Characteristics
Department	Client-server computing; enterprise databases; personal productivity applications.	Information is moved from paper to electronic form, managed by mainframes. Applications are added that exploit this information and support workers, often on decentralized computers. Decision-support functions are added by the ability of workers to access and manipulate information on their personal computers.
Enterprise	Business process reengineering; business transformation; enterprise resource planning; data warehousing; data mining; groupware.	Integration of information from across the enterprise is used to reengineer and automate business processes. Information is consolidated for decision making.
Inter-enterprise commerce	Electronic data interchange; electronic commerce; electronic business; supply-chain and supply-web management.	Information integration and business processes are extended to include other firms (both suppliers and customers). Decision making is enhanced by real-time input. The Internet enables smaller companies to participate in commerce applications.
Consumer commerce	Consumer electronic commerce.	Shareholders and the public are provided with information about the company. Consumers are provided with marketing information. Products and services are sold, and product support is provided over the Internet.

3.1.1   Customer Care

Software merchant software4u.com sees as a major competitive advantage its customer-care organization, which provides postsale support to its customers who have difficulty installing and using purchased software. Customers access this customer-care operation over the Internet, illustrating a consumer commerce application. Internally to software4u.com, customer care is organized into two departments, customer service and technical support, as illustrated in Figure 3.2.

The customer service department consists primarily of customer service agents—users who interact directly with customers by means of the suite of social applications described in "Social Applications" on page 21. Customers who wish to interact directly with agents can use a direct-immediate remote conferencing application, allowing them to talk to and see the agent (and vice versa), and also allowing the customer and agent to examine various documents and make sketches as they interact. Since customer service operates only during normal business hours, customers can also direct inquiries and complaints by

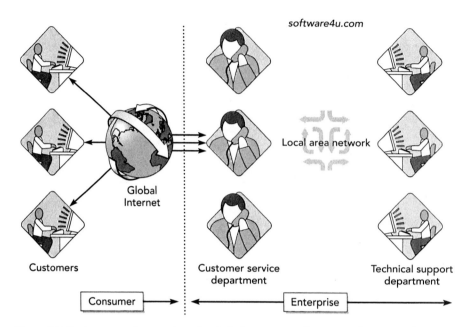

Figure 3.2 Customer service agents and technical support workers at a software merchant

the direct-deferred email application. In all cases, for purposes of efficiency, a customer does not know in advance which agent he or she will access, but rather all interactions are automatically directed to the next available agent.

During each interaction, the agent can access a digital library of documentation provided by the vendor of each software application the company sells. Numerous search and navigation tools have been provided to allow the agent to find information relevant to the customer's problem. In addition, software4u.com has discovered numerous problems commonly experienced by its customers that are not identified in the software vendors' documentation, and finds some of these problems occurring repeatedly. Thus, it has created its own knowledge base containing documentation of each and every problem encountered and the solution rendered, with sophisticated search tools allowing the agents to find relevant problems and solutions. Finally, because some problems require multiple interactions with the customer to resolve, especially when technical support has to be brought in, software4u.com has created a database maintaining an audit record of each customer interaction, from initial contact to problem resolution. For each separate interaction with the customer, the agent can refer to this historical record to find the status of the problem and the actions taken thus far to resolve it. This is particularly important because a different agent may be involved in each interaction. For each new customer interaction, the agent is automatically referred to the customer record associated with that specific customer.

Software4u.com is also concerned about reducing the cost of customer care and found that some of its more sophisticated customers are able to resolve their own problems without the assistance of an agent when given access to the same digital library of documentation and knowledge base of common resolved problems. Thus, software4u.com allows customers to access the digital library and knowledge base (although the customer is not allowed to directly change or add to the knowledge base). All queries to these information sources from both customers and agents utilize the Web, so customers can use their standard Web browser for this purpose.

The customer support agents are chosen more for their personality and customer empathy than for technical skills, although these are not, of course, mutually exclusive. Therefore, software4u.com has established a separate technical support department, where technicians can focus on challenging problems not addressed in vendor documentation or the knowledge base. In an illustration of information push, whenever customer service agents encounter a problem they can't resolve, they notify the technical support department, in the form of a message sent over the enterprise's local area network. This message includes a pointer to the appropriate record in the customer-interaction database, so the primary communication between agent and technician is through this permanent record. This notification is automatically routed to the next available technician with expertise in that software application. The technician assigned this problem then attempts to resolve it, and in rare cases may interact directly with the customer. The technician is expected to contribute to the knowledge base any solution to a previously undocumented problem, so that it can be resolved in the future without assistance from technical support. When a technician has solved the problem, she or he sends a notification to customer service, in the form of a message that includes a pointer to both the customer record and the new entry in the knowledge base. This notification is automatically routed to the next available customer service agent, who contacts the customer, conveys the solution, and follows up to be sure the problem was actually resolved.

As a further measure to reduce customer-care costs, software4u.com has also discovered that customers can sometimes assist one another in solving problems, even without assistance from technical support agents or technicians. Thus, it has made available to customers a forum in which they can discuss mutual problems. Technicians are instructed to monitor this forum whenever they have free time; that is, no immediate customer problem is pressing. These technicians can weigh in with assistance if appropriate, as well as identify new technical insights from customers (some of whom are more sophisticated than the technicians!). Software4u.com managers also monitor this forum, because it provides immediate feedback on customer-care shortcomings as customers use one another as sounding boards for complaints.

3.1.2   On-Line Bookselling

An on-line book merchant, books4u.com, sells a large selection of books directly to consumers over the network. Real-world examples of similar businesses include Amazon.com, Barnes and Noble, and Borders. The participants in a hypothetical new on-line bookseller books4u.com—the customers, book merchant, financial institution, and book distributors—are pictured in Figure 3.3.

Like most consumer commerce applications, bookselling builds on the Web, allowing potential customers to freely access information about available books using their Web browsers. This element is an information management application, and the various tools discussed in "Finding Useful Information" on page 41 can be helpful to customers. For a customer desiring a book with a specific author or title, books4u.com provides searching tools. A customer with less defined needs can browse or navigate through the available titles, which are appropriately organized and indexed.

Books4u.com uses other information management tools like those discussed in "Autonomous Information Sources" on page 46 to induce the customer to buy more books. It might allow customers to subscribe to an email information push notification service, informing them when new books become available in topics related to books they have purchased in the past. As the customer is searching or browsing, books4u.com may display other books commonly purchased on that topic—this is a primitive recommender system. It may provide customers other means to gain collective recommendations from other customers, such as discussion forums organized by general topics. Books4u.com also provides the option of invoking a remote conferencing application to discuss needs with an expert customer service agent (who acts a bit like the traditional librarian). However, to save costs, this option is offered only to the best customers, taking advantage of the customer purchase history stored in a customer database.

Once the customer orders one or more books by entering the information in a Web form, the application switches to an inter-enterprise e-commerce mode. The order includes two key pieces of information: what merchandise is bought and a payment or payment authorization. Chapter 14 discusses several options allowing a customer to make payment over the network—including a credit card or digital cash—that normally involve one or more financial institutions. For example, if the customer supplies a credit card number, books4u.com will want

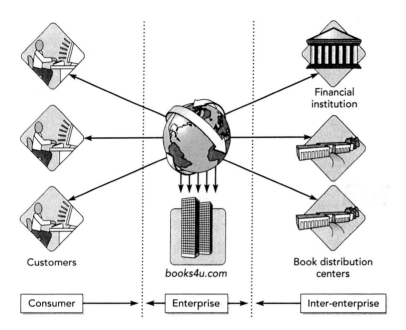

Figure 3.3 Individual and enterprise participants in an on-line book merchant e-commerce application

to obtain authorization for the charge, transferring the credit risk for nonpayment to the issuing bank for the customer's credit card. Books4u.com deals directly with its own "acquirer" bank—the bank it uses to clear its credit card charges—to obtain this authorization. The acquirer bank acts as an intermediary, contacting the issuing bank for the customer's credit card over the network to determine the customer's credit status. Both these interactions use a networked application operated by the credit card association for this purpose.

The final step is fulfillment of the order—getting the book to the customer. There are two options here. If the book comes in physical form, it is shipped via a package delivery service. Another option is to download the book over the network to a special reading appliance called an *electronic book* or *e-book*. (An *appliance* is a device dedicated to a particular function—as opposed to general purpose, like a PC.) The e-book is a battery-operated device that displays pages of the book on a screen (examples today include the Librius Millennium EBook and the Everybook Dedicated Reader).

In the case of a physical book, if books4u.com doesn't have the ordered books in its own inventory, it forwards the order to a book distributor. It finds one that is geographically close to the customer and has the books in stock by comparing the customer's location with available distributors from a distributor database and directly accessing appropriate distributors' inventory databases over the network to determine availability. This arrangement is formalized by a contractual relationship between books4u.com and its book distributors, which includes provision for the distributors to ship books directly to the customer and get paid by books4u.com. Monthly payments for merchandise from books4u.com to each ditributor use a networked application to initiate a funds transfer from books4u.com's bank account to the distributor's bank account.

3.1.3 On-Line Stock Trading

On-line stock trading—buying and selling stocks and other financial instruments by individual consumers—is growing rapidly. Existing brokerage houses (such as Charles Schwab) offer this supplemental service to their customers, and other start-up companies offer only on-line trading (such as E*TRADE). They offer the customer access to information regarding alternative investments and on-line advice on issues such as retirement saving and asset allocation. They also provide a brokerage account where securities can be held and allow a customer to buy, sell, and trade these securities. The major participants in a hypothetical on-line trading company stocks4u.com are pictured in Figure 3.4.

The stock trading application has some parallels to bookselling. The customer is offered information about investments, in part as an inducement to trade. In order to increase the diversity of information available (as well as to reduce legal culpability), stocks4u.com may acquire information from other information providers, especially those specializing in financial news, market price quotes, and research analysis on various investments. For this purpose, stocks4u.com creates a digital library of organized and indexed information gathered from those providers, presenting a unified view into these different repositories and adding searching, browsing, and navigation aids. Any information requested by the customer is first conveyed back through stocks4u.com— as opposed to referring the customer directly to the information provider (for example, by a hyperlink)—because the information provider wants to limit access to customers of stocks4u.com (and other on-line traders with which it has a commercial relationship).

When customers initiate a trade, they convey an order with specific instructions (chosen from a menu of options) typed into a Web form. In this case, no payment instructions are included in the order, since the funds will normally come from the customer's brokerage account held at stocks4u.com. The order is then conveyed to a stock exchange for execution. The stock exchange itself operates

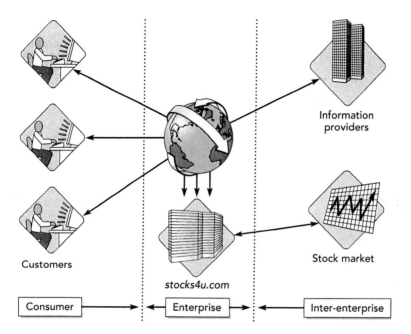

Information providers

Customers

stocks4u.com

Stock market

| Consumer | → | ← | Enterprise | → | ← | Inter-enterprise |

Figure 3.4 Participants in an on-line stock trading e-commerce application

an elaborate networked computing infrastructure to support the billions of daily trades worldwide.

Stocks4u.com has serious concerns about privacy and security. In this case privacy means preventing the customer's activity or financial status from leaking to third parties, and security means protection from adversaries such as thieves or imposters. Stocks4u.com's customers are sensitive to unauthorized access to brokerage account information. Both customers and stocks4u.com are concerned that unauthorized third parties be prevented from initiating trades or withdrawing funds from a customer's brokerage account. The lack of physical presence in each interaction between customers and stocks4u.com contributes to the paranoia about these problems, because this makes it simpler for an imposter. (A recent adage goes, "on the network, nobody can tell that you are a dog"—meaning that there are no physical or visual clues as to identity, unlike personal interactions in the physical world.) Fortunately, security technologies adopted by stocks4u.com (and discussed in Chapter 13) effectively alleviate these concerns for both parties.

3.1.4   Floral Delivery Service

The fourth and final application example is a hypothetical floral merchant flowers4u.com, which accepts orders for flowers and passes those orders to a

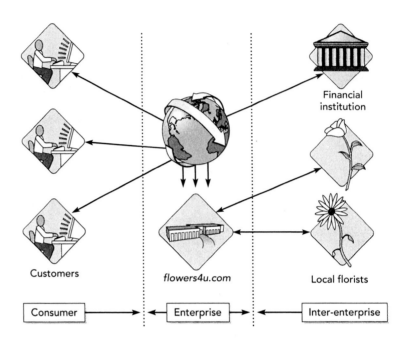

Financial
institution

Customers   flowers4u.com   Local florists

| Consumer | → | ← | Enterprise | → | ← | Inter-enterprise |

Figure 3.5 Participants in a floral delivery intermediary service

florist near the customer for fulfillment. Real-world examples include Roses.com and 1-800-FLOWERS. The major participants in this application are shown in Figure 3.5.

Major portions of flowers4u.com's business resemble the on-line book merchant, including ordering of flowers using a Web form (or by remote conferencing for good customers) and its payment options. The one major difference, which raises major challenges for flowers4u.com's technology professionals, is that flowers4u.com deals with 16,000 local florists (independent businesses contracting to flowers4u.com) for fulfillment of customer orders. Each of these florists is an independent small business, most of them with limited technology acumen. What flowers4u.com would like to do—once it identifies the florists geographically close to a customer—is present the customer with customized options from that florist, including some that tap into the creative energies of the individual florist. However, since many florists do not have the sophistication in Web publishing to pull this off, flowers4u.com maintains a database of which florists have published customized options, which it presents on a case-by-case basis to the customer, together with a standardized catalog of options available from all participating florists.

Flowers4u.com also faced the challenge of how to inform florists of ordered merchandise, given that most of these small operations have only a PC with

Internet connectivity. Initially, flowers4u.com tried publishing orders for each florist on an individualized Web page and depended on florists to access their orders frequently. However, it found that this information pull model did not work well, since many florists forgot to check orders for days or weeks at a time. It was decided that notification through information push was necessary. Flowers4u.com was tempted to send orders to florists by email, but was worried that some florists did not check their email very often either, and was also concerned about security (which existing email applications are lacking). The enterprise finally decided it needed to develop a custom messaging system by installing a custom application on the florist's PC. Orders were pushed directly to the screen of the florist's PC, and an accompanying audio alarm alerted the florist of the arrival of an order. If the florist's computer is turned off, not connected to the Internet, or flowers4u.com's custom application is not running, a service agent is automatically notified to call the florist on the telephone, and failing connecting that way, the order is automatically redirected to another florist. By these aggressive means, flowers4u.com was able to substantially reduce the average and worst-case delay from order to delivery, increasing customer satisfaction.

3.1.5   Observations

The organizational applications that have been described illustrate concrete uses of most of the social and information management applications discussed in Chapter 2. This is not surprising, as interaction among workers and access to and manipulation of information are central to all organizational missions. In fact, the conceptualization of an organizational application is in large part the creative merging and integration of generic applications serving individuals and groups and information management.

There are some new wrinkles, however. For example, several of these organizational applications utilize capabilities—such as the forwarding of notifications to groups of workers, with automatic routing to the next available individual—not addressed in Chapter 2. Many elements of these applications do not even involve users at all—they are automated operations that occur in the background, like the automatic bank funds transfers at the end of the month. Another important distinction is that these applications incorporate many elements that are ongoing and performed over and over—in business parlance, these are called *processes*. Processes can be defined and tuned in advance, as distinct from many nonorganizational contexts where user interaction and information access operations are often performed once and only once.

Finally, you should review the described organizations from the perspective of how they were carefully designed to take maximum advantage of networked computing technologies. If you had designed each organization to perform similar functions in the absence of networked computing, the structure and operation would likely have been dramatically different. The important lesson is that major gains in efficiency, speed, and accuracy require not only transcending the automation of existing processes but also conceptualizing new organizational structures and processes that make most effective use of technology. This presents both an opportunity and a challenge. The opportunity is dramatic gains in efficiency, speed, and accuracy, for both new and existing organizations. The challenge—and this is indeed a severe challenge—is to rethink and change an existing organization to take greater advantage of networked applications. Historically, many of the most successful applications of networked computing have been organizations designed from scratch to make best use of these technologies. This reflects the difficulties in making major changes in direction in existing organizations. Nevertheless, this is an increasing reality, and this book is meant to help you participate if and when presented with the opportunity.

Discussion

D3.1 For each of the four organizational applications described, discuss how it would have to be changed if networked computing were not available. Where are the major gains from networked computing, and how great are they?

3.2 Departmental Applications

The typical enterprise is divided into functional departments with specialties like accounting, manufacturing, purchasing, development, marketing, sales, and customer service. Similarly, governmental and educational organizations have functional departments like tax collection, motor vehicle bureau, admissions and records, and food service. The earliest departmental applications managed information within those departments, often replacing paper records. Often these departmental applications combine elements of social and information management applications. Two types of departmental applications are on-line transaction processing (OLTP) and workflow.

3.2.1 On-Line Transaction Processing

OLTP applications support workers (called service agents) who typically deal with outside parties—such as customers, governmental citizens, or students of a university—either in person or over the telephone. It may also support workers who gather and enter information within an organization.

EXAMPLE: *Customer service agents take orders, make reservations, take service or repair requests, help customers make deposits or withdrawals, provide customer support, or register students in courses. Workers in a warehouse use barcode readers to enter inventory information into an inventory tracking application. The book distributors in the on-line book merchant application likely use an OLTP application to keep track of the books in inventory (see "On-Line Bookselling" on page 66).*

The large volume of information managed by these applications typically resides in a *database management system* (DBMS) (described further in Chapter 4). A DBMS excels at managing the type of information common to such departmental applications, which includes numbers (bank accounts, employee ages, student identification numbers, etc.) and character strings (employee and customer or citizen or student names, etc.).

3.2.2 Workflow

A *workflow application* supports workers cooperating on ongoing repetitive tasks.

EXAMPLE: *In the customer-care application, the customer service agents interact with customers, gathering information about problems (see "Customer Care" on page 63). These problem reports are automatically routed to the technical support department. After resolving the problem, a technician generates a solution report, which flows back to the customer service group, where it is routed to an available telephone agent to inform the customer. This workflow application supports the flow of work from customer service to technical support back to customer service.*

Since the application coordinates multiple workers, workflow is another class of deferred social application, but one in which the tasks are ongoing and repetitive—not impromptu and extemporaneous like those discussed earlier in Chapter 2. There is often a delegation requirement, in which a number of workers fulfill a given task, and the choice balances workloads and accommodates work and vacation schedules.

3.2.3   From Centralized to Decentralized Computing

Over the decades, departmental applications often moved from centralized to decentralized computing. Through the 1970s, applications were typically acquired, deployed, and operated by a centralized information systems (IS) department and used centralized mainframe computers. As a centralized department itself, IS could insure a degree of uniformity to reducing support costs and also impose important discipline, such as the reliable backup of data to permanent storage media. OLTP and workflow could be supported by so-called dumb terminals wired directly to the mainframe. These terminals were primitive by today's standards, supporting only text-based interaction without graphics or pointing devices.

Since the operations supported by many OLTP and workflow applications are *mission critical*—an integral part of the enterprise, which often cannot function without them—they must operate correctly during business hours. In an increasing number of enterprises, this means twenty-four hours a day, seven days a week (known as 24 × 7). They must also be secure and reliable (see Chapter 9). The mainframe environment has been optimized to provide this secure, reliable, centrally managed computing environment. On the other hand, such centralized systems and their associated IS departments are, by themselves, rather inflexible [Wat95]:

- Workers and managers wanting customized information have to submit special requests, resulting in the infamous information system backlog—a long list of new applications and capabilities requested by departments and not yet acquired or implemented.
- Mainframes require large and expensive support staffs that tend to perpetuate the status quo.
- Since the IS department serves the entire enterprise and imposes a uniform solution, individual departments have little ability to streamline or increase their own efficiency—they do not control their own destiny.

Decentralized computing addressed these issues in a limited way by allowing workers to manipulate information in ad hoc and customized ways on their desktop (PCs)—especially using spreadsheets—without the involvement of an IS department. The networking of PCs allowed workers to retrieve information from mainframe OLTP systems for this purpose. The PC could also serve as a terminal replacement, connecting to the mainframe for legacy OLTP applications. Primary factors in the success of the PC were its empowerment of individual workers and the loosening of some constraints imposed by the IS department.

E X A M P L E :   *Back when stocks4u.com was a traditional broker and did not offer on-line stock trading, it used a mainframe to store and update records of its customers' brokerage accounts (see "On-Line Stock Trading" on page 68). This is a mission-critical application, as loss of data would result in errors in account records, and downtime would interrupt customer trading (alienating customers as well as reducing revenues). The mainframe environment was protected and reliable, just right for this purpose. Although at one time customers had account records available on paper, by going on-line, both workers (such as telephone customer service agents) and customers had customer records directly available on their PCs. This enabled, for example, customers to merge data from multiple accounts to determine their overall asset allocation. However, the account data still resides in the protected mainframe environment.*

Decentralized computing also empowered operational departments to acquire and operate applications themselves, based on relatively inexpensive microprocessor-based computers called *servers*, which could perform functions similar to mainframes. This led to *client-server computing* at the departmental level, where workers' PCs (called *clients*) could store, access, and manipulate information stored in these servers as well as in centralized mainframes operated by the IS department. Installing and managing applications within the departments added flexibility, and local control resulted in greater efficiency and streamlining of departmental functions. Client-server computing is discussed further in Chapter 4.

E X A M P L E :   *The customer-care application uses a server to store its digital library and knowledge base, and customer service agents can access these from desktop PCs acting as clients (see "Customer Care" on page 63). This application is not sufficiently critical to use a mainframe; thus less expensive (both to purchase and operate) PC-based servers are used.*

Client-server computing unfortunately also allows a proliferation of incompatible systems and applications across the enterprise. The computing environment became more heterogeneous, increasing maintenance and operational difficulties, and placing obstacles in the way of enterprise applications, as discussed next.

Discussion

D3.2 Discuss some workflow activity with which you have personal experience. What were the individual tasks, and how was the flow of work organized? How might this activity benefit from networked computing?

3.3   Enterprise Applications

The core mission of an enterprise is often the goods (including information goods) or services it provides to outsiders—such as the customers of a business, citizens of a governmental unit, or students of a university. Those goods and services provided externally usually require the cooperation and coordination of multiple functional departments across the enterprise. The overall coordinated set of activities and resources required to sell a good or provision a service is called a business process.

EXAMPLE: *A manufacturing process requires a flow of parts from suppliers, which in turn requires purchasing to order the parts and accounting to pay suppliers. Further, manufacturing must coordinate with sales to forecast demand and maintain manageable inventories, which in turn affects purchasing.*

Networked applications supporting business processes spanning departments are called enterprise applications.

3.3.1   Operations

The applications in Chapter 2 are directly applicable to enterprises—social applications can aid workers in collaborating or coordinating special projects, information management is a major activity in any enterprise, and education and training are important priorities. However, none of these types of applications directly supports the myriad repetitive activities in day-to-day operations. While departments each contribute to these operations, they frequently require the ongoing exchange of materials or information among multiple functional departments. A natural successor to departmental applications is enterprise applications facilitating these interdepartmental operations. Due to the greater geographic dispersal of departments, the network is an important infrastructure.

Business Processes

Organizational theory defines the business process as a stream of related activities starting with the acquisition of resources (people, capital, supplies, etc.) and resulting in a good or service in the hands of customers [Dav93]. A key term in the definition of a process is the *stream*, which indicates that the constituent activities are repetitive. This distinguishes them from the social and information management applications discussed earlier, which tend to be impromptu or ad hoc—each interaction or collaboration is different.

A more detailed view of the structure of a business process is illustrated in Figure 3.6. The process takes resources and services from suppliers and, ultimately,

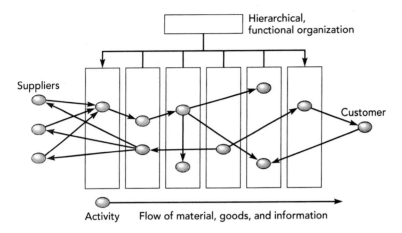

Figure 3.6 Illustration of a business process, which horizontally spans a typical vertical functional enterprise

provides goods or services to customers. The process requires coordinated activities within different functional departments, as well as the flow of material, finished goods, and information among them. It focuses on the activities to be coordinated, the resources required, and the pattern of information and material flows. While networked computing cannot directly provision the flow of people, material, or finished goods in a business process, it is ideal for controlling that flow and the manipulation of information supporting its coordination.

EXAMPLE: *In manufacturing, networked computing can support the flow of requests for material and parts from manufacturing to purchasing (so that suppliers can be notified), from receiving to accounting (so that suppliers can be paid), and from sales and distribution to manufacturing (forecasting the volume of production needed), among others. It can also coordinate their actions, such as matching manufacturing volume to sales forecasts.*

Business Transformation

Because a business process involves repetitive activities, it can be planned and optimized in advance. This *engineering* of the process has among its goals the following:

- Minimize operational cost (personnel costs, inventory and transaction costs, etc.).
- Reduce delays required from inputs to customer, allowing the process to respond more quickly to customers and to changes in the marketplace.

- Better quantify and minimize the costs associated with the overall process (as opposed to costs at the department level).
- Provide improved and more timely information to support business decisions.
- Make the process flexible, so products can easily be changed in response to marketplace needs, or even customized to individual customers' needs (called *mass customization*).

Used effectively, networked computing can provide considerable value in each of these areas. However, most existing processes were designed years ago—or arose in an incremental and ad hoc manner—and fail to make most effective use of information technology, and especially networked computing. It is popular to take a fresh approach to the design of business processes in a way that makes effective use of information technology. Called *business transformation* (or often *business process reengineering* (BPR) [Dav93]), where done effectively this has resulted in major savings and competitive advantage. Business transformation accounts for all aspects of a process, including the contribution and organization of workers, the flow of material, supplies, and finished goods, and the networked computing infrastructure and software. An essential issue in the design of a business process is what people do particularly well, what networked computing does particularly well, and how the two can work effectively together. This points out again that simply automating an existing process is rarely the most effective use of networked computing.

The phases of a business transformation consist of

- An *analysis* of business requirements and costs.
- A *design* that structures the individual activities and the flow of materials and information among these activities.
- A *development* of the management and worker organization, as well as computer systems and software.
- The *deployment* of the application, including worker training, and installing and testing of supporting information systems.
- The *operation* of the application supporting the production, sales, and distribution of goods and services.

The phases mirror the lifecycle of a networked application, as described in Chapter 9, and of course, the networked application is a part of and supports a business transformation. The design phase brings together managers (who understand the business goals and the organization and human resource challenges) and technologists (who understand the capabilities and limitations of the information technologies), but it benefits greatly from participants who understand both the management and the technology challenges. After reading this book, you will be prepared to participate effectively in this.

Enterprise Resource Planning

The computing component of many business processes was designed and implemented by an IS department working together with business units, often utilizing the services of outside consultants and professional services companies. Some of this custom design and implementation may be unnecessary because—while there are always local differences—there is much commonality among the processes in different companies.

EXAMPLE: *Financial accounting systems have a common purpose and operate under the same accounting rules within the same country. Human resource management (payroll, benefits, taxes, etc.) is reasonably standardized across many enterprises.*

It may be reasonable to purchase—rather than develop from scratch—an application to support a given business process. *Enterprise resource planning* (ERP) applications supply a networked computing application, with sophisticated configuration tools and options to customize to local needs. (The software methodologies making this possible are described further in Chapter 10.) ERP products are available for business processes that are fairly standardized across different companies:

- *Sales-force automation* supports the field sales force, with automated order entry, availability and delivery and pricing information, etc.
- *Document management* supports the massive documentation of designs, parts catalogs, etc.
- *Customer service and support* coordinates telephone agents and technicians supporting customers.
- *Manufacturing logistics* provides logistical support for the flow of materials and finished goods, inventory control, purchasing and payments to suppliers, etc.
- *Accounting* allows the company to keep track of cash flow, assets, profits and losses, etc.
- *Human resources* tracks employee history, salary and benefits, tax payments, etc.
- *Supply-chain management* coordinates with suppliers and customers, for example, in the supply relationships that support a finished goods manufacturer.

SAP: Largest ERP Vendor

SAP (Systems, Applications and Products in Data Processing), headquartered in Walldorf, Germany, is the largest ERP vendor. Others include PeopleSoft, Baan, and Oracle.

SAP's most recent product offering is called R/3. It incorporates many of the software technologies described in Chapter 10 (frameworks, components, cross-platform object communication). SAP's most successful products support manufacturing, accounting, logistics, and human resources. In 1998 it was in the process of expanding its applications to the extended enterprise with supply-chain management.

E X A M P L E : *Internally, books4u.com uses several ERP applications for managing its business, including its accounting and financial operations (see "On-Line Bookselling" on page 66). Fortunately, the ERP vendor has provided gateways that allow the book ordering application (which books4u.com developed internally to gain competitive advantage) to interact with it. This allows, for example, the bookings of customers' orders to enter books4u.com's internal financial systems directly and immediately, without manual intervention. The accounting system is thereby up-to-date and provides timely information to managers making decisions about adding workers or facilities.*

Purchasing an ERP application should be construed as implicitly adopting the design of the business process supported by that application—the configuration options do not support radical changes to the process itself. This has both benefits and downsides. On the benefit side, it is not necessary to pursue a long and costly process design—that has been implicitly provided by the vendor. Of course, it is necessary to adjust to that process, which usually means major reorganization of workers and their functions. A downside is that there is limited ability to accommodate local conditions in the enterprise, or to gain competitive advantage through a superior process design.

A key to ERP is *information integration*—meaning information required by the process and closely held within departments must be integrated into a single application. (Given the heterogeneity of computers and software in most enterprises, this is a severe challenge discussed further in Chapter 4.) In effect, an ERP application serves as a framework that allows information to flow automatically among departmental-level systems. ERP also provides several related functions:

- *Forecast and planning:* Effective operations dictate that many resources (such as real estate and worker head count) be planned well in advance, and suppliers may need considerable real time to manufacture and ship needed supplies. The ERP application can support these functions by providing historical information and future projections.
- *Control:* Efficiency can be improved by actively controlling the flow of goods to minimize inventory and manage accounts receivable and cash. ERP can provide feedback through the chain of activities in the process to control and coordinate them.
- *Real-time monitoring:* The ERP application can observe the business process as it is happening and present summary performance information. It can also highlight problems—such as weather-related transportation delays—that allow managers to react.

A downside is adapting processes to the ERP application—ideally it would be the other way around. Of course, this also avoids the burden of designing a process from scratch. Planning and deployment typically utilize experienced but expensive consultants (most accounting and consulting firms have entered this business). The considerations in choosing between a custom implementation and purchasing an off-the-shelf solution such as ERP are discussed further in Chapter 9.

A substantial obstacle to any major business transformation is the difficulty in replacing existing applications (see the sidebar "Legacy Applications"). A current example of the problems of legacy applications is the Y2K problem (see the sidebar "The Year 2000 Problem").

3.3.2   Decision Support

ERP forecasting and monitoring illustrate the important role of networked computing not only in operations but also in supporting managerial decisions. Networked computing offers capabilities of particular benefit to decision support:

- *Timely information:* The networking portion of networked computing communicates information around the world with negligible delay (seconds or fractions of a second). As a result, information supporting decisions is available practically "as it happens."
- *Data reduction and presentation:* In a typical enterprise application, the data is far too voluminous for a person to absorb in raw form. The computing portion of networked computing allows raw data to be aggregated and summarized, making the information it represents more useful.
- *Knowledge acquisition and management:* Networked computing can manage massive amounts of information and provide organization and search tools that aid workers in acquiring and managing the enterprise's knowledge assets.

Data warehouses and data mining are applications directed at decision support (see the sidebar "Data Warehouses and Data Mining" on page 83).

3.3.3   Knowledge Management

Knowledge is a key competitive asset of a modern enterprise. Historically, the acquisition and management of this knowledge was very informal. Most knowledge resided in the heads of managers and workers, or in large repositories of paper documents, and knowledge was shared among employees on an ad hoc basis. Modern trends such as downsizing and layoffs, higher turnover, and geographical dispersion of workers point to the need for more formal and

Legacy Applications

A serious constraint and obstacle to enterprise applications is the existence of legacy applications—those deployed some years ago using now-obsolete technology. In particular, preexisting departmental applications are an obstacle to enterprise applications. Integration of these applications is difficult because their design did not anticipate this type of change. Replacing them, on the other hand, is also difficult for several reasons:

- The information managed by a departmental application is frequently an important enterprise asset, and translating that information to a new application is difficult (see Chapter 9).
- Many departmental applications are mission critical, and trying to replace several of them at once is both logistically difficult and quite risky.
- Departmental applications are embedded within a larger business process, and either the process must be changed to fit the application, or the application must be molded to the process.
- Planning and deployment of an enterprise application require a major commitment of money and resources.

For these reasons, a business transformation project in general, and the decision to adopt an ERP in particular, is a major step for any enterprise, involving major expenses and risks that are potentially offset by the substantial benefits.

The Year 2000 Problem

Once applications are installed, they're often around a long time. Illustrating this is the Year 2000 (Y2K) problem. Many programmers in the 1950s and 1960s didn't anticipate their applications would still be operational forty years later, and they saved memory and storage (precious commodities at the time) by truncating years to the last two digits (assuming the first two are always "19"). As "January 1, 2000" is misconstrued as "January 1, 1900," havoc may result. These programs are written in old computer languages—and the original programmers have long since retired—so it is difficult to find and repair all instances.

The extent of Y2K points to the surprising number of legacy applications. Replacing a legacy application is time consuming and expensive and involves difficult logistical challenges. More sobering is the thought that new applications deployed today may have long operational lifetimes. On the positive side, Y2K has itself stimulated many replacements of legacy applications. Bypassing Y2K is one by-product of installing an ERP application, for example.

structured approaches to knowledge management [Ole98]. Networked computing can aid the acquisition of knowledge by providing workers with access to large information repositories that can be systematically searched or navigated, and with the aid of the network, this information can be widely dispersed throughout an enterprise. Recognizing the increasing importance of knowledge management, by 1998 40 percent of the Fortune 1,000 U.S. corporations had put knowledge management on a similar plane with the management of technology, money, real estate, and other corporate assets by creating a "chief knowledge officer" responsible for creating the infrastructure and culture of knowledge sharing and management [Ole98].

EXAMPLE: *Consider a customer service department in which service agents encounter and solve customer problems and enter this into an information base. This information is immediately available to all service agents, increasing responsiveness and efficiency in solving similar problems. This information—made immediately available to manufacturing and product development—can be used to discover flaws in manufacturing processes or improve designs.*

The customer support application knowledge base containing problems that have been encountered and their solutions is a compelling example of knowledge management (see "Customer Care" on page 63).

The term *knowledge warehouse* describes a large information repository (managed by a DBMS) that stores qualitative rather than quantitative information—such as work manuals, documentation, proposals, employee information, directories, newsletters—previously stored on paper. The knowledge warehouse is essentially a digital library as an enterprise application.

Discussion

D3.3 If you have experience with a business transformation project, describe the project, its goals, and its outcome. Was it a success?

D3.4 If you have experience with the deployment of an ERP application, describe both the benefits and the problems that were encountered.

D3.5 Discuss to what extent business processes are standardized across different companies and hence the viability of a "standardized" solution like ERP. Do you think it is a good or bad idea to change a business process to mold it to an ERP application? Compare to automation of an existing process or designing a new process without constraint.

3.4   Electronic Commerce

Once business processes within an enterprise employ networked computing, and decision-support tools are in place, there remains a major opportunity. A primary operational function of any enterprise—selling goods and services to other enterprises and to individual consumers—can also exploit networked computing, particularly with the growing ubiquity of the Internet. The selling of goods and services among enterprises comes under the general heading of commerce, and when supported by networked applications, it is called electronic commerce or e-commerce. E-commerce provides many of the same benefits for groups of enterprises and individual consumers as business transformation within the enterprise, including reducing costs (administrative and overhead), delay, and errors. E-commerce also opens up entirely new channels, such as selling goods and services directly to consumers over the Internet, and improves management decisions by providing more timely, complete, and accurate information [Kee97].

3.4.1   Types of E-Commerce Applications

Enterprises—such as companies, governments, or universities—engage in e-commerce, as do individual users. Enterprises, and occasionally individuals, serve as the creators of information goods or manufacturers of physical goods. Enterprises and individuals are also consumers, purchasing supplies for a manufacturing operation or personal use or consumption.

The basic transaction in e-commerce is the sale of goods or services. The seller might be a manufacturer, creator, distributor, or retailer, and the buyer might be an individual consumer or another enterprise. An enterprise might purchase the goods or services for internal use, or it may incorporate them into other goods or services that it sells. In addition to the buyer and seller, one or more intermediaries may assist in the transaction, for example, a search engine or directory, a catalog consolidator, an auctioneer, an escrow agent, or a financial institution that facilitates payment.

Three distinct types of e-commerce applications are listed in Table 3.4, classified as to whether the buyer and seller are individuals or enterprises. Although there are many commonalities, each of these types also presents unique challenges. Inter-enterprise e-commerce can be viewed as an extension of enterprise applications to involve two or more enterprises, and it involves many similar challenges to moving from departmental to enterprise applications. E-commerce involving individuals, on the other hand, has challenges similar to information access; indeed, information is a natural good to be sold on-line

Data Warehouses and Data Mining

Data warehousing and data mining are two applications tailored to decision support that address some limitations of OLTP applications. Decisions should take into account not only where things are now but also how they got that way, and they should use an enterprise-wide picture. A *data warehouse* is a very large nonoperational database (managed by a DBMS) that systematically captures information from a number of operational OLTP databases. It provides two major decision-support benefits:

- *History:* OLTP systems represent the present, but the day-to-day operational needs usually do not require maintaining a well-structured operational history. A data warehouse systematically captures the past. It is not updated on a transaction-by-transaction basis as in OLTP, but rather by periodically capturing snapshots of data from OLTP databases.

- *Consolidation:* OLTP applications typically don't present the total picture, because relevant data may be spread across major databases. Day-to-day operational needs may require only information for a single department or a single business process. A data warehouse consolidates information from multiple databases to gain an overall picture of the enterprise operation.

Overall, the goal of a data warehouse is to present a consistent and correct historical image of an entire enterprise, and particularly to uncover relationships among different parts of the enterprise that may not be evident from departmental databases.

Data mining is an application that uses advanced statistical tools to look for unexpected patterns in large amounts of data. Unlike database queries, data mining does not require the user to ask a question, but rather tries to identify what questions *should* have been asked. Its emphasis is predicting future trends and commercial opportunities by uncovering patterns within the massive data in a data warehouse. In a limited way, data mining helps workers extract knowledge from the information residing in a business process.

EXAMPLE: *Data mining is put to a number of uses [OHE96a], such as finding which medical treatments are most effective, uncovering the relationship of personal characteristics to voting patterns for courtroom jurists, relating credit card customer characteristics to the likelihood of default, finding risky behavior patterns for insurance companies, and analyzing stock prices.*

Table 3.4 Three types of e-commerce

Type	Description	Examples
Inter-enterprise	Many enterprises have commercial dealings with other enterprises—they both purchase and supply goods and services.	A manufacturer purchases raw material and parts, a school purchases books and supplies, a government purchases office supplies and automobiles.
Consumer	Many enterprises have commercial dealings with individual consumers, students, or citizens, who purchase goods and services.	An on-line bookstore sells books to consumers, a university may sell on-line courses, a government collects taxes from its citizens.
Interconsumer	Individuals engage in commercial transactions, typically buying and selling used goods, collectibles, or real estate. A third party may serve as an intermediary.	A newspaper offers classified advertisements to help sellers find buyers, an art gallery helps an individual sell a painting on consignment, a real-estate broker helps a seller find a buyer.

because it can also be immediately delivered there. Individual-to-individual commerce can be viewed as a social application, or at least, it can directly exploit social applications.

EXAMPLE: *Several examples in "Examples of Organizational Applications" on page 62 illustrate different types of e-commerce applications. The on-line bookseller, for one, deals not only with consumers ordering books (consumer e-commerce) but also with other enterprises (banks and book distributors).*

3.4.2 Steps in a Sale

Any commercial transaction involving a seller and a buyer involves the four basic steps shown in Table 3.5. Each of these steps—if completed over the network—presents its own challenges and opportunities. The matching of buyers and sellers is an information management challenge, the negotiation of terms and conditions is a social application, and the consummation raises issues of how payments are rendered and information goods delivered securely over the network. Customer service is typically some combination of a social and information management application. Each of these steps is now discussed in greater detail. There are also considerable distinctions in the challenges among the three types of e-commerce, as discussed later.

Matching Buyers and Sellers

There are two issues in the matching of buyers and sellers: How does the buyer find the available sellers (or a seller find willing buyers), and how does the buyer decide which seller to deal with? Making a buyer aware of willing sellers uses

Table 3.5 Four steps in a typical e-commerce transaction

Stage	Description	Typical mechanisms	Floral delivery example
Matching buyers and sellers	The seller makes the buyer aware of what is available for sale. This is partly an information management problem.	The seller has to make buyers aware of goods available, through mechanisms such as advertising, an on-line catalog, or recommender system.	Flowers4u.com buys advertisements on other Web sites. Once in its site, the customer's location is matched with local florists, and flowers4u.com presents the product offerings of those florists.
Negotiating terms and conditions	The buyer and seller reach terms and conditions on the sale, including price, delivery schedule, etc.	Negotiation is supported by work groupware applications. Alternatives to negotiation include fixed-price transactions and auctions.	Participating florists provide fixed-price product offerings, which the customer chooses.
Consummation	The agreed sale is completed by transfer of goods or services and payment.	The buyer conveys a firm order for goods and services based on the outcome of the negotiation, and the buyer conveys payment to the seller.	The customer places an order and payment authorization, which is conveyed to the local florist; it delivers the flowers to the customer.
Customer service	The customer may expect assistance from the seller in usage or repair or replacement of defective goods.	Customer service agents may assist the buyer (this can exploit social applications like remote conferencing or messaging). Alternatively, the seller may publish product information for access by the buyer.	Flowers4u.com has a customer service organization that acts on customer complaints. Many of these complaints are referred to the florist.

information management techniques. The seller usually takes the initiative by publishing information describing goods or services for sale. There are several approaches:

- *Catalog:* In this pull model, the seller publishes a catalog of goods and services for sale and makes it available for a large collection of willing buyers to access at their initiative. The Web is ideal for this purpose, and searching and navigation tools enable the buyer to find appropriate sellers.
- *Advertising:* In this push model, the seller makes a large collection of potential buyers aware of its goods and services for sale by attaching advertisements to other publications interested buyers may access. Advertising has become a substantial source of revenue for commercial Web sites, where the advertisement takes the form of a banner that also serves as a hyperlink to the seller's site.

- *Intermediary recommendation:* In this model, which is neither pull nor push, a buyer may be led to a particular seller or good or service by a recommendation from another satisfied buyer. This is an important role for recommender systems and also occurs informally in discussion forums.

Of course, transactions occasionally work the other way around: The buyer may publish his or her interest in purchasing a particular good or service. Publishers accommodate this in classified advertising, or companies sometimes publish a "request for proposal." In either case, a buyer invites willing sellers to step forward.

Networked computing offers value in all these mechanisms. The Web is a superb medium for either catalogs or advertising. Both the discussion forum and the recommender system offer mechanisms that are especially valuable to buyers in finding and evaluating goods and services for sale—mechanisms that are difficult to reproduce in the physical world.

Negotiating Terms and Conditions

The negotiation step is supported by social applications. This includes the general social applications described in Chapter 2 but, more often, social applications defined specifically for e-commerce.

An important aspect of the terms and conditions is the price. The most common approach in the physical world—goods or services offered at a fixed "take it or leave it" price—also applies directly to e-commerce. The prices are simply published in the catalog. Unlike the physical world where catalogs are printed, however, in e-commerce it is quite feasible to tailor a catalog, including the prices, for each customer. This may be based on estimates of the buyer's willingness to pay. Price discrimination—offering different prices to different customers—is discussed in Chapter 8.

> EXAMPLE: *Airlines, hotels, and other travel providers have long based prices on parameters such as willingness to stay over a weekend. Computerized reservation systems have allowed highly dynamic pricing structures based on not only willingness to pay but also the current status of reservations.*

Countering this trend toward price discrimination is the increasing information available to consumers about seller costs and the ability to more easily compare competitive products and sellers. Consumers thus empowered can drive prices toward seller costs, thereby reducing price variation.

> EXAMPLE: *Automobile dealers have traditionally practiced price discrimination by hardball negotiating tactics with each customer. However, the availability of*

dealer cost information on the network in the United States has driven many sales toward fixed pricing, or consumers may easily obtain competitive bids from multiple dealers.

Networked computing readily supports the auction, a specific mode of negotiation used more sparingly in the physical world (see the sidebar "Auctions").

Consummation

Once the buyer and seller have found one another and the terms and conditions have been negotiated, the consummation completes the sale. Typically it involves the following steps:

- *Order:* The buyer conveys an order to the seller agreeing to the terms and conditions.
- *Fulfillment:* The seller conveys goods to the buyer.
- *Payment:* The buyer conveys payment to the seller.

A major issue in this consummation is security, that is, preventing fraud or cheating on the part of the buyer or seller. The seller should not be able to repudiate an order, and the seller should be able to prove that goods or services were delivered. The buyer should be able to prove that payment was made. Security is an important issue in e-commerce—more so than in the physical world—because the lack of physical presence makes impersonation easier and eliminates one important mechanism for creating trust.

The security issues can get more complicated. An objective may be to insure that *both* fulfillment and payment will occur—absent this, either the buyer or seller can be cheated. In some circumstances, buyers may feel comfortable when dealing with a reputable merchant known to them, and sellers may have recourse (such as generating an adverse credit report) if payment is not received. Nevertheless, the security of the consummation can be considerably improved with the assistance of an intermediary trusted by both the buyer and seller—for example, an escrow agent. The seller may convey the goods to this intermediary (rather than the buyer), and the buyer may also convey payment to this same intermediary (rather than the seller). After verifying that everything is in order, the intermediary distributes the goods to the buyer and the payment to the seller.

Another interesting issue is how to convey electronic payments over the network and do this securely. There are security technologies addressing all these issues, as discussed in Chapter 13, and electronic payments are discussed in Chapter 14.

Auctions

An auction is a dynamic price negotiation involving more than one buyer or seller that operates under specific predefined rules. In the common *English auction* a seller makes an *open offering* of goods for sale, including all terms and conditions except price (such as delivery arrangements and method of payment). During the auction each buyer is informed of the highest previous bid price and has an opportunity to make a higher bid. The auction ends when no higher bids are received within a given time period. There are numerous other ways to conduct an auction.

Normal market mechanisms require a diversity of sellers and buyers to work effectively, so in the physical world the auction has traditionally been used where there are few sellers or unique goods or services are sold (such as paintings or antiques, real estate, or a construction project). The auction has also been used widely for selling used goods among enterprises (such as used automobiles).

The network readily brings together sellers and buyers to conduct an auction, and the precise rules lend themselves to automation. As a result, auctions have become much more popular in cyberspace than in the physical world.

Customer Support

Some products and services require ongoing postsale support, helping buyers learn features or solve problems. Historically this was handled by customer service agents in person or over the telephone. Networked remote conferencing applications enable richer interactions, for example, by displaying diagrams or pictures. For technical goods and services, the network enables agents to help customers in more direct ways, for example, by directly investigating options or configuring software remotely over the network. These customer support operations can be backed up by enterprise applications, for example, communicating "trouble tickets" to repair personnel or tracking product flaws and communicating them to manufacturing and design groups.

The larger opportunity is to increase productivity by giving buyers direct access to information archives where they can find solutions to common problems themselves. There is a trend toward free access to on-line information and a fee for access to customer service agents. Another trend in the support of software applications for individual consumers is not only to fulfill the order by downloading the software over the network but also to distribute new versions and upgrades over the network for automatic installation.

3.4.3   Role of Intermediaries

One advantage often cited for e-commerce is the elimination of intermediaries, or middlemen—layers of distributors and representatives between the supplier or seller and the consumer or buyer. Some intermediaries are indeed circumvented by direct dealings between buyer and seller over the network, which can strip costs, improve responsiveness, and reduce time to market for new products. There remain, nevertheless, compelling advantages to including intermediaries in some types of e-commerce transactions.

EXAMPLE: *Internet portal sites and search engines offer means for a buyer to find available sellers. The escrow agent described earlier provides a trusted connection between fulfillment and payment. An auction requires an auctioneer to enforce the rules. A financial institution may process a credit card payment or transfer of money between accounts.*

The examples in "Examples of Organizational Applications" on page 62 all include intermediaries. Books4u.com and book distributors act as intermediaries between the book publisher and consumer. Books4u.com's added value includes consolidation of books from many publishers and finding a local distributor for fulfillment. Stocks4u.com is an intermediary between consumer and stock market, maintaining a customer account and consolidating many investments. Flowers4u.com is an intermediary between the consumer and a local florist, again consolidating offerings and directing the sale to an appropriate florist for fulfillment.

Basic questions in e-commerce are what is the proper role of intermediaries, and what intermediary functions from the physical world can be eliminated? These and other issues are quite distinct in the three types of e-commerce, which are discussed next.

3.4.4   Consumer E-Commerce

Consumer e-commerce—that involving individual consumers on one or both sides of a commercial transaction—is an area of great activity. Consumer e-commerce allows merchants or even manufacturers to sell directly to consumers without intermediaries, corporations to interact directly with shareholders, government to provide services and benefits directly to citizens, and universities to sell educational material directly to individuals. This has become a major application of the Web, where consumers can easily access any seller using a standard Web browser.

Before the Internet, reaching consumers was limited to retail storefronts, printed mail-order catalogs, and the telephone. While the Internet cannot match the experience of seeing and handling goods in a retail store, compared to the catalog and telephone it offers a richer multimedia interaction, the potential for more tailoring of sales techniques and pricing to individual consumers (see the sidebar "Amazon.com: On-Line Merchant" for an example), and sales and transaction cost savings. A major advantage is the savings in travel time and costs to a consumer. Some opportunities afforded to consumer e-commerce by the suite of applications discussed in Chapter 2, as compared specifically to direct-mail catalogs, are listed in Table 3.6.

Without the personal exchange in a store or even a telephone conversation, impersonation and fraud are a serious issue in consumer e-commerce. It would be easy for an unscrupulous person to post a false storefront on the Web, claiming it represents a well-known brand name. Even more likely are unscrupulous customers attempting to avoid payment by impersonating someone whose credit information they have. Fortunately, there are security technologies, discussed in Chapter 13, that mitigate these dangers.

Another interesting issue for consumer e-commerce is the form of payment. Hard cash is not an option, but some of the same mechanisms requiring financial intermediaries used in retail stores—debit cards and credit cards—transfer readily to the network. In fact, new initiatives on the part of the credit card industry improve on the level of security.

Amazon.com: On-Line Merchant

A merchant that offers goods and services on-line gains an immediate global exposure and potential customer base—an opportunity unmatched in the physical world. An example of this is the bookseller Amazon.com (even its name reflects an exclusive on-line presence). Like any retailer, Amazon.com is an intermediary between the publishers, distributors, and customers, but since its customers browse on-line, Amazon.com need not maintain an extensive inventory. Rather, it passes many orders directly to distributors, as an illustration of an inter-enterprise application.

Amazon.com also illustrates how on-line retailing can offer new features and services. For example, each book the customer considers is accompanied by reviews from other customers (a recommender system), and additional sales are encouraged by listing related titles (based on both topic sales and customer behavior). The interests and behavior of customers can be monitored and presentations tailored accordingly. The customer can request email notification of books in categories of interest (an information push application).

Table 3.6 Comparison of consumer e-commerce with its earlier sibling, direct-mail catalogs

Consideration	Direct-mail catalog	Consumer e-commerce
Matching buyers and sellers	Seller must identify potential customers and invest in mailing catalogs.	Seller publishes product information, and buyer can find through searching, browsing, or navigating.
	Printed catalog can contain only text and pictures.	Multimedia product offering can be interactive and include audio, video, animation.
	Primary source of information about products is the catalog or seller representatives.	Recommender systems can be used to inform consumers about their choices or entice them to buy similar or complementary goods. With negligible shipping costs, samples of information goods can be provided.
Negotiating terms and conditions	Generally, all customers must be offered the same fixed price. The primary mode of price discrimination is versioning (see Chapter 8).	Price discrimination—basing prices on many variables such as customer characteristics or behavior, time or date, or current market conditions—is possible (see Chapter 8).
		Dynamic markets (such as auctions) offer an interesting alternative to fixed offering prices, particularly for goods with poor supply or limited demand.
	A limited set of versions of a product can be offered.	Mass customization can tailor goods to each order. Seller can integrate a product (such as a PC) for each customer.
Consummating the sale	Telephone agents and processing paper orders and payments is labor intensive.	Much order taking, payments, and customer service can be automated. Interacting with a human agent remains an option by using remote conferencing.
	Goods must be shipped by package delivery services.	Information goods and software can be delivered immediately over the network.
	Payment by credit card and check are the only options. Sellers are aware of credit card numbers.	For a credit or debit card purchase, financial information (such as card numbers) can be withheld from seller. Digital cash offers a cash-equivalent option. Lower transaction costs can make smaller payments economically feasible. (See Chapter 14 for further discussion.)
	Telephone agents can provide customer service.	Information about product support can be published for the benefit of buyers. Buyers can participate in discussion forums with other customers.

EXAMPLE: *Secure electronic transactions (SET)—an initiative of Visa International and Mastercard—is a more secure way for consumers to make credit card purchases over the network or in person. SET insures the consumer is the*

*legitimate cardholder (this is called authentication), precludes the merchant
from seeing credit card numbers or other financial information, and precludes
financial institutions from tracking purchases.*

Digital cash is another form of payment analogous to hard cash. Digital cash can
be stored in a computer and used to make direct payments to merchants. Alternatively, it can be stored in a *smartcard*—something that looks similar to a credit
card but has an embedded processor—and used to make cash payments personally or over the network. Some details of SET, digital cash, and smartcards
are described in Chapter 14. One opportunity is to reduce transaction costs to a
level that even payments of a thousandth of a cent (called a millicent) may be
practical, for example, in selling individual snippets of information on the Web.

3.4.5   Interconsumer E-Commerce

Consumers have always been able to sell collectibles or used merchandise to
other consumers, for example, in a consignment store or through classified
advertising in a newspaper or special-interest magazine. The Internet creates a
much larger and geographically dispersed base of potential buyers for an individual who wants to sell something.

The auction has emerged as a primary negotiation mechanism for one individual
selling goods to another. It offers the advantage of a structured negotiation
and, by pitting buyers against one another, is advantageous to a seller.

E X A M P L E :   *eBay is a successful on-line auction aiding individuals in selling to one
another. Each bidder typically negotiates terms (delivery, payment method,
etc.) with the seller before bidding and can inquire about the goods offered for
sale by email. Buyers and sellers can rate one another, and these ratings and
other details of each auction are available on the site.*

A major issue in individual-to-individual e-commerce is trust. The individuals
involved are not usually known to one another, and there are no ready ways to
verify identity or honesty. Auctions can be rigged by including false bidders, or
goods can be purchased but not paid for. These serious problems create a need
and opportunity for intermediaries (such as references or escrow agents) to participate in this type of e-commerce.

3.4.6   Inter-Enterprise E-Commerce

The dominant form of commerce among enterprises is *procurement*, in which
one enterprise purchases goods or services from another. Two varieties of

Table 3.7 Two types of enterprise procurement

Type	Description	Examples
Direct	Obtain raw materials and parts that are directly incorporated into products and services of the procuring enterprise.	An automobile manufacturer purchasing steel, a telecommunications company purchasing switches, a school purchasing textbooks, a telemarketing firm purchasing telecommunications services. Stocks4u.com procures order execution from the stock exchange, books4u.com procures book inventory and delivery services from book distributors (see "Examples of Organizational Applications" on page 62).
Indirect	All other procurements.	An enterprise purchasing office furniture, desktop computers and software, office supplies; a manufacturer purchasing equipment, maintenance, and repair; a consulting firm purchasing travel and entertainment; a research laboratory purchasing scientific supplies.

procurement—direct and indirect—listed in Table 3.7, are distinct from the standpoint of the opportunities and requirements for e-commerce.

Direct Procurement

Direct procurement has ongoing, consistent, and scheduled needs for materials and parts. Thus, the emphasis is on long-term supply relationships—trading long-term contracts and volume purchases for attractive terms and conditions. Enterprises typically have a number of suppliers, who themselves have their own suppliers. Not infrequently, two enterprises are each suppliers to the other. This set of relationships is called a *supply chain* or, more descriptively given the complex web of supply arrangements, a *supply web*.

In a supply web, the commercial relationships are typically long lived and ongoing. The phases of matching sellers and buyers and negotiating terms and conditions are infrequent, and they consume considerable time and resources. While amenable to social applications like remote conferencing, they do not lend themselves to special e-commerce solutions.

The consummation phase of direct procurement is an ongoing business process—one that happens to span enterprises. The functions—controlling and scheduling the delivery of supplies and paying for them—are similar to business processes within an enterprise. Thus, not surprisingly, ERP vendors are extending their products to manage supply webs. Not only can many similar benefits accrue to both supply webs and enterprise applications, but there is a major opportunity in seamlessly connecting the two, so that internal needs can be coordinated with external orders.

EXAMPLE: *Stocks4u.com engages in direct procurement from its information provider (see "On-Line Stock Trading" on page 68). It directly accesses information repositories in these companies as requested by its customers. Its monthly payments to those providers are automatic, directing bank account transfers over the network. Stocks4u.com uses an internal ERP application to manage its accounting and finances, and this is seamlessly connected to those transfers so that internal records are automatically updated.*

There are many differences and obstacles to managing supply webs as compared to enterprise applications:

- Supply webs lack the central administrative control that can make command-and-control decisions on choosing a single technical approach or application vendor.
- Firms must maintain a hands-off business relationship, and thus the information flowing must be restricted and controlled. Inadvertent disclosure of proprietary information must be avoided.
- Commercial relationships always have an associated payments process, which is often not a requirement of an enterprise application.

The administrative problem deserves elaboration, because it creates major requirements for the software solutions discussed later in this book. While enterprises can form bilateral coordination agreements with suppliers, each supplier has other customers and its own suppliers requesting similar coordination. Because of this web relationship, and since each enterprise can't afford a proliferation of systems, achieving the full potential of cross-enterprise applications requires that a large number of enterprises adopt compatible solutions. This is a major technical challenge, especially in light of existing legacy systems in each enterprise.

EXAMPLE: *The U.S. automobile companies (General Motors, Ford, and Chrysler) have been among the most aggressive in using supply-web e-commerce. They have formed the Automotive Network Exchange (ANX), connecting the automobile companies and suppliers. Members can use the network for e-commerce even if the automobile companies are not involved. The reach of the automobile company suppliers is great, so ANX could form the basis for a much broader e-commerce interest group [Jon97].*

Some emerging technologies, including XML (Chapter 15) and distributed object management (Chapter 16), are motivated in part by this problem of achieving compatibility across enterprises.

Dell Computer and Mass Customization

Dell Computer has eliminated traditional distribution channels, thus reducing costs in direct and indirect ways. Customers access the Dell Web site to view a product catalog and custom-configure a computer to their budget and requirements and obtain an immediate price quote. Once an order is input, it generates immediate feedback to various internal business processes—such as manufacturing and purchasing—and directly to parts suppliers. Illustrating mass customization, a computer is manufactured to specification *after* it is ordered, rather than retrofitted by a retailer, distributor, or customer.

Networked computing direct procurement has a long history, particularly in bilateral supply-chain relationships among large firms. *Electronic data interchange* (EDI)—the exchange of business messages in industry-specific standard forms—is a longtime e-commerce application. EDI replaces paper supply/customer documentation, such as purchase orders and invoices, with electronic messages. While previously available only to large firms willing to set up proprietary communication links, the public Internet and the Web make similar capabilities accessible to small companies.

Initially, EDI only included messages like purchase order and invoice, but did not arrange for payment. Electronic payments were the next phase of direct procurement e-commerce, allowing large companies to exchange payments using banks as intermediaries. Called *financial EDI* (FEDI), it authorized electronic funds transfers between bank accounts.

With EDI and FEDI, e-commerce had automated existing inter-enterprise business processes. The next phase—*integrated business logistics* [Kee97]—encompasses a broad swath of processes transcending buying and selling, including coordination of material flows, finished goods, services, and people. It focuses on efficiency, speed, accuracy improvements, and cost savings by changing the nature of business, that is, reorganizing it around networked computing technologies and particularly the public Internet.

E X A M P L E : *Dell Computer is a successful example of integrated business logistics (see the sidebar "Dell Computer and Mass Customization"). Based on a customer's order entered on Dell's Web site, manufacturing builds and ships a customer's computer, requiring no inventory of finished goods. A procurement process can respond quickly by transmitting orders to suppliers, minimizing inventory costs. When new pricing or product strategies are introduced, marketing obtains immediate feedback on their success [SAP97].*

Logistics is really just an extension of the internal business processes of an organization to span the commerce processes with other organizations with which it maintains a business relationship. Logistics using networked applications can reduce organizational barriers externally and flatten the internal management hierarchy of organizations, lowering barriers to customers and suppliers, and integrating internal operations with commercial partners. Logistics heightens customer expectations for speed, accuracy, customization, and cost.

Since ERP vendors are specialists in the automation of business processes, it is natural that they would expand their domain to processes spanning organizations. They call this *supply-chain management,* and it is an area of great activity. This class of cross-enterprise application extends ERP to controlling and monitoring the flow of materials, goods, services, and money through a supply chain. In its most extreme form, supply-chain management can create *virtual enterprises* [Gre96]. In this model of commerce, firms aren't tempted to accumulate all the specialties necessary for the manufacturing and marketing of products. Each individual product is designed, manufactured, and marketed by opportunistically pulling together (and later disbanding) an alliance of firms. In theory, virtual enterprises can react more quickly to market opportunities, and competitively chosen partners can deliver high quality, responsiveness, and low cost (compared to an internal supplier). The impact of networked computing on the boundaries among firms is discussed further in Chapter 8.

There are also opportunities to use dynamic marketplace mechanisms like auctions for direct procurement. These are especially useful for selling excess inventory or opportunistically finding bargains.

E X A M P L E :   *The FastParts Trading Exchange is a Web-based electronic marketplace that allows manufacturers, contract assemblers, component manufacturers, and franchised distributors to sell electronic components to one another. Companies with surplus components offer them for sale in an electronic marketplace with real-time negotiation. FastParts handles the payment and shipping of the parts and certifies sellers to insure quality. FastParts insures that the negotiation and transaction are anonymous, so companies cannot communicate competitive information.*

Indirect Procurement

Indirect procurement pursues the sporadic and opportunistic purchase of goods and services that indirectly support organizational objectives. Many miscellaneous items are purchased, often requiring individual management approval. Indirect procurement has many similarities to consumer e-commerce; often it is an individual in one enterprise ordering goods from a supplier to support his or her job function.

There are numerous opportunities to reduce cost and increase speed by exploiting networking. One trend is to use the Internet to allow workers to directly access the e-commerce sites of suppliers in order to explore options and make purchases. One example of this is Dell Computer, which maintains special e-commerce Web sites for certain customers. Another example is Boeing's PART.

E X A M P L E :   *Boeing's Part Analysis and Requirements Tracking (PART) system uses the Web to extend EDI to small airline customers. It streamlines Boeing's enterprise by allowing customers to search for obscure parts without help from Boeing workers. Significantly, PART also allows an airline's frontline workers (such as airplane mechanics) to directly search for and order parts without help from purchasing.*

Like direct procurement, there are opportunities to save costs by better monitoring of purchases to improve decision support. For example, an enterprise might aggregate purchases from different departments and obtain volume discounts.

EXAMPLE: *Desktop purchasing applications automate, aggregate, and monitor purchases. For example, Ariba offers a successful Operating Resource Management System (ORMS). Other vendors with similar products are Commerce One, Open Market, and Trilogy.*

On the supply side, distributors and suppliers are grouping together to make it easier for customers to adopt electronic procurement without requiring up-front investment. Intermediaries are aggregating product information from multiple vendors to provide an integrated electronic catalog.

Discussion

D3.6 If you have shopped for goods or services in cyberspace, how did the experience compare with visiting a retail store?

D3.7 How do you feel about auctions, both for shopping with a merchant or provider and for buying used goods from other cyberspace citizens?

D3.8 Discuss the similarities and differences between consumer commerce and inter-enterprise indirect procurement.

3.5   Critical Societal Infrastructure

Computing embedded in a plethora of products (such as automobiles and appliances) is "embedded computing in the small." Equally important is "embedded networked computing in the large," which focuses on networked computing embedded within critical infrastructure systems supporting society and the economy. The embedded computers supported by networks serve to monitor and control the infrastructure.

EXAMPLE: *The telephone network uses networked computing to automate and control the switching of telephone calls and also to detect equipment failures or traffic overloads and reconfigure the network accordingly. Similarly the electric power grid uses networked applications to control the flow of electricity and monitor failures. The air traffic control system depends on networked*

*applications to keep track of airplanes and provide controllers with the infor-
mation needed. Ground-based transportation systems—including railroads and
highways—depend increasingly on networked applications to increase capacity
and improve safety. The world's financial systems, including the flow of money
and financial markets, depend on a networked computing infrastructure.*

Although networked computing embedded in infrastructure predates enterprise applications, the two have some striking similarities. In one case, they control systems that are primarily technical and, in the other case, largely social,
although manufacturing is an intermediate case. In both cases, they control the
flow and allocation of resources, including payments.

Like other enterprise applications, there is also a trend toward e-commerce
applications in critical infrastructure.

E X A M P L E :   *One impact of telecommunication deregulation (discussed in Chapter 20) has been the fragmentation of the network service providers, so that
each network connection may require the coordination of complementary service providers. This necessitates payments among these providers for each unit
of end-to-end service provided. Recently, electric utilities have also been
deregulated in the United States, creating a dynamic market for electricity also
supported by e-commerce.*

Discussion

D3.9 Consider and describe the consequences if the electric power system
of a city fails for a day. Repeat for mass transit systems. How much additional cost do you feel is justified to insure reliability in such critical infrastructure?

3.6   Parallels between Social and Computing Systems

After reading this chapter, you should be convinced that networked computing
will be a critical element in the operation of most enterprises, whether they provide critical infrastructure functions, education, government services, or sell
products and services.

What is distinctive about organizational applications of networked computing—
including those embedded within critical infrastructure—is that the networked
computing technologies are only a *part* of a system, which also includes citizens
and workers, procedures, policies and laws, the flow of materials and finished
goods, and potentially many other nontechnological elements. To be most

effective, the technology should not be thought of as simply replacing and auto-mating existing functions (this is also illustrated by the historical example in "Electrification: Lessons from an Earlier Technological Advance" on page 5). The design of organizational processes should create a holistic combination of work-ers and technology, determining what is best delegated to technology and what can best be accomplished by people, and defining the nature of the interaction between the two.

Although not evident yet, there are remarkable parallels between the issues addressed in this chapter—how networked applications serve users and enter-prises—and how networked applications are *internally* organized and imple-mented, which is the subject of much of the remainder of this book. Examples of this abound:

- Enterprises (and other social systems) must delegate responsibilities to dif-ferent people, and networked applications must delegate responsibilities to different computers.
- People must communicate and coordinate themselves to accomplish defined tasks and so must the pieces of a networked application.
- People must figure out how to avoid conflicts when they share a common task or resource and so must networked computers.
- Society must allocate finite resources in efficient fashion—such as managing highway congestion, limited water and electricity—and so must the network and the computers attached to it.
- Social systems must cope with breakdowns, natural disasters, criminal behavior, and such occurrences, and so must computer systems.

You are urged to reflect on these parallels throughout the remainder of the book. Many of the same issues arise in social contexts and the internal imple-mentation of networked applications, and many of the solutions are directly analogous, or at least recognizable. This should help you navigate the many technical issues to be uncovered subsequently, and the book aids this by provid-ing numerous analogies. The ideas and concepts applied to the design of com-puter systems may also suggest similar concepts that can be exploited in the design of social systems, such as enterprises. There is doubtless much cross-fertilization that can occur between organizational theory and networked com-puting technology.

3.7 *Open Issues

Organizational applications raise a number of open issues, such as how they are invented and realized, and the impact they have.

3.7.1   The Productivity Paradox

Economists find it difficult to discern productivity gains in organizations that can be attributed to networked computing. Macroscopically, in the United States, overall productivity growth has slowed the last couple of decades just as networked computing became more prevalent. Microscopically, correlations between the financial results of individual firms and networked computing investments are difficult to discern. While this seems counterintuitive, there are a few relevant observations:

- Networked computing has its biggest impact on the service sector, where productivity is notoriously difficult to measure. One of its biggest impacts has been on customer service, which bolsters customer satisfaction rather than productivity.
- Much of the benefit is in quality, which is difficult to separate from productivity when measuring improvement. For example, networked computing enables solitary users to produce higher-quality documents (but perhaps consuming more time) and run financial projections not previously possible (but also consuming time).
- Most importantly, automating existing processes is not where the major productivity gains are expected. Rather, both the processes and the social dimension of the enterprises that incorporate them have to be reengineered to make most effective use of the technology [Wal89].

So, the question is "when will substantial and documented productivity gains from networked computing technologies appear?" Recent research is starting to yield preliminary evidence of productivity gains, but even more striking is the large variation in results among different organizations. This emphasizes that it really matters how networked computing is used, and the maximum benefits arise only with complementary investments in new strategies, new processes, and new organizations [Bry98]. This view is bolstered by some spectacular competitive successes (at the expense of their more traditional rivals) by companies organized from scratch around networked computing (such as E*TRADE, Dell Computer, and Amazon.com). All the hypothetical companies described in "Examples of Organizational Applications" on page 62 would be positioned very well against less technologically astute rivals.

3.7.2   How Are New Organizational Applications Invented and Developed?

Automation of existing processes does not fully realize the potential of networked computing. The biggest gains are achieved when application design is integral to the overall business process design, including human resource and organizational design. Application design is thus not primarily a technical activity, and yet technical issues (such as performance, cost-effectiveness, and flexibility) are also important. Thus, the traditional gulf between nontechnical and technical workers, where the former rely on the latter to define the applications and infrastructure and the latter rely on the former to define the application context, cannot meet the challenge of seamless interworking of the enterprise and its enabling networked applications. Can a collaboration of management with information technologists continue to work, or is a new cadre of technically astute managers (or managerially astute technologists) needed? In fact, one goal of this book is to help create precisely these individuals.

3.7.3 Better Accommodating Change

An obvious attribute of modern commerce is continual change. Firms recast their products rapidly, the product birth and obsolescence cycle shortens, reorganization is endemic, and networked computing penetrates more deeply. The boundaries of firms change with relentless mergers, acquisitions, and divestitures. These environmental factors place severe stress on information systems, which would ideally ease the path to change rather than inhibit it. An important objective—but one not achieved with the current state of technology—is flexible applications that readily adapt to changing needs. This is a serious challenge not only to the applications themselves but also to the infrastructure that supports them, and one that is arguably not met by today's organizational applications. Flexibility is an important requirement that should be kept in mind in the subsequent chapters. The conceptualization and design of any application should take into account future needs, the details of which usually cannot be anticipated.

Review

Organizational applications serve work groups, operations, commerce, decision support, information management, and consumer relationships. Over time they have expanded from the department, to the enterprise, to multiple enterprises, and to consumer outreach (as enabled by the Internet).

Departmental applications are realized using centralized and client-server computing, and they include on-line transaction processing (OLTP). Enterprise applications support a business process, and reengineering is a redesign of a business process to make most advantageous use of both workers and networked computing. For common business processes, enterprise resource planning (ERP) is a class of packaged, configurable, and extensible applications.

Enterprise applications generally support operations, forecasting and planning, and monitoring for decision support.

Enterprises find knowledge an asset with growing importance, and applications such as data mining and knowledge warehouses support the expeditious capture, organized archival, and dissemination of knowledge.

The commercial relationships among enterprises and with consumers are supported by e-commerce applications, which come in three distinct flavors: inter-enterprise, consumer, and interconsumer. Network computing offers some innovative new ways of conducting commerce.

An e-commerce transaction has four phases: matching buyers and sellers, negotiation of terms of sale, consummation, and customer service. Recommender systems are a good method of matching buyers and sellers, and auctions for negotiation of terms are common in networked computing.

Embedded networked computing is increasingly used for the control of critical societal infrastructure. This application has stringent reliability and security requirements.

Key Concepts

Evolution from departmental to enterprise to commerce

Departmental applications:

- On-line transaction processing (OLTP)
- Workflow

Business processes:

- Business transformation
- Enterprise resource planning (ERP)

Decision support:

- Data warehouse
- Data mining

E-commerce:

- Inter-enterprise, consumer, and interconsumer
- Matching buyers and sellers, negotiation of terms, consummation (fulfillment and payment), and customer service
- Direct and indirect procurement

Further Reading

There have been a number of books on business transformation and business processes. [Dav93] was an early influential book, and a more recent treatise is [Set98]. A textbook that essentially expands on this chapter and the next is [Lau99]. [Kee97] is a good introduction to e-commerce, with an extensive glossary.

Exercises

E3.1 List five types of information you believe should be stored in a mission-critical enterprise database for an insurance company. General categories of information will do; you don't have to get detailed.

E3.2 Repeat Exercise 3.1, but this time list at least five workflow applications that you believe would benefit the insurance company. Describe the general steps to the workflow and how information flows among those steps.

E3.3 Consider the "admissions and records" function of a university, which tracks a student from the time of application through graduation. Do a rough outline of the business process associated with this. What departmental activities are involved, and what is the flow of information among these activities?

E3.4 Suppose you are an insurance adjuster working with a customer (who has suffered a catastrophic loss) and with that customer's insurance sales agent to arrive at a settlement figure. Describe what considerations will come into play. What features of a groupware application supporting this settlement process do you believe would be useful?

E3.5 Suppose you purchase a book from books4u.com using a credit card (see "On-Line Bookselling" on page 66). List all the individual steps, from the time you first access the merchant's Web site until the purchase appears on your credit card bill.

E3.6 Consider the business relationship between a hypothetical car manufacturer and an outside supplier of its gasoline engines. Assuming that the routine business between these two manufacturers is conducted by interorganizational direct procurement e-commerce, list ten other capabilities you believe would be valuable to these two companies and could be supported by social or information management applications.

E3.7 Come up with some ideas to use unique networked computing capabilities with the goal of increasing sales and customer satisfaction, and describe how they would be valuable. Do this specifically for any two of the following:

   a. Selling golf equipment

   b. Selling music discs

   c. Selling gift certificates for manicures

   d. A matchmaking service

E3.8   For an on-line auction in which consumers sell items to one another, make a list of your ideas for how the application could give assurance to the buyer as to the trustworthiness of the seller. Do this specifically for one of the following types of goods:

   a. Used personal computers

   b. Rare coins

   c. Used music discs

E3.9   Describe some opportunities in the following categories that can be incorporated into the books4u.com organization (see "On-Line Bookselling" on page 66):

   a. ERP applications that are likely to be available and widely used across different industries

   b. Enterprise applications that may have to be developed specifically to match books4u.com's business

   c. Inter-enterprise applications that books4u.com may custom-develop to improve its efficiency in dealing with its enterprise partners

E3.10   Repeat Exercise 3.9 for stocks4u.com (see "On-Line Stock Trading" on page 68).

E3.11   Repeat Exercise 3.9 for flowers4u.com (see "Floral Delivery Service" on page 69).

Architecture

Architecture divides a
networked computing
system and application into
interacting functional
subsystems that can be
developed independently,
by different companies if
appropriate.

PART

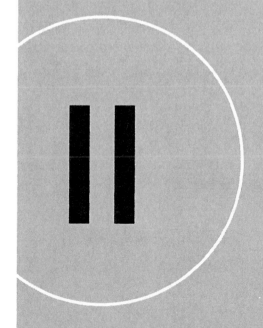

Information Technology

Chapter 2 and Chapter 3 gave an overview of the general classes of networked applications but did not discuss how those applications are actually realized. The technological basis of networked applications is information technology—the suite of computing and communications technologies that empower users and organizations to capture, store, communicate, and manipulate information. These technologies provide an infrastructure—those capabilities not specific to any application, but which support *all* applications—together with application-specific software.

ANALOGY: *A start-up in the physical world would be supported by an infrastructure, including highways, postal and package delivery systems, banking, accountants, and lawyers. This infrastructure is exploited by company-specific business processes.*

To conceptualize good applications, it helps immensely to have an appreciation for the capabilities and limitations of the infrastructure that supports them. This chapter gives an overview of the full suite of information technologies and how they contribute to networked applications. The first issue is how information technology represents its basic commodity—information. Then the equipment (computers and the network) and infrastructure software are described. Finally, the global Internet and its intranet and extranet cousins are described. This chapter, by giving a general introduction to these information technologies, can serve as a direct jumping-off point for many later chapters in this book.

The first topics of this chapter are the information that forms the heart of networked applications and how that information is represented in the computers and network. Then the equipment and software building blocks of the infrastructure are described. The important issue of how the application is mapped

A single bit can conveniently be represented by a *switch*, which is either on or off. Switches are easy to implement in modern electronics.

ANALOGY: *A common light switch is either on or off. It can store one bit of information, if you associate "off" with "0" and "on" with "1." The light can also be used to communicate information. For example, the light "on" might signal to somebody outside that you are at home, and "off" might tell them you are not at home.*

As this analogy suggests, bits are stored in computers by using tiny switches, and they are transmitted over long distances by sending pulses of light through strands of glass called *optical fibers*. Overall, bits can be manipulated, stored, and communicated much faster than physical entities (such as letters and packages).

onto the infrastructure is then followed by a description of the most ubiquitous network, the Internet.

4.1   Information Content

Just as the industrial economy deals with raw materials and finished goods, the emerging information economy focuses on the creation, capture, storage, retrieval, and manipulation of information and knowledge. "Information" in this context includes text and numbers, as well as other media such as art, video entertainment, games, money and financial instruments, and many other goods and services that don't have a physical presence. "Knowledge" means understanding and judgement based on large amounts of information, and it represents an intangible but critically important asset of most organizations.

Just as transportation and machinery form the technological foundation of the industrial economy, networks and computers are the technological foundation of the information economy. The basic commodity they manipulate is *information content*. What they actually do with or to this content depends on two things—the software controlling the computers and the actions of users or other external events.

4.1.1   Bits as a Building Block

In networked computing, information takes the form of *bits*. A single bit can assume the values "0" or "1." A collection of n bits can assume a larger number of values—2^n to be precise. Bits are universally used in information technology because they are conveniently stored, transmitted, and manipulated using modern electronics and photonics technologies (see the sidebar "Bits Are Easy to Manipulate, Store, and Communicate"). Physical goods, broken down into their most fundamental and indivisible elements, are composed of atoms. Atoms are the building blocks of the physical world, just as bits are the building blocks of computer-mediated information content [Neg96].

4.1.2   Information Is Represented by Data

Not all information in the physical world is composed of bits—for example, when you listen to the radio, the sound reaching your ears is a pressure wave in the air. However, it is possible to *represent* any information (including sound) by bits (see the sidebar "Any Information Can Be Represented by Bits"). In information technology, the term data is applied to any collection of bits that represents information. Representation means that the data temporarily takes the place of the information, in such a way that the original information can be recovered from it.

EXAMPLE: *If you ask someone if she has a million dollars, her yes or no answer is information. It can be represented in a computer by one bit—"1" represents "yes" and "0" represents "no." As a more sophisticated representation, the sound of that person's answer can be represented by data in the computer, communicated over the network in that form, and later, the original sound pressure wave can be recovered. This would capture not only the yes or no answer but also her voice inflection and emotion.*

Any representation of information by data is not unique, but is determined by a presumed *structure* and *interpretation* of the data. The structure refers to how the bits are arranged, and the interpretation refers to the significance of the bits to the user or application interpreting them as information.

EXAMPLE: *There are two ways to represent a yes or no answer by one bit—"yes" can be represented by either "0" or "1." The recovery of the yes or no answer from its representation as a bit requires knowledge of that interpretation.*

The collection of bits "101111" can represent the number "47," in the sense that "101111" can temporarily take the place of "47," and "47" can be recovered from "101111" by interpreting it as a base-two number, performing the calculation:

$$2^5 + 2^3 + 2^2 + 2^1 + 2^0 = 47$$

It is important to note that the data represents the number "47" only with the base-two arithmetic interpretation added. Without knowledge of this interpretation, "101111" could represent a lot of other things; for example, it could just as easily represent a number with the weighting attached to each bit reversed.

Additional interpretation might be added to the number "47" as the balance in a bank account in dollars. This illustrates that interpretation is often added incrementally—in this case, first the data represents a number, and second that number represents a bank balance.

The important point of this example is that data does not by itself represent anything meaningful. It is only when a structure is presumed and interpretation is added to the data that information emerges. This is illustrated in Figure 4.1, where information is first represented by data and subsequently recovered from the data. The representation assumes some specific structure and interpretation, which is necessary to recover the information.

Any Information Can Be Represented by Bits

Text such as you're reading now can be represented as bits by associating each character in the English language with a set of seven bits. Representation means that the original text can be recovered from the bits.

EXAMPLE: *Unique sequences of seven bits can be assigned to each of the letters in the English alphabet, for example:*

a ↔ 0000000,

b ↔ 0000001,

c ↔ 0000010,

etc.

Altogether, 128 characters could be represented this way—more than enough for the twenty-six letters of the alphabet and punctuation marks.

In a similar manner, bits can be used to represent all written languages, including those based on ideographs (such as Chinese). Because written language is formed of characters (in English or Arabic) or ideographs (in Asian languages), it is *discrete*. This means that it is represented by characters drawn from a finite alphabet. The alphabet can be small, as in English, or as large as the vocabulary, as in ideographs. Anything discrete can be represented as bits by simply associating an appropriate number of bits with each member of the alphabet.

Less obviously, a sequence of bits can also represent audio (such as a voice or music recording), images (such as pictures taken by a camera), and video. Unlike written language, these media are *analog* (meaning continuous, not discrete, in amplitude and time), but they can be approximated by bits with sufficient accuracy that a human couldn't tell the difference (see Chapter 20).

The representation of information by bits is a special case of a *digital* representation, meaning a representation in terms of numbers. A bit is just a digit with a base of two, but any other base (such as base ten) would be equally effective. In fact, "bit" is short for "binary digit."

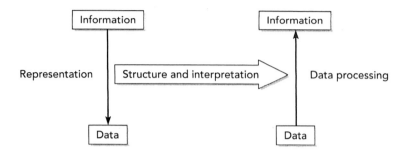

Figure 4.1 Information can be represented as data, and later recovered, but only if the data is accompanied by structure and interpretation

EXAMPLE: *Stocks4u.com stores its customer information, so that whenever customers log in, all the relevant information is available, for example, account information (stocks they own, cash balance) and contact information (name, telephone number, address, etc.) (see "On-Line Stock Trading" on page 68). All this information is represented as numbers and character strings, which in turn are represented as bits. The structure of this representation groups the bits according to these numbers and character strings. The interpretation specifies not only the number or character string, but also the significance of that number or character string to the application. For example, the cash balance is interpreted as dollars and cents, whereas for a stock, a number is interpreted as the number of shares.*

The last example illustrates how business information like a bank balance can be represented by data. Multimedia information, like audio and video, can also be represented by data.

EXAMPLE: *A picture, which is information because it conveys a scene that affects and informs the viewer, is shown on the left of Figure 4.2. (Although this picture is displayed on a page of this book, you can easily imagine it being represented in the memory of a computer and displayed on a computer screen.) This picture is actually approximated by square rectangles called pixels—each with an appropriate intensity—as evident in the blowup of a small portion of the picture on the right. The intensity of each pixel is then represented by eight bits, so that there are actually only 256 possible represented intensities. The original picture is 300 pixels high by 200 pixels wide, so it actually requires a substantial amount of data to represent it—480,000 bits to be exact. The amount of data required can be reduced substantially by compression, as described in Chapter 20.*

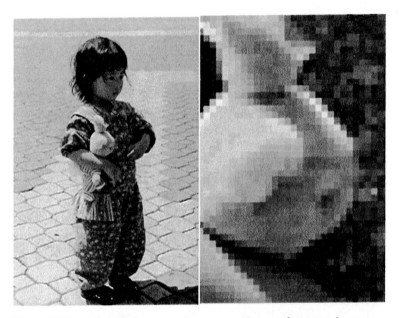

Figure 4.2 Illustration of the approximate representation of a picture by square pixels, each pixel intensity represented by eight bits of data

A matter of importance to information technology is the simplicity and universality of the bits composing data, and the fact that this data can represent all types of information. This makes possible computers, equipment, and software that can flexibly manipulate different types of information, and also combine different types of information as necessary. Older technologies (such as books or newspapers) lack this capability. In effect, bits are a *universal alphabet* for representing and manipulating all forms of information.

EXAMPLE: *In a remote conferencing application, information may consist of different media, such as audio to support a voice conversation, video to support video conferencing, and documents that are viewed and edited on the screen. Each of these information media can be represented by data, for example, for communication across the network. Because all data consists of bits and looks essentially the same, the infrastructure does not need to be aware of the different media. New media can be added without affecting the infrastructure.*

4.1.3   Data Processing

If particular data is known to represent information, then that information can be recovered from the data—if the structure and interpretation that should be applied to the data is known. This recovery is accomplished in a computer by *data processing.* Data processing is guided by a computer program—a sequence of processing steps guided by computer instructions—which embodies the presumed structure and interpretation of the data. Programming is discussed further in Chapter 11.

As implied by Figure 4.1, it is typical to capture information—for example, by a microphone, camera, or keyboard—and represent it as data in a computer's storage, communicate it over a network, and later recover the original information by data processing.

EXAMPLE: *If you are given the data "101111" and told that it has a structure as base-two arithmetic representation of a number with the least-significant bit on the right, you could easily recover the number "47" using a calculation like the equation on page 109, which is a simple example of data processing.*

Recovering the picture in Figure 4.2 from the data representing it requires, first, knowledge that the data is structured as eight-bit values—each such value interpreted as the intensity of a pixel—from which an intensity can be computed for each pixel value. Second, it requires the interpretation of 60,000 pixels as a 200 × 300 array. Armed with this interpretation, the data processing can reconstruct and display it as information in the form of a picture on a computer screen.

Note the two distinct elements in this example. The representation of the picture as data is stored in the computer memory (or perhaps a disk). The structure and interpretation is embodied in a computer program that guides the processing of this data to display the picture on the screen. Of course, the information technology can also manipulate and communicate the information—in its data representation—in ways described in the remainder of this chapter and much of this book.

EXAMPLE: *As a simple example, data may represent a picture in color, but in order to print the picture on a black-and-white printer, the representation may have to be converted from color to black and white.*

This perspective on data and information is distinct from the application perspective of "What Is Information?" on page 39, where information was defined from a user's perspective as patterns or meaning that influence the user in some recognizable way—such as changes in perspective, understanding, or behavior. Within the world of information technology itself, the information can be defined more narrowly as "structure and interpretation added to data." Of course, there is a connection between these differing perspectives. Often, the purpose of data processing is to offer information in a form that influences the user.

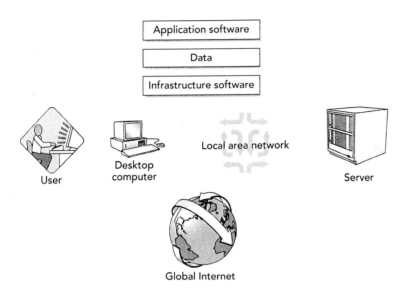

Figure 4.3 Building blocks of networked computing applications

Discussion

D4.1 Compare the representation of information in networked computing (collections of bits) with other ways to store or communicate information, such as books, videotapes, television, voice conversation, and facial expressions. Could information in those other contexts be represented digitally?

4.2 Building Blocks

Data processing requires both equipment and software building blocks. These include physical elements (user, computer, network, etc.) and logical and informational elements (information content, infrastructure and application software, etc.). The physical elements are illustrated in Figure 4.3 and briefly described in Table 4.1.

A networked computing infrastructure includes computers (for computation, information processing, and user interface), a network for communication among these computers, and a lot of software. This equipment and software requires administrative and operational support, and some of it is leased from and operated by service providers (see Chapter 9). None of the elements in Figure 4.3 and Table 4.1 is particularly useful in and of itself—except of course the users! All these elements must be combined in a *system* to accomplish the goals of the application.

Table 4.1 Description of the building blocks shown in Figure 4.3

Building block	Description	Typical function
User	Person who interacts with and derives benefit from a networked computing application.	Captures, enters, or retrieves information and directs its processing.
Desktop computer or host (or personal computer or client computer)	A computer directly accessed by the user that acts as an interface between user and application. A computer connected to the Internet is called a host.	Its screen displays windows, menus, graphics, graphs, etc.; and its keyboard, pointing device, camera, and microphone accept input from the user.
Server computer or host	A computer not directly associated with a user, usually missing a display, keyboard, or pointing device (except perhaps for administrative purposes). Often has substantial computing power and storage capacity and peripherals.	Stores, accesses, and manipulates large repositories of data, and realizes the logic of how the data is processed in light of user directives.
Application software	The programs running on the clients and servers realizing application functionality.	Embodies the unique functionality of the application (Chapter 10).
Data	The collection of bits representing—within the computer and network—the information manipulated by the application.	The form in which information is stored, processed, and communicated.
Infrastructure software	The programs running on the computers and serving many common needs for all applications.	Provides communication support (Chapter 12), manages resources (Chapter 15) and other functions.
Network	The communication infrastructure connecting the computers running an application. This may be a local area network (LAN) or a wide area network (WAN). The global Internet interconnects many networks.	Allows the different hosts to communicate data to one another (Chapter 18).

4.3   System Architecture

Any significant activity, such as a conference, business, or school, must be organized to be successful. Likewise, something as complex as a computing system also requires an internal organization to work properly (or to work at all). This organization takes the form of what technologists call a system. Roughly speaking, a system is something that puts together building blocks (such as those mentioned in the previous section) that interact to accomplish some higher-level purpose—a purpose that the building blocks themselves could not individually accomplish. Systems can be social (like an organization) or technical (like a networked computing system).

A more technical definition of a system is a composition of subsystems that cooperate to accomplish some higher purpose. A *subsystem* is an element within the system that performs some narrower well-defined function on behalf of the system and cannot be subdivided and still perform that function.

E X A M P L E :   *A telephone system, consisting of switches, transmission systems, and telephones is a system; these subsystems work together to provide telephone service. An electric power system consists of generation facilities, high-voltage transmission lines, and local distribution, and it provides power to the people. The computer infrastructure—computers and network—is a system. The government is a system consisting of executive, legislative, and judicial elements, and a bureaucracy, and provides various services to the citizenry.*

In practice, one person, group, or even organization cannot deal with the entire system as a whole. Thus, the purpose of decomposing the system into subsystems is so that the subsystems can be dealt with as individual units, independently of each other and independently of the system (insofar as practical).

4.3.1   Elements of Any Architecture

The *architecture* of a system encompasses its structure and organizing principles. An architecture has the three basic properties—decomposition, functionality, and interaction—described in Table 4.2. The basic purpose of architecture is divide and conquer—by decomposing the system into subsystems with more specialized functionality, the system can be designed, maintained, and updated more easily. Architecture is everywhere—in nature and social systems as well as computing systems (see the sidebar "Architecture Is Common").

Table 4.2 Basic elements of a system architecture

Property	Description	Government analogy
Decomposition	A partitioning of the system into individual subsystems that interact to realize the higher purposes of the system.	A government is partitioned into executive, legislative, and judicial branches.
Functionality	The specialized capabilities assigned to each subsystem supporting the overall system purposes.	The legislature makes laws, the executive enforces laws, and the judiciary determines the guilt or innocence of accused lawbreakers.
Interaction	How the subsystems communicate and cooperate to support the system purposes.	The executive branch informs the legislature of the need for new laws and brings accused lawbreakers before the judiciary.

Architecture Is Common

Architecture is a technique used by nature to construct physical and biological systems, as well as by people to construct buildings and social systems. The motivations are basically the same as computer systems—by dividing into subsystems with specialized functions that interact, the system becomes more manageable.

A building architecture is determined with its intended purpose (business, education, etc.) in mind. It is decomposed into rooms, halls, stairways, electricity, plumbing, etc.—their functionality determined by their specialized purpose. These subsystems interact in ways determined partly by connections (the hallway has doors into each room, and the stairs connect the floors).

Living organisms have specialized parts (cells, bones, organs, etc.), a specialized set of capabilities of each part, and ways those parts interact to achieve the overall functioning of the organism. While much of the history of biology has focused on understanding life in terms of chemical and molecular processes, architecture has recently become appreciated as a remarkable unifying and organizing principle across all forms of life [Ing98].

A business transformation project defines an architecture for a business process. It is decomposed into activities, with each activity having a specific functionality and a predefined cooperation (flow of information and resources) among them.

ANALOGY: The framers of the U.S. Constitution—who were the architects of the U.S. government—first decided on the roles and limitations of the federal government. Taking this "functionality" into account, they decomposed the government into executive, legislative, and judicial branches. Next, they determined the responsibilities and powers of each branch, along with their interaction.

Each of the building blocks in Figure 4.3 is, from an architectural perspective, a subsystem. The networked computing system composed of these subsystems, shown in Figure 4.4, is composed of two client hosts and a server host. Over the network, all these hosts can communicate with one another, but in particular, as shown by the dashed lines, each client can communicate with the server. With this architecture, a number of networked applications discussed in Chapter 2 and Chapter 3 can be realized by the addition of application software.

EXAMPLE: A user sitting at one client can send email to the user at the other client. Typically, the email will be stored in the server while it waits for the user to access it from that other client. The users can participate in a discussion forum, where the messages in the forum are stored in the server. Each of the users can independently access information that may be stored in the server—for example, by using a Web browser.

4.3.2   Emergence

The purpose of composing interacting subsystems as a system is to achieve the higher purposes of the system—purposes that could not be achieved by the subsystems in isolation. This higher-order behavior that emerges because the subsystems are composed is called emergence.

EXAMPLE: None of the subsystems of an airplane—such as an engine or cockpit—can fly. When they are composed into the airplane, the ability to fly emerges. A network in isolation would be fairly useless because there would be no data for it to communicate. Two computers cannot by themselves communicate with one another. When two computers are connected to a network, forming a system, the ability of the computers to communicate data to one another emerges.

4.3.3   Hierarchy

As illustrated abstractly in Figure 4.5, many systems have a hierarchical decomposition, meaning that subsystems are themselves systems with an internal decomposition into interacting subsystems. This is true of most systems, not only computer systems (see the sidebar "Hierarchy Is Common"). A computing

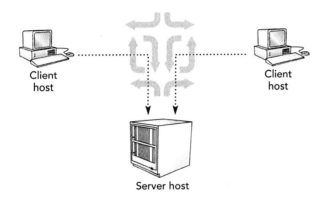

Figure 4.4 Architecture of a simple networked computing system

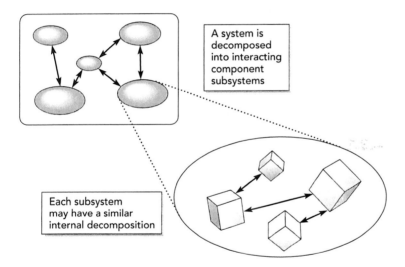

Figure 4.5 A hierarchical decomposition of a system into subsystems

system follows this hierarchical model. At the top level, the subsystems include hosts, network, and application and infrastructure software, but each of these subsystems is itself decomposed into internal subsystems.

This hierarchical organization is necessary to contain the inherent complexity of a computing system or any other system (see Chapter 10). The idea is that subsystems can be dealt with separately, and as independently as possible, but then those subsystems can themselves be considered systems and be similarly decomposed.

Hierarchy Is Common

Not only computer systems display hierarchy in decomposition. For example, biological organisms are composed of organs, those organs are composed of cells, and cells themselves have an elaborate internal structure. The universe as seen from Earth has galaxies, which are composed of stars, which are composed of molecules, which are composed of atoms.

The same is true of social systems. If the government is viewed as a system, each branch of government is a subsystem internally decomposed into its own subsystems (agencies, departments, etc.). All large organizations, including enterprises and universities, are decomposed hierarchically like this.

The idea of a subsystem is tied intimately to the organization of the computer and communications industries (see Chapter 7). If the subsystems are independent, they can be designed and manufactured (for hardware) or programmed (for software) by different companies. These subsystems can then be assembled into a system. Each subsystem supplier may itself have its own suppliers, and this is where hierarchy comes in, since each subsystem is then decomposed into its own subsystems.

EXAMPLE: *Each host has internal subsystems—one or more microprocessors (single-chip processing units), memory, and storage—that cooperate to execute a software program. A computer manufacturer such as Dell or Compaq purchases most of those subsystems from other manufacturers. Each of these is a system; for example, a microprocessor's functionality (running program instructions) requires an internal decomposition into subsystems (transistors, for example).*

Eventually, this hierarchical decomposition must terminate—an element in a subsystem can no longer be decomposed. In this case, the element is said to be *atomic*, meaning it can't be further subdivided.

4.4 Networked Computing Infrastructure

A networked application requires application software and the networked computing infrastructure. Each of these is a subsystem, and they interact to realize the application functionality. The application software is specific to the particular application (although it can also incorporate reusable elements called software components, as discussed in Chapter 10). The infrastructure is hierarchically decomposed into subsystems, which are generic and not designed with a particular application in mind. The cost of development and deployment of applications can be minimized by including within the infrastructure as much common functionality—things that many applications need—as can be identified. In particular, a networked computing infrastructure supports four important capabilities needed by most applications:

- *Communication across distance*—even within the same building—is supported by the network, which allows computers to communicate data to one another.
- *Communication across time* is provided by computer storage. Deferred social and information management applications permit users to participate at times of their choosing, so there is a need to temporarily or permanently store information. Business applications typically capture and manage mas-

sive amounts of data, which should be retained for later access over months and years.

- *Computation and logic* are defined by software programs. Most applications require internal logic governing how they react to user (or other) inputs, and many require numeric computations.
- *Human-computer interface*. Many applications (particularly social and information management) support users in their activity or job (including interaction, collaboration, information management, etc.). The application governs user interaction—this is called the *presentation*—by allowing the user to input data (through a keyboard, mouse, microphone, television camera, etc.) and extract information (graphics, video, audio, etc.).

The overall infrastructure and its relation to the application are illustrated in Figure 4.6 for the simplest of situations: a single client host supporting a single user, and a server host providing a portion of the application.

As mentioned in Table 4.1 on page 114, any computer connected to the Internet is—from the network perspective—known as a host. The terminology originates from the observation that the computer "hosts" the software (both infrastructure and application). Since this book is concerned with networked computing, all computers of interest are hosts. (The term host was also used to connote a mainframe in the earlier days of centralized computing, leading to some terminology confusion.) The desktop computer directly supporting the user is called a client host (or just client), and the computer not associated with the user is called the server host (or just server—see Table 4.1). The client and server hosts can communicate with one another over the network. Together, the network and computers form the equipment portion of the infrastructure. Equipment comprises *hardware* (electronics, circuit boards, and other physical realizations) and any embedded software bundled and sold with the hardware (increasingly, equipment functionality is realized by software as well as hardware). Much software is also sold separately, including infrastructure software (Chapter 6) and application software (Chapter 10).

If there are two hosts, as shown in Figure 4.6, the application functionality must be partitioned between them. The partitioning shown in Figure 4.6 is typical for this simple configuration. The presentation—everything particular to the interaction with the user, including the human-computer interface—runs on the client host. Other aspects of the application, such as data management, computation, and logic, may run in the server host. The portion of application software running on the client host is also called the client, and the portion running on the server host is also called the server. This application partitioning issue is discussed further later in this chapter.

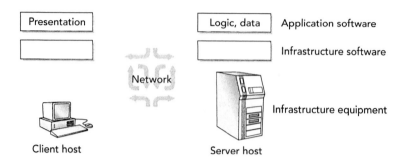

Figure 4.6 General structure of the infrastructure and application in the simplest case

4.4.1   Infrastructure Software Layering

A simplified view of the architecture of the equipment and software within a single host is shown in Figure 4.7. There are two parallel infrastructures, one supporting communication across distance (labeled "Communications"), and the communication across time (labeled "Storage"). Since these infrastructures act on behalf of the application, they are said to provide communication and storage services. The network equipment (discussed next) provides the host-to-host communication of data, and storage peripherals (such as magnetic disks and tapes) provide the storage of data. However, these functions require, in addition to the equipment, substantial infrastructure software. This software performs many important functions and is described in greater detail in Part V of this book.

A key idea embodied in the infrastructure software subsystem architecture is *layering*—a specific type of decomposition. The infrastructure is decomposed into layers, each of which depends on the layer below. Each layer is said to provide services to the layer above by building on services provided to it by the layer below and adding capabilities of its own. Also, each layer interacts with only the layers immediately below and above, so that each layer effectively isolates layers above it from layers below it. Thus, layering achieves additional capability by adding to the infrastructure, using what already exists rather than starting from scratch. (This superficially resembles the elaboration of brain structure in biological evolution.)

The software and equipment are layered; in particular, the software is thought of as "riding on top of" the equipment, utilizing equipment capabilities to run programs, communicate among hosts, etc. The software is itself layered, with two major layers shown in Figure 4.7—the middleware and the *operating system*. The operating system is familiar to all users of personal computers, who

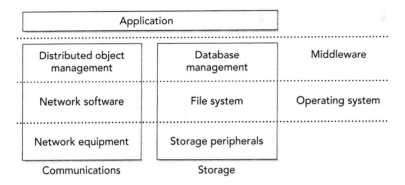

Figure 4.7 A simplified layered architecture of the infrastructure software and equipment

usually use the Windows, MacOS, or UNIX operating system. Without exception, every host has its own operating system, and in a networked computing system, different hosts may have different operating systems. The operating system is the most important piece of infrastructure software and has many invaluable functions (see the sidebar "Functions of an Operating System").

The middleware layer sits between the operating system and the application. It is optional—some networked applications will employ middleware, and others won't. There are different types of middleware, and any specific application will choose one or more types. One important middleware function is isolating an application partitioned across hosts from differences among operating systems on those hosts. Specific examples of middleware functions are distributed object management, which simplifies communications and is discussed in Chapter 16, and database management, which provides many capabilities in data storage and management and is discussed later in this chapter and in Chapter 15.

The architecture of infrastructure software, and the motivations and principles behind layering, are considered in greater depth in Chapter 6.

4.4.2 Communications

The communications subsystems in the infrastructure allow hosts to communicate over distance in the course of realizing a networked application. As shown in Figure 4.7, the main elements of this subsystem are the software managing this communication—within a host, this is one major function of the operating system—and separate network equipment, which itself includes considerable operational software.

Functions of an Operating System

The most visible part of the operating system (OS) to a user is the graphical user interface, which supports interaction between applications and users. However, there are many other important functions it performs behind the scenes that make it much easier to develop applications.

ANALOGY: *Your body has a somatic nervous system that lends you conscious control over voluntary actions (such as walking), and it also has an autonomic nervous system that controls ongoing, involuntary functions such as blood circulation and digestion. Your conscious activity is analogous to the networked application—those actions that are specific to the functioning of the application. The OS includes capabilities analogous to the somatic and autonomous nervous systems—allowing the application to perform its conscious activities and also regulating various behind-the-scenes functions.*

As shown in Figure 4.7, specific functions included in the OS are subsystems that manage communication and storage. Actually communicating data to another host or storing data locally involves many detailed low-level operations that are hidden from the application by the OS.

The OS has two other important functions. First, a host can do more than one thing at a time—this is called *multitasking*. For example, a PC can print a file at the same time it supports a user editing a document. This is especially important in networked applications that support many users, as the OS handles the myriad details that allow this to happen.

EXAMPLE: *Books4u.com has many customers browsing through its available books and making purchases at the same time (see "On-Line Booksell-ing" on page 66). Multitasking is what allows these customers to be accommodated, even if the supporting information management functions reside in a single host.*

Second, the OS manages various resources at the disposal of the host, determining how they are allocated among competing purposes. For example, both processing and memory resources must be allocated to the different operations happening simultaneously in multitasking. The OS is addressed in more detail in Chapter 17.

Network Functions

A computer network is to hosts what the public telephone system is to people, allowing hosts to communicate data as necessary to support the application. Any one host can communicate with any other host on that same network at any time. In the case of the world's largest network—the global Internet—this means that any host can communicate with tens of millions of other hosts. Each host on the Internet is assigned a *domain name* (for example, "info.SIMS.Berke-ley.EDU") that other hosts need in order to communicate with it.

Of course, limits must be placed to avoid chaos. One host requires *authorization* to communicate with another; it can't do whatever it pleases with another host without permission. Authorization must be accompanied by *authentication* that confirms the requesting host's identity. A host's owner controls which other hosts can access it and for what purposes. Techniques for authentication and authorization are discussed in Chapter 13.

ANALOGY: *The public streets enable Mary to travel anywhere in her car, includ-ing into her own garage. In principle, the streets allow any citizen to drive his car into Mary's garage, but only she is authorized to enter, and the garage door authenticates her by the key she carries.*

EXAMPLE: *A public Web server may authorize any host on the network to access its pages. On the other hand, access can be restricted, for example, to hosts in the same company. Another application running on the same host—one man-aging sensitive employee records—is only authorized to be accessed by the human resources department.*

The application partitions residing on different hosts may communicate by sending one another messages (very much like users communicate in many groupware applications). A message is the smallest unit of data that makes sense to the sender and recipient; by assumption, a fragment of a message is useless to the application.

EXAMPLE: *In an email application, one user sends an email message to another (note the use of the term message). The email message is the smallest unit of information that is meaningful to the sender and recipient. Delivering half the message to the recipient isn't useful. In the Web application, when the user requests a page of information to be displayed, that page is a message com-municated from the Web server to the Web browser.*

The network actually deals internally with packets rather than messages, where a message may be broken down into multiple packets (see the sidebar "Pack-ets"). Thus, it is called a packet network. The Internet is the most widely used (but not the only) packet network. The existing public telephone nework is not a packet network—it uses an alternative called circuits—but packet networks are capable of supporting voice telephony, and in the future they will likely supplant the existing telephone network.

People use the telephone network by initiating a "call" and holding a "conversation," and typically a given telephone participates in only one conversation at a time. The Internet differs from the telephone network in that one host doesn't have to "call" another host: It can simply send a message to one or to multiple hosts (or receive them from multiple hosts). It is also possible to set up something analogous to a "call" and hold a "conversation"—an ongoing bidirectional exchange of messages—in a service called a *session*. These options are discussed in Chapter 12. Managing the details of services likes these is one role of the operating system layer shown in Figure 4.7.

Network Topology

The network is a subsystem that has its own hierarchical decomposition into access links, switches, and backbone links. Consider the problem of carrying messages from one host to another. Although the application interprets the message as information conveyed from one place to another, the network considers it data. To communicate the data in a message from one host to another requires physical interconnections called *communication links*.

ANALOGY: *The wire that connects a residence to the telephone company's central office is a communication link. It carries the voice (using a telephone) and data (using a modem) from the residence to the central office, and also in the reverse direction.*

The detailed characteristics of communication links are discussed in Chapter 20. For present purposes, a link simply carries messages from one geographic location to another. It is impractical to directly connect each host with every other host by a dedicated communication link. In the global Internet, for example, there are millions of hosts, and having millions of connections to each host is nonsensical. This full interconnection is avoided by requiring each message to traverse multiple communication links, and by forwarding that message from one link to another using switching.

ANALOGY: *A city avoids having a dedicated street between each pair of garages by adding intersections (analogous to switches). Driving a car between two garages requires traversing multiple streets (analogous to communication links), and at each intersection, choosing one from among the (typically three) alternatives is analogous to switching.*

Packets

In practice, the network forwards not messages, but *packets*. A packet is typically a fragment of a message (a message may be composed of multiple packets), or a packet may be an entire message. A long message may have to be fragmented into packets and those fragments reassembled into the message at the destination. The reason for the distinction between packets and messages is related to performance, and this is discussed in Chapter 17.

ANALOGY: *A packet is analogous to a shipping container, which comes in a standard size. Something larger than a container must first be disassembled into pieces small enough to fit into multiple containers, shipped, and reassembled at the destination.*

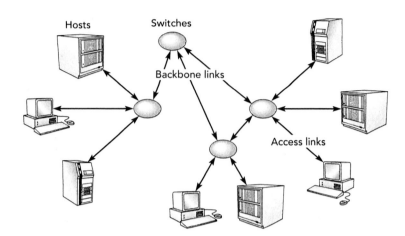

Figure 4.8 Introducing switches allows many hosts to be interconnected, with only one access link per host

A simple switched network is shown in Figure 4.8. Each host is connected to a switch by a single dedicated communication link, and switches are in turn interconnected by communication links. A message can be communicated between any pair of hosts with only *one* link connected to each host. The network has two distinct types of communication links:

- Each host has a single *access link* (analogous to a driveway), which interconnects it with the first switch, called an *access switch*. (This may be more complicated, as discussed in Chapter 20, but need not be of concern now.)
- Switches are interconnected by *backbone links*—defined as links not directly connected to hosts. Each switch is typically connected to at most a few other switches. The goal is to avoid—with switches as well as with hosts—an explosion of connected links as the number of hosts on the network grows.

There are also two distinct types of switches:

- An *access switch* forwards messages from an access link to the appropriate backbone link (and vice versa).
- *Backbone switches* forward messages from one backbone link to another.

The collection of backbone switches and backbone links are called the *backbone network*, and the access switches and access links are called the *access network*.

The particular pattern of interconnection of hosts and switches is called the *network topology*. (Topology is a branch of mathematics that concerns itself with, among other things, such interconnection patterns.) The primary requirement is that from each host to all other hosts there must be at least one feasible *path*—consisting of switches and connecting links—that a message can traverse. As in the simple topology of Figure 4.8, there may be more than one such path, implying that switches must choose from among feasible alternatives. Each switch forwards a message to an appropriate output link, bringing it closer to the destination host, and switches must be coordinated so that the message eventually arrives at the intended recipient host (this function is called *routing* and is discussed in Chapter 18).

4.4.3   Storage

Just as the network subsystem supports communication of messages over distance, the storage management subsystem deals with communication over time.

File System

An application often needs to store a package of data for some period of time. To support this, the infrastructure provides the file—a collection of data managed by a specific application (such as a word processor or spreadsheet). A file system is included among the functions of every operating system. It provides standard services related to creating and accessing files (see the sidebar "Functions of a File System"). A file plays a role in storage similar to that of a message in communication—the file system considers the file as data, while any structure and interpretation of that data is entirely the province of the application.

Database

In some applications, particularly those serving organizations, the data stored by the application takes certain standard forms involving numbers and character strings. A character is a single letter in the alphabet, such as *a*, and a character string is a collection of such characters, for example, "San Francisco."

EXAMPLE: *Employee or customer information would include character strings for name, address, city, etc., and numbers for telephone number, age, salary, etc. This information has to be retained over a period of time and hence is stored in a database.*

A *database* is a file containing interrelated data with a specific predefined structure. Specifically, a *data element* is a digital encoding of a character string or number, such as a customer name or telephone number. Each customer has the same set of data elements, although the *value* of the data elements will be different for different customers. The set of data elements corresponding to a

Functions of a File System

The file system organizes files in *directories*, or *folders*. Folders make it easier for the user or application to keep track of related files, by grouping them together under a single directory name.

All hosts, including clients and servers, have a file system provided by their respective operating system. It is common to have the larger storage in a server. By centralizing files there, systematic backup of data (by making copies on tape) prevents its loss due to equipment failure. Also, this allows data to be shared by multiple users, at their multiple clients. File systems are sometimes *distributed*, meaning there is a single hierarchical structure of files physically stored in different computers and accessed over the network. A file system does not know or care about what data is stored in the files—that is always managed by some application that "owns" the file. Many operating systems associate a file with a specific application through an extension to the file name (such as ".doc" for a Word document) or through information stored in a special place in the file itself reserved for the file system (as in the MacOS). That way, the file system can automatically invoke the application that embodies the structure and interpretation of the data in that file.

customer is called a *record*, and a database might contain a collection of records, one for each customer.

Another example of the structuring of data that is very common is a document, which is a collection of characters structured into paragraphs, headings and sub-headings, figures, etc.

Database Management System (DBMS)

Databases are common across many applications. There are also a number of standard operations performed on databases, such as storing new data and changing existing data, or searching for data meeting certain criteria. It is not necessary to reimplement all these operations in each application because of an infrastructure called the database management system (DBMS). The DBMS manages multiple databases holding massive amounts of data and can be purchased from a specialized vendor (such as Oracle, Sybase, Informix, or IBM).

> **EXAMPLE:** *The stock trading application stocks4u.com maintains the most recent bid and asking price of each stock on the world's stock exchanges (see "On-Line Stock Trading" on page 68). It would likely use a DBMS to manage a large set of current and historical stock prices. It would likely also use a DBMS to manage customer account information.*

The DBMS serves as the foundation of on-line transaction processing applications, which often manage large amounts of structured data. The capabilities of a DBMS include the following:

- The DBMS can isolate the application from changes in computer systems. In many situations the data itself—such as the customer data of a company—needs to transcend the replacement of a computer system by one from another vendor.
- The DBMS can provide many standard operations on data needed by many applications. Premier among these is the search, which in the case of a DBMS is called a *query*.
- Often a common data repository must be accessed by multiple users and applications, and thus it is appropriate to separate the database and its management from those applications. That way, applications can be added or removed without impacting the data. Also, the DBMS can take care of many complications arising when different applications try to access the same database at the same time.
- Frequently, data is a fundamental asset of an organization, and its safety and integrity are important. The DBMS provides many features that enhance the integrity of data. For example, it can prevent the loss of critical data when a computer fails.

Year	City	Accommodation	Tourists
2002	Oakley	Bed & Breakfast	14
2002	Oakley	Resort	190
2002	Oakland	Bed & Breakfast	340
2002	Oakland	Resort	230
2002	Berkeley	Camping	120,000
2002	Berkeley	Bed & Breakfast	3,450
2002	Berkeley	Resort	390,800
2002	Albany	Camping	8,790
2002	Albany	Bed & Breakfast	3,240
2003	Oakley	Bed & Breakfast	55
2003	Oakley	Resort	320
2003	Oakland	Bed & Breakfast	280
2003	Oakland	Resort	210
2003	Berkeley	Camping	115,800
2003	Berkeley	Bed & Breakfast	4,560
2003	Berkeley	Resort	419,000
2003	Albany	Camping	7,650
2003	Albany	Bed & Breakfast	6,750

Figure 4.9 A relational table

The relational DBMS is the most common type (see the sidebar "Relational Databases"). Other important capabilities of databases are discussed in Chapter 15.

4.5   The Internet

As described earlier, the purpose of the network is to allow computers to communicate with one another in the course of realizing application functionality. A number of networking technologies have been proposed and commercialized, but one has emerged as particularly important—the Internet.

Relational Databases

The relational DBMS exploits a mathematical model called relational algebra. In practical terms, this means data is organized in tables (with rows and columns). The table captures relationships among different data. While this model may seem limiting, it really is not, because of its ability to store and manipulate data in multiple columns, as well as in multiple tables. The application accesses the data in the database through the query.

E X A M P L E :   A relational table that stores data about tourism in four cities is shown in Figure 4.9. This table indicates the number of tourists by accommodation and year. Each row corresponds to a set of attributes (year, city, and type of accommodation). A typical query might be "tell me how many tourists stay in resorts in all cities further from San Francisco than Oakland." The application would recast this into the database query for the relational table in Figure 4.9 as "tell me how many tourists stay in resorts in Oakley and Albany." Since the database is not aware of the interpretation of the data, it cannot translate "further from San Francisco than Oakland" into "Oakley and Albany," but that would be inferred by the application, perhaps by consulting a separate geographical database.

Because all data is stored in relational tables, queries take standard forms that depend on this structure.

Historically, hosts were networked within buildings or campuses using one of several local area networking technologies.

EXAMPLE: *Ethernet is a LAN technology developed by Xerox Corporation and licensed to a number of vendors. Token Ring is an alternative LAN product designed and produced by IBM.*

Once hosts were networked by LANs, there was naturally interest in connecting these LANs by a wide area network. This would empower a number of networked applications such as those described in Chapter 2 and Chapter 3. Fortuitously, the U.S. government had supported a research effort to conceptualize and prototype a WAN technology that could interconnect existing LANs. The result was a new suite of internet networking technologies, where the "internet" refers to the feature of connecting existing local area networks. An *internet* (lowercase) thus designates a "network of networks," including standard ways to interconnect networks as well as equipment and software. Any network that uses these technologies is called an internet.

The Internet (uppercase) is a specific internet; namely, the large one that is global in extent, accessible to the citizenry, and subject to much attention in the news media. It arose first as a government-supported infrastructure for universities and national laboratories in the United States. Starting in the early-to-mid-1980s, commercial applications were allowed on this Internet, and it was gradually privatized. This Internet has become the most widely used WAN, and of particular importance for e-commerce applications is the fact that most enterprises and individuals can access it.

4.5.1   Intranet

The same internet technologies are used to construct private networks—called intranets—for exclusive use within an enterprise. An intranet and its suite of applications are often used to improve internal communications and collaboration while protecting proprietary information. Other proprietary network technologies and applications can be used for this purpose; however, this is becoming less attractive as the internet technologies provide a suite of existing solutions.

EXAMPLE: *General Motors Corporation deployed a satellite-based intranet connecting over 9,000 locations, including all its dealerships. It replaces many volumes of paper-based manuals and daily service bulletins with remote interactive access to the same information. Later, the same intranet will allow customers to customize automobiles and receive delivery in just a few days, or summon help if stranded on the road [Pan98].*

Inevitably, intranet users want access to the Internet from their desktop computers, for example, to exchange email outside the organization or to access the Web. For this purpose, the intranet is connected to the Internet—in a way that does not compromise internal proprietary information—using a *firewall* (see Chapter 13 and Chapter 18). The firewall creates a protected enclave by enforcing restrictions both on internal users' access to the Internet and on Internet citizens' access to the intranet. A pair of intranets and their connection to the Internet is illustrated in Figure 4.10. The dotted lines denote the boundary between intranet and Internet, and all communication links traversing those dotted lines are firewall protected.

E X A M P L E :   *Stocks4u.com maintains sensitive financial records in customer accounts (see "On-Line Stock Trading" on page 68). The last thing it would want is for its records to become available to nosy users on the Internet who have no reason to see them. At the same time, they must be available to the legitimate customer who owns that account. The intranet firewall balances those competing requirements, allowing legitimate customer access without compromising the privacy of that customer.*

There may also be firewalls internal to an organization to enforce restrictions on how employees in one department access resources in other departments. Firewalls and related security issues are discussed further in Chapter 13.

4.5.2   Extranet

Frequently an organization has two or more geographically separated locations—each with an intranet—and wants to join them in a single intranet. One option is private communication links among the locations, but this is relatively expensive. Another option is to connect the intranets through the Internet, as shown in Figure 4.10. This compromises the security of any messages traversing the Internet, because it's an unprotected domain outside the organization's administrative control. Confidentiality can be preserved using encryption (see Chapter 13), which can hide message content to anyone without a secret key.

A N A L O G Y :   *A bank has vaults to store cash securely, but it must sometimes transport cash through public streets (analogous to the Internet) from one vault (analogous to an intranet) to another. For this purpose, the bank creates a mobile protected environment with an armored car and armed guards to prevent theft. Access to the armored car requires a key (analogous to an encryption key), possessed only by the trusted guards.*

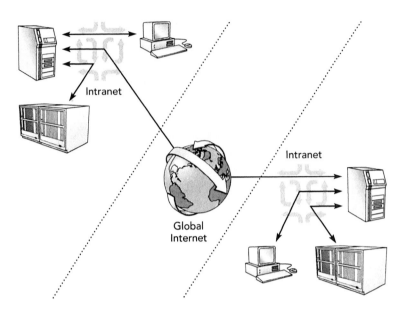

Figure 4.10 An extranet encompasses one or more intranets and the Internet

An Internet incorporated into an intranet, as shown in Figure 4.10, is called an extranet. Similarly, when different companies use the Internet to interconnect intranets for cross-enterprise applications like electronic commerce, this is also called an extranet.

EXAMPLE: *Flowers4u.com uses an extranet to connect its participating florists (see "Floral Delivery Service" on page 69). The extranet allows legitimate access by those florists to orders over the Internet while prohibiting access by unauthorized parties who might otherwise wreak havoc.*

The Automotive Network Exchange (ANX) electronic commerce initiative from U.S. automobile companies is based on a large extranet. The network— designed by Electronic Data Systems (EDS)—employs standard internet technologies. It offers numerous security and performance guarantees that insure that it is "business quality." Although the ANX is separate from the public Internet, it does connect many firms' intranets securely [Jon97].

An extranet also allows employees unfettered access to their company intranet while traveling, as illustrated in Figure 4.11. Individual hosts are allowed intranet access through the Internet. An extranet also allows individual consumers limited and secure access to intranet resources—for example, in selling goods over the Internet—while preventing theft of confidential information (such as credit card numbers). For this purpose, Web browsers support limited extranet capabilities.

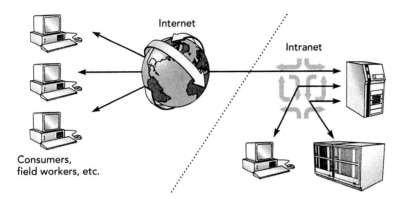

Figure 4.11 An extranet can extend an intranet to field workers and customers

4.5.3 Nomadic and Mobile Internet Access

As networked computing applications become widely deployed, network access becomes important not only at home and work but also while traveling. Access while traveling is called *nomadic access*. Access while actually moving—as in a car, bus, or train—is called *mobile access*.

E X A M P L E : *Today's telephone system provides nomadic access with pay telephones and mobile access with cellular telephones. There are some nascent services providing nomadic and mobile access to the Internet, but for the most part this is an infrastructure waiting to be built.*

Nomadic and mobile users want the same suite of applications as fixed users. Radio communications technologies supporting mobile access are more limiting than the fiber-optics technologies supporting fixed access (see Chapter 20). A technical limitation on portable devices is battery technology, which limits the time of operation and processing power.

Mobile and nomadic workers want unfettered access to their organization's intranet, and this is an important use of the extranet.

E X A M P L E : *A sales force is naturally nomadic, while sales automation applications enable the representatives to demonstrate on-line catalogs, check inventory and delivery schedules, and place orders. The latter functions require access to mission-critical business processes, where security and confidentiality are important.*

4.5.4   Internet Application Suite

While an internet is a "network of networks," it also provides a set of popular social and information management applications. When members of an organization speak of "having an intranet," they often refer to these standard internet applications as well as internet networking technologies. They are referring to most major social applications, including email, newsgroups, chatroom, list-server, and Web. The Web has emerged as an important enabler for many applications, as discussed further in Chapter 5.

Discussion

D4.2 Today many users use the telephone network with a modem to access the Internet. If you have experience with this, discuss some disadvantages of this approach and some problems you have encountered.

D4.3 Discuss problems that might arise if someone gained unauthorized access to the intranet of a bank or brokerage.

D4.4 Do you think mobile and nomadic computing are valuable to users? What types of applications might be popular, and what applications are not too compelling in a mobile/nomadic environment?

D4.5 In terms of what it allows and disallows, what capabilities would you like to see in a firewall?

4.6   *Open Issues

Information technology is ever advancing, and this raises many issues.

4.6.1   Pacing Change

Information technology is ever evolving. For example, the Web is a relatively recent success, and new capabilities are constantly being offered at the middle-ware layer. While presumably change is good at some level, as it represents the incorporation of new ideas and new capabilities, it is also a constant headache for individuals and organizations that use information technology. Some even express the sentiment that a slower evolution and more stability would be welcome. Equipment and especially software vendors need to be cognizant of the impact of change on their customers and make carefully considered trade-offs, taking into account both the benefits and problems of change.

4.6.2 The Future of Intranets

The intranet incorporates the idea of a protected enclave to control access to hosts and applications. This notion, which made good sense for the era of departmental applications, has become antiquated with the increasing popularity of inter-enterprise applications and e-commerce. First, it assumes that internal users are benign, and the only security threats come from external users. At the level of a department this is reasonable, but in an enterprise there is a need for simultaneous compartmentalization and unfettered access.

EXAMPLE: *Although a personnel department application that manages employee records should participate in enterprise applications, not all workers have a legitimate need to access it, for example, to satisfy their curiosity about their coworkers' salaries. Typically there will also be nonemployee contractors on the physical premises who should not receive the same access as many employees.*

Second, the protected enclave assumes that external users need only very limited and specific access to public servers. The trend, however, is toward inter-enterprise applications and collaborative applications among enterprises, implying the access requirements of outside workers may be similar to internal workers in some instances. For these reasons, the protected enclave idea is becoming increasingly limiting.

For the future, security technologies that protect individual resources rather than whole enclaves are needed.

ANALOGY: *Countries have border-control checkpoints that verify credentials of those wishing to enter the country. However, they do not rely on this mode exclusively. Internally there are many security arrangements for individual resources, such as the bank vault to protect a bank's precious metals and cash.*

4.6.3 Archiving Digital Information

Libraries and archives have preserved works of literature and many historical documents on paper media, but how will archiving of information represented in computer storage as data occur [Kah97]? Fortunately, data can be replicated and hence preserved (this is discussed further in Chapter 8). However, this raises two questions—one technical and the other economic:

- Recovering information from its data representation requires knowledge of the structure and interpretation of that data. It is thus not sufficient to archive data alone, which is the traditional role of storage subsystems. The data processing required to recover information is usually embedded in application software, which over time becomes a legacy application and may eventually disappear.

- Who does this archiving and who pays? Fortunately, publishing information on the network eases the logistical problem, as it can be systematically archived in a central repository.

The requirement that both data and associated applications must be archived is a technically feasible but daunting task. Does this mean that society must preserve instances of every computer platform and operating system in order to be able to run those archived applications? An alternative is to establish standards for information representation, so they are documented and reside in multiple applications and implementations, and may also be longer lasting. Examples of this include the SQL in the DBMS and the markup languages used to describe documents (see Chapter 15).

Review

The bit is the simple alphabet used by computers and networks to represent information of all types—documents, numbers, audio, images, video, etc. Built on this foundation, a large and complex infrastructure supports networked computing applications.

Data is a collection of bits representing information. That representation is not unique, so it presumes a given structure and interpretation. Information is recovered from data by data processing.

The infrastructure includes equipment and software and supports a wide range of applications. It serves four primary functions: communication across distance, communication across time, computation and logic, and the human interface.

Both an infrastructure and application have an architecture, which breaks them down into smaller, more manageable, pieces. More formally, an architecture is a decomposition of a system into subsystems, each with a narrower well-defined purpose and functionality. These subsystems interact to realize the higher purposes of the system. In a hierarchical decomposition, subsystems are themselves systems, unless they are atomic (cannot be further subdivided).

Common architectures for networked computing equipment incorporate modules such as computers (called hosts if they are connected to the Internet), communication links, and switches. A computer connects to an internet by an access link to an access switch. Access switches are connected to one another and to backbone switches by backbone links.

The infrastructure equipment and software use a layered architecture. Each layer utilizes services from the layer below and also hides it and other lower layers from the layer above. Major important layers are the equipment (hosts and network), operating system, and middleware. Visible functions of the operating system are managing the graphical user interface, communication (with networking software), and storage (with the file system software). Behind the scenes, the OS also manages memory, processing, and other resources, and it provides multitasking so that multiple applications or users can be accommodated in a single host.

An internet is a "network of networks," in which local area networks are interconnected by a wide area (or backbone) network. The (capital *I*) Internet is the global public internet. The internet technologies and applications can also be used to construct a private network, called an intranet. An extranet is an intranet securely connected to another intranet—or to a mobile or nomadic worker—through the public Internet. An intranet is an enclave protected from external threats by one or more firewalls.

Key Concepts

Data and information:

- Bits
- Representation
- Data processing

Building blocks:

- Hosts: client and server
- Network
- Information content

Architecture:

- Decomposition, functionality, interaction
- Subsystems
- Hierarchy and granularity

Infrastructure:

- Communication across time (storage) and space (network)
- Computation and logic
- Human interface

Operating system:

- Multitasking

Middleware

Networks:

- Communication links and switches
- Access versus backbone
- Messages and packets

Storage:

- File and file system
- Database and database management system (DBMS)

Internet:

- Intranet, extranet, and firewall

Further Reading

[OHE96a] is recommended as a general introduction to networked computing technologies.

Exercises

E4.1   For each of the following, describe at least two different ways to represent the pieces of information as a collection of bits:

    a. The name of one country in the world

    b. One day out of the week

    c. The current year by the Gregorian calendar

E4.2   How many different alternatives can be represented by the following number of bits:

    a. One

    b. Two

    c. Three

    d. An arbitrary number n

E4.3   Describe at least two ways Chinese ideographs could be entered on a keyboard. At your option, these methods can be interactive, using the computer screen and mouse as well as keyboard.

E4.4   You are given the task of finding a representation for a circle in a drawing application. The circle is to be displayed on the screen, and the user can edit the location and radius of the circle, both of which are expressed in units of pixels.

    a. Specify a data representation for the circle, trying to minimize the number of bits required.

    b. Describe how data processing would draw a circle on the screen, starting with stored data, following your representation.

E4.5 For a personal computer you use every day:

    a. Identify, either by name or by short description, one building block in your computer setup representative of application software, infrastructure software, storage, and communications.

    b. Which of the building blocks in *a* (there may be more than one) is supported by each of the following pieces of hardware in your computer: microprocessor, floppy disk, hard disk, network interface card, modem.

E4.6 You have probably used a kitchen to prepare a meal. Consider that kitchen as a system:

    a. Decompose your kitchen system into subsystems, and describe briefly the function of each subsystem.

    b. Describe how the subsystems interact (with your assistance) in a typical cooking task, for example, preparing pasta from your grandmother's favorite recipe.

    c. Describe the emergence of system behavior that is observed in *b*. What was accomplished that no single subsystem would have been able to do?

    d. Draw analogies between the subsystems in *a* and the subsystems of a computer system.

E4.7 Your PC has a file system, and that file system probably has a convention for naming files, including what folders they are in. Describe that convention and specify the purpose of its components.

E4.8 At your local software store you can buy a DBMS sold as a "PC application," either separately or as part of an "office suite of applications." In this chapter the DBMS has been described as part of the infrastructure—a middleware layer for storage. Explain the inconsistency in terminology. What perspective is the software store taking?

E4.9 Consider a box delivery service modeled after the United Parcel Service as an infrastructure available to business. It has many characteristics analogous to a networked computing infrastructure—for example, a box is analogous to a packet, a distribution center is analogous to a switch. Describe how the capabilities of a company like UPS are analogous to the following four elements. If there is no reasonable analogy, say why.

a. Communication across distance

b. Communication across time

c. Computation and logic

d. Human interface

Client-Server Computing

5

Chapter 4 mentioned two types of network hosts—clients and servers. The superficial distinction mentioned there is that a client is associated with a user and a server is not. A more fundamental issue is the following: A networked application is by definition distributed among two or more hosts, or else, it is not networked! Why should the application be distributed in that manner? How should the functionality of the application be partitioned among hosts? This chapter will begin to address the technical aspects of this issue. However, many of the motivations relate not to technology but to how organizations administer their networked computing infrastructure and networked applications, the discussion of which is deferred to Chapter 9.

Partitioning across hosts is the most fundamental architectural question regarding applications. The application can be considered a system that is decomposed into subsystems assigned to different hosts that interact over the network, as described in "System Architecture" on page 114. This chapter addresses this architectural question, focusing on the most common networked computing architecture, client-server, and a less-frequently used one, peer-to-peer. The applications discussed in "Examples of Organizational Applications" on page 62 will be used to illustrate concrete uses of client-server computing.

The idea behind client-server architecture is straightforward. Some hosts (the clients) are specialized to interact with users, presenting information to them and gathering input from them. These clients are typically desktop computers, exploiting the fact that most users already have these machines available. Other hosts (the servers) are specialized to manage large data repositories, process that data, and provide various other services related to the specific application. The form of interaction between clients and servers is primarily the users making demands on the clients, and the clients in turn utilizing functionality in the servers to satisfy those demands.

5.1 Two Host Architectures

Two simple alternatives are shown in Figure 5.1. The client-server architecture, which was introduced in Chapter 4, is attractive for many information access and organizational applications, and it was a natural outgrowth of earlier computing eras (see the sidebar "History of Client-Server Computing"). The peer-to-peer architecture is most appropriate for direct-immediate social applications. These alternatives illustrate that there is no single correct choice, nor are these choices limited to these two.

5.1.1 Client-Server Architecture

Clients are the hosts that directly support the user, and they are usually desktop computers (PCs or Macintoshes, but sometimes also UNIX workstations). Servers are hosts that do not interface directly to users, but provide services such as computation, logic, and storage to the networked application. It is typical for many clients to access a single server remotely across a network, and a server often has higher performance than a client, allowing it to serve those multiple clients. It is also common for a single client to access two or more servers, within one or more applications.

Client-server architecture is most suitable for information management applications, where the information is published on a server, which provides the storage and a single focus for update and administration. Users sitting at clients generate requests for information, which are passed to the server, and the client displays responses. Many clients can access this published information from the server. Clients can also access a variety of published information on multiple servers.

EXAMPLE: *The Web assigns information management functions to a Web server residing in a server host and the presentation to a Web browser residing in the client host. The user clicks a mouse to invoke hyperlinks, and these invocations are communicated over the network to the server host, which returns the requested page for the browser to display. A Web browser can access many Web servers. When the user invokes a hyperlink (by clicking highlighted text), this may cause the browser to shift to an alternative server host.*

OLTP applications, as a straightforward extension of information management (they add the element of updating the published information), are also appropriate for a client-server architecture.

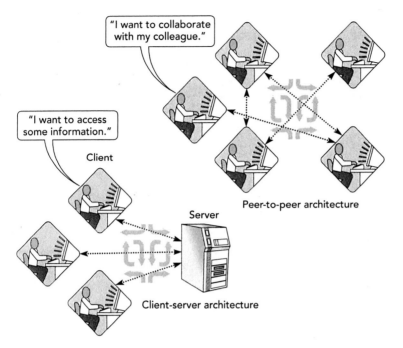

Figure 5.1 Two basic architectures for social and information management applications

In summary:

- The primary function of the client is to accept instructions from the user, make requests of the server, and display responses from the server for the user.
- The primary function of the server is to respond to such requests, typically from many clients.

This gives client-server architecture an *asymmetry* of function, where the client makes requests and the server satisfies requests.

EXAMPLE: *In an airline reservation system (a good example of an OLTP application), the travel agent is at a client, and the flight information is stored in a server. The travel agent can answer inquiries about flight times, which are accessed on the server.*

When a bank customer visits an ATM machine to get cash, she is the user, the ATM is a client, and the bank's central mainframe is a server. The ATM accepts customers' requests for cash, clears them with the server, and then issues the cash. This illustrates that a client need not be a PC.

such as word processing and spreadsheets could execute directly on the desktop computer, but users also wanted centralized capabilities previously supported by time-sharing:

- Social applications were enabled by multiple users accessing a centralized computer.
- Sharing information with other users—without carrying physical media such as floppy disks—is possible when users share a host. In addition, information stored on a central host allows collaborative authoring of documents.
- Centralized administration of widely used applications removes that burden on users.

These capabilities evolved—without giving up the advantages of desktop computers—in client-server computing. The server became the focus for the sharing and backup of information and centralized administration of applications, while users retained the ability to process information in personalized ways or install their own applications on desktop clients.

A server must be available at all times, waiting for requests from clients. Clients, however, can come and go, since they always initiate the interaction.

ANALOGY: *In a law practice, the customers are also called clients. The law office provides a service to multiple clients. A single person might be a client to both a lawyer and an accountant. A law office is always open for any potential client to request legal services, but the interaction is initiated by the client. Different clients may appear at different times.*

While the Web illustrates the client-server architecture for information management, it is also natural for direct-*deferred* social applications because there is a storage (communication across time) function naturally assigned to the server. The server also becomes a natural place to store information between the time it is generated and later accessed by users.

EXAMPLE: *An email application using a client-server architecture is illustrated in Figure 5.2. The user can input her messages into an email client program on the client host, and the result is sent to the email server program on a server host. The server stores each message during the time that elapses between the originating user composing and sending a message and the recipient user reading the message, and it also routes the message to the intended recipient (not shown). The recipient user can retrieve and view the message using his own email client. An example of an email client is Eudora, and an example of an email server is a POP server (where POP stands for "post office protocol").*

Client-server architecture is also appropriate for direct-*immediate* social applications, when there is application logic that naturally resides on a server, such as aggregation and consolidation of information from many users.

EXAMPLE: *In a chatroom application, illustrated in Figure 5.3, many users can participate at their respective clients. When a user types, each client sends the text to the chatroom server, which aggregates that typing and returns a single presentation back to all clients. Each user can see everything typed by everyone else.*

5.1.2   Peer-to-Peer Architecture

An alternative to client-server architecture is the peer-to-peer architecture, shown in Figure 5.1. There is no server but only desktop computers—called *peer hosts* because of their similarity of function—supporting the application and users. This architecture is attractive for some direct-immediate social applications, where no centralized application logic is needed.

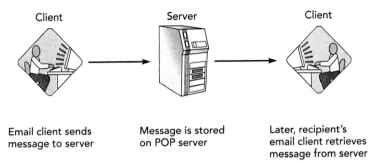

Email client sends
message to server

Message is stored
on POP server

Later, recipient's
email client retrieves
message from server

Figure 5.2 Using a client-server architecture to support an email application

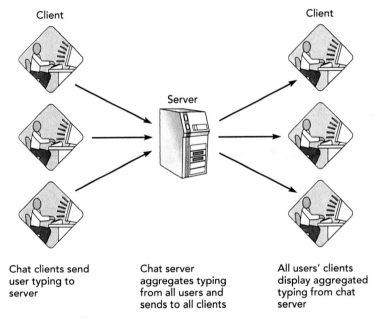

Chat clients send
user typing to
server

Chat server
aggregates typing
from all users and
sends to all clients

All users' clients
display aggregated
typing from chat
server

Figure 5.3 A chatroom application using a client-server architecture

EXAMPLE: *The peer-to-peer architecture is natural for audio and video conferencing. Data representing the audio or video is simply communicated over the
network directly from one peer to another.*

A distinguishing characteristic of the peer-to-peer architecture is the *symmetry*
of function—each peer provides essentially the same functionality—as contrasted to the asymmetry in client-server architecture. Architectures can also mix
client-server and peer-to-peer methods. For example, many direct-immediate

social applications involve an information management aspect and a multiuser interaction aspect. Their respective desktop computers may serve as both peers (to interact with other peers directly) and as clients (to access the information stored in a server).

EXAMPLE: *In remote conferencing, each user's desktop computer might act as a client to the server that manages the document edits coming from multiple users, while simultaneously acting as a peer for the voice and video aspect.*

A given desktop computer can be a client or a peer; it is the software that defines the role of the host in the application. There is no major distinction in the equipment between clients and servers, except as to the details of configuration (memory, storage, etc.) and performance and the requirement for user interface elements (display, keyboard, etc.) in the client.

Discussion

D5.1 Describe some parallels between client-server and peer-to-peer architectures and commercial relationships that arise in commerce.

5.2   Three-Tier Client-Server Architecture

The client-server architecture of Figure 5.1 is called *two-tier architecture*, where the first tier is the client and the second tier is the server. The combination of desktop computers and relatively inexpensive microprocessor-based servers enables individual departments to operate their own applications based on this architecture. However, the two-tier architecture does not recognize the special needs of a class of organizational applications that incorporate mission-critical databases.

EXAMPLE: *The stock trading application requires the maintenance of customer account records (see "On-Line Stock Trading" on page 68). Obviously, the integrity of these accounts is critical and requires extraordinary measures to insure they are not lost or damaged due to various problems that are inevitable, such as power failures or software crashes.*

Many OLTP applications fall in this category. Traditionally, mission-critical databases have been managed by a DBMS on a mainframe computer, an environment optimized for these requirements. At the same time, there is a desire to integrate these mission-critical databases into new client-server applications without sacrificing their desirable qualities. For this purpose, the *three-tier* client-server architecture was invented. This architecture is a marriage of client-server computing and centralized OLTP databases. The second tier is an application server, where unique application functionality resides, and the third tier is where the databases accessed by the application are managed. The three-tier architecture distinguishes three distinct functions in enterprise applications, as illustrated in Figure 5.4 and listed in Table 5.1. The essence of the architecture is to define the two types of specialized servers—shared data and application logic.

The application logic, which intermediates between shared data and presentation, manipulates the shared data. It also takes inputs and requests from the presentation, decides what needs to be done, decides what shared data should be accessed or must be updated, manipulates that data appropriately, and responds to the presentation. The shared data answers queries from the application logic, and the application logic determines what data is stored and what queries are needed.

There are several reasons to divide things this way:

- The presentation—dedicated to a single user—is natural to assign to the client for better interactivity.
- The application logic supports multiple users and thus is naturally assigned to a server. As the number of users increases, more application servers can be added, all accessing a common shared data server.
- The shared data server may support multiple applications and, by dedicating a host, can support more application users. It can also have a protected administrative environment for security and reliability (see Chapter 13).
- Keeping application logic out of the client is natural for applications accessed by the citizenry (like consumer e-commerce), since it avoids installation of special software.
- An alternative two-tier architecture would locate application logic and databases on a single server. This is reasonable in some less-critical circumstances. For reasons of security and reliability, however, these mainframes are not suitable as servers for general user access or running other client-server applications.

The three-tier client-server architecture has a many-to-one (or at least few-to-one) relationship at each level: There are many clients per application server and potentially multiple application servers per shared data server. There may or may not be more than one application sharing common shared data servers.

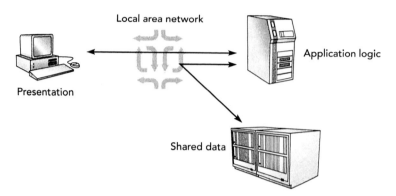

Local area network

Presentation

Application logic

Shared data

Figure 5.4 Three-tier client-server setup

Table 5.1 Partitioning functionality in three-tier client-server computing

Tier	Description	Analogy
Shared data	Manages mission-critical data shared by multiple applications. A database management system (often, but not necessarily, on a mainframe) accommodates searches from the application logic.	In a restaurant, the refrigerators store the ingredients (analogous to data). The kitchen prepares meals (analogous to information) on request from the waiters.
Application logic	Embodies the unique behavior and functionality of an application and runs in an application server. Frequently there are more than one application server per shared data server.	Operation of the restaurant requires offering the customer (analogous to user) choices, eliciting his order, satisfying requests. The waiter (frequently more than one per kitchen) serves the customer.
Presentation	Structures, formats, and displays information to the user by sight and sound. Receives user input and requests by voice, keyboard, or mouse.	The table service (dishes, plates, glasses) present the meal to the customer, who uses silverware to eat it. The customer verbally makes requests of the waiter.

5.2.1   Thin and Ultrathin Clients

The amount of application functionality to include in the client is controversial. One extreme is a lot—called a *fat client*—and the opposite is called a *thin client*. Three-tier client-server architecture, by keeping application logic out of the client, results in a thin client, which focuses only on the user interface and presentation.

There is increasing concern about the administrative costs associated with desktop computers—not the least of which is time users spend maintaining their own software. The thin client moves toward central administration and avoids separately administering and upgrading many desktop computers. This is one motivation for the network computer (NC)—a highly simplified desktop machine (see the sidebar "An Ultrathin Client: The Network Computer (NC)").

5.2.2   World Wide Web

The Web, while conceived as an information management application in its own right, has become the basis for a wider class of applications. It is a good illustration of the client-server architecture. The typical configuration—showing both the three-tier client-server host architecture and the software architecture—is shown in Figure 5.5. The Web browser includes capabilities useful for providing the user interface of many applications, such as formatted text and graphics, and various ways to capture user input, including forms, dialog boxes, and radio buttons. Rather than reimplementing these capabilities, applications can simply incorporate a Web browser as part of their presentation. This is a typical thin-client architecture, since the client has only the Web browser and no application-specific software. In the second-tier application server, a Web server is combined with application logic. For this purpose, Web servers include a *common gateway interchange* (CGI), which allows input from the client to be passed onto the application logic and the application logic to display information and forms in the Web browser. Finally, the application may incorporate a DBMS to manage databases in the third tier, often on a mainframe computer.

A major advantage to incorporating a Web browser is the reduction in development effort by incorporating the existing browser software. This also addresses a far more important practical problem: In an uncoordinated environment—such as individual consumer access to an intranet—getting application-specific programs installed on the client is logistically difficult and a deterrence to users. When applications require only a Web browser in the client, users find it very easy to get going because they need not install new software. In fact, there appears to be a larger trend emerging, in which stand-alone desktop applications are replaced by Web versions, where the application-specific software resides on the server. While this does require an Internet connection, it removes the burden of software installation and administration from the user, much like the NC.

Discussion

D5.2 What are some parallels and differences between the thin client and the dumb terminal connected to a time-sharing mainframe computer?

An Ultrathin Client: The Network Computer (NC)

Several approaches to the NC share a desire to simplify desktop computers and move users' data and applications to centralized servers with central administration. The hope is to reduce the lifecycle costs of the desktop computer. At its most extreme, the NC is a graphic-display engine. In this ultrathin client, even the presentation is moved to a server, and there is no application-specific software running in the client. Generic graphic-display capabilities can be exploited by all applications.

Many NC proposals include a suite of standard Internet applications—especially a Web browser—so it becomes a networked information appliance (an appliance is equipment with a specific purpose; see Chapter 7). Another approach is to allow application-specific presentation or logic to reside in the client, but dynamically load it into the client when needed (using mobile code; see Chapter 16).

The thin-client architecture limits a user's ability to install applications, so it is most appropriate when users deal with a limited set of standard applications (such as point-of-sale terminals, airline counters, and simple data entry). One weakness of the desktop computer—where the thin client or NC offers value—is security (see Chapter 13). Where a number of people may have physical access, restrictions on access to applications and data is easier when clients are thin.

Mobile or nomadic users may find the communication capabilities inadequate for a thin-client architecture. A thin client usually demands more communications to servers and thus is most appropriate in a local area net-work environment. On the other hand, the centralized administration of applications and user files in the thin-client architecture is an advan-tage if users are going to access these items from multiple locations, and particularly if they wish to access centralized enterprise databases.

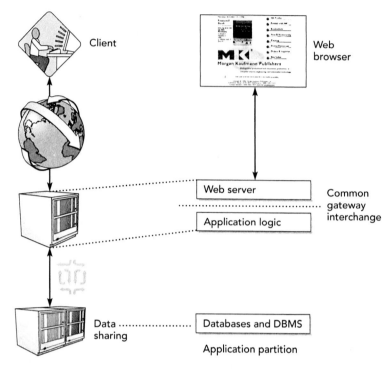

Figure 5.5 The Web incorporated into an application in the three-tier architecture

5.3 Application Examples

Examples introduced in "Examples of Organizational Applications" on page 62 serve to illustrate how networked applications can be partitioned across hosts. They also illustrate how the Web can be employed in such applications.

5.3.1 On-Line Book Merchant

The software architecture for books4u.com, focusing on how to serve a single customer, is shown in Figure 5.6. As in Figure 5.5, this application incorporates the Web browser and server in a three-tier host architecture. The functionality assigned to each tier is described in Table 5.2. The application logic is actually divided into two second-tier subsystems—customer logic that interacts with the customer to view merchandise and enter orders, and fulfillment logic to cause shipments of ordered merchandise. In the third tier are three categories of data-bases—past and present customers, available merchandise, and the status of past and present orders. There are communication links to book distributors to

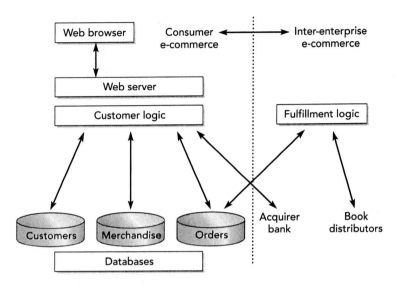

Figure 5.6 The software architecture for books4u.com and its customers

Table 5.2 Example of three-tier partitioning of application functionality for books4u.com

Tier	Functionality
Presentation	Manages placement and formatting of information about books on customer screen and interprets customer inputs based on the boxes checked or fields filled in.
Application logic	Takes inputs from the presentation, decides what database searches and actions are required, decides what information will be presented to the customer. Also interacts with financial institutions and book distributors as required.
Shared data	Manages mission-critical shared data, including customer information, book inventory and availability, and status of active orders and back orders. All queries for information from this shared data are initiated by the application logic.

check inventory availability and convey orders, and also to an acquirer bank for credit checks and credit card charges. The substantial information passing over these links probably justifies proprietary communication links, rather than using the public Internet.

In the course of browsing through the available merchandise and initiating orders, the customer logic not only determines what and how information is presented to the customer but also gathers information from customers. In the course of these interactions, it accesses and manages all three categories of databases. It may also authorize a credit card charge by interacting with the

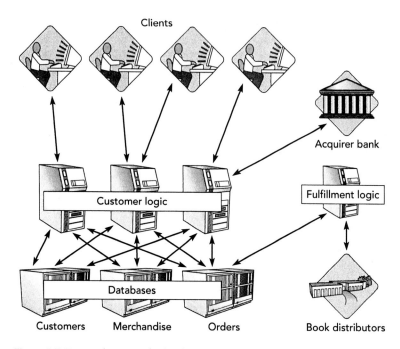

Figure 5.7 Host architecture for books4u.com and its customers

acquirer bank. The fulfillment logic is dedicated to fulfilling completed orders, causing books to be shipped to the customers. It systematically scans the order databases for completed orders, determining what book distributor is appropriate for each order and interacting with that distributor.

With this basic architecture, the question remains as to how the architecture is partitioned among hosts, in particular to insure that the application can serve a multiplicity of customers at the same time the customer base grows quite large. This property of the application is called *scalability* and is a major topic of Chapter 17. In understanding how to do this, it is first necessary to appreciate the concept of a *customer session*. This session consists of all the interactions between a customer (at his client host) and the application, from the time the customer arrives until he completes all orders and leaves.

A host architecture that achieves scalability (at least for moderate numbers of customers) is shown in Figure 5.7. There are two key ideas in this architecture:

- The customer logic for each customer session is dedicated to a single second-tier host—all interactions with a given customer while browsing merchandise and making orders is handled by that single host, as indicated in Figure 5.7. Each host can only handle a limited number of customers, but as

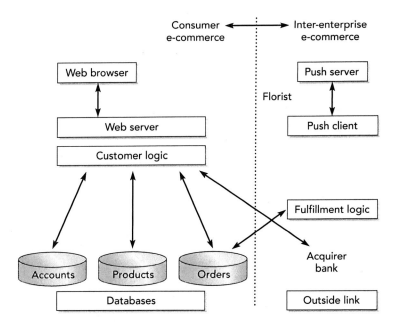

Figure 5.8 Three-tier software architecture for flowers4u.com, its customers, and its participating florists

customers increase, the numbers of second-tier hosts can increase to accommodate all of them—assigning different customer sessions to different hosts.
- A third-tier host is dedicated to each category of database, as labeled in Figure 5.7.

This method of partitioning the application will be discussed further in Chapter 17, but the basic reason is to simplify and minimize the communications required among hosts. There is a shared context for each customer session that requires keeping information about the particulars of the interaction with the customer throughout that session. For example, a record must be kept of the last book title displayed to the customer, so if the customer invokes a button labeled "order this book," the customer logic will know what specific book is to be ordered. The simplest approach is to keep all this session information together and manage it within a single host. Similarly, it is simple to group and manage all information about customers in a single third-tier host. For example, the customer logic always interacts with the same third-tier host regarding any customer information.

5.3.2 Floral Delivery Service

An appropriate software architecture for flowers4u.com, shown in Figure 5.8, is similar to the bookseller. The major difference is in the way fulfillment is

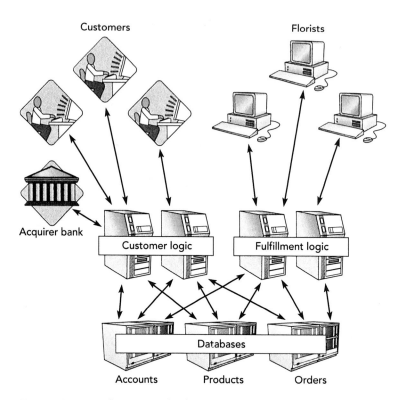

Figure 5.9 Host architecture and software partitioning for flowers4u.com, its customers, and its participating florists

handled. A large number of florists must maintain contact with flowers4u.com in order to receive orders. Since orders are pushed to the florist, the roles of client and server are reversed. A server is installed on each florist's PC—waiting at all times to receive orders—and flowers4u.com maintains a client that interacts with one of these servers whenever a customer order is placed. If this server is running at all times, the order can be passed soon after it is initiated by the customer.

Partitioning of an application host is shown in Figure 5.9. In this case the scalability of the fulfillment logic is an issue, since there are many florists. Thus, a dedicated second-tier host is assigned to a group of florists—however many it can reasonably handle—with hosts added as the number of florists increases.

5.4   *Trends in Client-Server Computing

Three-tier client-server architecture is only one of many possibilities for partitioning application functionality among hosts. A generalization is *multitier* client-server architecture, which structures the application in four or more tiers. The declining cost of servers based on microprocessor technology encourages approaches that trade off more hosts for other benefits such as better performance or reduced administrative costs. Another trend moving in the opposite direction is the growing popularity of mainframes as servers in a two-tier client-server architecture, driven in part by their rapidly declining cost. This illustrates that like the rest of computing, client-server computing is a moving target.

Discussion

D5.3 What are some obvious problems arising when trying to integrate legacy client-server departmental applications into an enterprise application?

5.5   *Open Issue: Beyond Client-Server Computing

Client-server computing is relatively mature, suggesting that a new phase of computing is near. The use of the Internet in commercial applications is a recent development, suggesting it is not yet mature. Both these observations raise questions of what comes next.

Client-server architecture is not an endpoint in the evolution of computing, but a stepping stone. But a stepping stone to what? The origin—and the strength as well—of client-server computing was in allowing users on desktop computers to access legacy applications on mainframes or other servers. It was a logical and incremental progression and not a clean break with the past.

There are two major unmet needs that the current client-server architectures do not address sufficiently:

- Organizational needs change quickly, and it is also important to quickly deploy applications supporting new business opportunities. This implies an ability to build new applications quickly—faster than if they are built from scratch. New applications need to be designed, implemented, and deployed by mixing and matching existing modules (databases, presentation, etc.). Client-server systems typically couple the tiers too closely to make this feasible, and one of the roles of additional tier(s) is to mediate in a way that is more flexible.
- Enterprise and cross-enterprise applications require data integration across different departments and different enterprises (see Chapter 6). Client-server computing has evolved primarily as a vehicle to support departmental applications and by itself does not supply the needed data integration.

Much more radical departures from the past are discussed in Chapter 16, such as distributed object management. These suggest an amorphous architecture, in which applications can search for interesting subsystems from a wide variety of sources and configure themselves more dynamically. There may also be mobile subsystems (called agents) that actively roam the globe looking for interesting goods or information on the user's behalf. This vision will entail a sophisticated infrastructure that doesn't exist today, as the client-server architecture is too simplistic to support it.

Review

Client-server architecture partitions the application across a client host, which is typically a desktop computer accessed by the user, and a server host. The client typically makes requests of the server, based on user input, which responds to those requests. There is an asymmetry of function, with the client initiating action and the server always available for requests from the client. Typically there are many clients for each server, and a client can access more than one server.

The three-tier client-server architecture defines two types of servers—one managing shared data (typically managed by a database management system) and the other running application logic. The client functionality is limited to the presentation—that portion of the application relating directly to obtaining direction from the users and presenting information back to them.

The Web is an important example of a client-server application. It has become common to integrate the Web as the presentation of a three-tier architecture. For this purpose, Web servers provide a common gateway interchange that allows application logic and shared data to be added.

Key Concepts

Client-server architecture:

- Two-tier architecture
- Three-tier architecture: presentation, application logic, shared data

Peer-to-peer architecture

World Wide Web:

- Common gateway interchange (CGI)

Further Reading

[OHE96a] is an accessible and excellent source of additional detail on the client-server software technologies, including current industry activity. [Wat95] covers the same basic material in much less technical detail, with the needs of managers especially in mind.

Exercises

E5.1 Give two examples from your personal experience of a two-tier client-server interaction that doesn't involve computers or networks. In each example, state several differences in the roles of the client and server.

E5.2 For each of the examples in Exercise 5.1, ignore how it is actually done in practice, and state a couple of different *possibilities* for the two-tier partitioning of functionality between client and server. State some considerations (scalability, administration, flexibility, etc.) that might be taken into account in choosing between these possibilities.

E5.3 If it makes sense, recast each of your examples in Exercise 5.1 as a three-tier rather than two-tier architecture. If it makes no sense, state why not.

E5.4 For each of the following applications, decide whether a two-tier client-server or peer-to-peer architecture is most appropriate, and state your reasons. If you choose client-server architecture, describe your partitioning of functionality between client and server:

   a. Newsgroup

   b. Calendar and scheduling

   c. Collaborative authoring

   d. Remote conferencing

E5.5 Describe what you believe would be an appropriate two-tier or three-tier client-server or peer-to-peer architecture for any two of the following applications. List the major functions assigned to each host in your architecture.

   a. An application for selling insurance to consumers through insurance company agents carrying mobile computers. The agents access information about policies, run financial projections, and enter customer orders.

   b. An application for issuing driver's licenses through a collection of local offices and a central motor vehicle bureau. Customers go to the local office to obtain new driver's licenses, and the bureau maintains central records.

c. An e-commerce application for selling published reports over the Internet.

d. An application for coordinating a manufacturer's inventory of parts with the manufacturing operations of one of its suppliers, keeping track of and controlling the flow of parts from the supplier.

e. An application for managing bank ATM machines and the centralized bank account records.

E5.6 Consider the stock trading application described in "On-Line Stock Trading" on page 68.

a. Describe a three-tier software architecture, including the partitioning of functionality among tiers.

b. Describe a host partitioning for this application that accommodates a large number of customers trading stocks at the same time.

E5.7 Consider the customer-care organization described in "Customer Care" on page 63.

a. Describe a three-tier client-server architecture to address this application.

b. Describe a host architecture that allows the computer company to provide customer service to a large number of customers. Use distinct servers to support the two departments involved (customer service and technical support).

c. Consider how a "pure" client-server architecture does not address the needs of this application because of the interdepartmental workflow aspect. How do the departmental servers need to interact to realize this functionality?

Modularity and Layering

The overview of information technology in Chapter 4 introduced the important concept of architecture as applied to networked computing systems and gave an overview of the infrastructure supporting networked applications, including both equipment and software. The infrastructure provides the environment within which networked applications run. The designers of the infrastructure have attempted to make it easy to develop and deploy networked applications, in part by hiding the details of common operations, such as storing and communicating data, and in part by incorporating in the infrastructure facilities needed by many applications.

ANALOGY: *In creating a new business, much existing infrastructure—such as real estate and telephone and transportation—is available and analogous to the computer and network equipment. A services infrastructure analogous to the software infrastructure includes package delivery, legal and accounting firms, and real-estate property management. Incorporating these existing capabilities rather than building them from scratch makes it much easier to build the business.*

For those contemplating using networked computing, and especially conceptualizing new networked applications, an understanding of architectural principles is important. Getting the architecture right is the most important step in the conceptualization and design of any system because it is the hardest aspect to change, and it influences everything that follows. The architecture is also the frontline defense against complexity, which is the most important limitation to what can be accomplished in software.

This chapter sets the stage by discussing why complexity is such a problem and by defining some proven and lasting principles of architecture design. These principles can be summarized in the single word *modularity*, and are illustrated in both the infrastructure software and in application and organizational contexts. Appreciating the infrastructure architecture also sets the stage for conceptualizing applications. Because they are realized by adding to this infrastructure, they simply elaborate or extend the infrastructure. This chapter describes in more depth one architectural approach underlying the infrastructure: layering.

The facility with architecture imparted in this chapter is important in appreciating the industry and standardization discussed in Chapter 7 and the architecture of networked applications discussed in Chapter 10. Also, the layered architecture of the infrastructure sets the stage for more in-depth coverage in Part V.

6.1   Software Complexity

A primary concern in application and infrastructure software design is complexity. As the number of distinct elements in a system increases, and as their interaction becomes more diverse and rich, the system's complexity increases. The most direct definition of a complex system is one that has too many elements and too complicated an interaction among those elements to be understood by a single person or a small group of people. This definition gets to the heart of the difficulties of complex systems—they are not only impossible for one designer to understand fully but also hard to design and maintain because of the large groups of people that must be coordinated.

Software systems are certainly not the most complex systems. The human brain or physiology or the global economy are vastly more complex. Software systems are, however, among the most complex systems that humans must *design*. (There are other systems with comparable complexity, such as nuclear power plants and, increasingly, even microprocessor chips.) There are many specific reasons why complexity is such an issue in software [Boo94]:

- The problem domain addressed by the application is often complex. An application can be no simpler than the problem it addresses.
- Software systems are designed top-down, from scratch. In even much more complex domains—such as the organization of an economy—top-down design has proven ineffective.
- Many other human activities are more constrained. For example, each economic agent operates under the constraints of laws and regulations, such as accounting standards, building codes, the uniform commercial code, etc. Although software suffers the curse of not being so constrained, a trend in modern software is to artificially impose more structure and standards.
- Human organizations are adaptable, because people are intelligent and adaptable. If some unexpected circumstance or problem arises, the people

in the organization can react (see the sidebar "Interfaces as Contracts" later in the chapter). In contrast, computers must be instructed in advance on how to deal with every eventuality. (In practice, a computer may just give up and turns the problem over to a human to deal with. This shouldn't happen often.)

- Most systems people deal with are continuous; they follow predictable paths. Software is discrete, and a program has an astronomically large number of possible conditions and jumps among them in complicated ways. It is not feasible to exhaustively test all possible conditions, and unpredictable or undesirable behavior is inevitable.

- An application software development is a large team effort (of tens or even hundreds or thousands of programmers), with all the management problems that result. (The popular culture thinks of programming as a solitary and antisocial activity, but this is far off the mark.) To be successful, the team must also remain in close contact with the societal or business context for which an application is intended.

- A networked computing system integrates equipment and software from many different vendors. Coordination, discipline, and a carefully conceived architecture design are necessary ingredients for success.

The complexity problem is accentuated for infrastructure software for two reasons. First, its design and development are spread over multiple vendors, adding coordination issues, and second, an infrastructure inherently has to evolve over time as application needs become more demanding. (An example is the evolution from individual and departmental to enterprise and commerce applications, which places great demands on the infrastructure.) The remainder of this chapter discusses how to restrain complexity through architectural techniques, drawing on application, organizational, and infrastructure contexts.

Discussion

D6.1 Discuss at least one complex system that doesn't involve software, such as the economy or human physiology. What makes this system complex? How are modularity, decomposition, and/or assembly manifested in this system?

6.2 Modularity

The architecture of a software system is important because it allows that system to be decomposed into smaller subsystems that can be dealt with separately. "Good" architectures have the properties of effectively limiting complexity and

Modularity in Organizations

Organizations have an architecture just as computing systems do, and they benefit from the same modularity principles. This can be illustrated by a bank and the interaction between three modules—a customer, the loan department, and the physical plant department.

A bank is a system providing financial services to its customers. A partial decomposition of a bank is shown in Figure 6.1. It has departments chosen so that each has relatively little concern about the internal operation of others. The loan department focuses on managing its loan portfolio, underwriting (assessing risk of a loan in the context of a portfolio), and issuing new loans, while the physical plant department maintains the buildings. There is interaction between departments, but it is less frequent and involved than activities within each department. For example, the loan department may report to the physical plant department that a room is dark, but it cares only that light is restored and not how this happens. The physical plant department concerns itself with details, such as diagnosing the problem. Similarly, the bank customer seeking a loan has well-defined "functionality" (such as filling out a loan application) but shouldn't be concerned with internal details in the loan department (such as the internal details of the approval process).

Each of the two departmental modules has an internal decomposition into subsystems. For example, the loan department is internally composed of a receptionist, an underwriter, a loan officer, etc. As there may be multiple underwriters and loan officers, there are finer-granularity

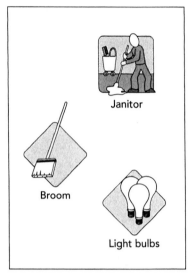

Figure 6.1 Partial decomposition of a bank into modules

providing for future flexibility and change. The term modularity denotes some of the properties of good architectures and is described in the following sections. Other desirable properties of architectures are discussed later in this chapter.

6.2.1 Properties of Modularity

Decomposition—the first and most important phase of architecture—is a divide-and-conquer strategy that allows subsystems to be implemented individually and, one hopes, even autonomously. It allows individual firms—without excessive coordination—to participate in the design, manufacture, and deployment of the infrastructure, and thus it affects the supplier industry organization as well as the technology.

The decomposition should be modular, which means the subsystems—called modules—have some special characteristics summarized in Table 6.1. The most important of these is *separation of concerns*: The internal concerns of one module are mostly not of concern to other modules [Boo94]. This allows the modules to be designed and maintained relatively independently by different design groups or firms, with minimum coordination.

It is useful to consider the human interface of a system from a similar perspective, because similar objectives apply—particularly the separation of concerns,

Table 6.1 Desirable characteristics that describe a modular architecture

Property	Desirable characteristics	Analogy
Functionality	The modules are chosen as distinct and natural functional groupings.	A government is modularized into executive, legislative, and judicial branches. Establishing and enforcing laws and sitting in judgement of lawbreakers are distinct and well-defined functions assigned to different modules.
Hierarchy	Each module can itself be a system—internally decomposed into modules that will not be visible externally.	The executive branch of government is decomposed into agencies and departments, each of which has an internal modular structure.
Separation of concerns	The functional groupings incorporated within each module are strongly associated and only weakly associated with functionality internal to other modules.	Law enforcement requires internal coordination, but its operations are of little concern to the legislature or judiciary.
Interoperability	Modules can successfully interact to realize the higher purposes of the system.	Law enforcement has well-defined procedures for bringing alleged lawbreakers before the judiciary, which results in their successful prosecution.
Reusability	Modules are defined, implemented, and documented independently of a specific system, so their design can be reused in other systems.	The concepts behind some modules in the U.S. government structure have been adopted by other countries, without the need to adopt them all.

modules associated with the loan officers (the "loan service group") and all underwriters (the "risk management group"). At a coarser granularity, the bank is decomposed into "customer services" and "business management" divisions, where the former groups modules dealing with customers (loans, withdrawals, deposits, etc.), and the latter encompasses internal functions (accounting, property management, physical plant, etc.).

because users should not be exposed to internal implementation details of an application any more than necessary. For this limited purpose, the users can be considered as "modules" and their "functionality" considered in the architecture.

EXAMPLE: *The architecture of a computer illustrates modularity. Figure 6.2 presents a simplified view, including major modules:*

- *A processor, which executes a program. A computer may include more than one processor (see Chapter 17).*
- *The memory, which stores program instructions and data currently being used.*
- *The storage—such as magnetic disks, CD-ROMs, etc.—keeps massive amounts of data, programs, etc.*
- *The network adapter connects the host to a network.*

The storage and network adapter are called peripherals—*because they assist the processor—and are connected to the processor by a bus (a very high speed connection shared by all the modules). Each of these modules has lots of internal activity, but their interaction with others is relatively straightforward.*

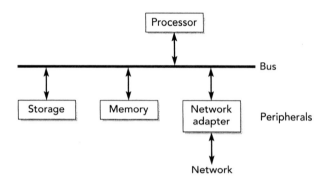

Figure 6.2 The simplified modularity in a computer system

> *Modules can be designed and manufactured by different firms because of that well-defined and well-documented interaction (see Chapter 7).*

Reusability reduces the overall cost and time for future developments but typically requires added analysis, functionality, or configurability. One major goal of the infrastructure is this design reusability—some vendors specialize in designing specific modules, which are resold to many companies to include in their systems.

6.2.2   Granularity and Hierarchy

Granularity determines the number of modules and the range of functionality of each. The architecture designer can choose a *fine* granularity—with many small modules—or a *coarse* granularity, with few large modules (these are usually called fine-grain and coarse-grain architectures, respectively). Each of these alternatives has advantages. A coarse-grain architecture is easier to understand at the architecture level, as there are fewer things to keep track of. A fine-grain architecture does a better job of "divide and conquer," dividing a system into more, smaller modules whose internal workings are simpler and easier to understand.

Since neither fine- nor coarse-grain architectures are ideal, architects look for ways to gain the best advantages of both. Hierarchy—meaning modules are themselves composed of internal modules—avoids defining a single granularity. This "decomposition within modules" architecture allows the system to be viewed at different levels of granularity, as appropriate.

EXAMPLE: *The single computer, whose internal composition into modules is shown in Figure 6.2, is itself a module (a host) in the larger client-server archi-*

tecture in Chapter 5. The overall hardware architecture is thus a two-level hierarchy. Each module in Figure 6.2 can be internally decomposed into modules in a third finer-grain level of hierarchy. For example, the processor has internal modules like "arithmetic unit," "address unit," etc. defined by the manufacturer of that module.

ANALOGY: *Political units are often composed hierarchically, such as (in the United States) nation, states, counties, and cities. Each political unit at one level of the hierarchy is internally composed of political units from the next lowest level.*

A single module will never be split across two or more hosts; it will reside in its entirety in one host. The interaction between application partitions on different hosts is forced to be an interaction between modules.

EXAMPLE: *In the three-tier client-server architecture, the application is split between three modules: presentation, application logic, and data sharing. These modules interact over the network in the way described here. These are typically very large grain modules, so each is hierarchically decomposed into smaller-grain modules.*

6.2.3   Interfaces

Each module must interact with others within the system. It is only through this interaction that the desired higher-level system capabilities emerge. The architecture designer should be thoughtful about this interaction to insure that the system operates correctly under all circumstances and is flexible enough to accommodate future change.

The interaction between modules focuses on an *interface* to each module. The interface is a key concept in computing, and it is well worth understanding both what an interface is and what it is not. Consider a specific module. The interface is the external view of this module, specifying what functions it performs and instructing other modules on precisely how to invoke those functions. Thus, the interface *is* those properties of the module that are determined at the time of architecture design. The interface is *not* a specification of how a module is actually implemented internally. In fact, there may be different versions of a module that share a common interface but are implemented differently, or the implementation may change over time without affecting the interface. This separation of functionality between a module interface and implementation is a key concept because it contributes to the separation of concerns that are integral to modularity.

Interfaces as Contracts

One aspect of law—writing a contract—has some similarity to the design of an interface. An interface is a form of contract that one module offers to other modules, promising to do certain things when asked and specifying certain protocols for accomplishing those things.

Much of the complexity of writing a contract is in anticipating every possible circumstance; similarly, the implementer of a module must anticipate every possible circumstance and give precise directions to the module on how to deal with it. The module implementer cannot assume that other modules will always follow the contract but, as in a legal contract, must deal reasonably with any misuse or abuse that may arise because other module implementers misunderstood the interface, or because they erred.

The lawyer's task is eased by several factors that don't benefit module designers. First, there is a "shared context" in the definition of legal terms, laws, and case law. Thus, some issues can be left to the "default" or a standard doctrine. Second, exceptional circumstances can be handled by applying human judgements in a court of law. The court considers the *intent* of the parties to the contract. Alas, computers and software are not nearly as sophisticated. Finally, a contract is usually written by one or a few attorneys, whereas software systems may be constructed by tens or hundreds or sometimes even thousands of programmers. This leads to a scale of complexity that demands strong management and high discipline.

Hardware Interfaces

Hardware interfaces, while also important, take a quite different form from software interfaces. They specify a physical wire or fiber and connector and the precise definition of the electrical or optical signals carried on that wire or fiber.

EXAMPLE: *An electric outlet is an example of a hardware interface. The interface definition includes the physical configuration of the compatible plug and socket, as well as electrical characteristics like voltage (110 or 220 volts), frequency (50 or 60 Hz), and maximum current in amps. In computers, the assorted jacks on the back (serial port, parallel port, monitor jack, power plug, etc.) are examples of interfaces. Each is associated with a set of physical (number of pins, geometry, etc.), electrical (voltage, etc.), and logical (order and meaning of bits) specifications.*

The reason for modularizing the system in the hardware domain is similar to software—so that different modules can be designed independently and provided by different companies, and a company designing and marketing a new subsystem sees a large potential market.

EXAMPLE: *If there was no well-defined interface for the electric socket, then either your electric appliances would have to be provided by the power company, or your computer company would have to supply power. By having a standard electrical interface, and*

EXAMPLE: *A familiar example of an equipment module is a printer. The interface to the printer does advertise to the computer what it does (prints pages) and how to invoke those functions (various control actions, a data representation of the document to print with a specified structure and interpretation, etc.). The interface does not specify anything about how the printer performs its functions. In fact, you are no doubt familiar with different types of printers, such as inkjet and laser, that use different technologies to perform the printing but have identical interfaces (hook up to the same computer in the same way). This separation of function from implementation allows your desktop applications to print without worrying about (or depending on) details about how the printing is actually done.*

A module interface is specified at the time the architecture is designed without making any assumptions about how the module will be implemented. Later, when the implementation of a module is turned over to somebody to implement, the interface specification is used as a starting point. It tells the implementers what functions have been promised to other modules and how those other modules have been told to invoke those functions.

How an interface works depends to some extent on whether it is a hardware or software interface, and even within each category it can work differently. The primary concern here is with software interfaces, although hardware interfaces are discussed in the sidebar "Hardware Interfaces." Software interfaces, which are harder to visualize since they have no physical manifestation, are the boundary between two software programs, or the boundary between two modules within the same software program. The type of software interface considered here follows the same client-server model discussed in Chapter 5. For purposes of the interface, each module is considered to be a server, which provides capabilities to other modules, and when other modules invoke those capabilities, they are acting as clients.

Actions

The nature of an interface to a software module can now be considered more precisely. For a server module, the key question is what it does. This can be expressed in terms of available actions that the module is prepared to take. An *action* is simply something specific (and documented) that the module does. Typically there will be a menu of actions that a module is prepared to take. Another module *invokes* a specific action to get something done, and later it may invoke other actions.

EXAMPLE: *It might be useful—within a larger software system—to have a module that provides the same capabilities as a pocket calculator—adding, subtracting, multiplying, dividing, taking square roots, etc. Whenever another module needs to do some arithmetic—for example, to add a deposit to a bank account—it can invoke the appropriate action or actions of the calculator module. The interface could be similar to that of a pocket calculator, except there are no physical keys or physical display. Its actions are things like "add numbers," "subtract numbers," etc.*

not having to deal with the logistics of providing power, a computer company sees a larger potential market.

Parameters and Returns

Usually, just telling a module what action to perform is not sufficient. There is a need to pass data to a module and receive data back from that module in the course of invoking an action.

EXAMPLE: *Asking the calculator module to add is not too useful unless you can also tell it what two numbers to add and get back the sum. The numbers to add are data passed to the module, and the resulting sum is data returned to the invoking client module.*

To address this need, every action has optional parameters and returns associated with it. Parameters are data that the server module expects to receive in the course of invoking that action, and which customize that action. Returns are data that the client module expects to receive back in the course of invoking that action.

Action Menus

A typical server module will have more than one action that it is willing to perform. Recall that the interface to a server module tells the world what it is prepared to do for other client modules. This takes the specific form of a list of actions it is willing to perform and, for each such action, not only what parameter values it expects when that action is invoked but also what returns it will pass back to the client when that action is invoked.

Thus, a complete interface specification, assuming there are *n* actions available, looks like this:

```
action-1: parameters → returns;
action-2: parameters → returns;
action-3: parameters → returns;
. . .
action-n: parameters → returns;
```

For each action, `parameters` is a list of specific parameter data expected by the module, and similarly, each `returns` is a list of specific return data promised back to the invoking module.

Interfaces and Organizations

Organizations illustrate interfaces as well as modularity. For the bank example of "Modularity in Organizations" on page 160, there are two interfaces—to the customer and between the loan and physical plant departments, as illustrated in Figure 6.3. The interface to the loan department expects certain standard actions, such as a request for a loan (from a customer) and the submission of a completed loan application (from the customer). Each request has predetermined responses, such as returning a blank loan application and responding yes or no to the loan request. Similarly, the physical plant department requires a standard submitted form to report a problem or a request for service (a "work order"). In each case, the department defines specific actions it is prepared to take.

When a customer makes a loan application ("invokes the loan application action"), she is a client of the bank, and the bank loan department is acting as a server to her. Similarly, when the loan department requests a service from the physical plant department ("invokes the work order action"), it is acting as a client of the physical plant department.

The loan department might define the following actions:

```
loan_request: name,amount
→ loan_application_form;
loan_application:
completed_application →
answer,loan_number;
request_for_funds:
loan_number,amount →
money;
```

The loan_request alerts the loan department that the customer is applying for a loan, with customer name and the amount of the loan as

EXAMPLE: *Some of the actions available at the interface to the calculator module, assuming it emulates a standard four-function calculator, would include*

```
clear: → display;
enter: number →display;
add: addend → display;
multiply: multiplier → display;
square_root: → display;
```

Most of these actions have a single parameter—the number to be operated on (corresponding to what would be punched on the keys of a physical calculator)—and a return, which is the numerical value resulting from the action (and would be displayed on a physical calculator). Actions may not have parameters or returns. For example, square_root *has no parameter because it takes the square root of whatever number is currently displayed. Similarly,* add *has only one number as a parameter because it adds that number to the displayed value.*

Some specific values can be put into these actions to see what the calculator module would do:

```
clear: → 0;
enter: 2 → 2;
multiply: 8 →16
square_root: → 4;
```

Significantly, the calculator interface specification reveals nothing about how the calculator performs these functions. These details are encapsulated, as in a real calculator. Behind the scenes, there are a number of possibilities—a mechanical contraption controlled by the computer, an operator operating an abacus, or more likely a software program running on that host. But the module will continue invoking the calculator's actions as long as the result is correct.

Although not a formal part of an interface, *documentation*—a description of the general functions of the module, as well as a description of each action, parameter, and return—is very important. The documentation is the primary resource helping a programmer incorporate a module into a system.

Another example illustrates that the interface between hardware and software may be specified similarly from the perspective of the software side.

EXAMPLE: *A computer system architecture would include the interface to the memory module in Figure 6.2. The two actions write data into the memory and read data from the memory:*

```
write: address,size_of_data,data_to_write ;
read: address, size_of_data → data_starting_at_that_address;
```

The parameter address *specifies a location in memory to store or retrieve the data (analogous to a street address). Either parameters or returns, or both, may*

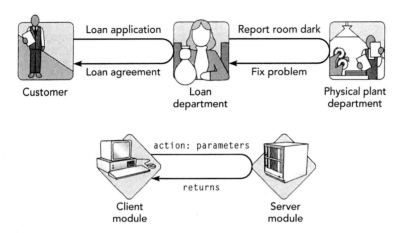

parameters. The loan department returns a `loan_application_form`, but also does other things internally (such as entering the customer in a database) that are not visible to the customer. The customer can then make a `loan_application` parameterized by the `completed_application_form`. After going through an elaborate internal approval process, the loan department returns an `answer` (yes or no) and a `loan_number`. The purpose of the `loan_number` is to identify the loan when the customer later makes a `request_for_funds`.

Figure 6.3 Examples of module interfaces in the bank example

be missing from selected actions, as in this example. There are other services the memory module might perform, such as

```
count_total_amount_of_data_stored: → number_of_bytes;
purge_all_data: → ;
```

Data Types

A typical action passes data from client to server modules (as parameters) and from server to client (as returns). In the discussion thus far, these parameters and returns were given descriptive names, which informs you or me of their purpose. This is clearly not enough for the modules involved. As described in "Information Content" on page 19, they must know the structure and interpretation of the data they are passed in order to deal with it reasonably. The data itself is just bits, but what usually matters is whether those bits represent text, numbers, pictures, or something else. The purpose of the interface action is to manipulate those bits in a manner specific to the information they represent.

EXAMPLE: *For the calculator module, in the action*

```
add: addend → display;
```

the client and server have to agree on what type of number the addend *and* display *data represent. Further, even if they agree that the addend and display are both numbers with a certain number of bits before the decimal place and after the decimal place, there is ambiguity as to how those numbers are represented as data. Without agreement on these issues, the result will not satisfy the intended purpose.*

Data Types

A specification of the structure and interpretation of a piece of data is called a data type. It specifies the range of values represented by a piece of data and the manipulations that may be performed on that data. The basic, or atomic, types represent data used in a wide variety of applications, the most important of which are listed in Table 6.2. Unfortunately, the details of representation of even these standard data types differ across computing platforms.

Table 6.2 Some widely used basic data types

Basic type	Information represented	Examples
Integer	Natural number, limited in size by the number of bits in its representation; can be manipulated by arithmetic operations.	The number of letters in the Roman alphabet is 26.
Float	Real number approximated by a finite number of digits in scientific notation. Usually it is written in the form nEm, which is equivalent to $n \times 10^m$ in scientific notation. The size of n and m are limited by the number of bits of representation. Can be manipulated by arithmetic operations.	π is 3.14159E0 (approximately); Avogadro's number (number of atoms in a mole) is 6.02E23, which in scientific notation would be 6.02×10^{23} (approximately).
Character	Single character from the Roman alphabet, including punctuation, digits, and special characters. Each key on a keyboard represents one character. Common representations are ASCII (8 bits) and Unicode (16 bits).	The word "Abe" has three characters: A, b, and e.
String	An ordered set of characters.	The name David can be represented by the string "David".

The *data type* was invented as a way for modules to agree on the structure and interpretation of data (see the sidebar "Data Types"). A type is attached to a specific parameter or return, and it specifies to both modules the structure and interpretation to be attached to that data when it is passed between modules.

The parameters and returns at an interface thus have three elements, as listed in Table 6.3: name, type, and value. The *name* is a moniker that is meaningful to people and also uniquely identifies a parameter or return. The *type* specifies to both modules the structure and interpretation to be used in processing that parameter or return. The *value* is the actual information represented by the collection of bits passed between modules in an action invocation. The name and type are fixed properties that never change—they are part of the interface specification. The value is typically different each time an action is invoked at the interface, depending on the information the modules wish to communicate.

The interface specification includes not only a list of parameter and return names but also a type associated with each of those parameters and returns.

EXAMPLE: *For the calculator module, the complete* add *action specification might be*

Table 6.3 Three properties of data passed through an interface

Property	Description	Examples
Name	A descriptive moniker that allows the data to be referred to multiple times and is also suggestive to a human.	`zip_code` is a customer's postal code; `customer_name` stores the name of a bank customer.
Type	Specifies the range of values of the data, as well as the manipulations that may be performed on it. The type itself does not specify a representation as data—that is, specific to the computing platform.	An `Integer` is a natural number that can fall in a specified range and be subject to arithmetic operations.
Value	The actual value from the range of values that the data represents at a given invocation.	23958 is the current value of an `Integer`.

```
add: float addend → float display;
```

where "`float addend`" specifies that the parameter with name `addend` has type `float`.

Protocols

Often an interface specification is expanded from a menu of actions to include expectations or restrictions on the order in which actions are taken. This defines a *protocol*. This will occur when sequences of actions accomplish higher-level functionality.

E X A M P L E :   *The four-function calculator actually requires two actions just to add two numbers and get a result. In particular, the first addend has to be entered, and then the* add *action has to be invoked with the second addend as a parameter:*

```
enter: addend-1 → display;
add: addend-2 → display;
```

The protocol further specifies that the result, the sum of addend-1 *and* addend-2, *is the* display *return for the* add *action.*

Protocols, an extremely important aspect of module interactions both within applications and within the infrastructure, are discussed again in Chapter 10 in the context of applications. (For example, protocols are an important enabler for security, as elaborated in Chapter 13, and network services, as discussed in Chapter 18.) Even a single action invocation is broken down into the steps of a protocol within the infrastructure (see the sidebar "Anatomy of an Action Invocation").

Anatomy of an Action Invocation

The invocation of an action at a module interface can be broken down into constituent steps. This recognizes a natural ordering: A module has to know an action has been invoked, along with the parameter data, before it can perform the computation necessary to determine the returns. This reality is illustrated in Figure 6.4, which shows the order of steps that actually occur in a module interaction. Fortunately, these steps—which constitute a simple protocol required for each invocation of an action—are buried within the infrastructure, so a module implementer doesn't have to worry about them. The protocol includes the passage of data in both directions bracketed by some computation by the server. Both the client and server modules are typically affected by the invocation—for example, each may have stored internal data that is changed.

The client sees only the *results* of the action—the returns specified at the interface—and otherwise has no visibility into what happens internally to the server. Similarly, the server sees nothing but the requested action and its parameters, with no visibility into the client—including even its interface!

When an action is invoked, the server is free to invoke one or more actions of *other* modules in the course of calculating returns. This is, however, *not* revealed as a part of its interface. It is one of those internal implementation details that is hidden. When a server does invoke the action of another module, it is acting *temporarily* as a client. Thus, modules will typically act—at different times—as either a

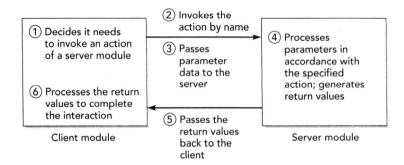

Figure 6.4 Details of a client-server interaction

Human Interfaces

The term interface also applies to the interaction between a user and a computer application. This is why a graphical user interface (GUI) is called an interface too. While this interface uses many elements comfortable to people, such as graphics, images, animation, sound, pointing devices, and keyboards, one of its foundations is the presentation of customizable actions in menus. Behind the scenes, the interface to application modules follows a similar client-server model. This is most visible in the standard approach in which the user is offered a list of actions, often in a pull-down menu, and selects one of them. Those actions may be parameterized (for example, by typing values in a dialog box) and may have returns (for example, something appearing on the screen as a result of the action).

E X A M P L E : *A bank ATM allows a customer to perform certain limited functions on her account—it offers a human interface to a bank customer. Although not presented to the customer in exactly this way, the ATM offers a set of parameterizable actions such as*

```
authenticate: account_number, PIN → available_actions;
show_balance: → account_balance;
withdraw: amount → cash, new_balance;
deposit: money → new_balance;
```

There are many more elaborate possibilities reflected in many applications. Some alternative forms of interface will be discussed in Chapter 10.

Messages

Interaction among modules using action invocations is not the only possibility. It is best described as a "tightly coupled" interaction, but there are more "loosely coupled" methods as well. The most common example is the message. As already described in Chapter 4, a message is simply a package of data that one module (the sender) communicates to another (the recipient), where the sender and recipient have an agreement between themselves as to the structure and interpretation of the data in that message. The message is much simpler than an action invocation, because there is no menu of actions and nothing is returned. It is a one-way communication rather than a two-way interaction.

A message is easily implemented using an action invocation. A module that wishes to receive messages can provide an action for that purpose:

```
receive_message: message_body  →;
```

Typically this is the only action such a module will provide at its interface. Note that there are no returns, because none is expected by the sender.

client or a server. The terms client and server refer to the distinct roles of the two modules in the context of a single action invocation.

In the client-server host architecture of Chapter 5, the terms client (server) refer to the *preponderance* of a host's interaction with other hosts, but do not necessarily restrict a host to always act as a client (server) with each and every action invocation.

Discussion

D6.2 Discuss how the architectural principles discussed here apply to organizational design. Does management—the designers of the organizational architecture—already use these techniques, or the equivalent? Could they benefit from a cross-fertilization of these ideas? Do they use other techniques that might benefit computing?

6.3   More on Layered Infrastructure Software

The architectural concepts of modularity and their interfaces aid the understanding and appreciation of the software infrastructure supporting networked applications. In particular, the infrastructure uses the specific layering form of modularity briefly described in "Infrastructure Software Layering" on page 120. Further detail on this general structure is given here, with a more detailed description of the infrastructure deferred to Part V of this book.

6.3.1   Goals of the Infrastructure

Well-principled architecture design as described is one goal in the design of the infrastructure, but there are other goals, such as

- Minimize the cost and maximize the performance (see Chapter 17).
- Minimize the effort required to develop and maintain new applications, in part by including capabilities in the infrastructure required by a wide range of applications (see Chapter 10).

Layering in Applications

Layering as a specific form of modularity is sometimes used at the top level of hierarchy in applications as well as infrastructure software. The three-tier client-server architecture is a simple example of layering, because the application module in the third tier (shared data) acts as a server to the second tier (application logic), and the second tier acts as a server to the first tier (presentation). Typically the first tier does not interact directly with the third tier. Thus, the tiers have all the characteristics of layers, although they are not called that.

Another example of layering in applications is software components and frameworks, which are discussed in Chapter 10. These can be thought of as an existing layer upon which the application is built.

- Provide capabilities to support the operation of the system and contribute to its trustworthiness and reliability (see Chapter 13).

The layered architecture described next was not designed top-down by a single individual or organization. It is the result of the evolution of computing systems over many years—an evolution almost Darwinian in nature because it has involved many hundreds of equipment and software suppliers and tens or hundreds of thousands of individual contributors. Interfaces play an important role in coordinating these many players. Interfaces are actually established through an industry process called standardization, described in Chapter 7. Some economic concepts that help explain the technological trajectory are deferred to Chapter 8.

6.3.2 Layering Principle

The specific form of modularity seen in the software infrastructure, at the top level of hierarchy, is layering, similar to the rings of an onion. This seems a relatively arbitrary choice for the infrastructure modularity, as certainly there would be numerous other possibilities. Layering as a form of modularity can be used in applications as well (see the sidebar "Layering in Applications").

Layering not only refers to an infrastructure decomposition into layers, but also includes important constraints on the interactions among those layers. In particular, the *layering principle* sets out some constraints (see Figure 6.5):

- Each layer is a server to the layer above, providing a standard set of actions but not revealing how they are implemented. Each layer documents its interface for the benefit of layers above, saying in effect, "Here are the actions I can perform to support you, but don't ask how I do them." As a result, the implementation of one layer can be changed without affecting the layers above. For example, a new networking technology can be introduced to the infrastructure (say, Ethernet replacing Token Ring) without requiring changes to the middleware layers or the application.
- Each layer is a client to the layer below, utilizing its available actions in the course of providing its services to the layer above it.
- Each layer is permitted to interact with only layers immediately above and below. Since each layer interacts only with the layer immediately below, that layer hides the layers below it.

Functionally, the idea is to provide increasingly elaborated or specialized services at each higher layer, with those services based on the services provided by lower layers and adding functionality. This approach is by no means unique to

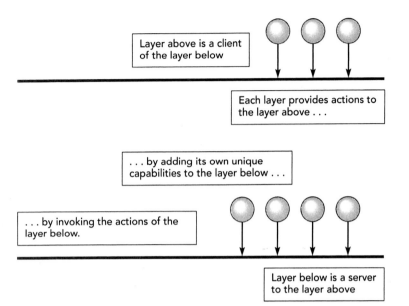

Figure 6.5 The layering principle in software/hardware modularity

Table 6.4 A layered architecture for the manufacturer of cyberwidgets

Layer	Functionality	Interaction with layer below
Assembly (third floor)	Assembles parts into finished cyberwidgets.	Requests specific parts as needed for assembly.
Inventory (second floor)	Stores parts awaiting assembly.	Indicates which parts are needed (in danger of starving assembly layer) or in excess supply (filling up allotted space). Requests and stores any parts that have arrived in receiving.
Receiving (first floor)	Coordinates the supply of parts, receives parts, and pays suppliers.	Orders and receives parts, unloading, counting, and authorizing payment.
Supply (external)	Manufactures and conveys parts to be assembled into cyberwidgets.	There is no layer below.

networked computing but is observable in the industrial economy (see the side-bar "Industrial Layering Example").

ANALOGY: *A manufacturing firm utilizes the services of a trucking company—a "lower-layer" service. The "action" of the trucking firm is to deliver material*

Industrial Layering Example

Consider a company that manufactures "cyberwidgets." The architecture of the company defines four layers—supply, receiving, inventory, and assembly—and a building designed around these modules. The inventory layer serves the assembly layer and is a client of the receiving layer, etc. The building has three floors, one for each of the receiving, inventory, and assembly modules. The supply layer encapsulates all the suppliers of parts assembled into cyberwidgets and is external to the building, but it interacts through the trucks and drivers they send. The interaction among modules follows the layering principle in that the module corresponding to each floor (one layer) makes direct use of the capability of the floor below, but no others. The four layers are described in Table 6.4.

The architecture of the building can support these layers by including means for each floor to make requests of the floor below (say, by an intercom system) and also means to convey parts to the floor immediately above (such as conveyor belts) in response to requests.

Each cyberwidget manufacturing plant layer has a specific functionality, which it fulfills by using capabilities of the layer immediately below. The assembly layer has a specific action it requests of the inventory layer,

```
send_one_part: part_ID →
part;
```

and the inventory layer has a specific action it can request of the receiving layer:

```
send_next_part: →
next_part;
```

The interface to each layer hides details of how it provides its actions. For example, receiving hides its supplier coordination functions, and inventory hides the amount of inventory stored.

This example has other features similar to the software infrastructure. For example, specific functions analogous to "supply," "receiving," and "inventory" are required in network computing (see Chapter 12). The coordination of supplier with assembly illustrates a problem in computing called flow control, described in Chapter 18.

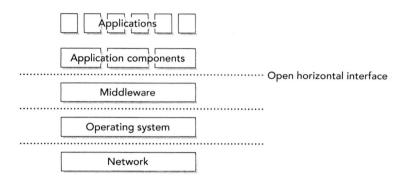

Figure 6.6 A simplified layered architecture for networked computing software infrastructure

given to it on time to the destination specified. It hides many details of its operations, such as warehouses, loading and reloading of trucks, tracking, etc. In turn, the trucking firm depends on a "lower-layer" railroad service. The railway's "action" is to transport a truck from one point to another, and internal details such as how it piggybacks a truck on a railroad car or accumulates railroad cars from many sources and hooks them together in a single train are not shown at its interface.

6.3.3 The Layers in a Computing Infrastructure

Figure 6.6 illustrates the major infrastructure layers in a networked computing system, in this case focusing on the communications (as opposed to storage). The functionality of each layer is summarized in Table 6.5.

How do the layers interact to get things done? Figure 6.7 shows application modules on two different hosts (A and B) interacting to realize a networked application. As much as possible, the infrastructure wants to make this interaction identical to how the modules would interact if they were on the *same* host—indicated by the dashed line. That way, the application implementer has to worry less about the fact the application is partitioned across hosts and has more time to dwell on the application functionality. The implementer also has more freedom to move modules around among hosts. There are some unavoidable complications of interacting between hosts—for example, the client has to tell the infrastructure on what host the server resides—but the infrastructure can achieve this ideal.

The way the infrastructure actually implements the interaction involves *all* the layers, as indicated by the solid line. Obviously, the network layer has to be involved, because it is the only means of communication between the hosts.

Table 6.5 Major layers in a computer infrastructure

Layer	Function	Analogy
Applications (Chapter 10)	Specialized functionality directly needed by a user or organization (such as electronic commerce, information retrieval, or collaboration).	A firm is in a particular line of business (such as automobile manufacture) and defines various processes tailored to the operation of that business (such as assembly lines).
Application components (Chapter 10)	Specialized modules incorporated by many applications and purchased as a product from an outside company.	All automobile manufacturers buy components, such as tires and batteries, from common suppliers.
Middleware (Chapter 16)	Hides the heterogeneity and distribution of operating system and network from the application. Also provides capabilities useful to a wide range of applications.	Professional services, such as accounting, law, private investigation, benefit all firms.
Operating system (Chapter 17)	Manages and hides the details of resources such as storage and printing. Also manages the details of interhost communications.	Resource management services such as janitorial, gardening are useful to firms.
Network (Chapter 18)	Communication of data from one host to another.	To support interaction among its different locations, a firm uses telephone and overnight package delivery companies.

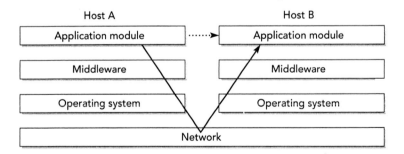

Figure 6.7 How the interaction of modules on different hosts is supported by the infrastructure layers

The operating system and middleware layers have their own important roles to play as well; in particular, they cooperate to pass data in both directions on behalf of the two middleware layers. The middleware layer may realize services more directly useful to applications, as described shortly. In practice there is no single middleware solution. An application implementer may be free to pick and choose among middleware alternatives, so there are other possibilities, some of which are discussed later (Chapter 12 and Chapter 16). For example, one mid-dleware option supports message services rather than action invocations.

EXAMPLE: *Different applications have distinctive needs, which can be matched by the choice of an appropriate middleware solution. For example, an interactive information access application has an inherent client-server structure: A user makes a request for information, and that information is returned. An email application has an inherent message-oriented structure: An email message is sent, but a reply is not necessarily expected. Thus, an information access application might choose middleware that provides an action invocation, and an email application might choose middleware that supports messages.*

The layered architecture, as described earlier, assumed that each layer acted exclusively as a client to the layer below. In the scenario of Figure 6.7, data is being passed downward through the layers in host A and upwards in host B. This is consistent with the client-server interaction if the data is passed as action parameters in host A and as action returns in host B. However, this is not the only possibility. The layering principle can be relaxed a bit by allowing each layer to act as a client of the layer above as well as below. (These are detailed implementation issues—you will be pleased that they are largely ignored in this book.)

In the coverage of the applications and infrastructure in Part IV and Part V, a top-down approach is followed: Each layer is examined successively—beginning with the application in Chapter 9—simplifying the layer below and describing what services it provides to the layer above. This approach is quite similar to how computer systems are actually designed and implemented. Typically, in any given host, the infrastructure layers are purchased from outside vendors, who do not display or even disclose their implementation, and it all works because of the layered modularity and documented interfaces.

EXAMPLE: *Intel focuses on microprocessors, Compaq on desktop computers, Microsoft on operating systems, and Iona on middleware. Each focuses on one layer of the infrastructure, providing an interface promised to layers above but not disclosing much more about implementation.*

6.3.4   Data and Information in Layers

The infrastructure—both equipment and software—concentrates on storage and communication of data. On the other hand, what the application presents to the user is usually information. Where and how does data get turned into

Table 6.6 How layers deal with data and information

Structure and interpretation of data	Storage	Communication
The lowest layers deal with data in its most primitive form: a package of bits. A package of data is a collection of a fixed and known number of bits, with a presumed ordering of those bits. (The term package is used only in this book.) This portion of the infrastructure does not interpret the data in a package in any way.	The file system stores and retrieves packages called files without interpretation—see "File System" on page 125.	A package of data called a message is communicated without interpretation—see "Communications" on page 121. Within the network layer, this message may be fragmented into packets—see "Packets" on page 123.
	The operating system layer, which manages both storage of files and communication of messages on behalf of an application, usually assigns no interpretation to them. In each case, these are the minimal packages of data that have significance to the application.	
The middle layers presume some structure for the data contained in a package. Typically data is structured into basic and user-defined types (described shortly). In some cases, additional structure may be presumed.	A relational DBMS presumes that the data is structured as basic and user-defined types and tables—see "Database Management System (DBMS)" on page 126.	Some middleware layers provide message or action invocation services, the latter with parameters and returns with basic and user-defined data types.
The application assigns additional interpretation to the data.	Within the application, data is interpreted within the specific application context; for example, a number may be interpreted as a bank account balance.	

information or information get turned into data? Who decides what representation is used for the information? The answers to these questions, while subtle, are crucial to understanding how the infrastructure really works. The specific structure and interpretation typically assigned to the data in different layers is described in Table 6.6. This table distinguishes between storage (where the storage and management of data is the primary concern) and communications, and it points out the parallels between the two. The goal now is to explain this table, both as to detail and the philosophy underlying it.

A Package of Data

The first observation is that the structure and interpretation of the data really do change in some substantive ways as the data moves through the infrastructure layers. As described in Table 6.6, there are two common structures for data supported in the infrastructure: the file (in storage) and the message (in communications), both of which are special cases of a *package* of data. (The term package, while not standard, is useful to emphasize the similarities between a file and a message.) Within the network, a message may be further fragmented into packets, which are reassembled at the other side of the network to reconstruct the message. As it moves through the infrastructure, data is often converted among these representations.

EXAMPLE: *A concrete example of how the infrastructure handles the communication of a page from a Web server to a Web browser is shown in Figure 6.8. The page is represented with the storage subsystem as a file—an ordered collection of bits with no presumed structure or interpretation. The file is retrieved at the behest of a Web server upon request by the Web browser by the file system residing within the operating system. The file is passed as a message (another ordered collection of bits with no structure and interpretation) by the Web server to the operating system layer for communication to the Web browser. That message is interpreted in the Web browser as a document—a string of characters with markers for paragraphs, section headings, etc. In fact, the browser has a particular way of interpreting a document using a particular markup language, HTML, described further in Chapter 15. The feature to note is that this structure and interpretation are unknown to the operating system and network, which structure that page only as a file or message. The Web browser processes the HTML representation to obtain a screen image for presentation to the user, using its known interpretation of the markup language.*

As the message is passed from operating system to network, its representation is further changed from a message to a collection of packets representing that message. (This description oversimplifies reality, but captures the essential idea.)

In this example, the infrastructure deals with the simple structure of the data as a package, not attaching any further structure or interpretation. A strong argument can be made that the infrastructure should never attach *any* interpretation to data it handles or manages, because to do so would make it unnecessarily dependent on applications, violating the separation of concerns idea. This idea has appeal, but is unfortunately undercut by the existence of different computing platforms, such as the mainframe, UNIX server, and desktop PC.

Responding to Platform Heterogeneity

There are instances where it is valuable to associate interpretations with data within the infrastructure, mostly as a way to deal with heterogeneity in computing platforms. The problem this addresses is that the different platforms were historically designed by different companies, with no compelling need to use common ways to represent information. This was fine for the centralized and decentralized computer eras, and even for many departmental applications, because the entire application could be limited to one platform. Unfortunately,

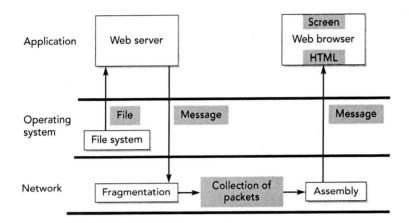

Figure 6.8 Processing from information to data and vice versa as a Web page passes through the infrastructure

in the modern enterprise and commerce applications the coordination required to impose one platform is impractical, and thus applications *must* span heterogeneous platforms.

The integration and communication of information across platforms is a mess to deal with since the application developer has to worry about where and what conversions to make—that is, *unless* the infrastructure can somehow hide this heterogeneity. The obvious solution is for the infrastructure to provide some automatic and transparent conversions between the different representations used on different platforms as information is communicated or stored. This is possible, but only if the infrastructure is aware of the structure and interpretation of the data assumed in the different platforms. This is a practical justification to associate some greater structure and interpretation to data stored or communicated in the infrastructure.

Fortunately, much of the information dealt with in applications (particularly organizational applications, where some of the greatest heterogeneity challenges arise) can be assigned standard data types such as numbers and character strings. Thus, a lot can be accomplished by making the infrastructure aware of the representation of a relatively small number of data types and their representations on the widely deployed computing platforms. The infrastructure is able to make conversions among the inconsistent representations of these standard types on different platforms, and it can do so automatically. This can actually be done in a way that does not require the different platforms even to be cognizant of one another's representations (see the sidebar "Two Ways to Convert Representations"). An example of a middleware layer that allows the

Two Ways to Convert Representations

As illustrated in Figure 6.9, there are a couple of ways that conversions between inconsistent representations can be performed. The straightforward way is simply to make a direct conversion from one platform to another. A more clever way is to define a common representation and convert from the source platform's representation to the common representation and back to the destination platform's representation. The second way is preferable because the infrastructure software on each platform does not need to know about the representation on all other platforms—it simply has to convert to and from the common representation.

The idea of converting to and from a common representation, rather than implementing all pairwise implementations, is used often. It reduces from $n \times (n-1)$ to n the number of distinct conversions necessary and allows new representations to be unilaterally added without affecting anything else.

A Middleware Example

The middleware layer illustrated in Figure 6.10 allows a client module to invoke an action of a server module, even though that server is on a different host with different representations for data types. (This type of middleware is called distributed object management (DOM); see Chapter 16.)

The middleware layer on the first host acts as a surrogate for the server module, accepting the action

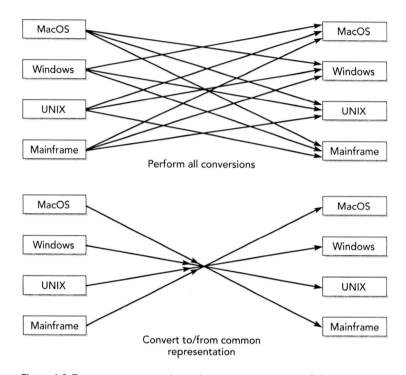

Figure 6.9 **Two ways to convert inconsistent representations of data types**

invocation of an action of a module on a different host, even one using a different computing platform, is described in the sidebar "A Middleware Example." This middleware layer predefines the data types it accepts for parameters or returns.

EXAMPLE: *The relational DBMS, which forms a middleware layer in the storage part of the infrastructure, as shown in Figure 4.7 on page 121, also presumes a standard set of data types. So that different platforms can access the same database, it can also perform conversions automatically.*

These middleware technologies enable data integration across enterprises, and hence they are one key to enterprise applications that incorporate legacy departmental applications and heterogeneous platforms.

EXAMPLE: *Stocks4u.com was a traditional broker before it entered the on-line stock trading business (see "On-Line Stock Trading" on page 68). Its starting point was therefore a set of legacy applications—one to manage customer accounts and another to manage trading orders. These separate applications were originally accessed by brokers employed by stocks4u.com rather than*

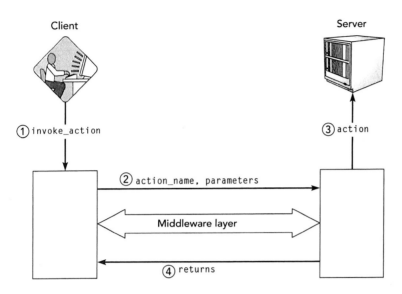

Figure 6.10 A middleware layer that allows a client module to invoke an action of a server module across heterogeneous platforms

customers, and newly purchased stocks from the order application were manually entered in the account application. One requirement for moving on-line was data integration across these existing applications. It was not feasible to replace them and begin from scratch. For example, the account and order applications both stored information about the customer who owned the account or initiated the order, but these legacy systems represented this information differently. The first step in this integration was therefore a new middleware layer that presented to the new application a unified view of these legacy applications, including automatic conversions into consistent representations of information.

The operating system and network deal with data as packages (collections of bits without further structure or interpretation), some middleware options attach standard data types, and the application is the primary place where the interpretation of data occurs. However, standard data types do not solve all issues of heterogeneous platforms because some applications have to deal with much more complicated representations.

EXAMPLE: *It is generally not reasonable to represent multimedia information, such as audio, video, and pictures, in terms of standard data types. Fortunately, information in these media arrived to computing relatively recently, and have had to deal with heterogeneous platforms from the start. Applications like remote conferencing and the Web use these media and are inherently*

invocation request. In particular, it may provide its own action,

```
invoke_action: module_ID,
action_name, parameters →
returns;
```

where module_ID specifies the server module, and action_name indicates the particular action to be invoked on that server. While the client is fooled into thinking it is invoking the action locally, the middleware arranges to invoke the action on the other host. This sleight of hand is arranged by sending the action_name and parameters as data through the operating system and network layers to the middleware layer on the other host, which acts there as a surrogate for the client. The action is invoked, and returns are captured and sent back to the first host as data to be returned to the client. The protocol is similar to "Anatomy of an Action Invocation" on page 170, except for the mediation of the two middleware layers.

The real sleight of hand is converting the representation of parameters and returns on one host to that assumed on the other host, if they are different. This is possible if parameters and returns are limited to standard data types known to the middleware, and the middleware is cognizant of their representations on different platforms. As described in "Two Ways to Convert Representations" on page 180, the data can be converted to and from a standard representation in the middleware on each host.

networked and have always assumed heterogeneous platforms. Thus, the approach for these media has generally been to choose a common representation across all platforms, obviating the need for any conversions within the infrastructure. This common representation is achieved by the standardization process discussed in Chapter 7.

More Layering Principles

With this practical backdrop, some general principles pertaining to how data and information are handled in the layered infrastructure can be stated. First, harking back to the definitions illustrated in Figure 4.1 on page 110, data is a collection of bits representing information, and information is structure and interpretation attached to data. This latter definition applies to the notion of information within the infrastructure, not from the perspective of a user (for which a different definition was given in Chapter 2).

The first principle is that in the infrastructure layers, the two complementary elements of information—data and its structure and interpretation—are dealt with differently. Data is passed from layer to layer as it is communicated or stored. Structure and interpretation are not passed from layer to layer, but rather are attributes of the layers themselves. More precisely, the structure and interpretation assumed within a layer is specified as part of the interfaces to that layer.

EXAMPLE: *A middleware layer like that described in the sidebar "A Middleware Example" on page 180 is free to define, at its interface to the application, the structure and interpretation it will apply to any data passed to that layer by the application. Typically this takes the form of some representation of an action and the parameters of that action. The middleware makes use of this structure and interpretation by forming any necessary conversions in representation for different platforms.*

The second principle is that additional structure and interpretation are added by each layer moving upward, or removed moving downward. That is, each higher layer makes more and more presumptions about structure and interpretation. The changing view of (often the very same) data as it moves through the layers is at the heart of the separation of concerns. Each layer avoids attaching any more structure and interpretation to the data it manipulates or passes than is necessary to realize its functionality, thereby reducing its mutual dependence on other layers and making each layer useful to a wider range of applications. The lowest layers, such as the file system and network, treat the information as a package of (unstructured and uninterpreted) bits. A little higher up—in the middleware layers—the structure and interpretation may be drawn from a limited repertory of standard data types.

The consequence of the second principle is that in the infrastructure, data and information are relative rather than absolute concepts, as illustrated in Figure 6.11. Information is defined as appropriate structure and interpretation attached to data *in the context of the current layer*. Moving down through the layers, data is being used increasingly as a representation of information; and moving up through the layers, structure and interpretation is incrementally added to the data to turn it into information.

EXAMPLE: *Consider a bank account balance. To the user, this is information that influences behavior, determining, for example, whether he can afford to purchase a new computer. It certainly does not have this connotation to the application that manages bank accounts in the bank, but it does have a particular interpretation—for example, the account balance increases or decreases as deposits or withdrawals are made. To the middleware or database layer, the bank account balance has an* Integer *data type, but with no further interpretation. It could be a bank account balance in pennies, or the number of angels on the head of a pin—it wouldn't matter. At the communication or storage layer, the data has no assumed interpretation, not even as a number. It is merely a collection of bits.*

The third principle is that there must be *consistency* to the structure and interpretation attached to data passed among layers. This doesn't mean all layers attach the same structure and interpretation; they don't. But it does mean that conflicting assumptions are ruled out. For example, one layer can't assume a structure and interpretation appropriate for a video medium and another, numbers and character streams.

The fourth principle is that the infrastructure must maintain the *integrity* of information. This means roughly that the data representation for information must not be changed in a way that corrupts the information it represents. Generally the goal of the infrastructure is to store, retrieve, and communicate information, not autonomously change it. This requires at minimum consistency between layers and also that each layer maintain end-to-end data integrity (see the sidebar "Data Integrity").

EXAMPLE: *In Figure 6.8, the representation of the same Web page by a file and by a message are consistent. They convey precisely the same data in different ways, one for storage and the other for communication. When the message is presented to the client host operating system layer by the network, the integrity constraint dictates that this message be identical to the one originally presented to the networking layer by the server host operating system. In turn, this requires that the fragmentation of the message into packets and the recovery of the message by assembly of the packets maintain this integrity.*

Data Integrity

Data integrity means that nothing is inappropriately lost or changed in the representation of information or subsequent recovery by data processing. The simplest form of integrity, at the lowest layers, applies to the package, such as a file or message (see Table 6.6). If a file is stored and retrieved, or a message is sent and received, the value of the bits, as well as number and ordering, must be preserved. If so, the file or message is said to have, or maintain, integrity. Integrity also applies to more complicated forms of representation and data processing.

EXAMPLE: *When a message is represented as packets in a packet network, this requires fragmentation of the message into packets at the source and reassembly from the packets at the receiver. The message will have integrity only if these steps—fragmentation, communication, and reassembly—are done correctly.*

A DBMS allows constraints to be placed on the data as part of its structure. For example, it might be specified that all the data values in a single column have to be unique (the same value cannot be repeated in different rows) or fall in a certain range of values. The DBMS then has the responsibility to maintain these constraints— maintain the integrity of the table—by rejecting any operation that would cause these constraints to be violated.

Integrity can also be compromised by unavoidable phenomena such as bit errors introduced in communication links (see Chapter 20) or by security threats (see Chapter 13).

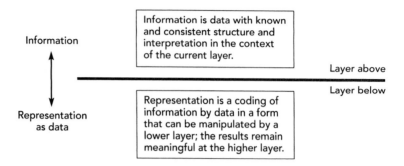

Figure 6.11 Relationship between data, information, and representation in a layered infrastructure

ANALOGY: *Differences in representation, consistency, and integrity can be seen in the print medium. To the printer, the information is simply a set of metal plates structured by page, with an ordering by page number. To the typesetter, the information has a finer structure, such as sentences and paragraphs. To the copy editor, the information has additional interpretation as sentences that are grammatically correct. To the author, the information should influence the perspective, understanding, or behavior of the eventual reader. The author is concerned that consistency and integrity of the information are maintained as it passes through the copy editor, typesetter, and printer. Consistency requires, for example, that the author and copy editor assume the same language. Integrity requires, for example, that the typesetter not make errors or surreptitiously modify the text prior to printing.*

6.3.5   The Horizontal Layer Interface

Given the layered architecture, a key aspect of the infrastructure is the *horizontal layer interface*, illustrated by the dashed lines in Figure 6.6, which defines how each layer interacts with the layer below and the presumed structure and interpretation of data passed between layers. In fact, it is largely through these interface specifications that consistency is achieved. Each layer interface is carefully documented, informing the implementers of the layer above precisely how to invoke its services, what information to provide, and how to represent that information.

These horizontal interfaces are said to be *open interfaces* when they are publicly available and not encumbered by any of the intellectual property protections discussed in Chapter 8. Thus, any vendor is free to design, implement, and sell software that builds on an open interface without fear of violating legal protections, assuming the vendor possesses sufficient documentation to do so. Open interfaces enable different layers of the infrastructure to be designed (and manufactured, in the case of equipment) by complementary vendors, and they also support competition among vendors at each layer, as discussed further in Chapter 7. Computing systems generously endowed with open interfaces are popularly called *open systems*.

6.3.6 The Spanning Layer

In reality, heterogeneous platforms lend some horizontal structure to each layer.

EXAMPLE: *This is illustrated by Figure 6.12, in which the layers are divided into modules at the granularity of an individual host. This heterogeneity arises not from the desire to have radically different functionality on different hosts, but from platform heterogeneity. The two heterogeneous layers shown in Figure 6.12 are the operating system (where there are several major OSs in the marketplace, including Windows 95/NT, MacOS, and UNIX; see Chapter 17) and the network (where there are a number of different technologies, such as Ethernet, wireless, and asynchronous transfer mode; see Chapter 18).*

Layers that are homogeneous in the horizontal direction, and can be assumed to be virtually ubiquitous on all computing platforms, have special significance because they divide the infrastructure into quasi-independent subsystems that can be developed and advanced separately, and because they hide any heterogeneity below. Further, such layers provide a built-in large market to vendors selling products at the layers both above and below, and thus they attract investment and industry competition. A layer with these characteristics is called a *spanning* layer [Cla97]. The following examples are illustrated in Figure 6.13.

EXAMPLE: *The internet protocol (IP) layer provides communication services to applications using a variety of network technologies (see Chapter 12). It is the foundation of the internet protocols and has reached such wide acceptance among consumers, universities, and many companies that it is virtually a spanning layer.*

The heterogeneity across different operating systems presents a problem to application developers who must produce different versions for each operating system. This creates a need for a middleware spanning layer above the operating system. One candidate is distributed object management (DOM) (see Chapter 16).

Discussion

D6.3 The middleware layer has analogies in the physical world. Discuss the mailroom operation in a company in those terms. Can you think of any other analogies?

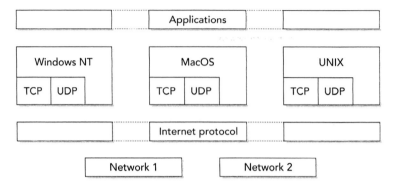

Figure 6.12 Platform heterogeneity gives horizontal structure

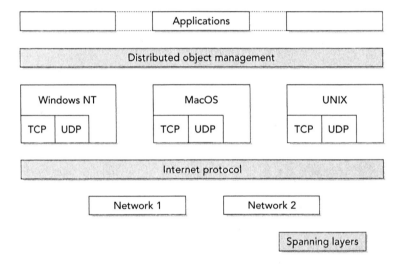

Figure 6.13 A spanning layer is uniform in the horizontal direction and almost ubiquitous

D6.4 Inherent in the layered infrastructure architecture is the possibility of a wealth of different applications sharing a common infrastructure. Discuss some of the advantages and disadvantages of this.

6.4   *More on Good Architectures

A more sophisticated view of system architecture leads to additional insights as to how architectures can be "better" in some dimensions. These ideas can be illustrated by the software infrastructure. Anyone designing applications should incorporate these ideas as well.

6.4.1   Abstraction

People use *abstraction* to make complicated things easier to deal with. Its proper use in architecture design makes that architecture more transparent and flexible to future change.

Abstraction is concisely defined as "generalization, ignoring or hiding details." In the context of architecture, abstraction is used to simplify the perspective of a module as viewed through its interface, focusing on the important overall goals of the system and avoiding becoming mired in a clutter of unnecessary details (see the sidebar "Example of Abstraction: The Flora"). Abstraction is also an important management technique in organizations (see the sidebar "Abstraction in Organizations").

Abstraction enables issues important to a system or module as a whole to be considered without being obscured by distracting details. At lower levels of hierarchy, those details are dealt with, but in a limited context that is constrained by the higher-level abstractions.

An important issue is choosing the appropriate abstractions and using them to make the system simpler and easier to deal with, but not so simple as to be unrealistic. As Albert Einstein stated, "Everything should be made as simple as possible, but no simpler." Architecture design incorporates abstraction as an integral part of decomposition. The avoidance of unnecessary detail allows architecture designers to focus on overall goals. Abstraction is most evident in module interface design—incorporating any abstractions in module interfaces, which should not reflect any unnecessary detail about the functionality of the modules. To do so allows unnecessary dependencies among modules (countering the goal of separation of concerns).

EXAMPLE: *In the Web browser-server example of Figure 6.8 on page 179, abstraction is evident at the horizontal interfaces. For example, an application can store and retrieve files knowing only their names and direct locations, but without knowledge of any details of how the file system works. One module composing an application can send a message to another module without knowing details of how this happens; for example, whatever the network does to deliver a message (such as fragment it into packets) need not be visible to the application.*

6.4.2   Encapsulation

An architecture focuses on the external behavior of the modules—as manifested by their interfaces—and how they interact. Implementers realize this interface using *encapsulation*—the assurance that internal implementation details are

Example of Abstraction: The Flora

Physical and social scientists abstract complicated and interdependent natural and social systems. To make the study of complicated systems feasible, they focus on the aspects most relevant to the investigation at hand, ignoring other less germane details. This is not limited to scientists; for example, consider the following perspectives on the flora taken by different occupations:

- The botanist classifies plants based on evolutionary family dependencies.
- The master chef studies a plant's taste and smell, whether it is edible or poisonous, how long it takes to cook, etc.
- The gardener is concerned with the adult size of the plant, what type of soil and climate conditions it favors, how much fertilizer it needs, etc.
- The pharmacologist looks for medicinal effects in each plant.

Although there is overlap and dependency, each profession finds germane a different aspect of the flora. Each is abstracting the flora to its own purposes.

Abstraction in Organizations

Abstraction and "management hierarchies" in organizations go hand in hand. Each higher layer in the management hierarchy takes an increasingly abstract view of the organization's architecture. To a top executive of the bank described in "Modularity in Organizations" on page 160, the loan department is a module that makes money for the bank by accepting loan applications and issuing loans likely to be repaid. This abstract perspective—when turned into reality by the manager setting up the loan department—has to be made concrete by setting up detailed steps for loan approval. Those details may actually change over time, based on experience, without affecting the view of customers.

When it comes to actually setting up the lower-level departments, there are a plethora of details handled internally. The manager of the bank loan department is responsible for determining the detailed processes *within* that department. The higher management views the department in abstract terms like "quarterly profit and loss," which hides much of its detailed functioning.

The organization also abstracts its interface to the customer. For example, the abstract view

```
loan_application:
completed_application →
answer,loan_number;
```

could be replaced by the more complicated series of actions:

```
loan_application:
completed_application →
application_number;
credit_check:
application_number →
good_or_bad_credit;
underwriter_advice:
application_number →
recommended_or_not;
loan_approved?:
application_number →
answer,loan_number;
```

By allowing the customer visibility into each stage of the loan approval process, this last design makes the customer dependent on those detailed steps.

invisible and inaccessible at the interface. This precludes other modules from becoming inadvertently dependent on those internal details, which would unnecessarily violate the separation of concerns and make the system less flexible.

Encapsulation is achieved by several means. Measures at the architectural design phase include insuring that both actions and their returns do not unnecessarily reveal internal details. Beyond this, it is important that bypassing the defined interface, somehow gaining "unauthorized" access to a module's internal details, be precluded. This requires support from a programming language (see Chapter 11).

ANALOGY: *Although the bank can insure that its standard customer interface (ATM, teller windows) doesn't allow access to its vault—the contents of which should be encapsulated—these measures alone cannot insure that a bank robber will not bypass the interface. The bank takes other measures, such as alarm system, combination lock, and guards.*

Encapsulation is also evident in the infrastructure architecture design and implementation.

EXAMPLE: *In the Web browser-server example of Figure 6.8 on page 179, the representation of a message as packets need not be made available to the application. If the Web browser sees only an incoming message and not the packets making up that message, it cannot become somehow dependent on the particular ways that messages are fragmented into packets.*

Abstraction and encapsulation are complementary. Both seek separation of concerns—the former by simplifying the external view and the latter by dogmatically enforcing these abstractions. Encapsulated details can be changed without affecting other modules, giving the design more flexibility. Abstraction is a tool of the architect, and encapsulation is a tool of the module implementer.

EXAMPLE: *The perils of violating encapsulation can be illustrated by many early PC applications that improved performance by writing directly to the video display of the computer, bypassing the operating system. This violation of encapsulation caused those applications to "break" if the computer manufacturer changed the video display in any way. For applications that followed the sanctioned route of doing all display actions through the operating system, changes in the display only needed to be mirrored in one place, the operating system.*

6.4.3   Flexibility

Change is a constant in organizations (see "Better Accommodating Change" on page 100). Thus, especially in organizational applications, the flexibility to accommodate unanticipated change is an important requirement. It is fair to say that achieving this is the exception rather than the rule—indeed, there is a lack of understanding of how to achieve this.

One important principle in interface design that helps is hinted at above: the *open-closed principle*. Interfaces should be *open* to extension, but *closed* to modification. "Closed to modification" means whatever capabilities are defined at an interface, and whatever information is visible at the interface, will never be changed, so that existing clients will never need to be modified because of such a change. "Open to extension" means that adding new capabilities should be possible without affecting existing clients. Together, these properties contribute to flexibility—without forcing changes to other modules unless they choose to take advantage of new capabilities.

Discussion

D6.5 Discuss the difference between microeconomics and macroeconomics. Is the difference primarily one of abstraction? Granularity?

Review

A modular architecture has a number of desirable properties that make systems easier to implement, maintain, and extend. Chief among these is separation of concerns in decomposition, so that modules can be implemented independently. The module interface reduces the dependency among modules, thereby freeing implementation considerations from the external view and making the implementation easier to change. The module interface defines a set of server actions, each of which is parameterized and returns values that can affect the client invoking the action.

The software infrastructure is composed of logical layers, where each layer provides services to the layer above utilizing the services of the layer below. The application itself is the top layer, while the remaining layers integrate many different applications. One of the major functions of some of the layers is to abstract and hide the heterogeneity of the infrastructure below.

In the infrastructure, information—recovered from data by data processing—is structure and interpretation applied to the data. Each layer makes minimal assumptions about this structure and interpretation in order to maintain generality. Thus, moving upward through the layers, information is added incrementally.

that provide visibility into the outcome of individual approval steps (such as the credit history report or the advice of the underwriter) and that the customer does not have physical access to the loan department premises (for example, by locking the doors at night).

Modularity and the Economy

The overall organization of the economy into distinct firms illustrates modularity. Each firm is more weakly associated with other firms and much more strongly associated internally. If two firms find themselves strongly associated—there is a dependence of function that cannot easily be disassociated—then they find it advantageous to merge, which changes granularity. There is hierarchy in both subsidiary relationships and internal organizations.

The interaction among firms is structured through a standard set of commercial relationships (purchase orders, invoices, bill of goods, etc.) under the control of law (contracts, Uniform Commercial Code, etc.). Each company presents a carefully designed interface to the outside world, such as toll-free number, advertising, lobby with receptionist, etc. It also encapsulates internal details by such measures as keeping proprietary internal telephone books, maintaining its own separate physical facilities, hiring security guards, etc.

The integrity of data must be maintained as it passes through the layers, and senders and receivers must maintain consistency in the structure and interpretation applied to data.

The horizontal layer interface is where interoperability among layers is assured by defining actions and their parameters and returns. The latter includes specification of the structure and interpretation of the data passed between layers. A spanning layer is one that is virtually ubiquitous and effectively hides the heterogeneity below.

Valuable architectural techniques include abstraction (simplifying the interface, hiding unnecessary details), encapsulation (dogmatically enforcing abstraction), and the open-closed principle (extending but not modifying an existing interface).

Key Concepts

Modularity:

- Interface—actions, parameters, and returns

Infrastructure layering:

- Network, operating system, middleware, application
- Horizontal interface
- Spanning layer

Data and information:

- Representation of information
- Structure and interpretation of data
- Consistency in structure and interpretation
- Basic and user-defined data types
- Data integrity

Abstraction and encapsulation

Open-closed principle of interfaces

Further Reading

An extensive discussion of architecture design can be found in [BCK98]. A much more technical introduction to the design of distributed systems is [CDK94]. Business process reengineering as described in [Dav93] is not dissimilar to the architecture design for software systems.

Exercises

E6.1   Books4u.com has hired you to design a modular architecture for its planned on-line bookselling service described in "On-Line Bookselling" on page 66. In fact, they appreciate that the principles of modularity apply both to their software design and to the design of their organization (for example, order fulfillment, marketing, finances, etc.). Separately for the software and for the organization, draw a modular architecture, indicating which functions are performed by each subsystem and the interfaces. If appropriate, employ hierarchy in your decomposition.

E6.2   Repeat Exercise 6.1 for any one of the following:

a. A bank or credit union offering money market and checking accounts to its customers

b. The X-ray department in a hospital

c. A grocery store

E6.3   List the appropriate actions, and their parameters and returns, for any two of the following examples of interfaces.

a. The interface between the post office and a citizen wishing to mail a package

b. The interface between a customer and your checkbook when you wish to pay a bill

c. The interface between a patron wishing to find and then check out a book on a particular topic and the local library

d. The interface between a hungry customer and a McDonald's restaurant

E6.4   Consider the `float` data type described in Table 6.2 on page 168.

a. Define a data representation of a value having this type.

b. Describe the processing required to recover this value from the data representing it.

E6.5   Suppose that two computer platforms represent a data type that is an integer having a range of values between 0 and 7. The two representations are shown in the following table. Describe two different data processing approaches to convert a value from the first to the second representation, such that information integrity is maintained.

Information	Representation on first platform	Representation on second platform
0	000	111
1	001	110
2	010	101
3	011	100
4	100	011
5	101	010
6	110	001
7	111	000

E6.6   Consider an email application, and in particular an email message sent from one user to another. Discuss the different representations for the same message within the application, the file system, and the network. Where does knowledge of these different representations reside?

E6.7   When you write a check to pay your rent, describe how the information integrity of the dollar amount on that check is assured. What keeps your landlord from just increasing the amount before cashing the check?

E6.8   For any two of the following, describe an abstract view, as well as the hidden details:

   a. A McDonald's restaurant from the perspective of a customer, from the perspective of a supplier of buns, and from the perspective of the corporate headquarters in Chicago

   b. A bicycle from the perspective of a rider, from the perspective of its manufacturer, and from the perspective of a police officer

   c. A subway system from the perspective of the rider, from the perspective of a train driver, and from the perspective of a train controller at headquarters

E6.9   For any one of the examples in Exercise 6.8, describe how encapsulation could be used to reduce dependencies.

E6.10   For the loan department described in "Abstraction in Organizations" on page 187, assume it made the credit report available to the customer at the interface. How would this violate encapsulation? Specifically, how would it make the design less flexible?

E6.11 For your chosen example in Exercise 6.10, describe how the open-closed principle would be applied.

E6.12 For a customer interface to the bank loan department, assume that the bank chooses to add an application fee to the interface to increase its revenues. Specify two ways of doing this, one following the open-closed principle and the other not. In specific terms, describe the advantages and disadvantages of each.

E6.13 Consider the interface that an automobile presents to its driver. Limit yourself to driving functions, not auxiliary functions such as the radio or the seat configuration.

   a. Describe this interface in terms of actions, parameters, and return values.

   b. Describe how abstraction is manifested in this interface.

   c. Describe how the design and manufacture of the automobile manifests encapsulation.

E6.14 Repeat Exercise 6.13 for the interface to a soft-drink vending machine. The machine offers four different kinds of soft drinks, all the same price.

Industry and Government Context

Government policy and the organization of the supplier industry, including economic and legal constraints, profoundly influence the direction of networked computing and applications.

PART

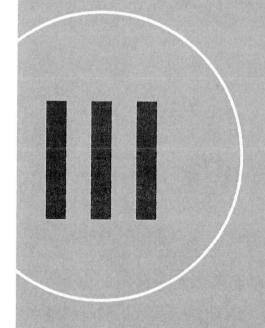

The Computer and Communications Industries 7

The past couple decades have seen increasing fragmentation of the computer and communications industries and, at the same time, increasing consolidation: This is the way the industry reorganizes itself in accordance with technological change and market opportunity. Still, the industry includes a number of suppliers of equipment, infrastructure and application software, and services (both professional and utility, like telecommunications). Networked applications must typically be assembled from a collection of off-the-shelf (equipment, software, and services) and custom-designed application-specific subsystems. Increasingly, the task of integrating these components and subsystems has been outsourced to professional-services firms.

This complicated industry structure implies that an appreciation of the structure of the supplier industries and the relationships and coordination among suppliers is integral to the acquisition of a networked application and its supporting infrastructure. This chapter discusses the industry players, their relationships, and how they coordinate themselves through standardization. This provides background information for acquiring new applications, which is addressed in Chapter 9, and more generally, acting as an informed customer of these industries. The current important developments in the communications industry are considered in Chapter 20. The industry context differs across nations, but this chapter emphasizes the situation in the United States.

7.1 Participants, Products, and Services

Networked computing is an industry with many different types of players, including suppliers of goods (equipment, software, information content) and providers of services (communications and computing operations, application development). Any networked application builds on products and services provided by these myriad players and must find ways to coordinate them successfully.

Recall from Chapter 6 that the *infrastructure* includes equipment and software available to and utilized by many networked applications—including the network, hosts, and infrastructure software. In contrast, *applications* provide specific capabilities and features serving individual users, groups of users, or organizations.

7.1.1   Components and Integration

There is a substantial difference between custom designing a subsystem—as part of a system design—and purchasing a subsystem as a stand-alone product from another company. In the former, the system functionality and interaction can be chosen freely to match the precise system requirements, and in the latter the subsystem must be accepted as is and the remainder of the system designed around it. A subsystem that is purchased as a product from an outside company is called a component.

> E X A M P L E :   *With rare exceptions, a networked application uses computers, peripherals, and networking equipment purchased from outside vendors. From the application perspective, these subsystems are components—the system must be designed around them, accepting their functionality and interaction as is.*

Components—particularly software components—are often highly configurable. Their suppliers have taken pains to provide a number of options and parameters that can customize the functionality to particular purposes. This increases the generality of the component, expanding its market.

> E X A M P L E :   *ERP applications are not monolithic applications that must be accepted in total or not at all, but rather are decomposed into components that can be mixed and matched (see "Enterprise Resource Planning" on page 79). These components are intended to fit in many different organizational contexts, so they have been made highly configurable. In fact, just their initial configuration, which must be carefully coordinated with the needs of the organization adopting them, is a major task.*
>
> *The DBMS is a large-grain software component that can be purchased from one of several suppliers (Oracle, Sybase, Informix, Microsoft) and incorporated into an application (see "Database Management System (DBMS)" on page 126).*

Components and their suppliers become available when the functionality of a subsystem reaches a stage of maturity at which it is well defined and accepted. At this stage, system designers often would prefer purchasing a component to undertaking the design of a similar subsystem. The task of taking these existing components, possibly adding custom-developed subsystems, and making them interact properly to realize the higher-level goals of a system is called *system integration*. As defined in "Emergence" on page 116, emergence reflects new capabilities and functions of a system that subsystems and components could not have provided by themselves. This emergence is a value added by the system supplier or system integrator and serves as the economic foundation of their business.

The industry supplying infrastructure and applications is thus organized as three groups:

- *Component suppliers:* Many companies specialize in supplying one component or a relatively small set of related components. In a hierarchical decomposition, each component may in turn incorporate components from other suppliers.
- *Custom subsystem developers:* These professional-services firms specialize in taking customer requirements and custom developing software to meet these requirements.
- *System integrators:* These professional-services firms specialize in implementing systems, typically assembling and integrating components (sometimes with custom-designed subsystems) to realize a system.

These categories are not mutually exclusive. Some companies perform two or all three services.

EXAMPLE: *A computer is a component that itself incorporates many internal components—microprocessor, disk drive, etc.—purchased from other companies. The computer manufacturer (Compaq or Sun, for example) is thus both a system integrator and a component supplier. A client-server application incorporates components such as client and server hosts and may add custom-designed application software. A user organization may purchase these components—hosts, network, application, etc.—and act as a system integrator to create an application.*

7.1.2   Suppliers, Providers, and Consumers

The many different application and infrastructure suppliers (those offering goods such as equipment, application software packages, and infrastructure software), service providers (offering services such as operation of a network or computing center), and consumers (purchasers of these goods and services), along with a variety of goods and services, are all listed in Table 7.1. Many firms are both consumers and suppliers.

There are several major categories of customers for networked computing–related products and services:

- *End-user organizations:* Virtually all medium-to-large organizations, and many small ones, integrate networked applications into their operations. These applications range from highly customized to fairly generic, and they incorporate equipment and software products from a number of suppliers. The applications can be managed by internal information systems departments, which specialize in the development, integration, and operation of networked computing; or increasingly, all or some of these functions are outsourced to professional-services firms.
- *Specific vertical industries:* In e-commerce, groups of companies within a given industry participate in shared e-commerce solutions, for example, for direct procurement. They can purchase a package of software and professional services to spread expertise and interoperable solutions.
- *Infrastructure service providers:* Network, computing, and middleware service providers purchase and deploy equipment and software, operate computer systems, and provide customer service and billing.
- *On-line merchants:* These firms sell information content or other goods over the network. They are customers of network service providers and equipment and software suppliers.
- *On-line service providers:* These firms sell services over the network, such as information searching and retrieval, financial planning, stock trading, and electronic banking. The dividing line between merchants and service providers is not clean, as information content is typically embedded in services.
- *Cyberspace consumers:* The Internet—because it is available to so many individual users—has created this new category of consumers. These consumers are customers of on-line merchants and service providers, and they desire communications (telephone service, email, etc.) and information access (the Web).

7.1.3 Types of Information Goods

Information in different media (such as text, audio, images, video) is the primary good stored, retrieved, and manipulated in a networked application. When this information is bought or sold, it is called information content. An important distinction should be made between static and volatile content. At its extreme, *static content* is created once and never changes, and at the opposite extreme,

Table 7.1 Suppliers, providers, and consumers of networked computing products and services

Supplier or provider	Description	Examples
Infrastructure equipment suppliers	Equipment includes computers, peripherals, and data and telecommunications switches. Increasingly, equipment suppliers specialize in each of these areas.	Computers: Compaq, Hewlett-Packard, Dell; data network: CISCO, Bay Networks, 3Com; telecommunications: Lucent, Nortel, Siemens
Infrastructure software suppliers	Infrastructure software includes operating system, database and Web servers, and middleware. Software is also embedded in network equipment.	Servers: Oracle, Netscape, Microsoft; operating systems: Microsoft, Apple, Sun; middleware: Iona, Microsoft; embedded software: CISCO, Lucent
Infrastructure service providers	Network transport of data, audio, and video, including Internet service providers (ISPs) and telecommunications providers. Increasingly, operation of networks internal to organizations and internal computer operation are outsourced.	Networking: MCI, America Online; telecommunications: AT&T, Sprint, MCI; computing: EDS, Computer Science Corp.
Application service providers	Infrastructure service providers sometimes bundle applications.	Telephony: AT&T, MCI; information indexing and searching: America Online; payroll processing
Content suppliers	Providing information content to consumers over the network.	Information services: America Online; entertainment video: TCI
Application software producers	Application software products sold to users and organizations without the option of modification or customization (colloquially called shrink-wrapped software).	Personal productivity suites: Microsoft Office; network management: Bellcore
Application framework producers	Partial applications—including components and frameworks—that speed application development (see Chapter 10), often with the aid of professional-services firms.	Enterprise resource planning: SAP, Baan, PeopleSoft
Professional-services firms	Systems integrators—who design and deploy infrastructure and applications incorporating products from a number of other suppliers—and custom application developers.	Systems integrators: Anderson Consulting, EDS; custom applications: Active Software
Industry-specific solutions	Organizational applications like e-commerce require the cooperation of companies within a given industry, for example, for direct procurement. Suppliers can provide a full range of software, professional services, and operational support for a specific industry.	Harbinger Corp. supplies full integrated solutions for e-commerce in vertical industries like petroleum.

volatile content continually changes, expands, and rapidly becomes obsolete. Most content falls somewhere between these extremes.

EXAMPLE: *Real-time stock quotes (representing the last trading price) are highly volatile content, whereas historical stock quotes (representing prices in the past) are static. A digital encyclopedia is static—but updated annually and requiring major revision every ten years or so. A movie is static—produced once and seldom modified thereafter.*

Much content has the characteristic that consumers don't want its entirety, but rather need to selectively narrow it to a relevant piece. Suppliers satisfying these consumers focus on indexing and searching, thus providing a *service* (searching for topical information) in addition to a *good* (the information itself). This can also be viewed as mass customization of an information good.

7.1.4 Types of Software Goods

Another good that is bought and sold is software—both application and infrastructure. There are two distinct approaches:

- The *software product*—sometimes called colloquially shrink-wrapped software—is developed with the hope that consumers will buy it (much like static content).
- The *custom-developed software application* is developed to a consumer's specifications and may have a single customer. The supplier and customer are the same if an information systems department develops and operates the application.

There are many intermediate cases of the two approaches. Custom-developed applications often incorporate components, because developing generic capabilities from scratch is much more expensive than buying them. Due to the escalating costs of software development, a new set of suppliers focuses on reusable software components and frameworks intended as a foundation for new applications (see Chapter 10). For example, ERP vendors sell customizable turnkey solutions for standard business processes, and a customer hires a professional-services firm to aid in the customization and integration into the particular environment.

The software product and services are another manifestation of the push versus pull distinction described in "Autonomous Information Sources" on page 46. In the product (push) model, the supplier defines and develops to a product specification and sells this off-the-shelf solution. In the services (pull) model, the customer provides a specification and commissions a supplier to develop an application to that specification.

Applications are not developed once and for all; once deployed, they move into a maintenance phase. Software products have a series of releases, each one fixing programming errors reported by customers and adding new capabilities and features or better performance. Custom-developed applications have similar maintenance needs.

Infrastructure software is normally sold as a product, as it is broadly deployed and not limited to a single organization. Customization of any sort is unusual; rather, the changing requirements of the collective consumers are incorporated into new releases. There are two categories:

- Infrastructure software *bundled within equipment* provides complementary functionality to the hardware (for example, the operating system supports the processor). It may be developed internally by the equipment supplier (Apple or CISCO) or by a separate supplier (Microsoft Windows bundled with a personal computer). In either case, although the software is bundled, new releases may be sold separately.
- *Unbundled* infrastructure software is sold separately. For example, middleware (see Chapter 16) and databases (see Chapter 15) are by nature deployed across a heterogeneous mix of platforms, and thus bundling with one and only one platform makes no sense.

7.1.5 Equipment

The equipment supporting networked applications includes computers and peripherals (like the network interface) closely associated with users and infrastructure equipment such as server computers and network switches. Equipment includes hardware (electronics, cabinets, power supplies, etc.) and frequently includes substantial embedded software—software that is specific and integral to the functioning of that equipment.

EXAMPLE: *Network switches must have considerable software for functions like choosing the appropriate outgoing communication link for each packet (see Chapter 18). That software is bundled with the hardware and sold as a unit.*

More so than software, equipment suppliers have long used a hardware component model, in which specialized component suppliers (such as microprocessor chip or memory chip supplies) sell to many equipment manufacturers.

Discussion

D7.1 What are some reasons it may be preferable to purchase a component rather than design a similar subsystem? The reverse?

D7.2 What are some reasons a company might purchase a service (like accounting or telecommunications) rather than provide that equivalent function internally?

D7.3 Discuss the differences in business models between firms supplying products, network and computing services, and professional services, in the networked computing industry.

D7.4 Outsourcing—leasing services and hiring professional-services firms in preference to internal organizations—is gaining in popularity. Discuss some of the factors behind this and also some of the disadvantages.

D7.5 Acquiring and deploying an application often requires dealing with a number of suppliers and providers. Discuss some of the challenges, especially if you have firsthand experience.

7.2   The Changing Industry Structure

As implied in the introduction to this chapter, the structure of the computer and communications industries is experiencing change. Major forces are the convergence of computing and communications in the context of networked computing, the changing application focus (moving from departmental to enterprise and inter-enterprise applications), and technological advances. The structure of the industry also exhibits a trend away from vertical integration, increasing fragmentation within each industry segment coupled with consolidation across previously separate industries, and has been markedly influenced by venture capital.

7.2.1   The Role of Architecture

The modularity of a computing system discussed in Chapter 6 is more than "merely" design choice; it also reflects or influences the industry structure. In order for components from different suppliers to be integrated into a networked computing system, they have to adhere to some common architectural assumptions. This implies, at minimum, a system or subsystem decomposition in which modules align with boundaries of firms, and common agreement on interfaces where products from different companies must be integrated into a functioning system. It is through these interfaces that firms coordinate themselves. This is one role of standards, discussed later in this chapter.

E X A M P L E :   *From the earliest PCs, interfaces were supplied for common periph-*
erals such as printers, modems, and monitors. This enables the customer to mix
and match peripherals, choosing the best supplier for each peripheral on the
basis of competitive feature, quality, and price considerations.

This decomposition is important because the range of technologies—including
integrated circuits, equipment, embedded software, infrastructure software,
application software, system integration, telecommunications service provision,
organizational design, among others—is simply too great for one company to
master. Generally, companies that specialize in one area are able to accumulate
greater expertise and provide higher quality at a low price. However, this
greatly complicates relationships in the overall industry. The most important
implication is that each company has to worry about both its competitors *and* its
complementers. Sometimes success hinges on getting complementary products
and services properly coordinated, as well as providing better feature, quality,
and price characteristics than competitors.

For example, a layered architecture for the infrastructure has great significance
for how the supplier industry for the infrastructure is organized. If accepted
interfaces between layers are available, there is a strong tendency for firms specializing in each layer to emerge. At each layer, users, vendors, and service providers may have alternatives for the layer below. Thus, this architecture focuses
competition at the level of alternative suppliers for each layer, and it may place
on the customer the burden of integrating the layers to assemble a complete
infrastructure.

7.2.2   From Stovepipe to Integrated Infrastructure

An architectural question with profound implications to the industry structure is
whether a single supplier provides an all-encompassing application solution
(called a *stovepipe* architecture), or whether this is split among suppliers. If the
responsibility is to be split, one obvious boundary is between an infrastructure
benefiting all applications (called an integrated infrastructure) and the applications themselves.

The telecommunications industry is where these alternatives are displayed most
strikingly, as illustrated in Figure 7.1. On the left, the stovepipe architecture
dedicates separate networks to different applications, for example, the telephone, television distribution, and data. Because each stovepipe architecture is
dedicated to one application, it typically bundles the application and infrastructure tightly together. This occurs on two levels: The infrastructure is designed

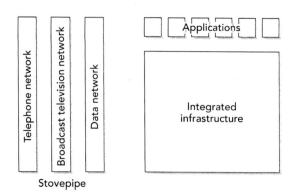

Figure 7.1 Stovepipe versus integrated architectures for the telecommunications infrastructure

specifically to support one and only one application, and each supplier typically bundles and sells the application and infrastructure together. This is sometimes termed a turnkey solution. An advantage to the customer is that only one supplier is involved, and that supplier takes full responsibility for making the application work. The stovepipe architecture focuses the competition on competitive turnkey solutions for each application.

The integrated infrastructure, on the right in Figure 7.1, separates the infrastructure from the application, and the infrastructure is designed to be general, supporting *all* applications. This allows suppliers to focus on just applications or just infrastructure. This architecture focuses competition on competitive integrated infrastructures and also on competitive suppliers for each application. The integrated infrastructure is a two-layer architecture—the applications are layered on an existing infrastructure. It is fairly easy to design and deploy a new application, because it does not require investment in a new infrastructure to go along with it.

Within the integrated infrastructure, it is also possible to use layered modularity, as described in Chapter 6 (a particular internal layering consisting of network, operating system, and middleware was described there). The infrastructure should be decomposed in *some* fashion, and layering is a decomposition that is consistent with the desire of the infrastructure to support integrated applications. The functionality is decomposed into natural functions—for example, networking (getting packets from one place to another) and supporting module interfaces (conveying action invocations and return values)—but each of those layers of functional grouping is designed to be general, supporting a wide range of applications.

The telecommunications industry has been evolving away from the stovepipe architecture and toward the integrated infrastructure architecture, although there is a ways to go.

EXAMPLE: *The telephone network was originally dedicated to one application—making voice telephone calls. The customer purchased that application and was not allowed to use the network for any other purpose. About thirty years ago, regulators in the United States decided to allow "foreign terminal devices" to be connected to the network, effectively allowing customers to purchase equipment supporting other applications (such as data transmission video conferencing) from suppliers other than the telephone company.*

The Internet was originally conceived as an integrated network in the sense that it always separated applications from infrastructure. Many applications have been added over the years without the need to make coordinated modifications to the network. However, the Internet does not yet achieve an integration across all applications—its capabilities for high-quality video with low delay are limited, for example.

A similar (although somewhat less striking) evolution has occurred in the organization of the computing industry. The mainframe computer was an environment optimized for mission-critical organizational applications, whereas the PC was optimized for personal productivity applications. Each was originally conceived largely as a turnkey solution by vendors—their goal was providing a complete solution to the customer—and hence each was a stovepipe. Even more striking examples of stovepipe architectures are the stand-alone word processor and calculator machines that preceded the PC.

As it turned out, however, the PC evolved into an integrated infrastructure architecture, as many non-PC suppliers soon offered a rich variety of applications. Very quickly, vendors differentiated themselves into those supplying the infrastructure and those supplying the application software. Further, the infrastructure adopted three distinct layers—the network, the desktop equipment, and the operating system—each with its own specialized suppliers. Each of these layers has been expanding the range of applications it supports, from personal productivity to social applications (the latter requiring multimedia capabilities, which is a substantial technical advance). Generalizing this, the trend toward three-tier client-server architectures in organizational applications represents a layered architecture (each tier is, in a sense, a layer) serving a larger class of applications and incorporating both the mainframe and PC.

In conclusion, it can be argued that both the computing and communications industries are undergoing an evolution from stovepipe to integrated infrastructure architectures and, further, that the integrated infrastructure is evolving toward an internal layering modularity. Both architectures are modular, allowing the development, supply, and ownership of the infrastructure to be divided among firms; and each allows competition—there can be competitive suppliers for each stovepipe, or competitive suppliers for the applications and infrastructure separately. So why such a strong trend toward integrated infrastructures and layering? Some economic forces encouraging these trends are summarized in Table 7.2.

Table 7.2 Forces driving the industry toward layering and away from stovepipes

Force	Description	Example
Economies of scope	A common infrastructure supporting a variety of applications allows sharing of development, purchasing, administration, operations, and billing costs.	The Internet is cheaper to operate than separate email and Web networks.
Economies of scale	An infrastructure supporting a variety of applications will have greater scale and thus have lower unit costs.	The Internet has more users—and hence is larger—than a network that supports only email or only the Web.
Incremental costs	Each new application—leveraging an existing infrastructure—need not justify the cost of an entire new infrastructure.	Users add applications to a PC for the cost of software.
Larger market	Because the infrastructure is in place, application suppliers see a large potential market with less risk. This consideration makes the spanning layer particularly important (see "The Spanning Layer" on page 185).	The Internet offers application developers a large number of users with Internet access.
Diversity of applications	A low incremental cost and larger market encourage greater application diversity, providing greater value to the users.	More users subscribe to Internet access or purchase a personal computer because of the large number of applications.
Competition	The user can mix and match complementary technologies across layers. The greater competition may reduce prices and increase quality.	The user can choose from among many Internet providers and PC vendors without changing applications.
Multimedia	Applications can incorporate different media (text, graphics, audio, video) at will.	Remote conferencing.
Single customer interface	In communications, the customer can deal with a single integrated services provider.	Today a user typically deals with separate telephone, television, and data providers.

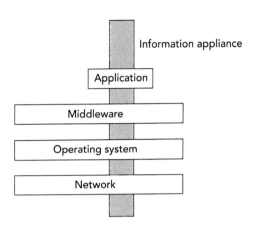

Figure 7.2 An information appliance captures a snapshot of an application and the layered infrastructure that supports it

Of course, the integrated and layered infrastructure architectures have disadvantages too. The burden is often on the customer to integrate the layers from different suppliers. Some customers would prefer to purchase a turnkey solution. This can be overcome with the use of a system integrator, either a third party or one of the vendors.

E X A M P L E :   *The difficulties users have integrating their personal computer with its various peripherals (modem, printer, etc.) partially offsets the advantages of greater competition. Vendors have responded to this in different ways, including Microsoft's "plug-and-play" automatic configuration and Dell's customization and configuration (see the sidebar "Dell as a Subsystem Integrator").*

Also, integrated solutions in computing have a reputation as being difficult to learn and use. Many believe that as a result of this, and the declining cost of electronics, there may be a movement back toward stovepipes in computing. This is manifested in the growing interest in information appliances (see the sidebar "Information Appliances").

7.2.3   Less Vertical Integration and More Diversification

Vertical integration and diversification, defined in Table 7.3, are two approaches available to companies wishing to expand their product offerings. These dimensions are independent choices—a company can become more vertically integrated, or diversified, or both. In the computer and communications industries,

Dell as a Subsystem Integrator

Layering—and more generally industry fragmentation—may require users to integrate complementary products to create a workable system. Particularly if there are numerous options available, this can make it difficult for the consumer to get everything working together.

While the success of Dell Computer has been attributed to its distribution model and customer service (see "Dell Computer and Mass Customization" on page 94), it also performs a valuable subsystem-integration function. Customers can interactively configure the desired peripherals, expansion cards, and software in their order, and Dell integrates these components and provides support.

System integration is a valuable service to the customer and a good opportunity for suppliers. Dell adds value only to the individual computer subsystem, but other firms (EDS and Anderson Consulting, for example) perform similar system integration functions for large networked applications.

Information Appliances

The information appliance (IA) is a stovepipe architecture that packages a single (or small number of) applications within a small, inexpensive, relatively easy-to-use package. An example is a cellular telephone equipped with email and Web browsing. As shown in Figure 7.2, an information appliance captures a stovepipe snapshot from the layered infrastructure. In effect, an IA represents a return to the stovepipe architecture while exploiting layering with open interfaces. With the decreasing cost of electronics, users can afford to purchase a collection of information appliances, rather than a single flexible (but more difficult to use) desktop computer.

IAs also have disadvantages. They tend to freeze functionality and standards at a point in time, forcing users to upgrade or replace them fairly frequently (making the manufacturers happy!). They also confront users with a proliferation of different user interfaces, and due to their limited display and keyboard power, they may have difficult user interfaces (like the infamous "VCR programming problem").

Table 7.3 Vertical integration and diversification

Strategy	Description	Examples
Vertical integration	A company is vertically integrated when it makes (rather than buys) all the subsystems in its products. It becomes more vertically integrated by acquiring suppliers that previously sold it components.	IBM makes everything from semiconductors to application software and provides professional services to install and operate applications. In acquiring Digital and Tandem, Compaq added a strong software and services business to become more vertically integrated. AT&T reduced vertical integration by divesting its equipment and computer subsidiaries. A system integrator is the least vertically integrated, as it purchases all its components.
Diversification	A diversified company provides products across different industry segments. It thereby achieves synergies, consistency of financial results, and provides customers with a "total solution."	By acquiring Tandem, Compaq also diversified by adding reliable OLTP software and servers to its product line. Telecommunications service providers are diversifying by accumulating telephone, cable television, wireless, and data networking assets.

there is a discernible trend toward more diversification and less vertical integration, although numerous exceptions among individual companies can be cited.

Diversification is encouraged by the customer's desire for a range of application solutions from a single supplier, simplifying the sales and customer support issues. Vertical disintegration is driven by the improved competitiveness of more specialized firms (pursuing either integrated circuits, equipment, infrastructure, or applications). Both are driven by the forces behind the integrated layered architecture as well. Companies that specialize in one infrastructure layer are inherently diversifying across a wide range of applications and are not vertically integrated in the sense that they are supplying only a part of the whole system solution.

This trend is driven by some of the forces illustrated in Figure 7.3. The firms of an industry constitute a "modularity of suppliers," but the boundaries among firms are driven by economics and marketing issues more than by technology. Some factors of particular importance in the computer industry include the following:

- A firm's boundaries are strongly affected by the relationship of internal and external coordination and transaction costs. These costs are decreasing both internally and externally, due in part to networked computing (particularly enterprise and cross-enterprise applications described in Chapter 3). The

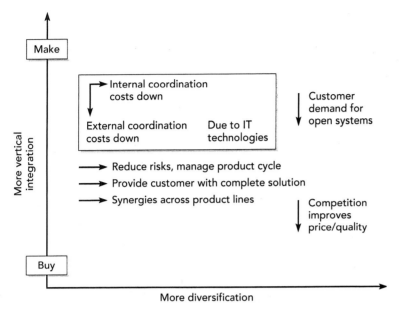

Figure 7.3 The arrows illustrate some driving forces in the computer industry that encourage diversified firms but discourage vertical integration

reduction in internal coordination costs encourages diversification, since it reduces the added costs of managing a diverse product line. The reduction in external coordination costs reduces the attractiveness of vertical integration, since the coordination of the complementary components of a product across firms becomes easier.

- Less vertical integration is favored by many customers for two reasons. Customers would prefer competition among suppliers for the different vertical components of a product because it reduces prices and improves options and quality. In addition, this competition opens the possibility of mixing and matching product components, reducing the lock-in that customers experience (lock-in will be discussed further in Chapter 8). Disadvantages are the need for the customer to integrate solutions from different suppliers and the fragmentation of customer support.

- More diversification is favored by customers, if the products offered are complementary, because customers can reduce their own coordination costs by dealing with fewer suppliers.

- Two factors related to the management of an individual firm favor diversification. Individual products tend to be cyclical, with periods of high expense (during new designs) and high profit (early after product introduction, when the product is more differentiated from competitors). Diversification improves the consistency of financial results, which managers favor. Also, there may be synergies across product lines, such as common expertise and design tools, economies of scope (like the sharing of design groups across product lines), and economies of scale (as in production, sales, and distribution).

All the "trend arrows" in Figure 7.3 point in the direction of more diversification (more buying and outsourcing) and less vertical integration, and indeed these trends are readily observable in the computer industry. Of course, there are exceptions that can be cited as well.

EXAMPLE: *The acquisition of Digital by Compaq resulted in a greater diversification of product mix, manifested particularly by the expansion of Compaq into professional services. It also increased vertical integration, as Digital was more involved in microprocessors and networking.*

In telecommunications and networking, the issues are somewhat different because of the emphasis on services rather than products. Nevertheless, the trends are similar.

EXAMPLE: *In the United States, the former Bell telephone companies have divested both a major software development arm (Bellcore) and an equipment manufacturing arm (Lucent) in order to concentrate on their service provider function and move away from vertical integration. There is a wave of mergers among service providers, in part because each provider wants to offer customers a fully diversified set of services (wired and wireless, telephony and data) on a global basis.*

7.2.4   Venture Capital and Start-Ups

Venture capital arguably plays a larger role in networked computing than in any other industry in the United States—except perhaps biotechnology—and is one powerful force behind vertical disintegration. Venture capitalists (VCs) fund new companies in the hope they become public companies with high valuation. These investments are risky, and thus VCs diversify—each VC funds multiple start-ups, and each start-up is typically funded by multiple VCs.

Why is this model so successful? Here are a few observations:

- The barriers to entry, particularly in software, are lower than in many industries. Large capital investments are not needed from the VC, and the needed human capital is rewarded by equity. Thus, venture capital focuses on those parts of the business that have low barriers to entry, including application

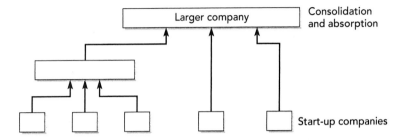

Figure 7.4 A process of absorption and consolidation creates new products in start-ups and moves those products into diversified firms

software, semiconductor design (where fabrication can be outsourced), and equipment design (where manufacturing can be outsourced).

- The trend from stovepipe toward layers with open interfaces allows small firms to fully participate with complementary products, without having to provide a total system solution.

- The technology and the industry move very rapidly, but size can be a disadvantage if slow decision making is the result. In addition, large companies with their installed bases find it more difficult to overcome supplier lock-in (see Chapter 8).

- Start-ups have often proven financially lucrative to early employees as well as investors, and large companies cannot offer a comparable upside. Thus, start-ups sometimes have an advantage attracting the top talent necessary to bring a new idea to fruition.

Some start-ups succeed fabulously, others fail and go out of business, but a common process is the absorption of start-ups into larger companies, as illustrated in Figure 7.4. It is increasingly common for new products to be developed by start-ups, often with collaborative marketing, sales, and distribution agreements with other firms. Moderately successful start-ups are often purchased by larger firms pursuing diversification, while wildly successful start-ups are taken public.

7.2.5 Computing/Communications Convergence

Convergence occurs when once-independent product categories or whole industries become—through the evolution of technology or the marketplace—either competitive or complementary. The evolution from centralized to networked computing has resulted in major convergence (see "The Evolution of Computing" on page 2).

The overriding convergence—between the telecommunications and computer industries, as a result of the networking of computers—illustrates both competitive and complementary forms of convergence. When users demand networked computing applications, they require both computers and communications, which become complementary.

EXAMPLE: *Computer equipment manufacturers believe the unavailability of high-speed Internet residential access is stifling their business opportunities. Home computers—rather than business computers—have often been technology drivers because major applications are multimedia and games, which require high processing speeds. These stand-alone applications will be extended over the Internet, but the full potential will not be achieved until residences have higher-speed connections. The obstacles are discussed in Chapter 20.*

At the same time, networked applications become competitive with traditional applications from the telecommunications industry, such as telephony, facsimile, and video conferencing.

EXAMPLE: *Internet telephony provides a two-way voice capability similar to the telephone network, but using the Internet (see Chapter 20). Internet telephony is directly competitive to the telephone network, but is often much cheaper, particularly for international calls where telephone rates sometimes far exceed costs. Some telephone companies complain that Internet telephony is not subject to the same regulatory environment as the traditional telecommunications carriers, and thus the competition is unfair.*

Another example of competitive convergence is the information appliance, which often provides similar applications to those available on a desktop computer (see "Information Appliances" on page 209). For example, cellular telephones with email and Web browser capabilities compete directly with notebook computers.

The computer/communications convergence is irrevocably changing both industries. The computer industry today encounters many more difficulties achieving interoperability—a stand-alone turnkey no longer offers much value—and thus is becoming heavily involved in standardization (discussed next). The telecommunications industry is being driven away from stovepipe networks. Together, these influences make the two industries more similar.

Discussion

D7.6 Discuss some of the problems a consumer experiences in integrating products from different vendors. How will these difficulties encourage stove-pipe architectures? Diversification of suppliers?

D7.7 Do you think information appliances are a serious competitor to desktop computers, or complementary? Why?

D7.8 Some say expectations for convergence of communications, computing, and consumer electronics are overblown. Do you think these are serious trends? Do you think future companies will continue to specialize in one of these areas, or pursue two or three?

D7.9 Some would say that venture capital is ultimately destructive because it bleeds good people away from large companies and universities. Discuss the merits of this charge.

7.3   Standardization

The successful integration of components from different suppliers (examples are the infrastructure layers or the application and the infrastructure) requires those suppliers to define and adhere to common interface definitions. This raises a daunting problem: At each interface, the products of different suppliers must be *interoperable*—they must work together correctly. To achieve this, there must be a single standard interface definition, so that *each* product can be interoperable with *all* products that may interact with that interface. The solution is to standardize the interface, through the process of *standardization.* A standard is a specification generally agreed upon, precisely and completely defined, and well documented, so that any supplier can implement it. Standardization is common in many industries and professions. For example, standards are set for the legal profession by the Uniform Commercial Code and for the accounting profession by the Financial Accounting Standards Board.

Standardized interfaces offer value to customers, as they allow customers to mix and match products from different vendors complying with the standard. This creates market pressures on suppliers to create and adopt standardized interfaces. Standardization applies to software, to hardware (see the sidebar "Hardware Standards"), and to the representation of information. With respect to the latter, data is often exchanged among applications or among modules of a single application. To allow the information to be properly recovered from this data, both the sender and recipient must agree on the structure and interpretation. This is another role for standardization—an agreement on a standard struc-

Hardware Standards

The standardization of hardware is at a more mature stage of development than that of software and is thus an area of less current concern and activity. Here the problem arises more from the existence of multiple standards. Where they must be incorporated into a common networked computing infrastructure, applications must somehow accommodate their heterogeneity. It is acceptable for different types of computers to participate in a networked application (although such heterogeneity does introduce complications), because the software layers abstract and encapsulate the computer's internal hardware (this is elaborated in Chapter 15 and Chapter 16).

EDI Standards

Electronic data interchange (EDI) requires enterprises to exchange standard business messages (see "Inter-Enterprise E-Commerce" on page 91). Its success depends on standardization of the formats (structure and interpretation) of these messages. These EDI standards illustrate standards attached to data and the importance of standards internal to inter-enterprise applications (as opposed to infrastructure).

EDI was stimulated by a standard, ANSI X12 [Kee97], which specifies the formats for the exchanges of many standard business messages, including the invoice (X12-810), tax information reporting (X12-826), purchase order (X12-850), notice of employment status (X12-540), mortgage appraisal request (X12-261), and many others.

Without ANSI X12 (and an equivalent European standard, EDIFACT), EDI would be far less prevalent. The significance of standards like ANSI X12 is that many businesses can exchange messages without prior coordination or negotiation of formats beyond simply specifying the name of the standard they are using. They can purchase rather than develop software to generate and interpret messages particular to specific business partners. Another example of application standardization is electronic payments (see Chapter 14).

Document Standards

One of the most common forms of information is the document, which contains words, pictures and drawings, and structural elements such as

ture and interpretation (see the sidebar "EDI Standards" and the sidebar "Document Standards" for important examples).

7.3.1   Reference Models and Interfaces

In the context of systems, an architecture defines a modularity, including decomposition, functionality, and interaction. All these elements of the architecture can be standardized, enabling modules to be integrated even though they may be implemented by different groups or vendors. The internal implementation of modules is not standardized, both because it is unnecessary and because the implementers should be given maximum freedom.

In standardization activities, decomposition and interaction are together called a *reference model*. The reference model is a critical starting point because it determines where interfaces are placed in the system, and the location of those interfaces further defines the boundaries of competition.

The layered infrastructure architecture is an important reference model. After agreeing on a common reference model, both the functionality and interaction of the modules is specified. These standards focus on the interfaces, specifying what actions are available in each module as well as how a module is expected to interact with other modules.

E X A M P L E :   *In the case of software modules, the interface standard will specify a set of actions, parameters, and return values, which are called* formats. *A format is an example of a specification of a structure and interpretation of data. In addition, there are often constraints or expectations on the protocols—the order of action invocation. Once a reference model is established, the standardization process focuses on the detailed specification of interfaces, including formats and protocols. A goal is to leave room for vendors to differentiate their products based on the standards, for example, with proprietary extensions.*

7.3.2   Industry Organization and Standardization

The dynamics of standardization are influential in determining the direction of networked computing, as well as winners and losers among vendors. Standards place constraints on the viable organization of the whole industry. From a customer's perspective, modules provided by different vendors can be purchased and integrated, but only if those modules have standardized interfaces adhered to and supported by the vendors. Recall from Chapter 6, a system generously endowed with standardized open interfaces is termed an open system.

EXAMPLE: *Open system strategies that have been successful are the PC (with standardized interfaces for expansion cards, monitor, keyboard and mouse, and peripherals), the UNIX operating system (which Sun Microsystems developed into a business), and the Internet (which CISCO developed into a business).*

For two companies' products to interoperate requires a standardized interface. For companies to divide a computing and communications system among themselves requires agreements on the location of interfaces. While modularity and interfaces are important within proprietary systems as well, "opening up" interfaces to standardization and making them available to other firms are weighty strategic decisions. Inserting a standardized interface defines the boundaries of acceptable competition. It enables different companies to supply complementary products, and it often results in unexpected innovation as companies find new ways to exploit standardized interfaces.

EXAMPLE: *Both electric power and telephone industries once restricted the connection of "foreign" devices. Opening up these systems with standard interfaces (the electric outlet and telephone jack, both accompanied by electrical standards) resulted in a wealth of innovation in complementary products (electric appliances, modems, answering systems, for example). The standard interfaces in the PC have allowed many innovative peripherals.*

On the other hand, proprietary interfaces moderate competitive pressures for a dominant system supplier in the short run, but invite strong competition at the system level from better modularized systems solutions in the long run.

EXAMPLE: *Sun Microsystems and CISCO have pursued an "open systems" strategy, embracing standardized interfaces. Many customers favor them because they feel less locked in and can mix and match products from different vendors (see Chapter 8). Other companies, such as IBM (in earlier decades) and Microsoft, have had success providing full system solutions with mostly proprietary interfaces (Microsoft only in the operating system and applications software). However, IBM had to largely abandon this strategy as the open systems vendors attracted away customers.*

Some economic foundations for standardization are discussed in Chapter 8.

7.3.3   The Standardization Process

Any formal standardization process requires a recognition of need by a standards body, industry organization, or government. A *standards body* is an organization set up for the express purpose of promulgating standards (see the

paragraphs and headings. The publication of documents on the network and subsequent successful viewing by users depends on standardized document representations. Several important document standards have emerged:

EXAMPLE: *Word processors are used by individuals to author documents. They represent the document in a file format, and that file can be published directly, as long as the user accessing the document possesses a compatible word processing application. Microsoft Word has emerged as a de facto standard.*

EXAMPLE: *Postscript (PS) and Portable Document Format (PDF), both from Adobe Systems, have emerged as de facto standards for representation of documents that need only be displayed—by users possessing the application that displays the document, called a viewer. The advantage is that any word processor can be used to author the document, but a PS or PDF document cannot be edited by the user accessing it.*

EXAMPLE: *The Web is associated with standards called markup languages for the representation of pages. Two of these are HTML and XML, which are discussed further in Chapter 15. Both are variants on an ISO de jure standard, SGML. An advantage of XML over HTML is that it separates the structure from the presentation of the document. Both formats can*

*be edited by any user access-
ing them, given the appropriate application. In the future,
word processors may increasingly use XML as an internal
representation.*

International Organization for Standards (ISO)

ISO is an international, nongovern-
mental federation of national standards bodies from more than 100
countries—one from each country
(the American National Standards
Institute (ANSI) in the United States).
Its stated role is to "promote the
development of standardization and
related activities in the world with a
view to facilitating the international
exchange of goods and services."
The technical work is carried out in a
hierarchy of some 2,700 technical
committees, subcommittees, and
working groups with representatives
of industry, research institutes, government authorities, consumer bodies, and international organizations.
They come together as equal partners in the resolution of global standardization issues.

ISO standards are not always successful in the marketplace. For example,
the "Open Systems Interconnection
(OSI)" was a very elaborate standard
for networking protocols that has
been supplanted by the Internet protocols.

sidebar "International Organization for Standards (ISO)" for an example). The standards process also requires the commitment of monetary and human resources by a set of participating companies. A standards process may pro-duce a single standard and dissolve, but more often there is an ongoing process of refinement and extension.

EXAMPLE: *The Internet requires complementary technologies and the coordina-tion of a set of hardware suppliers (such as CISCO, 3Com, and Bay Networks), service providers (such as MCI and AT&T), and application suppliers (such as Netscape and Microsoft). These companies—together with university research-ers—cooperate in a process of continuous refinement through the IETF (see the sidebar "Internet Engineering Task Force (IETF)").*

A typical organization of the standards process is illustrated in Figure 7.5. The sanctioning body commissions ad hoc standards committees for each specific standard it pursues. A large number of companies may choose to participate in the process or in specific committees of interest. Each committee holds periodic (typically quarterly) meetings for debates, arguments, and negotiation, with the objective of arriving at an agreement on reference model, interfaces, and proto-cols. The details vary widely among different standards bodies.

As part of the process, there may be implementation, testing, and refinement, usually performed by the participating companies or organizations. (Standards not benefiting from these activities are usually not as successful.) Thus, the pro-cess is partly a collaborative design process. Companies have several incentives to contribute to the design phase of a standard:

- One company doesn't have the necessary range of expertise to complete a design by itself. This is particularly true with integrated layer architectures, where many applications have to be served well. Thus, different companies contribute expertise to different parts of the design.
- Companies may benefit financially through patent protection and royalties if they maintain ownership of some technology (see Chapter 8).
- Companies want a standard to be high quality, as it may constrain the indus-try in the future.
- Companies can get products to market faster if their contributed technology is adopted. They not only have expertise but also may have prototype imple-mentations. Often the most profitable period in a product's lifecycle is early, before competitors have entered the market.
- Companies gain intelligence on competitors.

Finally, an important part of the finalization of the standard is its detailed docu-mentation.

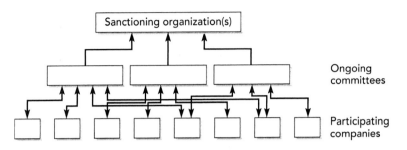

Figure 7.5 Typical standards process

An increasingly popular approach in computing is a *technology web*, which is a set of companies informally coordinating complementary technologies without a formal process. (This isn't related to the Web information access application, except that the companies enhancing the Web are themselves a technology web.)

E X A M P L E :   *The desktop personal computer is based on Intel microprocessors, the Microsoft operating system, various hardware suppliers, and various application software vendors—the Wintel technology web. Intel is particularly active in promulgating hardware interface standards through its Architecture Laboratory, and Microsoft is similarly concerned with software interface standards.*

While the formal standards process is at times slow, technology webs support a rapid continual technology refinement. A technology web is typically open only to a small set of suppliers (often only one supplier for each of the complementary technologies), while most standards processes welcome all comers.

Two distinct types of standards—de facto and de jure—are described in Table 7.4. The computer industry advances very quickly, so the de facto standard is increasingly popular.

7.3.4   Who Controls and Who Enforces Standards?

A question with commercial, legal, and political implications is who controls and enforces standards. These issues heavily influence the competitive outcomes in the industry, and standards are increasingly a battleground for supremacy in the industry [Sha98].

As described in "The Horizontal Layer Interface" on page 184, many standards are open (publicly documented and unencumbered by intellectual property restrictions). For them, the primary "enforcement" is the marketplace, which

Internet Engineering Task Force (IETF)

The IETF is a "large open international community of network designers, operators, suppliers, and researchers concerned with the evolution of the Internet architecture and the smooth operation of the Internet." The internet technologies that are in direct competition with the OSI standards promulgated by ISO (see the sidebar "International Organization for Standards (ISO)") have won hands down in the marketplace. The reasons are several. The Internet standards have been developed incrementally from simple beginnings, always accompanied by a working implementation funded largely by government research budgets. OSI, in contrast, attempted a complete "paper" design without implementation. As a result, the Internet standards reached the marketplace much faster and were distributed for free as part of the Berkeley UNIX system. The result is that the Internet standards had already developed a large suite of applications before the OSI standards could be completed. This is an illustration of the importance of "time to market" and winner-take-all effects (see Chapter 8).

Table 7.4 Two types of standards

Type	Description	Examples
De facto standard	A technology so commonplace that it is a standard in practice, even if not recognized by any formal body. It can be established in a couple of ways: • *Market power:* Some product categories have winner-take-all effects, resulting over time in a dominant solution (see Chapter 8). • *Voluntary cooperation:* Companies recognizing the need for interoperability voluntarily work together to recommend standards.	Market power: Windows operating system and the Hayes command set. Voluntary cooperation: internet protocols (Chapter 12), Java (Chapter 16), and CORBA (Chapter 16).
De jure standard	A standard established by a formal process organized by government, an industry association, or standards body. It may actually be mandated by law.	ISDN telephone interface; X.500 directory service; GSM digital cellular telephone.

favors products complying with the standard, in part because they are interoperable with complementary products.

A de facto standard may in principle be available for use by anyone, but there may be a dominant proprietary *implementation* (an example is Adobe's Post-Script). Although a competitive vendor is permitted to build a standard-compliant product, the dominant vendor hopes the development cost would be prohibitive and market acceptance would be minimal.

EXAMPLE: *Competing implementations have occurred — contrary to the wishes of the dominant supplier — in the PC BIOS (code embedded deep within the bowels of a PC implementation). Originally designed by IBM, it was successfully reverse-engineered and implemented by Phoenix Technologies. Another example is the Intel Pentium microprocessor, which has been cloned by Advanced Micro Devices and others. They created a design independently by replicating the functionality and specifications and without using the original design.*

De jure standards are rare in the computer industry, but they occur in communications, which is often subject to government regulation (see Chapter 20). The regulatory process may dictate a single standard but leave it up to industry to determine its details.

Standards can also be *proprietary*—restricted by copyright, trade secret, or patent law (see Chapter 8). Sometimes such a standard is only intended to be used by companies who have joint ownership or who license the technology to one another. It may seem strange to call this a standard, but it does share the purpose with all standards of coordinating complementary products of different suppliers.

A standard may be publicly documented but incorporate patented ideas and require adopters to pay royalties. In this case, companies contributing technology to a standard are able to retain patent rights, but are obligated by the standards organization to freely license the technology to all comers for a "fair, reasonable, and nondiscriminatory" royalty.

7.3.5 Why Open Standards?

Since no company can claim ownership or collect royalties on an open standard, why would companies participate in the development of such a standard? They do so only with some reluctance, and many considerations come into play.

Some open standards did not arise in the commercial sector, but were developed through academic research. The basic internet protocols are an example of such a standard. When such a standard is available and widely used—aided by the availability of a cost-free implementation—it becomes difficult to overcome due to some economic effects discussed in Chapter 8. Customers also encourage open standards, because they can be implemented and enhanced by multiple vendors, which enhances competition, improves features and quality, and reduces cost. As a result, proprietary technologies may have difficulty competing with an open standard.

EXAMPLE: *There are proprietary alternatives to the internet standards—such as X.25, Frame Relay, and ATM—but the weight of interoperability concerns and economic factors (Chapter 8) precludes them from making significant inroads.*

In other cases, companies may cooperate on open standards because they perceive a compelling need that transcends immediate commercial interests. For example, a single company may not deem itself capable of defining, developing, and promulgating an entire system concept. Standardization then becomes a collective activity, with the development and marketing of components relegated to individual companies. The standard may specify the minimum required for interoperability, allowing component suppliers room to provide added features, better implementations, or lower prices.

Sometimes a company can expand its market and derive increased revenues and profits when its product is standardized and there is a viable market in complementary products. This observation has a strong basis in economics discussed further in Chapter 8.

Object Management Group (OMG)

An important voluntary cooperative standardization effort is the *Object Management Group (OMG)*, which focuses on object-oriented systems (see Chapter 11) and enterprise computing. The OMG includes over 700 software companies that have found it in their best interest to join together to promote cross-platform standards, so their products can participate together in enterprise applications. Strictly speaking, the OMG is not a standardization body, but rather simply makes recommendations as to the best technologies. Thus, it views its charter as the cooperative promulgation of de facto standards. The process followed by OMG is to identify areas that need standardization, request participating companies to contribute, evaluate those contributions by a technical committee, and make a final recommendation. Occasionally they ask members to merge their best ideas into a single proposal.

EXAMPLE: *The Apple Macintosh computer is a proprietary and well-conceived product, but Apple's fortunes have been declining while that of PC suppliers such as Compaq and Dell are rising. The company with a proprietary "total system solution" may be at a long-term competitive disadvantage.*

In other cases, a company develops a technology as only one element of a larger product, but later it becomes a de facto standard with longevity.

EXAMPLE: *The Hayes command set for controlling modems was originally a small part of the Hayes modem products but became a de facto standard for virtually all modems. IBM developed the original PC architecture in part to serve as a platform for its software products. IBM was never a significant factor in PC applications (although it has had some recent successes), but the PC architecture became a de facto standard.*

The networked computing era places more of a premium on interoperability across different companies' products and greatly expands the scope of the "system." As a result, standardization is growing in importance, even where companies recognize they may reduce *direct* proprietary or competitive advantage. Often companies expect to succeed with superior (or even exclusive) implementation of a standard, or from enhancements and extensions, or from complementary products. Their participation in the standards process gives them the advantage of early market entry and a more successful market overall.

A common strategy is to define an open standard deliberately designed to be extensible. Then, participating companies can benefit from the market power of the open standard while adding proprietary value.

EXAMPLE: *The Motion Picture Experts Group (MPEG) was convened by ISO to standardize a format for digital video. MPEG standards are the basis for video coding in computer multimedia and also digital television systems worldwide. An MPEG decoder should display video represented by the MPEG standard, even though the encoding may have been performed by a product from a different firm. The standard specifies only the formats of the bit stream (see Chapter 12) representing the video and leaves considerable room for suppliers to improve both the coding and compression process (see Chapter 20) and the decoding process.*

7.3.6 Standardization Has Downsides Too

There are disadvantages to standardization. As compared to proprietary technology development, the standardization process can be slow and cumbersome. When standardization proceeds without the benefit of working experimental prototypes, it may be nonfunctional or too expensive to develop and manufacture.

The most serious problem is that once a standard is established, it is difficult for new technologies to displace it. This may stifle further innovation or new entrants.

EXAMPLE: *Governments have been known to establish de jure standards for the purpose of national advantage. For example, they may prohibit the importation of a product (such as computers) to stimulate a domestic industry with proprietary standards (for example, the "Panda" computer in China). Such policies have usually resulted in an industry that falls behind the state of the art, and they are usually deleterious in the long run.*

It is, fortunately, possible for a superior technology to overcome a widely adopted standard, but its advantages (in functionality and/or cost) must be substantial. In recognition of this problem, many standards in networking and computing establish an ongoing process of upgrade, improvement, and extension, which offers an opportunity for further innovation without discarding the standard altogether. Examples include the internet protocols and MPEG.

EXAMPLE: *The MPEG standard has passed through two phases (with more on the way), and each one extended functionality and performance. Each new phase is backward compatible, so that an encoder and decoder conforming to any of the phases of MPEG are interoperable. Another example of this backward compatibility is the voiceband data modem standards emanating from the CCITT. The IETF follows the same methodology where possible.*

Discussion

D7.10 What standards do you see around you? Why are these standardized? What was the process by which these standards were developed?

D7.11 What are some examples of business strategies in computing that are centered around standardization? How effective have these strategies been?

D7.12 Discuss some examples of standards you believe have stifled innovation.

7.4   *Open Issues

The computing and communications industries have mutated more than most. Experimentation to find the most successful approaches in the marketplace has been constant.

7.4.1   Industry Organization

The computer industry has shifted toward a more fragmented industrial organization in which different vendors contribute to a horizontally layered infrastructure and a diverse set of applications exploiting this infrastructure. While this began in the era of decentralized computing, networked computing is recasting both the computer and communications industries again. Networks and enterprise and commerce applications put a premium on interoperability across heterogeneous computing platforms—something much less an issue in an earlier era where each computer platform was essentially an independent commercial marketplace. Standardization efforts like the IETF and OMG—each with wide industry participation—are concrete manifestations of this. The infrastructure for distributed applications can no longer be developed and deployed by individual companies or even small groups of companies; it has to be an industrywide effort.

In this respect, the computer industry is becoming more like the telecommunications industry, which has always emphasized standardization on a global basis. However, the telecommunications industry is also reorganizing, as described further in Chapter 20. Major mergers are creating consolidated global telecommunications service providers offering a diversified portfolio of end-to-end services to multinational corporations. Telecommunications companies have traditionally offered turnkey applications such as telephony and video conferencing (which they call "services") rather than general-purpose infrastructure. This directly collides with the computer industry, where applications are typically sold independently of infrastructure.

This picture is complicated by the growing importance of information appliances, which represents a return to stovepipe solutions. This is driven by the rapidly declining cost of hardware and by usability issues.

The final outcome is not clear. What is the most effective industrial organization for the computer industry in the networked computing era, and for the telecommunications industry in an era of globalization, greater competition, and the growing importance of computer-mediated applications? The organization of both industries will be much different, and the two industries may become more consolidated.

7.4.2 The Best Standardization Processes

There has been a striking shift in the standardization process over the past couple decades. Rather slow and cumbersome international standardization bodies have been displaced to some extent in the networking and computing technologies by much quicker and more agile processes such as technology webs, consortia, and more informal organizations promulgating de facto standards. At the same time, the importance of standardization has increased in computing, with the advent of networking and greater emphasis on enterprise, cross-enterprise, and consumer applications. Rapid standardization tends to give poor-quality and limited results that require subsequent refinement and extension. This situation continues to evolve. There is no perfect process, and everything is a trade-off. Where will it go in the future?

Review

Subsystems purchased as is from another company, possibly with many configuration options, are called components. System integration involves the assembly of components, making them interact properly to achieve higher-level system functionality.

There are a variety of suppliers of goods and providers of services in the domain of networked computing. Goods include equipment, software, and information content, and services include computing and networking and professional services (such as system integration or application development).

Industry trends include the integrated layer instead of stovepipe architectures (the information appliance is an exception), less vertical integration and more diversification, and convergence between the computing, communications, and consumer electronics industries.

A standard is a set of commonly agreed upon and well-documented specifications. Standardization is an important mechanism for coordination and collaborative design among complementary suppliers, and it increases the value of those products to customers. A number of standards are promulgated by government, standards bodies, industry groups, and technology webs.

Standardization assumes a reference model and then proceeds to define and document the interface between modules within this reference model. The layered software infrastructure is an example of a reference model and interface standardization.

Open standards are available to be implemented by any company without restriction and are often demanded by customers. It is also possible for standards to have proprietary content (restricted by copyright or patent law) and require licensing under "reasonable, necessary, and nondiscriminatory" terms.

Standards can inhibit innovation by precluding the entry of new ideas and approaches, but they can be overcome by significant technical advances.

Key Concepts

Components and system integration

Suppliers and providers:

- Product suppliers
- Service providers
- Professional services

Standards:

- Standardization process and organizations
- De facto and de jure standards
- Open standards

Architecture: stovepipe and integrated layers

Boundaries of the firm: vertical integration and diversification

Convergence: complementary and competitive

Further Reading

Textbooks on management information systems such as [MBD99] and [Lau99] discuss the organization of the industry from the perspective of an end-user organization. Many strategies relative to using standardization as a competitive tool are discussed in [Sha98].

Exercises

E7.1 Look at a PC you own, and list all the components (subsystems purchased from suppliers by the PC manufacturer) you see or know about in two categories:

   a. Hardware components

   b. Software components

E7.2 Using the definition of component from "Components and Integration" on page 198, for each of the following, give two examples, and justify your answer:

    a. Component useful for the software infrastructure

    b. Component useful for software applications

    c. Component useful for equipment manufacturers

E7.3 For each of the types of suppliers listed in Table 7.1, page 201, give two more examples (not listed) of such a supplier or provider. You may want to browse the Web for ideas.

E7.4 For each of the following, give two examples, and briefly justify your answer:

    a. Suppliers who gained competitive advantage primarily through better coordination with their complementary suppliers

    b. Suppliers who gained significant market success primarily by outperforming their competitive suppliers on feature, quality, or price

    c. Suppliers for whom both complementary supplier coordination and execution were significant competitive advantages

E7.5 Two concepts of industry organization were discussed: architectural alternatives (stovepipe, integrated layering) and product strategies (vertical integration, diversification, convergence).

    a. Discuss the relationship between stovepipe and integrated layering—to what extent are they independent issues, and where are they coupled?

    b. Repeat a for integrated layering and convergence.

    c. Repeat a for vertical integration and diversification.

    d. Repeat a for vertical integration and convergence.

    e. Repeat a for diversification and convergence.

    f. Discuss the relationship between these architectural alternatives and product strategies—to what extent are they independent issues, and in what respect are they coupled?

E7.6 For each of the following examples, state whether it can be viewed as an example of stovepipe, integrated layer architecture, vertical integration, diversification, or computing/communications convergence. If it is an example of more than one, state this. Give a brief justification for your answer.

    a. Public telephone network

    b. WebTV

    c. Notebook computer with modem

    d. Cellular telephone with integrated Web browser

    e. Personal digital assistant

    f. Operating system with bundled or integrated Web browser

    g. Computer manufacturer with professional-services organization

    h. Cable TV system that provides integrated Internet access and telephone service

E7.7 For two of the following examples, think about and describe briefly the benefits and disadvantages of each option.

    a. Pocket calculator versus desktop computer spreadsheet program

    b. Voice telephone service via the telephone network versus via the Internet

    c. Stand-alone word processor versus desktop computer word processing program

    d. Television viewed on a TV set versus on your desktop computer screen

E7.8 An example of computing/communications convergence would be the desire of three industries to provide Web browsing capability in their products: computer (desktop computer), telecommunications (phones equipped with screens and keyboards, particular cellular phones), and consumer electronics (television set). Putting yourself in the position of the consumer, discuss the advantages and disadvantages of each. Do you think they will all be successful?

E7.9 For any two of the following industries, list five to ten standards—either de facto or de jure—associated with that industry:

    a. Automobile industry

    b. Electric power industry

    c. Book publishing industry

    d. Telephone industry

E7.10 Suppose there is an industry effort to create a standard user interface for word processing programs, so that all programs would provide a common set of features, with the same look and feel. Following the open-closed principle of interfaces described in "Flexibility" on page 189, individual vendors would be free to add features, so long as they preserved the common way of performing the operations specified in the standard.

a. What would motivate Microsoft, Corel, or Red Hat to participate in this process?

b. Why might they choose *not* to participate?

c. Are the answers to *a* and *b* different, based on the companies' current market share in the word processing or operating systems market?

E7.11   For each of the following items, discuss why a supplier might want to participate in the standardization and later adopt the resulting standard. Then discuss why a supplier might *not* want to adopt a standard.

a. The format for storage of word processing documents on disk

b. The graphical user interface to a word processing program

c. A method of cash payment over the Web

E7.12   For each of the items in Exercise 7.11, explain the relative advantages of an open, proprietary, or available standard to

a. The user or consumer

b. The supplier or firm providing the product or service.

E7.13   Give three examples of standards that you believe are out of date and inhibiting innovation. If you cannot think of three examples, discuss what conclusions you might draw about the characteristics of that industry.

a. In the information content industry

b. In the software industry serving social or information management applications

c. In the infrastructure software industry

d. In the software industry serving organizational applications

e. In some other industry outside computing or communications with which you are familiar

E7.14   Give three examples of standards in the computing and software industries that you believe resulted in dramatically greater success for the standardized function or technology, compared to the alternative of proprietary competitive solutions from different suppliers. Explain why the function or technology would have been far less successful if it had not been standardized, in your view.

Economics and Policy

8

The computing and communications industries are subject to some unusual economic effects that have distinct imprints on these industries. Appreciation of these imprints aids in understanding the structure and anticipating future evolution of these industries and their products. These effects will be referred to throughout the remaining chapters, especially beginning with the infrastructure in Part V.

In addition, the government has a substantial impact on this industry in supporting long-term research and protecting intellectual property rights. Networking is also raising increasing issues for policy makers. Policy issues and government actions are having a substantial impact on networked computing (for example, affecting which products can be exported from the United States and placing restrictions on the business practices of companies) as well as on networked applications (for example, placing restrictions on the dissemination of information about users to protect privacy). Thus, the government context is an important backdrop for the industry and applications.

8.1 Obstacles to Change

While networked computing evolves quickly, there are actually substantial obstacles to change in this industry. As a rule, these obstacles buttress dominant technical legacy solutions or suppliers, thus creating obstacles to the entry of new technology or suppliers. They create winner-take-all effects that reduce the diversity of products and solutions, and path-dependent effects that prevent the market from adopting the best technologies. Surprisingly, without these obstacles the technologies might change even more quickly than they do. In considering the challenges faced by suppliers and consumers later in the chapter, it is helpful to understand these broad industry forces.

Metcalfe's Law

This is a simple illustration of network externalities (named for Robert Metcalfe, the inventor of Ethernet). It estimates the total value of a computer or telecommunications network in terms of the number of connections it can support. If there are n users (or telephones or facsimile machines or computers) connected to a network, then they can each connect to $n - 1$ others. The total number of distinct connections is thus $n \times (n - 1)$. (Actually, this counts each bidirectional connection twice. The actual number is half this.)

The total value of a network, if it is presumed to be proportional to the number of connections it supports, is thus proportional to n^2. The purpose of switching is to reduce the number of communication links required to support all these connections from n^2 to something more like n, the number of access links. (Backbone links benefit from tremendous economies of scale and are thus relatively unimportant in the cost picture.) This makes the economics of networks very favorable, as the total value per unit cost increases as n. This may explain why companies want to enter the networking business!

8.1.1   Network Effects

When the value of a product or service to an individual consumer depends on the number of other consumers adopting it, this is called a network effect or network externality. "Network" refers to the fact that the different instances of the product are logically connected (or possibly physically connected through a network). "Externality" denotes an impact one consumer has on another without a compensating payment.

E X A M P L E : *You probably don't particularly care how many other consumers own the same automobile as you, as long as there is a sufficient critical mass of cars so that parts are available and mechanics know how to fix them. In the case of fashion, you may actively seek out clothing and colors not worn by too many other consumers.*

A particular fashion often has *negative* externality if its loss of uniqueness causes it to have less value. Many networked computer products have *positive* externality [Eco96]: The value to each consumer, or to consumers collectively, increases with the number of adopters.

E X A M P L E : *The telephone and the facsimile machine exhibit strong positive externality. The value of a telephone (facsimile machine) depends on how many other people you can call (fax) (see the sidebar "Metcalfe's Law"). To illustrate network effects without a physical network, a word processing program offers an individual user more value when there are many other users with whom he can share files. A computer programming language offers greater value when widely used, because it is easier to find qualified programmers and complementary development tools. An operating system offers greater value when widely adopted because it attracts a greater diversity of applications. In each case, you can consider a logical network of word processing users or programmers or application developers who all derive positive benefit from the fact that they share a common product.*

There are two types of network effects, as listed in Table 8.1—direct and indirect. In terms of the impact of network effects on the marketplace, two concepts should be understood: critical mass and positive feedback. Early in the lifecycle of a product or service with network effects—when there are few adopters—its value (as measured by consumer willingness to pay) may be lower than the supplier's costs, so that a supplier cannot sell to the consumer at a profit. If the supplier overcomes this—say, by selling at a loss to get sufficient adopters—then eventually the willingness to pay will exceed the supplier's cost. This is called a *critical mass* of adopters.

Table 8.1 Two types of network effects in networked computing

Effect	Description	Examples
Direct	The value of a product or service depends on the number of other users available to participate.	The value of a packet network depends on the number of users connected to the network and available to participate in social applications.
	The value of a product or service depends on the number of complementary products with which data can be shared.	The value of a word processor depends on the number of compatible word processors with which files can be shared. The value of a Web browser depends on the number of compatible servers.
Indirect	The value of a product or service depends on the availability of software or content. A widely used product or service attracts more complementary software or content.	A large number of Web browsers attracts many information publishers. A large number of Microsoft Windows platforms attracts many application suppliers. Large numbers of music CD players attracts many available titles.

After a product adoption exceeds critical mass, this increases its value to consumers further, thereby attracting new adopters, further increasing its value. This "success breeds success" phenomenon—called *positive feedback*—often results in dramatic and rapid market penetration. Positive feedback works in the reverse direction also: For a product losing adopters, there is increasing downside momentum because the value of the product is decreasing. Existing users derive less and less value—and become more likely to defect—while the product attracts few new adopters.

The result of critical mass and positive feedback can be a winner-take-all effect, where a product category "tips" to a dominant supplier [Sha98].

EXAMPLE: *The declining market share of the Apple Macintosh operating system and the rise in market share for Microsoft Windows illustrate positive feedback and a winner-take-all effect. No doubt in part this is due to poor execution by Apple and good execution by Microsoft, but it is also because Macintosh users find fewer applications available (particularly in their local store) and increasingly have difficulties sharing files with colleagues. Similarly, Windows draws increasing focus from application developers.*

*Economic Model of Network Effects

A simple qualitative economic model that explains the impact of network effects for a hypothetical product (the widget) is shown in Figure 8.1 [Eco96]. The consumer demand $p(k, n)$ is plotted. Ignoring the argument n for an instant, $p(k, n)$ is defined as the price at which consumers in aggregate will purchase k

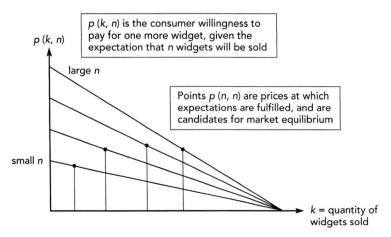

Figure 8.1 The demand for widgets, which has a network effect, depends on the consumer expectations of the total number of widgets sold

widgets. In order to sell more widgets, the supplier has to reduce the price, so this curve decreases with k.

The second argument n is defined as the consumers' collective expectation of the number of widgets that will be sold—the number of other adopters. In the presence of network effects, each consumer attaches a value to widgets that depends on the number of other adopters. For positive consumption externalities, the larger n, the more a typical consumer will be willing to pay for a widget. Thus, if n is large, the demand curve p(k, n) is higher (consumers will buy the same number of widgets at a higher price), and if n is small, the demand curve p(k, n) is lower. Thus, there is a family of demand curves parameterized by the consumer expectations.

Shown in Figure 8.1 are the points at which consumer expectations are exactly fulfilled—the actual sales and adoptions k equal the expectations n. Only these points are candidates for market equilibrium, because elsewhere the consumer expectations either exceed or underestimate reality, eventually increasing or decreasing demand after consumers realize their expectations are inaccurate.

To predict a product's success, the supplier's cost has to be considered, as shown in Figure 8.2. For simplicity, the supplier's unit cost is assumed constant (no economies of scale). Sales divide into three regions:

1. For low production, the adoptions are below critical mass, as evident from a consumer demand below the supplier's cost. In this region the supplier cannot recover its costs without driving down sales.

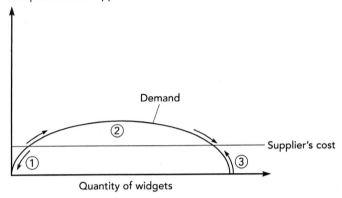

For one more widget, demand
(consumer's willingness to pay)
compared to the supplier's cost

Figure 8.2 In the presence of network effects, the quantity of goods sold divides into three regions—below critical mass, positive feedback, and oversold

2. In the middle region, demand is above the supplier's costs, so the supplier has an easy time gaining adopters at a profit. The number of adopters typically grows rapidly because of positive feedback.
3. Eventually, at high volumes most consumers who need widgets—even given the large adoption rate—have purchased one, and additional sales can't cover the supplier's costs.

Of course, if the supplier's cost is above the peak of demand, there is no region of positive feedback: Technology has to advance, or the demand has to increase, before critical mass is possible. Alternatively, an existing product benefiting from positive feedback is difficult to displace by an otherwise superior product, which has to somehow overcome critical mass.

EXAMPLE: *The facsimile machine was invented in 1843 and first demonstrated in 1851. It was more than a century later, in 1974, that the first international standard was established and it became a viable consumer product because of the declining costs of electronics. Once it reached critical mass in about 1980, the market grew dramatically, and millions of fax machines have been sold.*

Standardization and Network Effects

Strong network effects are a driver of de facto standards. A technical solution unencumbered by intellectual property restrictions, which gains a modicum of success, tends to be adopted by other suppliers wanting to offer greater value to *their* customers. The solution becomes more successful with time and eventually becomes dominant, establishing the de facto standard.

Network Effects in Enterprise and Commerce Applications

The Internet technologies—originally developed by government-supported academic research projects—were widely available in the free Berkeley UNIX operating system. This attracted many complementary applications. By the time similar commercial networking became commonplace, the Internet had a large cadre of users (providing direct network effects) and a set of widely used applications (providing indirect network effects). Other commercial and proprietary networking solutions, even those that had been standardized (such as the OSI protocols) never attracted a critical mass of users or application developers. The rest is history. The Internet has experienced phenomenal growth as it passed critical mass. Its success can be attributed in part to network effects, as the standards became widely deployed and a useful suite of applications was developed.

The Internet also illustrates network effects in applications. Although it doesn't by itself create application interoperability, it is a great enabler that allows applications on heterogeneous platforms—all of which support Internet access—at least to communicate. This in turn has served as the basis of both enterprise and commerce applications. The Web applications built on the Internet—together with the Internet itself—have enabled consumer electronic commerce. Because these application advances all leveraged the spanning layer provided by the Internet, they occurred almost simultaneously—following closely behind the explosive growth of the Internet.

EXAMPLE: *The Hayes command set for controlling a modem from a personal computer was initially defined by a successful modem supplier, Hayes. Suppliers of communication software included an option to use that command set because there were many Hayes modem adopters. Later, other modem manufacturers became "Hayes compatible" because the communications software packages supported it. Eventually, the Hayes command set became a de facto standard.*

A premier example of a de facto standard arising out of indirect network effects is the IBM personal computer. IBM did not successfully maintain intellectual property protection, and other suppliers exploited the critical mass and resulting application availability by producing compatible computers. IBM retained copyright of the operational code stored in read-only memory, but the functionality (not the design) was independently copied by Phoenix Technologies. Because IBM sold many PCs, complementary applications and peripherals were widely available, increasing the value of the PC to users. Other suppliers quickly "cloned" the PC product. IBM temporarily tried to abandon the PC (and the competition it generated) by designing a new and enhanced product, but was forced to return to the original design due to network effects. Today, the PC is a de facto desktop computer standard, and the greatest beneficiaries are Intel and Microsoft (original suppliers to IBM) and not IBM itself.

A de facto standard can also be a product of academic research, particularly if an implementation of the technology is made widely and freely available and attracts complementary content or applications. The Internet is an excellent example of this as well as the power of positive feedback, both in terms of the network and its applications (see the sidebar "Network Effects in Enterprise and Commerce Applications").

All these de facto standards arose in a messy fashion, creating losers among the suppliers and consumers who chose dead-end technologies. Today suppliers recognize the importance of network effects and sometimes form consortia or use other means to define a dominant technology rather than waiting for the market to determine it. Their goal is to stimulate the market (and hence revenues and profits) more quickly and avoid stranded investments (which neither pay off nor can be recovered).

EXAMPLE: *The Automotive Network Exchange (ANX) electronic commerce initiative from U.S. automobile companies is based on standard internet technologies. Many companies associated with the automotive industry are candidates to join ANX. Cross-enterprise applications are subject to direct network effects, but these companies may form a critical mass, creating de facto standards. Clearly the founders of ANX have this in mind.*

The fundamental identity driving decision making in products with network effects is

$$\text{revenues} = \text{market share} \times \text{size of market}$$

It is possible for revenues to increase for one supplier, even as market share is ceded to other firms, as long as the total size of the market is increased sufficiently as a result of positive feedback. The implications of this identity are both profound and complicated by the observation that supplier strategies affect the two terms, market share and size of market, differently.

EXAMPLE: *The digital versatile disk (DVD)—a format for storing digital data on an optical storage medium—resulted from industry cooperation because the manufacturers felt it necessary to define a single standard before the product came to market. They were driven by content suppliers, who felt that incompatible products would confuse consumers and reduce the total market.*

Both the OMG and the IETF are cooperative efforts to define de facto standards. In each case, companies cooperate to define a common solution in a marketplace where direct network effects would likely cause the market to tip to a dominant solution anyway.

This is not an entirely benign trend, as there is value in a winning solution from among competing choices arising because of market forces—as opposed to vendor collaboration—as it may result in cost, performance, or features advantages. In fact, the telecommunications industry—where network effects have always been dominant and "standardization before implementation" has historically been assumed—is actually experimenting with different processes.

EXAMPLE: *The Advanced Television Systems Committee (ATSC) is a consortium of television manufacturers and broadcasters who joined to choose a high-definition television standard for the United States. The standardization process was unusual for this industry, with different groups of companies implementing competing approaches and then merging the best features of each.*

Even more unusual was the decision of the Federal Communications Commission not to encourage or allow a single standard for the digital cellular telephone. Rather, service providers were allowed to deploy whatever technology they chose, hoping the marketplace would choose a superior de facto standard. The short-term trade-off is that a given phone doesn't work in all locations, but the hope is that consumers will benefit from a superior system in the long run. Even a proliferation of cellular standards benefits from the network effects of the telephone system—at least they can all make calls to one another.

Success of the Web

The Web is a de facto standard that has established a whole new industry and increasingly forms the basis for network applications. The origins of its success are easy to see with hindsight. Information access has indirect network effects, and the availability of a browser encouraged a rush of complementary content—publishing in this format guaranteed a large potential audience. Of considerable importance was the ability of almost any user to inexpensively publish content, creating a demand for browsers even before significant commercial activity in content. Netscape and Microsoft provided free browsers to create critical mass and stimulate demand for their complementary server products (for which they charged).

Arguably the greatest credit should go to the Internet itself, which by creating an open spanning layer enabled new applications such as the Web to be globally deployed with a minimum investment for both developers and users and no change or addition to the network itself.

Value of Locked-in Consumer

The supplier has an opportunity to sell upgrades, aftermarket products, etc. at higher-than-competitive prices to a locked-in customer. Of course, the supplier can't charge too much, or the consumer may switch anyway. Thus, the size of the premium prices and profit opportunities is directly related to the consumer's switching costs, which the supplier must evaluate carefully in setting prices.

A locked-in customer represents a tangible monetary value to a supplier—something the supplier can take to the bank. Under certain assumptions, the present value of future profits due to a consumer's lock-in is equal to the consumer's switching cost [Sha98]. The present value takes into account the time value of money by discounting profits in future years in accordance with prevailing interest rates.

Finally, note that this is an oversimplified view of network effects—they do not always lead to market inertia, and there are many subtleties [Kat92].

8.1.2   Lock-in

A networked application comprises a system composed of complementary, interoperable pieces (such as application software, processors, operating systems, network, and peripherals). There are also intangible assets, such as time invested in learning the software and organizations set up to administer it. Networked applications are more diverse than many other goods—say, automobiles. An automobile is a stovepipe "transportation application"—due to de facto standardization—and once you learn to drive one automobile, you can probably drive any other.

Lock-in means a user or organization can't change one piece of a system in isolation, except by replacing it with a direct substitute. Multiple complementary tangible and intangible assets are one source of lock-in [Far88]. (Others, such as contractual relationships, are of less interest here.) In the presence of this form of lock-in, either many complementary pieces have to be changed in a coordinated fashion, or one piece must be replaced with a direct substitute. Lock-in is a barrier to selling new products, since a locked-in customer has to consider the tangible and intangible costs of making complementary changes as well. This is often so daunting and expensive that customers simply keep what they have. Suppliers with a locked-in customer have an advantage over potential competitors.

Of course, lock-in isn't absolute; it comes in degrees. A user who simply wants to switch word processing applications will have an easier time than a user who wants to switch from a PC to a Macintosh. The degree of lock-in is quantified by the consumer's *switching costs*. Let's say that a consumer is considering a new supplier for a product. The switching costs are over and above the replacement of that product, typically including the cost of replacing complementary assets, and including less tangible costs such as worker training or downtime during the conversion.

Suppliers can take advantage of lock-in by successfully charging their customers higher prices than competitors for upgrades or complementary products (see the sidebar "Value of Locked-in Consumer"). Thus, suppliers have a strong incentive to encourage lock-in of their own customers. An important impact of lock-in is the roadblocks to new technologies it engenders.

EXAMPLE: *Many large corporations, even today, store mission-critical information in database systems such as IMS, IDMS, and VSAM, even though these are considered inferior to modern relational databases.*

However, lock-in is not entirely negative for the customer, who benefits from a long-term relationship with a single supplier. A locked-in customer—especially a major one—often has considerable influence over the evolution of products.

Supplier and Industry Lock-in

Suppliers can suffer lock-in too. Because each supplier is also creating a product that is only a piece of an overall system, it must pick and choose among complementary products.

EXAMPLE: *An application supplier has to choose a language and set of design tools, an operating system and computer platform, quite possibly a set of software components, a set of network protocols, etc. An equipment supplier has to choose among possible interfaces, integrated circuit components, etc.*

All these choices of complementary products have the potential for switching costs and lock-in. A supplier can also suffer lock-in to its own proprietary technologies. This comes in a number of forms, for example, the attraction of a lower incremental cost of upgrading a current product compared to creating a new one, or the need to continue supporting customers with legacy products. Customer lock-in also creates supplier lock-in if the supplier can't convince customers to switch and has to continue supporting the old product. The costs of doing so are a deterrent to developing and supporting new products.

EXAMPLE: *In the shift from centralized to decentralized computing, the suppliers of centralized computers (mainframe and minicomputers) were destabilized. Some never recovered. Even where they recognized the broad impact of the technological change, lock-in to existing products was difficult to overcome.*

Digital Equipment Corp. experienced difficulty in making the transition from its proprietary VMS operating system to industry-standard UNIX. It delayed making the transition and later was forced to maintain two operating systems. Competitor Sun Microsystems benefited from supporting only a variant of UNIX.

The lock-in of suppliers to existing technologies is one source of success for start-ups in computing and networking. They need not overcome the baggage of an installed base and the various forms of lock-in. In fact, many successful start-ups have been founded by employees leaving established firms after they can't prevail with new product ideas.

EXAMPLE: *Tandem Computer established the market for on-line transaction processing servers with high availability (see Chapter 9). The founders came from Hewlett-Packard, where they had tried and failed to convince management to pursue this product opportunity.*

Open Systems and Lock-in

Lock-in drives open systems standards. In the centralized computing era, computer systems were closed and proprietary, with equipment, software, and even applications from a single supplier. The result was consumer lock-in, to the advantage of suppliers and mostly to the disadvantage of customers. This vertically integrated approach serves mature industries (such as automobiles and appliances) relatively well, but it was too inflexible for the rapidly evolving computer and telecommunications industries because consumer and supplier lock-in ran counter to rapid technological change.

The open systems response places interfaces that separate the concerns on the two sides of the interface, allowing suppliers to upgrade products more independently. (Of course, they should do compatibility testing to verify interoperability.) Similarly, open interfaces allow customers to mix and match products from different suppliers. This increases competition—presumably improving the combination of quality, features, and price—and reduces switching costs. On the other hand, the customer becomes the system integrator, which is sometimes troublesome, particularly with immature technologies.

Open standards, however, represent a form of lock-in for the *whole industry*. As technology advances, switching costs may be daunting for everyone if it seems advantageous (in terms of capability or features) to abandon one open standard in favor of another. One response is to define an evolutionary standards process that incorporates a process of "continuous backward-compatible improvement." These types of open standards activities are increasingly common in the industry and represent a collective, ongoing design process.

EXAMPLE: *The evolution of internet standards illustrates the role of "continuous improvement." IETF has recently standardized a new version of its basic design, the Internet Protocol (IP), which will be described in Chapter 12 and Chapter 18. This new version (called IPng or IP.v6) includes many enhancements, but conversion of the entire network at one instant would not be feasible either technically or financially. Thus, the new standard had to be backward compatible and had to coexist with the old standard for some time. Such constraints may result in design compromises and added costs or lower performance.*

8.1.3 *Path-Dependent Effects

The cumulative effects of the described obstacles to change—particularly lock-in and network effects—is that the industry as a whole has considerable memory. Many standards have a lifetime greater than expected, in light of rapid technological change. Many of these legacy standards appear, in retrospect, almost accidental and old-fashioned.

E X A M P L E :   *The IBM PC platform, which became a de facto industry standard, illustrates industry lock-in. Consumers experience lock-in to this platform through their investments in software applications, add-on boards, and myriad other accessories. Intel and Microsoft experience lock-in through their accumulated investments in the microprocessor and operating system development. Indirect network effects cause the platform to have greater value to consumers because of the large number of complementary products on the market (applications, add-on cards, experienced technicians, training courses and books, etc.). Even superior competing approaches have difficulty establishing themselves because they have to overcome all these advantages. Making improvements to the platform is difficult because of the coordination of complementary products. Recognizing the latter, both Intel and Microsoft have invested in platform improvements, even in technological areas where they do not benefit directly.*

At any time, the marketplace does not necessarily allow the best or lowest-cost solution to dominate. Many seemingly minor or innocuous decisions by IBM in the original PC design remain today, even if better approaches would be available. This tendency of seemingly inconsequential decisions as a part of a standard (even de facto standard) to be irreversible and impact the marketplace much later is one example of *path dependency*—the ultimate consequence of obstacles to change. Path dependency is a market failure that can prevent the best or most cost-effective solutions from achieving success.

Discussion

D8.1 Are there industries other than networked computing in which network effects are a big factor? If so, what are some examples? Is there anything about networked computing that particularly distinguishes it?

D8.2 Repeat D8.1 for lock-in.

D8.3 Are there obstacles to change other than network effects and lock-in?

D8.4 Discuss the strategies a supplier might use to establish a new de facto standard in a product area with strong network effects.

D8.5 Discuss the strategies a supplier might use to overcome customer resistance due to lock-in.

Microsoft vs. Everybody Else

The greatest battle in the software industry is between Microsoft, which gains increasing dominance of several product categories, and the other suppliers. It illustrates well the forces of network effects and lock-in.

One of Microsoft's primary allies is network effects. Obviously Windows and Office maintain a strong position due to network effects, but the remaining competitive battle is for the corporate "back office." Microsoft is attempting to establish its NT operating system in competition with UNIX by exploiting the fragmentation of UNIX and resulting adverse network effects. The success of Microsoft's back-office server products will clearly depend on the success of NT, just as the Office application was established in part because of Windows. On the other hand, Microsoft concluded it couldn't overcome the momentum of the Internet and thus fully embraced Internet standards rather than going its own way.

The rest of the industry is using open standards as a way to battle Microsoft, pointing out to corporate customers the dangers of lock-in to Microsoft. In the interest of open standards, they are doing some extraordinary teaming, such as OMG's CORBA and Sun's Java. If it were not for competition from Microsoft, it is not clear the rest of the industry would find teaming nearly so attractive.

8.2 Challenges for Suppliers

In networked computing, there are a variety of goods and services, such as infrastructure software and equipment, application software, system integration, custom application development, information content indexing and searching, and communications (see Chapter 7). Suppliers of these goods and services face many challenges and risks that are different from those of other industries. In particular, information and software as economic goods have some special technical and economic properties. Understanding these is helpful to being a successful supplier or informed customer.

8.2.1 *Technical Properties of Information

Information can be captured in *discrete*, or *digital*, form, meaning it is represented by a set of symbols from a discrete alphabet. In computing, that alphabet is bits, and all information is represented by a collection of bits (see "Data and Information in Layers"on page 176). A basic property of information represented digitally is that exact replicas—equivalent to the original representation in every respect—can be created, simply by making a copy of the data. In contrast to the manufacture of physical goods, this replication is very cheap.

The following example illustrates that there are different representations of information with dramatically different characteristics, particularly when viewed over a long period of time.

EXAMPLE: *The paper in books physically deteriorates over time. To preserve a book, one approach is to make copies (say, on a photocopying machine). These copies also deteriorate, so more copies can be made from the original—which has deteriorated further in the meantime. Or more copies can be made from the copies, but since each copy is only a good approximation, the quality deteriorates further. Inevitably, the quality will become unacceptable, despite our best efforts. An alternative is to create replicas of the book, say, by a group of monks transcribing the words from the book onto new paper. Each replica faithfully preserves the original words, assuming the monks don't make any mistakes. The replica is a perfect rendition of the original author's thoughts and words without the same physical form.*

The paintings in an art museum also physically deteriorate over time. Contemporary artists can "touch up" these paintings or create a copy as they may have appeared originally. However, unlike the works of literature, there is no way to recover a perfect rendition of the original. We will never know precisely what the original painting looked like.

The distinction of this example is in copying, the work in its physical form is reproduced, with any physical flaws reproduced as well; in replication of data, the data is copied to a new physical rendition, but without affecting its ability to represent information. (While this distinction is important, the terminology used here is not standard.)

E X A M P L E : *If a musical performance represented digitally is copied from a CD-ROM to the memory of a computer, a replica has been produced. The physical form is very different (semiconductor memory versus optical pits on the disk), but the information represented (music) is identical.*

Many very old original literary works have been preserved (in content, not in form) by repeated replication. A copy of a book by Chaucer (the first author available in English literature) available in today's library is faithful to the original, not in form but in content (assuming those monks did their job carefully). In contrast, as paintings can only be copied, they have deteriorated in content, or else changed in form (such as a rendition or photograph).

What is the difference between a work of literature and a painting? The literature is represented by language, which in its textual written form is discrete. This means it is composed of a string of characters (in Western languages) or icons (in Chinese, for example) having a finite set of possibilities (twenty-six plus punctuation in the case of the characters of the English language). The monk has a good chance of recovering the original characters and words, even from a manuscript that has physically deteriorated, because there is a small and finite set of alternatives to choose from for each character. Furthermore, there is *redundancy*, meaning that only certain sequences of characters form feasible words. Thus, an individual character in a word can be lost, but the original word may still be recoverable. On the other hand, the painting is represented in its medium as a continuum, with infinite possibilities. Thus, after minor deterioration of the painting, there can be no hope of recovering the original.

A N A L O G Y : *The date on a calendar is discrete, but the time of day is a continuum. It is not possible to build a clock that tells the time exactly, as there is always some measurement error. On the other hand, the measurement error would have to be very large to get the date wrong because there are only 365 possibilities (in most years). Thus, a clock can tell us the date with complete accuracy, but time as only an approximation.*

A continuous physical representation of information (like a painting) is called *analog*. Any discrete or digital representation can be represented precisely in terms of bits by associating a string of bits with each discrete symbol (in the

Digital Information as One Basis of Life

The digital representation of genetic information and replication is fundamental to the propagation of life. As animal species reproduce, they carry genetic information digitally, in the form of the genome. The genome consists of a string of symbols (called base pairs), each of which assumes one of four values (four amino acids). From one generation to the next, the vast majority of these base pairs are faithfully replicated (after suitable combining of mother and father, with occasional errors or mutations). The only reason this is possible across hundreds and thousands of generations is because of regeneration (and replication in the case of multiple offspring); otherwise impairments would rapidly accumulate through the generations. Even in modern living animals, much of the original genetic information from the origins of a species (and even predecessor species) is faithfully represented in the genome.

Regeneration of Data

When a replica of data is created by estimating the discrete symbols in the original, the result is called a new *generation* of the data, and the process is called *regeneration*. Regeneration is easily expanded to create multiple exact replicas of the data, by simply performing regeneration repeatedly—this is replication. Replication is an important advantage of digital or binary representations of information, because it allows an unlimited number of people to possess the same information in its precise, original form. A replica is different from a copy, which retains any flaws in the physical representation and may introduce new flaws as well.

Regeneration has two other important advantages. Information can be preserved precisely over time by occasionally regenerating it. This works even if there is deterioration of the physical medium storing it. Information can also be preserved precisely when communicated over distance by occasional regeneration, even when there are physical mechanisms causing its deterioration.

EXAMPLE: *A long-distance telephone call used to be distinguished from a local telephone call by the "hissing" that accompanied the voice. That was due to the deterioration of quality as an analog representation of the voice was copied (by amplifiers) repeatedly to carry it long distances. The modern telephone system represents voice digitally and regenerates it repeatedly to carry*

manner described in "Any Information Can Be Represented by Bits" on page 109). An analog representation can be *approximated* by a digital representation (see Chapter 12).

EXAMPLE: *In its physical form, sound is represented as a pressure wave in a physical medium such as air or water, which evolves continuously in time and has a continuously changing pressure. Sound can be stored on magnetic tape or a vinyl record by capturing the evolution of pressure (with a microphone) as an electrical analog and then recording this electrical signal. Similarly, a scene captured by your eyes can be represented on film (by a camera). In both these cases, the representation is analog, like the original sound or image. Any of these representations can be approximated by a digital representation, with sufficient accuracy that people won't notice that they are viewing or listening to an approximation.*

While analog representations have been widely used and are quite natural, they inevitably and irreversibly deteriorate over time. If a digital representation is created as an approximation, then its deterioration over time can be prevented by occasional replication (see the sidebar "Regeneration of Data"). However, this doesn't suffice to preserve the information unless the structure and interpretation of the data is also preserved.

8.2.2   Economic Properties of Information

Because it can be freely replicated, digital information as a good has some unusual economic properties. There are three distinct phases in the supply of content:

- *Creation:* Content has to be created or updated. This may require *authoring* (as in the case of a document, encyclopedia, music score, or movie script), *producing* (as in a movie or music performance), or *collection* (as in the case of content that reports on some external phenomenon, such as the stock market). The creation of some content combines authoring, producing, and collection (such as news reporting).
- *Replication:* Once it has been created, one replica of the content is generated for each customer.
- *Distribution:* Content replicas have to reach the consumers. In networked computing, replicas can be inexpensively distributed over the network or by physical transport of magnetic or optical storage media (as in a CD-ROM).

ANALOGY: *Creation is analogous to design, and replication is analogous to manufacturing in the world of physical goods, such as automobiles or watches. Distribution is common to all goods.*

Table 8.2 Economic comparison of information and physical goods [Var95]

Property	Information content	Physical goods
Replication or manufacturing cost	Replication and distribution cost is small in comparison to creation cost.	Manufacturing and distribution costs are significant, even for relatively small production volumes.
Economies of scale	Unit costs decrease rapidly with sales volume, because the major costs are one-time creation.	Economies of scale are limited by a significant manufacturing cost component.
Cost recovery	Creation costs are sunk; that is, they cannot be recovered if there are no sales.	Some start-up costs (such as manufacturing capital equipment and real estate) can be recovered if there are no sales.
Value judgement	Content is an experience good, meaning the consumer must see it to judge its value.	A consumer can often judge the value without seeing the good (for example, if it is consumable, such as motor oil).

it long distances. For that reason, there is no noticeable deterioration in quality with distance.

The ability to regenerate data is arguably the most important advantage of digital representations. A caution, however: Regeneration applies only to data, but to be useful the structure and interpretation must be preserved over time and distance as well.

Although these steps parallel those for physical goods, there are some significant differences, as listed in Table 8.2. Supply economies of scale give substantial advantages to a high-volume supplier, which has significantly lower unit costs. While this is true in most manufacturing industries, it is more extreme for information content. The observation that creation costs are *sunk* (they cannot be recovered if there are no sales) and content is an *experience good* (it must be seen before it can be judged) together make content creation quite risky. This can be overcome to some extent by building the reputation of the supplier (it turned out excellent content in the past) or through recommendation (see "Third-Party or Collective Recommendations" on page 43).

Economic characteristics differ significantly for the suppliers of static and volatile content. Suppliers of static content deal with risk by diversification: They invest in a portfolio of content creations and recover most of their costs from their winners, leveraging the strong supply economies of scale that create high profits for these winners. Suppliers of volatile content often avoid risk by selling information by subscription; that is, a consumer receives a continuous stream of updates for a fixed price. The investment in updating volatile content can be based on an accurate estimate of subscription revenues, and as a result, volatile content is a relatively low-risk business not as dependent on diversification.

EXAMPLE: *No book publisher would specialize in only books about mutual funds. On the other hand, Morningstar Mutual Funds successfully specializes in providing volatile information about mutual funds by subscription.*

Forms of Recommendation

The use of recommendations in filtering out useful information has many rich possibilities in cyberspace. The recommender system, which accumulates and summarizes the collective recommendation of many users (either explicitly or through observing their behavior) is the most sophisticated form, but there are many simpler possibilities.

EXAMPLE: Viral marketing *is an approach that makes it easy for users to make recommendations to their friends. A user visiting a Web site is invited to supply the names and email addresses of acquaintances who may be interested in that site's content. An email message is then automatically pushed to those acquaintances, inviting them to visit that site on the user's recommendation. The email message includes a hyperlink, making it easy to do so. The name refers to the "infection" of users by others.*

Of course, forms of recommendation from the physical world, such as reviews or the branding of information (by a respected publisher), can be easily repeated in cyberspace.

An intermediate case is the provider of information searching and indexing services. The indexing is part of the content creation costs, and searching is a cost of providing service. While typically more costly than content replication, automated searching is still inexpensive (at least compared to the manufacture of physical goods). This business thus enjoys substantial supply economies of scale, and at high volume, the largest component of unit cost is often searching. Thus, these providers are emphasizing services.

8.2.3   Software as a Special Case

Software is a particular form of information that informs and controls the behavior of a computer (rather than a person). From a supplier perspective, it is similar to information content. As will be seen later, it is distinctive on the demand side.

From a supplier cost perspective, software is similar to information content, typically falling between the static and volatile extremes. The representation of software—like information—is data (in the case of software representing low-level processor instructions). Thus, replication is inexpensive, creation costs are significant, and there are strong supply economies of scale.

During development, software products have supply-side characteristics similar to static content: They are an experience good, and the costs of development (analogous to content creation) are sunk. Thus, software product development is risky, and suppliers respond by diversifying. On the other hand, the custom development of software—sold only once—benefits from no economies of scale. The high creation cost must be offset by the consumer's control over the features. Since consumers' needs are rarely unique, it is common to gain greater supply economies of scale by making an application configurable for each consumer's needs. The creation costs for software can also be reduced by utilizing reusable components and frameworks (see Chapter 10).

Creating custom or customized applications is relatively low risk, since development is undertaken on contract, with specified milestones, deliverables, and payment schedule. On the other hand, the supplier's profits are capped by the poor supply economies of scale. As a result, professional-services organizations typically retain some ownership of custom applications, so that all or part can be sold to others. Over time, they may develop a portfolio of customized products, resulting in a hybrid product-services model (like the ERP applications).

Software maintenance and upgrade costs are significant—whether the application is custom or a product. Charges for upgraded releases of the software—resembling the creation of volatile content—often represent a major source of supplier revenue, whether upgrades are sold by subscription or by new release.

Unlike volatile content, there may be no subscription, but the supplier usually receives a steady stream of revenue from upgrades to offset the maintenance costs. Customer lock-in may create an implicit subscription.

8.2.4   Equipment

From the supply perspective, the equipment involved in networked computing shares common characteristics with other durable goods. Unit manufacturing costs are a substantial portion of the total cost, and supply economies of scale are thus more modest. Development and manufacturing costs are substantially reduced with reusable components. The semiconductor component suppliers operate under special rules (see the sidebar "Semiconductor Manufacturers: Moore's Law").

Infrastructure software bundled with hardware—which typically provides a considerable portion of the functionality—has the economic characteristics of software products. Until recently, equipment suppliers tended to think of their bundled software as a cost of business rather than a profit opportunity in its own right. This is changing as companies realize that software is a significant valued added.

8.2.5   *Protecting Investments with Intellectual Property

As emphasized above, content and software both have a large cost of creation and low cost of replication. This is a double-edged sword. On the bright side, this leads to strong supply economies of scale and hence large rewards for successful products. On the dark side, it creates an opportunity for *piracy*—the large-scale unauthorized replication of information or software for sale through licit and illicit channels. Piracy creates a competitor who unfairly avoids the cost of creation—the major cost. Piracy reduces the economic incentives for the creation of content or software, and it is thus in the best interests of society to discourage it. Piracy is discouraged by granting *property rights* to the creator, and this is a normal and necessary function of government. Since content and software don't have a physical manifestation, they are called *intellectual property*. The laws governing intellectual property (copyrights and patents) are discussed later in this chapter.

8.2.6   Selling Content and Software

Content and software suppliers face special pricing challenges that affect industry outcomes (see [Sha98] for a discussion of pricing strategies). First, consider

Semiconductor Manufacturers: Moore's Law

While the chapter emphasizes the suppliers of information and software, a critical underpinning for the networked computing industry is semiconductor technology. This technology has followed a remarkable progression predicted by Intel's Gordon Moore. He said that the capability of integrated circuits with the "same area" (which translates to roughly the same cost) would increase geometrically with time, doubling every eighteen months. This is exactly like compound interest, with an annual interest rate of 58 percent. At this rate, $10,000 in savings would grow to $10 billion in three decades.

What is the driving force for Moore's law? It isn't technology or physical laws, since physical limits haven't been reached. Rather, it is related to the business model of semiconductor firms and their limited (but substantial) ability to make investments in research and development and new factories. Incremental advances have to be made (a factor of four in capability for each generation of technology is typical) so that existing product revenues can support the development of the more advanced technology, with the returns on investment accruing in a reasonable period of time (a delay of several years is typical). Thus, the rate of technological advance is limited by the rate at which current revenues justify new investments and the limited time horizon required of that payoff.

If unlimited resources were available, could technology advance faster than Moore's law? Probably, at least in the long term, although it would still take time for the inventions and refinements to occur.

Standardization and Competition

While there are powerful forces behind standards, including taking advantage of network effects and reducing customer lock-in, standardized products become commodities, not differentiated from competitors' implementation of the same standard. Fortunately, there are ways around this. Standard interfaces don't necessarily limit functionality, especially if they are designed for extensibility. An infrastructure with standard interfaces does not limit application functionality. In the infrastructure, vendors can strive for better quality and performance metrics (see Chapter 17) and can also try to incorporate more functionality into their products. Winner-take-all effects reduce competition, even for standardized products.

EXAMPLE: *Microsoft Windows illustrates these strategies. Microsoft has continually improved performance metrics and incorporated more functionality, such as the graphical user interface and Web browser, to provide greater value. Even as you would expect the operating system to become a commodity, it has succeeded in becoming dominant through winner-take-all effects.*

the nature of competitive markets. An idealized economic model is "perfect competition," in which there are many suppliers of a comparable product and no single supplier has control over the price. In such an idealized market, the price theoretically approaches the supplier's marginal cost (including incremental cost of production and a normal return on invested capital). Suppliers attempt to gain an edge by driving their costs lower than that of competitors.

EXAMPLE: *Perfect competition is a good model in agriculture, in which a large number of producers can't easily distinguish their products and the price is dictated by the market.*

Strong supply economies of scale preclude such perfect competition in content and software. The incremental replication cost is practically zero, so that a supplier of a substitutable product that sells a higher volume is able to undercut a competitor's price, gain market share as a result, and eventually become dominant. As necessary, a dominant supplier can undercut the price of any new entrant that has lower sales volume. Once one supplier achieves dominance, the basic assumptions of "perfect competition" are not valid.

EXAMPLE: *A few widely used and mature applications have a "standard" feature set (word processors, for example), making product differentiation difficult. Rather than perfect competition, a dominant product emerges and is difficult to displace because of its supply economies of scale. While it is relatively easy to develop a competing product, the dominant supplier has much lower unit costs. Lock-in and network effects also contribute to these winner-take-all effects.*

All suppliers want to differentiate their products—to limit competition and improve profits—but it is essential for content and software suppliers [Sha98]. Each must strive for sufficiently distinct features and performance to attract its own loyal customers. These considerations run directly counter to standardization (see the sidebar "Standardization and Competition").

Rejecting perfect competition, consider the opposite extreme of a dominant supplier. How should it price its product? Can it charge anything it pleases? Certainly not, as there are at least two pricing constraints. First, it must keep the price low enough to discourage the entry of competitive suppliers of a substitutable product. (In practice, it has to worry about products that are similar, if not exact substitutes.) This is called *limit pricing*. Second, it can't charge more than consumers are willing to pay, which depends on the value the consumer places on the product.

With limited competition, a profit-maximizing supplier charges as much as it can. It doesn't base the price on creation costs nor replication or distribution costs, but rather the consumer's willingness to pay. Called *value pricing* [Var95], this allocates the costs of creating new content or software among consumers based on the value they derive, which makes social and economic sense. However, it does imply price discrimination, which raises many practical issues.

Value of Content

An important consideration in pricing information content is the value attached to it by consumers [Tag95]. Because information is an experience good, the supplier's reputation is important, since that is often the basis of choice. Where content is authored (as in works of literature), the consumer may attach more weight to the author than to the publisher. As a result, content suppliers choose authors carefully to protect their reputation. Consumers may also depend on the recommendations of others.

For volatile content sold by subscription, the consumer is willing to enter a longer-term purchase agreement. Timeliness frequently affects value, and networked computing is an ideal medium, commanding higher prices than the same content distributed by slower means.

The value of content is reduced when there is too much of it, making it difficult for the consumer to find useful information. Content customized to the consumer's needs thus offers high value [Sha98] and is another strength of networked computing because it can make a dynamic and user-specific presentation of content. Distribution over the network makes customization relatively easy if the customer's interests are known or can be learned. Customers can be queried, or their choices captured and analyzed. Information providers providing searching capability are customizing. Similarly, a key to selling content is gaining the attention of the consumer in an increasingly information-rich environment.

It is often possible to get third parties to pay for content through advertising support, and this is an increasingly popular revenue model on the Web. In spite of the fact that an advertiser derives little value from each consumer—after all, relatively few respond to the advertisement—the low replication costs make this a viable means of support. Advertising targeted to consumers most likely to respond offers greater value to the advertiser and is possible by observing the information accessed by the consumer to target advertising in this way. Thus, customized content can serve as the basis of customized advertising, increasing the advertiser's willingness to pay.

Characteristics such as timeliness, customization, and low distribution cost suggest that the networked distribution of information offers greater consumer value than print media. While not yet established in the marketplace, this means of distribution may become dominant in the future.

Value of Software

While it is similar on the supply side, software differs considerably from information content in the value proposition to the consumer. A software application provides the user assistance in some task, including communication or collaboration with other users. From the user perspective, application software performs a service, replacing administrative assistance, travel, or alternative services.

EXAMPLE: *A word processor with voice dictation assists the user in creating a written document, providing functionality similar to a secretary taking dictation and transcribing the result. It is important for what it* does; *that is, its behavior. Similarly, a collaborative application replaces travel, another service.*

From an economic perspective, software is very much a hybrid between goods and services: The supplier cost structure is similar to information goods, while the value to the consumer is characteristic of services. In establishing the value to the customer—and hence the pricing—the factors listed in Table 8.3 should be considered. Information service providers that provide indexing and searching should take into account similar factors.

Some factors in Table 8.3—such as functionality, usability, and quality—are intrinsic to the application itself, while others can only be evaluated in the customer's context. To take full advantage of the latter, the supplier must *price discriminate*, charging different consumers different prices. In this respect, software products are quite distinct from custom-developed applications, for which there is a single customer and price is determined by negotiation. Price discrimination is more difficult for products, but can be achieved by versioning and other means.

Usage is an interesting value factor to implement. It can be measured by metrics such as the number of transactions handled, the number of users, the number of customers served, etc., but this requires monitoring within the application and billing (with supplier access to a customer's hosts). The ubiquity of the global Internet makes usage-based billing technically feasible. In business applications, usage pricing has traditionally depended on cruder metrics such as the maximum number of hosts running the application (which ignores the utilization of

Table 8.3 Factors affecting the value of a software application to the customer

Factor	Description	Examples
Usage	How much the application is utilized.	Hours per day, number of simultaneous users, number of occasional users.
Functionality	Capabilities provided that users might otherwise have to do for themselves.	Voice rather than keyboard input for a word processor, user customization of menus.
Quality and performance	Attributes that make the application better than other applications with similar functionality.	Time to perform a calculation, graphics with higher visual impact, consumes less disk space.
Usability	Ease of use and learning.	Speed of accomplishing task, lower training time or cost.
Impact	Tangible benefits of the application to the customer's organization or environment.	Cost reduction, increasing competitiveness, higher productivity, greater market share for the customer's product or service.

those hosts) or the maximum number of users accessing the application (called a floating license).

Infrastructure software offers a value proposition more like traditional goods. The value of infrastructure software can't be easily separated from infrastructure equipment. They are frequently bundled and sold together. It is increasingly common for end-user organizations to outsource the design to a professional-services organization and, often, the operation of the infrastructure to a service provider (see Chapter 9). In this case, the consumer of infrastructure products is a service provider rather than an end-user organization.

*Price Discrimination and Versioning

A challenge in value pricing is that willingness to pay often varies widely among consumers, so it is difficult to establish a single fixed price without significantly reducing revenues. If the price is set high, each sale derives high revenue, but sales will be restricted to the small number of consumers with high willingness to pay. If the price is set low, unit sales will be larger, but each sale derives low revenue. Profit-maximizing behavior usually results in a relatively high price, which is undesirable from a social perspective, since relatively few consumers benefit. This is particularly unfortunate for software and information goods, given their low cost of replication.

The social benefit of many sales can be balanced against the supplier interest in large revenues if the supplier practices price discrimination—charging different prices based on the consumer's willingness to pay.

Quality and Features of Shrink-Wrapped Applications

Some users complain that software products have poor quality and excessive features, making them hard to use. If true, this is likely due in part to the industry tradition of fixed pricing. Keeping development groups employed requires steady revenue, which requires a steady stream of new products, an expanding customer base, or new releases sold to existing customers. There is thus pressure to frequently produce new releases with added features and a disincentive to improve quality if it lengthens the release cycle.

If software pricing were usage based, there would be greater incentive for high quality. Revenues would depend less on new features and releases and more on retaining users and getting them to use the application more. It would also better align pricing with value, benefiting suppliers. With the ubiquitous Internet, it is technically feasible to include usage monitoring and billing in software applications, but there might be customer resistance. Do you think it might become more common?

Auctions and Price Discrimination

The buyer auction is the ultimate form of price discrimination, because each customer pays a different price. Further, that price is determined by the second highest willingness to pay among all those bidding, as the winning bidder has to pay at least this amount. By making the consumer surplus small, the auction method of determining price is quite favorable to the seller. By avoiding the need to get bidders together physically, networked computing makes it relatively easy to gather a large number of bidders, which is also favorable to the seller.

E X A M P L E : If there are two users, and user A is willing to pay $150 while user B will pay only $50 for the same information or software, the supplier can charge $150 and sell only to user A (with a revenue of $150), or it can charge $50 and sell to both users (with a revenue of $100). Obviously, the producer will choose the former, and user B is deprived. With price discrimination—charging both users what they are willing to pay—the supplier gains more revenue ($200 rather than $150) with very little cost penalty for cheaply replicated information or software.

The revenue foregone from high-willingness-to-pay users with fixed pricing is the *consumer surplus*—the difference between what a consumer would be willing to pay and the price [Var87]—which is *potential* revenue from that consumer that is forever lost to the supplier. Price discrimination strategies are therefore directed at trying to reduce the consumer surplus. How can this be pulled off? One approach is usage-based charges, as discussed previously. Another is to estimate the willingness to pay by observing consumer behavior.

E X A M P L E : The airline cost structure is similar to that of information goods. The airplane, its fuel, and the crew all represent fixed costs independent of the number of passengers on the plane. The marginal cost of another passenger is thus very low, as long as the plane isn't full. Airlines observe customers' behavior, such as whether they are flying during the week or staying over the weekend, or how far in advance they are making the reservation, and they price-discriminate accordingly. Many passengers flying during the week are business travelers with higher willingness to pay than vacationers, who are willing to stay over a weekend.

Information goods sold over the network are ideal for this sort of price discrimination, because the supplier often can discern characteristics about the consumer that are correlated with willingness to pay. This is particularly true if the supplier can maintain a longer-term relationship with each consumer and observe and capture his or her behavior. For example, attributes such as zip code, what type of credit card is used, past buying patterns, etc., all correlate with willingness to pay. Price discrimination can also be keyed to where a consumer shops or works, for example, offering schools or students or senior citizens a discount. Consumers probably don't relish price discrimination, but it does benefit consumers with lower willingness to pay.

Price quotes over a network (or by telephone) are also ideal for price discrimination from the perspective that each consumer doesn't see prices quoted to other consumers. But if it is necessary to publish prices for all to see—as with shrink-wrapped software in a store—then the price has to be more uniform.

Even in the case of published prices seen by all, price discrimination can still be practiced by product *versioning*. In this time-honored strategy, a portfolio of similar products is offered, with individual versions differentiated by quality or features or performance and price [Var97a]. Consumers are induced by the careful choice of prices to self-select, so consumers choose a version according to their willingness to pay. It has the significant advantage that the consumer voluntarily chooses the version and price, avoiding possible consumer annoyance with other price discrimination strategies.

E X A M P L E :   *Airlines use versioning, offering different classes of service (coach, business, first) at different prices. Their pricing tries to induce travelers with a high willingness to pay to choose a higher class, while keeping the grade of service in the cheaper classes low enough not to tempt them. First-class flyers don't complain about the high price, because they voluntarily chose that version.*

Software is particularly easy to version. A full-featured and high-performance version—sold at a high price—can be modified to have fewer features and lower performance by selectively removing features or adding wait states. Contrary to the airline example, lower-priced versions of software or content actually incur *added* costs to the supplier, even though they carry a lower price [Var97a]. Versions of information services are easily created by varying parameters such as resolution, timeliness (adding delay), or customization.

E X A M P L E :   *Adobe sells a less-capable version of Photoshop—its image processing application—to makers of digital cameras, who bundle it with their camera. IBM's and Dragon Systems' voice dictation applications come in versions distinguished by vocabulary size or specialization.*

U.S. stock quotes are available for free on the Web with a twenty-minute delay, but they are also sold by brokers with less delay. The Central Intelligence Agency consumes voluminous U.S. taxpayer dollars to scan and digest voluminous public information from around the world and condense it into targeted reports, suggesting that their customization provides high value to the government and taxpayer.

The key to making versioning work to the advantage of the supplier is the choice of prices. The trick is to keep the consumer with high willingness to pay from choosing the lower-value versions, which requires a high-value price lower than might otherwise be the case.

Versioning may also become common in selling network services, such as Internet access. As discussed in Chapter 18, network services with different performance and quality characteristics (and associated pricing) will become available.

Network services also have "high fixed cost, low variable cost" and require sophisticated pricing strategies to achieve profitability in a competitive market.

Discussion

D8.6 Recall some information or software goods and services you have purchased lately, and think about the seller's pricing strategy. How do they relate to the strategies discussed here?

D8.7 Discuss consumers' acceptance or resistance to pricing strategies based on usage and impact—the two factors that may vary significantly across customers.

D8.8 Repeat D8.7 for price discrimination based on observation of customer behavior or estimates of customer willingness to pay. Do you think different prices for different customers is fair?

8.3   Government Roles

Thus far, the industry and its challenges have been emphasized. Governments also play a number of roles affecting networked computing, particularly since it is having an increasing impact on society. The evolution of the industry thus depends on government policies, laws, and regulation, and that influence is growing. While the general issues are universal, details differ across nations, and this section emphasizes the United States.

8.3.1   Protecting Intellectual Property

In "Protecting Investments with Intellectual Property" on page 247, the importance of intellectual property to suppliers of networked computing was emphasized. The granting and protection of property rights is a government role. Governments grant limited-term exclusive property rights to inventors and creators to control exploitations of their works. Although creative work doesn't depend on such rights, the incentives to make such investments would be greatly reduced without them, given the high cost of creation and low cost of appropriation.

The primary forms of protected intellectual property are technological innovations (protected by patents) and the original works of authorship (protected by copyright). Mere expenditures of time, money, and energy don't insure protection by patent or copyright law. A copyrighted work must be original (have a modicum of creativity), and a patented invention must be novel, useful, and nonobvious to someone skilled in the art. Furthermore, the inventor must apply for a patent and persuade a patent examiner that the specific claims defining the scope of the invention are sound.

Although not discussed further, there are also *trademarks* and *trade secrets*. The trademark—by granting exclusive use of a name—gives a supplier the incentive to make the necessary investment so its reputation developed over time is for high quality and good value. The trade secret protects from theft and appropriation a proprietary formula, method, or device that gives a company an advantage over competitors.

Copyrights

The copyright encourages the creation or authorship of original works of information content or software by granting to the author exclusive control—including the right to sell or license—over its replication. The intent of copyright law is to prevent others from appropriating, replicating, or displaying a work without the permission of the copyright holder. However, there are significant limitations on these rights. One is a *fair use* defense against charges of infringement, which may include actions such as making a copy for students in a class. A copyright does not prevent others from *independently* creating or authoring similar works, even based on the same facts or ideas. However, an author does maintain control over a *derivative* work—one based on or derived from another work (for example, a movie based on a novel). A copyright is in force for a long time—typically fifty years beyond the author's lifetime.

The copyright law encourages not only the creation or authorship of works—by giving them protections that enhance their commercial value—but also their orderly dissemination and use under the control of the copyright holder.

In the United States, an original work is eligible for copyright protection when reduced to tangible form—such as storing to a computer disk or printing on paper—which is called *fixation*. It is not necessary to attach a copyright notice (although a notice increases the legal rights, particularly in other countries, and is thus advisable). The digital representation of information and its dissemination over computer networks have raised sensitive new issues in copyright law. Some say major revisions of copyright law are needed, while others contend that current laws—interpreted in the new context—are adequate.

EXAMPLE: *In the United States, a National Information Infrastructure Task Force's Working Group on Intellectual Property Rights addressed this issue [Oke96]. Their conclusions, while comforting to those deriving income from works published on the Internet, have raised consternation from a broad cross-section of interested groups, who fear that every substantial work on the Internet will carry license fees. For example, the group recommended that a con-*

Intellectual Property as a Strategic Tool

Complex strategies revolve around intellectual property (IP) as a competitive tool. Patent rights allow the holder to decide whether to allow others to use an invention or not, and under what terms. Companies not allowed to use an invention may be able to circumvent it by using different techniques, but that may increase their design costs or slow them down. If they do license it, they may be disadvantaged by license fees, but may also invent improvements and patent those. A copyright is circumvented by independently achieving similar functionality, but it does force a competitor to incur similar creation costs and slow its market entry.

EXAMPLE: *The first spreadsheet program was Visicalc. Since it was an immediate success, the functionality was soon copied by competitive programs, such as Lotus 1-2-3.*

The first IBM personal computer depended on the copyright of software included in read-only memory (called the "BIOS") to prevent competitors from creating clone products. The functionality of the BIOS was soon copied by Phoenix Technologies—and sold to competing suppliers—by carefully isolating the designers in a "clean room" environment without access to anything but the product specifications.

In both examples, firms relied on copyright, which other companies eventually circumvented. Patent rights are more fundamental, since they can prevent a competing product from exploiting the invention.

sumer purchasing a digital copyrighted work cannot sell that work to another— a right available to a magazine or book purchaser. The group also failed to clarify the meaning of fair use in digital media and cautioned against redefining fair use before the technology matures.

The uncertainty about copyright law is somewhat of a damper on the commercial networked distribution of information. However, a more serious and very legitimate concern is the difficulty in *enforcing* copyright laws in digital media (both networking and storage). Some content providers may have overreacted to this enforcement problem in ways that jeopardize consumer acceptance.

Copyrighting Software

Software can be copyrighted and usually is. The copyright enables the holder to exercise legal control over replicating the software, which the holder can exploit to license the software to the public. A *software license* lays out specific terms and conditions under which the software can be used or disseminated. There are some creative license provisions—for example, *freeware* (software given away but for which copyright is retained) and *shareware* (software for which payment is voluntary)—made economically feasible by free replication and inexpensive distribution. Another licensing option is *copyleft*, which restricts the ability to make derivative works unless they are distributed free of charge. However, not all license provisions are necessarily enforceable, as there are limitations imposed by the copyright laws.

A movement gaining some momentum is *open source software*. This is similar to freeware, except that it has much greater commercial ramifications, a viable business case and marketing plan behind it, and an established process for software development and modification involving many volunteer programmers. The idea is to create a software development process that makes use of this volunteer programming talent, peer review, and rapid evolution of source code, resulting in high quality and state-of-the-art features. The license for open source software must guarantee the right to read, redistribute, modify, and use the source code freely.

EXAMPLE: *The most successful open source effort to date is the Linux operating system. This variation on UNIX was created by one individual but is now upgraded through an established process. Red Hat software and others sell support for Linux, and there are those who believe it is a serious competitor for Microsoft's Windows. If it is to become a competitor, the key is the indirect network effect of application software availability.*

Netscape, following this example, has made its source code available for its client Web browser software under an open source licensing arrangement. The

*business case behind this is Netscape's sale of complementary server soft-
ware—it was never expecting to derive much revenue from its client anyway. Its
hope is that its client will evolve more quickly and maintain higher quality under
the open source license, and the enhanced success of the client will contribute
to the success of the server applications.*

Infringement occurs when users or organizations ignore or violate copyright
holdings. Egregious infringement—for example, setting up a large factory to
produce and sell large volumes of goods through licit and illicit channels—is
piracy. Piracy remains a major problem in spite of copyright laws. Individual software companies and the industry as a whole devote considerable effort to
uncovering infringement and piracy.

EXAMPLE: *The Software Publishers Association (SPA) is a trade association of
software publishers in North America and Europe that works to eliminate software copyright infringement through various means. It conducts an education
campaign to inform users and organizations about the copyright laws, their
provisions, and their importance, and maintains hotlines for reporting abuses. It
aggressively pursues suspected abuses through legal action. The SPA estimates that in 1996, 43 percent of the worldwide replicas of software applications were pirated.*

Over the years, software publishers have incorporated various technical mechanisms into the software representation in an attempt to defeat infringement and
piracy. These mechanisms are usually invasive and annoying to legitimate licensees, and are relatively easy to defeat for determined adversaries. Relatively
secure mechanisms for this purpose would require hardware support, and such
options are available, although it is not clear computer manufacturers will be
motivated to include them at extra cost.

Patents

A patent is a grant from the government of the right to make, use, or sell an
invention for a fixed period of time after filing (twenty years in most countries).
Exactly what is an invention? Informally, it is an idea that is both *novel* and practically *useful*. A patentable invention must have sufficient novelty over the "state
of the art" to justify the grant of a monopoly and must not be obvious to one
"skilled in the art." Like other forms of property, a patent can be used to
prevent others from using the invention or can be licensed for compensation
(called a *royalty*).

The patent encourages research and development by rewarding an inventor with
exclusive limited-term rights, allowing him or her to exploit the invention for
commercial gain or by deriving royalties. Less obvious is the public interest in

Some patents are fundamental and
can't be readily circumvented. Others are easy to circumvent but slow
down a competitor. In intermediate
cases, circumventing patents may
force competitors to increase the cost
or reduce the functionality of their
products.

Patents and Standardization

As discussed in "Standardization" on page 215, competing firms increasingly participate in consortia or standardization efforts to define interface standards. This mechanism allows multiple suppliers to participate in designing and marketing complementary interoperable products in a system context. Patents are a major issue in such efforts. Many different arrangements are possible. A common approach is for all parties to agree—as a condition for participation—to license patents freely on "reasonable and equitable" terms. "Reasonable" means roughly to charge royalties sufficient to recover research and development expenses but not exclude competitors, and "equitable" means that differences in royalties charged different companies must be justified.

In a small consortium, patent rights are a key element of the negotiations, including the negotiations on exactly what is included in the standard.

EXAMPLE: *The DVD standard was agreed upon by two groups of companies. Each group had collaboratively created its own standard but decided that a single standard was necessary. They each brought patent rights to the negotiating table, and royalty arrangements were an integral part of the negotiations on the technologies incorporated.*

seeing that inventions are publicly divulged—when the patent is issued or (in some countries) applied for—so that others can improve on them. Without patent protection, inventors might keep inventions secret, even as they are exploited in commercial products. The limited term of the patent gives the inventor a reasonable period of exclusivity while eventually removing exclusive property rights and putting the invention in the public domain for the benefit of all.

Viewed in economic and social terms, the patent system is a trade-off. The maximum benefit to society would accrue if inventions were *public goods*, meaning that they are owned by nobody (or, equivalently, owned by everybody). That way, inventions would be exploited by competitive suppliers, benefiting the public. The economic problem with public goods is *free riding*, where companies have little incentive to invest in research and development to create and develop inventions. Thus, the patent system gives the inventor ownership for a limited period of time (to motivate research and development expenditures) but moves the invention into the public domain after a period of exclusivity (to encourage widespread use).

It is common for patent licenses in the computing and communications industry to be exchanged (called *cross-licensing*) rather than sold. The strategy of many large companies is to file patents aggressively on many inventions to build up a portfolio to exchange with other companies. Each company is motivated to invest in research for both defensive and offensive reasons, and the inventions that result are often available to many companies for exploitation. Critics argue that this approach creates an unfair barrier to small companies excluded from the "web" of large-company cross-licensing agreements. On the other hand, many small companies and start-ups (and their venture capital funders) view patents as an important asset and are more likely to try and exploit them exclusively.

Software Patents

Patenting ideas embodied in software is controversial but has important ramifications for industry. Since software is an expression of an algorithm, it is subject to copyright law. Should it also be possible to protect the algorithms embodied in software by patents if they meet the "novel and useful" criteria? Traditionally, scientific principles and mathematical formulas were not eligible for patenting. Software was considered an expression of a mathematical formula and thus could not encompass patentable inventions. This led to a basic quandary: Much of the same functionality can be achieved in hardware or software, so why could hardware embody patentable inventions but not software? In the United States, courts have succumbed to the notion that software can embody patentable inventions. Officially, they are not called software patents, but rather "patents on methods or processes that can be embodied in computer programs," where the words "computer programs" could well be replaced by "digital hardware" without any essential distinction. There are significant practical difficulties with software patents (see the sidebar "Difficulties with Software Patents").

8.3.2   Government Policies and Laws

Technology has tremendous power to do good, but also has bad side effects. For example, automobiles transport people efficiently, but they also kill pedestrians. Society tries to accentuate the positive contributions while containing the negative, using public policies and laws as a tool. The important questions are what activities must be constrained by public policies and laws, how should those policies and laws be structured, and what technological and societal measures can be put in place to enforce them?

Networked computing has spawned some capabilities of concern to government policy makers. None of these is limited to networked computing, but the issues are rendered more immediate and serious by networked computing technologies and their expanding importance. Advocates of individual freedom and unfettered innovation would not restrict the use of technology. Some concerned by individual privacy and the protection of children would restrict the use of technology.

Privacy

Personal privacy is threatened in many ways by networked computing. Bringing ordinary transactions on-line creates a wealth of information about personal habits and preferences. Further, by making databases available on-line, information about individuals—previously available from public sources—becomes easier to access. In nomadic computing, the network has to know the movements of users, and that information could be tracked. These are viewed by some as abuses of privacy, and they would place legal restrictions.

In the United States, opposition to a national identity card has been based on privacy concerns. On the network, the equivalent is important to avoid fraud or mistaken identity across a network (see Chapter 13), since physical mechanisms for authentication (such as a person's face) are not available. Can a network "digital identity card" survive these forces of opposition?

Some strategies for providing greater value to consumers of information content—such as observing user behavior and tailoring content accordingly—also raise privacy concerns. For example, databases containing personal preferences and habits of individual citizens might be gathered and sold. However, there are big differences in approaches to these problems.

Difficulties with Software Patents

Software patents are quite controversial, in part because of some practical difficulties. How is it determined whether a "method or process embodied in a computer program" is novel? If the invention has been described or used before, it isn't. Thousands or even millions of programs have been written, and many techniques used are embodied in the code with no separate documentation or publication. Searching a database of past patents isn't effective, since software patents were only issued starting about 1981.

EXAMPLE: *In 1993, an infamous patent was issued in the United States to Compton's New Media, which described techniques for access to a multimedia database that had long been used in the industry. This raised a firestorm of protest, on the basis that the patented techniques were already widely used in the software industry, and the patent was quickly rescinded by the Patent Office.*

The software industry moves much more quickly than the patent system. The diffusion of basic knowledge is also extremely rapid, as programmers move from company to company fairly quickly. The industry (including both software companies and law firms) has formed the Software Patent Institute (SPI) to address these issues. The most interesting initiative of the SPI is to form a database of software technologies to assist the U.S. Patent Office in identifying the novelty (or lack thereof) in patent applications.

On the other hand, patents offer the same advantages to software as to other technologies. They reduce the motivation to maintain trade secrets, which are not revealed to be improved on by others. Most "inventions" in software arise in the course of development projects, where they are both used and disclosed quickly and can be quickly appropriated by others. Patents are important to the funding of start-ups (see "Venture Capital and Start-Ups" on page 212), so software patents are a stimulus to this proven method of bringing new ideas to market.

It has been argued that a new form of intellectual property protection for software is needed that provides less vigorous protection for software functionality than a patent [SDK94].

E X A M P L E : *The European Union has issued a directive that regulates what information can be collected on individuals and limits the uses of that information. The United States prefers to defer to industry self-regulation—with uncertain results thus far—except in the case of collection of information from children on-line. Differences in approach are problematic on the global Internet, leading to disputes among governments.*

Content Regulation

Should the government place restrictions on information content published in cyberspace? This issue arises in several contexts.

In the physical world, it is relatively simple to withhold certain products and services from children. For example, merchants can put questionable merchandise on a high shelf, or they can easily recognize an underage consumer and refuse a sale. These measures don't work on the network.

E X A M P L E : *In 1996 Congress passed the Communications Decency Act, which banned "indecent" material from the Internet for the protection of children. There were several problems with this act, including the vagueness of the word "indecent" and the questionable jurisdiction of the United States over the Internet citizenry of other countries. The law was struck down by the U.S. courts as violating the "freedom of speech" provisions of the Constitution. The courts ruled that the Internet would be subject to the broadest interpretation of "freedom of speech" also applied to newspapers and magazines, as opposed to more limited interpretations applied to radio and television broadcasts.*

This law—while not the solution—addressed a real problem. An alternative approach is for users or organizations to voluntarily add filtering software to their browsers.

E X A M P L E : *The World Wide Web Consortium has defined a Platform for Internet Content Selection (PICS) standard, in which a Web site can provide self-rating of content or there can be third-party rating [Res95b]. Concerned individuals or organizations can install software that block sites with selected ratings.*

There are civil liberty concerns that PICS might be applied in a draconian fashion by some organizations, thus restricting free speech without constitutional protections. For example, protecting children from "indecent" material is not controversial, but should it be acceptable for a politically conservative private university to block student access to liberal causes (or for a liberal school to block conservative views)?

Content regulation arises in other contexts. For example, governments have attempted to restrict the right of hate groups or political opposition groups to express their views. In all these cases, the global Internet undermines the ability of governments to regulate content except by placing access restrictions at national borders—an expensive and difficult proposition.

Law Enforcement and National Security

There is potential for problems when criminals or rogue nations utilize networked computing technologies for illegal ends. Criminal enterprises can benefit from these technologies, just like legal enterprises. Of particular concern [CST96a] is technology that insures confidentiality—such as encryption (see Chapter 13)—that compromises law enforcement tools such as court-ordered wiretaps. Forms of digital cash (see Chapter 14) could aid money laundering. Governments also want to prevent the availability of effective encryption technologies to other governments, which might foil electronic eavesdropping as a tool for furthering national security.

E X A M P L E :   *The U.S. government has restricted the export of cryptographic technologies, products, and even related technical information by including them on the U.S. Munitions List maintained by the State Department. Computer and software companies in the United States assert that these controls hamper their export of advanced software products (and benefit overseas competitors without similar restrictions) and potentially stifle electronic commerce. Such government intervention may have hampered the security of public networks, making industrial espionage easier.*

Public policy in these areas is in a fluid state, with eventual outcomes unclear.

Antitrust Law

Products in networked computing and software have economic characteristics that encourage winner-take-all outcomes, such as network effects and lock-in. Companies increasingly cooperate in setting industry standards. The acquisition of smaller companies is used as a faster alternative to internal development of complementary technologies. All these observations attract the attention of government policy organs charged with preserving competition in the industry. For example, in the United States, antitrust laws penalize certain business practices that are deemed to undermine competition. In the United States a monopoly is not illegal per se—for example, if it arises out of natural economic forces or fair competitive practices—but blatant attempts to monopolize through what are considered unfair business practices are illegal. These may include acquiring competitors, entering into agreements that unreasonably restrain trade (price fixing among competitors, for example), or tying the availability of one product in which a firm has market power to the customer's agreement to acquire a second product [Sha98].

One easily applied tool of antitrust law is blocking mergers, where the market concentration that results is deemed to reduce competition. It is more difficult to separate already existing dominance due to winner-take-all economic forces from dominance due to predatory business practices. However, legitimate monopolists operate under greater restrictions on business practices to prevent them from unfairly extending this monopoly. Further, in computing, players that appear to be dominant at one point are often undercut by later technological discontinuities.

EXAMPLE: *IBM was sued under the antitrust laws in the 1960s, as it was a dominant firm in both computers and applications at the time. However, the shift to decentralized and networked computing severely undercut its dominance.*

In view of this, the antitrust apparatus has focused in the case of computing on preventing dominance in one product category from being used unfairly to further dominance in a complementary category.

EXAMPLE: *Microsoft's dominant position in desktop operating systems is viewed by many as a natural consequence of positive feedback in an industry with network effects. Although this dominance has not been directly challenged by antitrust officials, Microsoft has been accused of unfairly leveraging its operating system dominance to create a dominance in some applications. For example, in 1997 Microsoft was sued by the U.S. government, which claimed it violated antitrust laws by forcing computer manufacturers, who have essentially no choice but to bundle the Windows operating system with their desktop computers, to also bundle their Internet Explorer Web browser. The United States claimed that the browser is an application, and thus Microsoft's actions were unfairly penalizing suppliers of competitive applications. Microsoft claimed that it was merely innovating to the benefit of its customers.*

A policy dilemma is that product dominance has short-term benefits for the user, who sees better integration and ease of use. Longer term, however, it can deter new ideas and better implementations from entering the marketplace. Antitrust laws will likely have growing influence on the industry evolution, whether by outright enforcement or by indirect influence on business practices.

Telecommunications Regulation

Insight into the relationship of antitrust law and networked computing results from examining the telecommunications industry. In the United States, AT&T became dominant in telecommunications in the early part of the twentieth century. However, rather than invoking antitrust law, the government deemed tele-communications to be a *natural monopoly*. The justification was the impracticality of investing in duplicate telecommunications infrastructures, just as duplicate national highway systems make no sense. In fact, in many countries telecommunications networks have been government owned, like the highways or the postal system. Another justification was a desire to extend service to all citizens (called universal service), which would likely not be the goal of a profit-maximizing enterprise. A third justification was network effects, in the expectation that a single network would offer more value to all its users.

The U.S. government agreed in 1921 to officially sanction AT&T's monopoly status and keep monopoly power in check (and achieve other social goals—see Chapter 20) by industry regulation. Recently regulation has been a tool to reintroduce a competitive environment in long-distance services, as it was decided that a natural monopoly no longer existed due to new technologies and the large volume of traffic. Today, regulation is being used to create competition in local access (see Chapter 20).

While the natural monopoly justification may have been real, the monopoly and focus on universal service also slowed the adoption of innovative technologies and services. To address this, the U.S. government returned to the antitrust laws.

EXAMPLE: *AT&T was sued by the U.S. government under the antitrust laws in 1949 and again in 1974. In 1949, the primary goal was to divorce the equipment manufacturing division from the rest of the company. This was unsuccessful, but the 1974 action resulted in the 1984 dismemberment of the company into seven "regional operating companies" and AT&T Corporation itself, which retained long-distance service and equipment manufacturing. This arrangement proved a problem for the equipment division: Competitors in services were reluctant to buy AT&T equipment. Thus the equipment division was voluntarily divested as Lucent Technologies in 1996, the action sought by the government in 1949.*

Divestiture and related decisions, such as making facilities available for lease by competitors and rules for interconnection, have revitalized innovation in tele-communications. There remain problems, however, as discussed in Chapter 20.

Discussion

D8.9 Are software patents a good or a bad idea? Is there any justification for treating software differently?

D8.10 Discuss the trade-off between free speech and protecting children.

D8.11 What limitations should be placed on the use of information gathered in the course of electronic commerce?

D8.12 Discuss the trade-offs between security in electronic commerce and restrictions on encryption in the interest of law enforcement and national security.

D8.13 Is there such a thing as a "natural monopoly" in either telecommunications or networked computing today? Is this cause for new antitrust laws or new regulatory regimes?

D8.14 Discuss the difference between winner-take-all effects and natural monopoly.

8.4   *Open Issues

The changing nature of the industry and the societal discontinuity introduced by the Internet raise many unresolved issues.

8.4.1   Sovereignty and the Global Internet

Political units are organized around geography, because historically, interaction and socialization have been limited by geography. While the Internet is global in reach, governments and laws are territorial. When two users (or a supplier and a consumer) access the network in different jurisdictions, they are each operating under different laws. Increasingly, groups coalesce around interests or expertise without regard to geography. Territorial laws and policies are increasingly ineffective in the face of this globalization. How, for example, do you enforce tax laws, restrictive policies on content, or prohibitions against encryption on a global network? When commerce and information retrieval are conducted globally, how do the political institutions regulate and tax the transactions? How do they control access of their own citizens to material they may consider subversive or offensive? How do authoritative governments maintain control in the face of free information flow, or if they restrict that flow, what impact does it have on their economy? Certainly the impacts are not all positive, nor all negative, but surely they are very real.

The solution may be delegation of more government functions to international institutions, continuing a trend of the past century.

8.4.2   The Language of the Internet

Since the Internet is global, an important question is whether there will be a dominant language for collaboration and commerce on the Internet, or whether a diversity of languages will be preserved [Oud97]. There are strong network effects in language and positive feedback effects that tend to result in a dominant language. Many multinational companies and conferences choose English as the "official" language. On the other hand, native speakers of other languages would properly like to preserve their languages for Internet content and commerce. A technical solution would be automatic translation, but unfortunately this technology is not yet sufficiently accurate.

8.4.3   A New Partnership

Many business and societal issues and problems emerge from networked applications, some of which have been discussed in this chapter. Doubtless there are many more. As with earlier technologies, the technology itself can mitigate many problems it creates. Further, there is an opportunity to coordinate new applications with changes in organizations, thus making more effective use of networked computing and minimizing adverse factors.

What is needed is a new partnership between technologists and other disciplines—such as law, economics, public policy, business, etc.—to address problems and opportunities. Those responsible for policy or legislative initiatives need greater understanding of technology (I hope this book can help) and its side effects, and greater warning of potential problems and issues so they can be properly debated. Technologists must take a greater interest in the societal impacts of their work, which expand tremendously with the networking of computers. Technologists should draw attention to problems and feasible solutions, and they should work to mitigate undesirable side effects. Business and organizational experts should collaborate with technologists to define more effective means of melding applications with their societal and organizational context. Most of all, a new partnership will allow all the interrelated public, organizational, and technological issues to be properly and expeditiously addressed.

Review

When the value of a product or service to the consumer depends directly or indirectly on the number of other adopters, it has network effects or externalities. For example, Metcalfe's law predicts that the total value of a communication network increases in proportion to the square of the number of users on that network. Network effects are a major motivation for standards, which may increase the size of the total market and thus benefit each participating supplier.

When many complementary products form a system solution, a customer experiences switching costs in moving from one product to another, resulting in lock-in. The present worth of future increased profits from a locked-in customer is, under some conditions, equal to the switching costs. Customers encourage open standards, in part to increase competition and reduce lock-in.

Information can be represented in a continuous physical form (analog) or discrete form (digital). Analog representations can only be copied imperfectly, and thus over time (or space) information is inevitably lost. Digital representations can be exactly replicated. Copying or replication and communication of information is inexpensive relative to manufacturing and distribution in the physical world, leading to larger supply economies of scale.

The information creation costs are sunk, and information is an experience good, implying a large risk for the author and publisher, which can be mitigated by creating a diversified portfolio. An exception is volatile information or software upgrades that can be sold by subscription, where revenues are more predictable.

Software and information have similar challenges to a seller, but to a buyer software is valued for what it does; that is, it has the characteristics of a service, not a good.

Large economies of scale imply that information and software must be well differentiated from competitors and should be priced based on the value to the customer, not on costs. The value of information can be increased by filtering, searching, and customization. The value of software is related to usage, functionality, quality and performance, usability, and impact. Value differs widely among customers, and thus price discrimination is advantageous to the seller. This can be done by estimating customer characteristics or by versioning.

Intellectual property protections are important to suppliers because knowledge, information, and software are easily appropriated. Forms of property rights include technological innovations (patents), original works of authorship (copyright), names (trademark), or proprietary information that would help a competitor (trade secret). Software patents are recent and somewhat controversial.

Public policies are an area of increasing concern in the networked computing era, particularly in view of the major societal impact of the technology. Areas of contention include individual privacy, protection of children from adult material, and encryption in the hands of lawbreakers and foreign adversaries. Winner-take-all effects lead to issues of maintaining competition through antitrust actions or other means. The regulatory environment for telecommunications is changing rapidly.

Key Concepts

Network effects or externalities:

- Direct and indirect network effects
- Metcalfe's law

Lock-in:

- Switching costs

Path-dependent effects

Information representation:

- Analog versus digital
- Copying versus replication

Selling information and software:

- Creation costs, sunk costs, experience good
- Subscription and advertising support
- Value pricing
- Versioning

Intellectual property:

- Copyright
- Patent
- Trademark
- Trade secret

Further Reading

A beginning text with a modern treatment of information economics is [Var87]. [Sha98] is a recent book that overlaps this chapter, focusing on the strategic implications to managers in the computing and communications industries, as well as customers of those industries. It also has a discussion of government policy issues, especially as they affect business strategy. [OHE96a] contains much valuable information about specific products and vendors in client-server computing. [Eco96] is a good introduction to network effects, and [Dif97] is an excellent view into government policy implications for the industry.

Exercises

E8.1 For each of the following, give three concrete examples from the domain of networked computing and networked applications not mentioned

Economics and Policy

in the chapter:

a. Direct network effects

b. Indirect network effects

c. Customer lock-in

d. Supplier lock-in

e. Winner-take-all effects (either technology or product category)

E8.2 Consider the consumer demand for a product with direct network effects.

a. Sketch a typical demand curve (collective consumer willingness to pay versus quantity sold) for a fixed expectation on the total adoptions. Intuitively, what properties will that curve have?

b. Repeat a for a curve characterizing—at a fixed volume of sales—how the willingness to pay will vary with expectations.

c. Repeat a for a curve characterizing—at a fixed willingness to pay—how the sales vary with expectations.

E8.3 Concisely answer the following questions:

a. Does vertical integration make it easier or harder for a company to achieve customer lock-in?

b. Does product diversification make it easier or harder for a company to achieve customer lock-in?

c. Does the presence of a widely used open horizontal interface between two layers make vertical integration more or less attractive to a company?

d. The text describes lock-in as resulting from complementary assets. Suppose that a vendor sells a single product for which there are no complementary products (though there may be some near substitutes). Is there any way for a vendor to create consumer lock-in for such a product?

E8.4 Which of the following examples of information have an analog representation, and which digital?

a. A photograph

b. An image on a Web page

c. The temperature reported in the daily newspaper

d. The temperature on a mercury thermometer

e. The price of the last trade on the stock market

E8.5   For a supplier of music content:

a. Give as many reasons as you can think of why the vendor would prefer to sell and distribute that content in analog form.

b. Repeat a for digital form.

E8.6   What, in your opinion, are pricing and versioning strategies most advantageous to the seller for each of the following products or services sold over the network? Briefly justify your option.

a. Restaurant reviews and recommendations

b. Architectural plans for swimming pools

c. Software application for managing investment portfolios

E8.7   For each of the examples of Exercise 8.6, analyze whether advertiser support might suffice to cover the supplier's costs and make a profit, and justify your answer. If you believe it would, what types of advertisers would you solicit?

E8.8   For each of the following, what form of intellectual property protection would be suitable for preventing appropriation by other suppliers:

a. A method of protecting information content from piracy

b. The name of a new word processing application

c. The specification of an internal module interface for an application

d. A song commemorating the anniversary of the invention of the computer

e. A new technique for protecting the privacy of music sold over the network using encryption

E8.9   For each of the following forms of intellectual property protection, describe the *differences* in the kind of things that can be protected and the nature of that protection.

a. Patent and trade secret

b. Patent and copyright

c. Copyright and trade secret

E8.10   Discuss briefly the motivations of an individual or organization that writes a new piece of software and chooses to offer it to others using the following types of licenses. Emphasize both the similarities and differences.

a. Freeware

    b. Shareware

    c. Open source

    d. Copyleft

E8.11 When a copyrighted work is sold to a consumer, should that consumer be allowed to resell that work to another consumer? Discuss your opinions on this question for the print and digital media, from the following perspectives:

    a. Technical

    b. Economic

    c. Legal

E8.12 Suppose you have been hired as a lobbyist for the American Library Association (ALA). Congress has expressed a desire to keep so-called harmful-to-minors materials from reaching children over the Internet and has proposed legislation that includes a requirement that libraries install software filters on at least some of their public access terminals. Your organization has taken a strong position against the use of software filters or other access restrictions on materials in libraries. Your political advisors tell you that if you want to keep the legislation from passing, "you can't stop something with nothing." Discuss alternative actions you would suggest to Congress, and discuss their benefits.

Making It Happen

There are many options and challenges in acquiring a networked application in an organization.

PART

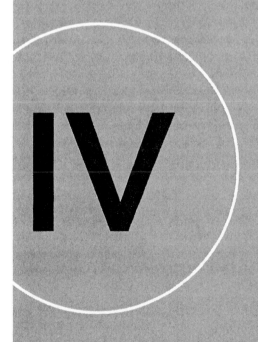

IV

Applications and the Organization

Applications were discussed in Chapter 2 and Chapter 3 from the perspective of the users and organizations benefiting from them. One important point emphasized in Chapter 3 is that organizational applications are integrally tied to the processes within an organization, and those processes need to be reconsidered in order to make most effective use of networked computing. The complete lifecycle of the application—its conception, fruition, and maintenance—is irrevocably tied to the organizational mission.

The rationale for networked computing, as contrasted to alternatives like centralized computing, is largely related to how organizations work. Applications don't just happen, they have to be conceptualized by someone who recognizes a need, the needs must be analyzed to determine requirements, and the software has to be written. Most business applications are developed (or at least customized) for a rather specific need of an enterprise and its business partners. One of the most critical of these needs is the application availability—how much of the time it must be functioning correctly, and when and how it can be maintained. To insure that the application meets organizational needs, works correctly, meets availability objectives, has adequate scalability and performance, and is sufficiently flexible and maintainable, it is important to follow a rigorous development process. Further, the maintenance and upgrade of the application software is an ongoing process.

Application software can be acquired in a number of ways, each with strengths and weaknesses from organizational, technical, and business perspectives. The business arrangements and associated technical approaches that surround the acquisition of application software are rapidly evolving. There is a trend toward the outsourcing of application development and the reuse of software across different applications, and this is supported by new and evolving software development methodologies (see Chapter 10).

A single chapter cannot cover these challenging topics in a comprehensive way, but this chapter will survey many considerations to take into account in the acquisition and operation of applications in organizational contexts.

9.1 Organizational Rationale for Networked Computing

Why should applications be networked rather than centralized? Social applications—which require that every user has a desktop computer (client or peer) to support the human-computer interface and presentation—are inherently networked, because sharing a single computer for this purpose misses the point. What about other applications, particularly organizational? While networked computing has compelling advantages, the rationale is a bit complicated. Two important justifications are scalability and administration.

9.1.1 Scalability

Scalability is the ability of an application to support increasing levels of *activity* and *capability*. For example, information management or consumer electronic commerce should have no inherent limitation on the number of users or consumers, or on the amount of information or goods and services for sale. The activity and capability of an application should not self-limit because of some technological bottleneck. A single computer has limited capability, and as the level of activity increases, it eventually exhausts some resource (processing power, storage capacity, etc.). Scalability requires at minimum multiple hosts and hence networked computing.

E X A M P L E :   *A Web server may initially use a single host, but as the number of users accessing the server increases, eventually the communications capability or processing power is exhausted. A second host can accommodate more users, then a third, a fourth, etc.*

A N A L O G Y :   *In principle, a company could hire a single employee, but as the company grows, eventually that employee can't keep up and it is necessary to hire more employees. Ways must be found to divide the work among those employees, and doubtless they will need to interact.*

Scalability also means the costs of the infrastructure grow no more quickly than key application activity and capability performance attributes. This aspect is addressed later, in Chapter 17.

9.1.2 Administration

Administration refers to the ownership and operation of an application and the infrastructure supporting it. This administration requires workers to install, operate, and maintain the application. Thus, the cost of the infrastructure—the emphasis of scalability—is only the tip of the iceberg. Equally or more important are the administrative costs—salaries, professional services, etc. Even where a single host may achieve the required performance, this may not be desirable or cost effective from an administrative perspective. Some administrative justifications for networked computing are listed in Table 9.1.

In the centralized computer era—when computers were large and expensive—it was important to fully utilize computers, for example, by sharing them over many applications. Today, the cost of a substantial microprocessor-based server (including storage and peripherals) is comparable to a few months loaded salary. Salary costs being generally dominant, minimizing them is paramount, even if this means more hosts than technically required. Two administrators maintaining the same host—or worse, sharing a single host across two or more administrative units—introduces complications. So it often makes sense to dedicate servers to individual administrative units or even single applications.

EXAMPLE: *In the customer-care application, the organization chose to administer two separate servers, one for the customer service department and the other for the technical support department (see "Customer Care" on page 63). Each department hired its own computer system administrator, each of whom had full control over one of these servers. This may not have been justified by the computing load, but it simplified the administration.*

Having said this, there can also be compelling reasons to centralize, such as an enterprise database that must be shared among applications, as in three-tier client-server computing. Thus, in practice there is often a mixture of centralization and distribution.

For cross-enterprise applications, the impact of the administrative boundaries on the partitioning of application and data becomes much more constraining. Compartmentalization—allowed access to data and applications by internal users while keeping out external users—is an overriding consideration. It is enforced not only by using administratively separated hosts, but also by other access control means such as firewalls in intranets.

Table 9.1 Administrative justifications for networked computing

Issue	Description	Analogy
Specialization	Each department finds it advantageous to administer its own dedicated infrastructure. Today, hardware is inexpensive in relation to salaries, so it makes sense to minimize administrative expenses by proliferating computers with more specialized functionality, if that reduces administrative costs.	An enterprise is broken down into specialized functional units (departments).
Compartmentalization	For cross-enterprise applications, it is not administratively practical to share computing resources. Each company owns and operates its own hosts, permitting them to interact by communicating over the network. This also makes it easier to allocate costs to each company.	Even when two companies need to cooperate, each hires its own workers rather than sharing them.
Locality	It is desirable to store information near where it is captured or created (administratively and geographically) and generate the presentation near where it is used (drawing upon multiple sources) (see Chapter 10).	A factory is located near transportation hubs and natural resources, but a retail outlet is located near customers.
Sharing	Information is needed by many users and applications. It should be maintained and updated in only one place, but made available to users and applications across an entire enterprise.	A firm may have many customers.
	Conversely, each user or department should be able to access information maintained by multiple sources.	A firm may have many suppliers.
Security	Information must be reliable, available, and protected against unauthorized access while making selected information accessible from the outside. A single host can selectively make information or interaction available to other hosts. This is much more secure than sharing a host (see Chapter 13).	A firm wants its own dedicated building. Locating two firms in the same building is less secure.
Availability	A networked application must be working correctly when the users need to interact with it. Availability refers to the time (usually expressed as a percentage) that an application is working correctly. Many organizational applications have stringent availability objectives. This may dictate, for example, redundant hosts that serve only as a backup.	

9.2 Acquisition Options

Some distinct approaches to developing or otherwise acquiring application software are listed in Table 9.2. These are not mutually exclusive choices; rather, they can be combined in various ways.

Table 9.2 Approaches to acquiring application software

Approach	Description	Comments
Purchase	Buy an existing application, and configure it for local requirements.	Often termed commercial off-the-shelf (COTS), this is the minimum-cost approach, because development cost is split among multiple deployed applications. The organization and its processes must be molded to the application. Since other organizations have purchased the same application, there is little opportunity to gain competitive advantage.
Outsourced development	Hire another company to develop the application to specification.	With a fixed-cost contract, this carries low financial risk. However, the developers may not be as familiar with or concerned about detailed organizational requirements. There is opportunity to reengineer the process along with the application. Simply automating existing processes is rarely the best solution. The contractor's experience with similar applications improves the chances for success. The contractor can apply its experience to other contracts, reducing but not eliminating competitive advantage.
Internal development	Develop the software application in an internal information systems department.	This approach is most likely to result in an application closely matched to needs. However, this responsiveness may come at the expense of greater time-to-completion and development cost. The development organization is well positioned to maintain the application and manage future upgrades and extensions.

EXAMPLE: *Most custom-developed business applications incorporate a commercial DBMS into a custom development, and ERP is an example of a commercial off-the-shelf (COTS) acquisition that is configurable and customizable. Software components and frameworks provide a way to mix and match COTS and custom with a finer granularity (see Chapter 10).*

As intimated in Table 9.2, the appropriate path to acquiring application software is a critical tactical and strategic decision—one that balances risks (failure, cost overruns, delays, failure to meet organizational needs), cost (development, maintenance, and upgrade), and the flexibility for future upgrades and extensions. The dimension most difficult to manage is the trade-off between meeting precise requirements on the one hand and cost and risk on the other. This is reflected in terms of two dimensions discussed in the following subsections.

9.2.1   Make vs. Buy

The decision to make (internal or outsourced custom development) versus buy (purchase existing application) is usually driven first and foremost by the availability of a suitable application package to purchase. For functions that are fairly standardized across organizations, this is likely to be the case. Although such packages are usually configurable to some extent, this option means adapting the organizational processes to the application—ideally it would be the other way around.

Internal development is most likely to meet the precise requirements, but that benefit usually comes at a higher price (both monetary and risk). It is difficult for an internal development group to resist closely tracking expanding requirements, resulting in longer development cycles and more assumed risk. Outsourced development lies somewhere between—generally, requirements are flexible, but have to be fixed at the start of the project (the developer will resist changes thereafter).

9.2.2   Purchase Terms and Conditions

When development is outsourced, a major issue is the terms and conditions of the contractual arrangements. There are two diametrically opposed options: *fixed price* and *time-and-materials pricing*. In the fixed-price model, the acquirer contracts to pay a fixed price for a finished application that meets specific acceptance tests. In time-and-materials pricing, the acquirer pays an hourly rate for the developer's actual time spent, plus other costs.

The fixed-price model has low risk to the acquirer, but does not readily accommodate requirements changes. Also, as discussed in "Challenges for Suppliers" on page 242, the developer will strive to couple the negotiated price with the value of the application to the acquirer, rather than to development costs. With time-and-materials pricing, the risk of cost overrun is transferred to the purchaser, but price is directly coupled to costs. This model better accommodates changing and expanding requirements but can increase time-to-completion and risk.

Many large projects combine these elements in various ways. An outside software developer may have modules already implemented that can form the basis of the application. In that case, the modules can be licensed (essentially a fixed-price purchase) and combined with integration services and custom module development on a time-and-materials basis.

These conflicting goals result in a constant quest for the best mixture of COTS and custom-developed technology and the best contractual terms and conditions. Software components and frameworks appear promising as a way to better balance the conflicting goals (see Chapter 10).

Discussion

D9.1 Discuss and compare the business model of a software product supplier, a custom application developer, and a systems integrator. What issues do they have in common, and how do they differ?

D9.2 From the perspective of a company wanting to acquire a customized application, discuss in more detail some of the considerations in choosing internal development or outsourcing.

9.3   Application Lifecycle

The acquisition of an application is only one step in its complete lifecycle, which includes other important phases such as deployment, operation, and maintenance. It is particularly important to recognize during the acquisition phase the requirements and constraints emanating from the later operational and maintenance phases. The conceptualization, development, deployment, and maintenance of a business application must satisfy many stakeholders and (sometimes conflicting) objectives. The stakeholders whose influences and needs should be taken into account in application development include the following [BCK98]:

- *Management:* Within the application development organization—whether the development is internal or by a professional-services company—management will be concerned about the cost and time to completion.
- *End-users:* The users of the application and their management will be concerned about their cost of acquisition, features, quality, administrative and operational costs, and flexibility to meet changing requirements. There may also be different criteria applied by management and users.
- *Operators and administrators:* The staff who manage the ongoing operation of the application are concerned about how it is partitioned across hosts and when and how it can be brought down for upgrades and maintenance.
- *Maintenance organization:* The staff maintaining the application features to track changing requirements, whether internally or contracted out, are concerned about the maintenance costs and resilience to adding new features.
- *Suppliers and customers:* If a business application impacts suppliers and customers, they will be concerned about features, ease of use, etc.

9.3.1   Lifecycle Model of Development

Assuming an application is developed internally to an organization, and keeping in mind the needs of stakeholders, this section describes the phases in the application lifecycle [Boo94] [McC97] [Lau99]. Many large application developments ultimately fail: The application is never deployed due to a number of

Automated Development: CASE Tools

A *tool* is a customized software product that automates many of the details of some aspect of software development. Computer-aided software engineering (CASE) tools can automate some or all aspects of a life-cycle development process [MBD99]. There are different types:

- Upper-CASE tools can aid the earlier phases of the lifecycle, for example, a database of system specifications, report and documentation generators, graphical representations of architectures and project management tools. (Yes, this is a pun, demonstrating that software professionals do have a sense of humor.)
- Lower-CASE tools provide high-level descriptions of architecture and functionality and can automate some of the translation to software code.
- Integrated-CASE tools combine lower- and upper-CASE.

Many of the same issues arise for CASE as for packaged applications, on a different dimension. In adopting a set of CASE tools, you are adopting a development methodology, just as adopting a packaged application means adopting a business process. Much flexibility is lost, typically to the chagrin of technology professionals. There are also difficulties with the integration of different CASE tools. While some major successes have been reported, thus far their promise has exceeded reality.

causes, such as not meeting requirements, not having adequate performance, or the need has gone away. But avoiding this requires at minimum a well-thought-out and well-executed process. The lifecycle model discussed now consists of seven distinct stages. It describes an elaborate process that is appropriate for large and complex projects. However, a caution is in order: The process is never as clean and linear as might be implied here. At a minimum, these phases overlap, and they may even have to be repeated if the outcome of a later stage is not satisfactory.

Conceptualization

Conceptualization establishes the basic objectives. In a business application, this is an aspect of understanding and refining the business process or commerce, taking into account the organization of workers, the application functionality, and the interaction of workers and application. The conceptualization includes vision (what new function is to be accomplished?) and assumptions (what are fixed points that cannot be changed?). Typically, a business case has to be formulated to convince management that the investment in the development and deployment of the application is warranted. Important objectives include activity and capability performance parameters and how those parameters may evolve over time.

A great opportunity is lost if existing processes are simply automated. Thus, an important aspect of conceptualization is rethinking the complete organizational processes, that is, the context of the networked application as well as the application itself. Keep this in mind as the remainder of this lifecycle discussion focuses on the networked application.

A useful validation tool is low-cost experiments. Using whatever means available, stitching together a prototype to validate basic ideas and assumptions is worthwhile. The human-computer interfaces to the application can be roughly prototyped and tried out on real users. The earlier major problems can be identified and addressed, the more likely the project will be successful. A prototype is also useful for selling the vision to top management.

Analysis

Once it is decided to move ahead, the next phase is the analysis of the application in its organizational context. The analysis is best described by its outcome, which is a description of what the application does in a form that can be reviewed by stakeholders, and in detail sufficient to allow them to make suggestions for change and judge whether development is advisable. It considers the application implementation details only to the extent necessary to validate the analysis; that is, establish that the behavior of the application meets reality.

A useful technique to use during analysis is *scenarios*. A scenario represents a typical usage of the application, and it specifies external events and the actions of both the people and the application in response to those events. The scenarios chosen should also represent a reasonably complete set, so that no major objectives are neglected.

Analysis does not result in highly detailed specifications. That is best reserved for a process of "iterative refinement" during the design evolution phase. It is important to avoid moving ahead with architecture design before the analysis phase has reached sufficient maturity, or at least the analysis may have to be revisited after greater understanding is developed in the architecture.

One of the major requirements for modern business applications is flexibility to meet changing needs. The business environment will change as new products and services are introduced or organizations are split or merged. Thus, it is a mistake to overanalyze the near-term needs and ignore or compromise the needed flexibility. In the analysis and architecture phases, a major consideration should be somehow accommodating future changes and extensions that cannot be anticipated.

Architecture Design

The application is a system performing the specific functions identified by analysis. The system architecture phase requires the decomposition of the application into hardware and software subsystems, the functionality of those subsystems, and their interaction, as described in "System Architecture" on page 114. Often, the application itself is only one subsystem embedded within a larger social or business system. Often, this larger system context will include more than one networked application.

Architecture is critical because it forms the basis of a divide-and-conquer strategy in the subsequent design evolution phase, where individual subsystems are farmed out to different programmers or groups of programmers. One goal is to make subtasks as independent as possible, avoiding excessive coordination. Insufficient attention to or poor design of the architecture is a frequent cause of project failure. At the other extreme, a poorly conceived architecture can constrain the programmers excessively, so the application cannot meet objectives or has insufficient flexibility.

An application architecture is primarily of concern to the implementers; it is not generally visible to or of concern to users. Its primary role is structuring the development process.

Development Evolution

Although not evident from the previous description, the outcome of architecture design is often a software program that is a very incomplete implementation of the system, but incorporates major subsystems without details filled in. A major activity in the application development is programming, in which the nascent architectural description is successively refined into a prototype of the production system. Usually it is best to avoid going directly from architecture to production system, but rather to start with the architecture and incrementally add detailed capabilities through successive refinement.

ANALOGY: *This incremental development is analogous to the development of an animal from an embryo. The embryo is not a miniature form of the animal, but initially differentiates into only three types of tissue—ectoderm, mesoderm, and endoderm—each of which in turn further differentiates into the numerous tissue types and organs.*

Both the architecture and development evolution phases are described further in Chapter 10.

Testing and Evaluation

Testing an evolving implementation is crucial to uncover shortcomings and flaws [KFN93]. It does not await a complete production system, but rather is an integral part of the design evolution. With a well-conceived architecture, subsystems can be tested independently, with many problems uncovered and repaired. The merger of interacting subsystems—called *integration*—requires further testing of their successful interaction. At this stage an evaluation should also be made of whether the application meets its goals defined in the analysis phase. This is not simply a matter of establishing correct operation but also establishing that it will have the intended impact on the organization.

Once the first prototype of a production system is available, it can be tried out in an environment that approximates the intended usage, called an *alpha test*. Major problems needing repair are often identified at this stage, so it is "off-line," and users must be cooperative and tolerant. Once the problems are shaken out and repaired, it is typical to move to a second phase of testing, called the *beta test*, in an environment as close as possible to intended operational conditions. Ideally, beta testing is performed in a production context but, again, with cooperative and tolerant users. After completing beta testing, the application is ready for deployment.

Deployment

For a business application, the deployment phase includes the establishment of the human organization and the hardware infrastructure (network, hosts, and installation of software on the hosts) and user training. Not infrequently, deployment requires a conversion from some previous operational process and includes extensive planning to avoid major problems and outages, as well as special measures to convert and import relevant data to the new application. Deployment requires advance planning that is every bit as rigorous as design of the software, and total deployment costs frequently exceed the development cost.

Operations, Maintenance, and Upgrade

Once successfully deployed, the application moves into the operations and maintenance phase. Operationally, vigilance of human administrators is necessary to take care of problems as they arise, and especially to maintain security (see Chapter 13). In addition, an application requires continual maintenance by a group of programmers, for two reasons. First, no amount of testing can detect and repair all problems, but inevitably more arise in the operational phase, where conditions not anticipated in testing may arise. Evaluation in the operational phase may uncover fundamental problems, such as failure to meet all functional requirements or user needs. Further, the performance aspects of the application, as it grows to accommodate more users or transactions, is difficult to test fully. Problems must be repaired as they are observed. Second, the operational requirements typically evolve with time, and thus continual development is required to add new capabilities or change functionality to meet changing needs. One reason the architecture design is critical is that a well-conceived architecture is far easier to maintain (both repair and upgrade).

9.3.2   Alternative Development Methodologies

The lifecycle model is appropriate for large complex projects that are developed internally to an organization. Alternative models may be appropriate for other circumstances.

If the application development is outsourced, the lifecycle model has to be modified to take into account the role of two organizations (the end-user and developer) and the formalities of their relationship. The developer will become heavily involved during the analysis phase and will take the lead in the architecture and development evolution phases. One recipe for success is to break down the formalities as much as possible, at least at the working level, for example, by locating developer personnel at the end-user site and involving the developer early in the conceptualization.

Purchasing an application package may eliminate the early phases of the lifecycle—after all, the conceptualization and analysis were performed during the development of the application. However, it is rarely this simple. The application package only provides the software—the necessary changes to the organization still have to be understood, planned, and implemented. There are likely many options for configuration, customization, and mixing and matching of different application modules. This moves conceptualization and analysis to a different plane, but does not eliminate these phases entirely.

The lifecycle model is formal, expensive, and relatively inflexible. While there may be no avoiding it for large projects, at least two alternative methodologies are available for smaller and simpler projects: prototyping and end-user development [Lau99]. The *prototyping* approach moves the development evolution earlier by building an early prototype of the application. End-users can actually try out the prototype, and their hands-on feedback can enhance the iterative refinement. If the application is simple enough to make this work, prototyping is effective because more immediate end-user feedback can directly influence the design.

> E X A M P L E :   *One reason the Web is increasingly used as a basis for application development is its suitability for rapid prototyping. For example, user interfaces can be built and tried out quickly by simply incorporating a Web browser. Even if an entire application is not prototyped, doing just the user interface and seeking end-user trial and feedback is worthwhile.*

The *end-user development* methodology takes this idea further, actually having end-users do their own application development. While limited in applicability, this approach is made increasingly viable for simple applications by the availability of automated tools and major application modules. CASE tools aid the traditional lifecycle process, but there are also more friendly and limited tools accessible to end-users. In the future, the component software may allow greater end-user programming by allowing them to integrate a wealth of available components (see Chapter 10).

> E X A M P L E :   *Many tools exist for generating Web-based interfaces, such as Microsoft FrontPage and Macromedia Dreamweaver. Coupled with tools for connecting Web servers to standard DBMS interfaces, simple applications can easily be developed.*

Discussion

D9.3 Discuss appropriate roles for the management, the end-user organization, and the development organization in each phase of the application lifecycle.

D9.4 Approximately how long would you expect the phases of an application lifecycle to last? Which phases are more likely to overlap, and which less likely?

D9.5 How does a networked application lifecycle differ from the lifecycle of a business process? A product or service? An organization chart? The relationship with a supplier or customer?

D9.6 Many application developments are failures, in the sense that the application is never deployed. What kinds of things may have gone wrong?

D9.7 Discuss some desirable characteristics of the relationship between a captive application software development group and its internal customers. In what ways should that relationship differ from an outsourced developer? Consider the entire application lifecycle, not just initial acquisition.

9.4 Examples

The considerations overlapping the application design and the organizational needs discussed in this chapter can be illustrated by the organizational applications described in Chapter 3. Both the organizations and the development scenarios below are hypothetical; they are simply intended to illustrate the many different scenarios that occur in application acquisition.

9.4.1 Customer Care

When software4u.com decided to set up its customer-care operation, it expected that this application would be needed by many merchants, at least in roughly similar form. Scouring the market, it found two small start-up software companies who specialized in application packages for customer-care operations. Although these packages had never been sold to a software merchant like software4u.com, they turned out to be a reasonable match to software4u.com's needs. However, one major feature they did not have was the knowledge base to store customer problems and solutions. After investigation, software4u.com decided that low cost and rapid start-up dictated COTS solutions. Therefore, it decided to design its customer-care operation around one of the existing applications packages from a small company, Customer Solutions, compromising on some capabilities that it had hoped to incorporate. Essentially, the application it purchased from Customer Solutions determined the details of its customer-care business process. This saved time and effort, although it may have sacrificed some features and efficiency.

Software4u.com was determined to implement the knowledge base, however, so it purchased that application separately. Fortunately, Customer Solutions had encountered similar special requirements from its customers before, and so it had an internal development group devoted to contract customization services on a time-and-materials basis. It was reasonably cost effective because it was already up to speed on its own application. Thus, Customer Solutions was able to integrate the knowledge base with its application on behalf of software4u.com. Later, Customer Solutions was so impressed with this capability that it purchased this integration back from software4u.com in order to sell it as an option in its standard application package.

9.4.2 On-Line Bookseller

Books4u.com was a start-up company, so acquiring its e-commerce software was a key step in its business strategy. Since it was the third firm to go into the on-line bookseller business, its first step was to contact the first two firms to see if they might be willing to license their software. In spite of the potential revenue opportunity, neither was anxious to help a potential competitor, so they both declined. However, books4u.com found that one of those existing implementations had been acquired on a fixed-price contract from an outsourced developer, Creative Solutions. Figuring that Creative was at minimum experienced with developing this application, books4u.com contacted them. It turned out that Creative had used some existing modules and had also retained joint ownership of some of the software it had custom-developed for bookselling, and it was willing to license these pieces to books4u.com to reduce the cost of a fixed-price development contract.

In return for a substantial fee, Creative sent three professionals to participate in a two-month conceptualization phase at books4u.com. This brainstorming resulted in many innovative features that would not only give books4u.com a competitive advantage but were also deemed feasible to implement. A second fixed-price contract was let to Creative to do the analysis, creating a detailed set of requirements and a development plan. Based on this plan, Creative was willing to set a fixed price and timetable for the development of the entire application. The negotiation of the contract was complicated by the many intermediate milestones and deliverables, and by contingencies should those milestones be missed. However, after a month of hard negotiations with considerable give-and-take, a contract was signed, and Creative got down to work developing the books4u.com's e-commerce application.

9.4.3 Stock Trading

Stocks4u.com was started by a traditional broker entering the e-commerce business. A major feature of its business plan was to make use of the existing systems for tracking customer accounts, orders, and stock trades. Networked applications being a major enabler for the financial services industry, stocks4u.com already had a large internal information systems organization that would be able to develop the e-commerce application, incorporating these legacy systems.

As a way of shaking out innovative features, and also understanding some of the challenges of data integration across these legacy applications, the first step was a rough prototype of the customer interface. This was tried out on focus groups, including some of its technology-savvy customers, and their feedback was used to refine the ideas. This combined conceptualization and prototyping exercise resulted in major new requirements for the application. With this revised concept in hand, stocks4u.com embarked on an internal lifecycle development process. The integration with legacy applications turned out to be so complicated that the time for implementation was underestimated by many months, and the costs ballooned to more than double the original estimates. Nevertheless, the development was successfully completed.

Stocks4u.com was so successful with its new e-commerce business that the customer base ballooned rapidly. It was quickly discovered that the scalability of the application was inadequate to meet the demand, especially on high trading volume days. Business was lost and customers were alienated. As a result, the information systems department at stocks4u.com has been fully engaged in upgrading the application to match an expanding customer base and demand. No small part of the original implementation has been abandoned in order to enhance scalability. Even today, the technologists are not sure precisely how their application will be able to meet the expected demand six to twelve months in the future, but it seems clear that its current three-tier client-server architecture will not be up to the task. Thus, stocks4u.com is working closely with a major computer manufacturer to explore alternative architectures for the next generation.

9.4.4 Floral Delivery

Flowers4u.com is a start-up company pursuing a new business model. Its requirements, and especially the need to interoperate with 16,000 small business partners, were unique, so flowers4u.com was forced to develop most of its e-commerce application from scratch. To minimize development effort, and minimize time from business concept to operations, it leveraged Web-based technologies as much as possible. For example, it purchased Web server technology from Netscape and a commercial DBMS from Oracle. The Netscape products included e-commerce security software (see Chapter 13).

Expecting its business model to evolve rapidly over time, fine-tuning its approaches to dealing with local florists, expanding into new services, and expanding its business to other goods, flowers4u.com decided to acquire its own in-house development group. To gain a fast start, the group first hired part-time contract programmers and has since hired a dozen full-time professional programmers. Since the start of the company, this group has been continuously improving and developing flowers4u.com's e-commerce application. For example, its experimentation with different ways to push orders to the florists evolved through several stages, all involving software development.

Typical of (initially) small start-up companies, flowers4u.com used the prototyping approach to application development. It first prototyped the customer and florist interfaces and tried them out on family members and cooperating local florists to refine their ideas. Then it added the database and e-commerce software, first obtaining a rough prototype and subsequently refining it. Now that flowers4u.com has grown into a substantial company, and its applications have grown, it follows a more disciplined lifecycle development methodology. Its ongoing plan involves completing a new version of its applications each six months, hoping to stay ahead of potential competitors.

9.4.5   Observations

These hypothetical examples illustrate several points. First, there are many ways to acquire an application, and they are not easily categorized—often a combination of approaches is used. Second, change is a constant, and this is especially true of businesses that depend heavily on networked computing and e-commerce. Thus, application development is not a one-time activity, but more often a process of continuous change and improvement. Third, legacy systems are often a serious constraint, as well as an obstacle. Even applications developed today are not particularly tolerant of change, but legacy applications are even less so. Fourth, developing an application achieving the desired functionality is not sufficient—it also has to have adequate performance and scalability. This is difficult to achieve while meeting time and budget constraints and interoperating with legacy applications.

9.5 Open Issue: Best Development Methodology

The development of software applications—a scholarly discipline called software engineering—has traditionally focused on the problem of managing groups of professional programmers and supporting them with proper methodologies and tools. One of the major issues is productivity, and a related issue is shortages of trained and interested professionals. While there have certainly been productivity gains, they haven't been dramatic. Can more attention and resources applied to this problem yield major improvements? One possible answer is software reuse. In Chapter 10 some new methodologies based on components and frameworks are discussed. These may improve professionals' productivity, expand the possibilities for end-user programming, or in some cases eliminate programming altogether.

Review

Some applications—particularly social applications—naturally require networked computing to access geographically dispersed users. Others, including many departmental and enterprise applications, make use of networked computing for different reasons. The two most important reasons are scalability (need to provide a growing capability) and adherence to administrative boundaries.

An application can be acquired by purchasing a packaged application, often with numerous configuration options, or developing it either internally or by outsourcing the development to a professional services firm.

The formal lifecycle development methodology includes conceptualization, analysis, architecture design, development, testing, deployment, operation, maintenance, and upgrade. Alternative methodologies for less ambitious application developments include prototyping and end-user development.

Key Concepts

Application acquisition:

- Purchase
- Internal versus outsourced development

Application lifecycle:

- Conceptualization and analysis
- Architecture design, development refinement, testing

- Deployment
- Operation, maintenance, and upgrade

CASE tools

Prototyping

End-user development tools

Further Reading

A number of books discuss the management of information technology in organizations, including [MBD99] and [Lau99]. The process of developing new applications is discussed by [BCK98], [McC97], [Pre96], and [Boo94], where the latter served as the basis for the description here. Testing methodologies are discussed in [KFN93].

Exercises

E9.1 Discuss the specific rationale for using networked computing (as opposed to centralized computing) for each of the following applications:

    a. A portal Web site that provides indexes and entries to many other sites (like Yahoo!)

    b. A calendar and scheduling application for a large corporation

    c. An ERP application that schedules manufacturing inventory and production and sales, feeding sales forecasts to govern inventory and production

E9.2 List all the risk factors for both the buyer and the seller that you can think of for the following application acquisitions:

    a. Internal development

    b. Outsourced development with fixed-price contract

    c. Outsourced development with time-and-materials contract

    d. Purchase software product

E9.3 For any one of the following applications, assume you are charged with its conceptualization. Consider and describe briefly a process that might be suitable for assessing the needs of the users of the application. In each case be clear about who the users are. If there is more than one distinct category of users, repeat for each such category.

a. Computing support of a food service organization in a large organization (keeping track of inventory, employees, customer payments, etc.)

b. Support a help-desk organization in a computer manufacturer (as described in "Customer Care"on page 63)

c. Automate a library's card catalog system (support library patrons wishing to find a book by author, title, or topic)

E9.4 For any one of the following applications, pretend the application does not yet exist. Pretend further that you just came up with the idea for this application, and carry out the conceptualization and analysis phases and document your results for each phase. Feel free to steal ideas from versions of this application you may be aware of. Feel free to consider a "lightweight" version of the application to keep the work within reasonable bounds for a homework exercise—the main point is to understand the separation of the conceptualization and analysis phases.

a. Calendar application to keep track of your schedule

b. Application to originate and read email

c. Application to synchronize files between a desktop and laptop computer

E9.5 For each of the following applications, describe concisely how it might be tested after implementation and prior to deployment:

a. Bank account customer transaction and record keeping

b. Web-based book retailer

c. Manufacturing, shipping, and inventory control between a manufacturer and one of its parts suppliers

d. Sale of information stored in a database on the Web

Application Architecture

A s described in Chapter 9, one option for acquiring a networked application is to develop rather than purchase it. The application should be subjected to the design, implementation, and maintenance stages described in "Application Lifecycle" on page 279. One of those stages, and the general topic of this chapter, is defining the architecture of the application. General architectural principles useful for this purpose were described in Chapter 6. The architecture lays the groundwork for the development evolution, and in particular, it is important to the separation of concerns that allows the application development to be partitioned among development groups while minimizing coordination overhead. Architecture is also the stage at which an opportunity to reuse existing components and avoid implementing everything from scratch is created. It is also a key to achieving flexibility—an increasingly important requirement for organizational applications.

You may ask, "Why do I need to know about this—won't technologists take care of this for me?" This is a reasonable question, and indeed you may be able to get along fairly well with no clue as to how applications are designed (or programmed, as discussed in Chapter 11). Equipped with an understanding of architecture, however, you will be in a much better position to interact with technologists in carrying your application ideas to fruition. The application architecture should be carefully aligned with the context of the application itself, and both you and the technologists will be in a far better position to work together effectively to do this right if you share a common understanding and terminology.

Of course, it is also true that the application software development has to focus on much more than achieving the desired functionality, which is the focus of this chapter. The development addresses other issues such as performance, flexibility, and maintainability. In addition, the various stakeholders have to be concerned about the costs, the risks, and the time-to-completion of the development process. Thus, the issues addressed in this chapter form the core, not the totality, of the important design considerations.

10.1   Major Considerations in Architecture Design

Before embarking on a detailed architecture design, there are a number of major decisions to be made and considerations to be taken into account. Acquiring an application is in fact not a binary decision between purchase and development; there are many intermediate possibilities. One major asset of any organization (and many individuals) is the store of information that has been accumulated over time and forms the basis for operations and decision making. How this information, and its representation as data in the networked application, is to be acquired and stored is a major consideration that often transcends individual applications. These and related issues are discussed in this section.

10.1.1   Decomposition vs. Assembly

In acquiring a new application, it is normally advantageous to reuse as much existing technology as feasible without compromising short- or long-term objectives. This often results in using a mixture of off-the-shelf components with custom-developed software modules. The extreme cases are illustrated in Figure 10.1 and defined in Table 10.1: decomposition and assembly. They differ as to how the modularity is established.

- *Decomposition* chooses the application modularity without constraint. The overall system functionality is decomposed into natural functional modules, emphasizing desirable architectural properties such as the separation of concerns and future flexibility.
- *Assembly* builds the application from purchased software components, which were described in "Components and Integration" on page 198. (Assembly is also called "composition," but that term is avoided here because it is so close to "decomposition.") Assembly is highly constrained by the availability of such components and their functionality and interfaces.

Modules arising from decomposition must be implemented, and components must be purchased or licensed. In either case, they must then be integrated (made to work together) and tested to finish the application development phase.

EXAMPLE: *A common methodology for business applications is to incorporate an off-the-shelf database management system (DBMS) and add custom-*

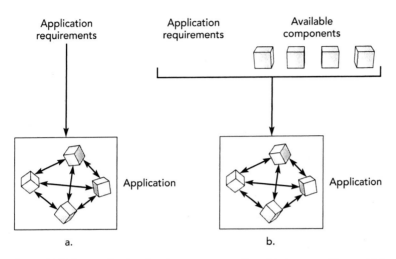

Figure 10.1 Two application development approaches: (a) decomposition and (b) assembly

Table 10.1 Three methodologies for developing an application

Approach	Description	Comments
Decomposition	Starting with application requirements, do an unconstrained decomposition into interacting modules. Custom-implement and integrate those modules to realize the application.	This is the most common approach today, particularly when developed in one organization in its entirety. Decomposition is supported by the object-oriented programming methodology discussed later in this chapter.
Assembly	Find software components (subsystems available for purchase) that approximate application requirements. Assemble and integrate those components to realize the application.	The components are usually purchased from outside vendors and locally configured. Vendors try to provide many configuration and customization options to increase their market.
Mixture	Usually an application is developed by assembling custom-designed modules with purchased components.	For example, ERP applications provide a framework and components—with a high degree of configurability—but also allow custom modules to be added. Often an experienced professional-services firm is hired to design the business process and configure the ERP components.

designed application logic. *The application logic module is itself developed by either assembly or—more likely today—decomposition. This illustrates that if the modularity is hierarchical, then at each level of hierarchy the development of the next lower level can use decomposition or assembly.*

Enterprise resource planning (ERP) applications emphasize assembly over decomposition. The application is mostly provided in modules that can be mixed and matched. Each module can be configured and extended by adding internally developed modules.

ANALOGY: *Establishing the modularity of a software application is analogous to organizing a company. Making the company self-contained—developing all its departments from scratch—is decomposition. Outsourcing every function—development, marketing, manufacture, sales—is assembly. In practice, the two approaches are mixed. Manufacturing may be outsourced, but marketing will be performed internally.*

Assembly and decomposition as development methodologies support the distinct business models discussed in Chapter 9: Decomposition is custom development, whereas assembly uses COTS, with the added step of integration of the purchased components. Assembly in its purest form is not likely because if all the components can be purchased to assemble an application, it is likely that a turnkey application can be purchased. Thus, some custom development is usually associated with assembly, and in reality the possibilities span a continuum between decomposition and assembly. Assembly may be used for an initial prototype, followed by internal development to refine either application functionality or performance.

Decomposition: Objects

For systems or subsystems that are developed rather than purchased, the most common approach to decomposition is *object-oriented programming* (OOP). The basic unit of application modularity is called an *object*. Objects have well-defined interfaces that support abstraction and encapsulation, as described in "*More on Good Architectures" on page 186. As in any form of decomposition, there are three implementation phases: architecture design (decomposition of the application into objects), implementation (programming of the objects), and integration (testing and modifying objects so that they interoperate). OOP as an architectural tool is described in this chapter. Later, when programming an application is considered in Chapter 11, OOP as a programming methodology will also be described.

Assembly: Software Components

Although OOP is currently popular, in computing there is always something new on the horizon. Today one new trend is *component software*. Like objects, components form the basic modularity of the application, but the programming methodology is quite different. Components for the application are presumed to preexist and are sold by outside vendors. The application is assembled from these existing components, often adding custom-implemented modules. This will be called *component-oriented programming* (COP) here—a terminology that is nonstandard.

EXAMPLE: *Today components are widely available to construct graphical user interfaces, which have become largely an assembly operation for most simple applications. Powerbuilder from Powersoft is an example of a development environment for user interfaces.*

In the future there will be available components representing typical business entities, such as the customer, account, invoice, and purchase order. A business application might then be assembled from these components, together with a DBMS. The development process will focus on configuring and integrating these components into a working application, rather than implementing modules.

In COP, the architecture phase takes the form "how can existing, available components be incorporated into the application?" Ideally, the development is largely focused on the integration of components, although it will typically be necessary to custom-implement some customized subsystems.

Assembly offers considerably less freedom than decomposition. The application architecture is constrained by the desire to use existing components, and there are likely constraints on functionality and performance imposed by available components. For this reason, COP is viable only if there is a vibrant market in components, so that each development has available a reasonable diversity of components at a quality and price improved by competition [Szy98]. Today this market largely does not exist, except for some very large-grain components like the DBMS. However, the industry is working intensively on the underlying technology and standards that will enable a component marketplace (see the sidebar "Component Standards").

In business terms, the difference between OOP and COP is a make-or-buy decision. OOP focuses on decomposition into internally implemented and integrated modules, while COP focuses on assembly, configuration, and integration of purchased components.

10.1.2   Software Reuse

The size and complexity of new applications is growing dramatically, and as a result, the costs of software development and the length of the development cycle are often unacceptable. It is imperative that ways be found to contain the required effort and at the same time make applications more flexible. A key to

Component Standards

Today there are emerging three competing component de facto standards: CORBA from the Object Management Group, Java and JavaBeans from Sun, and DCOM from Microsoft. Each comes from a different perspective and strength: enterprise applications for OMG, the internet technologies for Sun, and the desktop applications from Microsoft [Szy98]. Each is working to expand its domain and hedging by providing bridges to the others.

The success of these competing standards will reflect secondary network effects, as described in "Network Effects" on page 232, much like the operating system. Each is working hard to achieve critical mass, where positive feedback kicks in. Application developers will prefer the standards with the largest repository of available components, and component vendors will prefer the environment with the largest market for applications. Positive feedback will create a tendency toward a winner-take-all effect. This is a classic standards war in its infancy.

Reuse in Industry

Reuse is an important source of productivity gain across industries—indeed, it is a foundation of the industrial revolution.

The use of a common infrastructure is well established. A new business can make use of a wealth of existing or available resources, such as buildings, furniture, computers, accounting and human resources software packages, and workers with relevant experience. It can also count on an existing infrastructure, such as roads, telephones, postal system, data networks, overnight package delivery services, and consulting services.

The industrial revolution moved away from handcrafted products (the way much software is developed today) to the use of standardized interchangeable parts that are analogous to software components. For example, an electronic equipment manufacturer incorporates a number of components and integrated circuits that are purchased from other vendors.

Strategies analogous to the software framework are also commonplace. For example, each car manufacturer has relatively few automobile platforms—a basic design for all models of a similar size. It consists of a steel frame, components (such as suspensions, engines, etc.) that fit to that frame, and associated production equipment. New models can be designed quickly and inexpensively by cosmetic modifications and additions to an existing platform.

reducing the cost and development time is *software reuse*. This takes a number of different forms, all with a common objective:

- The entire application can be purchased, often in a form that is highly configurable or customizable to meet distinct end-user needs.
- All the capabilities provided by the software infrastructure need not be reimplemented in each application. Most of the activity in adding capability to the infrastructure is at the middleware layer, which is discussed in Chapter 15 and Chapter 16.
- Software components can be licensed and assembled into an application together with custom-implemented modules.
- A *software framework* is an established application-specific architecture—usually accompanied by components designed to fit into that architecture—that can be modified and extended.

Reuse is a time-honored technique—see the sidebar "Reuse in Industry." Software reuse using components and frameworks is promising for both vertical industries and common business functions across industries. A vibrant market in components, frameworks, and middleware addressing both these opportunities is developing.

EXAMPLE: *Many business applications share common elements, such as the customer, address, invoice, payment, etc. Components supporting these common entities can be used in many different applications. ERP applications provide a mixture of components and frameworks. Each ERP application, such as supply-chain management, accounting, or human resource management, is a specific framework designed to support this business process, together with a set of objects or components that fit within that framework. Each framework and constituent components are configurable and can fit different business requirements. On the other hand, each tightly constrains the business process that it automates, as there are limits to this configurability.*

Reuse is more difficult than it might appear. Actually achieving reuse requires discipline and a business process focused about that goal [JGJ97]. Developing reusable software is more expensive and takes more time than developing single-use software, and that added time and expense has to be initially budgeted, taking account of long-term benefits, often to short-term detriment.

10.1.3 Location of Data and Processing

Information is the basic commodity of networked applications and is represented by data within the infrastructure. Recall from Chapter 4 that the infrastructure supports four key capabilities on behalf of the application: communication across

space, communication across time, computation and logic (together called processing), and the human-computer interface. Data is communicated across space
and time, data is manipulated by computation and logic, and the information
presented at the user interface is represented by data. All these basic functions
include data as an integral element.

Networked applications have four fundamental tasks: the acquisition of data, the
storage of data, the processing of data, and the presentation of data. A fundamental architecture question, therefore, is where is data acquired, stored, processed, and presented? Since the equipment supporting the application consists
of hosts and network, this is a question of which hosts acquire data, manage the
storage of that data, process that data, and present it to users. The answers to
those questions determine the pattern of data transport over networks and have
the greatest impact on performance parameters of the application, which is discussed further in Chapter 17. For example, communicating data across the network takes time—a time that increases with the size of the data that must be
transported—which in turn delays its processing. Processing data available on
local storage media is, in contrast, much speedier.

EXAMPLE: *In the three-tier client-server architecture, shared data, application
logic, and presentation are functional groupings assigned to different hosts. As
a result, data has to be transported from shared data to the application logic
tier to be processed, and from application logic to the presentation tier to be
presented to the user. Similarly, data acquired from the user passes in the other
direction. While this has a cost in terms of transporting data across the network
several times, it also has benefits. The shared data may be administered in one
place and yet be made available to multiple applications. The opposite
extreme—storing data on a client computer so it can be processed and presented entirely locally—has serious disadvantages. When multiple users need
access to overlapping data, it is difficult to maintain consistency among the
multiple copies.*

This example illustrates some of the considerations that need to be taken into
account in partitioning both data and processing across hosts. Questions that
should be asked include

- Is it more advantageous to store data near where it is acquired, or where it is
  processed, or where it is presented?
- How many different users need access to the same stored data? How many
  different applications?
- How important is the data to the users and organization? Should it be managed in a highly protective environment like a mainframe, or can a greater
  possibility of loss or corruption be traded against other benefits?

Partitioning in Organizations

Organizations have always faced data and processing partitioning issues. Before networked computing, these issues manifested themselves as the partitioning of paper records and workers acquiring and processing those records. Consider an organization processing large volumes of paper records. It faces choices like distributing the records into small pieces—each managed by a single worker and stored in that worker's desk drawer—or maintaining a centralized records vault in the basement. In the latter case, each worker must retrieve records from the vault, process them, and immediately return them.

In considering the trade-offs, a manager defining the organization will consider that the distributed records model is expeditious and time efficient for the individual worker, but raises significant coordination issues. For example, if two workers need to access the same record for different purposes, how will that work? If a copy is made, suddenly there exist two (possibly inconsistent) copies of the same record. The centralized model allows records to be better safeguarded—the vault can be fire protected, the records can be logged as they leave or enter, and backup copies can be systematically maintained in case a record is accidently destroyed. Also, the centralized vault makes coordination more straightforward—the keeper of the vault can check replicas out to two or more workers and keep track of location and modifications.

- Is it acceptable to replicate the data and store it in two or more hosts at the same time? If so, what happens if those replicas are each modified by processing, so that they are no longer replicas?
- How volatile is the data—how fast does it change with time? With less volatility, it makes more sense to replicate the data in different places to gain faster access.

EXAMPLE: *In the customer care-application of "Customer Care" on page 63, the primary data acquired by the application falls in these categories:*

- *Data represents information gathered about customer problems. Once this data is acquired, it may be appended but does not change.*
- *Data represents activities relating to the resolution of a particular customer's problem. Again, this data is appended as the problem is resolved, but it does not change.*
- *Data represents the knowledge base with solutions to customers' problems that have been encountered and resolved in the past. This data is nonvolatile, although it grows and accumulates.*

Customer problem data is captured from the customer by the service agents, and customer resolution data and knowledge base data is generated by the technical support department. Logically, customer data flows from service agents to technicians, and resolution data flows in the opposite direction. It must be accessible to both, but not to the customer. The knowledge base is made available to both service agents and technicians, and possibly also the customer via the Web.

The partitioning of the processing needed by the application across hosts raises similar issues. One consideration is the location of processing in relation to the data that is processed. Another is how an adequate aggregate processing capability can be achieved, given that it must be partitioned across hosts. These are scalability issues that are addressed in more detail in Chapter 17. Nor are they unique to networked applications (see the sidebar "Partitioning in Organizations").

10.1.4   Data as an Asset

As discussed in Chapter 3, information and knowledge are often among the most significant assets of an organization—they have significant asset value. Much of this information and knowledge is represented by data acquired, stored, and manipulated by information technology. Of course, there may also be printed records, and the knowledge and experience of employees is of utmost importance.

Often data is viewed as an asset to be managed independently of applications that acquire and manage it. Some compelling reasons for this are listed in Table 10.2.

EXAMPLE: *The on-line stock brokerage stocks4u.com of "On-Line Stock Trading" on page 68 accumulates considerable data that should be treated as a separate asset. Information about customers is needed for many purposes, including authorizing their login, maintaining account information, and relating orders to customers. Account information must be kept for a number of years for auditing and tax purposes, aside from its near-term operational significance.*

Like other companies in the on-line stock brokerage business, stocks4u.com sees its information technology as the strategic core of its business. It maintains an advantage over competitors by upgrading existing products and adding new products and capabilities, all based on its information technology. Thus, it must contend with a constantly changing mix of applications, but they all generate, access, and manipulate a common pool of data. That data is a core asset of the company.

The DBMS is designed in part to meet this need. There are a number of advantages to placing a layer of storage middleware between the storage/file system and the applications:

- Since data is not managed directly by the application, it assumes an identity separate and apart.
- A DBMS contributes to software reuse by embedding common functionality needed by many applications.
- Hidden behind the DBMS interface, a lot of detailed issues of data partitioning and replication can be encapsulated. If an application crashes or fails, the DBMS can prevent irrevocable loss of data.
- Vendors can add capabilities such as data mining, OLAP, and data warehousing by focusing on interfaces to a small number of DBMSs rather than a large number of applications.
- The DBMS can coordinate multiple applications in accessing a common repository of data.
- Applications can be eliminated, upgraded, or replaced without impacting the data.

Because of these compelling advantages, the DBMS is a component that is integrated into many applications. It is discussed further in Chapter 15.

Table 10.2 Characteristics of data that give it value independent of applications

Characteristic	Description	Examples
Asset	Data underlies information and knowledge, increasingly important assets for many organizations. Data's value is enhanced by decoupling it from specific applications.	Customer and employee information, inventory and order information.
Common source, shared resource	A given set of data originates from a single source and yet may be exploited by multiple applications. Rather than replicate this data within each application, which leads to coherency problems among those replicas, it may be centrally managed.	Customer information is incorporated into many business processes (such as sales management and accounts receivable); sales information is used to forecast production (as in supply-chain management and marketing strategy).
Interaction	The exchange of data with standard formats is a powerful mechanism for interaction among applications. If centrally managed, the update of data by one application immediately becomes available to all applications sharing that data.	Information about customer purchases can later be used to forecast sales, guide manufacturing; a knowledge base of problem reports in customer support can be used in the development of new products.
Decision tool	Data captures the condition of a business and is valuable as a tool for tactical and strategic decision making.	Sales information can be used to divest products or stimulate related product development.
Archival	Data captures the history of a business, invaluable for discovering trends.	Data warehousing.
Searching or mining	Data can be systematically searched, browsed, or mined to uncover useful information.	Data mining and OLAP.

Discussion

D10.1 Does the decomposition versus assembly issue arise with other products or services that a company may have to acquire? Give some examples and discuss the comparison to software.

D10.2 Assembly and reuse as viable strategies depend on the similarity of functionality and interaction that can be practically imposed on modules across different applications. Discuss the feasibility of this for social, information management, and business applications.

10.2 Object-Oriented Architectures

The decomposition approach to designing an application usually takes the form of object-oriented programming (OOP). The basic unit of modularity in OOP is the software object, which encapsulates both data and the processing that manipulates that data. Each object models some well-defined and self-contained functionality within the application, with the objective of separation of concerns among the different objects. Objects interact to achieve the higher-level functions of the application.

OOP is supported by object-oriented programming languages, representative examples being C++, Java, and Smalltalk. A *programming language* is a way to describe the operation of applications in a way the computer can understand and act upon. This chapter concerns OOP as an architectural technique, and some programming considerations in OOP are deferred to Chapter 11.

Recall that an architecture incorporates three elements: decomposition, functionality, and interaction. OOP follows precisely this approach. The decomposition is into objects, and the functionality of each object is displayed at an interface. The interaction of objects results because one invokes functionality provided by another.

10.2.1   Objects and the Application Context

An important idea behind OOP is to align the decomposition of objects with the physical and informational entities that form the application context. The architectural challenge is to define software objects within the application architecture that mirror these real-world entities, making the transition from the physical or logical context to the application as seamless as possible. To understand this further, real-world entities will be discussed, followed by software objects, followed by the relationship between the two.

Physical and Information Entities

Looking around the real world, you probably see many entities. In common usage, this means things that have a distinct identity, as separate from other entities, serve some useful function by themselves, but sometimes also serve higher purposes by interacting among themselves. (These entities might also be called "objects," but to avoid confusion with software objects, "entities" is used.) Some entities are purely informational—they need not have a physical manifestation—while others inherently have a physical manifestation.

E X A M P L E :   *A clock is a physical entity that keeps track of time, but it is most useful if it interacts with a person, who observes that time. A purchase order is an informational entity that expresses the desire to purchase a specific product or service from a vendor, but it is most useful when it interacts with that vendor, who then ships the product or provides the service. A bank account is an informational entity that serves as a repository for money and also reflects its time value (that is, compounds interest), and it is most useful when it interacts with its owner, who makes deposits and withdrawals. In this pragmatic view, even a person (say, a customer or employee) can be considered an entity that interacts with the surrounding physical and logical world.*

Some entities can be customized or configured (like the clock, where the current time can be set), and other entities are immutable (like a brick). Other entities are dynamic, meaning some characteristics change with time. Usually the customization or observed change in an entity can be captured by *attributes*—changeable properties owned by the entity. The *behavior* of an entity describes the manner in which its attributes change, particularly as time passes and as it interacts with other entities. Often, there is a direct coupling between this interaction and behavior.

E X A M P L E :   *A clock is an entity that serves to tell the time. One of its attributes is the time it displays on its face, which reflects the passage of time. Another attribute is the energy remaining in its battery, which decreases with time and determines how long it will continue to tell the correct time. One of its behaviors is to change its display attribute. A person can interact with the clock to set its time (change its display attribute to some desired value).*

In summary, an entity in the real world has at least two characteristics: its attributes and its behavior. It is these two characteristics that should be captured in software objects.

Software Objects

Software objects also have attributes and behavior, and they interact with other objects to realize some higher-order function. Some terminology surrounding objects is summarized in Table 10.3 and will be explained subsequently. The important point is that software objects can mirror physical and informational entities in the real-world context of the application. This correspondence between application context and software makes applications more natural to design and implement.

E X A M P L E :   *In commerce, customers and suppliers exchange goods for payment, where the payment can be a simple cash transaction or a more formal exchange of purchase order (authorization to ship goods and promise to pay), invoice (demand for payment), and payment. In electronic commerce, except for physical goods, each of these entities from the physical world can be mirrored by software objects. There may be a software object mirroring the purchase order, another mirroring the invoice, and another mirroring the payment.*

Table 10.3 Definitions of terms relating to software objects

Term	Definition
Object	A module at the lowest level of hierarchical decomposition in an object-oriented programming methodology.
Attribute	A numerical value or other data that represents some externally visible information about an object. Some attributes can be changed, others are only observable.
Method	An action available at an object interface. Other objects interact with it by invoking this method, passing parameters, and receiving returns. Parameters and returns can be either data or objects.
Interface	The set of all methods and attributes of an object, usually accompanied by documentation as to the functionality of the object and its methods.
Class	That which is in common among a set of objects with the same interface and functionality.
Instance	All objects sharing the same class share the same implementation and are called *instances* of that class.

In addition, within the electronic commerce application, there are likely to be other objects mirroring each customer, supplier, and good being shipped.

The attributes of these objects customize them to a specific purpose. For example, attributes of a purchase order include a description of the goods being purchased, the agreed price, the name and address of the supplier (recipient of the purchase order) and the customer (originating the purchase order).

The structure of a software object is shown in Figure 10.2. An external perspective is shown on the left—consisting of its interface and documentation—and an implementation perspective is on the right. An object has an interface that serves two purposes: It provides guidance to another interacting object, and it provides guidance to the implementer as to what attributes and methods have been promised.

What does the object interface look like? As described in "Modularity" on page 159, an object offers a set of actions, each with parameters and returns, which are called *methods*. In addition, objects may have attributes, which are numerical values or other data that is visible outside the object. Methods will be provided to examine (and sometimes change) an attribute. One useful enhancement of object interfaces is that a parameter or return can be an object, or it can be data, as described in Chapter 6.

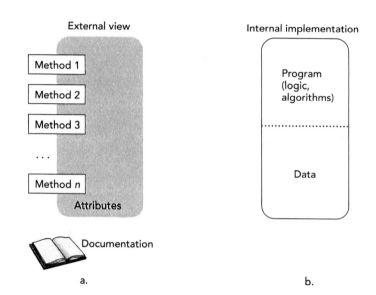

Figure 10.2 (a) External and (b) internal views of a software object

EXAMPLE: *An object mirroring a bank account will contain data representing attributes such as the account balance, the account number, and the customer owning the account. The actions include setting or examining customer information, reading the account balance, or making a deposit or withdrawal from the account. Setting customer information might be handled in two ways: There could be a series of methods setting customer attributes (name, address, etc.) individually, each passing data representing that attribute as a parameter. Alternatively, there might be a single method that passes a single object mirroring the customer, and that object would include all those customer attributes.*

Internally, an object consists of data managed by the object. This includes the attributes and frequently other data as well. It also includes the processing logic that implements the methods, processing the data in the object. Through encapsulation, the details of the implementation, such as how the methods work and how the data is structured, are hidden from other objects.

One object interacts with another by invoking one of the methods at its interface, providing parameters and receiving returns. This is the same approach to interaction as described in "Interfaces" on page 163.

ANALOGY: *A pocket calculator provides an example of a physical entity. It provides a set of actions: add, subtract, multiply, divide, and clear. Each action is accompanied by a set of parameters, which are typically a pair of numbers to add, subtract, multiply, or divide. Each action has a return value, which is the result of the arithmetic operation, and appears on the calculator's display. A software object mirroring the pocket calculator will be considered shortly.*

In OOP, every module in an application architecture is an object that interacts with other objects. This means many things that you might not think of as having "actions" must be cast into this form. The only way to interact with an object is through its methods, even for simple things like directly examining or modifying an attribute.

E X A M P L E : *A software object mirroring a driver's license would have the attributes such as name of the person, picture (which is a digitally represented image), address, date of birth, and license number. The way these attributes are established in the first place, or changed, is through a set of methods that change attributes. For example:*

```
set_name: new_name → status;
set_birth_date: new_birth_date → status;
```

In these methods, the returned status *simply indicates whether the action was successful or describes some exceptional condition that may have occurred.*

A method may encapsulate much behind-the-scenes processing not visible at the interface. The set_birth_date *method, beyond changing the attribute, would doubtless do error checking. For example, it would check that the month is an integer between 1 and 12, and it would check that the date is reasonable (for example, a birth date more than 130 years ago or in the future might be rejected and that fact noted in the* status *return value). The method might also cross-check the birth date against government birth records for the holder of the license to be sure it matches.*

In an interaction between two objects, the object that invokes a method of another is called the *client object*, and the object whose method is invoked is called the *server object*. These are often shortened to just client and server—terms used in computing wherever one entity takes an action in response to a request from another entity and also used to describe hosts in Chapter 5. In OOP, the request from the client takes the form of a method and parameters of that method, and the response is the returns.

Relationship of Software and Real-World Entities

The previous section used the term "mirroring" to describe the relationship of an entity in the real world and a corresponding software object. This term will now be clarified by examining more carefully that relationship. In fact, it can

Table 10.4 Relationships between software objects and the real world

Relationship	Description	Examples
Representation	Applies only to an informational entity—one that need not have a physical manifestation. Temporarily replaces that information with the expectation that the information it represents can later be recovered.	A software object can represent a customer's bank account; another can represent an invoice; another a purchase order.
Proxy	Interfaces to and acts as a surrogate for a physical entity, acting on its behalf within the software application. Proxies can also act on behalf of informational entities, such as another application.	A software object can be a proxy for a customer, gathering information and directions from that customer and offering them to other objects in the application; another can interface to a sensor (for example, a thermometer), gathering information about the environment.
Model	Predicts the behavior of a physical entity for purposes of control or coordination.	A software object can turn the past position and velocity of a train (provided by a proxy object) into a prediction of the future location; another can turn past temperatures from a blast furnace into a prediction of when the metal will melt.

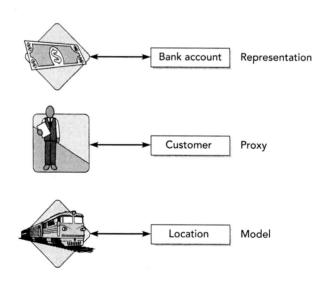

Figure 10.3 The relationship between physical or logical objects and software objects can take several forms

take several distinct forms, as listed in Table 10.4 and illustrated by example in Figure 10.3. Each of these relationships will now be discussed in more detail.

Representation Objects

Many real-world entities, especially in business applications, are informational and do not necessarily have a physical embodiment. They can, however, be represented as a physical entity, often as a printed document. These types of informational entities can also be represented by software objects. In each case, the representation is a temporary stand-in for the information.

EXAMPLE: *A bank account can be represented by a printed document (account statement) on paper or as a software object that manages information about the account balance and history of deposits and withdrawals. A unit of monetary value can be represented by cash (a coin or paper bill) or as a software object that manages information about the value and what institution stands behind that value.*

In each case, one representation can easily be turned into another. The monetary value in a software object representing a bank account can be withdrawn (turned into a software object representing monetary value) and then turned into a physical cash representation (by an ATM).

There is a fundamental difference between the physical and software object representations of an informational entity. Often a physical representation is passive—it can be examined, but it doesn't have any behavior. The software object can have behaviors, stimulated by invoking its methods. This is a powerful advantage for the software object, because it implies that it can do more than represent information—it can also manipulate that information through the data processing provided by its methods.

EXAMPLE: *A document representation of a bank account—the account statement—cannot do deposits or withdrawals. A software object representation can have a method that does a deposit and another that does a withdrawal, each at the request of another object.*

Proxy Objects

While the software object representation of an informational entity is the most common case, it is not applicable to physical entities; typically they cannot be represented in software. An example is people, who are important to many applications in roles of user, customer, worker, etc. People cannot be represented by software objects, in the sense that the software object is a stand-in for the person. Not only is it not possible for software to represent the physical presence, but it also cannot represent the consciousness or actions of a person. Nevertheless, it is common to capture the directions or insights of users in an application. This is the purpose of a *proxy object*. A proxy object interacts with the entity it is acting as a proxy for, gathering information about its actions and providing information to it, in a way that is expected by that entity. That interaction is not likely to be the standard way in which software objects interact. In the case of a software object acting as a proxy for a person, for example, the interaction might take the form of a keyboard and graphical user interface.

EXAMPLE: *In an ATM banking application, there could be a* Customer *proxy object for each customer that walks up to the ATM and engages in a transaction. This software object would be responsible for asking the customer questions (such as "what is your PIN" and "would you like to make a deposit or withdrawal") and capturing the customer's responses. This* Customer *object would then interact with the rest of the application to effect the appropriate actions as directed by the customer.*

What is the purpose or benefit of a proxy object? There are at least a couple of important purposes. First, the remainder of the application interacts with the proxy conventionally—a method invocation—rather than having to interact directly with a physical entity. This is important because physical entities interact differently from software objects. They typically do not have method invocations, but require means such as a keyboard and screen. That "unconventional" interaction is encapsulated in the proxy object and the proxy object alone. Second, proxy objects aid in the encapsulation of application implementation details from the perspective of a physical entity outside the application. Since all interaction is through the single proxy, the physical entity does not see any details of the internal architecture of the application.

EXAMPLE: *Allowing the customer of an ATM to interact directly with all relevant software objects in the application makes all those objects visible to the customer and requires that they are all cognizant of the "unconventional" ways of interacting with a customer. Each of these is undesirable in terms of the architectural principles discussed in Chapter 6.*

Modeling Objects

A third type of software object is the model. Although physical entities cannot be represented by software objects, it may be possible to predict aspects of their behavior through the application of scientific or mathematical principles. This is called a *model*. The model may be able to predict how the object behaves in the real world, but it will never replace it by performing the equivalent function.

Modeling is important in applications that have to coordinate or control physical entities. The model object and proxy object are complementary in that case—the model predicts the impact of certain control actions, and proxies interact with the physical entity to effect those actions.

EXAMPLE: *In an automated highway system, the application may control various parameters, such as traffic light timing. For this purpose, the application may model the behavior of automobiles as they pass through the traffic lights. By observing the location and speed of automobiles at one time, a modeling object for each automobile may accurately predict when that automobile will arrive at the next traffic light. A proxy object interacts with the traffic light to insure that it is green when the automobile arrives. The model and proxy objects interact (using the standard ways for software objects to interact) to coordinate two physical entities, the automobile and traffic light.*

10.2.2   Objects as Information Entities

Data can represent information, but to recover that information through data processing, the structure and interpretation of the data must be known. An object not only encapsulates data but also encapsulates knowledge of the structure and interpretation of that data. Thus, it can be argued that an object is an informational rather than data entity.

In practical terms, an object has methods that process the data it encapsulates. These methods embody the structure and interpretation of the data. This isolates interacting objects from having to be aware of the structure and interpretation of data in a software object—indeed the data is encapsulated and hidden from view—or how to process that data to extract information.

EXAMPLE: *A software object that manages an image such as that in Figure 4.2 on page 111 not only encapsulates the data representing the image, but also probably has a method that is able to display the image on the screen—in effect, turning it directly into information. Other objects don't have to know the internal image representation, which can be changed at will without impacting other objects.*

As this example suggests, the encapsulation of both data and its structure and interpretation in objects is a powerful advantage, eliminating the burden otherwise placed on other parts of the application if they had to be aware of these representations. As an architectural tool, this encapsulation enhances the separation of concerns.

10.2.3 Class

In both the physical world and networked computing, there are frequently two or more entities or objects (often *many* more) that have much in common.

EXAMPLE: *A house typically has a clock in each room, where all the clocks have the same functionality but differ only in cosmetic ways. They may also differ as to the current value of their attributes, such as displayed time (if they are set differently) or energy stored in the battery.*

A typical bank will have a large number of savings or checking accounts with the same interface (methods and attributes) and same internal implementation, and differing only in the current value of their attributes. Each account has a different owner, a different balance, a different date of last deposit, etc.

A *class* is defined as the set of characteristics shared by a set of objects. In practical terms, a set of objects that share the same interface (methods, parameters, and returns), and have the same implementation, are said to be instances of the same class. The process of creating a new object with a given class is called *instantiation*. (OOP is known for somewhat prosaic terminology.) Under identical circumstances, each instance of a given class will have identical behavior. However, each instance has likely had a different history of interaction and hence does not behave identically.

EXAMPLE: *Class* Bank_account *describes a set of objects that represent bank accounts, one instance for each customer. Each instance has been provided a different customer name and account number, and each has encountered a different history of deposits and withdrawals. Hence, presented with a new method invocation, each instance would likely behave differently.*

If a bank has customers Joe, Mary, and Sylvestor, each of whom has an account at the bank, then the application may have three objects that are instances of class Bank_account. *One of them represents Joe's* Bank_account, *so its* Customer_name *attribute is "Joe."*

In practical terms, a class has a name and includes a description of an interface and a program implementing objects in that class. The class allows a single implementation to represent all objects that are instances of that class and thus achieves software reuse. The implementation of the modules in the application architecture requires implementation of each class, not each instance.

The class plays the same role for an object as a data type plays for data. They both specify how to use or interact with the entity. The class describes what methods are available—which implicitly conveys the structure and interpretation of encapsulated data, since that is embodied in the methods—and the data type describes the structure and interpretation of the data. The interface to a class must specify the class or data type of an object or data passed as a parameter or return.

10.2.4   Visual Architecture Modeling

OOP lends itself to visual representations of objects and the pattern of interaction among objects. Similarly, a diagram can show classes and relationships among those classes. A visual modeling language provides a standard way to do this, much as building architects represent architectural features in their blueprints. Visual modeling has two major advantages:

- Programmers can communicate ideas to one another, and document their architectures, using these diagrams.
- Visual modeling tools can assist the designer in generating and manipulating these visual representations.

E X A M P L E :   *The Unified Modeling Language (UML) is a standard modeling language [Har97]. A simple example of a UML diagram is shown in Figure 10.4. This diagram displays some classes, and the relationships among these classes are represented by arrows.*

Of course, once a visual representation of the architecture is complete, each object class must be implemented and then the object instances integrated and tested before there is a working application.

10.2.5   Dealing with Legacy Systems

OOP methodologies have become popular over the past couple decades, but applications created previously used different architecture and programming methodologies. In enterprise computing, this represents a problem and a challenge, since there is a need to integrate different data and applications at the department level into applications automating business processes. It is usually not cost effective, nor even advisable, to replace all these legacy applications. In an operational system, making radical changes is both expensive and risky.

If legacy applications need to be integrated with an application that utilizes OOP, it is possible to encapsulate them within objects in the new, integrated application. Whatever interfaces were built into the legacy application can be recast as an object interface within the OOP application.

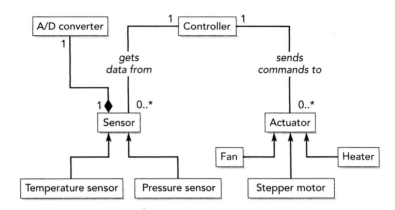

Figure 10.4 UML diagram applied to a building's climate control system

ANALOGY: *Rather than replace an old building, a cheaper and quicker approach is to renovate it. By adding a veneer of new paint, ceiling tiles, and exterior siding, the basic structural elements of the building can be preserved while making the building appear to be new.*

However, the problem of partially replacing legacy applications, or integrating them with other applications, is usually much more difficult than this analogy suggests. Here is a better one.

ANALOGY: *In trying to renovate and cosmetically tune your house, you discover that (by basic architectural concept) it will never really meet your needs. A better approach would be to tear it down and start over. Unfortunately, there is the problem of where you live in the meantime.*

Business applications, especially, must be operational at all times—the business depends on it. Changing a portion of a legacy application—or integrating it with another—is an extraordinarily difficult challenge akin to rebuilding an ocean liner while it crosses the ocean.

Discussion

D10.3 What are some disadvantages of the encapsulation of data and processing together in objects?

D10.4 If you have experience with programming using a methodology other than OOP, discuss how that methodology differs and some advantages and disadvantages of each.

10.3   Components and Frameworks

Software reuse has the objective of reducing the cost and risk of developing new applications by either adopting the architecture of similar applications, but using components shared with other applications, or both. While reuse was one of the original motivations for OOP, in practice it does not achieve much reuse because its methodology does not impose sufficient discipline. Without that discipline, which will be clarified shortly, managers and programmers must make conscious decisions to follow a disciplined process and pay the price in increased cost and delay. That conscious trade-off of long-term benefit at short-term detriment is difficult and rarely achieved.

Software components and frameworks offer hope for much greater levels of reuse. The basic idea is quite old (see the sidebar "Components, Frameworks, and the Industrial Revolution") but conceptually difficult to pull off in software because of its complexity. Nevertheless, it is worth the trouble. Some promises of component/framework technology include

- *Quality and reliability:* A component or framework used in many applications has been more thoroughly tested and has accumulated more operational experience.
- *Time to deployment or time to market:* Application development reverts to assembling components within a framework, possibly adding custom-designed components. Much of the module implementation is avoided.
- *Low cost:* Components and frameworks benefit from being employed in multiple applications, over which their development cost can be amortized.
- *Flexibility:* Components can be upgraded or replaced, or their assembly modified, to upgrade the application.
- *Competition:* In a market for components, different vendors will compete within each component category, increasing quality and reducing prices. The ability to mix and match components may reduce customer lock-in, as described in "Lock-in" on page 238.

10.3.1   Software Components

Software components are reusable modules assembled to construct an application. Components (as well as frameworks) are usually developed, maintained, and supported by an outside vendor, as a separate business opportunity. The costs of creation and maintenance are amortized across many uses, justifying the additional cost of the more disciplined development process required to make them truly reusable. Purchased as a product, they have to be accepted as is, although they may be highly configurable. The application developer may

Components, Frameworks, and the Industrial Revolution

The idea of components and frameworks for the physical world dates to the industrial revolution. Before that, products were handcrafted, meaning each instance of the product was individually fabricated by a craftsman. One innovation leading to the industrial revolution was standardized, interchangeable components.

EXAMPLE: *A particular automobile is a standard assembly of components (motor, steering wheel, axle, etc.) glued together by a standard framework (steel frame and shell). To put out a new model, the designer may minimize effort by making a modification to an existing framework and adding new sheet metal. The manufacturer also uses many of the same components for different cars. Much of the new car design is reused from the older design.*

Standardized components in a reusable framework led to remarkable increases in efficiency:

- The effort required to generate a new design is dramatically reduced.
- There is a natural decomposition into component and system manufacturers. Each is more specialized, which separates their concerns and improves their individual performance.
- Production of a large number of nominally identical components can be automated, increasing productivity and achieving higher economies of scale.

In computing and networking equipment, integrated circuit components

purchase or license components from a number of vendors and assemble them into an application together with custom-designed modules.

EXAMPLE: *An example of a software component is an editor. Many desktop applications require editors of different types, for example, text editors, drawing editors, and organization chart editors. Even simple forms entry (as in a Web browser) requires an editor. Rather than developing custom editors for each application, it makes sense to develop editor components for each medium (text, drawing, and organization chart) and assemble them into many applications.*

How does a component differ from an object [Szy98]? A primary difference is that since a component does not arise from decomposition of a specific, single application, it is harder to anticipate what other components it may have to interact with, including components from other vendors. This requires a considerably more disciplined approach to defining the ways in which components interact. Another challenge is that the purchaser of a component, unlike an object, will not have access to its internal implementation, that being the proprietary intellectual property of a vendor. Encapsulation must be practiced much more dogmatically with components than with objects. Components should reduce the programming skill level required of application developers (component assemblers), while concentrating the skilled programmers in component implementation. Finally, OOP may or may not be used to develop a component, and if OOP is used, a component may be hierarchically decomposed into multiple objects.

Components are not just a different style of programming; they represent a different industrial organization (see the sidebar "Components, Frameworks, and the Industrial Revolution"). Components move away from vertical integration, as applications are no longer developed monolithically but assembled from components provided by outside suppliers. Earlier examples of this include the DBMS (see Chapter 15), and the long-standing tradition of buying rather than making infrastructure software (principally the operating system and networking software).

Some detailed characteristics of components are listed in Table 10.5 together with analogies from the industrial or work world.

The standards and metadata have the greatest opportunities and challenges. Mixing and matching components from different vendors demands standardization. Metadata allows components to discover the useful services (methods, parameters, and returns) of other components, allowing them to adapt to one another. This capability makes it easier to envision different components inter-

Table 10.5 Characteristics of software components [Kri98]

Characteristic	Description	Analogy
Modifiable	Components can be modified as they are incorporated into an application, without access to their implementation.	Parts bought from a vendor can be machined to change their characteristics prior to assembly.
Events	Components respond to action requests (through a method invocation) and also can issue notifications of changes in selected attributes. Other components can subscribe to these notifications.	An assistant might be prepared to interrupt your meeting if an important call comes in. You indicate to your assistant what calls require notification.
Standards	Components adhere to predefined component standards.	Interchangeable parts like screws and nuts can work together, even if they come from different vendors, but only if they adhere to standards of diameter, thread dimensions, etc.
Metadata	Components can describe themselves so that other components can discover how to interoperate with them.	Parts bought from a vendor are accompanied by paper documentation of their features.
Hierarchy	Two or more components can be assembled to form a larger-grain component. A component can be assembled from other components.	An engine is a component of a car, but is itself an assemblage of components (pistons, gears, etc.).

are also assembled in frameworks (printed circuit boards). Until recently, software has been mostly hand-crafted, but software components and frameworks will change that.

acting properly without that specific interaction having been anticipated in their design.

Designing Components

In the component model, the programming task is split into two parts. The first is the implementation of the components themselves, and the second is the assembly of components into applications. These two tasks require different approaches. Component implementation uses a *systems programming language* that allows the programmer to directly express algorithms and data structures, starting from the computer's basic capabilities (see Chapter 11). Most widely used systems programming languages today are object-oriented. They allow the programmer to specify the interfaces and implementation of object classes, instantiate objects, prevent any violation of encapsulation, etc. Programming in such languages requires considerable skill and patience.

Scripting and Visual Assembly

Component assembly should require less effort and less sophisticated programming skills than implementing objects or components. Approaches include visual and scripting assembly. An environment for component assembly, as well as modification of components or implementation of new components, is called an *integrated development environment* (IDE).

EXAMPLE: *A number of software companies are marketing IDEs, including Microsoft's Visual Studio, IBM's VisualAge for Java, and Symantec's VisualCafe.*

In *visual assembly*, the components are displayed on the programmer's screen graphically, including displays of metadata, documentation, and configuration. The programmer assembles components by dragging and dropping visual icons representing them. A visual language for components is similar to the UML for objects described earlier in this chapter.

ANALOGY: *A building architect specifies the assemblage of components such as bricks, sinks, windows, etc. The architect specifies their arrangement and interaction by a blueprint, which is analogous to a visual programming language. The design and detailed specification of the components are left to their individual manufacturers, in a process analogous to systems programming.*

Scripting assembly uses a textual scripting language specifically designed for gluing components together [Ous98]. The most popular scripting languages are Visual Basic on the desktop and Tcl, Perl, and JavaScript in the server. Languages, including scripting, are covered in more detail in Chapter 11.

10.3.2   Software Frameworks

Assembling components is still considerable work, because the developer must learn about available components, make choices, and do integration (including testing). There remains the need to create an architecture that meets application needs by deciding what components are to be assembled and how they are to interact.

Frameworks allow an application to be developed with much less effort by providing a preexisting architecture as well as components within that architecture. A framework can be thought of as a prepackaged application that can be both customized and extended.

ANALOGY: *Legos come in a set of components that can be combined in different ways. It is not a framework, because the burden is on a child to decide what to build and how to combine the components to achieve that end. A Barbie doll is more like a framework. Barbie can be dressed up in different ways, but Barbie is still basically Barbie no matter how she is dressed. The ways in which*

Barbie's components are combined is predetermined, but there is some freedom to mix and match components (blouses, shoes, for example).

Frameworks generally allow modification or extension of components or the framework itself, as well as the addition of custom components.

Example: Compound Document

The *compound document* is a successful framework allowing a number of components to share a common document window, including two competing standards—OpenDoc and Object Linking and Embedding (OLE).

Before the compound document, each window in the graphical user interface was managed by a single application, such as a spreadsheet, word processor, or drawing editor. Data could be cut and pasted from one window to another, but once pasted it couldn't be modified. As a result, applications were driven toward more and more features, with duplication of some of those features among applications.

In contrast, a compound document splits a window into arbitrary areas, each managed by a different component. When the user interacts with a specific area, for example, by clicking in it with the mouse, the controlling component is notified (through an event) by the framework and manages that interaction. Special menu items corresponding to the currently active component are also displayed. This allows limited-functionality components to share a window and different full-functionality applications to be assembled from these components.

E X A M P L E :   *In Figure 10.5, a presentation graphics editor, an organization chart, and clip art share a window. Also included is a bitmap picture not managed by a component. Areas controlled by components may overlap, but the framework insures that only one component (the foreground object) is presented to the screen.*

Discussion

D10.5 Discuss the future of the software component industry. What are some opportunities, and what are some obstacles? Why has it taken so long to get going?

D10.6 Some say that software components will reduce the importance of programming in application development. Do you believe this?

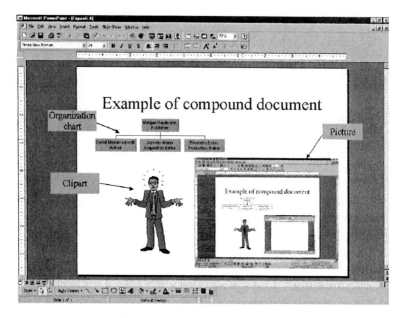

Figure 10.5 Example of a compound document

Review

The complexity of a system increases as the number of interacting modules and the complications of those interactions increases. Complexity is one major consideration in the design of the architecture and management of the development process.

A software application can be acquired by purchasing a product (also called commercial off-the shelf, or COTS), through internal development, or through outsourced development. Outsourced development can be under a fixed-price or time-and-materials contract.

In practice, applications are acquired with a mixture of decomposition (design modules and do a custom implementation and integration) and assembly (purchase modules and integrate them). Object-oriented programming supports decomposition, and component-oriented programming supports assembly. A large-grain component commonly assembled into applications is a database management system (DBMS).

A key architectural choice is the partitioning and replication of data, and the relationship between processing and data. Two diametrically opposite approaches are tightly coupled processing and data (as in object-oriented programming) and loosely coupled processing and data (as in the DBMS).

Objects are the smallest granularity modules in an object-oriented programming methodology. They have a well-documented interface with methods and
attributes. Class is what is in common among a group of objects. All objects
sharing an identical interface and implementation are instances of the same
class.

Objects can be used to model (predict the behavior of) physical entities or represent (take the place of) logical real-world entities. Objects can also serve as a
proxy for a physical entity, such as a person or a sensor, gathering information
from the entity and presenting it to other objects in the application.

A component is a module purchased from another vendor and intended to be
used in a variety of applications.

Key Concepts

Decomposition versus assembly

Location of data and processing:

● Data partitioning and replication

Data as an asset:

● Database management system (DBMS)

Object-oriented programming:

● Object: attribute, method, interface
● Modeling, representation proxy
● Class: instance and instantiation

Component-oriented programming:

● Scripting and visual assembly

Frameworks

Further Reading

The definitive references on software objects and components are [Boo94] and
[Szy98]. Many business and nontechnical issues are also covered in [Szy98]. Both
these books are long and detailed, but well written, accessible, and highly recommended. Although both books discuss the application software development process, a more detailed treatise on application architecture and the
application lifecycle is [BCK97]. [JGJ97] discusses software architecture in the
context of achieving reuse.

Exercises

E10.1 What are examples of design by decomposition and by assembly for each of the following product categories?

    a. Restaurant meals

    b. Interior decoration of a house

E10.2 For any two of the following, describe the application context in which data is acquired, the context in which that data is processed and a bit about the nature of that processing, and the context in which it is presented as information to the user:

    a. The customer-care application of "Customer Care" on page 63

    b. The on-line book merchant application of "On-Line Bookselling" on page 66

    c. The on-line stock trading application of "On-Line Stock Trading" on page 68

    d. The on-line floral delivery service of "Floral Delivery Service" on page 69

E10.3 For each of the following, describe any data that you believe should be considered an asset managed separately from the specific application, either because it may outlive the application or may need to be shared with other applications. State your reasons.

    a. The on-line book merchant application of "On-Line Bookselling" on page 66

    b. The on-line floral delivery service of "Floral Delivery Service" on page 69

E10.4 Give two examples of each of the following:

    a. An informational entity in the real world, outside a networked application

    b. A physical entity in the real world

E10.5 For each of the following ideas, give two examples of physical entities in the real world that illustrate the idea:

    a. Attributes that are made available for examination but not modification to the outside world

    b. Attributes that are both made available for examination and subject to modification by the outside world

   c. Attributes that govern the future behavior, but are encapsulated—not made available for examination or modification

   d. Behavior

   e. Ways to interact with an entity that are analogous to methods

   f. Interfaces for interaction with other entities that are well known and specified

   g. Analogies to the class for physical-world entities

   h. Multiple instances of a given class

   i. Instances that interact with other instances of the same class

   j. Instances that interact with instances of different classes

E10.6 Repeat Exercise 10.5 for informational entities in the real world, outside a networked application.

E10.7 For each of the following ideas, give two additional examples from specific applications (examples not mentioned in the chapter). Briefly describe how the example works within that application context.

   a. A software object that is a representation of an informational entity

   b. A software object that is a proxy for a physical entity

   c. A software object that is a proxy for an informational entity

   d. A software object that is a model of a physical entity

   e. A model object and a proxy object that could interact to control one or more physical-world entities

E10.8 Which classes shown in Figure 10.4 on page 314 do you think are likely to

   a. Be a proxy object mirroring a real-world object

   b. Be a representation object mirroring the real world

   c. Be a model object mirroring the real world

   d. Have no direct relationship to the real world

E10.9 For any two of the following contexts, define a set of three to five software components that you believe will be useful in a diversity of applications. Briefly describe each of these components in terms of their attributes and methods.

a. Relating to students in a university

b. Relating to employees in a company

c. Relating to customers of a stockbroker

d. Relating to financial instruments

Programming an Application

Once the architecture of an application is determined—including basic decisions about where data is acquired, processed, and presented and what components are purchased and subsystems developed—the next phase is the implementation of those subsystems that are not purchased off-the-shelf, followed by subsystem integration. This chapter concerns the implementation phase, which is the creation of software in the form of a *computer program*. The program is the means by which the programmer tells the computer precisely what to do and how to communicate the results back to users.

The computer embodies many ideas, but the most powerful is programmability: Unlike earlier products, the functionality of a computer isn't determined at the time of manufacture, but is determined later by the software that is added. This makes the computer almost infinitely extensible. What can be accomplished with a computer is limited primarily by the programmer's imagination—and pragmatic constraints such as complexity and cost—rather than physical limitations.

This chapter considers some programming issues. The notions of algorithm and protocol discussed in the first section and the ways of locating things in the second section play fundamental roles in several of the following chapters.

11.1 Algorithms, Protocols, and Policies

Modules that interact correctly to achieve the higher-level system goals are said to be interoperable.

EXAMPLE: *The communication software and a modem connected to the computer are interoperable if the software is able to successfully establish a data connection and communicate data remotely using that modem. The interoperable client and server partitions of an application work correctly together. Interoperable objects interact to correctly achieve an emergent function.*

Interoperability is enabled by four elements—algorithms, protocols, formats, and policies—defined in Table 11.1. Protocols and policies govern the steps the modules follow to work together, algorithms work internally to the modules to realize the required behavior, and formats govern the interpretation of communications between the modules.

EXAMPLE: *Traffic signals coordinate drivers by establishing a protocol that prevents two cars from occupying the same space at the same time. The protocol is accompanied by policies (laws) that require drivers to follow the protocol. Drivers also follow the protocol that they drive on the right (or left) side of the road to prevent head-on collisions, again backed by policies.*

Within an application with a common administration, where all modules are considered benign and trustworthy, policies do not play a major role. Adherence to the established protocols is a given. On the other hand, in an application with uncoordinated elements, particularly in consumer electronic commerce where the entire citizenry is able to participate, it cannot be assumed that all modules follow established protocols. There may be adversaries deliberately violating established protocols for nefarious or harmful purposes. For this reason, policies and the enforcement of those policies are an important element of security measures, which attempt to counter these threats. Security is discussed in Chapter 13.

For every situation that arises, an algorithm or protocol must specify a well-defined action; it is not acceptable to "give up." Because there are usually many different feasible scenarios, algorithms and protocols can be quite complicated. In fact, considerable design effort is devoted to dealing with the exceptional or unusual situations that seldom occur.

EXAMPLE: *A slightly more complicated protocol coordinates you and your mailperson. To send a letter, you put it in your mailbox and raise the flag (otherwise the flag is down). The mailperson opens the mailbox and removes the letter if the flag is up. In any case, the mailperson puts incoming mail in the mailbox. If the flag is down and there is no incoming mail, the mailperson doesn't open the mailbox at all. The protocol is accompanied by policies, such as "nobody but the mailperson or owner can put items in or take items out of the mailbox."*

Table 11.1 Four elements critical to achieving interoperability among interacting modules

Element	Description	Example
Algorithm	A sequence of predefined steps designed to accomplish a specific task. A single computer program realizes an algorithm. Each module internally uses an algorithm that determines its contribution to a protocol, as well as other behavior.	A taxpayer follows a specified set of steps to fill out tax forms, such as "to determine the tax, if your adjusted gross income (AGI) is more than $20,000, take 10% of the AGI. If the AGI is less than $40,000, take $2,000 plus 15% of the difference of the AGI and $20,000."
Protocol	An algorithm performed cooperatively by two or more interacting modules, consisting of a sequence of communications from one module to another. The protocol coordinates the behavior of the modules to achieve interoperability.	A taxpayer and the government tax agency cooperatively follow a protocol. For example, the taxpayer fills out forms and mails them with a check, and the agency returns a check if there is a refund or sends notification of tax due, and the taxpayer returns that with a check.
Format	Each communication in a protocol includes information needed by the recipient module represented as data. The format defines the structure and interpretation of that data (see "Data and Information in Layers" on page 176).	The tax form and check sent by the taxpayer each have predefined formats.
Policy	A specific set of allowed and/or disallowed behaviors. The most fundamental policy is that interacting modules must follow the predefined protocol.	A taxpayer with income is required to file a tax return, and pay taxes due, by a certain date. The agency is required to treat all taxpayers equally.

11.1.1   Algorithms and Flowcharts

It is common to present simple algorithms in a *flowchart*, which visually displays the steps in the algorithm, with arrows indicating the order in which they are executed.

E X A M P L E : *A simplified algorithm engaged in by one player of the board game Monopoly is shown in Figure 11.1. It specifies the set of steps that a player must follow in one turn. You can easily imagine a computer program that plays Monopoly and follows an identical set of rules.*

An important aspect of algorithms is conditional steps (represented by a triangular box in a flowchart) where the next step differs depending on the result of a decision or test. The algorithm does not follow the same sequence of steps each time it is executed, but rather the actual sequence differs depending on

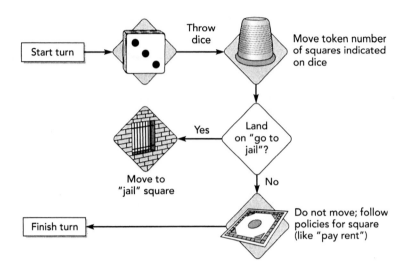

Figure 11.1 Flowchart of the algorithm for one player in one turn of Monopoly [Oak96]

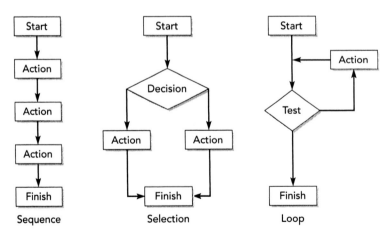

Figure 11.2 Three building blocks for algorithms

those decisions or tests. Three building blocks for algorithms are shown in Figure 11.2. The *sequence* gives a sequence of steps that are always followed in the same order. The *selection* allows the sequence of steps to be modified based on a decision, and the *loop* allows steps to be repeated over and over until some test terminates those steps.

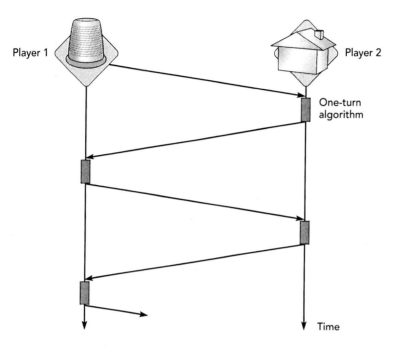

Figure 11.3 Protocol interaction diagram showing the protocol engaged in by two Monopoly players

11.1.2   Protocols and Interaction Diagrams

A protocol is also an algorithm, but one engaged in by two or more distinct entities. It can be represented visually by a protocol interaction diagram.

E X A M P L E :   *The protocol in Monopoly is illustrated by an interaction diagram in Figure 11.3. The protocol in this case is extremely simple—it alternates from one player to the other, with each player executing the one-turn algorithm of Figure 11.1.*

The interaction diagram shows (by horizontal arrows) the interactions that occur between the entities and, by the passage of time (from top to bottom), the order in which those interactions occur. An important point to note about the example in Figure 11.3 is that the algorithm that each player engages in on one turn is complementary to the protocol. In particular, at the end of each turn, each player cedes control to the other player, and that player begins executing his algorithm.

In Chapter 6, the protocol was described as a prescribed sequence of interactions among modules. While this definition is correct, it is incomplete because it fails to capture the characteristic that the sequence of steps is not always the same—it depends on circumstances. Like the selection and loop constructs in an algorithm, the protocol can take different paths depending on a decision or test.

EXAMPLE: *In the stock trading application stocks4u.com in "On-Line Stock Trading" on page 68, in the case of a customer order to purchase a stock at a price no higher than some limit, the host in stocks4u.com may interact repeatedly with the stock exchange to inquire about the current price. The first time the price is below the limit—but not on any previous inquiry—stocks4u.com then follows up by submitting a buy order and makes no further price inquiries. This is an example of the test-and-loop algorithm illustrated in Figure 11.2. The number of times the price inquiry is made depends on the outcome of those inquiries.*

Protocols, formats, and policies are complementary, as they together govern module interaction. The standardization of interfaces focuses on these three aspects. To achieve interoperability, modules must know the details of all relevant protocols, formats, and policies and correctly implement them in internal algorithms. The implementers of modules then define encapsulated algorithms that correctly realize the protocols and formats.

11.1.3   Three Common Protocols

Three simple but very common protocols executed between a client module and a server module are listed in Table 11.2 and illustrated by an interaction diagram in Figure 11.4. The *request-response protocol* is the type of interaction between modules described in Chapter 6 and is manifested specifically in the object method invocation described in Chapter 10. The *send-receive protocol* is a simpler variation in which no response is expected, and the *publish-subscribe protocol* is a more complicated variation in which the number of responses is not known in advance. It may range from zero to many, and the responses are not immediate but occur at times determined by circumstances and not knowable in advance.

EXAMPLE: *The protocol between stocks4u.com and the stock exchange as described in the previous example uses a repeated set of request-response interactions to track the price of a security. A simpler approach from the perspective of stocks4u.com would be to use a publish-subscribe protocol instead. Stocks4u.com would submit a single subscription to "tell me the first time the price of the stock drops below this limit," and it would hope for (but not count on) a single response.*

Table 11.2 Three simple but widely used protocols

Protocol	Description	Common application	Analogy
Send-receive	One module sends a message to another, which receives it.	Inform or direct another module.	Send a letter or email to a friend.
Request-response	One module (the *client*) sends a *request* to another module (the *server*), and the server returns an immediate *response*.	Obtain *information* or a *service* from another module. Forms the basis of client-server computing (see Chapter 5).	Send an order form to a catalog retailer, expecting to receive goods by return post.
Publish-subscribe	One module (the *subscriber*) sends a *subscription* to another module (the *publisher*), and the publisher returns responses. Neither the number or time of the responses is known in advance.	Can be used to obtain information on an ongoing basis with a single subscription. Can also be used to obtain notification of a single event.	Send subscription order to a magazine, receive back multiple issues; request notification of a bounced check from the bank.

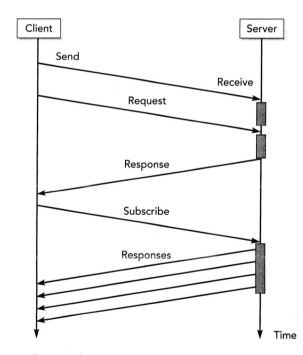

Figure 11.4 Three simple protocols widely used in applications

The Hypertext Transfer Protocol (HTTP)

HTTP is a request-response protocol that governs the interaction of a Web browser (the client) and a Web server (see "World Wide Web" on page 36). The four basic steps are shown in Figure 11.5. The request is initiated by the user clicking on a hyperlink. The most common request is for an HTML or XML document (see Chapter 15), which is returned to the browser and displayed.

A hyperlink is a highlighted piece of text associated with a *uniform resource locator* (URL). The URL has three parts representing the protocol (in this case HTTP), the name of the host desired, and the name of the desired document on that host.

E X A M P L E :   *A typical URL is* http://www.sims.berkeley.edu/ index.html, *where* http *denotes the protocol,* www.sims.berkeley.edu *is the name of the host, and* index.html *is the name of the HTML document requested.*

The request has a defined format that includes a *directive*, which is a description of the capability of the client and the resource that is desired. The "client capability" is a description of what types of data the browser can display (including using "helper" applications), which helps the server satisfy the request. The response format includes a status indication, a description of the document it is returning, and the document itself.

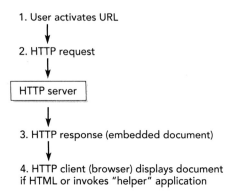

1. User activates URL

2. HTTP request

HTTP server

3. HTTP response (embedded document)

4. HTTP client (browser) displays document if HTML or invokes "helper" application

Figure 11.5 The HTTP protocol that forms the foundation of the Web

In the customer-care application of "Customer Care" on page 63, after gathering the information from a customer about a problem, the service agent stores the information in a database and then notifies the technical service department of that problem. No immediate response is expected of technical service, so a send-receive protocol can be used.

As this example suggests, all three simple protocols are widely used in applications. The send-receive protocol is most appropriate for workflow applications, where work requests are simply forwarded to the applicable group or individual. The request-response protocol is useful to make a request for information or service and expect a single response with the results of that request. A publish-subscribe protocol is most useful for requests to be informed about some event or events of interest, without the trouble of making repeated requests.

For all these protocols, interoperability requires that each message, request, response, and subscription have a defined format understood by the recipient. Each protocol supports a different type of interaction. HTTP, the basis of the Web, uses a request-response protocol (see the sidebar "The Hypertext Transfer Protocol (HTTP)"). The publish-subscribe protocol is the most complex, as the number and timing of responses are determined by circumstances. It often requires a prior *discovery*, where the subscriber determines that there is an appropriate publisher to which to subscribe. There may also be an *unsubscribe* defined in the protocol to stop the flow of responses.

Discussion

D11.1 **In the context of a classroom, are any algorithms used? Protocols? Policies?**

D11.2 Discuss the relationship of protocols as defined in computing and as used in diplomacy.

11.2   Locating Things

Aside from how modules interact, another important issue in application programming is locating things. An application may be partitioned across two or more hosts, so that some interactions among modules are internal to a host, and some are external. In order to interact with a server, a client must first locate it. This is a general issue in networked computing—there has to be some way of locating any entity for the purpose of interacting with it. For example, to send a message to a user, you must specify who the user is or where she can be found.

The problem is actually split into two pieces:

- A client somehow specifies the location of a server to the infrastructure.
- Given this location information, the infrastructure takes responsibility for directing interaction to that server.

In this division of responsibility, every client does not have to know how to direct communication to servers; this is a function every client needs and is better delegated to the infrastructure. On the other hand, the client does have to indicate its intentions to the infrastructure, which can then act properly on its behalf.

There are three ways of locating something: a name, an address, and a reference. All three represent the location of a server as data, and that representation is known to both the application and the infrastructure.

A N A L O G Y :   *The name and address are in general use. Every person is given a name, which is a convenient way to locate or speak to that person. In a crowded room, yelling "Joe" allows everybody with that name to identify himself. An alternative technique is to identify someone's street address or telephone number, both of which are examples of addresses. The appellation "my mailperson" is a reference—a designation of a particular person without specifying his name, address, or even his location.*

11.2.1   Names

A *name* is an arbitrarily chosen and unique symbolic representation of an entity, usually chosen for the convenience of people to remember or guess. A name is usually represented by a character string.

E X A M P L E :   *Each host on the Internet has a name—called its domain name—that is chosen hierarchically according to administrative domains. For example,*

Name Services

Although they all uniquely specify locations, names or references are much more appropriate than addresses for applications. From an application perspective, it is undesirable to have to worry about the topological location of a module; that is best left to the infrastructure. On the other hand, an address is necessary for the infrastructure to actually direct interaction to a server.

To aid the application in avoiding managing addresses, the infrastructure may provide a *name service*. This is a special server that maintains a database of names and addresses. (For example, a relational database would store this information in two fields—one for name and the other for address.) Provided with a name, the name service provides the corresponding address.

A variation on name service returns a reference rather than address. This is preferable for modules that move, since that reference takes the burden of keeping track of a changing location. Mobile objects—objects that can move from one host to another— are discussed in Chapter 16, and mobile computing can result in hosts that change location as well.

`info.sims.berkeley.edu` *is the domain name of a host within the name* `info` *within a school* (`sims`) *of a university* (`berkeley.edu`).

This idea of a naming hierarchy is very common in computing and can be applied to modules within a host, or even to users having accounts on a host, as well as to hosts.

EXAMPLE: *The so-called email address of a person with an account named* `joe` *on host* `info.sims.berkeley.edu` *would be represented as* `joe@info.sims.berkeley.edu`. *The hierarchy is "a user with account name* `joe` *on host* `info` *in school* `sims` *within university* `berkeley.edu`." *The term email address is a misnomer—it is a name, not an address!*

11.2.2   Addresses

An *address*—usually represented as a number—specifies a path to reach the topological location of the entity, or it represents equivalent information from which that path can be inferred. The address can therefore be used to directly route communication or interaction to a module, since it specifies the topological location where that module or user is connected to the network.

EXAMPLE: *Each host on an Ethernet has an Ethernet address, which is a number uniquely assigned to it on the network. Each host on the Internet has an IP address—a number uniquely assigned to it and from which a path through the network to reach the host's topological connection point to the Internet can be inferred. IP addresses and finding paths through the network are discussed in Chapter 18.*

Typically, applications are not required to deal directly with addresses, which can be obtained from names (see the sidebar "Name Services").

11.2.3   References

The *reference* abstracts the location of a module, enabling another to interact with it without explicitly keeping track of either its name or its address. A reference is especially valuable to interact with something that is changing location, since the reference itself keeps track of the location, removing a burden from the client.

EXAMPLE: *The telephone number of a "wired" phone is an address, because it specifies the topological point of connection of the telephone to the telephone network. The telephone number of a cellular phone is a reference, because the*

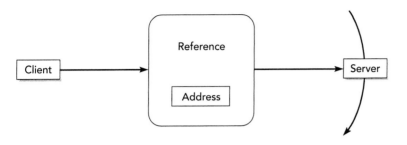

Figure 11.6 A reference keeps track of the address of a server, allowing the client to interact with it without knowing its location

> *topological point of connection may move, but the phone number nevertheless locates it. In that case, the telephone network keeps track of where the phone accesses the network and automatically redirects calls to that point.*

A reference can be thought of as a replacement or stand-in for purposes of interaction, as illustrated in Figure 11.6. A client interacts with the reference rather than the server it represents. Behind the scenes, the reference internally keeps track of the address of the server—even if it changes location—and thus can redirect interaction to the actual server's location.

A module must have a single address at any given time but can have more than one name (called *aliases*) or more than one reference, as long as they all resolve to a single address.

11.3 *Programs and Languages

The implementation of system modules is mostly a matter of programming. The computer program is a representation of the programmer's detailed instructions to a computer. A program is written in a systems programming language, intended to be transparent to the programmer and also meaningful to the computer. The remaining aspects of system implementation include the integration of modules and testing, as described in "Application Lifecycle" on page 279. As another illustration of network externalities, at any given time there needs to be only one or two dominant programming languages (see the sidebar "Dominant Programming Languages").

One way to understand programming better is to examine the analogy to writing a creative novel, with programming analogous to the actual writing phase— putting words to paper and editing them—as described in Table 11.3. An important distinction between writing a novel and programming is that any reasonably sized application typically requires a large collaborative team of

Dominant Programming Languages

Programming languages exhibit indirect network effects. A language that is widely used has considerable advantages because of reduced training costs and the availability of experienced programmers, good programming tools, and libraries of already implemented modules.

There is usually competition among vendors in providing compilers, interpreters, and toolkits for any given language. While it is possible to obtain intellectual property protection of languages, due to these network effects, languages that are highly successful are generally those that are not so encumbered. Java is an interesting case study discussed further in Chapter 16.

In spite of these winner-take-all effects, the popularity of a programming language does wane quickly, to be replaced by a new dominant language. This is currently happening in OOP, from C++ to Java. The advantages of a new language must be compelling, making programmers enthused to learn it. Vendors of new languages make sure they are compatible, in the sense that modules written in different languages can be mixed within any given application.

Table 11.3 Analogy between writing a creative novel and programming an application

Lifecycle stage	Writing a novel	Programming an application
Conceptualization	Brainstorm on possible contexts and plots for the novel and develop a coherent theme.	Brainstorm on the possible benefits of the application and develop coherent goals and outcomes.
Analysis	Study the historical context for the proposed theme, and refine the major characters, plot twists, and outcomes.	Study the application context in depth, and develop detailed scenarios.
Architecture	Develop detailed storylines, including minor twists and turns of the plot and the relationship of characters.	Develop the decomposition of the application into modules, and establish the functionality and interaction of those modules.
Development	Commit the actual words to paper.	Write the actual program, implementing individual modules, and integrate those modules.
Testing	Run the spell and grammar checker. Have friends read the manuscript and suggest ways it can be more compelling. Have editors proofread the manuscript and point out flaws and inconsistencies in plot as well as typographical errors.	Execute the application in its context, and check that the various features work as intended.
Deployment	Produce, publish, and sell the novel.	Purchase and integrate the equipment and software, train workers, and make a transition from the previous process.

programmers, while a solitary author might write a novel. Thus, contrary to popular perception, programming is a distinctly social activity. Also contrary to popular perception, programming is at the same time logical and creative, again like writing.

11.3.1   Imperative vs. Declarative Languages

English and other human languages are not very suitable for communicating instructions to a computer for several reasons. These languages have considerable ambiguity and require a shared context, both of which confound the computer. They are also not as adept at describing the precise algorithmic nature of what the computer excels at as are languages defined for this specific purpose.

Early *imperative* computer languages were tied to the needs of the computer, specifying primitive actions (such as add or multiply) that a computer can follow almost directly. Tied closely to how the computer itself works, imperative languages are inadequate for programming large, complex applications. Modern *declarative* languages directly express appropriate abstractions for the problem domain, with less regard for the immediate needs of the computer. These are also called high-level languages.

EXAMPLE: *An instruction booklet from the income tax authority is written in an imperative style. For example, it reads, "add up all sources of dividends and interest and enter on line 10, then add line 9a and line 9b and enter on line 11," etc. "Interview-style" programs (such as TurboTax) are declarative, asking direct questions like "Did you have any consulting income this year? Did you have any medical expenses this year?" If your answer is yes, you proceed to a series of related questions, or if no, you skip to the next category of income or deduction. This interview program then translates your answers into the imperative style the tax authority demands.*

There is really only one practical way to program a large application, and that is to use a high-level language. If the program project exploits object-oriented programming, then the language should specifically support this methodology.

11.3.2 Object-Oriented Programming Language

Systems programming languages that are object-oriented provide language support for object interfaces (methods and attributes) and the instantiation of classes and interaction among the resulting objects, and they enforce encapsulation.

Recall that an object encapsulates data together with methods that process that data. The first task in object implementation is to describe the structure of data stored in objects and passed as parameters and return values at the object interface, by specifying the name and data type for each data element. Systems programming languages support basic and user-defined data types—the latter by assembling basic types with other user-defined types. Then an OOP systems programming language enables detailed specification of the processing of data (computation and logic) in the implementation of each method. Primary tools are conditional and control statements specifying algorithms, including the specific building blocks illustrated by the flowcharts in Figure 11.2 on page 328.

ANALOGY: *The data types and algorithm have analogies in cooking. A recipe (analogous to a program) for spaghetti starts with a description of the ingredients, such as the flour, the tomatoes, etc. (analogous to basic data types). It specifies more complicated "user-defined" ingredients such as noodles. It also specifies the specific steps in preparing spaghetti—such as "roll the dough,"*

Other Programming Issues

Programming languages must deal with a number of issues. *Memory management* allocates memory resources (allocated by the operating system from a central pool) to house data created and manipulated in a program. Memory has to be returned to the central pool when no longer used (called, humorously, *garbage collection*).

It is advisable to always check for exceptional (unanticipated) conditions whenever performing any operation (for example, attempting to divide by zero). *Exceptions* are a mechanism to deal with such circumstances systematically.

Many programs perform concurrent (overlapped in time) tasks. This raises many issues that can be addressed by a programming language. For example, critical sections of code are allowed to be executed to completion without conflict with concurrent tasks. Issues related to concurrency are discussed in Chapter 17.

"cut the noodles," "boil the noodles," etc. (analogous to an algorithm). These steps specify what the cook does, and in what order, including the decisions that have to be made and the impact of those decisions.

11.3.3   Scripting vs. Systems Programming Languages

Some systems programming languages play the dual role of implementing modules and specifying the patterns of interconnection and interaction of modules. This is generally true of OOP languages such as Java and C++. However, it is also possible to use different languages for the two purposes. This is especially true for the component-oriented programming discussed in "Components and Frameworks" on page 315, because the component implementation is separated from the assembly and integration of the components. Thus, integrated development environments for components usually provide ways to assemble and integrate components, including both scripting and visual representations.

11.3.4   Program Execution

The representation of a program authored by the programmer (the *source code*) is quite different from the representation required for execution in the computer (an *executable*). The former is a textual or visual representation that is easily comprehended and manipulated by people, and the latter is represented as a series of elemental steps that directly control the processor hardware. A translation from source code to executable is required. There are two basic ways of doing this—*compilation* and *interpretation*—described in Table 11.4. This is not an either/or distinction—for example, Java utilizes a combination (see Chapter 16). It is typical for systems programming languages to be compiled and scripting languages to be interpreted [Ous98].

Discussion

D11.3 Discuss the distinctions between data as a representation of information, and a program as a representation of data processing. What are the similar and differing needs in these two cases?

D11.4 As discussed in "Critical Societal Infrastructure" on page 96, it is becoming increasingly difficult to separate a networked application from other aspects of a critical system, such as the organization of workers, materials, and goods. How do you think this can be addressed? Should programmers learn more about the application environment? Should organizational specialists learn more about programming?

Table 11.4 Program compilation vs. interpretation

Mode	Method	Analogy
Compilation	A one-time translation of the source code into an executable. Later, that executable can execute on one or more computers as many times as desired.	A book is translated from German to English once. The English edition is published in multiple copies, to be read many times in that representation.
Interpretation	Translation of the source code on the fly, as it is executing. The translation is repeated each and every time the program executes.	A speech in German in the United Nations is translated into English as it is being made. An English speaker listens to the translation simultaneously with the original speech.

Review

An algorithm is a sequence of steps for accomplishing a given goal, a protocol is a distributed algorithm that serves to coordinate two or more entities, a format is a specified structure of interpretation of the constituent messages, and a policy is a definition of allowed and prohibited actions and behaviors. Simple algorithms can be represented visually by flowcharts, and protocols by interaction diagrams. Standardization of module interfaces focuses on protocols, formats, and policies, and implementers of modules focus on algorithms realizing that interface. Simple but widely used protocols are the send-receive, request-response, and publish-subscribe.

Entities can be located by name, address, or reference. A reference stores an address internally and redirects interaction with the reference to the entity being referenced. Objects usually locate one another by reference.

Programming languages allow the programmer to express instructions to the computer. Imperative languages are directly tied to the computer itself, whereas declarative languages express abstractions from the application context. Systems programming languages are used to implement modules (object classes in the case of OOP languages), whereas scripting languages can be used to compose modules. Programs can be compiled once and executed many times, or interpreted each time a program is executed.

Although the method invocation directly supports a request-response protocol, simpler or more complex protocols can be realized using the message. Common examples include the send-receive (message) and publish-subscribe (event notification).

Key Concepts

Interoperability:

- Algorithm
- Protocol: send-receive, request-response, publish-subscribe, session
- Policy

Location:

- Name, address, reference
- Name services

Programming languages:

- Imperative versus declarative
- Compiled versus interpreted
- Systems programming versus scripted
- Object-oriented

Further Reading

The definitive reference on OOP is [Boo94]. The management of software development projects is quite challenging. It is briefly described in Chapter 9 and is the subject of many books, including [Pre96], [You97], and [McC97].

Exercises

E11.1   Give three real-world examples of the following:

    a. Algorithms

    b. Protocols

    c. For each of your examples, do policies play a role? If so, what is their role?

E11.2   For each of the following, does it require a protocol (*distributed* algorithm coordinating two or more entities) or just an algorithm? Why?

    a. Bank customer obtaining money from an ATM

    b. Bank customer balancing his checkbook

    c. On-line customer purchasing a book

    d. Professor setting grades for students in her class

E11.3   Using a flowchart, specify an algorithm for any two of the following. Feel free to use any of the basic algorithm building blocks shown in Figure

11.2 on page 328. Construct the easiest algorithm that works—don't be concerned with efficiency.

    a. Calculate the sum of the first 1,000 non-zero integers.

    b. Search a list of student names in a class to determine whether a particular last name is on the list.

    c. Starting with an alphabetized list of students in a class with grades A, B, C, D, and F, reorder that list from highest grade to lowest.

E11.4 Using a protocol interaction diagram, specify a protocol for any two of the following:

    a. Two students determine whether they are the same age and, if not, which is older.

    b. Three students create a list of their names ordered by their ages.

    c. Two students collaborate on writing a project report.

E11.5 For each of the following, give three examples from the real world:

    a. A send-receive protocol

    b. A request-response protocol

    c. A publish-subscribe protocol

E11.6 Which of the three protocols listed in Exercise 11.5 do you believe is most useful and appropriate for each of the following actions? Why? If more than one would be applicable, indicate how.

    a. Determining the current time

    b. An alarm clock

    c. Informing a child it is time to leave for school

E11.7 Give three examples from the physical or information world for each of the following:

    a. Name

    b. Address

    c. Reference

    d. Name service

E11.8 A cooking recipe is sometimes used as an analogy to a computer program. Describe briefly some ways in which a recipe is similar to and differs from a program.

E11.9 For each of the following features of common desktop applications, describe how you believe they are declarative languages—express directly the elements of their intended application domain.

   a. Describing the calculation of one cell of a spreadsheet

   b. Macro language for a spreadsheet

   c. Email filtering

   d. Setting options in a Web browser

Infrastructure

The networked computing infrastructure provides many common capabilities for the benefit of all networked applications.

PART

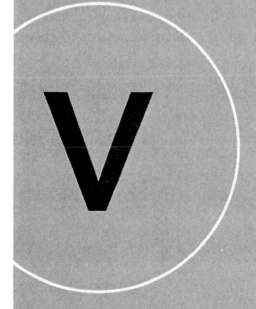

Communication Services

In networked applications, data and processing are distributed across networked hosts. For this purpose, the infrastructure and application have a layered form of modularity, as discussed in "More on Layered Infrastructure Software" on page 171. The application is layered on the infrastructure, which provides many capabilities needed by the application. The three basic types of infrastructure are processing, storage, and communication. This chapter focuses on the communications infrastructure. The storage infrastructure is the topic of Chapter 15, and the processing infrastructure is discussed in Chapter 17.

A *service* is a dynamic capability (such as communications from one host to another) provided by the infrastructure for the use and benefit of applications. Communication services are necessary for distributed application modules to interact with one another. Data must be conveyed from one application module to another as an integral part of that interaction, and it must often be conveyed in the reverse direction as well. For this purpose, the infrastructure provides a set of communication services for the benefit of applications. A single communication service cannot meet all needs, which is why there is more than one type.

ANALOGY: *In the physical world, common communications mechanisms include the postal letter, the postal letter with return receipt, the registered letter (with guaranteed delivery), and the telephone call (which supports a conversation). Each of these services meets a distinct need when supporting geographically distributed activities, such as a supplier-customer relationship.*

How does the communications infrastructure decide what services to provide? One possible goal is to hide—insofar as possible—the distributed nature of the application in order to simplify development. This means communication services among hosts should support the interaction of modules in a way that is similar to how they interact within hosts.

EXAMPLE: *The infrastructure may allow one module to invoke an action (a method in the case of an object) on another module, even though it is on a different host—this is called a remote method invocation (RMI). In fact, RMI can be realized by a communications middleware layer in the infrastructure by passing data representing the desired method and parameters in one direction and data representing the returns in the other direction. This might work as described in "A Middleware Example" on page 180.*

The infrastructure can never completely hide the distribution of an application across hosts, because the developer must consciously choose how the application is partitioned. Performance and scalability issues will also depend on this partitioning, as well as the performance characteristics of the communication services, as discussed later in Chapter 17 and Chapter 18.

Trying to hide the application host partitioning may not be the right answer in other circumstances. For example, for inter-enterprise or social applications executing across different administrative domains, use of "simpler" communication services may make sense, because they require less coordination across the infrastructure, which is also spread across administrative domains. Also, the remote action or method invocation is not the right form of interaction for many purposes, such as conveying the video or audio medium that is incorporated in a direct-immediate social application. Understanding what communication services are valuable, and how they match different application needs, is the topic of this chapter.

Different types of communication services are discussed first in generic form, so that the range of possibilities can be appreciated. Later, the specific services provided by the Internet, which fall in the same generic categories, are described. The network is the foundation of the communication services; and other functions of the network, mostly relating to its role of accommodating many simultaneous users and applications, are discussed in Chapter 18.

12.1   Generic Communication Services

As in the physical world, no single communication service is suitable for all purposes. Some communication services most useful to applications, and the role of protocols in realizing those services, will now be described.

The major generic services to be discussed in this section are summarized in Table 12.1. An application is free to choose which service it utilizes and is free to mix them within a single application as appropriate. It is important to recognize the distinction between the service as seen by the application, and the issues

Table 12.1 Some useful communication services

Service	Description	Analogy
Message	A message with a pre-agreed format is sent to another module to inform or direct. The recipient is available to receive messages at any time.	Judge Sylvia issues a subpoena to Bob, which is served on Bob in person.
Message with multiplexing and queueing	Like a message, except there can be multiple senders for a single recipient. The recipient need not be available to receive messages, but can retrieve them later, after they were sent.	Alice, Harry, and June all send postcards to Bob. The postcards languish in Bob's mailbox until he retrieves them.
Message with reply	A message is coupled with an obligatory reply, also with an agreed format. The reply may return useful information or merely confirm an action or indicate a status.	Alice mails an order for tickets to a broker, who sends them back by return mail; Alice sends a letter with return receipt requested to Bob. The return receipt confirms the letter was received.
Conversation	A sequence of messages possess a shared context. A conversation may be one-way (one module is always the sender and the other always the recipient) or two-way.	Alice telephones Bob. Each makes utterances in each direction, forming a conversation.
Broadcast	A one-way conversation in which there is a single sender and two or more (often a multiplicity) of recipients. Each recipient receives every message.	Television or radio broadcast to the public; a newspaper or magazine that sends out multiple issues.

involved in its internal implementation (see the sidebar "Abstraction of Communication Services"). In the next section some concrete services provided by the internet are described. True to form, they generally map into the categories in Table 12.1.

Application modules use protocols to govern their interaction, as described in "Algorithms, Protocols, and Policies" on page 325. The central idea of the communication services is to support specific application protocols. For this reason the protocol associated with each service is highlighted in the following.

12.1.1   Message Service

A *message* is a one-way communication of information from one module to another. The message itself simply consists of a collection of data representing that information. Receiving a partial message is of no value to the recipient; so a message service will deliver the entire message or not deliver it at all.

**Is a Message Delivered
for Sure?**

Sending a message is "open loop,"
like sending a letter. The sender does
not receive an acknowledgment that
the message was delivered. Can the
sender be sure the message arrived?

The reliability of message delivery
depends on the infrastructure investment. Messages can be delivered reliably when everything is running
correctly. However, it requires more
work to insure that messages are not
lost in computer crashes or hardware
failures. There are elaborate middleware solutions to deal with such scenarios, as discussed in Chapter 15. A
simpler solution is for the application
to request a confirmation message
from the recipient and consciously
deal with lost messages.

A N A L O G Y: *Although your postal
letters are delivered most of
the time, you accept that they
occasionally aren't. If it is critical to know, you purchase a
special return receipt requested service, or ask the recipient
for confirmation.*

E X A M P L E: *An email application would use a message service. Whatever one
user types is sent (as an atomic message) to the recipient. More generally, messages are commonly used in social and work group applications.*

*For the benefit of the application layer, the communications infrastructure layer
might provide an action*

`deliver_message: recipient, message_body → status;`

where `recipient` *identifies who is to receive the message, and the returned*
`status` *confirms that the message was delivered (or discloses a reason why it
wasn't). To be able to receive messages in this way, a module might provide an
action*

`receive_message: message_body → ;`

The infrastructure layer accepts the message with the `deliver_message`
action and arranges to find the `recipient` *and deliver the message using that
recipient's* `receive_message` *action.*

Another important characteristic of a message service is that one message does
not share a context with other messages—each message is self-contained and
stands on its own. An application can create its own context for a group of messages, but the message service provides no assistance to this end.

E X A M P L E: *A pair of users may want to discuss a controversial topic by email,
sending messages back and forth. The users create the shared context themselves, using phrases like "replying to your last idiotic statement." The message service is not aware of the context and treats each message
independently.*

*A message service would be used for notification applications. A message is
the appropriate service for flowers4u.com discussed in "Floral Delivery Service" on page 69 to notify a local florist of a customer order. There is no shared
context among different orders, and no returned information from the florist is
necessary. Flowers4u.com would like to be notified if the message is not delivered—possibly indicating that the florist is not available to fulfill the order—so
it can convey the order to an alternative florist.*

One subtle consequence of the "no message context" is that a message service
will not promise to deliver messages in the same order as sent. If the messages
have no shared context, then they also have no order (in time) from the perspective of the message service. It is also possible that a message is never delivered (see the sidebar "Is a Message Delivered for Sure?").

ANALOGY: *If someone sends a number of postcards home over the course of a
trip, the postal service will not necessarily deliver them in the order sent. The
postal service is unaware of the common context of these postcards (the trip).
It may even fail to deliver them all.*

Message services raise a couple of important issues. Does the service guarantee
delivery of a message? The answer to this question is a complex one (see the
sidebar "Is a Message Delivered for Sure?"). Can a recipient receive messages
from multiple sources? The answer is undoubtedly yes, and this leads to the
idea of multiplexing. Must a recipient always be available to receive a message,
at any time? This question suggests that there are two distinct flavors of message services—an immediate form, in which messages are delivered as sent,
and a deferred form, in which messages may be delivered later. The deferred
form leads to the idea of queueing discussed next.

12.1.2   Message Queueing and Multiplexing

The simplest message service would allow a given sender and recipient to communicate messages that are delivered as they are sent. This service presumes
the parties participate in the send-receive protocol discussed (along with the
request-response and publish-subscribe) in "Algorithms, Protocols, and Policies" on page 325. As will be seen, this simple service can be useful for direct-
immediate applications, especially for the transport of audio and video. For
most purposes, however, message services need enhancements such as multiplexing and queueing.

EXAMPLE: *Message-oriented middleware (MOM) is a class of infrastructure software providing message services that include multiplexing and queueing. It is
discussed further in Chapter 16.*

Queueing

Queueing, illustrated at the top of Figure 12.1, deals with a situation in which a
recipient may not be prepared to receive a message at all times (perhaps
because it is busy doing something else). A message is sent to a queue (which is
another module) associated with the recipient, rather than to the recipient
directly. The message can reside in the queue as long as necessary, and the
recipient retrieves messages waiting in the queue whenever it chooses.

EXAMPLE: *The queueing of messages is used in deferred user-to-user applications such as email or voicemail. The message service can queue an email message until the recipient reads it.*

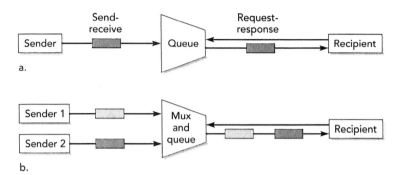

Figure 12.1 (a) Queueing allows sender and receiver to work independently, while (b) multiplexing allows two or more senders for the same recipient

> *Queueing is not appropriate for the local florist order notification by flowers4u.com, which wants no uncertainty in how long it takes to fulfill the customer's order. On the other hand, in the customer-care application of "Customer Care" on page 63, the customer service department expects that a technician will not be available to solve a customer's problem at all times. Thus, it is appropriate to use a message with queueing service for that notification to the technical support department.*

The message with queueing service illustrates how protocols must be assembled to realize more sophisticated services. As shown in Figure 12.1, this service internally requires an intermediary module called a queue and combines the send-receive (between sender and queue) and request-response (between recipient and queue) protocols. The fact that the queue is available at all times to receive a message frees the recipient from that burden; in fact, the recipient retrieves messages from the queue at its own convenience.

Typically, a number of messages might accumulate in the queue awaiting retrieval by their intended recipient. A message service might provide *prioritizing*, where some messages waiting for a recipient are presented ahead of others. The priority might be set by the sender, or it might be related to the identity of the sender.

Multiplexing

It is common for one module to receive messages or messages with reply requests from multiple sources. For example, a Web server will typically receive requests from many Web browsers. Multiplexing, illustrated at the bottom of Figure 12.1, merges messages for a given recipient from more than one sender. Those messages are stored in a single multiplex and queue to be retrieved by the recipient when desired. The multiplexing function frees the recipient from

dealing with the complexities of multiple senders—for example, the simultaneous arrival of messages from two or more sources—while allowing the recipient to deal with messages sequentially. Queueing can exist without multiplexing
(although this is unusual), but multiplexing requires queueing, since messages
from two or more senders arriving simultaneously requires all but one of them
to be stored while the others are retrieved.

A N A L O G Y: *The postal service provides a message service with multiplexing and
queueing. Your mailbox is a queue for letters awaiting your opening and reading them. It also multiplexes messages—mail from many senders arrives in your
mailbox. Multiplexing is also analogous to the merging of many highway lanes
into fewer lanes. Unless traffic is light, this results in a backup (queue) of cars
waiting to merge.*

E X A M P L E: *Figure 12.2 shows an example of a workflow application—the processing of purchase orders—that can utilize multiplexing and queueing. A number of workers may generate purchase requests that are multiplexed and
queued for a single administrative assistant. A number of these assistants may
forward these requests to a single purchasing department (again they are multiplexed and queued). If that purchasing department internally has a number of
agents, they may all retrieve requests from the single queue as they free up
time to process them. The agents then forward the requests to the receiving
department (where they are again multiplexed and queued), so that the
department is alerted to the future arrival of the purchased goods.*

*The customer-care application uses a multiplexing and queueing service to
notify the technical service department of a customer problem. This is because
the technical service department wants a single queue for incoming problem
reports. Technicians within the department, as they are freed from dealing with
a prior problem, access the highest-priority message—that priority having
been set by the customer agent based on the attributes of the customer from
the customer database. As each trouble task is completed, the technician notifies the customer service department by sending a message. The priority of
that message is set the same as the trouble report message. The next available
agent in customer service retrieves the highest-priority notification waiting and
informs the customer of the problem solution.*

12.1.3   Message with Reply Service

Some applications need a guaranteed and immediate reply to a message—the
reply is a message in the opposite direction, from recipient to originator. Typically
this occurs when the originating module is blocked, awaiting information or the
results of a service request from another. *Blocked* means unable to continue the

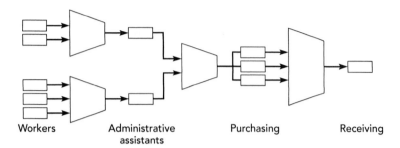

Workers   Administrative   Purchasing   Receiving
                  assistants

Figure 12.2 Multiplexing and queueing in a workflow application; the retrieval of a message from a queue is simplified to a single arrow

task that initiated the message because a reply is required. A message with reply service creates a shared context for the original and reply messages. There is an ordering—the reply message follows the message—and the reply is specifically identified to the sender as a response to the message, freeing the sender from identifying a reply from all the other incoming messages.

The message with reply service illustrates how communication services can place burdens on the modules that utilize them. It assumes the sender is blocked, waiting for the reply, so a recipient participating in this service is asked to reply as soon as possible. The service is immediate—it is assumed the recipient is able to accept a message and generate an appropriate reply at any time—and thus does not require queueing.

EXAMPLE: *When a student is studying for an exam and has a question, she may send an email message to the teacher, who replies at his leisure. If he is too busy, he may not reply at all, as there is no obligation to do so. This is the message service. While the student is actually taking the exam, she will expect a reply to her question, and she will expect it as soon as possible. She will use a message with reply service.*

EXAMPLE: *User-directed information access applications like the Web would use a message with reply service. When a user requests a piece of information, he is expecting the information to appear, and as soon as possible. The user instruction is sent to the Web server as a message, and the server is expected to reply as soon as possible with the Web page for display (because the user cannot do anything else until the reply is received). The reply is identified to the Web browser as a response to the message.*

The stock trading application discussed in "On-Line Stock Trading" on page 68 uses a message with reply service for a customer order. The customer submits an order to buy or sell a specified number of shares, and the reply includes an estimated price and confirmation number. The message with reply service iden- tifies the reply to the customer application, simplifying its task.

The message with reply service presumes the request-response protocol.

The message and message with reply services underlie the push and pull mod- els of information access (see the sidebar "Supporting Push and Pull").

Remote Method Invocation

A variation on the message response service is the remote method invocation (RMI). A standard way for objects to interact is the method invocation, as described in "Software Objects"on page 304. Recall that an invocation takes the form

`method: parameters → returns;`

where the `method` specifies the action to be performed by the server object, `parameters` configure or specialize that action, and `returns` convey the results of the method back to the client. As shown in Figure 12.3, the method invocation can work the same whether the client and server objects reside in the same or in different hosts.

EXAMPLE: *Any client-server application that is designed using OOP can use RMI as the form of interaction between objects residing at the client and objects residing at the server.*

Because the RMI requires communication of data representing parameters and returns between objects, RMI must be supported by a communication service. In the manner described in "A Middleware Example" on page 180, the client and server objects can be fooled into thinking that they are doing a method invocation like any other. The name of the action and the parameters can be conveyed as a message, and the returns can be conveyed in a reply. RMI is thus closely related to a message with reply service.

Behind the scenes, the RMI service requires substantial infrastructure. *Distrib- uted object management* (DOM) and *distributed component platforms* (DCP), two middleware technologies that provide an RMI service, are discussed further in Chapter 16. Because the form of object interaction is transparent to whether the objects are on the same or different hosts, DOM and DCP make building distributed applications much more like centralized applications. DOM and DCP also provide services that deal with special needs of such applications, such as the location and naming of objects (since the host needs to be identified as well as the object on that host) and security issues.

Supporting Push and Pull

Recall from "Autonomous Informa- tion Sources" on page 46 that the pure push model allows a source to determine what and when it sends information—this is supported by a message service. The broadcast also supports a pure push model for a continuing stream of information. The message with reply service supports the pure pull model, when a recipient makes a request (as a message) and then receives the requested informa- tion (in a reply).

There are intermediate cases. The message with queue service gives the source the freedom to choose what is sent, but the recipient chooses when to receive it.

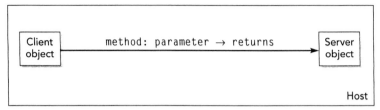

Method invocation

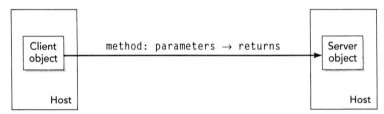

Remote method invocation (RMI)

Figure 12.3 Conceptually, an object method invocation can work the same way for two objects on the same host, or on different hosts

Timing and Concurrency

While the message service may appear as just "a message with reply service that is missing the reply," this understates the difference. This is better understood by examining the timing of the underlying protocols, which describes not only what happens but when.

A protocol interaction diagram for RMI is illustrated in Figure 12.4. This diagram shows the evolution of time (from top to bottom), the specific steps in the protocol, and the time at which they occur. The horizontal arrows represent each individual communication, the direction of that communication, and the time it takes (because of delays getting data through the network and other factors discussed later). The client object is blocked from the time it initiates the request until it receives the response. Recall that blocked means the client object is inactive because it is awaiting its response, keeping it from doing any other work. Components of this blocked time include network and processing delays for the request, the time to invoke the method and compute return values on those arguments in the server, and finally, the delay in the values returning to the client.

Blocking is not necessary, as seen in Figure 12.5. In the send-receive protocol, the sender is not blocked if it is not expecting a reply—it is free to go off and do other work. Since the sending and receiving objects are working on different tasks at the same time, they are said to be working *concurrently*. A request-

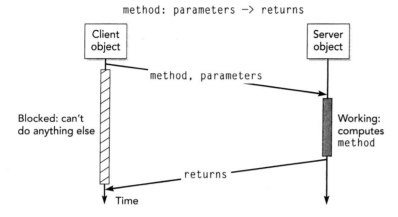

Figure 12.4 Protocol interaction diagram for a request-response protocol

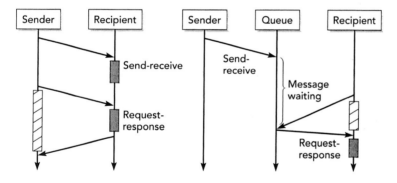

Figure 12.5 Protocol interaction diagram comparing timing of three protocols

response protocol—such as a message with reply or an RMI—does not allow the interacting objects to work concurrently during the course of their interaction. This distinction is important, because overall, more work may be completed when objects are able to work concurrently.

A comparison of two communication services in Table 12.2—message and messages with reply—illustrates why neither service (or more generally no single service) meets all needs. Each choice has advantages that might be compelling in certain circumstances.

ANALOGY: *The distinction between message and message with reply is similar to deferred versus immediate social applications. If the sender and receiver are considered to be users, then almost exactly the same considerations apply.*

Table 12.2 Relative advantages of two message-based services

Factor	Message	Message with reply
Transparency	Sending a message from one module to another would be similar within a host or across hosts.	For OOP, a method invocation both within a single host and across hosts is similar.
Applications	Natural for some applications, such as workflow. Many messages with one reply, or many replies for one message, are possible.	Naturally supports client-server computing. However, the service supports only one reply per request.
Sender blocking	The sender is not blocked, so it is possible to continue working on a different task.	The sender is idle waiting for the reply. This may not be as big a disadvantage as it seems, however, because of a technique called multitasking discussed in Chapter 17.
	If a reply message is expected, the message context has to be stored and later recalled.	Blocking and waiting for a reply is logically simpler, because the sender simply resumes where it left off.
Reliability	There is no automatic confirmation that the message is delivered.	Sender can easily detect if the message is not delivered, or if the recipient is not available or does not exist.
Recipient availability	If there is queueing, the recipient can access the message whenever it desires.	A recipient has to accept a message at any time and is expected to respond as quickly as possible.

12.1.4   The Conversation

Sometimes application modules desire to hold a *conversation*—a series of messages in both directions forming a single coupled interaction.

ANALOGY: *A telephone conversation between Alice and Bob consists of a series of utterances, first from Alice to Bob, then a reply from Bob back to Alice, then from Alice to Bob, etc. Rarely does a conversation consist of just one utterance (which is amenable to a message) or just one utterance with one reply (which is amenable to the message with reply).*

All the messages within a conversation share a *context*: Each message has an interpretation that can be interpreted only in that context; that is, the interpretation of one message depends on the messages that preceded it and affects the interpretation of messages that follow it.

E X A M P L E : *An application that accesses a database repeatedly to store data and make queries benefits from a conversation. The queries are ordered; if one query changes the database, later queries should reflect those changes.*

A conversation has a couple of important properties. Since each message is significant to interpreting what follows, it is important not to lose any messages—they must all be delivered. Also, it means that messages must be delivered in the same order as sent. Although an application can manage a conversation itself by building on the send or the request-response protocols, this is complicated since those protocols do not preserve an ordering of messages and may not even guarantee delivery of all messages. Thus, it is very helpful to have a communication service that supports a conversation. Such a service is called a *session*, which provides an often bidirectional sequence of messages, guaranteeing delivery of messages in the same order as sent.

E X A M P L E : *In the stock trading application of "On-Line Stock Trading" on page 68, the execution of a customer's limit order (purchase a stock, but only when the price falls below a threshold) could use a conversation between stocks4u.com and the stock market. This is because the stock price needs to be checked periodically, so the conversation would consist of repeated queries for a price followed by returned prices. The strategy for determining the right time to buy could become very confused if the stock prices arrived out of temporal order, and thus the ordering property of the session is a simplification.*

The protocol implicit in a session is pictured in Figure 12.6 and has three phases: establishment ("let's agree to converse"), conversation, and release ("let's stop conversing"). Their purpose is as follows:

- The establishment is the phase where the parties agree to communicate with a shared context. It also causes the infrastructure to allocate resources needed to support the session.
- During the conversation phase, it is typical for many more messages to flow in one direction than the other, and sometimes the conversation is unidirectional.
- The release is where the parties agree to stop conversing, and any allocated resources within the infrastructure are released.

Since the messages composing a session are usually bidirectional, and there is no coupling between messages in one direction and the other, the modules engaging in a session are called peers rather than client and server—this distinction was introduced in Chapter 5. There is, however, an asymmetry in the establishment phase—one peer originates the session. Release can be initiated by either peer.

Some Advantages of a Conversation

The conversation offers significant advantages for some applications:

- Where communicating objects have need for a continuing communication (analogous to a telephone "conversation"), a conversation creates a context for that communication. This removes a burden from the application—the context of each arriving message is identified by the communication service.

- A session protocol offers considerable advantages when authentication and confidentiality are required, as discussed in Chapter 13.

- Messages in a session stream can include sequence numbers, providing an easy way for the recipient to detect lost messages.

- A session protocol may have less overhead in the network if routing can be done once per session rather than once per message. Routing is discussed in Chapter 18.

- Sessions can be associated with quality-of-service (QoS) attributes determined during establishment. These QoS attributes offer predictable performance parameters to the application (such as the delay in delivering a message, or the frequency of lost messages). QoS is discussed in Chapter 18.

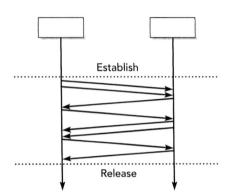

Figure 12.6 A session consists of establishment, a sequence of back-and-forth messages, and release

EXAMPLE: *A telephone call is analogous to a session. Establishment starts when the originating party picks up the phone and dials, and ends when the receiving party picks up the phone to answer. The two parties talk during the conversation phase. Release is initiated by either party hanging up the phone. Establishment serves to allocate a connection through the telephone network to support the conversation, and release causes that connection to be removed.*

The conversation has many other advantages over messages (see the sidebar "Some Advantages of a Conversation"). An isolated message that is not part of a session is sometimes called a *datagram*.

Multimedia Transport

The session serves as the foundation for multimedia transport. As you know, multimedia applications incorporate combinations of audio, video, animation, images, graphics, data, and other media. Audio, video, and animation can be transported over the network, as long as they are represented digitally. Certainly people don't talk digitally, nor are the microphone or camera outputs digital. However, these media can be converted to digital by an audio or video *coder*, and back from digital by a *decoder*. Coders also *compress* the medium—which means represent the medium with fewer bits—therefore consuming less storage and communication resources, as discussed in Chapter 20. Once the audio or video is digital—represented by data—it can be communicated over the network by forming it into a sequence of messages.

There are two distinct cases, depending on whether the application is immediate or deferred:

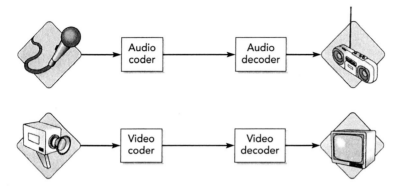

Figure 12.7 Audio telephony, video conferencing, and other immediate applications require that the audio or video medium be transferred over the network in real time

- *Live audio or video:* In immediate applications such as remote conferencing, the recipient is listening to the audio or viewing the video as it is being created, as illustrated in Figure 12.7. From the perspective of the communication service, this audio or video is called *streaming* (like water continually passing by in a stream).
- *Store-and-playback audio or video:* In deferred applications such as information access, the audio or video is stored in a host and "played back" as the user watches it. An option, illustrated in Figure 12.8, is to temporarily store the audio or video in the user's client and play it back locally. If there is insufficient local storage in the client, or for other reasons, the audio or video may instead be played back by streaming from a remote host.

E X A M P L E :   *Broadcast television requires approximately one megabit per second to represent with high quality. One hour of video at this rate would require 450MB of disk storage. This is a substantial portion of the storage capacity of a typical personal computer. Streaming video can shift this storage requirement to a server.*

How is the audio or video content partitioned into messages? Since the user probably perceives the entire audio or video presentation as atomic, it is natural to think of it as a single message. In the store-and-playback case, this is acceptable—the entire content is transported to the client as a message, and once received in its entirety, the playback begins. In the live case, however, the presentation must be divided into multiple messages.

E X A M P L E :   *When Alice calls Bob, he answers, "Hello," and she replies "Hi, this is Alice," and he replies, "Hi Alice." The entire piece of the conversation from*

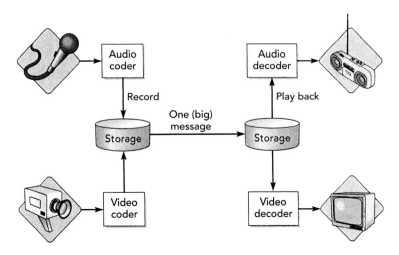

Figure 12.8 Audio or video information access and other deferred applications have the option of storing the medium on a local host before playback

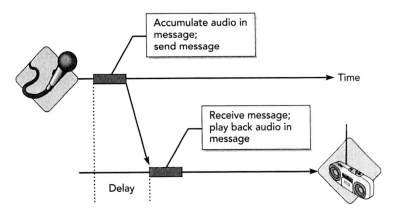

Figure 12.9 Streaming audio or video is captured in a stream of messages, which can be transported across the network in a session

Bob to Alice including "hello" and "hi Alice" could not be transferred as a single message, since Alice would never have a chance to inject her "hi, this is Alice" in response to the "hello."

Streaming audio or video—splitting the audio or video into a sequence of messages transported using a session—is natural for the live case, as shown in Figure 12.9. The coder divides the presentation into "natural" units, such as single utterances in the case of telephony, and sends each unit as a message. Since messages may be delayed by different amounts by the network, the relative timing of messages may have been reconstructed at the receiver. To reconstruct the original timing (for example, the time between utterances), the service has to include *synchronization* information.

Multimedia applications frequently incorporate more than one medium, such as audio *and* video, or often multiple audio and video streams in a multiway conference. This generalizes the notion of session to multiple, logically connected streams. The service also has to support synchronization of these streams, to make sure, for example, that video and its associated audio are time aligned.

12.1.5   The Broadcast

The *broadcast* is a one-way version of a conversation. Rather than a peer relationship between participants, it has an asymmetrical sender-receiver relationship. This leads directly to a fundamental characteristic of the broadcast—there can just as easily be many recipients as a single one, each recipient receiving a replica of the information from the sender. This depends on the easy replication that is a property of information represented by data. Because all the recipients must be available and receiving the broadcast at the same time, it inherently supports immediate applications.

EXAMPLE: *Remote learning with multiple students is an application of broadcast if it is cast as an immediate application (the students are viewing the presentation as it happens). Remote conferencing often involves multiple participants, and each participant may wish to hear (or see) all the other participants, which can use a broadcast from each participant.*

Relative to the session, the broadcast is simultaneously a specialization (one-way rather than two-way) and a generalization (multiple recipients).

There are two ways to create multiple replicas of the messages originating from the sender:

- *Simulcast:* The sender creates the replicas and creates a separate session for each recipient. This composes a broadcast to multiple recipients from a set of peer-to-peer sessions, one for each session. This places a burden on the sender, and to the sender, simulcast is much different from a session.
- *Multicast:* The multiple replicas are created by the communication service rather than the sender. From the sender's perspective, multicast appears to be a one-way communication session.

Multicast is a service recently made available by the Internet and is discussed further in Chapter 18.

Origins of the Internet

The local area network (LAN), specifically Ethernet, allowed interconnection of hosts within a building. Its
biggest application was allowing
users to log in and access files in different hosts, which allowed them to
send email to one another, etc. It
demonstrated the value of interconnecting hosts and allowed development of an early suite of networked
applications.

In the early 1970s, the U.S. Defense
Advanced Projects Research Agency
(DARPA) funded research into wide
area computer networking. Since
LANs already existed, this project
interconnected existing LANs, rather
than designing from scratch a new
end-to-end network. It resulted in the
internet protocols, which have been
extended and refined in the IETF.

Wide area networking was also stud-
ied by ISO, resulting in the open systems interconnection (OSI) standards.
The differences in process are striking. OSI defined an elaborate and
complete protocol suite *before*
implementation, whereas the internet protocols arose from university
research projects that developed,
prototyped, and tested them incrementally. The internet used a process
of continuous improvement by
researchers, rather than top-down
design.

The most telling difference was the
availability of prototype internet
implementations in freeware distribu-
tions of Berkeley UNIX. A number of
applications were developed and
refined at the same time as protocol
refinement. The applications
impacted the protocols, and vice
versa, in an empirical environment. By
the time OSI implementation started,

Discussion

**D12.1 If you have had direct experience with a workflow application, com-
puter based or otherwise, describe its purpose, your experience with it, and
the role of multiplexing and queueing.**

12.2   Internet Communication Services

The most popular communication services today are provided by the internet
suite of networking technologies. The process by which the Internet arose and
gained popularity is informative (see the sidebar "Origins of the Internet"). The
internet provides specific variations on all the generic communication services
already discussed. There is nothing fundamental about the specific internet services; they are simply design choices.

Internally, the infrastructure is layered. Communication services, including the
internet protocols, are internally layered. This means that elaborated and specialized services can be deployed by adding a layer—leveraging an existing service
on an existing network—rather than building it (service or network) from scratch.
The internet services are layered as illustrated in Figure 12.10. Each layer provides a communication service at its interface; however, because protocols play
such an important role in networking, these are sometimes called protocol layers
because of the fundamental role of protocols in their implementation. More than
one service option can be defined at each layer, if needed to meet distinct application needs.

E X A M P L E : *TCP and UDP are two "transport layer" services implemented using
the IP service, which is the foundation of the Internet. Two more specialized
services, RTP and IIOP, are implemented by adding a layer to UDP and TCP,
respectively. An application is free to use any of these services (TCP, UDP, RTP,
or IIOP) directly.*

These services are de facto standards from the IETF, with the exception of IIOP,
which is promulgated by the OMG. Further details on how the internet services
are implemented is given in Chapter 19.

12.2.1   Internet Protocol (IP)

The internet is a "network of networks." The internet technologies did not
begin from scratch, but rather built on existing local area networking technologies. Those technologies (such as Ethernet, Token Ring, and Asynchronous
Transfer Mode) are shown as the bottom layer, labeled "subnetworks," in Figure
12.10. The *Internet Protocol* (IP), which forms the *internetworking layer*, can be

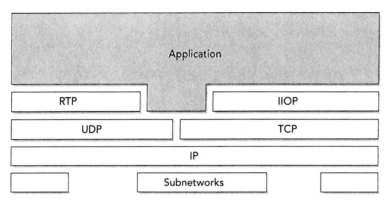

the Internet was already soundly established and included a suite of compelling applications. Because of network externalities and lock-in, as discussed in "Obstacles to Change" on page 231, OSI lost, illustrating the power of early to market and positive feedback with winner-take-all effects.

Figure 12.10 The Internet suite of protocols, including those supporting datagrams, sessions, and the remote method invocation, are implemented within the middleware operating system and networking layers

viewed in two complementary ways. First, it is a protocol for interconnecting subnetworks, with the result that end-to-end communication services are possible in spite of the heterogeneity of the underlying layer. Second, IP is a spanning layer that hides this heterogeneity through a standard interface decoupled from specific networking technologies. IP is accessed by applications through an intermediary transport layer (UDP or TCP). Transport services customize the generic but limited service provided by IP to particular application needs.

12.2.2   User Datagram Protocol (UDP)

UDP is the most basic internet transport service. UDP provides a datagram, which is similar to a message, but with one important difference—the number of bits in a datagram is limited. If an application wishes to send a message too long to be a UDP datagram, it must split up that message.

The service provided by UDP is quite similar to the postal service postcard analogy: Each UDP datagram is independent, and UDP does not recognize any shared context. UDP does not promise to deliver a datagram (although it obviously tries its best), and it does not promise to deliver datagrams sent to the same recipient in the sending order. UDP provides multiplexing and limited queueing. In order to receive datagrams, the recipient has to request them from the UDP layer.

UDP is rarely used directly by end-user applications, in part because it offers no session services, cannot be used to transport arbitrarily sized messages, and does not promise delivery. The most important role for UDP is as the layer that supports RTP and other protocols for multimedia streaming layers, as discussed shortly. While UDP does not offer the session protocols needed for streaming multimedia, these are realized directly in RTP.

12.2.3   Transmission Control Protocol (TCP)

TCP offers a type of session (called a TCP *connection*), although like UDP it does not directly support messages. Rather, TCP delivers a stream of bytes (each byte is eight bits of data) delivered reliably and in the same order they are sent. There is an establishment and a release phase to the protocol. There are two ways to communicate messages by TCP:

- *One message per connection:* To send a single message, a single TCP connection can be established and disestablished. The message is sent as a stream of bytes (with the constraint that the message must have an integral number of bytes). This high-overhead approach (due to an establishment for every message) is most useful for sending long messages.
- *Application-defined message protocol:* Multiple messages can be sent per TCP connection if the application is willing to define its own protocol to do so. Fortunately this is simple, for example, by defining a special delimiter byte that separates messages.

TCP doesn't offer multiplexing, although a recipient can open separate connections to multiple senders. It does provide queueing, as the recipient can ask for any data that has been received and is provided all the bytes that have arrived on that connection. Since it offers more facilities, such as reliable and ordered delivery, TCP is simpler to use than UDP. These facilities are discussed in Chapter 18.

EXAMPLE: *TCP is the workhorse of networked applications that use the Internet or an intranet or extranet. For example, the Web uses TCP to underlie its own HTTP protocol described in "The Hypertext Transfer Protocol (HTTP)" on page 332. The messages in both directions are conveyed by defining a "message begin" and "message end" string that delimit the message, and then transporting that message as a stream of bytes using TCP.*

12.2.4   Internet Inter-ORB Protocol (IIOP)

UDP and TCP allow communication in both directions to flow independently, but they do not directly support a message with reply service. The association of a message and its reply would have to be created by the application. Similarly, UDP and TCP don't directly support the remote method invocation.

The OMG has defined a de facto standard called IIOP that provides RMI directly and transparently across the network. IIOP is a layer above TCP; it allows a series of RMIs to another host on a single TCP connection. See the sidebar "RMI Can Be Layered on Messages" to see how this layering is implemented.

12.2.5 Streaming Multimedia

As applications become more sophisticated, and especially as they incorporate streaming audio and video and similar media, there is an expanding need for protocols supporting complex combinations of real-time streaming media, such as audio and video, and also complex sessions incorporating simultaneous audio and video streams.

E X A M P L E : *A multipoint video conference may have a number of users partici-pating, each originating video with its associated audio, which is broadcast to all the users.*

The IETF and W3C (World Wide Web Consortium) are standardizing protocols supporting these complex multimedia sessions (see the sidebar "Internet Streaming Multimedia Protocols").

E X A M P L E : *Real Networks distributes a player for streaming audio and video and complementary servers and media-coding algorithms. Consumers can down-load a player and then view a variety of video and audio content, including both live content and repositories of store-and-playback content. By distribut-ing the player for free, it creates a large community of viewers, which encour-ages content suppliers. The resulting secondary network effects have made Real the dominant supplier. Real can then sell the servers to those suppliers, creating revenues and profits.*

Discussion

D12.2 Discuss the process leading to the internet protocols, including government-funded research and de facto standardization. Has it been effective, or could the Internet be much better today if a different process had been used? If it has been effective, why?

D12.3 Using the internet protocols as a concrete example of layering, dis-cuss this methodology—building new capabilities on what already exists. What are alternatives? What are the strengths and weaknesses of layering?

Review

Communication services provide capabilities that are of direct use to applica-tions but are stripped of implementation details. Widely used services are the

RMI Can Be Layered on Messages

An RMI consists of a request of the form (`action, parameters`) and a response in the form (`return_values`); each can be embedded in a message. The pro-cess of packing a list of data items (parameters and return values) in a message is called *marshalling*.

The request message must include a host and object identifier (so the invo-cation can be routed to the correct object). The message body must include a `method` identifier (so the right method can be invoked on that object) and the `parameters`. The response message includes the `return_values`, and the ser-vice binds the response with the request to the client object.

Marshalling is greatly complicated if the two objects are running on differ-ent platforms in different languages, since the representation of data is likely to be different. There is there-fore a conversion necessary some-where in the infrastructure (see Chapter 16).

Internet Streaming Multimedia Protocols

The most basic protocol for multi-media streaming is the *Real-time Transport Protocol* (RTP), which included message sequence and tim-ing information allowing a recipient to reconstruct the relative timing of messages. RTP normally utilizes UDP, because of its minimum delay, although there are other possibilities (such as TCP, with its reliability but higher delay). RTP also includes a def-inition of *mixers* and *translators* with the network that allow the coding to be changed or firewalls penetrated.

Associated with RTP is the *Real-time Streaming Protocol* (RTSP) that allows applications to control sessions incorporating multiple RTP sessions; in essence, RTSP controls a remote multimedia server and is intentionally similar to HTTP, which controls a remote Web server. Multipoint applications often use broadcast services, where recipients may enter and leave dynamically as time passes. The *Session Description Protocol* (SDP) provides a way for such "conferences" to be advertised, as well as ways for hosts to enter and leave them. The *Synchronized Multimedia Integration Language* (SMIL) is a W3C standard that allows the composition of complex combinations of media from a multimedia server.

message (which supports an application send-receive protocol), the message with reply (which supports a request-response protocol), and the conversation and broadcast (which can use a session protocol). The broadcast is a specialization of a conversation to one-way interaction, but a generalization to multiple recipients.

In message services, the infrastructure can supply multiplexing (retrieving messages from multiple senders) and queueing (freeing a recipient to retrieve a message later than sent). These are particularly valuable in workflow applications. A useful service built on a message with reply is the remote method invocation (RMI), which simplifies application programming by making the interaction among objects appear location independent.

The message and message with reply services have one major difference—with the message, the sender does not have to block while waiting for a reply, and the recipient does not have to be available at all times to receive and immediately respond to a message. On the other hand, the sender of a message with reply gets verification that the message was received and acted upon.

The internet illustrates variations on all these services. It is constructed from layers, where new services are implemented by specializing (adding a layer) to the previous. Each layer is called a protocol layer, because it implements a protocol between peer entities that makes use of the service provided by the layer below. The most popular protocol layers are TCP (a type of session) and UDP (a type of message), both layered on IP, which achieves interoperability between subnetworks. Recently, protocol layers have been added to support multimedia and multicast services, including RTP layered on UDP for supporting a real-time conversation.

Key Concepts

Communication services:

- Message: multiplexing and queueing
- Message with reply and remote method invocation (RMI)
- Conversation and broadcast

Multimedia:

- Live versus store and playback
- Streamed versus stored

Internet: IP, UDP, TCP, RTP

Further Reading

[CST94] is a good introduction to the Internet, and especially some of the problems facing it in the future. [Pet96] and [Wal96] are excellent recent books on networks and their design philosophy, although both focus on low-level details omitted in this chapter. [Bak97] covers distributed object management and the remote method invocation.

Exercises

E12.1   For any two of the following applications, describe a protocol that you believe is most appropriate to serve as its foundation, in terms similar to Figure 12.1 on page 350. Justify your choice.

  a. A direct-immediate messaging system

  b. A direct-deferred messaging system

  c. An email application

  d. Stock price notification application

E12.2   For each of the following, choose the most appropriate generic communication service, and justify your answer. If it naturally combines two or more services, so state.

  a. Remote conferencing (audio and video components)

  b. Posting to newsgroup

  c. Retrieving messages from newsgroup

  d. Sending email

  e. Retrieving email

  f. Participating in chatroom

  g. Broadcast video

  h. Video on demand

  i. Accessing electronic library

E12.3   For each of the following, give one situation from your recent experience (in either the real world or on the network) where this communication service would be appropriate, and state your reasons:

  a. A message

  b. A message with reply

    c. A conversation

    d. A broadcast

E12.4 Examine a recent email message you have received. Examine the elements of the message—including header information—and briefly describe their purpose. (Note: Some email viewers allow you to hide headers, so be sure you are looking at all the headers.)

E12.5 Compare each of the following situations to a message session. In particular, are there phases analogous to establishment, conversation, and release? If so, what are they?

    a. A work group holding a meeting to discuss their project

    b. Accessing an internet service provider using a modem to retrieve your email

    c. Using a laptop computer on an airplane

E12.6 For any one of the following, list the steps of a protocol based upon messages that accomplishes the given collaborative task.

    a. Obtain bids from three automobile dealers on a new car you want to purchase, inform the dealers of your decision, and order the car from one of them.

    b. Serve as an auction house to sell a rare painting to a group of individuals.

    c. Serve as an agent for a hotel serving a customer making a reservation.

E12.7 Give three examples (not mentioned in the chapter) of applications where the multiplexing and queueing of messages is useful.

E12.8 Based on your knowledge at this point:

    a. List factors you believe would make a remote method invocation (on an object in another host) slower than a local method invocation (on an object in the same host).

    b. Describe a feasible naming convention for locating objects on a remote computer.

E12.9 Repeat Exercise 12.2, except choose a specific internet protocol rather than abstract communication service, and justify your answer.

E12.10 Assume you are provided a message communication service. Describe how you would turn this into a message session.

Trustworthiness

13

Amission-critical networked application must be trustworthy. This means it works correctly, almost all the time, and is secure against various external threats and natural disasters. As the applications of networked computing expand to encompass critical infrastructure, business applications, and electronic commerce, trustworthiness becomes a crucial issue for business and the larger society. The impact of failures or inappropriate penetration could be widespread and damaging. Trustworthiness thus becomes one of the most important design and operational considerations.

Violations of trustworthiness come in many forms. The application can crash due to software bugs or hardware failure, or it can succumb to deliberate vandalism. The application may run correctly, but fail to protect proprietary information, or improperly allow an imposter to masquerade as a legitimate user. Two major facets that contribute to trustworthiness are listed in Table 13.1.

A networked application is only as trustworthy as its weakest link. One of those links that should not be forgotten is the human element. Both reliability and security depend on competent and honest operators, who faithfully follow established policies and procedures and make good operational decisions. A critical component of security is operational vigilance for unusual or suspicious activity. Humans are a major defense against problems, and human failings are a major cause of breakdown. Humans are also the primary security threats—the vandals, thieves, counterfeiters, and imposters among the citizenry are few in number, but nevertheless a reality. The possibility of access to the Internet by any citizen creates a serious security threat to balance its wonderful benefits.

As with functionality and performance, there are trade-offs between costs and development time and the objectives for availability and security that can reasonably be achieved. Thus, consideration of these trade-offs is an essential

Table 13.1 Facets of trustworthiness in networked computing systems

Factor	Description	Analogy
Availability	The application operates correctly, all the time, even in the face of inevitable equipment and facility failures and natural disasters. This assumes no deliberate internal or external threats or vandalism.	A bank's financial systems should be designed and managed such that in the course of normal operations customers are served well and no financial errors are made. This includes contingency plans for floods, earthquakes, and other disasters.
Security	The system continues to operate reliably and protects its confidential information in the face of aberrant or malicious behavior on the part of outsiders.	The bank designs its facilities and operations to prevent criminal behavior such as robberies, sabotage, and theft of confidential information about its customers.

aspect of the conceptualization and analysis phases of the application lifecycle, as discussed in "Application Lifecycle" on page 279.

This chapter discusses availability, followed by security. Both availability and security require a systems approach, combining many complementary elements to achieve goals. An issue of special significance to e-commerce is electronic payments, which have especially severe security requirements and are discussed in Chapter 14.

13.1   Availability

The most fundamental issue in trustworthiness is whether the application is running correctly. The all-encompassing measure of this important attribute is *availability*—the fraction of the time an application is running. Availability is reduced by *downtime*, which is a period an application is not doing its job for any reason. Downtime may be due to scheduled maintenance (including installation of software upgrades, or fixing of bugs or configuration errors or problems), hardware failures, software crashes, power failures, or malicious attacks by vandals. Availability is usually expressed as the percentage of time the system is available. The relationship of downtime and availability is shown in Table 13.2.

The impact of downtime depends on when it occurs and how long it lasts and, of course, the nature of the application itself.

EXAMPLE: *Downtime specifically scheduled for system maintenance at a less critical time (such as 2 a.m. Sunday morning) has much less impact than downtime during a period of normally high usage. A short downtime may have less impact than a long downtime.*

Table 13.2 Relationship of downtime to availability [Ber97]

Downtime	Availability
One hour per day	95.8%
One hour per week	99.41%
One hour per month	99.86%
One hour per year	99.9886%
One hour per 20 years	99.99942%

> Downtime during times of market trading is especially damaging for stocks4u.com (described in "On-Line Stock Trading" on page 68), because customers may be unable to take advantage of short-term price moves. Outside of normal business hours, availability is less critical. On the other hand, flowers4u.com (described in "Floral Delivery Service" on page 69) can save both design and operational costs with more relaxed availability objectives—its customers can more easily try sending their orders again later.

There are two aspects to availability covered in the following sections. One is the intrinsic reliability of the application and the infrastructure that supports it in the absence of any external threats, and the other is the ability of the application to face explicit security threats.

13.1.1   Intrinsic Reliability

The intrinsic reliability of an application refers to its ability to run correctly in the absence of external threats or deliberate attempts to undermine it. Numerous problems can compromise reliability, including software bugs and hardware failures.

Software Bugs

A major source of unreliability is flawed computer programs. Software applications and the infrastructure that supports them are very large, complex, and can experience an astronomically large number of possible conditions. Although any application is subjected to extensive testing, including alpha- and beta-site testing with actual users, it is simply not possible to thoroughly test *all* possible conditions. Thus latent program errors (colloquially called "software bugs") are inevitable.

ANALOGY: *The transportation system works well most of the time, but occasionally there are accidents.*

These bugs are observed and corrected as they are observed, as part of maintenance and new releases. Serious flaws may be manifested at the time of installation, in which case it may be necessary to roll back to a previous release. Serious bugs can cause the application or computer system to *crash*—meaning an unrecoverable error necessitates restarting from scratch.

EXAMPLE: *The Nasdaq stock exchange upgraded the software on both its primary and backup computers (for compatibility) in July 1994. This caused their systems to crash, and the exchange was forced to halt trading for two hours while the previous release was restored [OST97].*

Bugs in their most benign (but most difficult to detect) form don't cause crashes, but "merely" cause incorrect results.

EXAMPLE: *Early versions of the Pentium processor were found to encounter errors in floating-point arithmetic, caused by a bug in its "microcode" (software embedded within the chip). Although rare, once the bug was detected, Intel was forced to supply replacements to many customers.*

Configuration and Operation

Every application has to be configured during installation for its local conditions, and during its operations innumerable decisions are made by its operators. Even the best-laid plans of its designers are dependent on vigilance and competent decisions during installation and operation.

EXAMPLE: *A telephone switching center in New York City inadvertently went on battery backup (during a power system overload compounded by a backup generator failure) in September 1991. The designers had included alarm bells and warning lights to warn of this condition, but they were ignored by operators for six hours until the batteries discharged. Because the center was crucial to local air traffic control, 400 flights were canceled, and tens of thousands of passengers were inconvenienced [OST97].*

Emergent Behavior

Recall that emergent behavior arises from the interaction of subsystems, supplementing the functionality of individual subsystems. Most emergent behavior is the necessary and desirable result of integrating subsystems, but there can also be undesirable forms of emergent behavior. Even though a large application may be assembled from individual modules whose behaviors are individually well understood, complex interactions sometimes result in surprising and unanticipated emergent behaviors. These are not a bug or error per se, but rather a natural phenomenon that can be beneficial, but is most often undesirable or even destructive.

ANALOGY: *A system as complex as the worldwide economy exhibits emergent behavior, such as business cycles and recessions, that cannot be well anticipated or explained in terms of the behavior of individual economic actors. On the other hand, by studying the behavior of the system in the large (in macroeconomics), insights can be gained, if not complete understanding.*

Undesirable forms of emergent behavior can cause crashes, but more benign forms cause deterioration in performance or functionality. Prevention of emergent behavior or even of recurrence is difficult. The widespread replication of the same technology seems to increase the likelihood of emergent behavior (see the sidebar "Diversity, Reliability, and Security").

Cost of Reliability

There is a trade-off between the economic impact of downtime and the cost of high reliability. In many critical applications, such as an air traffic control system or telephone network, the social and economic cost of downtime is so great that extraordinary measures (and costs) are undertaken to insure high availability (one hour per twenty years is achieved in telephone switching systems). In many other applications, relaxed availability objectives may be traded for lower cost. For example, 99 percent availability might be acceptable in a typical business application, if the downtime comes in many short periods rather than one long failure per week, or if it could be scheduled at less critical times (for example, 2 a.m. Sunday morning) [Ber97].

Downtime is not the only impact of application crashes or aberrant behavior. There may be permanent loss of data, which has its own economic or social cost. The issues are thus how often downtime occurs, what the restoration time is, and how much if any data is lost. All this must be evaluated, of course, in the context of the specific application.

There are sources of downtime other than crashes or failures. Applications require maintenance and upgrade, and by far the easiest way to do this is by deliberately taking the application off-line. While this can be scheduled at opportune times, unfortunately, as availability requirements increase in many organizational applications, the opportunities for scheduled maintenance are shrinking or disappearing altogether. Increasingly, maintenance on an operational application is a requirement.

Diversity, Reliability, and Security

A diversity of technologies and vendors may increase the likelihood of either downtime or security holes, in part because the operators have less familiarity with each individual technology. On the other hand, in the absence of such diversity, problems that do occur can be more severe.

ANALOGY: *Genetically diverse animal populations are more robust to disease. If all animals in a population were genetically identical, they could readily succumb to the same disease.*

When an application incorporates multiple identical copies of the same program, minor errors can spawn serious problems because of subtle interactions among the multiple copies. In this regard, software components are a double-edged sword. On the one hand, widely used components are more thoroughly tested and thus have fewer bugs. On the other hand, since they are distributed more broadly, they might interact in surprisingly destructive ways.

EXAMPLE: *A small flaw in a software upgrade in a telephone switch in New York City in January 1990 cascaded throughout the country, causing over half of the telephone traffic to be blocked in the AT&T nationwide network for over seven hours [OST97]. The same upgraded software had been replicated across the country, and the replicated flaw interacted, causing each switch to crash the switches with which it interacted.*

Similarly, if a security flaw is exploited in a particular technology, the damage is potentially more severe if that technology is widely deployed.

Other Uses of Data Replication

There are a number of motivations for data replication besides aiding in fault tolerance. Replication can improve performance by keeping a replica of data "closer" to where it is needed. In networked computing, usually "closer" means "on this side of a communications bottleneck," which leads to the idea of caching described in Chapter 20.

ANALOGY: *If you are living in a two-story house and don't appreciate the time and effort to run up and down the stairs, you might purchase two copies of a book you are reading and keep one copy on each floor. That way, a copy will always be at hand.*

Similar issues arise when users collaborate on common information, as in collaborative authoring. The data must be replicated, one copy for each user. Replication of data where the copies are all being modified at overlapping times means that changes to one copy must be propagated as soon as possible to the other copies. A similar issue is document *version control*. When multiple users are making changes to a document, there is need to recover older versions of the document if not all users agree with the changes.

Many of these issues come under the general heading of concurrency control, which is discussed in Chapter 17.

High availability requirements can increase the costs of development and equipment, as well as the cost of worker training or salaries (such as hiring more skilled operators). Development costs are increased by greater attention to recovering gracefully from unusual conditions and more time and attention paid to program correctness and testing. Avoiding downtime even during inevitable failures of hardware and communication links requires *fault tolerance*, where a failed piece of equipment is automatically replaced by a redundant replacement. Some useful technical tools for increasing availability are listed in Table 13.3.

For example, if one processor fails, then switching to a redundant processor will prevent loss of data, if there is a replica or if the data is persistent. Data replication has many uses besides fault tolerance (see the sidebar "Other Uses of Data Replication"). Data replication and equipment redundancy are both required to achieve complete fault tolerance. A spare processor must have replicated data if uninterrupted operation is necessary. In less stringent applications, some loss of data is acceptable, so the application can be reinitialized. An alternative to data replication is data persistence, one of the strengths of the DBMS. The DBMS commits changes to the data on magnetic disk or other nonvolatile storage, so committed data isn't lost in a crash. It is seldom possible to preserve *all* data in a crash, because something will be in process in volatile storage. Thus, it is usually necessary to roll back to some consistent state when initializing the application. This is one role of transaction processing, which is discussed along with the DBMS in Chapter 15.

13.1.2 Security: Countering Deliberate Threats

Intrinsic reliability addresses unintended or natural problems. Security addresses hostile threats from citizens (including workers internal to an organization) with nefarious purposes, such as vandalism (corrupting data or disrupting operations) or theft of data or services. The greatest external threats arise when hosts are connected to a network, especially the global Internet, since this allows virtually anybody to attempt access. Various means have been developed to counter these threats, although not yet with complete effectiveness.

ANALOGY: *Once access to bank branches is given to the general public, both customers and bank robbers can enter. Countermeasures such as glass partitions, surveillance cameras, and alarms can deter criminals, but also create a less friendly and functional environment for the customer.*

This analogy illustrates two downsides to security. First, it is expensive—like high availability, high security increases design costs, capital investments, and

Table 13.3 Techniques for fault tolerance and graceful crash recovery

Feature	Description	Analogy
Equipment redundancy	Provide backup equipment (hosts, network switches, communication links, etc.). Upon failure of the primary, switch to the redundant backup. Improving availability by redundancy is expensive (see the sidebar "How Effective Is Redundancy?").	Keep a spare car in the garage. If you have car trouble, get a ride home to use your spare car.
Data replication	Keep replicated copies of data. Upon loss of data, restore from the replica (losing changes in the interim).	Leave a spare copy of your income tax returns with a friend. In case a fire destroys either copy, use the spare.
Data persistence	Persistence is a property of data that outlives the program that created it. Upon a crash, data can be recovered when the program is restarted. This is discussed further in Chapter 15.	Take written notes at a meeting. In case you can't remember what happened, fall back on the notes.

operational costs. Second, security is invasive—there is a trade-off between helping legitimate users accomplish their purposes easily and preventing vandalism or theft. Connecting a host to the Internet, for example, reflects a desire for citizens (such as customers or traveling employees) to access applications, but security measures designed to foil undesired intruders can be inconvenient for these legitimate users.

Good security requires an understanding of both the inherent vulnerabilities of the application and the nature of potential threats. Unfortunately, such comprehensive understanding is infeasible, so vigilance and continual learning of new threats are necessary [OST97]. Security is an ongoing process, requiring frequent reevaluation and added measures to counter newly identified threats [CST98a].

EXAMPLE: *CERT is a clearinghouse located at Carnegie Mellon University that "studies Internet security vulnerabilities, provides incident response services to sites that have been the victims of attack, publishes a variety of security alerts, researches security and survivability in wide-area-networked computing, and develops information to help you improve security at your site."*

Two aspects of security are easy to overlook, so they should be emphasized up front:

- An individual security measure is rarely effective in isolation. Security is by nature a *system* composed of many complementary measures, and they are only effective in concert.

How Effective Is Redundancy?

Assume that a component of a system has a constant failure rate λ. This means that over a small interval of time Δ, a fraction $\lambda\Delta$ of the remaining components still working will fail, on average. The average time to failure for a single component is then $\mu = 1/\lambda$.

EXAMPLE: *If the average time to failure of a given computer is ten years, then the probability of a given computer failing in a year is 1/10, or the probability of it failing within one hour is $1/(10 \times 365 \times 24)$. The assumption is that this probability is the same after any elapsed time, assuming of course the computer has not already failed prior to that time.*

Replicating these components n times so that they back one another up—any one of which can keep the system operational—should increase the reliability as measured by the average time to system failure, which is the average time to failure of all n components. This can be statistically modeled if one additional assumption is made: The failure of one component has nothing whatsoever to do with the failure of another component (they are said to fail independently in the statistical sense). With this assumption, the average time to system failure is

$$\mu \times \left(1 + \frac{1}{2} + \frac{1}{3} + \ldots + \frac{1}{n}\right).$$

Thus, the second redundant component only extends the average time to system failure by $\mu/2$, the third by $\mu/3$, etc.

EXAMPLE: *To double the average time to system failure requires four redundant components. To double it again (to four times that of a single system) requires thirty-one redundant systems.*

Although the average time to failure can be made arbitrarily long, this becomes increasingly expensive as redundancy is added. The payoff (measured by increase in average time to failure) decreases as $1/n$ for the nth added system. Intuitively, the reason is that the average lifetime of one component is μ, so it becomes increasingly unlikely for any components to last significantly beyond μ.

Availability, Security, and the Market

High-availability computer systems were pioneered by Tandem in the 1970s, and since then other vendors have entered the market. These systems are used in mission-critical organizational applications, where downtime is expensive.

The market is arguably less effective in fostering security. Threats are diffuse and difficult to characterize, and the cost benefits of security are difficult to quantify. Much core technology (the UNIX operating system and the internet technologies) was developed in a benign environment of trusted users (the university research community) and thus was originally lax on security.

The most effective market mechanism for promulgating good security is to make sure the risks (and costs) of security breakdowns are borne by those in the best position to deploy the security necessary to counter

- People are as important as technology to good security. Although people external to an organization or administrative domain can be a security threat, employees or other "insiders" are a much greater threat, as they have greater opportunity for mischief. Conversely, worker training, competence, and vigilance (fortunately more the norm than dishonesty and maliciousness) are the most important ingredients of effective security.

13.2   Security Measures

How can the myriad external threats to networked computer systems be countered? This is the role of security measures covered in this section. First, the security measures in the postal system, a physical-world analogy, are examined because they illustrate some of the requirements in a familiar context. Following that, some pillars of security in network applications are introduced. The remainder of this chapter will discuss both how these pillars work technically and how they are combined in a system to achieve a variety of objectives.

13.2.1   Postal System Analogy

The analogy to the postal system—which encounters in the physical world many of the same security objectives and issues as networked computers—illustrates some security measures that can be taken, as well as some weaknesses. Features of postal system security are illustrated in Figure 13.1, focusing specifically on sending a document through the mail.

Assume that Alice wants to send a message (using a postal letter) to Bob. To begin, Alice writes her message on paper using permanent ink, making it difficult to modify surreptitiously. This provides assurance to Bob that the message was not modified in transit by some third party, say, Eve. (The fictitious names Alice, Bob, and Eve are commonly used by computer security people to distinguish the participants in a security protocol.) Formally, the paper and permanent ink provide evidence of the *integrity* of the message. Also, to assure Bob that Alice was the source of the message (and not Eve pretending to be Alice), Alice may affix a signature that Bob can check against a copy of her signature that he keeps in his files. The signature provides *authentication*, which means a provable identification of Alice. Alice may also not want Eve to read the message, which she would like to keep *confidential* (between her and Bob). For this purpose, Alice seals her message in an envelope to keep away prying eyes.

During transit, the postal system maintains *physical security*, allowing access only to postal workers, who are presumed honest and trustworthy. Once it arrives, Bob can unseal the envelope to read the message and examine the sig-

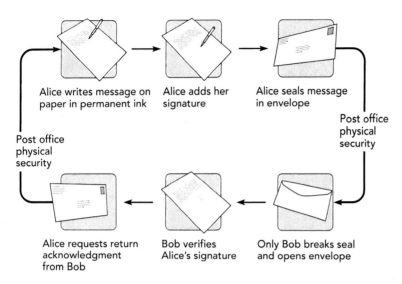

Alice writes message on paper in permanent ink → Alice adds her signature → Alice seals message in envelope

Post office physical security

Post office physical security

Post office physical security

Alice requests return acknowledgment from Bob ← Bob verifies Alice's signature ← Only Bob breaks seal and opens envelope

Figure 13.1 How the postal system provides security features in a message from Alice to Bob

those risks.

EXAMPLE: *In the United Kingdom, by law, the risk of a disputed transaction from automatic teller machines is borne by the consumer, whereas in the United States it is borne by the bank. As a result, banks in the United States have deployed much stronger ATM security measures.*

nature to authenticate Alice. He may notify Alice (using a return letter) of successful delivery. Later, Bob may find it necessary to prove in court that Alice sent him the message (for example, if it is a legal contract). For this purpose he would produce the message and argue that since it was written in permanent ink on paper—and thus difficult to modify without detection—and contained Alice's signature, Alice must have sent it. The inability of Alice to later deny she sent the message is called nonrepudiation.

If Bob is unable to verify Alice's signature because he does not have an authoritative original copy that he can trust, he has several contingencies. He might ask Alice to send him a copy of her signature separately; however, this is inherently suspect, because Eve could easily fool Bob by sending him her forged signature of Alice. Thus, to be safe Bob must have the assistance of a *trusted authority*. For example, he might request a replica of Alice's signature from the government and then compare it to the signature on Alice's letter. Alternatively, he might ask that Alice have her letter notarized—the notary public is also relying on an authority in checking some credential that Alice provides, such as her driver's license or passport.

Some of these security measures would falter if they had not been combined in a security system. For example, Alice might be able to repudiate the message if she had not been authenticated (she could claim somebody else sent it) or if she could claim the message was altered in transit (the message didn't have integrity).

Security Analysis and Planning

Security threats are numerous, and security measures can be invasive to users and expensive to implement. As a practical matter, it is necessary to focus efforts on the most likely and damaging threats in a particular circumstance. For this reason, it is important, as part of the conceptualization and analysis phase of the application lifecycle, to include a *threat analysis*. What are the most likely threats, and in what areas can the greatest damage be wrought? What security measures are cost effective in relation to the potential damage? As part of this process, it may be determined that some threats cannot be countered—or should not be countered—because of contradictory considerations such as ease of use or cost. In that case, a plan for *damage control* and *recovery* should be formulated. There should also be contingency plans both to detect and deal with the inevitable unanticipated security threats. These plans should include both damage control and the augmentation of security measures.

Even with all these measures, the postal system has inherent vulnerabilities. Bob's mailbox—in order to be accessible to a postal worker—is also accessible to any passerby (such as Eve) who can steal a letter or insert a forged letter. The address and return address on the envelope may allow Eve to determine that Alice sent Bob a message, even if she can't examine the contents. To counter many threats of this type, where technical measures are ineffective or usability concerns intervene, the government has established *legal sanctions*—including laws against the theft of mail from, or insertion of unauthorized mail into, a mailbox. If Bob is especially worried about these threats, he could rent at extra cost a post office box, which restricts access to his mail (by giving him an exclusive key) and thus maintains physical security all the way from Alice to him.

13.2.2   Examples of Threats

There are many potential security threats that should be anticipated—insofar as possible—and countered with security measures (see the sidebar "Security Analysis and Planning").

Many security threats and measures in the physical world must be transferred to networked computers. Messages crossing the network, whether they originate with a user (an email message, for example) or with an application (a module-to-module interaction), are data (a collection of bits). This is a security challenge, because the infrastructure, in order to manipulate and process those bits (replicate them, for example), must inherently be able to observe and modify them. Without additional measures, there would be no way to prevent a message from being examined or modified in transit, or to detect that this happened. In particular, there are four specific threats to a message communicated through the network, as listed in Table 13.4.

All these security threats can be duplicated on the Internet unless additional security measures discussed in this chapter are taken. For example, both the contents of messages and their internal identification of sender and recipient are represented by bits, which can by their very nature be observed or modified without detection. It is possible to pretend to be a different host by faking the sender identification information (this is called *spoofing*).

ANALOGY: *It is easy to put a deceptive return address on a postal envelope. You are wise not to trust the return address as a form of authentication, but to look for a more secure authentication of the sender (such as a signature) inside the envelope.*

Table 13.4 Security threats to messages communicated using the network [Sta99]

Threat	Description	Example
Interruption	The delivery of a legitimate message is prevented.	An employee might prevent his manager from submitting his performance evaluation.
Interception	A message is observed by an intruder and its contents noted.	An employee might violate the privacy of another employee by observing her evaluation as the manager submits it.
Modification	A message is modified before it is passed to the recipient.	An employee might change his evaluation before it is submitted.
Fabrication	A message is fabricated, including a false identity for the sender.	An employee might fabricate a good evaluation for himself or a bad evaluation for a coworker and make it appear to come from the manager.

Sometimes security policies are based on network addressing, which is not wise. For example, a firewall might admit unrestricted access to a particular network address, thought to be associated with a trusted employee working at home. This simple approach offers low security, because under some conditions network addresses can be spoofed (one host masquerading as another).

Networked computers are susceptible to more subtle threats beyond those listed in Table 13.4. One threat, particularly in a network environment, is the *computer virus*. This is a piece of executable program that can "infect" computer files, self-replicate, and cause damage (see the sidebar "Computer Viruses").

Like vandals that might break into a post office, hosts are also susceptible to *intrusion* by unauthorized access through the network. Ways are needed to prevent these intrusions by admitting authorized users and preventing access to others. Frequently it is desired to provide *conditional* access to some applications but not others.

EXAMPLE: *A Web server is often intended to be accessed by anybody on the Internet. At the same time, there may be other applications or stored information on the same host that should have restricted access.*

Even if access is denied to any but authorized users, others might gain entry by mimicking an authorized user. To counter this attack, there have to be user authentication measures analogous to the signature in the postal system. Similarly, if legal contracts are "signed" over the network, or orders for goods

Computer Viruses

Between executions, programs are stored in a special *executable* file in the computer storage (such as magnetic disk). During these dormant times, executables are vulnerable to infection by a virus. A virus attaches itself to an executable (called a *host executable*) in a way that causes its own execution each time the host executable is run. The virus then replicates itself by attaching itself to other executables, and it may also consume resources or destroy data. Transporting an infected executable to another computer will likely cause other files there to be infected.

A N A L O G Y :   *In biology, a virus is an infectious agent that can multiply by replication only in living cells of animals, plants, or bacteria and can consume resources or act destructively. Similarly, computer viruses infect computer systems and can multiply by self-replication.*

One way a virus can attach to an executable is shown in Figure 13.2. The virus adds a block of instructions—consisting of the virus body and payload—at the end of the file. The *body* is a program replicating the virus, and the *payload* is a benign or malicious action. By putting a new "jump" at the beginning of the executable, the virus ensures that its body and payload are executed. After executing the body and payload, another "jump" returns execution to the original program. Upon each execution, the virus body executes (searching for and infecting other files), the virus payload executes (with some benign

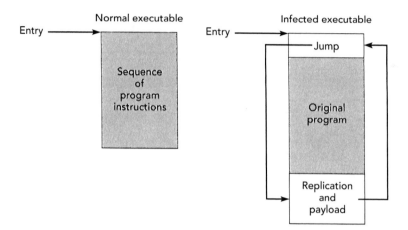

Figure 13.2 One way a computer virus can attach itself to an executable

placed, a forgetful or unscrupulous user might later repudiate the transaction unless there are security measures to prevent this.

A malicious attacker may mount a *denial of service attack*, injecting vast amounts of artificial work or communications that cause a host or network to become overloaded and degrade the performance for legitimate users or crash the application altogether.

E X A M P L E :   *In 1988, a student at Cornell University unleashed a "worm" on the Internet that resulted in a denial of service to a large number of UNIX hosts. A worm is similar to a virus, except it replicates by exploiting operating system vulnerabilities to get itself installed and executed on another computer. It was not intended as a denial of service attack, but due to a programming error, the worm replicated far more than intended, swamping the infected computers.*

This discussion of threats is meant to give you the impression that security is a daunting but important problem. There are many threats to contend with, some obvious and many subtle. Fortunately, there are some effective tools to deal with many of them, as discussed in the remainder of this chapter.

Discussion

D13.1 Discuss the measures taken to achieve trustworthiness in a noncomputer system familiar to you (such as a transportation or electric power system, or a bank). What are some similarities and differences to networked computing?

D13.2 Discuss further the human element to system trustworthiness. What measures can and should be taken on this dimension?

13.2.3 Pillars of Security

The security of networked applications builds on some analogous measures to those noted in the postal system analogy. Because they are so fundamental, I call them *pillars* of security. Like pillars in the physical world, they are discrete structures that support much of the security infrastructure. Also like pillars in the physical world, they are rarely effective in isolation, but must be employed in a coordinated way. These pillars, listed in Table 13.5, are very sophisticated and capable of achieving a much higher level of security than in the postal system analogy. However, some of them are unfortunately also invasive (in cost or convenience or usability) to legitimate users—one of the costs of security. Among other things, these security measures raise burdensome administrative and operational issues.

These pillars of security must work in concert as part of a coherent security system. They must also be backed by well-trained and vigilant operators, a coherent set of established security policies, and ultimately, by criminal laws and penalties. Overall, security is only as good as the weakest link.

13.3 Confidentiality

A primary pillar of security is confidentiality. Insuring the confidentiality of either stored or communicated data requires a *confidentiality protocol*. The foundation of confidentiality is encryption technology, which is introduced in this section and revisited later in the chapter.

Suppose Alice wants to send a confidential message to Bob while preventing an eavesdropper (Eve) from reading the message. The idea is for Alice to lock a message so it can only be unlocked by Bob, who has the unlocking key. Eve is unsuccessful in unlocking the message because she does not possess Bob's unlocking key. The protocol uses an *encryption* algorithm to lock the message and a complementary *decryption* algorithm to unlock it—each requiring the special encryption or decryption key. Although there are simple encryption algorithms, those with adequate security are quite sophisticated and complex (see the sidebar "Simplistic Encryption Algorithms").

ANALOGY: *In the physical world, a lockbox can be used to provide confidentiality. The lockbox requires an unlocking key to open. To be analogous to encryption, a special lockbox that requires two keys—a locking key to lock and an*

or malicious action), and finally, the host program executes.

Viruses must be taken seriously whenever an executable is moved from one host to another, using a floppy disk or transferring over the network. Fortunately, there are excellent utilities for detecting and eradicating viruses.

Simplistic Encryption Algorithms

A couple of simplistic encryption algorithms will illustrate the basic idea behind them. Suppose a text message is to be encrypted. A *substitution algorithm* would use a table of substitutes for each individual letter. For example, a partial substitution table might be

Letter	Substitute
a	r
e	j
y	b

in which case "yea" would encrypt to "bjr." A *transposition algorithm* would move letters around according to a predetermined permutation pattern. For example, in three-letter words the first letter might become the second, the second the third, and the third the first, so that "yea" would encrypt to "eay." Of course, substitution and transposition could be combined to yield better security. The decryption algorithm simply reverses these operations. The encryption key in this case is the substitution and/or transposition tables.

Although simple algorithms like this were used in the ancient world, they are easy to analyze and reverse by statistical techniques. For example, the letter e occurs most frequently in English text, so its substitute could easily be detected by examining a large sample of encrypted text. Nevertheless, some modern algorithms use sophisticated variations on the basic techniques of substitution and transposition.

Table 13.5 Pillars of a computer security system

Capability	Description	Analogy
Authentication	Messages received over the network may be received from anyone and anywhere. Authentication enables a recipient to verify the identity of a sender.	On paper documents, a signature is appended. The recipient of a telephone call may be able to identify the caller by recognizing her voice.
Message integrity	A message is data that may easily be modified as it crosses the network. Message integrity insures that the message has not been modified since originated by the sender.	Paper documents created in permanent ink are difficult to modify without detection. While additions are possible, they are difficult to achieve without detection.
Confidentiality	A message passing through the network might be read by an eavesdropper. Confidentiality insures that a message can only be read by the intended recipient.	The sender of a letter encloses it in an envelope to keep away prying eyes. A postcard, on the other hand, does not provide confidentiality.
Nonrepudiation	A sender might later claim never to have sent a message. Nonrepudiation enables a recipient to prove (in court if necessary) that the sender did originate the message.	A recipient of a document (purchase order or contract, for example) will require a signature on it, so he can later prove the identity of the sender. Additional assurance is provided by signing two copies of the document, one kept by the sender and one sent to the recipient.
Access control	A host connected to the Internet will be vulnerable to theft or vandalism by unauthorized parties. Access control restricts access to hosts, or particular applications, to authorized and authenticated users.	Postal patrons are allowed into the public area of the post office, but only postal employees can enter secure areas where mail is sorted. Employees are authenticated by a picture badge.

unlocking key to open—must be assumed. First, Alice locks a message in the lockbox to protect it from being read by Eve. Second, Bob unlocks the lockbox to obtain the contents—the message from Alice.

Encryption comes in two distinct flavors: symmetric and asymmetric. These are analogous to two distinct types of lockboxes, depending on the relationship of the locking and unlocking key, as illustrated in Figure 13.3.

- *Symmetric locking and unlocking key:* The lockbox requires identical keys to lock and unlock the lockbox. There are two replicas of this key; one is held by Alice and one by Bob. Alice puts the message in the lockbox, which she locks using her replica of the key. Bob uses his replica of the key to open the

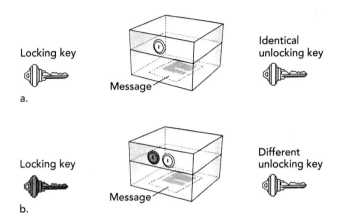

Figure 13.3 Two types of lockboxes, which are analogous to an (a) symmetric and (b) asymmetric encryption system

lockbox and retrieve the contents. Lacking the key, Eve is unable to view or modify the contents.

- *Asymmetric lock and key:* The lockbox has two *different* keys, a locking key to lock the lockbox (possessed by Alice) and an unlocking key (possessed by Bob) that unlocks the box. Alice's key cannot unlock the box—it can only lock it. Only Bob's key can unlock the lockbox to recover the message—once it has been locked.

The symmetric lock and key is conceptually simpler, but there are advantages to the asymmetric lock and key, as seen shortly.

13.3.1 Symmetric vs. Asymmetric Encryption

The lockbox analogy illustrates a confidentiality protocol for the two cases in Figure 13.4. The requirements for confidentiality are different in the two cases:

- *Symmetric encryption:* The locking and unlocking keys are identical. Bob and Alice must each possess a replica of this key—sometimes called a shared key—but Eve must not.
- *Asymmetric encryption:* The locking and unlocking keys are different. Eve must not possess a replica of the *unlocking* key, but it doesn't matter if she possesses a replica of the locking key, because that would not allow her to unlock the message.

The last statement is important, but to be valid an additional important assumption is necessary: It must be computationally impractical for Eve, possessing a replica of the locking key, to turn that into a replica of the unlocking key. Fortunately, this is feasible.

Trusted Systems

Authors and publishers making a living from creating information content are reluctant to distribute that content in digital form because of the ease of replication. Copyright laws are effective against large piracy operations, but not individuals distributing free replicas to their friends and neighbors. Encrypting the data representing copyrighted information would seem to be a solution; however, if a consumer is provided a decryption key to legitimately view the information, then she can also replicate and disseminate the information after it has been decrypted.

A solution to this dilemma is a *trusted system*—equipment that can be relied on to follow prescribed rules [Ste97]. An example would be a viewer of written material or a player of audio or video that would allow legitimate viewing or playing but refuse to make unauthorized replicas. The usage rights associated with particular content can be expressed in a language designed for that purpose and passed to the trusted system, which can be relied on to enforce them. The types of usage rights include transport rights (rules for copy, transfer, or loan), render rights (viewing, printing, and playing), derivative-work rights (extracting and editing for other publications), and backup-copy rights. Trusted systems can provide similar combinations of freedom for the customer and protection for the author that exist in the physical world.

EXAMPLE: *Divx is a product that turns a DVD video player into a trusted system. It allows consumers to trade a lower price for video disks for restrictions, such as a restricted time interval to play a disk. The player*

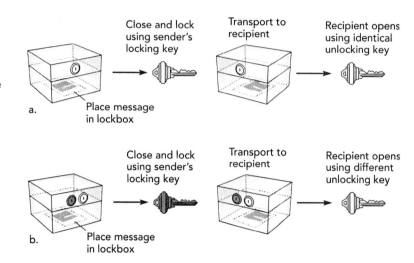

Figure 13.4 Using a lockbox to preserve confidentiality through (a) symmetric and (b) asymmetric encryption

In the asymmetric case, it is permissible to distribute replicas of the locking key publicly. Bob, who wishes to receive confidential messages from many people (including Alice), can publish his locking key to the citizenry (in directories or on his Web home page), so *anyone* can send him a confidential message. Bob need not worry that Eve will then possess the locking key, since it will not help her unlock a message sent by Alice (or anyone else). For this reason, the asymmetric locking key is called a *public key* and the asymmetric unlocking key is called a *secret key* (since only Bob can possess it).

The symmetric encryption system raises a practical quandary: Who (Bob or Alice) originates the secret key, and how do they get a replica to the other? Remember that Eve could observe the key if it were sent over the network. This logistical problem makes the asymmetric system more attractive for use in uncoordinated administrative domains.

EXAMPLE: *If Bob is a merchant selling goods over the network, literally anybody is a potential consumer who might buy Bob's goods, including Alice. If Alice wants to use her credit card to make a purchase, she would like to avoid its interception by Eve, who might use it improperly to make her own purchases. The asymmetric confidentiality protocol is preferred, since Bob can simply publish his public key, and Alice can use it to encrypt her credit card number. Eve, who does not possess Bob's secret key, cannot view the credit card number. Of course, Eve too is a potential customer of Bob.*

Encryption can also be used to protect intellectual property distributed in digital form, over the network or not (see the sidebar "Trusted Systems").

13.3.2   Encryption Algorithms

As shown in Figure 13.5, in networked computing a message to be sent confidentially is data called *plaintext*. (This terminology is a holdover from an earlier age when predominately text messages were encrypted—today, such a message may well not represent text.) The encryption algorithm is a mathematical algorithm that accepts the plaintext and a key, and transforms it into *ciphertext*—from which the plaintext cannot be recovered without knowledge of a secret key. The key, plaintext, and ciphertext, like any other information, are all data (a string of bits). A parameter of great interest, because it relates directly to the security of the encryption, is the size of the key (number of bits).

The legitimate recipient, possessing the secret key, can apply a decryption algorithm to recover the original plaintext. The confidentiality protocol requires the sender to encrypt the plaintext, transmit the resulting ciphertext to the recipient, and the recipient to decrypt it. Confidentiality depends on only the recipient—or possibly both recipient and sender—possessing the secret key. Confidentiality does *not* depend on the secrecy of the algorithms—in fact, they should be standardized and publicly divulged so everyone can use them.

In the symmetric confidentiality protocol, the same secret key *SK* is used by sender and recipient. Using the notation $E_K(P)$ to denote encryption of P using key K, it can be written as

$$E_{SK}(P) \rightarrow C, \; D_{SK}(C) \rightarrow P$$

The asymmetric confidentiality protocol is similar, except that two keys are used: Bob's secret key *BSK* (which Alice and nobody else should possess) and Bob's public key *BPK* (which Bob can distribute freely):

$$E_{BPK}(P) \rightarrow C, \; D_{BSK}(C) \rightarrow P$$

E X A M P L E :   *The most widely used de jure symmetric encryption standard is the data encryption standard (DES), formally called DEA-1 by ISO. A widely used de facto asymmetric encryption standard is RSA, named after its inventors Rivest, Shamir, and Adleman [RSA78].*

Strictly speaking, recovering the plaintext from the ciphertext is not impossible—it is just intended to be very hard. Eve can apply any of several known attacks on the ciphertext in an attempt to discover the secret key or the plaintext (see the sidebar "Attacks on Confidentiality Protocols").

While asymmetric encryption appears much more desirable than symmetric—it avoids the need for distribution of a secret key—it has an important disadvantage. Available asymmetric encryption algorithms require roughly a thousand times more computational effort than symmetric encryption and decryption

communicates by telephone, so that the terms and conditions can be modified, and the consumer is later billed. It is marketed as a DVD rental replacement, but without the need to physically return disks.

Trusted systems can be endowed with the ability to recognize other trusted systems and convey content securely using confidentiality and authentication protocols. Trusted systems can prevent unauthorized replication but not copying, as those terms are defined in "Technical Properties of Information" on page 242. A user could still capture an imperfect copy using a camcorder, camera, microphone, or copying machine. However, *digital watermarks* (special invisible but detectable patterns) can be embedded in some types of content, allowing a publisher to trace the source of illicit copies.

Attacks on Confidentiality Protocols

An important task of the designer of encryption algorithms and protocols is to anticipate and foil attacks that Eve may apply. It should be established that attacks are *computationally impractical*. This means not possible, using a computer that Eve can afford, within a period of time that would make the plaintext useful to her.

EXAMPLE: *If the computation took ten years with the fastest commercially available computer, Alice and Bob might consider that acceptable confidentiality—by the time the plaintext could be recovered, it would be useless to Eve.*

For the symmetric protocol, the primary attack is to try all possible secret keys. The feasibility of this attack depends on the *key length* (number of bits in the key) and the speed of available computers. The key length can be made sufficiently long to foil this attack for any desired period, for a particular computer technology.

EXAMPLE: *For a 128-bit key, there are $2^{128} \approx 3 \times 10^{38}$ different keys. If a computer could try 100 million keys per second (a rough estimate for today's fastest desktop computers), this attack would take 3×10^{30} seconds, or 10^{21} centuries—a very long time!*

DES uses a 56-bit key, which is considered inadequate today. Fortunately, there are ways to apply DES twice or three times, each with a different key, to increase the effective key length. An Advanced Encryption Standard (AES) is currently being standardized as a

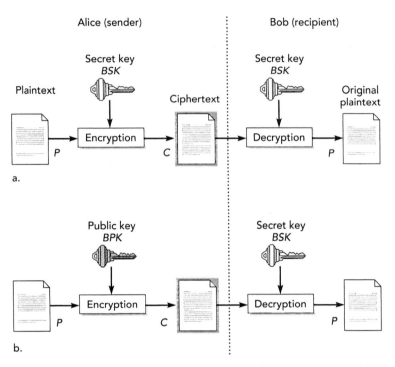

Figure 13.5 The (a) symmetric and (b) asymmetric confidentiality protocol hides a message from viewing to anybody without the secret key (*SK*)

(partly because larger keys are required). Thus, symmetric encryption is superior for "bulk encryption" of large amounts of data and is widely used for this purpose. Asymmetric and symmetric encryption can be combined in useful ways, as described later.

13.4   Authentication

Another pillar of security is *authentication*—verifying the identity of a party over the network. Encryption is useful for authentication, as it is for confidentiality.

If Bob receives a ciphertext purporting to be from Alice, he should be very suspicious. The ciphertext might actually have originated from Eve or another imposter seeking to impersonate Alice. Compared to the personal interaction of the physical world, impersonation is easy over the network.

EXAMPLE: *When Alice visits an Unlimited store in the local mall, there are a number of clues that this is likely to be a legitimate business—such as the store, the sign out front, etc. Over the network, Alice should be skeptical of a seller claiming to be Unlimited, since an unscrupulous person (such as Eve) could more easily set up a Web site claiming to be Unlimited and collect money* *from Alice without delivering the goods. In its store, Unlimited authenticates Alice by requesting a picture identification or credit card. Over the network, Eve might more easily impersonate Alice, and Alice might then have to pay for goods actually ordered and received by Eve.*

Authentication allows Bob to verify that the person claiming to be Alice is in fact Alice. In practice, both Bob and Alice each authenticate the other. Examining how authentication is done in the physical world gives some clues as to how it can be done over the network:

- Bob could compare a person's face with Alice's picture shown in her picture identification card, and if it matches authenticate her as Alice. This authentication depends on Alice's physical characteristics.
- If a person can produce Alice's credit card—and the issuer of the credit card confirms that Alice has not reported it stolen—Bob might authenticate that person as Alice. This authentication depends on the person presenting something that only Alice should possess.

In both these cases, authentication depends on a trusted third party, called an *authority*—either the issuer of Alice's picture identification, or the issuer of her credit card. In fact, it is impossible to authenticate Alice without the aid of an authority. Depending on Alice to authenticate herself without verification by a trusted authority is inherently suspect.

13.4.1 Biometrics

The two physical-world authentication techniques have analogs in networked computing. The first, based on a person's physical characteristics, is called *biometrics*.

EXAMPLE: *If Bob wants to authenticate Alice, and has obtained some unique physical characteristics of Alice from a trusted authority (her picture, her fingerprint, or the pattern of the iris of her eye, for example), then Bob can verify that physical characteristic.*

Biometrics requires a trusted way to gather the biometrics data on the person being authenticated. This is most widely used to authenticate a person entering a controlled physical facility such as a bank vault, computer center, or automatic teller machine, where the biometric data is gathered under the complete control of the authenticator. More generally, it might depend on the gathering of biometric data by a trusted system.

replacement for DES. For RSA, the recommended key length is about 768 bits for personal use and 1,024 bits for corporate use.

Asymmetric keys are much larger than symmetric keys, since the attacks are different, and there are shortcut attacks that Eve can mount. She may try to recover the secret key from the public key. Alternatively, because Eve possesses the public key, she can use a *chosen plaintext* attack. She can encrypt any plaintext she suspects using the public key and see if it matches the ciphertext. This would be particularly valuable if she suspects a particular message, such as "attack at dawn." (However, this is easily foiled by adding some random bits to the plaintext).

Eve might be even more sneaky and try to obtain a secret key by deception, or by physically breaking into Alice's or Bob's premises, or rummaging through their trash.

13.4.2   Secrets

Asking the person claiming to be Alice to produce something that only Alice should possess, as confirmed by an authority, is the most practical authentication technique over a network. In the physical world, that "something" is a picture identification, credit card, or other physical object. Over the network, that something can't be a physical object and thus must be a *secret*. A secret is data—or something that can be represented as data, such as a password—that only one person knows. A password is a nonsensical string of characters (letters, punctuation marks, numbers) that the person has chosen and committed to memory.

Authentication proceeds by challenging a person claiming to be Alice to produce Alice's secret. There are several subtleties in doing this securely:

- It is a bad idea for Alice to give her secret to Bob for purposes of authentication, since Bob could later use it to impersonate Alice.
- It is doubly bad for Alice to send her secret to Bob over the network, as Eve could intercept it and later use it to impersonate Alice (and Bob would have it as well).
- There must be an authority that Bob trusts to verify Alice's secret.

There are thus two valued properties of an authentication scheme based on a secret:

- Alice should be able to prove she has a secret without revealing it.
- Bob should be able to verify the secret with an authority he trusts and without actually knowing the secret.

While these requirements might appear impossible at first glance, in fact they can be achieved using asymmetric encryption keys. In this approach, Alice's secret can be her secret key *ASK*, and Bob can make use of Alice's public key *APK* to force her to prove she possesses *ASK*—without himself possessing *ASK*. Bob can also check the validity of *APK* with an authority, who tells him "Yes, *APK* is Alice's public key." Of course, Bob would be wise to authenticate that authority also!

The protocol for verifying that Alice possesses the *ASK* corresponding to *APK* depends on a property of the asymmetric confidentiality protocol: the roles of the two keys can be *reversed*. Alice can encrypt a plaintext using her secret key *ASK*, and Bob can decrypt the resulting ciphertext using Alice's public key *APK*, and the original plaintext is recovered. This reversed protocol does not provide confidentiality, since anybody with *APK* can recover that plaintext. It is the basis of a *challenge-response* protocol, in which Bob—making use of *APK*—chal-

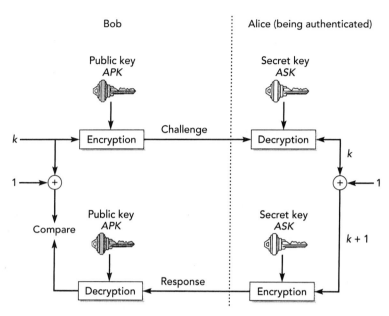

Figure 13.6 A challenge-response protocol requires the party being authenticated to prove she possesses a secret key *SK*

Challenge-Response Protocol

The commonly used challenge-response authentication protocol is illustrated in Figure 13.6. Bob (the suspicious party) generates a plaintext representing random integer k, encrypts it using *APK*, and sends the resulting ciphertext to Alice with the challenge to respond with $k + 1$ encrypted by *ASK*. In order to meet that challenge, Alice has to decrypt the message using *ASK* to obtain k, add one, and encrypt the result using *ASK*. Both require Alice to possess *ASK*. Bob, knowing *APK*, can decrypt the response from Alice to confirm that it is, in fact, $k + 1$. This protocol depends on the reversal of the role of the public and secret keys in the asymmetric confidentiality protocol, since Alice encrypts her response with her secret key and Bob decrypts it with her public key. Notice Alice does not reveal *ASK*, nor does Bob possess it.

Symbolically, this challenge-response protocol can be summarized as:

1. Bob generates a random integer k and sends $E_{APK}(k) = C_1$ as a challenge.
2. Alice determines $D_{ASK}(C_1) = k$ and responds with $E_{ASK}(k + 1) = C_2$.
3. Bob calculates $D_{APK}(C_2)$, and if the result equals $k + 1$, Alice is authenticated.

lenges Alice to prove she possesses *ASK*, and Alice's response to that challenge convinces Bob that she does indeed possess *ASK* (see the sidebar "Challenge-Response Protocol").

ANALOGY: *The challenge-response protocol is a sophisticated version of a protocol familiar from spy movies. Suppose spy Helen is given a secret code word "limabeans" before she leaves headquarters. Another spy, wishing to authenticate Helen in the field, challenges her to present her code word. When she presents "limabeans," her identity is established. Of course, this spy-movie protocol is ridiculously weak, because anybody can obtain Helen's secret by just asking her!*

13.4.3 Digital Certificates and Certificate Authorities

Bob's authentication of Alice depends on knowing her public key *APK*. Of course, Bob must obtain *APK* from an authority or have it verified by an authority.

This works like the driver's license authentication analogy in the physical world. Alice presents Bob with a credential called a *digital certificate* (analogous to a driver's license) issued to her by a trusted *certificate authority* (CA), which is

Certificates and a National Identity Card

U.S. citizens have always resisted a "national identity card" because of privacy concerns. In the physical world, it has been possible to get by without one. However, authentication on the network for general purposes such as electronic commerce requires the equivalent in networked computing—the digital certificate. Are the citizens finally ready to accept this?

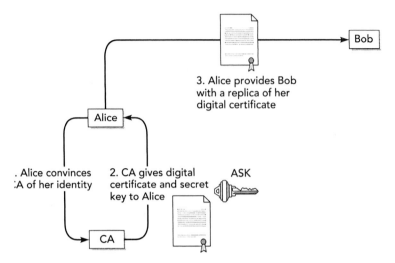

Figure 13.7 Alice uses a digital certificate to provide an authenticated public key to Bob

analogous to the motor vehicle bureau. The digital certificate supplies APK to Bob in a way that he can trust, presuming he trusts the authority.

The CA is a company or government agency that specializes in issuing digital certificates. The protocol that Alice uses to obtain one and later use it is shown in Figure 13.7. (The driver's license bureau of the physical world could be substituted for the CA without any difference in the protocol.) The three steps are as follows:

1. Alice proves her identity to the CA (for example, the CA might require Alice to appear in person and present her birth certificate, social security card, and driver's license). The CA then generates a new unique matched pair of asymmetrical encryption keys (ASK, APK) on her behalf. The CA gives the secret key ASK to Alice (which she must *keep* secret), as well as a digital certificate (ADC) that contains both her identity and her public key APK.
2. To supply her public key APK to Bob (or to anyone else), Alice supplies the digital certificate (ADC) provided her by the CA.
3. Presuming that Bob trusts the CA, he can use the APK he obtains from the ADC to authenticate Alice and send her confidential messages.

EXAMPLE: *The most prominent CA is VeriSign, a company that specializes in security and makes money by issuing certificates. Like all CAs, VeriSign maintains strict internal security practices. For example, revealing Alice's secret key to a third party would be an egregious security breach.*

In security, there is often a catch. What is to prevent someone from making his own digital certificate and claiming it comes from the CA? For example, why can't Eve manufacture a digital certificate that attaches her own public key to Alice's identity? Alternatively, why can't Eve modify Alice's digital certificate to substitute her public key for Alice's? If Eve can do either, she can fool Bob. These problems are circumvented using a digital signature, described in the next section.

13.5   Signatures

Important pillars needed to fill out the security picture are message integrity and nonrepudiation. Recall that the integrity of a message sent by Alice is the assurance that the message was not modified in transit to Bob (analogous to a paper document written in permanent ink), and nonrepudiation allows Bob to prove in court that Alice sent the message (analogous to a signed document). Integrity is necessary for nonrepudiation, since without integrity Alice can always repudiate a message by simply claiming it was modified after she originated it. Integrity and nonrepudiation are employed by a CA to convince Bob of the validity of a digital certificate it issues.

Consider a message sent by Alice to Bob, and assume that Bob has Alice's public key APK. How can Bob be sure that a plaintext message from Alice has integrity, and how can he prevent Alice from repudiating it? Like the challenge-response protocol, these capabilities are based on the reversal of the asymmetric confidentiality protocol—encryption with the secret key followed by decryption with the public key. This capability is used to create a *digital signature*, as illustrated in Figure 13.8. The signature S is simply the plaintext message encrypted by Alice's secret key ASK. When Bob receives both the signature $S = E_{ASK}(P)$ and the plaintext P, he can verify the signature by decrypting S using APK, and comparing the result to P:

$$D_{APK}(S) \equiv P$$

If they are equal, Bob knows that only Alice could have generated both the plaintext message *and* the signature, because that requires possession of ASK. Eve, who intercepts the signature, can recover the plaintext from it (she probably has APK too), but doesn't have the means to modify the message and generate a new signature because she doesn't possess ASK. The signature by itself does not provide confidentiality, but integrity and confidentiality can easily be combined using a more complicated protocol, as described shortly. A digital signature is usually implemented differently from the way just described in order to reduce the computational requirements (see the sidebar "Message Digest").

Message Digest

The digital signature is described in "Signatures" on this page as the plaintext encrypted using the signer's asymmetrical secret key. This form of signature has the problem that the plaintext may be large, requiring a large computational effort to encrypt with the asymmetric algorithm. In practice, the digital signature is based on a *message digest* (MD). The MD of a plaintext is first calculated, and then that MD is encrypted using the signer's secret key. The MD is a concise summary of a plaintext, and thus its encryption requires less computational effort.

The MD always has the same number of bits (typically 128 or 160), regardless of the length of the plaintext. Since the plaintext can be bigger than the MD, the MD does not uniquely specify the plaintext—it is possible for many plaintexts to have the same MD. However, the MD has some characteristics that make it useful:

- An MD is one-way, in the sense that given a specific MD, it is computationally infeasible to find a plaintext with that MD. Thus, that a given MD corresponds to a given plaintext can be verified, but the plaintext cannot be recovered from the MD.
- It is computationally infeasible to find two messages with the same MD (this is called the collision-free property). Thus, in practical terms, if an MD is verified for a given message, it can be assumed that MD was generated from that message.

As a result of these properties, the MD can be relied upon as a concise summary of the plaintext, and it can be substituted for the plaintext in the digital signature algorithm (and other purposes).

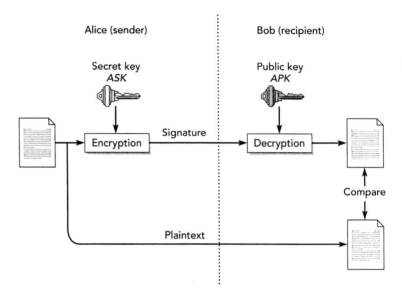

Figure 13.8 The digital signature is an encrypted version of a plaintext using an asymmetrical secret key

The plaintext and signature can also prevent Alice from repudiating the message. If Bob keeps a copy of the plaintext and also a copy of Alice's digital certificate, he can prove in court that encrypting the message required *ASK*—which could only be done by Alice—and that the message was not later modified by someone else. Alice's only defense would be that *ASK* was accidently revealed to someone else before the message was sent, but her case is weak if she did not report this to an authority.

Establishing the authenticity of the digital certificate also depends on integrity and nonrepudiation. The digital certificate includes the following parts:

1. Alice's identification information (name, address, etc.)
2. Alice's public key *APK*
3. The CA's signature for the concatenation of 1 and 2, using its own secret key

ANALOGY: *If the CA is analogous to the driver's license bureau and the CA-issued digital certificate is analogous to a driver's license, its digital signature is analogous to the seal authenticating the license and the plastic encasing the driver's license that prevents it from being modified.*

The last important detail is that Bob requires the CA's public key to check its signature on Alice's digital certificate. This is usually addressed by building it into Bob's software.

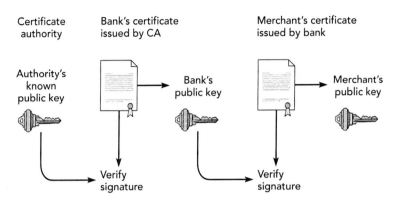

Figure 13.9 A chain of trust from a merchant to the merchant's bank to a trusted certificate authority

E X A M P L E :   *Web browser software includes the public keys of a set of CAs (and the user can add more). This allows the browser to check the authenticity and integrity of any certificate issued by one of those CAs. The browser can obtain authenticated public keys of Web servers from certificates supplied by those servers and use these public keys to check the server's authenticity, check the integrity of messages from it, send confidential messages to the server, etc.*

In practice, there is usually a hierarchy of CAs (see the sidebar "A Chain of Trust").

All these protocols may sound complicated, but it is important to note that they are embedded in software applications, so the user need not deal with them directly. The purpose of this discussion has been to understand what security protocols can accomplish and what assumptions are necessary to assume they are trustworthy.

13.6   Security Systems

Just like the postal system analogy, a system assembling the complementary pillars of security can achieve multiple objectives. For example, Alice and Bob probably desire a combination of confidentiality, authentication, integrity, and nonrepudiation. The pillars can be combined in various ways to achieve protocols for this purpose.

As an example, assume that Alice and Bob possess their own secret key and a digital certificate providing the public key of the other, and that they have both checked the authenticity of the public key by verifying the signature of the CA. If Alice attaches her signature to a message (by encrypting it or its message

A Chain of Trust

A single, global CA known to everybody is not only logistically difficult—it would be difficult for a single authority to deal with worldwide authentication—it is probably not politically feasible either (what country will relish using a CA in another country)? Fortunately, it is easy to use a hierarchy of CAs. Bob may accept a certificate from an authority he has never heard of, if that CA is in turn certified by another CA he trusts. There may be a chain of trust extending through several authorities until it reaches an authority that he does know and trust.

A N A L O G Y :   *A notary public—a professional dedicated to authentication—typically relies on a certification of Alice's identity by birth certificate, driver's license, etc. Bob relies on authentication by the notary public because he is confident that the notary will responsibly demand proof of Alice's identity from authorities that Bob does trust.*

The following example reveals the details of how a chain of trust works.

E X A M P L E :   *As shown in Figure 13.9, suppose an on-line merchant supplies a digital certificate issued by its bank. Anticipating that Bob may not know or trust this particular bank, the merchant also supplies a certificate issued by a well-known CA that certifies the bank. If Bob knows that CA and has a trusted copy of its public key, then Bob can verify the CA's signature on the bank's certificate. This certifies the bank and its public key, so*

Bob can now check the bank's
signature on the merchant's
certificate. That certifies the
merchant's public key, so Bob
can now use it to authenticate
and communicate confiden-
tially with the merchant.

Example of a Combination Protocol

Suppose Alice wants to communicate a plaintext P confidentially to
Bob, but Bob insists on first authenticating Alice and later verifying the
message integrity. The following
combination protocol can achieve
this objective.

First, Alice generates a signature S
using her secret key:

$E_{ASK}(P) = S$

Next she combines the plaintext and
signature to obtain a new message
$M = P \cup S$ (here "$\cup$" means to con-
catenate the data from each to generate a larger data). Alice then encrypts
this new message using Bob's public
key BPK and sends the resulting
ciphertext C to Bob:

$E_{BPK}(M) = C$

Bob can now recover M, and hence P
and S, by decrypting C using his
secret key BSK,

$D_{BSK}(C) = M = P \cup S$

from which both P and S can be
recovered. Finally, Bob verifies the
signature S using Alice's public key
APK:

$D_{APK}(S) \equiv P$

This assures Bob that the message
originated with Alice. Eve, not knowing BSK, is unable to obtain M, and

digest with her secret key) and encrypts the message concatenated with signature using Bob's public key, then Bob can be sure of confidentiality and also the
integrity of the message to Bob (see the sidebar "Example of a Combination
Protocol").

13.6.1 Confidential Sessions

While Alice sometimes wants to send just a single message to Bob, she may also
want to engage in an extended conversation with him. This is supported by the
session communication service described in "The Conversation" on page 356.
Although a confidentiality protocol based on asymmetric encryption avoids
logistical problems of key distribution, and is practical in an uncoordinated public administrative environment, asymmetrical encryption and decryption require
considerably more computation than symmetrical. Thus, it would be desirable
to use symmetrical encryption to insure confidentiality, thereby reducing the
computational load, while still avoiding the logistical problems with symmetric
keys. This can be done by generating a secret key for the exclusive one-time use
in this session, called a *session key*. If Bob, for example, generates this session
key randomly, he can feel comfortable sharing it with Alice because he will
never use it again.

This is the idea behind the *digital envelope*. Symmetrical encryption and
decryption are used for all messages in the session. The session key is conveyed
by an asymmetrical confidentiality protocol as part of session establishment,
thus insuring that only Alice and Bob possess the secret session key. This is
called a digital envelope because it provides a framework for confidential sessions, analogous to how an envelope protects confidentiality of a postal letter.
The protocol is described in more detail in the sidebar "Session Keys."

E X A M P L E : *Netscape defined an open de facto standard called* secure sockets
layer *(SSL) that adds authentication, confidentiality, and integrity to sessions
using the internet's TCP. This protocol is widely used, particularly for secure
connections between a Web server (such as retail, brokerage, and banking
sites) and the browser. SSL's operation is indicated by a "key icon" in the lower-
left corner of a Netscape Navigator window. The protocol has been adopted
and extended by the IETF, which calls it Transport Layer Security (TLS).*

SSL/TLS forms the basis for security that can be achieved in today's Web environment in e-commerce applications (see the sidebar "Web Browser Security").

13.7   Example: Stock Trading Application

Of the applications discussed in "Examples of Organizational Applications" on page 62, the one with the most critical security requirements is stocks4u.com. As part of its initial business planning, considerable effort was devoted to threat analysis, as described in the "Security Analysis and Planning" on page 378, and unusual vigilance is exercised in the operations. Focus groups were conducted to determine what threats were most troubling to customers, regardless of the accuracy of their perception. As a result, not only were security measures instituted, but also, where possible, they were made visible to the customers to provide assurance, especially in areas of greatest concern.

Confidentiality is important to customers, and avoiding imposters is important to both stocks4u.com and its customers. As a starting point, SSL/TLS was utilized because it is already supported by Web browsers. This allows the browser to authenticate stocks4u.com's server and to set up a confidential session based on a secret session key and symmetric encryption. Stocks4u.com advertises its strong security measures with a "security" link on its home page.

Unfortunately, SSL/TLS cannot authenticate the customer to stocks4u.com, so a password is used. In a sense, this is more secure than a secret stored in the customer's computer, as long as the customer commits it to memory and doesn't write it down. Since the password is entered after a secure session is established, it cannot be stolen over the network. Once the password is checked, stocks4u.com and the customer have each authenticated the other, and the remaining business transactions can proceed confidentially.

A different security challenge faces the stock exchange and stocks4u.com, since the threats in this arena potentially have much greater impact. Major fraud could be committed, or a denial-of-service attack could literally close the exchange temporarily. The exchange established a set of security policies and procedures that applied to all its brokerage partners. Because of the closed nature of this inter-enterprise e-commerce, a digital certificate and public key infrastructure is not necessary or appropriate. Rather, secure sessions are established between the exchange and its brokerage partners over the Internet, establishing an extranet using symmetric session keys. To improve security, no session and session key is allowed to last more than one hour. The authentication and digital envelope associated with these sessions are established using a shared secret key that is conveyed between companies by courier (on paper) the first day of each month. The number of secret keys to manage is modest because the brokers communicate only with the exchange, not with one another.

hence P, so confidentiality is maintained.

Subtle security lapses can arise. As the protocol is described, Eve could observe and make a replica of Alice's double-encrypted message, and resend it to Bob later. Bob would be fooled into thinking this second message came from Alice, even though it was actually from Eve. This is called a *replay attack* and can be foiled by using a more secure challenge-response authentication protocol.

Session Keys

Alice and Bob can avoid sharing a secret symmetrical encryption key if Alice generates a random secret key called a session key (SK). Next, as part of the session establishment protocol, she sends the session key to Bob, while keeping it confidential, by encrypting it with Bob's public key BPK:

$$E_{BPK}(SK) = CSK$$

Bob can then obtain the session key by decryption using his own secret key:

$$D_{BPK}(CSK) = SK$$

Bob and Alice now both possess SK, but nobody else does. SK is now used to encrypt all session messages in both directions.

As part of session establishment, before exchanging SK, Bob and Alice will authenticate one another, using a challenge-response protocol. This protocol has advantages in addition to computational efficiency:

- The session key is used only once, for the duration of a single session. Although Alice has revealed SK, she will never use it again, so she doesn't mind revealing it to Bob.

- Permanent asymmetrical keys are used little, minimizing their vulnerability to discovery.
- The session key provides a continuing authentication and integrity for every message in the session. Since the session key is held by only Alice and Bob, Bob knows that each message in the session can only have been generated by Alice and was not changed.

Web Browser Security

In today's Web, there is the desire to create a secure environment, for example, for electronic banking and retailing. Since consumers do not normally have digital certificates, authentication of the user today depends on passwords. On the other hand, it is reasonable to insist that the server obtain a digital certificate. For this reason, bidirectional authentication is usually provided in the following way today:

- The server provides a digital certificate, and the Web browser software encapsulates the public keys of a standard set of certificate authorities. Thus, the browser can obtain an authenticated public key of the server from the server's certificate.
- The browser can generate a random session key and send it confidentially to the server by encrypting it with the server's public key. This provides a digital envelope, by which the browser and server can confidentially communicate for an entire session using symmetric encryption. (In SSL, the session is provided by the Internet TCP.)

13.8   Open Issues

Trustworthiness is arguably one of the least mature areas of networked computing and also one that raises contentious policy issues.

13.8.1   Increasing Vulnerability

Networked computing integrated into vital societal functions carries vulnerabilities. Even technological security, such as that discussed here, cannot by itself be completely effective. Physical security, employee integrity, operational vigilance, and many intangibles are involved. Further, not all possible threats can be anticipated, so the update and addition of security measures throughout the lifecycle of an application is inevitable.

Most unsettling is the observation that network breakdowns or break-ins can be massive, with much wider impact than physical breakdowns or break-ins. Further, the magnitude of the risks are difficult to quantify, and as a result the insurance industry has not been active in offering means for spreading these risks as it has in other human activities.

How will these problems be addressed? One clear need is additional research, seeking more effective security systems and greater robustness and reliability. Another need is for a much more vigorous response on the part of government and law enforcement, especially in developing more effective means for deterrence, detection of illegal or harmful activities, and investigative techniques.

13.8.2   National Security and Law Enforcement Needs

Government policy and laws applying to cryptographic technology must make some difficult trade-offs, and this is an area of strong disagreement between governments and industry [CST96a].

On the one hand, strong encryption technology—the basis of all the security tools discussed—is extremely important to networked applications, especially electronic commerce. A credible threat to any country is economic espionage, which can be countered by maintaining confidentiality in commercial network traffic. The government has a law enforcement obligation to counter domestic and foreign threats to commerce and industry, and thus should encourage encryption technology. On the other hand, the government relies upon electronic eavesdropping to address legitimate national security threats and to conduct court-ordered wiretaps in criminal law enforcement and prosecution. These require a government to decrypt intercepted messages, which motivates it to keep "strong" encryption away from criminals, terrorist organizations, and foreign governments. (Here, "strength" is generally related to the number of bits in the encryption keys.)

Thus, governments have encouraged encryption technology that is sufficient to counter threats by adversaries with limited resources, but are not so "strong" as to thwart the government itself. One strategy employed by the U.S. government has been to legalize any and all encryption within the country, but disallow the export of strong encryption technology. Industry complains that this makes U.S. software less competitive globally and stimulates viable overseas competitors. A U.S. government response has been to propose "key escrow" schemes that allow a back door for "authorized" access to encrypted information by forcing keys to be deposited with an escrow organization under legal obligation to disclose them in national security and criminal cases. Illegitimate use of the escrow keys would be discouraged both by splitting keys into two parts that are deposited with two organizations and by legal sanctions. Industry has found these proposals unsatisfactory, arguing in part that individuals and businesses should be afforded the strongest protections available in the technology. Also, these proposals are difficult to implement globally, across multiple jurisdictions. These policy issues are far from settled and will doubtless be debated for some time.

13.8.3 Theft and Piracy of Software and Information

A concern on the part of sellers of information and software is the ease of replication and unauthorized dissemination over the network. Security measures such as encryption provide sellers some tools to enforce license provisions. However, there are limitations, since information must be decrypted in order to be read or viewed, opening opportunities for copying, if not outright piracy. Like other security measures, encryption is also inevitably invasive to the consumer. Some strategic issues for sellers are discussed in [Sha98].

Review

A key objective for networked applications is availability, which depends on reliability, security, and various operational issues. Intrinsic reliability refers to freedom from crashes and incorrect results due to software bugs and equipment failures. Security refers to protection from malicious attacks or theft. There is a trade-off between these trustworthiness factors and cost (development, equipment, and operational).

- The user has not yet been authenticated, but this can be achieved by asking that user to provide a password (previously set by the user). Since the session is encrypted, the password is protected.

- The user's credit rating can be assured and payments made by asking for a credit card number, which is also confidential because of the digital envelope.

In the future, it would be desirable for consumers to possess digital certificates and secret asymmetric keys to support a more secure bidirectional authentication.

Final Defense: Legal Sanctions

No matter how secure a site is, it is possible for an intruder to gain access by surreptitious or fraudulent means. An extreme example would be breaking and entering a physically restricted facility, but there are other ways, such as a confidence game or blackmail. In these cases, the intruder may have broken federal or local laws and can be apprehended and prosecuted.

EXAMPLE: *A particularly notorious individual who gained surreptitious access to many systems is Kevin Mitnick [Haf95], who was convicted of a felony.*

Laws and legal sanctions are the ultimate protector of computer systems.

Security threats include monitoring of communication, unauthorized access, impersonation, theft of service, and vandalism. Many of these threats are accentuated by the anonymity of the network. Security capabilities can insure confidentiality, authenticate users or hosts, insure message integrity, and prevent the sender from repudiating a message.

A basic security tool is encryption. Encryption of a message followed by decryption recovers the original. Encryption and decryption can use the same keys (which must be kept secret) or different keys (asymmetric case). In the asymmetric case, one key can be public without compromising the other secret key or confidentiality. Alternatively, the secret key can be used for authentication (challenge-response protocol) or a digital signature for integrity and nonrepudiation (calculate a message digest followed by encryption with secret key). A public key must be confirmed by a trusted authority, usually by a digital certificate signed by that authority.

Carefully conceived security policies should be established and enforced through the security tools and other measures such as access control (authorization lists and authentication) and firewalls. Policies are backed up by laws and legal sanctions.

Key Concepts

Trustworthiness:

- Intrinsic reliability: software correctness, equipment redundancy, data replication
- Security

Security protocols:

- Confidentiality
- Authentication
- Data and message integrity
- Nonrepudiation

Security tools:

- Encryption: symmetric and asymmetric
- Public and secret keys
- Authentication: challenge-response protocol
- Integrity: digital signature
- Digital certificate and certificate authority

Security policies:

- Access control
- Firewalls

Further Reading

An excellent overview of the various compromises to trustworthiness is [CST98a], and its implications to critical societal infrastructure are summarized in [OST97]. [Ber97] gives a good practical picture of computer system reliability. [Sch96] is an excellent compendium of security protocols, while [Sta99] is a broad overview of security techniques. Cryptography policy is discussed in great detail in [CST96a].

Exercises

E13.1   Which of the following systems would you expect to have redundancy and fault tolerance? How would you expect them to do this? Why?

   a. An electric power system

   b. A telephone system

   c. A subway system

   d. An air traffic control system

   e. A local residential Internet service provider

E13.2   For each of the applications in Exercise 9.5, discuss the availability requirements. Roughly estimate what requirements would be suitable, and rank the applications from highest to lowest availability.

E13.3   For each of the applications in Exercise 9.5, list between five and eight of the most serious security threats that you believe should be addressed in the application design.

E13.4   You are running a major mainframe center with an enterprise database. What intrinsic threats would you worry about that might prevent you from gracefully recovering from a fault or natural disaster? Describe what measures you might take to insure your ability to get the application up and running after such an event, without loss of data.

E13.5   Assume you are supplying video-on-demand services—the networked equivalent of a video rental store where the video is displayed on a customer's computer screen. List all the security requirements you believe necessary to avoid:

a. Theft of service—a customer viewing your video without paying your normal fee

b. Theft of content—a customer creating and reselling a pirated copy of your video

E13.6 Presume an intruder to your networked application is not malicious but is motivated by personal gain. List five to ten generic ways that intruder might be able to benefit financially from successfully penetrating your system.

E13.7 For each of the following applications, discuss the importance, if any, of confidentiality, data integrity, authentication, and nonrepudiation. In each case, the application is to be implemented entirely over the network.

a. Sending an order to purchase shares of stock to a stockbroker

b. A spy in the field sending what she learned back to the spy agency's offices

c. A transaction between a manufacturer and a parts supplier consisting of purchase order, order confirmation, invoice, and payment

d. A consumer order for a book from a Web-based book merchant, confirmation of that order by the retailer, and the payment from consumer to book merchant

E13.8 Encryption for confidentiality offers message integrity, since if the encrypted message is altered, it will not decrypt properly. Consider the threat of an evil hacker, Darth, who can not only eavesdrop on your network connection but also alter the messages that are sent. Decide whether Darth can successfully alter a confidential, encrypted message from Alice to Bob, without Bob realizing it, and back up your conclusion, for the following cases:

a. Symmetric encryption

b. Asymmetric encryption

E13.9 Discuss briefly the relative merits of the metal-keyed versus combination forms of locks in the physical world.

E13.10 Discuss the problem of loss of a secret key. What measures could be taken to guard against problems caused by this? Repeat this for

a. Symmetric key

b. Asymmetric key provided by a certificate authority

E13.11 You should worry about a digital certificate being compromised. For example, the certificate authority might have its secret key stolen, allowing the thief to issue bogus certificates. Describe at least two ways to deal with this contingency.

E13.12 Is it better to have a government agency act as a certificate authority, or is it better to leave this to private companies? Cite some advantages and disadvantages of each.

E13.13 Assume you obtain your Web browser by downloading it over the Internet. Discuss possible security loopholes associated with depending on the browser certification of CAs.

E13.14 In the United States, there has long been discussion of a "universal identification card," and the idea has generally been rejected on the basis of privacy concerns and Big Brotherism. Discuss how a digital certificate may be similar to or different from an identity card. Should there be similar concerns about certificates in terms of privacy and "big government"?

E13.15 Describe how authentication might be done using symmetrical encryption. Under what conditions would this be possible and useful?

E13.16 How do the properties of the message digest described in "Message Digest" on page 391 contribute directly to the security of the digital signature?

E13.17 Before you give your credit card number to a mail- or phone-order merchant, how do you "authenticate" the merchant? (Your initial reaction may be that you don't, but chances are you do, perhaps subconsciously.)

E13.18 Discuss the properties of the following challenge-response protocols, each of which determines whether you possess a specific secret key. If either possesses any weakness, is there a simple way to fix it?

    a. I challenge you with a random integer (in plaintext), and you respond with that integer encrypted using the secret key.

    b. I challenge you with a random integer encrypted using the secret key, and you respond by returning the integer (in plaintext).

E13.19 Invent and describe a new challenge-response protocol for authentication that has the same properties as the one described in "Challenge-Response Protocol" on page 389.

E13.20 Suppose you are going to design and market a "fingerprint recognizer" to authenticate another user across an untrusted domain. An obvious problem you have to avoid is an imposter capturing an image of a fingerprint, which he can use rather than his own fingerprint. Devise a scheme for your product to insure the integrity of a fingerprint.

E13.21 You decide, as a business opportunity, to provide a registration service that allows people to register documents without revealing their content, and later prove that they are the author. (Such a service might be useful for the enforcement of copyright laws.) Suppose Alice registers a document with you, and later Eve claims to have written that document. Alice should be able to use your service to prove that she is the real author. Design and describe these aspects of your service:

    a. What information would Alice have to send you in order to register her document?

    b. What information would your service retain?

    c. What information would your service send back to Alice when she registers her document?

    d. How would your service help Alice later when she wants to prove that she is the author?

E13.22 Describe why encryption of the message digest using a secret key is needed in the digital signature. That is, what bad things happen if a public key were used instead?

E13.23 For encrypting a signed message, the alternatives are symmetric and asymmetric encryption. Discuss the role the digital signature plays in message integrity in the two cases, highlighting any differences.

E13.24 Describe some of the things an intruder able to spoof network addresses in your intranet from the public Internet might be able to get away with if authentication depended completely on network addressing.

Electronic Payments

Electronic commerce, which was discussed in Chapter 3, has especially sensitive security requirements, because it involves the transfer of money, and compromised security can result in large economic losses. In addition, general acceptance of e-commerce depends on confidence in its perceived security against various threats—theft of money and credit card numbers, being stuck with charges made by others, etc. It is wise for a merchant and a customer to authenticate one another—so that the customer is not duped by an unscrupulous merchant, and the merchant is assured of payment—and the merchant also needs nonrepudiation of a customer's order. All these features can be achieved using security capabilities discussed in Chapter 13.

One security issue is unique to electronic commerce: electronic payments. The ramifications of a security lapse in electronic payments are severe—the possibility of widespread forgery or theft. Payments can potentially compromise privacy if they allow merchants or financial institutions to indirectly track purchases. Privacy benefits from insuring that ordering information be available only to the merchant, and that the customer's financial information remain with the financial institution. These objectives place challenging requirements on an electronic payment system. This chapter discusses some electronic payment options, as well as a bit about how these objectives can be achieved.

14.1 Some Benefits to Electronic Payments

In the physical world, payments are made by cash, credit cards, debit cards, and personal checks. Credit and debit cards can be used on-line, presuming appropriate authentication and confidentiality. Electronic funds transfers from one bank account to another, which work like a check, can also be used. There are, however, reasons to consider innovative alternatives:

- It may be possible to improve user convenience.
- Added security measures can reduce the vulnerability of all parties to fraud, even below what is acceptable in the physical world.
- A credit card payment, having a substantial transaction cost, is not economic for small purchases. Particularly in the sale of on-line information, there is a desire for small payments, (for example, fractions of a cent, often called *micropayments*). Thus, payment mechanisms with a small transaction cost are desirable.
- Many consumers are concerned about privacy and don't relish any ability of merchants or financial institutions to track their purchases.

The parties involved in payments are the customer, the merchant, and financial institutions. There are potentially billions of customers, millions of merchants, and thousands of financial institutions. Typically, there is a single designated financial institution associated with the merchant and a different one associated with the customer. The customer wants a payment mechanism to work with any merchant, regardless of the financial institutions involved—thus, payment mechanisms require industrywide standardization.

14.2   Types of Payments

There are two basic approaches to payments, whether electronic or not:

- *Account authorizations* linked to purchases (such as checks, credit and debit cards), in which payment is transferred from financial institution to merchant, drawing upon the customer's account (a debit) or as a loan to the customer (a credit).
- *Tokens of value* carried by the consumer, such as cash or stamps. These tokens must have either intrinsic monetary value (like the rare metal in a coin), or they must be backed by a financial institution or the government (like a stamp or a bill, which in the case of the United States is formally called a Federal Reserve Note). In the latter case, it must not be possible for unauthorized parties to counterfeit tokens. Tokens are directly exchanged for goods and services.

EXAMPLE: *A postage stamp is a token of value that can be exchanged for a single specialized postal service. It is affixed to the item being mailed. A stamp is an example of a small payment (although not a micropayment), and transaction costs are reduced by the sale of a book or sheet of stamps, aggregating the purchase in a single transaction.*

Account authorizations are a natural for e-commerce, as these authorizations can be conveyed as secure messages among consumer, merchant, and financial institution. Less obvious but no less real is the opportunity to use tokens of value in e-commerce—not in the form of tokens with intrinsic value, but the form backed by financial institutions. An example discussed later in this chapter is digital cash. Digital cash tokens of value are represented by data, so they can be stored or transported in the networked computing infrastructure just like any other data. Payment may be made by transferring a token directly from consumer to merchant. There is also a third option, the prepaid smartcard, discussed later. In this case a reservoir of monetary value is stored in a card that looks like a credit card. The consumer can tap that value by inserting it in a terminal owned by the merchant, where a secure transfer of value from card to merchant occurs.

14.3   Credit or Debit Card Payments

The physical-world form of payment that is most easily and naturally transferred to e-commerce is the credit or debit card. Each card has a unique identity represented by the card number, and consumers can make a payment by providing that card number together with a payment authorization. This results in a transfer from the customer's account to the merchant's account in the case of a debit card, or a loan to the customer paid directly to the merchant (again likely by account transfer) in the case of the credit card. This section discusses some potential disadvantages of this form of payment, followed by a description of SET, a standard that addresses these disadvantages.

14.3.1   Problems with Card Payments

Credit or debit card payments are common for payment by telephone or over the network. In their simplest and most common form, these card transactions have some disadvantages—some reflecting the physical world and some new:

- Security depends in part on the secrecy of credit card numbers. Having stolen that number, a thief can make unauthorized purchases. In the physical world, this is countered by requiring a signature from the cardholder and physical possession of the card (which is hard to forge), but this form of security is not easily transferred to the network. Theft of card numbers can be stolen by eavesdropping, but this can be countered by confidentiality protocols, such as the secure sockets layer. More fundamentally, as in the physical world, credit card numbers are subject to theft by an unscrupulous employee of a merchant.

- Because no signature is involved, a consumer making a payment authorization over the network can rather easily repudiate the transaction.
- As in the physical world, purchases made using cards can be linked to the identity of the customer. It is therefore feasible for a merchant or financial institution to track purchases of a particular individual, raising privacy concerns.

All these disadvantages can be mitigated by appropriate use of the security tools discussed in Chapter 13. In fact, a considerably higher degree of security can be achieved than in the physical world. Authentication of a customer can be more secure than a physical signature, the identity of the customer can be kept from the merchant, and the merchant can be protected by nonrepudiation of the customer's order. These features are included in an electronic credit/debit payment standard called SET, which serves as an example of the possibilities.

14.3.2   Secure Electronic Transactions (SET)

SET is a standard for on-line credit/debit card transactions established by Visa and Mastercard. In a conventional credit card transaction, the consumer deals with the merchant, and the merchant deals with the financial institution. The consumer provides credit card information to the merchant, who both authorizes the charge before fulfilling the consumer's order and submits it to the institution for payment. A key shortcoming addressed by SET is the availability of the credit card information to the merchant, which enables the tracking of purchases and increases the possibility of theft of credit card numbers.

SET logically partitions the transaction into the order and the payment authorization. The *order* for goods and services—and fulfillment of that order—is conducted between the consumer and the merchant. The *authorization for payment* is conducted between the consumer and the financial institution, which credits that payment to the merchant. This partitioning insures that the merchant has no visibility of credit card or financial information, and the financial institution has no visibility of the order, both preserving consumer privacy. The protocol uses previously discussed security features, including authentication and confidentiality.

SET includes two more subtle features. First, the authorization actually passes through the merchant, so that the consumer has the appearance of dealing only with the merchant. This authorization is encrypted, and the merchant lacks the secret key necessary to view it. Of course, the merchant does obtain confirmation from the financial institution that it will receive payment before order fulfillment. Second, the merchant is protected by a linking of order and authorization so that the customer cannot later repudiate the purchase, for example, by claiming that the payment was for other goods never delivered. This uses a variation on the digital signature, called a *dual signature*, which allows both merchant and financial institution to verify (and prove) the linking. These features illustrate both the use of security tools covered earlier and more advanced options.

*SET Chain of Trust

Although the customer deals directly with the merchant, also involved in the transaction are the *acquirer* institution (which clears the merchant's financial transactions), the *issuer* (which extends credit to and bills the customer), and the *association* (Visa or Mastercard). The authorization flows from consumer to acquirer to issuer. Each participant has a secret asymmetrical encryption key that is used for authentication, and a public key that is authenticated by a digital certificate. The SET standard itself has a public key and issues digital certificates to the associations. The chain of trust flows back to SET as follows:

$$\text{Consumer} \leftarrow \text{issuer} \leftarrow \text{association} \leftarrow \text{SET}$$

$$\text{Merchant} \leftarrow \text{acquirer} \leftarrow \text{association} \leftarrow \text{SET}$$

Actually, each participant has two keys and two certificates, one for authentication and one for establishing a session key.

*SET Order-Authorization Protocol

SET includes complex protocols for registering merchants and consumers and distributing certificates. The heart of SET is the order and payment for goods. The major steps illustrated in Figure 14.1 are initiate, purchase, authorize, and capture:

- *Initiate:* The customer conveys his identity and association, and the merchant returns a unique `transaction_ID` (which is used to link the phases of the protocol). This return value is signed by the merchant, insuring integrity.
- *Purchase:* The customer conveys his order and authorization, which both include the *bid*—the amount he is willing to pay—and are signed using a special dual signature algorithm. This signature prevents the customer from repudiating the combination of order and payment authorization—including their linkage—but without revealing the order to the financial institution or the payment authorization to the merchant.
- *Authorize:* If the merchant accepts the bid, it requests authorization from the acquirer, which in turn obtains authorization from the issuer (which determines the consumer's authorized credit balance).
- *Capture:* Finally, the merchant issues a capture to the acquirer, which in response issues a capture to the issuer. Of course, the merchant should also

Many Questions about Digital Cash

New tokens of value, such as digital cash, raise a number of questions. One obvious one is who will back the value. Is it backed by the financial institution, as in a demand deposit withdrawal; or is it backed by the Federal Reserve Bank, as in paper money; or is it backed by somebody else? What happens if a token is lost or stolen? Can the value be restored, or is it irrevocably lost? Can the thief spend it, and if so can the thief be traced? Another issue is whether digital cash is subject to regulation, and if so by whom and for what societal purpose. For example, value tokens add to a nation's money supply, the size of which is tracked and controlled by a central bank to preserve monetary value. What is the impact of the global reach of the Internet and electronic commerce? Who pays for the underlying infrastructure and operation of a digital cash system, and how do they recover those costs? Is it the government recovering costs through taxation (or selling the cash they manufacture), or financial institutions through fees? Does digital cash replicate the anonymity of coins and bills, such that purchases cannot be traced?

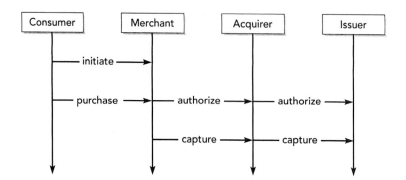

Figure 14.1 The SET order-authorization protocol involves the merchant and acquirer and issuer financial institutions

initiate fulfillment—supplying the goods purchased—although this is not part of the SET protocol.

14.4   Digital Cash

Another on-line payment mechanism, *digital cash*, is a token of value in networked computing—analogous to bills and coins in the physical world—that can be directly exchanged for goods or services. There are many economic, business, and policy issues raised by any new token of value (see the sidebar "Many Questions about Digital Cash"). There are also interesting technical issues.

There are two quite different contexts for consumer purchases using electronic tokens of value: in person or on-line.

- The customer can convey digital cash on his or her person, much like the cash carried in a wallet or purse, using a prepaid smartcard. A smartcard looks like a credit card, but has an embedded processor and memory, which is why it is called "smart." A smartcard's cash can be replenished at a bank's automatic teller machine, and later that value can be transferred to a merchant's terminal. Desirable security features include a tamper-proof card and mutual authentication by the smartcard and terminal (see the sidebar "Types of Smartcards").
- Digital cash can be stored in a computer and used to make payments across the network. The cash can be replenished over the network.

14.4.1   Challenges for Digital Cash

Like all information in networked computing, a token of value in a digital cash system must be represented by data. Presumably, this data represents numerically the monetary value, as well as possibly other things. This raises some troubling questions:

- *Forgery:* How can counterfeiting of bogus cash be prevented? Anybody can create arbitrary data, so how are unauthorized parties prevented from creating data that would fool a merchant or financial institution into thinking it was a valid token of digital cash?
- *Multiple spending:* Like any information represented digitally, a token of digital cash can easily be replicated an arbitrary number of times. How, then, can a holder be prevented from spending it multiple times, cheating a merchant or financial institution?

The first issue is rather easily addressed by security tools that already exist. Someone accepting digital cash must be convinced of its monetary value, and the party that stands behind that value—called the issuer, and typically a financial institution—must be trusted by the merchant and must not be able to later repudiate its value. The authenticity of the digital cash can be established by a digital signature from the financial institution, insuring the integrity of the value (it hasn't been changed since issued) and authenticating the issuer. Since only the issuer can generate a verifiable signature, counterfeiting is prevented.

A consumer obtains digital cash by taking an account withdrawal in digital cash. (Financial institutions love this idea, because to them it is an interest-free loan!). The consumer can then spend the digital cash, and the merchant can verify its authenticity and the credibility of its issuer by checking the digital signature. For this purpose, the merchant is provided a digital certificate from the issuer, providing a trusted copy of the issuer's public key.

The second problem, multiple spending, is more difficult. Since digital cash is data, unlike coins and bills it is easy to replicate. What, then, is to prevent the consumer from spending it more than once? This requires a policy dictating that digital cash can be spent only once, as well as a means of enforcing that policy. One of the implications of this policy is that, unlike physical cash, a party who accepts payment in digital cash is not allowed to turn around and use it as payment to a third party. There is no way to distinguish this action from double spending.

Enforcing the single-spending policy requires, first, a way of detecting multiple spending. This is achieved by including a unique identifier in each token. The identifier is a big number, just like the serial number on a physical bill, and since a digital signature is attached, the integrity of that identifier is assured. Replicas of a given token can then be detected by comparing identifiers: If two or more digital cash tokens carry the same identifier, then they are improper replicas.

Types of Smartcards

The simplest form of smartcard—containing primarily memory and minimal processing—is functionally similar to a credit or debit card with magnetic stripe. The extra hardware can be used to provide, for example, password or PIN protection for memory access. This type is limited to working in a closed single-provider environment, and since it cannot authenticate the terminal, it is vulnerable to an imposter that queries the owner for a password and then captures the smartcard memory to create a counterfeit card. To avoid this, the terminal should be authenticated by a challenge-response protocol, which requires processing in the card.

Authentication can be based on a shared secret, but this is possible only in a closed single-financial-provider administrative environment. Smartcards that either create or carry digital signatures can be authenticated using publicly available information. A signature-carrying card is loaded with signatures along with stored value—so the secret underlying the signature is not stored in the card—while a signature-creating card creates signatures within the card itself based upon an encapsulated secret key.

These smartcard systems all associate a unique identity with each card and can therefore be used to trace transactions. A more sophisticated digital cash protocol can avoid this pitfall.

While the identifier provides a means of detection, the more difficult question is where and when are identifiers checked? Only if identifiers are checked by a single party can replicas be detected. The obvious choice for this party is the issuer, because it is the issuer who must also "make good" on converting the cash token to "real" value and who suffers economic loss with multiple spending.

With this assumption, a simplified digital cash protocol is shown in Figure 14.2. The consumer purchases digital cash by exchanging "real" money (physical cash or a withdrawal from her account) for a like value in digital cash. In effect the cash is an IOU from the issuer, promising to pay any merchant who redeems the digital cash, and the payment to the issuer in exchange for the cash is an interest-free loan from the consumer. The consumer can make a payment to the merchant using the digital cash, who in turn redeems it with the issuer. In fact, the merchant is wise to redeem the digital cash before crediting the consumer for payment. The issuer, before accepting the redemption, verifies that the cash has not been previously spent, by comparing identifiers with previously redeemed tokens.

To enforce the single-spending policy, therefore, a token must be redeemed with its issuer the first and only time it is spent. Digital cash is thus different from physical cash in that a merchant accepting payment in the form of digital cash cannot spend that digital cash again—it must be redeemed with the issuing institution. The "real" money flows from consumer to merchant through the issuer, while the digital cash is a representation of that payment that the consumer actually presents to the merchant. In contrast to the physical world, to prevent multiple spending, a financial institution must be involved in every digital cash transaction.

14.4.2   Privacy and Digital Cash

Just like credit and debit cards, and unlike cash in the physical world, digital cash raises privacy concerns. The involvement of the issuer in every digital cash transaction may make it possible to track a consumer's purchases—even through multiple merchants—by matching the identifiers of issued and spent cash. This undermines one advantage of cash, which is spending anonymity—the inability to discern later the identity of a consumer who engaged in a specific transaction. On the other hand, complete spending anonymity would undermine the ability to hold a consumer accountable for trying to violate the single-spending policy.

What is needed is a *conditional* form of anonymity, obscuring the identity of the consumer to the issuer and merchant when the cash is presented for payment

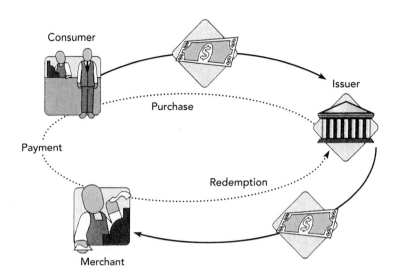

Figure 14.2 A simplified digital cash protocol; the trajectory of the digital cash token is shown by the dashed line

the first (legitimate) time, but identifying someone who attempts to cheat by multiple spending. This privacy issue is addressed by *anonymous* digital cash (see the sidebar "Privacy and Anonymous Digital Cash").

The basic idea behind anonymous digital cash is to hide the identifier of a token from the issuer when issued, while still insuring that it is unique. Double spending can still be detected, since the issuer can check for replicated identifiers without knowing what those identifiers are in advance.

Discussion

D14.1 What are the advantages and disadvantages of credit cards versus digital cash? What are the contributors to transaction costs, and which is likely to be cheaper? Which is likely to garner greater consumer acceptance?

D14.2 Discuss the issues raised in the sidebar "Many Questions about Digital Cash."

Review

Electronic payments—an important enabler to electronic commerce—have stringent security requirements. The most widely used payment mechanism for consumers—credit and debit cards—can be compromised by theft of card numbers, especially at the merchant, and raise privacy issues. Secure electronic

Privacy and Anonymous Digital Cash

There is a tension between the desire of consumers for privacy in their purchases on the one hand, and a societal interest in preventing tax avoidance and money laundering on the other. The latter encourages audit trails for monetary transactions. Already, with the level of credit and debit card purchases, a great deal of information is becoming available about the spending patterns and lifestyles of many consumers. If in an electronic commerce system *all* purchases are logged and traced, the private lives of individuals would be an open book to financial institutions. For example, if every purchase of gasoline, payment of toll on a highway, and minor purchases of snacks and drinks were logged, it would be possible to track the location of individuals almost as effectively as by surveillance.

David Chaum is the most eloquent and persistent advocate of privacy in electronic transactions and has developed protocols for anonymous digital cash. He has written [Cha91]:

We are fast approaching a moment of crucial and perhaps irreversible decision, not merely between two kinds of technological systems, but between two kinds of society. Current developments in applying technology are rendering hollow both the remaining safeguards on privacy and the right to access and correct personal data. If these developments continue, their enormous surveillance potential will leave individuals' lives vulnerable to an unprecedented concentration of scrutiny and authority.

transactions (SET) is an example of a more sophisticated protocol applying security tools to enhance privacy and minimize theft.

Digital cash represents monetary value by data tokens of value backed by an issuer financial institution. Each token has a unique identifier allowing double spending to be detected, and includes a digital signature by the issuer to prevent repudiation. It must be redeemed by the issuer. Tokens of value can be conveyed physically by a smartcard or over the network.

Although the issuer can potentially track consumer purchases, sophisticated digital cash protocols can provide spending anonymity and greater privacy for the consumer.

Key Concepts

Account authorizations versus tokens of value

Credit and debit cards:

- Secure electronic transactions (SET)
- Issuer and acquirer
- Chains of trust
- Dual signature

Digital cash:

- Issuer
- Identifier and issuer signature

Further Reading

Payment systems and protocols are discussed in more detail in [Mah97] [Lyn95]. Digital cash is covered in [Way97] and SET in [Dre99]. See [DLM96] [War99] [VLB98] for a discussion of policy, business, and economic issues related to new payment systems.

Exercises

E14.1 Discuss what happens internally in a bank's accounting systems if you do the following:

   a. Arrive at a branch with a traveler's check (issued by that same bank) and some cash and deposit them in your checking account

   b. Arrive at a branch with your credit card (issued by that same bank), take a cash advance on that card, and deposit that cash advance in your checking account

E14.2 Describe briefly how a bank makes money with the following services (if they do):

a. Providing your checking account

b. Issuing you a credit card

c. Issuing you a debit card

d. Selling you traveler's checks

e. Cashing your payroll check

E14.3 In what ways might a financial institution make money by issuing and depositing digital cash?

E14.4 The SET root certificate authority signs its own signature using a secret key. All SET software is provided a replica of the SET root public key. Are there any problems or vulnerabilities with this scheme? Either argue that there are or not, or if there are problems, state their nature.

E14.5 Compare digital cash to traveler's checks.

a. In what ways are they similar?

b. In what ways are they different?

E14.6 Suppose you are the bank and detect that the same digital cash was deposited in your bank twice either because (a) the consumer spent it twice with two different merchants, or (b) a merchant deposited it twice. Discuss what requirements on the design of the digital cash protocol would be necessary to distinguish these two cases.

E14.7 Consider "money laundering," say, by drug dealers:

a. What purpose does it serve?

b. Which of the following services might be useful to someone wishing to do money laundering: cash deposit, electronic funds transfer, traveler's checks.

c. Would spending anonymity in digital cash be useful to a money launderer? If so, how? If not, why not?

E14.8 Compare digital cash with spending anonymity and hard cash with respect to the possibilities for sales tax evasion by a dishonest merchant.

E14.9 Using the digital signature, I can produce a "digital check." I generate a message consisting of the bank account, the amount of the check, and the identity of the recipient, and then sign the message and send it to the recipient. The recipient can present the check to the bank for payment.

a. Describe how the bank can ensure that the recipient and only the recipient can cash the check.

b. Unlike paper checks, the recipient can make as many copies of the check as she likes. How can I prevent her from cashing the check multiple times?

E14.10 What are the relative merits of digital cash and a debit card employing SET for purchases on the Web?

a. From the perspective of a consumer

b. From the perspective of the merchant

c. From the perspective of a financial institution

E14.11   A consumer is provided with a merchant's digital certificate. What exact sequence of steps does the consumer's software follow to obtain an authenticated public key for the merchant, and what information does that software need?

Data Sharing

As discussed in Chapter 10, information (represented by data within the computing and networking infrastructure) is the basic commodity of information technology. One important function of applications is to acquire, store, examine, and manipulate information. A broad range of applications—especially organizational applications—have similar requirements for the storage and manipulation of data, and those requirements can be captured in reusable infrastructure software. The sharing of data is also a common way to integrate distinct applications, so that data management becomes a form of communication across both space and time.

The database management system (DBMS) is a large-grain software component that performs many of these functions. Since it intermediates between the operating system and file system and applications, it can be considered a form of storage middleware, as described in "More on Layered Infrastructure Software" on page 171. It provides many common functions and permits the sharing of data among applications.

Aside from shared access to a DBMS, another common form of information sharing among applications is through the exchange of messages. A long-standing example is the electronic data interchange (EDI) that is discussed in Chapter 3 and is widely used for standard business messages such as invoices and payment authorizations. More recently, the structured document has gained currency as a way of sharing information. The Web in particular has given momentum to the sharing of documents quite apart from the DBMS, as it is largely based on a document model. The Extensible Markup Language (XML) is a recent standard that is being adapted to the Web as well as general information-sharing purposes.

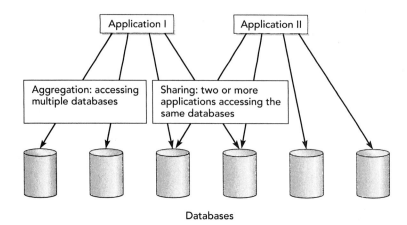

Figure 15.1 Two types of multiple database accesses: aggregation and sharing

This chapter discusses the DBMS and XML in more detail and describes another form of middleware called transaction processing. This deals with several problems arising when an application accesses multiple repositories of data, or two or more applications share a repository of data.

15.1   Database Management

The DBMS (see "Database Management System (DBMS)"on page 126) is a large-grain infrastructure component available commercially. It manages large amounts of data on behalf of applications and is typically the foundation of the third tier of the three-tier client-server architecture described in Chapter 5. The DBMS is particularly relevant to organizational applications. Most organizations have a body of mission-critical data, including records of employees, customers, inventory, etc. This data must be shared among applications and, as important assets of the organization, must outlive applications that create it and the upgrading or replacement of infrastructure equipment and software.

As shown in Figure 15.1, there are two complementary relationships between applications and databases. In the *aggregation* relationship, two or more databases are accessed by a single application. This type of relationship is displayed by all the examples that were covered in "Application Examples" on page 148. In the *sharing* relationship, two or more applications access a common database.

A DBMS bundles many capabilities related to mission-critical data and the applications sharing it, as listed in Table 15.1. Of these properties, persistence is the most fundamental and important. Mission-critical data must be reliably pre-

Table 15.1 Important capabilities of a DBMS

Capability	Description
Structured data model	Databases offer structured ways of storing data that capture the relationships among data and enable standard queries to examine or modify it. This reduces the required functionality within the application, thereby reducing development cost and time.
Persistence	When an application is no longer executing (because it crashed or was stopped), the data stored directly within the application may be lost. In contrast, persistent data outlives the application that created it. In most applications requiring database capabilities, it is a critical requirement that the data be long lived (decades or longer), even in the face of system crashes or the upgrade or replacement of applications or the DBMS itself.
Transaction support	Both the aggregation and sharing relationships raise issues and problems. In the aggregation case there is often needed coordination of resources managed by the different databases. In the sharing case, conflicts and harmful interactions can result in loss or corruption of data. The resulting problems and threats are addressed by transaction processing, which is a middleware technology supported by the DBMS. Transaction processing is discussed in this chapter for the aggregation case and again in Chapter 17 for the sharing case.
Access control	A database allows control over who can examine or modify data. This function, in a more general context, is discussed in Chapter 13.
Encapsulation	The DBMS determines the physical partitioning of the databases across hosts, and may also replicate data in multiple hosts, all to achieve the required performance characteristics. These physical structuring factors are encapsulated and hidden from applications—which are presented with a logical model of data structuring separated from its physical structuring—so the application does not become dependent upon them.
Scalability	Since the needs of many applications expand with time, a database can improve its performance (such as the number of queries per unit time) as applications require. See Chapter 17 for more discussion of scalability.

served for decades, even as applications and DBMS servers come and go. Persistence is achieved in part by maintaining the data on nonvolatile storage—storage that is not lost in a power failure or a computer crash—and in part by managing it in the protected environment of the DBMS. Another important feature is the logical structuring of data that separates concerns by allowing application developers to focus on the application logic and the DBMS to deal with physical structuring issues. A third important feature is the treatment of data as a separate asset that outlives specific applications or even upgrades and changes to computer systems, as discussed in Chapter 10.

15.1.1   The Relational Model

The relational logical model for data structuring uses a relational algebra based on a solid mathematical foundation (set theory and predicate calculus) (see "Database Management System (DBMS)" on page 126). In practice, a relational DBMS (RDBMS) stores data in *tables* with rows and columns, which is easy to understand. This concept was presented by a concrete example in Figure 4.9 on page 127.

> EXAMPLE: *The table shown in Figure 15.2 illustrates information relevant to employees, specifically labeling the columns and rows. The columns, also known as fields, have identifying labels, and represent the employee's attributes. Each row, also known as a record, represents an individual employee.*

As described in "Data and Information in Layers" on page 176, the DBMS relies heavily on the idea of defining a set of standard data types supported at the interface. Those data types may be represented differently on different computing platforms, such as second- and third-tier servers, with automatic conversions as necessary. Thus, the interface to the DBMS specifies the name and data type that apply to each field (column) in a table. The data types can be atomic types like those listed in "Data Types" on page 168, or they can be user-defined data types called *domains*. A domain is an assembly of atomic data types and other domains and can include additional aspects of representations such as constraints on values, formatting information, and comments.

Typically a database will include two or more related tables. This capability contributes to an economy of expression by representing collections of related data compactly.

> EXAMPLE: *Two related tables containing information about departments and employees in an organization are illustrated in Figure 15.3. The tables are related because one of the fields in the employee table is the employee's department, and armed with that information, other information about that employee's department can be examined. For example, a list of other employees in that department can be obtained from the employee table by extracting all records with that department number. The name of the department can be determined from the department table.*
>
> *If all the information in the two tables in Figure 15.3 were combined in a single table, the total amount of data would be increased substantially because of duplications. For example, the department name would be duplicated many times, once for each employee.*

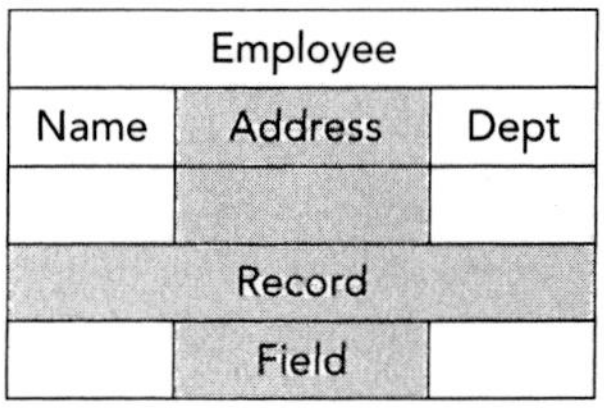

Employee		
Name	Address	Dept
Record		
	Field	

Figure 15.2 Sample relational table storing employee data

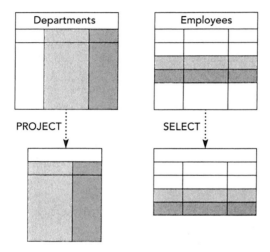

Figure 15.3 Two operations that perform data manipulation in SQL

The relational model specifies a suite of *operations* or *operators* that can be performed on tables. Each operation accepts one or more tables, produces as an output another table, and in the process does some useful manipulation. Because the result of each operation is a table, operations can be freely combined—the output of one operation is input to the next operation—to form more complex operations. These operations are expressed by commands in an internationally standardized *structured query language* (SQL). Operations that take as input two or more tables allow the information in tables to be combined in useful ways.

EXAMPLE: *As shown in Figure 15.3, two simple SQL commands, PROJECT and SELECT, both produce a smaller table. The PROJECT operation removes fields, and the SELECT operation removes records, each based on criteria included in the arguments to the operation. For example, the SELECT operation would be used to find all the employees in a specified department.*

Data Warehouses and OLAP

Often an organization will have multiple operational database management systems, but needs to develop a "big picture" of the overall operation—not only a snapshot at one time but also historically (see "Data Warehouses and Data Mining" on page 83). Since a data warehouse can store huge amounts of data, ways to analyze this massive data are needed. *On-line analytical processing (OLAP)* presents multidimensional views of data stored in two-dimensional relational tables.

E X A M P L E : *A three-dimensional view of the data stored in the two-dimensional relational table in Figure 4.9 on page 127 is shown in Figure 15.4. While this representation is equivalent in supporting queries, it is often better suited to the presentation of data to a human who wants to understand relationships or trends in the data.*

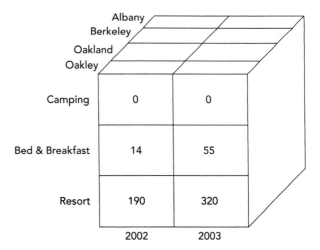

Figure 15.4 An OLAP presentation of the data in Figure 4.9

The JOIN operation combines the fields from two tables, resulting in a third table with a larger number of fields. It is based on a comparison of a field in one table with a field in the other table sharing a common domain. The combination is performed in a way that insures that those two columns in the joined table have the same values for the fields on which the JOIN is based.

SQL forms a standardized interface between an application and an RDBMS that is supported by many database vendors. Customers prefer this, because a database vendor or the computing platforms can be changed without impacting the applications or losing the persistent data. While SQL is more complicated than the form of interface (a menu of actions with parameters and returns) described in Chapter 6, it is composed of "statements" that are similar to actions.

Examples of more advanced uses of databases are discussed in the sidebar "Data Warehouses and OLAP."

Application Logic and Tables

The application logic is typically programmed using the object or component architecture described in Chapter 10. The application logic therefore encapsulates its own data within objects, and the DBMS is not the only repository of data. However, the application-encapsulated data is usually more transitory—intermediate values rather than final results, or temporary duplicates of data obtained from the databases. Any data that must be persistent—recovered after the application logic crashes, for example—must be written to the database by the application logic.

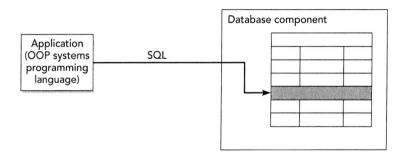

Figure 15.5 Application logic written in conventional programming languages manipulates relational tables by forming SQL queries

The application logic interacts with the database (to store, examine, and manipulate data) through SQL statements. As shown in Figure 15.5, a typical mode of interaction between application logic and a database table is, on one record at a time, to access that record, examine or manipulate it, and write it back to the database if it has changed.

The application designer determines which data is stored in objects and which is stored in the DBMS, often including duplication between the two—especially in the case of proxy objects whose role is to interact with the database and present an object interface to the remainder of the application logic. Factors to consider were listed earlier, such as persistence and data sharing.

*Objects and Tables

Objects and relational tables are not as different as they might appear. They actually have a natural correspondence that aids in understanding both, as well as appreciating more fully how they can work together. Each has strengths and weaknesses, and they are complementary, as manifested in the three-tier client-server architecture.

An object instance corresponds to one row of a table, and an object class corresponds to the structure of the table—its fields (names and data types). These two correspondences are illustrated in Figure 15.6. Among the similarities:

- A table specifies a set of fields (columns), which correspond to the attributes of an object. The table and its internal fields specify a structure for the data in the table that is similar to the attributes of an object class.
- The records (rows) in a table correspond to different instances of objects with the same class.
- In the object model, the data follows no uniform structure throughout the application—objects with different classes can have different internal data

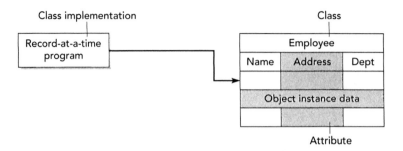

Figure 15.6 Some correspondence exists between the object and the relational database model

structures and interact with one another. The relational model similarly allows different tables to be defined and manipulated separately or jointly.

The two models also have important differences:

- The object model allows arbitrarily complex data representations to be defined as part of a class by the program code representing the methods, whereas the relational model specifies that data must consist of certain basic and user-defined data types.
- Objects can encapsulate data, making it inaccessible or accessible in a controlled way through methods, while all the data in a table is visible to the application logic. This provides greater flexibility—the ability to change internal structuring of data as needed—to the object model.
- Methods can embody the structure and interpretation of encapsulated data, turning it into information. Tables include only standard data types, which are relatively lightweight specifications of structure and interpretation.
- The object model imposes a uniform structure on the partitioning of the application logic—a set of interacting objects. The relational model imposes no structure on the application logic, other than specifying an SQL interface to the database.
- Since data in table entries has certain basic types and domains, it is relatively easy to define the application-independent SQL queries that manipulate the data. Such queries are difficult in the object model, as there is no uniform structure imposed on the data nor a limitation to standard data types.

Ultimately OOP and the RDBMS are complementary. The object model is designed to impose a particular structure on the application logic, and the relational model is designed to impose a certain structure on data manipulated by the application. The object model's strength is in structuring the application logic, and the relational model's strength is in structuring persistent data separate from any application and allowing applications to work together through the sharing of data.

15.1.2   *Extending the DBMS

The relational DBMS predates the popularity of OOP, and thus the alignment of their data structuring models is not as close as it might be. As a result, some new categories of DBMS products are emerging that provide an even closer correspondence between the models (see the sidebar "Extending Databases to Objects: ORDBMS and ODBMS").

Discussion

D15.1 Discuss the considerations that an application developer should take into account in choosing among the competing database technologies.

15.2   Documents and XML

Documents (such as memoranda, proposals, and articles) are widely used by organizations and individuals. Documents also encompass forms widely used in commerce, such as purchase orders and invoices. They serve as one foundation of interaction, collaboration, and commerce among individuals and organizations. Repositories of documents can be an important business or personal asset.

The DBMS is able to manage documents, like other data. However, relational tables do not naturally represent the internal structure of documents. Today's DBMS can store documents in their entirety, but the *internal* structure of a document is not visible to the DBMS. This is somewhat at odds with the recent success of the Web, which focuses on the presentation of information to users based on a document model. Unlike SQL and the DBMS, documents are appropriate for sharing information among organizations and with consumers.

EXAMPLE: *Whereas a DBMS typically stores business information, such as names and addresses, the Web document emphasizes the representation and formatting of documents consisting of text, images, audio and video clips, etc. Of course, documents can be stored in the DBMS, and this is one of the expected common applications of the ORDBMS. Thus, the difference is really in the representation of a document as seen by the client. In the ORDBMS, the representation is via SQL, and in the Web the representation is narrowed to the specific needs of documents.*

Extending Databases to Objects: ORDBMS and ODBMS

The RDBMS and OOP have some disadvantages:

- The RDBMS is able to store and manipulate only a small set of standard data types, such as integers and character strings. Today's applications need more complex data, such as images, audio, and video.

- The absence of direct support for persistence in OOP creates complications, including the need to store mission-critical data in a DBMS. But the relational model does not directly support complex structures of data possible in objects.

- The application programmer must learn and use two programming languages: the OOP language and SQL.

Two new database product categories deal with these shortcomings: *object-relational DBMS* (ORDBMS) and *object DBMS* (ODBMS). The ORDBMS extends the RDBMS to include the ability to store and retrieve complex objects while retaining (and extending) SQL as the interface. The ODBMS abandons SQL and simply adds persistence directly to objects. There are merits and downsides to these approaches:

- The ORDBMS preserves existing applications and databases, but allows them to be extended as desired into the world of complex data. Thus, the ORDBMS avoids many switching costs and offers a less radical migration path.

- The ODBMS is missing the structured query operations of the RDBMS. Also, the persistence is less useful long-term since the persistent data is more difficult to reuse in future applications.

- The ODBMS eases the programming task, avoiding the extra step of deciding which data is persistent and consciously forming database operations. Rather, it essentially makes all data persistent.

The ORDBMS vendors have significant switching costs in moving from RDBMS to the ORDBMS. Both vendors and customers have made huge investments in RDBMS technology, and this will be difficult for ODBMS vendors to displace.

The battles in this product category illustrate the immaturity of software technology. The RDBMS arose independently of and prior to the object model, and the two are mismatched in some ways. The marketplace will shake out an eventual winner, but before it does there may be some new technology on the horizon.

Applications across Organizational Boundaries

For applications spanning administrative domains or mixing and matching modules developed by different organizations and vendors, standardization is important to interoperability. There are several generic ways to do this:

- As in standards for EDI (described in "EDI Standards" on page 216), the formats of data shared across application elements can be standardized.
- The SQL standard allows the description and querying of data represented in the relational model in an application-independent way.

Not infrequently, documents represented in the Web are actually stored in a DBMS. In this case, the Web server accesses the DBMS to retrieve the requested document through the standardized common gateway interchange (CGI). This is an example of a three-tier client-server model.

15.2.1 Markup Languages

A markup language represents a hierarchical structure for a document—for example, sections, subsections, sub-subsections, sidebars, and images/figures—by attaching identifying *tags* to individual words, paragraphs, etc. Markup languages allow documents to be exchanged among applications, which can interpret them using the common language. They also enable authoring tools that present specialized author interfaces, but use a common representation that can be shared with others.

ISO has developed a standard called the Standard General Markup Language (SGML). SGML is considered too complicated for "everyday" uses, and thus the Web standards use a simplified subset of SGML, initially the Hypertext Markup Language (HTML). HTML has proven quite limiting because it focuses on the presentation of documents, rather than representing their internal structure. W3C, the World Wide Web Consortium that creates de facto standards for the Web, has defined a new markup language called XML (see the sidebar "eXtensible Markup Language (XML)"), still staying within the confines of SGML.

> E X A M P L E : *There are a number of specialized "HTML editors" (such as Adobe PageMill and Microsoft FrontPage) that allow users to generate HTML documents without knowing the language. These editors present a standard "what you see is what you get" document-editing interface. Standard word processors and page layout applications (such as Microsoft Word and Adobe FrameMaker) offer the option of generating an HTML representation and soon will support XML.*

XML opens up many possibilities for building business applications using the Web. If the lingua franca of communication between a business application and its presentation becomes XML, then XML supports an open interface between client-server tiers much like SQL, as shown in Figure 15.7. The application logic can generate the presentation in standard XML and access data using SQL. HTTP and CGI become standard protocols for supporting the multitier architectures, and XML and SQL become the standard formats for the messages passed between tiers.

Beyond just building applications, the XML-enhanced Web can be the basis for new businesses, as one Web site can seamlessly incorporate other Web sites.

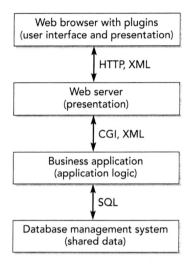

Figure 15.7 XML and SQL as the interface languages in multitier client-server applications

Businesses can be layered on top of one another much the same way the software infrastructure is layered.

E X A M P L E :   *Businesses might enter the Web-based "wholesale" sales of specialized goods, representing their catalog and pricing in XML. Various other businesses could then set up "retail superstores" that aggregate these wholesale goods in various ways, add a price markup, and sell directly to consumers. Because the wholesale goods are described in XML, the retailer can flexibly incorporate these descriptions into its own catalog, changing the presentation to conform to a uniform "look and feel." All this could happen dynamically and automatically as the consumer browses the catalog.*

XML or similar markup languages have tremendous potential for many applications requiring documents and for the exchange of information among applications using messages formatted in a markup language. Nevertheless, XML does not offer a complete solution, because there remains the question of the interpretation of various XML tags. For such messages to have meaning, those tags must be subject to agreement, which in turn suggests standardization. Many industry-specific standards can be expected, extending and replacing the EDI standards discussed in "EDI Standards" on page 216. Direct support of XML can also be expected in future database products, as well as document-authoring applications.

- XML is a language for expressing the representation of documents. This allows the standard to be extended by any programmer and yet be immediately available to all.
- Component standards (including, for example, W3C Document Object Model) allow the interoperable elements in an application to encompass algorithms and programs as well as data.

More sophisticated approaches—which will arise in the future—are important in enterprise and cross-enterprise applications, such as electronic commerce. They also lend efficiencies in the form of reusability, and create a market in which some vendors focus on the creation and sale of application components and others combine these components in new ways to create innovative applications.

eXtensible Markup Language (XML)

XML [Lau98] will govern document and data representation on the Web in the future. The term "extensible" refers to the language's ability to define new markup tags customized to particular purposes. XML focuses on expressing document *structure* rather than the presentation (formatting and display). As a result, a single document can be formatted and displayed in many different ways, depending on the needs of the user (as defined by the application).

XML also enhances information searches. (A simple example would be to search top-level section headings, or the document title, rather than all the text in the document.) The standard includes the *Resource*

Description Framework (RDF), which allows the description of metadata about the document suitable for searching and similar purposes (see Table 2.8 on page 44).

A Document Object Model (DOM) defines standardized interfaces to documents thought of as objects. RDF and DOM allow documents to be treated as specialized components (see "Software Components" on page 315), making documents active entities rather than static data. Clever application developers will build in many customized features using these standards.

Discussion

D15.2 In the operation of businesses, discuss the relative importance of the relational and document model for structuring data. Do you think the latter might supplant the former to some extent?

D15.3 Brainstorm further on opportunities brought about by a standard such as XML. Can you come up with other application ideas?

15.3   Transaction Processing

Networked applications are by definition distributed over multiple hosts. For example, if the application is decomposed into objects or assembled from components, those objects or components may actually reside on different hosts and interact through remote method invocations or by sending one another messages. An application may aggregate data from databases managed on different hosts, or a given database may offer shared access from applications on different hosts. This reality introduces many complications. For example, one host may crash, resulting in the loss of only a portion of the application. How does the application recover gracefully from such a catastrophe? Different applications sharing a common database may perform operations that conflict with one another, compromising the integrity of each. How are such conflicts avoided?

A general framework for thinking about such questions is to think of an application as coordinating a set of distinct *resources*. Often these resources are physical or logical entities with economic value, such as bank account balances or financial instruments or goods being bought or sold. However, within the networked application these resources are represented by data, which often resides in a database but may also reside temporarily in other entities, such as a message queue.

E X A M P L E :   *A travel reservation system manages resources like airline seats, hotel rooms, rental cars, and other resources. The current status of airline seating is represented by fields in a database in the airline reservation system, while the hotel rooms are kept track of in a database in the hotel chain's computers.*

In this context, the DBMS can be thought of as a *resource manager*, not just of raw data but rather the resources represented by that data.

Transaction processing greatly simplifies application development by consistently handling—within the infrastructure and removing that burden from the application developer—many problems that arise in the management of complementary resources as well as the shared access to resources [Ber97]. Transaction processing is incorporated into middleware products and is supported by DBMS products in ways that will be seen shortly.

15.3.1   Example: Travel Reservations

A travel reservations application illustrates the challenges addressed by transaction processing. One challenge is achieving consistency in the allocation of complementary resources.

EXAMPLE: *Planning a trip requires coordinated reservations for hotels, airplanes, rental cars, etc. The managed resources are airplanes seats, rental cars, and hotel rooms. For consistency, the rental car and hotel reservation must coincide with arrival of the airplane, on each of multiple legs of the trip. If consistent reservations are not available (for example, there is no airplane seat that day), then the hotel and rental car reservations should not be made.*

How is a situation like this handled? One approach is to make sure an airline reservation is made before a rental car and hotel reservation. However, there may be no rental cars available—or perhaps no hotel rooms—on the day of arrival. So there is *no* feasible order for reserving resources that guarantees consistency.

Another approach is to take two passes: Confirm availability of all resources (without reserving them) and then return to lock them in. This approach is undercut if there are other unrelated reservations of the resources being made at the same time. (If two sets of reservation actions are overlapped in time, they are said to be *concurrent*, as discussed in Chapter 17.)

EXAMPLE: *If the travel reservations application confirmed the availability of consistent airline seat, rental car, and hotel availability, when it returned to lock them in it might find the airline seat was the last available and in the meantime was given to another customer.*

Other things can go wrong. For example, the crash of a participating host or application might leave the reservations partially incomplete.

EXAMPLE: *The travel reservations application might think it had locked in a reservation for an airline seat, but not be informed that an airline's host crashed and lost the reservation before the database update was completed. At the airport, the customer would discover the problem.*

It would be quite complicated to deal with all these cases in the application, which are accentuated by the participation of distinct administrative domains (the airline, rental car company, and hotel company).

Similar issues arise in a number of networked applications. Later in the chapter, two more—distributed databases and electronic commerce—are discussed. Transaction processing deals with these issues in a generic way, by capturing solutions to the common problems, simplifying application development, and contributing to software reuse.

15.3.2   Role of Transaction Processing

Transaction processing simplifies application development by coordinating multiple resources and the shared access to common resources in a systematic and consistent way. Examples of applications where transaction processing has been used include [Gra93]

- Service management and billing (electric power, telephone)
- Financial (stock market, bank ATMs)
- Reservations (travel, theatre)
- Manufacturing (inventory, purchasing, billing)
- Process control (manufacturing plants, networks)

These application domains share the characteristic that resources (often represented by information stored in databases) are managed on different hosts. Transaction processing addresses some generic challenges:

- Managing the various resources in a consistent way is impossible. For example, one resource is just not available or cannot be allocated in a way consistent with other resources.
- Two operations can try concurrent access to shared resources. This can result in conflicts—incorrect results caused by interference between the operations. This issue is revisited in Chapter 17, which discusses some consequences of concurrency.
- A system crashes, so a collective resource action is only partially completed. This may leave the distinct resources in an inconsistent state.

Dealing with these problems within the application itself is complex. Since these problems are common across a wide range of networked applications, transaction processing can provide a single middleware solution.

15.3.3 What's in a Transaction

In everyday language, a transaction is a series of related reciprocal actions or communications between two people (such as a bank teller and customer). Users also participate in transactions with information systems (such as a customer using an automatic teller machine). One of the earliest commercial applications of computing—on-line transaction processing (OLTP) systems—manage large numbers of these transactions.

More recently, the term *transaction* has been formalized in computing to have a specific meaning: It is a group of related resource management actions that are atomic; that is, they are all completed successfully (called a *commit*), or the resources are left as if none of the actions had ever happened (called an *abort*).

E X A M P L E :   *In the travel reservations system, if all the consistent reservations constituting a complete itinerary are grouped together as a transaction, then by definition consistent reservations in the itinerary were successful, or alternatively, no reservations were made—it is as if they had not even been attempted.*

The transaction processing takes care of insuring atomicity. The application logic can group together a set of resource actions as a transaction and not have to worry about all the complicated issues arising when some actions are successful and others aren't, because that can't happen. The application logic must still deal with the possibility of an abort, but that is simpler: Abort is the same as if the transaction hadn't been attempted.

E X A M P L E :   *In the travel reservations application, either a consistent set of reservations was successfully made, or none of the reservations was made (as if they had not been attempted). There are no intermediate cases to worry about.*

Internal to the transaction processing middleware, there are many possibilities to deal with. Of course, it would be even easier to declare that a transaction always completes successfully. Unfortunately, this isn't realistic: A number of unavoidable problems can cause an abort, such as a system crash or a request for a resource that simply isn't available.

E X A M P L E :   *A travel agent may make most of the reservations, but there is a leg of the trip where transportation is not available. Rather than leaving this incomplete itinerary, the agent should reverse the other reservations, not burdening the customer with this.*

The ACID Properties of Transactions

The acronym ACID is often used to describe four important properties of transactions:

- *Atomicity:* All the components to a transaction either complete together or all are aborted; there is no such thing as a partial completion.
- *Consistency:* A transaction must leave the system in a consistent state at the end of the transaction, or it must abort, returning all resources to their initial state.
- *Isolation:* Concurrent transactions are allowed, but they don't interfere with one another (this is discussed in Chapter 17).
- *Durability:* (or persistence). A transaction leaves the resources in a permanent state after it commits—a state that outlives the transaction.

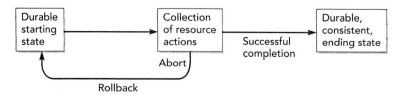

Figure 15.8 A transaction consists of a sequence of resource manipulation tasks logically coupled to one another, which either succeed or fail as a unit

The structure of a transaction is illustrated in Figure 15.8. There are only two possible outcomes of a transaction: Either the transaction completes in its entirety, or it fails. In the latter case, the resources are left in precisely the same state as if the transaction had never even been attempted.

EXAMPLE: *From your perspective, there are two acceptable outcomes of your attempt to plan an itinerary through the travel agent. The hoped-for outcome is that all the reservations are successfully completed so that the itinerary is consistent. That is, your flights arrive in each city the same day as the rental car and hotel reservations in that city, and outgoing flights are coordinated with the last day of those reservations. If it turns out to be impossible to complete a consistent itinerary, say, because one leg of the flight is unavailable, then you want none of the reservations to be made and paid for.*

This example captures pretty well what a transaction is. What the transaction avoids is a situation where some resource actions are completed but others failed. In practice such a possibility would greatly complicate the application logic, which would have to be prepared to unwind the resource actions that had been completed or be left in an inconsistent and unwanted state.

As shown in Figure 15.8, a transaction starts and ends in a consistent, durable state. The *state* of a resource manager is a set of conditions (for example, the reservations for a traveler in the travel reservations system). A state is *consistent* when resources are not at odds with one another (for example, the day of arrival and hotel reservation are consistent), and it is *durable* if it outlives the transaction that created it. By definition, the intermediate inconsistent, transient states—corresponding to only a portion of a transaction's resource actions—are not durable. If something goes awry in the midst of a transaction (such as the unavailability of a resource or the crash of a resource manager), it is aborted. In that case, there is a *rollback* to the initial durable state. The hoped-for outcome is that all the consistent resource actions in the transaction are successful, so the transaction is declared successful and the resource managers are left in the second consistent, durable state.

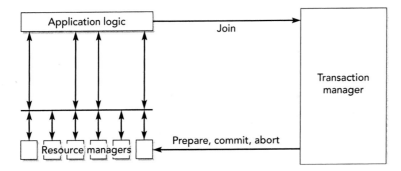

Figure 15.9 Architecture of the application, transaction manager, and resource managers

15.3.4   Transaction Processing Architecture

The *transaction processing monitor* is a middleware product that coordinates a set of resource managers involved in the transaction and serves as coordinator of the application and these resource managers. Often those resource managers are databases managed by a DBMS, but there are other possibilities (such as message queues). To benefit from transaction processing, both the application and the resource managers must conform to a predefined architecture (shown in Figure 15.9) and a set of policies and protocols:

- *Architecture:* The application logic and distinct resource managers that are being coordinated must be distinct and visible to the middleware transaction manager. Typical resource managers are database servers and message queues. Commercial products in these areas conform to the policies and protocols necessary to participate in transactions.
- *Policies:* Each transaction initiated by the application must be registered with the transaction manager. Each resource manager must be prepared to roll back all actions related to a given transaction and also participate in the appropriate protocols.
- *Protocols:* When the application logic declares the transaction complete (the last resource action), the resource managers participate in a voting (prepare-commit-abort) protocol with the transaction manager. The transaction manager informs the application logic as to successful completion (a commit) or abort of the transaction.

When the application logic registers a transaction (a *join*), it is provided a unique transaction identifier (ID) that it uses to identify each resource action. Each resource manager has to be prepared to roll back to the initial durable state in case of an abort; to be prepared for that, the resource manager must keep track

TP protocol standards are important
for two reasons. Consistent with the
open systems philosophy, they
increase competition by allowing
customers to mix and match elements
(databases, MOM) from different
vendors. In addition, in applications
like electronic commerce, it is increasingly common to run transactions
across company and administrative
boundaries, where detailed coordination is not practical.

OSI TP is a de jure standard established by ISO (see "International
Organization for Standards (ISO)" on
page 218). Like many ISO computing
standards, it is not widely implemented, largely because it came
along slowly. OMG (see "Object
Management Group (OMG)" on page
221) is defining a de facto standard,
Object Transaction Service (OTS),
as part of its CORBA standards
(see Chapter 16). Many database
and MOM vendors plan to
implement OTS.

of all resource actions and be prepared to reverse them. When the application
declares the transaction complete, the transaction manager conducts its voting
protocol. If all resource managers agree that the transaction was completed
successfully, they are told to wrap up the transaction (a commit). If one or more
of them don't agree (or fail to respond), the transaction is abandoned (an abort),
and each resource manager is directed to roll back.

In order to enable resource managers and applications from different vendors
to participate together in transactions, standards are required (see the sidebar
"Open Transaction Processing Standards"). Some special complications arising
when two or more transactions are concurrent within the same resource manager (concurrent transactions) are discussed in Chapter 17.

15.3.5   *Transaction Protocols

To participate in a transaction, a resource manager must have these capabilities:

- It must allow *locking* of resources to prevent conflicts. This prevents resource
  conflicts when two or more concurrent transactions attempt to modify a
  resource, by allowing one transaction to complete (reach a consistent, durable state) before the other transaction is allowed to modify that same
  resource (see Chapter 17 for clarification of this class of issues).
- It must be prepared to roll back; that is, restore the consistent state that
  existed before the transaction began. This requires the *logging* of resource
  modifications and built-in logic to access that log and reverse its actions.
- It must participate in the voting protocol with the TP monitor and the other
  resource managers. This protocol serves to coordinate their actions so that
  they all complete the transaction or they all roll back to the initial state.

A common voting protocol is the *two-phase commit*, illustrated in Figure 15.10.
This protocol is initiated by the TP monitor when it is informed by the application that all resource actions in that transaction are complete. The protocol has
two phases, with two possible outcomes:

- *Prepare:* The TP monitor asks all resource managers if they have successfully
  completed their responsibility in the transaction. If one or more resource
  managers fails to respond (perhaps because they have crashed), or if one or
  more votes no, the transaction is aborted; otherwise, it is committed.
- *Commit:* With the unanimous agreement of the resource managers, the TP
  monitor informs each resource manager of a commit. The resource managers then wrap up, for example, by destroying any logging information that
  was intended to aid rollback.

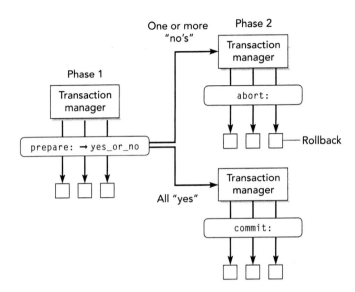

Figure 15.10 The two-phase commit transaction protocol

- *Abort*: In the absence of agreement, the TP monitor declares an abort and instructs all resource managers to roll back.

15.3.6 Examples

Transaction processing benefits applications requiring coordination of resources across hosts, and for which reliability and availability are important, as discussed in Chapter 13. In pragmatic terms, such applications generally incorporate multiple databases and message queues, often across administrative domains (see the sidebar "Open Transaction Processing Standards").

Automatic Teller Networks

A simple application of transaction processing is an automatic teller machine (ATM) network [Ber97]. The implementation of such a network would define transactions such as Deposit, Withdrawal, and RequestBalance. Each such transaction involves at minimum a database in the bank owning the ATM and a database in the bank with the customer's account. Defining these operations as transactions insures the consistency of these databases, so both banks have a consistent and durable view of the results of the transaction, and money is not destroyed or created.

E-Commerce

An important application of transaction processing is electronic commerce [Tyg96]. A typical transaction would be a Purchase, which includes an order, a payment authorization, a fulfillment of the order (delivery of goods from merchant to customer), and a payment (from financial institution to merchant) (see Chapter 14). The transaction involves resources in both the merchant and a couple of financial institutions. A number of problems arise if a Purchase is not atomic, such as the customer pays for merchandise but doesn't receive it, or a merchant ships the merchandise but never receives payment.

Stock Trading

Another application is a customer stock trading system at a brokerage house. It may have to access roughly ten different stock exchanges [Ber97], where a typical transaction is ExecuteTrade. Obviously it is important that databases in the brokerage (crediting or debiting a customer account) and at the stock exchange end in a consistent and durable state after each trade.

Discussion

D15.4 Discuss the relationship between what a (human) travel agent does versus transaction processing middleware for an automated travel reservations system.

D15.5 Discuss ways an application can deal with an aborted transaction.

15.4   Example: Stock Trading System

The stocks4u.com stock trading application discussed in "On-Line Stock Trading" on page 68 illustrates some challenges in database management and transaction processing.

15.4.1   The Databases

Stocks4u.com maintains three major databases: *accounts* (information about customers and the current holdings in their accounts), *products* (information about financial products available for sale), and *orders* (information about pending and executed orders made by customers). The accounts and orders databases are managed by a DBMS in the protected environment of separate mainframes, while the products databases are less sensitive and run on microprocessor-based servers.

As examples of relational tables, here are some of the columns (fields) in the accounts database:

- *Customer table:* Name, address, telephone number, tax identification number, password

- *Account table:* Account number, customer tax identification number
- *Security position table:* Account number, security name, quantity, date purchased

The stocks4u.com Web site allows the customer to examine an up-to-date statement of current positions. This is provided by an "account statement application" that was developed by stocks4u.com. To log in, the customer must authenticate himself using a tax identification number and password. From the customer table, the application determines the name and tax identification number for the on-line statement. The tax identification number and the SELECT operation of SQL yield a smaller table listing all the accounts for that customer. Using record-at-a-time processing, the application then examines one row (account) at a time. For that account, the application examines the positions table, using the account number and the SELECT operation to obtain a smaller table with one row for each position for that account. The application uses record-at-a-time processing to extract the information about each securities position (name and quantity). The application also obtains the latest price of that security by sending a message to the stock exchange.

Having completed these steps, the account statement application is prepared to present the account statement to the customer. Following a prescribed format, it generates an XML document that structures information about accounts and lists all securities positions for each account. That XML document is sent to the Web browser for presentation to the customer.

15.4.2   The Transactions

In developing their full application suite, stocks4u.com considered where transaction processing would increase reliability and simplify development. The critical e-commerce component of their application is the order to buy or sell a security and the execution of that order. It was decided that these two operations are separate and should be structured as independent transactions. The key consideration was the granularity of atomic operations that fail or abort. On reflection it became obvious that an order could commit and yet its execution fail, so these should not be part of the same transaction. For example, the customer might specify a minimum price for selling a security position, and that price might never be available before a "time-out" period had elapsed. Thus, the order and execution were divided into four tasks for a sale (a purchase would be similar):

- *Order entry:* The customer places an order, and it is confirmed by stocks4u.com. Later, the customer can examine the status of the order.

- *Price query:* The order application requests (by sending a message) an event notification from the stock market when the current price of the security is above the specified minimum sale price. The price query times out after a fixed period of time has elapsed.
- *Sale execution:* When notified of a favorable price by the market, the application sends a sell order to the market and awaits notification of execution and the price of execution.
- *Records update:* Once notified of a successful execution, or a failure to execute, the fourth step is to update the order database and send a notification to the customer.

Of these steps, the order entry, sale execution, and records update must be atomic. Examples of violations of atomicity that result in poor service or financial loss include the following:

- If the customer enters the order information, but the order database is not updated to reflect that (perhaps the database crashed just then), the order is lost and the customer is under the mistaken impression that it will be executed if possible.
- If a sell execution message is sent to the market, but execution notification is never received, the application is left to wait indefinitely, not knowing if the sale occurred or not.
- If the application is notified of a sale, but it never reaches the order database, the customer account will never be credited with the proceeds from the sale.

Thus, it was decided to structure the sale as three transactions: `Order_entry`, `Sale_execution`, and `Records_update`. Since each of these is atomic, each can be assumed to be completed successfully or else aborted and left in a consistent state as if it had never been attempted. The final question is what the application does upon the abort of a transaction:

- Upon an aborted `Order_entry`, the customer is notified to "try again later."
- Upon an aborted `Sale_execution`, the application returns to the price query step, awaiting another opportunity to sell at an acceptable price.
- An aborted `Records_update` must be repeated until it is successful, or the `Sale_execution` that preceded it must be rolled back, or otherwise the account will not be debited the security position and credited the sale proceeds.

Although the `Sale_execution` and `Records_update` seem like logically distinct tasks, they must fail together or succeed together. Therefore, stocks4u.com decided to use a more sophisticated form of transaction called a *nested transaction* [Ber97]. A nested transaction Execution is composed into the two *subtransactions*. The nested transaction allows the results of a Sale_execution to be made available to the Records_update as if it had committed, but without forfeiting the right to later abort the Sale_execution should the Records _update abort.

15.4.3 Inter-Enterprise Messages

The stock exchange must conduct e-commerce with a number of brokerage houses such as stocks4u.com, exchanging messages with them for purposes of giving direct price quotes and price quote notifications, accepting orders, and giving order execution notifications. The stock exchange and its cooperating brokerages thus set up an industry standards committee to decide on a common set of formats and protocols. It was decided to utilize XML documents as the basis for these messages by defining a set of ordering tags specifically for this purpose. This had several advantages:

- Many programmers already experienced in XML were available for hire.
- A number of software tools for extracting information from XML documents were available off the shelf.
- Like any XML document, these messages can easily be displayed directly in a Web browser in a nicely formatted form—no poring over prosaic and anachronistic low-level message formats.

15.5 *Open Issue: Future of the DBMS

While the ODBMS is a radical departure from the RDBMS, the more evolutionary step of the ORDBMS has been more successful. However, the existence of data warehouses illustrates that large distributed databases—ones that could manage all the data for an enterprise—are not yet practical. Future progress can therefore be expected in the dimensions of expanding the richness of the supported data types and the size and distribution of related databases.

Review

The relational model (in practical terms) structures data in tables with rows (records) and columns (fields). All data in a column has the same specified data type, which can be a basic or user-defined type (domain). Tables are manipulated by operations, which take one or more tables and return another table. SQL is an internationally standardized language used as an interface to relational and object-relational databases.

A markup language represents the hierarchical structure and formatting of a document by attaching tags to paragraphs. The form is the basis for document management in the Web. Internationally standardized markup languages for the authoring and manipulation of documents are HTML (which emphasizes formatting) and XML (which emphasizes structure).

A transaction is a series of resource actions that are all completed successfully, or the resources are left in the same state as if the transaction had not been attempted. Transaction processing middleware coordinates transaction-supporting resource managers (such as database management systems) to realize transactions. It uses transaction processing protocols (such as the two-phase commit). Resource managers must realize locking and rollback features to participate in transactions.

Key Concepts

Database management system (DBMS):

- Relational, object-relational, and object

Structured documents:

- Markup languages: HTML, SGML, XML

Transaction processing:

- Transaction: atomicity, consistency, isolation, durability
- Two-phase commit protocol
- Resource managers: locking, logging, rollback

Further Reading

There are a number of books on database management, with [Con98] and [Mar95] representative examples. [Ber97] is a good general reference on transaction processing and computer system reliability in general, while [Gra93] is the most authoritative and extensive reference on the subject.

Exercises

E15.1 For one of the following, define a set of relational database tables that you believe would be useful to the application. For each table, list three or four of the most important fields.

   a. The customer-care application of "Customer Care" on page 63

b. The on-line book merchant application of "On-Line Bookselling" on page 66

c. The on-line floral delivery service of "Floral Delivery Service" on page 69

E15.2 For the application you chose in Exercise 15.1, discuss in specific terms the importance of each of the factors mentioned in Table 15.1 on page 417 to that application. If one of those factors is not important, state the reasons.

E15.3 For the application you chose in Exercise 15.1, give two specific instances where the following could be useful:

a. The SQL SELECT operation

b. The SQL PROJECT operation

c. The SQL JOIN operation

E15.4 For each of the following, give situations within any one of the applications listed in Exercise 15.1 in which the type of database technology would be useful:

a. ODBMS

b. ORDBMS

E15.5 For one of the applications in Exercise 15.1, describe briefly all the uses of messages formatted in a markup language like XML that you can think of.

E15.6 For two of the following, describe in specific terms how some or all of the basic ideas of transaction processing are manifested:

a. A marriage ceremony

b. An escrow agent in a real-estate transaction

c. Arranging a mutually acceptable time for a meeting

d. Negotiation and execution of a legal contract

E15.7 For one of the applications listed in Exercise 15.1, decide how transaction processing could make the application more robust and easier to develop. In particular:

a. Define a set of no more than two or three atomic transactions that would be useful.

b. Describe how the application would deal with an abort of that transaction.

   c. Describe a couple of ways in which the application would be less
      reliable or more difficult to develop if it did *not* use transaction pro-
      cessing.

E15.8   List all the underlying causes you can think of (but no more than ten)
that could cause a transaction to abort.

E15.9   Discuss how transactions might work in an interorganizational application. Is this type of application a strong argument for standardization of
transactions protocols?

Communications Middleware

16

Infrastructure layering was discussed in "More on Layered Infrastructure Software" on page 171. Middleware is a software infrastructure layer that falls between the application and the operating system. Its primary purpose is to hide heterogeneity either above or below—allowing legacy applications to work together, or hiding the heterogeneity of the infrastructure from the application developer. The DBMS and transaction processing covered in Chapter 15 can be considered a form of storage middleware. This chapter focuses on middleware devoted to communications.

Layering allows elaboration of specialization of an existing infrastructure (consisting of the layers below), and middleware is a good illustration. While the lower infrastructure layers (operating system and network) have existed for some time and have a fairly established (albeit evolving and expanding) set of capabilities, middleware is a diverse and changing software product category where much innovation in infrastructure software occurs. Just as there are different communication services for different purposes, as described in Chapter 12, there are different middleware solutions serving different categories of applications.

ANALOGY: *Companies providing new services built on an existing infrastructure would be analogous to middleware. Examples include the FedEx overnight package delivery (built on an existing airport and highway infrastructure) and the Schwab OneSource mutual fund marketplace (that consolidates the offerings of many mutual funds on a single statement). Note that these examples serve quite different and specialized purposes—a characteristic of middleware.*

Middleware is assuming more importance as an enabler for enterprise and cross-enterprise applications. Many such applications must integrate legacy departmental or enterprise applications, which are heterogeneous both at the application level and at the infrastructure level (platforms and languages).

Middleware is one approach to mitigating these incompatibilities by performing the necessary automatic conversions within the infrastructure. Middleware is also viewed as an enabler of more flexible applications that can adjust to changing needs—another important requirement for the future.

Middleware can serve many purposes, either singly or in combination, including

- *Abstraction and complexity management:* Middleware can isolate an application from heterogeneous operating systems and networking protocols. For example, middleware might allow an application to be transparently ported to different operating systems—or even run across hosts with different operating systems—without imposing onerous application development effort. In this role, middleware potentially becomes a spanning layer.
- *Location independence:* Middleware can partially hide the application partitioning across hosts, making it appear to the application developer as if the application were running on a single host. This simplifies application development and makes that partitioning more configurable, for example, allowing the number of participating hosts to be automatically adjusted according to performance requirements as discussed in Chapter 17.
- *Software reuse:* Middleware can incorporate generic functions useful to many applications—especially in a networked environment—thus reducing application development cost and time.
- *Software portability:* Middleware can provide a uniform execution environment, so that one application program can run on different platforms with minimal reprogramming.
- *Mobile code:* In a form of dynamic portability, program execution can be moved from one host to another. This can have several advantages related to performance and interoperability.
- *Interoperability:* Middleware can simplify interoperability by predefining formats and protocols for common tasks. It can also allow legacy applications or modules to interoperate by performing the necessary conversions between different formats or protocols they presume.
- *Scalability:* Middleware can support scalability by automating load balancing or parallelism, as discussed further in Chapter 17.
- *Reliability:* Middleware can simplify the application's task in dealing with software crashes or exceptions. The transaction processing discussed in Chapter 15 is an example of this.
- *Resource coordination:* Middleware can prevent conflicts resulting from manipulation—at the same time or overlapping times—of common data by different applications. Again, transaction processing is directed at this goal.

There is no single widely accepted middleware solution, especially not one providing *all* the capabilities listed. Also, there is no precise boundary between
capabilities provided by middleware (adding an infrastructure layer above existing operating systems) and distributed operating systems (enhancing the operating system layer to manage two or more hosts). Different approaches are
vying for dominance, and maturation may or may not bring widely accepted
solutions. However, when applications span administrative and organizational
boundaries, middleware provides a way to address the heterogeneity of the
resulting computing environment. Thus the emergence of social and electronic
commerce applications is stimulating some ambitious de facto middleware standardization efforts that may lead to greater uniformity.

Middleware is not only a software product capability, but is also frequently
developed on an ad hoc basis to meet specific needs. For example, an organization wanting to integrate some legacy departmental applications into an enterprise application may accomplish that with minimum changes to the legacy
application by adding a custom-developed layer of middleware.

This chapter doesn't attempt to catalog and discuss all flavors of middleware,
but rather focuses on some important generic capabilities of value to applications and illustrates them with specific middleware products and product categories. The capabilities here are of sufficient general interest that they can be
incorporated into a variety of middleware software products. A broadly encom-
passing definition of middleware is assumed; that is, some capabilities discussed
here might be considered by some vendors as a part of distributed operating
systems rather than middleware.

16.1   Messaging and Queueing Middleware

Although transaction processing was a great advance in networked applications, it doesn't provide a complete solution in many applications. It is particularly difficult when the task defined as a transaction spans a considerable length
of time, such as minutes to days. One problem that arises is the resource locking
required to insure the isolation of concurrent transactions—an issue discussed in
Chapter 17. For long-lived tasks this resource locking is not feasible, because
the performance penalty would be unacceptable. There are many other practical obstacles to long-lived transactions spanning multiple departments in an
organization, two of which are heterogeneous departmental systems and the
unavailability of the needed resources simultaneously. The latter is particularly
an issue in transaction systems involving workers in helping satisfy requests. A
way to circumvent these issues while still benefiting from transaction processing

is to split a request into multiple transactions and introduce queueing and messaging between those transactions. These *multitransaction workflow* [Ber97] systems are deferred rather than immediate applications. Problems that arise, such as the failure of a particular transaction, must then be directly dealt with by the application.

Message-oriented middleware (MOM) supports the messaging and queueing needs of multitransactional systems. Because MOM emphasizes queueing, appropriate applications for MOM include those that

- Can tolerate deferred processing
- Have long task lifetimes, especially those involving workers working with information technology
- Allow the availability requirements to be relaxed by deferring tasks
- Deviate from the simple client-server model, such as requiring many-to-one or one-to-many communications, or requiring many responses to a given request or a single response to many requests.

E X A M P L E : *The book distributor working with books4u.com described in "On-Line Bookselling" on page 66 would benefit from MOM in its inter-enterprise e-commerce with the book distributors. The book distributor receives orders (represented in XML) from many book merchants and queues them. An application then scans these orders to distribute them to the warehouse geographically close to the customer. As workers in the warehouse become available, they each access and fulfill the next order in that warehouse's queue.*

It would be advantageous if each book merchant working with the distributor layered its e-commerce application on the same MOM. This would create a uniform environment for all the book merchants and distributors, simplifying interoperability across enterprises. However, it proved impossible to coordinate this with all the book merchants—who deal with other distributors as well—so MOM is used only internally to the distributor.

This last example illustrates one of the difficult challenges of middleware in inter-enterprise and consumer applications. Since there is no single widely adopted middleware solution, the level of coordination required of all the participants in the application is difficult to achieve. Unfortunately, network effects work against the widespread penetration of such a solution.

Discussion

D16.1 Discuss how MOM could be used to advantage by student project groups.

16.2   Mobile Code, Objects, and Agents

Until recently, as a practical matter it was necessary to manually install software on a host in order to run it. The idea of mobile code removes this restriction, allowing a program to be moved to a host and immediately executed there without manual intervention. This idea, with a couple of enhancements called mobile objects and mobile agents, is explored in this section. The implications range beyond the technical—mobile code has important implications to both the network effects and lock-in that were discussed in Chapter 8. In fact, it may herald a major transition in both the computer and communications industries.

With *mobile code* (MC), as illustrated in Figure 16.1, a program is sent to a target host (as a message) and then executed there. This is possible because a program, like any other information, is represented by data and hence can be stored as a file or communicated as a message. When a message containing mobile code is received at a host, it can be executed there. The term "mobile" here, while commonly used, is something of a misnomer—the code does not actually move while it is executing. Rather, the code is replicated, communicated to another host, and then executed there.

The biggest obstacle to the simple idea of mobile code is the differing representations and the interfaces between a program and the infrastructure across computing platforms. Restricting mobile code to a single platform would greatly reduce the utility, except within closed administrative domains. This obstacle is addressed by the Java technology described shortly.

The idea of mobile code can be enhanced by conveying data along with code. This makes particular sense in conjunction with object-oriented programming, since objects tightly couple the code implementing the object with the data managed by the object. *Mobile objects* (MOs) convey object instance data (the data encapsulated in an object and constituting its state) along with the code (object implementation). MC allows object classes to be instantiated on a host and executed on that same host, while MO allows already instantiated objects that are executing to be moved dynamically among hosts.

The idea with both MC and MO is that computation can be dynamically moved where it is most advantageous. The program code does not need to be preinstalled on the host where it is to run.

16.2.1   Advantages of Mobile Code

Although the MC and MO ideas are simple, the advantages are subtle, and implementation faces numerous challenges.

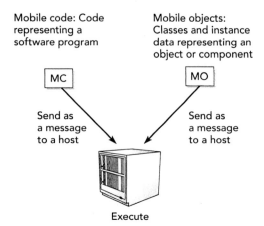

Figure 16.1 Mobile code (MC) and mobile objects (MO) allow a program execution to be moved from one host to another

Interactivity and Scalability

Some advantages of MC and MO are illustrated in Figure 16.2. One advantage is that MC and MO can dynamically move processing cycles from one host to another. There are two important performance implications. First, if the presentation (or a portion of it) is moved to a client, the user will experience faster response, because each user interaction will not experience the latency of messages sent over the network. For example, animations executed in a server but presented in a client are generally not satisfactory. However, the message conveying the MC will typically be large, resulting in a noticeable latency to get it to the client.

EXAMPLE: *Java (an MC system discussed shortly) has been successfully used in the Web. The MC (called a Java applet) is retrieved from a Web server and executed in the browser. Flowers4u.com described in "Floral Delivery Service" on page 69 decided to enhance the sales appeal of its customer presentation by displaying animated pictures of the merchandise, including flowers sprouting and growing into bouquets. The limited Internet access rates of many customers precluded doing this animation on the server, so flowers4u.com downloaded a Java applet to the Web browser, where the animation exploited local processing.*

Another advantage of MC is that it allows computation to be moved dynamically to whatever host is appropriate, based not only on interactivity considerations but also on available resources. This is particularly valuable in moving computation from a server to a client, because clients automatically scale in pro-

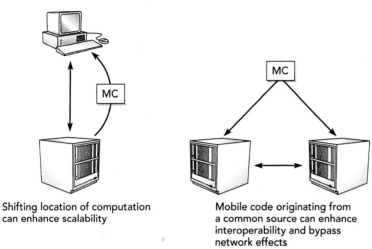

Executing program closer
to user can enhance interactivity

MC

MC

Shifting location of computation
can enhance scalability

Mobile code originating from
a common source can enhance
interoperability and bypass
network effects

Figure 16.2 Advantages of mobile code include interactivity, scalability, and interoperability

Mobile Code and Objects

MC is invariably used in the context of objects or components. The object or component offers a convenient unit of code to transport to another host, where it can interact with other objects or components already residing there.

Considering the object approach, in technical terms MC is a class or assembly of classes—which are instantiated and executed in the target host—while an MO is an object or assembly of objects. A class includes its implementation (a program in some appropriate language), which is transported to the target host in a message. An object includes both the class and the data stored in the object, all of which can be enclosed in a single message.

portion to the number of users. See Chapter 17 for additional discussion of performance issues such as this.

ANALOGY: *A company running short of workers—instead of hiring more—might train its customer's workers to perform the same functions. As the number of customers increases, the total workers' capability expands accordingly.*

Interoperability

As shown in Figure 16.2, one powerful benefit of mobile code is interoperability. In a distributed environment, installing interoperable pieces of a distributed application on the hosts—and keeping them updated with compatible upgrades—is a daunting administrative hassle. At minimum, the application need must be anticipated so the software can be installed. Mobile code can bypass these issues: If the distributed pieces are sent from a single source using MC, then interoperability is easier, and the need does not have to be anticipated. This is particularly advantageous interorganizationally, where coordination is more challenging. The interoperability of MC also bypasses network effects (see the sidebar "Mobile Code and Network Effects").

EXAMPLE: *MC is part of the proposal for the network computer discussed in "An Ultrathin Client: The Network Computer (NC)" on page 147. A major*

Mobile Code and Network Effects

As discussed in "Network Effects" on page 232, new direct applications are difficult to establish due to direct network effects. Early adopters derive very little benefit and have low willingness to pay. By aiding interoperability, mobile code can bypass this problem [Mes96a], since one user's license can permit her to opportunistically provide another user with compatible MC.

ANALOGY: *In the genesis of the facsimile machine, imagine that fax was implemented in software. Even if another user had no fax, if you could send a fax machine (as MC) followed by a fax, network effects would be lessened. Even the first adopter would derive full benefit.*

Applications with strong network effects are the most compelling for

MC, including direct-immediate applications with the peer-to-peer architecture described in Chapter 5.

If the licensing and pricing of mobile code is done like phone calls, the originator pays the license fee (and it is free to the responder). Alternatively, usage-based fees could be paid by both originator and responder.

argument in favor of the NC is the reduction in administrative costs in avoiding the configuration of individual clients.

Jini is a set of standards built on Java mobile code and proposed by an industry consortium led by Sun Microsystems that is designed to enable the interoperability of information appliances. The idea is that each appliance would accept MC, enabling it to interoperate with other appliances to collaborate on common tasks. Java also allows information appliances to be upgraded over the network, reducing their obsolescence.

Information Access

MOs provide an intriguing way to implement information access applications, as illustrated in Figure 16.3. The conventional approach has been to move data to join the processing, resulting in the shuttling of data about the network. An alternative is to leave the data in place and move the processing by using MOs. The reason this is an application of MOs rather than MC is the ability of an MO to "sweep up" information and carry it along with it. Also, an MO carries with it state, which allows it to adjust its itinerary depending on what it finds.

ANALOGY: *You might send an assistant (mobile assistant) to visit all the libraries in town seeking particular information, rather than browsing the on-line catalog and having a book sent to your office. The mobile assistant can browse the stacks, looking inside books and possibly finding something not evident from the catalog entry. The assistant can accumulate and bring back information in his briefcase.*

An MO that has the ability to adaptively adjust its itinerary (the host that it visits) is called a *mobile agent* (MA) or *intelligent agent*. An intelligent agent has four sets of capabilities [Woo94]:

- *Autonomy:* It contains all the code and data necessary to determine its itinerary and its execution. It is not dependent on additional facilities provided by hosts aside from those that allow it to execute.
- *Interaction ability:* It can interact with other agents or its environment.
- *Reactivity:* It can adjust its actions based on what happens in its environment.
- *Proactivity:* It can initiate actions by itself.

The capabilities of the intelligent agent open up a number of interesting possibilities. Intelligent agent technology originated in artificial intelligence, where you can imagine sophisticated humanlike qualities such as adaptation to the environment and higher-level cognitive functions. More mundane applications

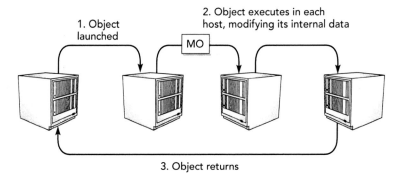

Figure 16.3 Information access using a mobile object

include generalizations to user-driven information access, such as cruising the network to gather or disseminate information.

16.2.2   Mobile Code and Object Middleware

To be practical, mobile and intelligent agents require a middleware infrastructure that supports them. As an example of the capability needed, an agent must have the authority to move itself from one host to another, and at each host it must receive appropriate processing and storage resources to complete its task. *Mobile code middleware* addresses one key issue—software portability—and other issues, such as security. Executable code is not easily portable from one host to another, as there are differences in computer instruction sets and operating systems. A lot of the advantage is lost in a network environment if MC can execute on only one specific platform (such as UNIX, Windows, or MacOS). The mobile code middleware provides a platform-independent abstract machine to the mobile code, so that it can execute anywhere. In addition, it is dangerous to execute code from an untrusted source, and MC middleware can enforce security policies that restrict sources of MC or the action available to the MC.

Discussion

D16.2 Discuss the software licensing issues in mobile code and mobile objects. In particular, how could one user distribute licensed mobile code to another?

16.3   Distributed Object Management

Two objects (or components) can interact even if they reside on different hosts, for example, by using a remote method invocation (RMI), as introduced in

Competing Distributed Object Visions: DCOM and CORBA

Two de facto distributed object management standards are engaged in a classic standards war. In terms of strategies and models for industrial organization, they are dramatically different. DCOM is promulgated by Microsoft, which controls the dominant Windows platform. CORBA is developed by OMG, an industry consortium with more than 700 participating companies.

DCOM, not being "designed by committee," is today more real, but it doesn't benefit from the give-and-take and infusion of ideas from a multiplicity of companies. CORBA is more ambitious in its goals, including platform independence, and in its aspirations to subsume other middleware functions such as transaction processing and mobile code.

The healthy competition between two standards will result in shorter time to market. On the other hand, network effects are strong, and two standards may confuse the marketplace and slow down adoption.

Chapter 12. Interacting objects executing on different hosts are called *distributed objects*. Exploiting this capability, applications can be decomposed into distributed objects (or assembled from distributed components), which are partitioned across multiple hosts. Distributed objects introduce practical difficulties. For example, how can RMI be made to work even if the hosts have different operating systems, or the objects are implemented using different languages? How can an object on one host identify objects on another host, or maintain a reference to such objects? It doesn't make sense for every application developer to address these and similar issues independently. Rather, distributed objects require distributed object management (DOM) middleware. To the application developer, the major benefit of DOM is that it makes a distributed application appear more like a centralized application, as the interaction among objects is similar whether objects are distributed or reside on the same host.

ANALOGY: *Two companies will have difficulty collaborating on a project if one uses English and the other Spanish. A service to facilitate this collaboration is an automatic translation from English to Spanish and Spanish to English that is transparent to the employees involved.*

As illustrated in Figure 16.4, without DOM (at the top), application software has to be ported to different platforms, and it has to provide its own object interaction communications (using, say, TCP/IP). With DOM, the application programmer uses RMI for object interaction, and interoperability is achieved regardless of platform and language.

EXAMPLE: *Two pieces of an application, one written in the Java language on a Windows NT platform, and the other written in C++ running on a UNIX platform, would be interoperable (could invoke one another's methods).*

This also allows more flexibility in partitioning an application across hosts without affecting its architecture or functionality. Two standards are competing to become de facto standards (see the sidebar "Competing Distributed Object Visions: DCOM and CORBA"). The most compelling need for DOM is in enterprise and inter-enterprise applications, since these encounter the greatest platform and language heterogeneity. Such applications should be easier to develop and manage because of DOM, which has the potential to provide an infrastructure similar to the Internet but richer and with higher levels of abstraction. Unfortunately, like all middleware solutions, such a standard must overcome network externalities, which have thus far stifled attempts to establish a widespread public infrastructure. DOM has, however, been quite successful in some enterprise applications where there is common administrative control.

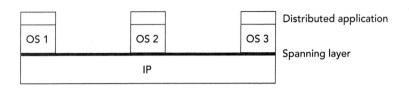

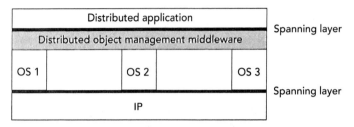

Figure 16.4 DOM middleware adds a spanning layer isolating the application from its distribution and heterogeneous operating systems and languages

EXAMPLE: *DOM has been adopted by the telecommunications industry as the foundation for software that manages many large public networks. For example, TCSI supplies a SolutionCore platform for the development of such network management applications that incorporates the CORBA standards, together with SolutionSuites application frameworks.*

The proponents of DOM have ambitious goals, subsuming capabilities discussed earlier in this chapter (messaging services, transaction processing, and mobile code). There is hope for realization of this vision—it has the support of the largest software companies and a viable standardization process—although it has proceeded so quickly that many important capabilities (transaction processing, for example) seem to be afterthoughts.

16.3.1 One DOM Standard: CORBA

The integration of data across enterprises (or cross-enterprise) relates to the communication, representation, and interpretation of data. DOM addresses these problems, and the architecture of one DOM platform—CORBA from OMG, shown in Figure 16.5—illustrates how [OPR96] [Sie96] [Ran95] [Bak97]. Also see the sidebar "The OMG Process" for a discussion of how CORBA standards are developed.

16.3.2 Changing Data Representations

The first issue is how data is communicated between two objects (the protocol) and how it is represented (the formats). A request-response protocol is associ-

The OMG Process

The process used by OMG has similarities to the IETF. Officially the OMG doesn't call itself as a standardization body, but rather a consortium of companies cooperating to define a DOM architecture and interfaces within that architecture. The stated goal is designing "a common architectural framework for object-oriented applications based on widely available interface specifications." The hope is that the open interfaces will be implemented by multiple vendors.

Once the OMG decides a given interface is needed, it issues a request for proposals and guides the refinement of proposals submitted through comment and consensus, sometimes by suggesting that companies work together to integrate their best ideas. Unlike the IETF, proposals need not be accompanied by a working implementation, but companies with successful proposals must agree to market a commercial implementation within one year.

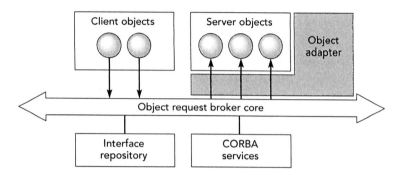

Figure 16.5 The architecture of CORBA

ated with RMI. The formatting issue is also important, because different platforms and languages can use different representations for standard data types.
CORBA deals with the latter issue by defining standard data types that it supports and then performing automatic conversions between different representations within DOM.

> EXAMPLE: *Conversions between different representations of data types partially
> address one primary obstacle to the integration of data across an enterprise.
> Partitions of applications can share information, as long as the information con-
> forms to the standard data types supported by CORBA, and can maintain data
> integrity through these conversions.*

All the issues relating to the heterogeneity of object languages and platforms is
finessed by communication through an intermediary—the *object request broker*
(ORB). The ORB arranges whatever translations are necessary to allow a client
object to perform an RMI on the server object. Internal to the ORB is a communication protocol and a universal format for marshalling of method parameters
and return values. The flavor of this protocol built on the internet TCP/IP is IIOP,
described in "Internet Inter-ORB Protocol (IIOP)" on page 364.

> ANALOGY: *The ORB is analogous to an English-to-Spanish translation service
> that is invoked automatically whenever two companies collaborate.*

It is possible for many vendors to implement and sell CORBA-compliant ORBs.
The goal is to allow objects managed by different ORBs—even from different
vendors running on different platforms in different languages—to interact
through RMI, and to share other resources and services. Thus, the emphasis of
CORBA is interoperability, but not portability (see the sidebar "Portability vs.
Interoperability").

A remote client object can invoke a method on a local server object as intermediated by the ORB. Also included is an *object adapter*, which manages local objects, such as invoking them when their methods are called and routing each RMI to the appropriate object. Aside from communication protocols and formats, another issue is how a client object specifies the location of a server object and how it knows that object exists in the first place. Dealing with the first issue (and deferring the second), each object in the DOM is assigned an *object reference* when it is created. This reference is unique and stays with the object even if it moves to a different host or is temporarily stored on disk. Thus, a server object can use that reference as long as it likes. This *location transparency* is especially important for mobile objects.

16.3.3   Interface Discovery

The common interpretation of data among objects implemented by different programmers in different languages is an issue. How does one object know the names, parameters, and return values of another object? CORBA provides two forms of assistance: an interface definition language (IDL) and an *interface repository* (IR).

A N A L O G Y :   *IDL and IR are analogous to a memorandum that describes to the employees of two companies the precise ways in which they will collaborate. This memorandum is not a part of the collaboration itself, but rather documents in advance how it will take place.*

IDL is a language defined for the express and limited purpose of describing the interface (but not the implementation) of an object's class. The implementation is presumed to be in a systems programming language (such as Java or C++). The steps in implementing a class would be as follows:

1. Describe and document the class interface using IDL.
2. Automatically translate the IDL description into a template in the implementation language (called a language *binding*).
3. Use that template as a starting point for implementing the object class.

IDL also serves as documentation for the class interface that can be published. (You can imagine a whole library of interface specifications and many pleasant evenings spent poring over them.) More interestingly, IDL serves as the basis for *discovery* of the interface, so that a client can interoperate with an object without knowing its interface in advance. A given ORB publishes IDL descriptions of the classes it harbors in a database called the interface repository (IR).

Portability vs. Interoperability

Network effects and lock-in—introduced in Chapter 8—are related to the portability and interoperability discussed in this chapter. The objective with *portability* is to avoid customer lock-in by building application elements that are easily moved from one platform to another. Java provides portability for a single language but does not promise interoperability with application modules written in a different language.

Interoperability bypasses network effects by allowing application elements to work together even though they were developed on different platforms in different languages. CORBA offers interoperability (an object in one ORB can be a client of an object in another ORB) but does not promise portability: Generally an application developed on a vendor's CORBA-compliant ORB can't easily be moved to a different ORB. Although the interoperability of two ORBs is assured by IIOP, the ORB itself is not standardized. In fact, ORB vendors have no strong desire for portability because lock-in benefits them.

Thus, mobile code and DOM are complementary concepts: Mobile code emphasizes portability, and DOM emphasizes interoperability. Thus, it is common for CORBA vendors to support the Java language and mobile objects written in Java.

A N A L O G Y :   *The telephone network emphasizes interaction among people no matter what their location (interoperability). The transportation system emphasizes moving people from one location to another (porta-*

bility). The two are comple-
mentary—more of one tends to
lead to more of the other.

The ORB offers *dynamic binding* of objects. First, a client object can discover a class interface through the IR, which means find its methods as well as the names and data types of the parameters and return values. Armed with that information, a client can interact with any object that is an instance of that class. This is in contrast to a conventional OOP language, in which object interfaces must be compiled into the program. Dynamic binding allows new classes (not just new objects) to be added to an executing application as it executes.

16.3.4 Services

A DOM like CORBA also captures as *object services* common facilities needed by many applications, contributing to software reuse. Representative CORBA services include

- *Lifecycle and relationship services:* Lifecycle services specify standard interfaces for operations common to all object systems, such as `create`, `destroy`, `move`, and `copy`. Relationship services provide standardized ways of composing objects into larger modules.
- *Naming and trader services:* The object reference allows interaction with an object once it is known, but ways of finding objects are needed. The naming service, when provided the name of an object, returns a reference to that object. The trader service allows objects to be found by function rather than name or reference. The trader service is also being standardized by ISO.
- *Security services:* These specify the standard security capabilities of authentication, access control, and confidentiality.
- *Transaction services:* These provide standard interfaces to transaction processing, as discussed in "Transaction Processing" on page 426.

16.3.5 Interoperability among ORBs: IIOP

Each organization will select, install, and administer its own ORB, implying that a given distributed application might span ORBs from different vendors, or separately administered ORBs from the same vendor. This requires interoperability among ORBs (see the sidebar "Portability vs. Interoperability"). CORBA has defined a *General Inter-ORB Protocol (GIOP)* that defines the payload of messages among ORBs. GIOP can be implemented on top of any reliable transport protocol, but the most common is the internet (GIOP over the internet TCP is called IIOP and was briefly described in "Internet Inter-ORB Protocol (IIOP)" on page 364).

16.3.6   Horizontal and Vertical Facilities

DOM also encourages the specification of standard *facilities*, which are much like application components and frameworks described in "Components and Frameworks" on page 315. Horizontal facilities are frameworks that are useful across a wide range of applications, and vertical facilities are frameworks of interest within a limited application domain or industry. The existence of DOM is expected to create a marketplace for a variety of plug-in components and frameworks.

Discussion

D16.3 Discuss the new possibilities for cross-enterprise and commerce applications enabled by DOM. Is the opportunity new applications, or easier development of existing applications?

D16.4 Given the existence of interoperability standards, discuss how CORBA-compliant vendors will compete against one another. Are there winner-take-all effects in this market?

16.4   Open Issues

Middleware is still an emerging software product category; so much remains to be resolved.

16.4.1   Middleware Service Providers?

Telecommunications, discussed further in Chapter 20, has always featured a service provider that planned, deployed, and operated telecommunications facilities as a public infrastructure. While companies have traditionally provisioned their own computing and internal networking, it is increasingly common to outsource networking and occasionally computing facilities. The question arises, will the rising importance of middleware expand the role of service provider? Today the Internet provides at least one service—domain name services, discussed in Chapter 18—not traditionally provided by telecommunications networks. An expanded suite of services could include many things, such as MOM and DOM, encryption key distribution and escrow, directory services, and payment mechanisms.

A public infrastructure supporting mobile or nomadic computer users suggests more strongly the need for supporting middleware services, if users are to be afforded comparable services regardless of location. Advocates of ultrathin clients like the network computer (NC) also advocate a major role for a service provider in which the user provides only a platform for application execution, but all storage is maintained centrally. Another manifestation of this trend is free services, such as email, provided on Web sites with advertiser support.

Which part of the distributed computing environment is a public infrastructure, and which part should be provided by users for their own needs? Who will design, construct, and operate the public infrastructure needed for distributed applications, and how will it be paid for?

16.4.2   Middleware Spanning Layer?

A spanning layer offers considerable benefit in hiding heterogeneity in the underlying infrastructure in a way that offers vendors a large market for tools and applications, as described in "The Spanning Layer" on page 185. The emergence of a spanning layer (standardized and ubiquitous, supported by many vendors) would be very beneficial in hiding platform heterogeneity and enabling enterprise and cross-enterprise applications. Unfortunately, as we have seen, there is considerable differentiation in the goals and capabilities of middleware solutions, and there are many possibilities not discussed in this chapter. Will a single middleware solution arise through the power of positive feedback in a market like this with direct network externalities? If so, it is likely to encompass all the capabilities discussed here—messaging, transactions, distributed objects, mobile code—and more. The two emerging solutions described in "Competing Distributed Object Visions: DCOM and CORBA" on page 450 show promise, but will the market eventually tip to one of them?

16.4.3   Middleware vs. XML and the Web

Both Java and CORBA were established with the vision that they could become a spanning layer that might mitigate the severe coordination difficulties for applications spanning administrative domains, such as interorganizational and consumer commerce. A ubiquitous layer of middleware that hides the underlying heterogeneity could not only make such applications much easier to develop and maintain but also contribute to flexibility. Of course there are severe obstacles inherent in the network effects—how does such a solution survive the build-up period before it can achieve critical mass and benefit from positive feedback?

There is a less radical approach to achieving interoperability across administrative domains, and that is to allow applications to share documents, as described in Chapter 15. The mode of interaction becomes the message, where the message formats follow an international standard such as XML, supplemented by industry-specific standards defining XML tags for specific purposes. This is an evolutionary approach, migrating from the long-established electronic data interchange, as described in Chapter 3. The availability of standard tools to interpret such messages makes it fairly easy to build the interpretation of such messages into new or even legacy applications. The alignment with the Web technologies also makes this approach attractive.

So far, the middleware approach seems to be losing ground, except in closed administrative domains where network effects are easily overcome, and XML seems to be gaining momentum as a standard for interorganizational applications.

Review

Middleware is an infrastructure layer falling between the operating system and the application. It has many purposes, such as using existing lower-layer capabilities in new ways and hiding the heterogeneity of networked hosts. There is no single middleware solution, but rather different middleware for different purposes.

Message-oriented middleware (MOM) supports workflow applications by providing messaging, queueing, and multiplexing facilities.

Mobile code (MC) middleware allows programs to be transported to a new host and executed there, even on a different platform. MC contributes to interactivity (by locating execution close to the user), scalability (by moving execution to a lightly loaded host), and interoperability (by allowing users to participate in an application without needing preinstalled software).

Mobile objects (MO) are MC that in addition carry data (state). Supported by MO middleware, agents can travel around the network gathering information and adaptively choosing their next destination.

Distributed object management (DOM) is a middleware layer that hides heterogeneous platforms and languages from object-oriented networked applications. DOM allows objects to interact transparently by RMI, whether they are on the same or different hosts, and offers various other services and facilities of value to applications. An interface description language (IDL), used to describe object interfaces, enables discovery of those interfaces and dynamic binding.

Key Concepts

Middleware

Message-oriented middleware

Mobile code

Mobile objects

Distributed object management:

- CORBA, IDL, IIOP

Further Reading

[OHE96a] is an excellent general reference on middleware technologies, including those discussed in this chapter. [OHE96b] gives a more complete description of distributed object management in particular. [Fla96] is a recommended reference on Java, especially for those with prior programming experience. Although there is not yet an ideal reference on CORBA, [Bak97] can be recommended (although it emphasizes one vendor's products).

Exercises

E16.1   Discuss the relationship of MOM to the postal service. What if anything does the postal service provide that MOM doesn't, and vice versa?

E16.2   Suppose a piece of mobile code is totally untrusted (you don't know who created it or what it does), so you want to restrict its capabilities. Consider policies on the following types of operations and indicate, first, what undesired actions by the mobile code might be precluded, and then what legitimate purposes might also be undesirably restricted as a side effect.

   a. Network access

   b. File system access

   c. Method invocation on other, nonmobile objects residing permanently on your computer

   d. Method invocation on other, mobile objects residing on other hosts

E16.3   You want to buy a new car. Suppose you want to build an application that allows different car dealers to bid against one another for your business. Describe how you might use mobile agents in this application.

E16.4   Discuss the similarities and differences among the following forms of platform independence. In particular, what distinct capabilities are required of the middleware to support each one?

   a. "Write once, run anywhere"

b. The ability of one object to invoke the methods of another object, where the objects are on different platforms but use an ORB from the same vendor

c. The same as *b*, except that the two objects run in the ORBs from different vendors

E16.5 Discuss any administrative or logistical problems you might encounter in using DOM for each of the following applications:

a. Network management for a large telephone network

b. E-commerce between companies in the automobile industry and their suppliers

c. Consumer e-commerce

Performance

Organizations are concerned with the level of activity supported by their networked applications, and users are concerned with the speed and responsiveness they experience.

PART

VI

Scalability

In most networked applications, there are performance and quality objectives, which, if violated, adversely impact their utility to users and organizations. These objectives strongly depend on the specific application context. Not meeting them may reduce the quality of the user experience, or cause annoyance, or worst of all cost money.

EXAMPLE: *After clicking on a Web hyperlink, time spent waiting for display of the linked page is wasted. Displaying poor-quality (muddy or distorted) video in a video conference will reduce the quality of the experience. Delaying execution of a stock trade may cost the stock4u.com's customers money (see "On-Line Stock Trading" on page 68).*

Applications are rarely static in their performance objectives. Often they must support a growing demand in terms of number of users or volume of transactions or data processed, while maintaining adequate response. These issues become particularly important in enterprise and commerce applications, where the total demands can grow to monstrous proportions. Scalability is the characteristic of application architectures that can grow in this way with the addition (but not replacement) of resources and at reasonable cost.

Identifying performance and quality objectives is an important part of application needs assessment, as described in "Application Lifecycle" on page 279. These objectives then have direct impact on the architecture and design of the application—especially the mapping of application functionality onto multiple hosts. The network and communication links also affect performance and quality, as discussed in more detail in Chapter 18 and Chapter 20.

17.1   Metrics

The performance and quality of networked applications are measured by metrics, often quantitative in nature. In the operation of a networked application, *performance* refers to quantitative measures such as the aggregate number of users accommodated and the speed of response to each user. *Quality* refers to subjective measures of the user experience, such as the fidelity of audio or video reproduction. Important quality metrics also include program correctness and reliability, as described in Chapter 9. Performance and some quality attributes can be objectively measured, while other quality attributes require subjective assessment, asking users to rate their experience.

A N A L O G Y :   *Analogous questions could be asked about a work group completing some repetitive task (such as processing license applications). How many applications is the group processing per week? How often do they make mistakes? How satisfied are the applicants with the experience?*

It is usually not meaningful to address the performance or quality of an application as a *whole*, as there are many constituent aspects and perspectives. These questions need to be decomposed, like other aspects of computing. The overall assessment of performance and quality is a judgement that aggregates many considerations.

17.1.1   Performance

Although performance can be quantitatively measured, requirements must be related to the user or organizational needs. Like availability and security, there is a trade-off between performance and cost, so it is important to understand not only what performance is adequate, but also what is sufficient.

A N A L O G Y :   *What are the performance characteristics of a rope? When used to tow a vehicle, the correct metric is the force it can exert without breaking. If used to rappel down a mountain, an important metric is length. It is inefficient to use a really long rope to tow a vehicle, or the strongest rope to rappel down a mountain.*

The first step is to divide the application into individual tasks. A *task* is a small, manageable collection of actions that are not usefully subdivided—similar to the transaction described in "Transaction Processing" on page 426, but without necessarily imposing the formal properties of atomicity and consistency.

EXAMPLE: *In Web browsing, one task consists of the hyperlink being clicked and the resulting retrieval of a new page. The task is complete when the page is displayed, and in the meantime the user is idle. In stock4u.com's trading system, the execution of a stock trade with the exchange would be a task.*

ANALOGY: *A complete application is analogous to the work group in social applications. Like the work group, it has the goal of completing some well-defined project. A task is then analogous to a task group spun off from the work group. Looked at in this way, achieving high performance in the networked application faces similar challenges to achieving high productivity and output from a work group.*

For some tasks, an important performance parameter is *completion time*. For *repetitive* tasks, the number of tasks completed per unit time (called the *throughput*) may hold the greatest interest. Not infrequently both are important.

EXAMPLE: *For a Web browser, the individual user is concerned about individual task (information request and response) completion time. The task throughput for one user is dominated by the time he spends reading the retrieved material, and hence is not relevant to application design. However, the Web server supports a large number of users making requests, and the number of users served is directly related to task throughput.*

For stock4u.com's trading system, the throughput must exceed the largest expected daily volume of trades divided by the trading hours, or else some customers won't be served on busy days. The execution time for a market order is important (lest the stock price change), but the fulfillment time is not (since the customer is not waiting, and it has no impact on the price).

ANALOGY: *For a bridge authority, a single task would be one car passing over the bridge. The driver of that car is primarily concerned with completion time, but the bridge authority is primarily concerned about the throughput (which directly relates to its toll revenue).*

For repetitive tasks, are completion time and throughput related? Naively, you might assume that reducing the completion time and increasing the throughput go hand in hand. Although they are related, there is a third parameter, concurrency, that changes the balance, as illustrated in Figure 17.1. Shown are two cases:

- In the first case, the execution of tasks overlap in time (said to be *concurrent*), for example, if multiple hosts are working cooperatively on the tasks. The completion time for each task is long, and yet the throughput is high.

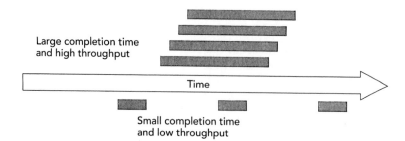

Figure 17.1 Relationship of task completion time and throughput for repetitive tasks

- In the second case, the tasks are not concurrent; each task is completed before the next task begins. Because of a large idle period between the end of one task and the beginning of the next, the throughput is low, and yet the completion time is short.

EXAMPLE: *In the Web browser, the user waits for a new page to be displayed before clicking on a hyperlink on that page, so the tasks that make up the viewing of successive pages are inherently not concurrent. The user probably stops to examine and read each page, leaving a substantial gap between tasks. Even if task completion time is short, task throughput is dominated by user behavior and not by computing system performance.*

Stock4u.com's trading system has a set of hosts performing trades concurrently. Each new order would be routed to an idle host, decoupling throughput from completion time.

In summary, the trade-off between throughput and completion time depends on the level of concurrency and other factors such as inactive time waiting for external events. As will be seen later in this chapter, the trade-off is also affected by irregularities in task arrival times or task processing time.

17.1.2   Quality

Important quality metrics relate to the *subjective* quality of audio, images, and video media. Any audible or visible elements not present in the original source (such as noise or distortion) are called *artifacts*. ("Artifact" means man-made or artificial. In this context, artifacts are artificially introduced by the computer system or network.)

E X A M P L E :   *Distortion causes an audio signal to sound unnatural, while noise is a "hissing" component most evident when the audio is silent. For images and video, artifacts take the form of visual effects such as unnatural mosaic patterns, fuzziness caused by lowered resolution, etc. Artifacts are introduced by compression algorithms designed to reduce the bit rate necessary for representing the source (described in Chapter 20) and by impairments introduced within networks (described in Chapter 18).*

Another common detrimental artifact in direct-immediate applications (telephony or video conferencing, for example) is the *delay* between the original source and reproduced signal. Delay in excess of approximately 0.25 to 0.5 seconds makes a two-way conversation difficult. In deferred applications (such as audio or video on demand or broadcast), delay is less critical.

E X A M P L E :   *For streaming audio or video, the data representation of the source is split into messages and transferred across the network, as illustrated in Figure 12.9 on page 360. There are two sources of delay between the original and reproduced sound or video: the time to accumulate the data that makes up each message and the latency that the message suffers across the network.*

The components of message latency are discussed further in Chapter 20.

17.1.3   Contributors to Performance and Quality

The factors listed in Table 17.1 contribute strongly to performance and quality. While technology and equipment both improve in cost and performance characteristics over time, for an application developer the goal is achieving adequate performance in *today's* technology and equipment. The application architecture is thus the primary consideration. In Table 17.1, as in the remainder of this chapter, the restaurant analogy of Table 5.1 on page 146 is used frequently. One important point made in this table is that the underlying electronics and communications technologies are advancing rapidly, promising improving cost-performance characteristics for some time to come.

Discussion

D17.1 Discuss your experience with the Web, and the phenomenon known as the "world wide wait." How does this impact the utility or experience? What do you think may be impacting performance?

D17.2 If you have any experience with video displayed from a computer CD-ROM and video transmitted over the Internet, compare the quality of these

Table 17.1 Determinants of performance and quality

Factor	Description	Analogy
Software architecture	The architecture of the application determines the partitioning of the application onto multiple hosts, which determines processing resources. It also addresses the relative location of data and processing. These both impact the communications overhead.	A restaurant can organize its kitchen and table service in various ways. For example, gourmet and fast-food restaurants are organized quite differently.
Technology	Electronics, magnetic and optical storage, and fiber optics are rapidly advancing. Application performance benefits directly from these technology advances. One metric not subject to technology advance is the speed of light propagation delay, which is considered in Chapter 20.	Agriculture and food preparation technologies reduce the cost of food over time, thereby reducing the cost of restaurant meals.
Equipment	Computing systems and networks exploit technology to provide processing, storage, and communications services to applications. Their performance is determined by both technology and their internal architecture and design.	Kitchen equipment such as microwave ovens and conveyor belts substitute for labor, improve speed, and reduce costs.

sources with the video you see on your television set. What might account for any differences?

D17.3 Similarly, if you have experience with Internet telephony, compare its quality to your telephone. What might account for any differences?

D17.4 Have you had experience with a telephone call in which the delay was noticeable? If so, describe the impact it had on the conversation.

17.2   The Role of Concurrency

Since technology is fixed at any point in time, the application designer must look elsewhere for handles on the performance and quality metrics. One such handle is the equipment, which at any given time allows trade-offs between performance (such as processing speed and communication bit rate) and cost. Another important determinant of performance is the application architecture. If improved performance metrics are desired, one important architectural tool is concurrency. Recall that two tasks are concurrent when they overlap in time. Two important motivations for concurrency are listed in Table 17.2.

In many applications, concurrency is unavoidable due to functional requirements.

Table 17.2 Two motivations for concurrency in networked applications

Motivation	Description	Analogy
Intrinsic functional requirements	The application requirements may require concurrent tasks, such as multiple users working independently.	In a restaurant, multiple customers are ordering and eating their meals at one time.
Performance objectives	A single host or communication link may not be fast enough to meet task completion time or throughput requirements.	A fast-food restaurant may find that one cook cannot serve up meals fast enough, so more cooks are hired. A single waiter may not be able to serve all customers, so more waiters are hired.

EXAMPLE: *Many applications support multiple users simultaneously. Stocks4u. com's trading system allows many customers to enter orders at overlapping times. If each such order and execution is considered a task, then they must be concurrent.*

In other applications, concurrency is dictated by performance objectives. If one host can't provide needed throughput, it may be possible to increase that throughput by assigning tasks to multiple hosts. If the performance of a single host or a single communication link is inadequate, the only option is to get more things happening at the same time, and that implies concurrency.

EXAMPLE: *In an email forwarding and routing application, the entry, sending, and delivery of one email message is a task, and the primary performance objective is throughput. As the number of users and messages increases, eventually one host can't accommodate them. Throughput can be increased by adding a second host, assigning half the messages to it. The tasks on the two hosts are then concurrent.*

Often the two motivations in Table 17.2 go together: A *large* number of users performing tasks simultaneously requires concurrency for both functional *and* performance reasons.

17.2.1   Concurrency with Multiple Hosts

If task throughput must be increased, adding hosts to work on tasks concurrently may help. A couple of simple approaches (for two hosts) are shown in Figure 17.2. As tasks are initiated, they can be routed to different hosts, or alternatively, they can all be routed to a single host, but that host can delegate those tasks it is unable to accommodate.

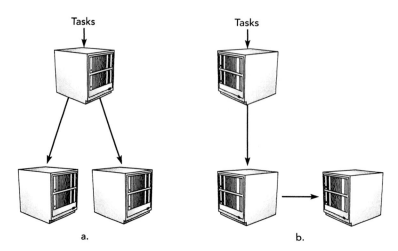

Figure 17.2 Task throughput can be increased by (a) routing or (b) delegation of tasks to multiple hosts

EXAMPLE: *It is common for a Web server to route requests from different users to multiple hosts. For example, stocks4u.com has dozens of hosts handling trading. Each new customer who initiates a trading session is automatically routed to the host that currently has the lightest load.*

Often life isn't this simple. A frequent obstacle is dependency among tasks, so delegation to different hosts creates communication overhead that limits throughput. Another constraint is the location of data needed by tasks, which may also create communications overhead.

17.2.2   Concurrency in a Single Host

Concurrency in a *single* host is necessary if concurrency is an intrinsic requirement and a single host offers adequate performance. Tasks can be concurrent in the same host using *time-slicing*, as illustrated in Figure 17.3 (for only two concurrent tasks—a larger number is possible). The idea is simple: the host alternates execution back and forth between tasks (each switch is called a *context switch*), working on the first for a while and then the second for a while, and then returning to the first. Although the two tasks are never executing simultaneously, they are concurrent because their execution overlaps in time.

ANALOGY: *A single waiter can serve multiple tables in the restaurant by dividing her time among the tables. First she fills the water glasses at one table, then switches to bringing a meal to another table, then switches to bringing the*

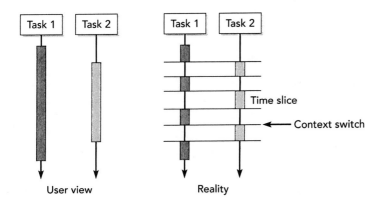

Figure 17.3 Time-slicing allows concurrent tasks in the same host

Different Forms of Multitasking

There are two forms of multitasking: *cooperative* and *preemptive*. In cooperative multitasking, tasks must periodically and temporarily give up control voluntarily. In preemptive multitasking, tasks need not worry about this, as context switching is invisible to tasks. The operating system invisibly preempts every task whenever it wishes to pass control to another, and later restores the first task without its realizing that it was interrupted.

check to a third table. Considering the start-to-finish service to one customer as a task, she is performing concurrent tasks by context switching.

Performing concurrent tasks in a single host—called multitasking—is an important feature of modern operating systems. Because computers are very fast, multitasking is not evident to a user, who perceives that a host can run different applications concurrently without apparent impact on one or the other.

E X A M P L E : *Multitasking allows a personal computer to overlap the printing of a document with some activity supporting the user, such as editing a document. The user may not be aware that there is a concurrent printing task, because the computer is fast enough to keep up with both the user's requests and the printer needs, while dividing its attention between the two.*

One important motivation for multitasking (aside from intrinsic application requirements) is *fairness*. On a single host, the alternative to multitasking would be to execute tasks sequentially, one after the other. This may be "unfair" if one task has a very long completion time, shutting out other tasks. The impact of concurrency on fairness is illustrated in Figure 17.4. The individual time-to-completion of each task is inevitably greater (since the computer is switching among them). Nevertheless, a short task may complete sooner—because it is allowed to start sooner—if the tasks are concurrent. Exactly the same idea applies to communications (see the sidebar "Why Networks Use Packets").

E X A M P L E : *Without multitasking, a user would have to wait for a document to completely print before doing anything else. This could be a long time. The user would prefer to "edge in" other tasks, even at the expense of increasing printing time.*

Why Networks Use Packets

Multitasking has a precise analogy to the communication of messages. Like a task, a message isn't useful until received in its entirety. Consider sending two messages across a communication link, as illustrated in Figure 17.5. Each message consumes the link for a period of time proportional to the number of bits in the message. A very long message, given exclusive access to the link, may delay the arrival of many other shorter messages.

EXAMPLE: *If a message payload includes a very large executable file, it may be many megabytes in length. On a slow link, this might take many minutes to transmit.*

To address fairness, messages can be communicated concurrently by fragmenting each message into *packets*. As shown in Figure 17.5, two messages arriving simultaneously must contend for the same link, and if the communication of the long message is completed before the shorter message starts, the shorter message's arrival is delayed. Packetization allows the two messages to be communicated concurrently, by interleaving packets. (Of course, another approach would be to add parallel communication links.) Because messages are fragmented into packets, a network such as the Internet is called a "packet network."

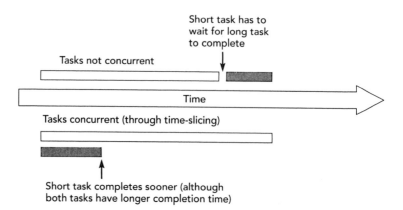

Figure 17.4 Multitasking in the same host contributes to fairness

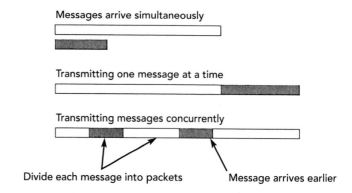

Figure 17.5 When messages are fragmented into packets, contending messages can be communicated concurrently by interleaving of packets

> *If stocks4u.com's trading system forced each order to the market to complete before allowing a new order to initiate, an order that waited some time for the right market price would back up many other orders. Especially for orders that may take considerable time to complete, it is important to permit other orders to execute concurrently.*

Multitasking does not magically create more processing resources, it simply divides them up differently. In fact, due to overhead in context switches, it actually results in a reduction of total processing available to the tasks themselves.

17.2.3 Resource Conflicts and Transactions

While concurrency is important for meeting requirements or improving performance, it introduces many subtle complications into application development.

One of the most important is the *resource conflict*, which is an incorrect result due to an adverse interaction between two concurrent tasks manipulating the same resource. The prevention of conflicts is an important role of transaction processing, which was introduced in "Transaction Processing" on page 426. Transaction processing prevents these conflicts, which is the goal of the transaction *isolation* property (see "The ACID Properties of Transactions" on page 429).

ANALOGY: *In the restaurant, when a customer orders a glass of milk, the waiter goes to the refrigerator, removes the bottle of milk, pours a glass, and replaces the bottle. Suppose two waiters do this concurrently. What could happen is the second waiter goes to the refrigerator while the first waiter is pouring, and concludes incorrectly the restaurant has no milk.*

EXAMPLE: *Suppose George is withdrawing $100 from a joint bank account at one ATM, and concurrently his wife Linda is depositing $100 into the account at another ATM. After completion of both transactions, the bank account should be unchanged. However, consider what might happen with the common account information manipulated by both transactions:*

- *George's transaction reads the account balance.*
- *Linda's transaction reads the account balance.*
- *George's transaction subtracts $100 and replaces the balance.*
- *Linda's transaction adds $100 and replaces the balance.*

The end result is that the balance ends up $100 too large, making the bank unhappy. It could easily work the other way, with the balance $100 smaller, making George and Linda unhappy. In either case, the result has no integrity—money has been created or destroyed purely as a result of transaction conflict.

The goal might be to prevent concurrent transactions from interacting at all, but this is impossible. In fact, even tasks that are *not* concurrent and execute sequentially may interact if they manipulate common resources.

EXAMPLE: *If one transaction reserves the last seat on a flight, there is no seat available to give to another transaction trying to reserve a seat on the same flight, whether concurrent or not. The first transaction has affected the second. The best hope is to avoid an unnecessary conflict, such as neither transaction getting the seat, or both getting the same seat.*

In transaction processing, concurrent transactions are isolated from one another in the sense of *serial equivalence*, as illustrated in Figure 17.6. The result of two concurrent transactions is precisely the same as if the transactions were sequential; that is, one followed the other. Serial equivalence says nothing about the *order* of the transaction equivalence—it could be the first followed by the

Concurrency Control

Concurrency control for long-lived tasks is important, particularly for social applications.

EXAMPLE: *In collaborative authoring, two or more users may edit the same document concurrently. Locking of the document while one user is editing it may be unacceptable, because the authors wish to finish it quickly and don't wish to adjust their schedules to others.*

Locking is an example of a *pessimistic* concurrency control protocol: If concurrent manipulation of common resources may possibly result in a conflict, preclude that possibility by the prior locking of resources. Where the performance limitations of locking are unacceptable, as in the collaborative authoring example, there are other options [CDK94]. An alternative is an *optimistic* protocol: Since concurrent manipulation of common resources will often not result in an actual conflict, let them go ahead unabashed. In the (hopefully unlikely) event that a conflict does occur, detect that after the fact and force the concurrent transactions to roll back and abort, undoing the conflicts and restoring a consistent state.

A third approach is based on ordering transactions. Each transaction is given a number that orders its starting time relative to the other transactions— just like the "take a number" protocol used by some customer service operations. Thus, given two transactions, one is unambiguously "earlier" than the other. A concurrency control protocol forces the transactions to consistently manipulate common resources in accordance with this ordering. To simplify the protocol

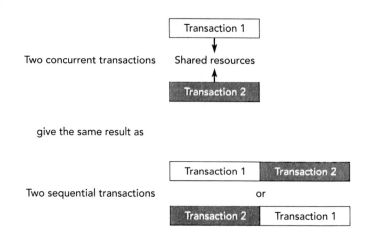

Figure 17.6 A transaction provides serial equivalence to concurrent transactions

second, or the second followed by the first—but merely that the result will be equivalent to one or the other of these two cases. The two concurrent transactions many affect one another, since the first transaction may affect some resource that impacts the second.

EXAMPLE: *If two concurrent transactions attempt to book the same last-remaining airline seat, serial equivalence dictates that one will obtain the seat and the other won't. The transaction that actually obtains the seat has affected the other. Serial equivalence doesn't indicate which transaction will be lucky.*

Serial equivalence can be achieved using *resource locking*. One transaction applies a lock to resources during periods of possible conflicts, preventing another transaction from conflicting.

ANALOGY: *One waiter might lock the refrigerator while pouring a glass of milk, so that a second waiter will not even be able to check for milk availability until after the milk bottle is returned.*

The isolation property of concurrent transactions, while a great simplification for application development, implies that long-lived transactions (minutes, hours, or days) are difficult. They may lock resources for long periods, preventing other transactions from completing expeditiously. This effectively destroys concurrency, including its benefits in increasing throughput or fairness. There are more sophisticated approaches not requiring locking—such as hoping that conflicts will not arise but being prepared to roll back if they do—that can make more long-lived transactions feasible (see the sidebar "Concurrency Control").

17.3   *Scalability as a Performance Consideration

An application is *scalable* if its performance metrics can improve, as necessary and essentially without limit, by adding equipment (more hosts, more network connections, etc.) and without the need for replacement of existing equipment. Further, equipment cost should increase at most linearly with performance metrics, so that the cost per unit measure of performance is constant or declines. Most (but not all) networked applications require scalability to accommodate a growing user base.

EXAMPLE: *An application supporting the purchase or sale of stocks should be able to accommodate increasing sales volume, essentially without limit. An application supporting requests for location of packages in a package delivery service should be able to accommodate more requests as the customer base increases.*

There are two keys to scalability. First, processing needs to be partitioned across multiple hosts in such a way that more hosts can be added as necessary. Second, close attention has to be paid to the location of data relative to processing and to the overhead of communications.

A number of other characteristics have to be right. The most important are the following:

- All the hosts have to be kept busy. "Busy" is measured by a performance metric called *utilization*, which is the fraction of time the host is doing useful work—a utilization of 1.0 means the host is busy all the time. To the extent the utilization is below 1.0, application performance metrics for n hosts cannot approach n times a single host.
- Communication among hosts must be kept in check. There is message latency in this communication, or equivalently a blocked period for a remote method invocation, and the application partitioning must consider the performance implications of this latency.
- Operational data *originates* from a single source, but is typically *used* by multiple applications, implying one-to-many communications. Similarly, in decision support, data originates from many operational sources, but must be aggregated in one place, implying many-to-one communications. The storage and communication requirements for such data must be taken into account.

A number of typical problems arise that can adversely affect scalability. These are described in the following subsections.

somewhat, a transaction is allowed to modify a resource that was last modified by an "earlier" transaction, but if it tries to modify a resource last modified by a "later" transaction, it fails and must abort.

Scalability in Production

Networked application scalability has a close analogy to the production of goods and services [Var87]. A production process has inputs (raw materials, labor, capital goods, etc.) called the *factors of production*, and outputs a quantity of finished goods. When that output quantity increases as fast or faster than the factors of production, the production has *constant* or *increasing returns to scale*. This desirable property (analogous to scalability) implies a constant or decreasing cost of factors of production per unit output; that is, economies of scale. The factors of production are analogous to hosts, networking equipment, wide area network services, software licenses, etc., and the production is analogous to the number of users served, or transactions per unit of time, or other performance metrics.

17.3.1 Blocking

One common way to delegate work from one host to another is the remote method invocation. This service invokes some action on the server, but the client is blocked while waiting for the reply, which reduces its utilization and defers continuing the remainder of the task. On the other hand, a message service (not demanding an immediate reply) allows the client to continue working immediately after delegating work to a server.

EXAMPLE: *The workflow (purchase order processing) application of Figure 12.2 on page 352 illustrates the delegation of work to other hosts (and in this case workers too) using a message service. Each host (and worker), after delegating the next stage of one repetitive task, can immediately move on to the next task.*

Two objects interacting remotely will incur greater overhead than if they were local. One manifestation is a greater delay in interaction across the network—this is discussed in Chapter 20. The application partitioning should take this into account by minimizing communication overhead and mitigating its impact.

17.3.2 Duplicated Work

Scalability requires a partitioning of tasks onto hosts, but this is rarely straightforward because of dependencies among tasks. One possible problem is creating more work *in aggregate* because of the partitioning, typically because a given operation must be artificially repeated n times (or at least more than once) just because there are n parallel work units.

ANALOGY: *Suppose the government birth certificate bureau finds that a single clerk can't handle the load and so hires n clerks. However, an inept manager splits the birth certificate records randomly among the clerks, so each client must talk to multiple clerks to find his records, and there is a large duplication of effort. A competent manager divides the birth records alphabetically, so a client goes directly to the right clerk.*

17.3.3 Faulty Load Balancing

If scalability is to be achieved, each host must be well utilized, which requires *load balancing.*

ANALOGY: *A fast-food restaurant will increase the number of order takers with the expected customer load, but all order takers must be kept busy. Fortunately the arriving customers—who join the shortest line—perform their own load balancing.*

As this last example suggests, queueing is effective for load balancing if arriving tasks can observe the tasks waiting in queues and join the shortest one (this is a valuable function provided by message-oriented middleware). In general, delegating work to the currently least-utilized host is effective, but may be upset by dependency among tasks.

A N A L O G Y :   *In the fast-food restaurant, each order placed must also be picked up. If there is a single pickup worker, as the number of order takers is increased, there will develop a long line at pickup. This load balancing problem can be overcome by assigning each worker to both order taking and pickup.*

Load balancing problems typically arise because of these task dependencies, causing some tasks to wait on others.

E X A M P L E :   *In processing repetitive stock trades, suppose there are two subtasks for each trade: executing the order on a stock exchange, and making appropriate changes to a customer account. If the execution and the account transaction are assigned to different hosts, load balancing depends on them both consuming the same processing power. If one requires significantly more processing, that host will be more heavily loaded.*

17.3.4   Congestion

In many applications, the workload varies irregularly or randomly with time.

E X A M P L E :   *In the purchase order processing workflow application of Figure 12.2 on page 352, the number of purchase orders generated will vary day by day. In a stock trading system, the number of trades will vary minute by minute, driven in part by current market conditions (such as the balance of buy and sell orders).*

An unfortunate consequence of these fluctuations is *congestion*, which is a transient shortage of resources due to temporarily high arrivals.

A N A L O G Y :   *Highway congestion results from too many cars trying to use the highway (a finite resource). It results in increased delays for cars reaching their destinations.*

Congestion results from too many tasks contending for a host's computational resources, or from too many messages contending for a network's communication resources. It impacts performance directly by delaying task initiation, or increasing task completion time, or in the case of communications, delaying the

Modeling Congestion

The following simple model of congestion illustrates its impact. Suppose processing tasks arrive at a server at irregular times and have irregular processing times. An analogous situation (modeled the same way) is packets that have irregular transmission times (due to different packet sizes) arriving at a switch. The processing time for a task or transmission time for a packet is called the *service time*. The time between arrival of a task or packet and the beginning of service is called the *waiting time*—this is the period when earlier arrivals are being processed or transmitted.

By making certain assumptions about the statistics of arrival and service times, assuming the server deals with only one job at a time and tasks or packets are serviced in the order of arrival, the average waiting time can be related to the average service time,

Average waiting time =

$$\frac{\rho}{1-\rho} \times \text{Average service time}$$

where ρ is the *utilization* of the server—the average fraction of time it is occupied processing jobs. (If you know probability theory, this assumes independent Poisson arrivals with independent exponential service times—the so-called M/M/1 queue.) The important point is that the average waiting time increases rapidly as the server becomes fully utilized. The problem is the irregular arrivals—sometimes the arrival rate temporarily exceeds server capacity and arrivals "pile up" in the queue. Overall, as we increase average throughput (proportional to utilization), average completion time (waiting time plus service time) also increases.

time of a message arrival at its destination. The most important point about congestion is that processing and communication resources have to be sized in anticipation of the peak load, which means that most of the time they are underutilized.

Congestion impacts scalability since, as the load grows and some resource becomes congested, that congestion inhibits performance. Possible points of congestion should be anticipated and ways incorporated to increase those resources as load increases. Congestion of one resource can limit performance, even if other resources are not congested.

A general characterization of congestion depends on modeling the task or message arrival times and the task completion or message transmission times (see the sidebar "Modeling Congestion"). It is normal for arriving tasks or messages to be stored in a queue and serviced in the order of arrival—thus, they have to wait their turn. The prediction of the sidebar "Modeling Congestion" is that the average throughput of tasks or messages can be increased—resulting in an increase in the average utilization of the congested resource—but only at the expense of an increased time waiting for servicing. In the presence of load fluctuations, the average utilization of resources must be kept below 1.0, which emphasizes again that processing and communication resources will not always be fully utilized.

EXAMPLE: *As the number of people trying to use the highway to commute to work increases, both the utilization of the highway and the throughput of cars actually getting to work also increases. However, this is at the expense of greater delays experienced by each driver. These greater delays are caused in part by sojourn time waiting at traffic lights, highway entrances, toll plazas, etc.*

Congestion in Processing

Consider the situation in which tasks are arriving at a given host to be processed. Both the arrival times and the task completion times are irregular, as illustrated in Figure 17.7. The important point is that irregularities contribute to fluctuations in host utilization. Resources such as host processing capacity must be sized to meet anticipated peak demand.

EXAMPLE: *The rate of orders in a stock market trading system is irregular, depending on the actions of numerous individual investors and market conditions. The completion time of an order is also irregular, depending on how easily a buyer or seller is found. Electronic mail messages arrive irregularly, although there are some patterns—for example, more arrive during the day than at night. Similarly, the time spent reading each email message is irregular.*

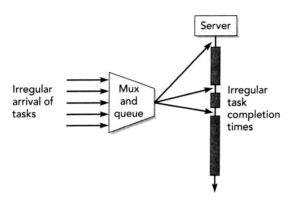

Figure 17.7 Multiplexing and queueing of tasks for a server

The model in the sidebar "Modeling Congestion" applies: Subject to assumptions about statistics of arrival and completion times, it suggests that attempting to increase host utilization, with a commensurate increase in the throughput of completed tasks, results in longer average task sojourn time waiting for the processing of earlier-arriving tasks to be completed. In some cases sojourn time is not a performance problem, but in many cases it adversely affects scalability. For example, there may be incomplete tasks elsewhere in the application awaiting the results, slowing their throughput or increasing their completion time.

EXAMPLE: *In the stock trading system, if the trading portion of the application delegates the trade to a system in the stock exchange and awaits the results, its own throughput will be affected if the stock exchange trade takes longer.*

The analysis in the sidebar "Modeling Congestion" applies to the *average* waiting time; in fact, there are fluctuations about this average. The temporary increases in waiting time at times of especially heavy workload are manifestations of congestion. During these periods, the aspect of performance that deteriorates is the *task latency*—the total time from arrival of a task until it is completed—including both sojourn time and completion time.

ANALOGY: *If a bank has a single bank teller, then the bank must insure the teller works at less than full utilization (has some idle time). Otherwise, the queue of customers outside the door would grow without limit. (In practice, some arriving customers, observing the long line, would choose to go away mad, violating the modeling assumptions.)*

EXAMPLE: *If the utilization is 0.5, the average waiting time is equal to the average service time. If the utilization is increased to 0.9 in order to increase the throughput by 0.9/0.5 = 1.8, the average waiting time balloons to nine times the service time. The average completion time increases fivefold.*

Likewise, increasing the utilization of a communication link also increases packet latency, because packets must wait longer to be transmitted. This model offers no hint of what happens if the arrival rate is higher than can be accommodated ($\rho > 1$). What happens is the waiting time increases to infinity, or in practice, waiting space is finite and tasks or packets must inevitably be discarded.

There is a direct trade-off between the task latency and task throughput. As the throughput is increased, the latency increases and can get arbitrarily large. This leads to the following principle:

> When the arrival times and completion times of tasks are irregular, the average host utilization and average task throughput can be increased by allowing tasks to wait in a queue until they can be served, albeit at the expense of increased task completion time (waiting time plus service time).

How best to deal with congestion in processing depends on the relevant performance metrics. At its simplest, if the task latency is the most important factor (as in an application that must interact with users), then server utilization must be kept low. If, on the other hand, the task throughput is paramount without regard to latency, utilization can be increased. Most situations are greatly complicated by dependencies among tasks.

Congestion on Communication Links

Sharing a host among tasks is analogous to sharing a communication link among messages or packets. Like a host, a communication link has a finite peak capacity, and the portion of that capacity consumed by messages depends on both arrival rate and message length (synonymous with task throughput and completion time). Thus, congestion issues arise in communication links in entirely synonymous ways.

Mitigating this congestion is a function of the network. It utilizes tools synonymous with those previously discussed for hosts:

- The network associates queues with each communication link. Packets can temporarily arrive faster than they are accommodated on the link, with the excess packets queued. Later, when packets are arriving more slowly, the queue can be emptied.
- Like multiple hosts, the network can provide multiple links for packets to travel, even between the same source and destination. Like load balancing in hosts, the network tries to balance the packet load on the alternative links.
- The network provides congestion information to the hosts that allows them to mitigate that congestion (analogous to highway traffic reports on the radio).

As in processing, communications congestion manifests itself by increased message latencies—defined as the time elapsed from when a message is sent until it is received in its entirety by the recipient. There is a direct relationship between message throughput and message latency, and like processing, the best strategy depends on the performance objects of the application. Congestion in networks is discussed further in Chapter 18.

A similar principle applies to communication links as processing:

> When the arrival times and service times of messages or packets are irregular, the average communicating link utilization and message or packet throughput can be increased by queueing packets awaiting transmission. However, a price is paid in an increase in average message and packet latency.

Congestion in Storage

Getting data from where it originates or is modified leads to communications congestion. Particularly in decision-support applications—where data from many operational systems is aggregated—congestion can also occur in storage systems.

E X A M P L E :   *Data warehouses have so much data pouring in that the accumulated data can be outrageously large (many terabytes and even petabytes). Such large amounts of data cannot be accommodated by disk storage and thus must rely on so-called tertiary storage devices (such as magnetic tape). Tertiary storage suffers much greater access time than disk, and thus applications that rely on tertiary storage suffer from scalability problems.*

17.3.5   Role of Application Architecture

Scalability may not matter in some applications if the performance requirements are modest in relation to current technology and it is certain they will not grow. Such situations are, however, rare. Usually an application is designed with the expectation of success, the demands may increase, and it is difficult to predict where performance requirements will saturate.

Fortunately there is much that can be done to aid scalability. As the modularity of the application is determined, the architect should be aware of the obstacles to scalability that have been discussed. The following steps are helpful:

- The application should be modularized so that as the workload grows, it can be split into more and more submodules that can be assigned to different hosts.
- Care should be taken to minimize communications requirements among submodules and also dependencies among tasks delegated to submodules. This depends heavily on what performance metrics are important.
- Duplication of effort across hosts should be avoided. For example, indexes should be established so that tasks can be parceled out directly to the hosts

best able to complete those tasks (with low utilization or able to satisfy data requirements locally).

- Scheduling of tasks should be effective in balancing computational and communications requirements, avoiding "hot spots."
- In the face of irregularities in computational and communications requirements, the utilization of both hosts and communication links should be adjusted to limit congestion. Approaching full utilization of processing and communication resources to approach the maximum possible throughput will result in deterioration in latencies.

Addressing all these issues is difficult enough in architecture design, but it is far more difficult to modify the architecture of an already operational application.

Designing High-Performance Systems

The following are typical steps in designing a high-performance and scalable application architecture:

1. Break the application down into small, atomic tasks, where each task will be assigned to one host (to avoid communication overhead).
2. Characterize the resource requirements of each task. For example, how much processor execution time and memory and storage space does it consume? This step is best left to an expert with detailed knowledge of the internal workings of computer systems.
3. Analyze the communication patterns among tasks and in particular the communication burden on the network created by assigning tasks to different hosts.
4. Understand the scheduling constraints on tasks. What tasks depend on the prior completion of others? This determines how much parallelism is possible—if one task must be completed before another, there is completion-time advantage to assigning them to different hosts.
5. In light of these constraints, tentatively assign tasks to different hosts in a way that attempts to achieve the maximum parallelism and minimizes communication requirements. Establish prioritizing in each host—what tasks should be completed most urgently, because results are needed by another task?
6. Analyze the proposed host assignment in terms of hot spots—points of congestion in either processing or communication—as well as underutilized resources. What bottlenecks will ultimately limit overall application performance? Remember that performance is evaluated in terms of application requirements, such as response time to users. Attempt to modify task assignments—or add communication or processing resources—to eliminate these bottlenecks, thus improving overall performance.

Throughout all these steps, the scalability of the design should be evaluated. Specifically, how can processing and communication resources be added to improve performance as needed? This may lead to additional design modifications.

A similar design methodology can be used in designing the organization supporting a business process. In that case, hosts are replaced by workers, but many similar considerations apply. The best outcome will be achieved by considering the tasks assumed by workers and by networked computing together, as they often have mutual dependencies that affect the overall performance and efficiency of the business process.

17.3.6   Role of Mobile Code

The mobile code described in "Mobile Code, Objects, and Agents" on page 445 can aid scalability, since it allows computation to dynamically move among hosts, even where the necessary software code does not previously reside. This provides added possibilities to locate computation where there is low utilization, or reduce communication overhead, or both. For example, in client-server applications the server becomes congested as the number of users (and clients) grows. The number of clients expands directly with users, so scalability is enhanced if load can be shifted there.

E X A M P L E :   *Web browsers can directly support the user interface (text, graphics, dialog boxes, etc.) but generally not anything specific to an application (presentation or application logic in the three-tier client-server architecture). There are problems if these elements must execute exclusively on the server. First, any interaction between user and application suffers from message latencies, slowing response time. Second, presentation services are limited to those directly supported by the browser. Third—and this is the scalability argument—the server becomes congested as the number of users increases. Mobile code can avoid all these problems by dynamically moving presentation and application logic specific to the application to the client. (This was an early application of Java.)*

Another example arises in data-intensive applications. It is not practical to move massive databases around to different hosts, so there are only two other possibilities: Access the data over the network (which is the point of the three-tier client-server architecture), or move application logic to the host where the data is stored. The latter trades lower communication overhead for additional load on that host.

A N A L O G Y :   *A worker needing repeated access to a body of records can be phys-*
ically co-located with the records, rather than using company mail to make
requests for and receive those records.

The most compelling application of mobile code is in applications that span
administrative domains. From the perspective of scalability, flexibility in locating
computation is desired, but it may be administratively difficult or impossible to
insure that needed software is installed. In principle, mobile code allows computation to be located anywhere.

Discussion

**D17.5 Using the same terms defined here for networked computing, discuss
the scalability of manufacturing operations for a large company. Consider
capital equipment and salary costs in relation to product revenues.**

17.3.7   Example: Stock Trading Application

Stocks4u.com has experienced rapid growth in its base of customers as business has been stolen from traditional brokers. In addition, the low cost of on-
line trading has stimulated demand. As a result, the scalability of stocks4u.com's
systems are continually stressed by rapid growth in customers and activity per
customer. The high security of the application accentuates processing demands
because of the processing-intensive encryption and authentication.

The central approach for achieving scalability is to partition customer sessions
across hosts. New customer logins are assigned to the least-utilized first-tier
customer logic server. This approach also contributes to availability, since a
crashed application server merely reduces the total processing resources in the
pool—redundancy and concurrency go hand in hand. However, due to significant fluctuations in the processing requirements of each customer, to maintain
reasonable interactive response requires that the utilization of each customer
logic server be kept considerably below 100 percent. In practice, there are
major fluctuations in trading activity from day to day, so the total processing
resources must be allocated in anticipation of extremely heavy trading days, and
as a result the utilizations are quite low most other days.

Trades are assigned to separate order processing servers that manage interaction with the stock market over an extranet. As this function has less stringent
requirements for task completion time, these hosts can have higher utilization.

17.4 *Operating Systems

The operating system (OS) is the portion of the software infrastructure primarily responsible for supporting concurrency, such as managing and scheduling tasks in multitasking, and packetization and scheduling of messages in communications. Some of the important functions of an OS were described in "Functions of an Operating System" on page 121. The major operating systems today are listed in the sidebar "Today's Operating Systems." The major capabilities of the OS are now described, particularly as they relate to performance issues.

17.4.1 Processes

When a single program is written and compiled, it executes as a *process*, which provides an executing environment that abstracts many details of the physical host and its peripherals. The operating system supports multiple concurrent processes through multitasking (see the sidebar "Different Forms of Multitasking" on page 471). This allows concurrent programs on the same host through time-slicing. The process hides from each program the existence of other concurrent programs (unless it wishes to interact with them). With preemptive multitasking, a program is not aware that it is being suspended to do a context switch to another program.

E X A M P L E : *You doubtless have experience starting two or more applications on a personal computer, such as an email application and a word processor. Each application is a program executing as a separate process.*

This example illustrates one motivation—running multiple applications—for having multitasking and processes. Another is the need for concurrent tasks on one host within a single application, typically because of an intrinsic application requirement (such as supporting multiple users). A third motivation is mitigating the blocking that programs experience while they wait for an external request. Structuring an application as concurrent processes allows a host to do useful work (in other processes) even when one process is blocked waiting for an external request to be satisfied. Thus, this blocking does not necessarily result in lowered host utilization, as long as there is other useful work to be performed.

E X A M P L E : *A task needing information from a remote host may need to wait for a time before receiving a response. Meantime, other tasks can continue their work, increasing host utilization.*

Today's Operating Systems

Three widely used operating systems for servers and desktop computers are UNIX, Macintosh OS, and Windows.

UNIX is relatively easily ported to different hardware platforms, so incompatible variations are provided by several vendors. A freeware version called Linux has become popular for desktop computers.

MacOS and Windows are each tied to a particular microprocessor. MacOS has lost significant market share, in part because Apple Computer pursued a proprietary hardware/OS strategy, and in part because it has lost its technological edge (for example, it has cooperative but not preemptive multitasking).

Windows is the dominant desktop operating system, and Microsoft is also making it a vibrant competitor to UNIX with a modern version called Windows NT.

Operating Systems and Winner-Take-All Effects

Several factors discussed in Chapter 8 contribute to winner-take-all and path-dependent effects for operating systems:

- *Indirect network externalities:* A dominant operating system attracts a large base of application developers, offering users a large suite of applications. It is easier to share files and run direct applications for users with the same operating system.

ok486   17   Scalability

- *Path-dependent effects:* New entrants must match the expanding accumulated investment to provide competitive features and maturity. As with all software, large supplier economies of scale reduce the unit costs for an operating system with high market share.
- *Lock-in:* Users accumulate application software for a particular operating system and gain familiarity with its operation and administration, increasing switching costs.

Over time, it is inevitable that one operating system gains dominance, like the "natural monopoly" tendencies that have long dominated telecommunications policy.

EXAMPLE: *In 1998, Windows had a 90 percent market share for new desktop computers. In 1998, the U.S. government filed an antitrust suit against Microsoft, not on the basis of the Windows near-monopoly (which is legal), but alleging illegal business practices by tying other applications and services to Windows to extend that monopoly.*

Middleware layers and the thin-client model may reduce the visibility of the operating system over time. This could give an opening to other operating systems.

What Is the Difference between RPC and RMI?

An RPC allows a function call on the program running as a process, whereas a remote method invocation (RMI) allows the invocation of a method on an object. The RMI thus provides considerable value over

17.4.2   *Other Operating System Functions

Aside from multitasking and processes, the operating system has other important functions:

- *Resource management:* The OS manages memory, file and storage space, network access, and peripherals, attempting to assure fairness to the processes it manages. This includes arbitration of near-simultaneous requests for the same resource from two or more processes.
- *Protection:* The OS protects machine resources and other processes from errant processes. Each process is encapsulated and prevented from doing disruptive things to other processes and host-manage resources, contributing to reliability and availability. In particular, the OS enforces a set of policies about what each process is allowed to do and not do.

A simplified architecture of an operating system is shown in Figure 17.8. Each process is associated with a block of memory (separate from the memory allocated to other processes). The *kernel* is where the important functions of the OS itself reside. The OS achieves protection by mediating access to central resources (disk, peripherals, network, etc.) through the kernel. For efficiency, a process can access its own dedicated memory (called its *address space*) without going through the kernel.

As illustrated in Figure 17.9, each process invokes methods on the kernel to accomplish typical operations such as accessing a file, sending a message to another process, or communicating over the network. Execution within a process is called *user mode*, and execution in the kernel is called *kernel mode*. A process is blocked (not executing) during kernel mode. Sometimes this may be for a relatively long period of time, for example, if some remote resource is being accessed.

EXAMPLE: *A Web browser running in a process may send an HTTP message requesting a page from a remote Web server because the user clicked on a hyperlink. It may take some time for the page to return, and meantime the client process is blocked.*

This blocking simplifies programming, because from the perspective of the process it just does a kernel call, which returns after some indeterminate time. The process does not have to worry about finding something else to do in the interim. On the other hand, blocking is problematic at times, because external requests can slow it down. This is one reason multithreading was invented—see the sidebar "Multithreading." Multithreading supports concurrent active

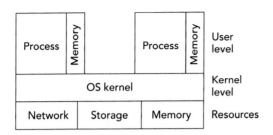

Figure 17.8 A simplified operating system architecture

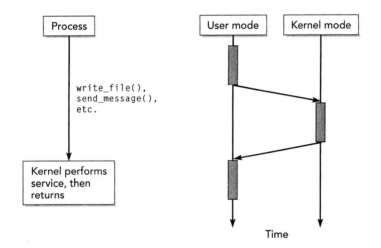

Figure 17.9 A kernel call is blocked while the calling process waits for completion of the operation and a return value

objects within a single process with less overhead than concurrent active objects in multiple processes.

Discussion

D17.6 Discuss the future of the UNIX, Macintosh, and DOS/Windows/NT operating systems. Do you believe there is a role for all three for the indefinite future? Will new operating systems arise?

D17.7 Discuss the merits of the lawsuit brought by the U.S. Department of Justice against Microsoft with allegations of unfair extension of its Windows near-monopoly to applications.

D17.8 What are some distinctions between a single-host operating system and one that is specifically designed to support networked computing?

RPC, in that it directs the procedure call to a particular object within the process.

As described in "Message Service" on page 347, RMI is typically constructed from messages. In reality, RMI is layered on top of RPC, which uses messages. Using RPC to implement RMI requires a standard argument containing a reference to the object, as well as the method to be invoked in that object.

Multithreading

Splitting an application into a large number of processes creates an unacceptably large overhead, because each context switch requires significant processing. *Multithreading* allows independent centers of activity (multiple active objects) *within a process* with much less overhead. Overhead is lower because multithreading offers less protection, and threads communicate through shared memory rather than messages. (In technical language, they run "in the same address space.") Since all the threads in a process are part of the same program—written by the same programmer or group of programmers—this reduced protection is acceptable.

EXAMPLE: *An example of a typical use of threads is shown in Figure 17.10. A Web spider creates a database of Web pages that can be used in search engines by systematically navigating all URLs on the Web. For each URL, it obtains the page content, extracts keywords, and stores those keywords as well as URLs in a database. Due to the message latencies in the Internet, the time it takes to access each*

URL is quite large relative to the speed of a host, so this navigation may take a very long time if done serially. Rather, a separate thread can be created for each URL request outstanding. If there are n threads, there can be n concurrent URL requests in progress, increasing throughput.

Threads have only recently been integral to operating systems, and thus they are not well supported by languages. An exception is Java, which has direct language support for threads.

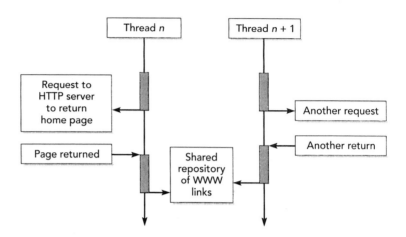

Figure 17.10 A Web spider illustrates a natural use of threads

Review

Application performance can be evaluated by decomposing it into atomic tasks and applying performance measures such as task completion time and task throughput. Concurrency—overlapping tasks in time—is a primary tool for increasing performance as well as meeting intrinsic application requirements such as accommodating multiple simultaneous users.

The subjective quality of video and audio is affected by audible and visible artifacts introduced by compression and by network performance factors such as loss, corruption, and delay.

Tasks are concurrent when they overlap in time. Concurrency can uncouple task throughput from completion time, allowing each to be adjusted independently. Two methods for achieving concurrency are by executing tasks on different hosts and multitasking (time-slicing on a single host). Multitasking not only supports intrinsic application requirements for concurrency, but also contributes to fairness among competing tasks sharing a host. Multitasking is supported by modern operating systems through the process and the thread. Similarly, packetization in networks achieves concurrency among messages on a single communication link, contributing to fairness.

Concurrent tasks that access common resources can result in resource conflicts. Transaction processing achieves isolation of concurrent tasks (specifically, serial equivalence) through resource locking.

An application is scalable if its performance can be improved arbitrarily by adding equipment resources, not replacing what is already in place. Usually the objective is a linear increase in equipment costs with improvements in measures of performance. Scalability is an important objective of application architecture design. Numerous processing and communications bottlenecks can impact scalability. Typical problems to be aware of are blocking on external requests, duplication of work as it is assigned to multiple hosts, and load balancing across hosts. Congestion caused by variations in processing or communications loads impacts scalability by forcing tasks or messages to wait for service or transmission, thereby increasing task or message latencies. Mobile code is a useful tool for improving scalability by allowing processing to be off-loaded to clients without prior software installation.

The operating system infrastructure layer manages host resources (memory, storage, communications, peripherals) and manages concurrency. A process presents an abstract machine to an executing program. The operating system manages multiple processes through multitasking and protects processes from one another, in part by separating their address spaces. A single process can have multiple threads that communicate through common memory (a shared address space) and thus impose lower overhead (but less protection).

Key Concepts

Performance:

- Tasks: completion time versus throughput

Quality

Concurrency:

- Multitasking, packetization
- Isolation of concurrent transactions: serial equivalence
- Scalability
- Work duplication, load balancing
- Congestion

Operating system:

- Process, thread
- Remote procedure call (RPC)

Further Reading

[Sil97] and [TWW97] are excellent references on operating systems, with much more detail than given here. [Hwa98] discusses scalability, primarily from a hardware perspective.

Exercises

E17.1   Give two examples of computing tasks that are

  a. Repetitive

  b. Not repetitive

E17.2   For two of the following applications, list three to five repetitive individual tasks that are a part of the application:

  a. On-line bookseller

  b. Web browsing

  c. On-line stock trading

  d. Collaborative authoring

E17.3   Give two examples of application tasks for which

  a. Task completion time is the appropriate performance metric

  b. Task throughput is the appropriate performance metric

  c. Both are important

  d. Neither is important

E17.4   Discuss the typical performance issues in the following generic classes of applications, from the user perspective:

  a. Information retrieval

  b. Groupware

  c. Workflow

  d. Electronic commerce

E17.5   For any two of the following examples of workflow, divide the overall project into tasks, and briefly describe each task.

  a. An instructor assessing students' performance in a class through examination

  b. A restaurant serving a customer

  c. A citizen receiving a driver's license at the motor vehicle bureau

  d. The tax authority processing tax forms mailed in by citizens

  e. A health insurer processing claims sent by doctors

E17.6   Give a real-world analogy to each of the following:

  a. A resource conflict in concurrent tasks

  b. The completion time of a task reduced by parallelism

    c. The throughput of a repetitive task increased by parallelism

    d. The throughput of a repetitive task increased by pipelining

    e. A single worker performing two or more concurrent tasks through time-slicing

E17.7 As mentioned in "Resource Conflicts and Transactions" on page 472, transactions are short lived because of problems with resource locking in long-lived transactions.

    a. Give an example of an application in which long-lived transactions would be useful.

    b. Discuss how this long-lived transaction could be divided into shorter-lifetime transactions.

    c. In *b* how would the application deal with an aborted transaction? Repeat for each short transaction.

E17.8 You are collaborating with a colleague to edit a report. You are each using the same word processing program. Since the result is time critical, you edit the report concurrently.

    a. Describe how you might coordinate your activities so that (1) your edits don't conflict and (2) you can successfully merge your edits at intermediate points in time to yield a single version of the report incorporating both your changes.

    b. Relate your answer in *a* to the techniques discussed in the chapter.

E17.9 You are organizing a factory, and one of your goals is scalability: You want the factory to be able to expand production by adding workers. Each of the following issues might be an obstacle to this scalability. For each issue, give a physical-world example of where this issue could be an obstacle:

    a. Time spent in communication among the workers

    b. Forcing workers to duplicate one another's work

    c. Unbalanced load of the different workers

    d. Congestion caused by irregular work arrivals

    e. Congestion caused by irregular work completion times

E17.10 Consider and discuss the challenges in achieving scalability for any two of the following applications. What measures should be used to define scalability? What obstacles can you anticipate?

    a. On-line stock trading application

    b. On-line bookstore

c. A purchasing department workflow application

d. On-line auction

E17.11   A server is presented with repetitive tasks in a manner consistent with the assumptions used in "Modeling Congestion" on page 478.

a. If the objective is an average task completion time (waiting time plus processing time) no more than five times the average task processing time, what is the maximum server utilization?

b. If the task throughput objective requires 80 percent server utilization on average, what is the average waiting time in relation to the average task processing time?

E17.12   Intuitively, if you had *n* servers working in parallel, and effectively balanced the loads of those servers, do you think those servers' utilization would need to be greater, lower, or about the same compared to a single server, for the same average task completion time?

E17.13   For each of the following tasks, describe how to partition the task into processes or threads in order to achieve an appropriate concurrency in a single host:

a. At a client user interface, accepting user input (mouse clicks or keystrokes) while displaying an application output to the user on the screen

b. In a collaborative authoring application, accommodating multiple users concurrently editing the same document

c. In a remote conferencing application, capturing audio and video from a local user and simultaneously playing the audio and video from a remote user

E17.14   For the Web search engine example of "Multithreading" on page 487, define one task as requesting a document with a particular URL, receiving that document as a response, and storing the relevant information in the database. Discuss the practical limits on the throughput of these tasks even if assigned to multiple threads. At what point does adding more threads not offer an improvement in throughput?

Collective Issues in Networking

18

The most elementary and fundamental role of the network—carrying messages from one host to another using switches connected by communication links—was described in "Communications" on page 121. The internet technologies, manifested most visibly by the public Internet, are most popular today, in part because they allow existing LAN networks to be incorporated into a WAN by internetworking, as described in "The Internet" on page 127. The communication services supported by the network, such as message, message with reply, session, and broadcast, were outlined in Chapter 12, together with concrete examples of internet services. As mentioned in "Why Networks Use Packets" on page 472, for reasons of fairness—one large message can't delay others inordinately—long messages may have to be fragmented into smaller packets for network transport.

Aside from this elementary role of conveying packets from one host to another, the network has a number of other functions. These mostly relate to the overriding observation that the network handles communications for a large number of users, applications, and hosts simultaneously. While this raises opportunities to improve the cost economy of the network through resource sharing, it also raises knotty issues related to the division of limited networking resources among potential uses during times of congestion. There are closely related pricing and cost recovery issues, such as the economic and business basis of increasing the capacity of an overly congested network. These and related topics are the subject of this chapter.

18.1 Functions of a Network

The network performs some important functions besides empowering hosts to find and address one another and transporting packets from one host to another.

It allocates limited communication resources to different applications and users, and ultimately, it controls quality metrics of interest to the application.

18.1.1   Sharing Communication Links: Statistical Multiplexing

In the network topology of Figure 4.8 on page 124, backbone communication links are shared among hosts, users, and applications. This sharing is the essence of the favorable economics behind a public network.

ANALOGY: *Although it is an overused (and sometimes misleading) analogy, the network shares some characteristics with the public highway system. The highways connect everybody's parking lot or garage (except for the small problem of the oceans) and are shared by all citizens. A better analogy—and the one used here—is the railroad system. Like the Internet, in the United States the railroad system is privately owned, but ownership and use are shared by a number of companies, and the system transports a variety of goods for the benefit of every segment of the economy.*

Any specific communication link may forward packets from a number of hosts to a number of other hosts, depending on the network topology. Sharing reduces the number of communication links and thus serves to reduce the unit communication costs. It also implies packet queueing and multiplexing at each link, since packets arrive from many different hosts. Queueing allows packets arriving from different sources at the same time (this is called packet *contention*) to be accommodated by delaying them as necessary.

Figure 18.1 illustrates the queueing and multiplexing function within a network switch. Packets are stored in queues as they arrive, and the switch chooses one packet at a time to be transmitted on the link, thus performing multiplexing.

The dynamic sharing of a communication link in the network is called *statistical multiplexing*. Specifically, the communication capacity of a given link—called the bit rate, or sometimes inaccurately the bandwidth—is constant and is measured in bits per second (bps). On the other hand, the packets multiplexed on the link vary in their demands on the link, depending on what the application and users are currently doing. The demand on the link is best characterized by the average bit rate required to support the aggregate packets from all sources, which is the product of the average packet size (in bits) and the average rate of arrival (in packets per second).

EXAMPLE: *A typical voiceband data modem connecting a personal computer supports a bit rate of 33,300 bps, while a switched Ethernet LAN may have a*

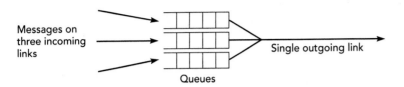

Figure 18.1 A switch stores incoming messages in queues and sends them to outgoing links one after the other (special case of three input links and one output link shown)

capacity of 100 million bps or even 1 billion bps. If the average packet size is 8,000 bits, then the modem can accommodate at most $33,000/8,000 = 4.125$ packets per second; whereas an Ethernet can accommodate up to 12,500 or 125,000 packets per second.

In practice, both the packet size and the rate of packet arrival are irregular—as is their aggregate bit rate demand—so that at some times the packets may be arriving too fast (or may be too big), and at other times they can easily be accommodated by the link. In the former case, packets accumulate in the queues, and in the latter case, the queues are gradually emptied. Statistical multiplexing works well as long as the aggregate average bit rate demand is less than the link capacity.

Statistical multiplexing actually demonstrates economies of scale—it is more efficient to multiplex more sources of traffic on a high bit rate link, in the sense of an improved trade-off between throughput and latency (see the sidebar "Advantage of Statistical Multiplexing").

18.1.2   Packet Forwarding and Routing

The network must find a route from source to destination host—consistent with the network topology—for each packet. To support this function, each packet looks like the following:

Header	Payload

The two data elements of the packet are a packet header and packet payload:

- A *packet header* includes information meaningful to the network, such as the address of source and destination hosts, the size of the payload, etc.

Advantage of Statistical Multiplexing

Statistical multiplexing improves the trade-off between the utilization of communication links and packet latency. To see this, the proper comparison has to be made. Consider the simple case of N identical sources of traffic. In statistical multiplexing these N sources are aggregated and switched onto a single communication link with bit rate R. The opposite of statistical multiplexing would be to divide that communication link into N lower-speed links, each with rate R/N, and dedicate one of those links to each source. (This approach is called time-division multiplexing).

In "Modeling Congestion" on page 478, it was pointed out that the total average latency of a packet at a switch is, for a simple model for source traffic, proportional to the average packet transmission time and a term that depends on the utilization ρ—the fraction of the link bit rate used on average. This latency is N times lower for statistical multiplexing. The reason is simple. All else being equal, the utilization is the same for statistical and time-division multiplexing, but the higher bit rate link reduces the average packet transmission time, and hence average latency, by N.

This can be interpreted another way. For the same average packet latency, statistical multiplexing can achieve a higher utilization and hence higher throughput and time division.

- The *packet payload* includes data to be delivered to the recipient. For example, it might include a message (or fragment of a message) that should be delivered to an application or user.

The network has no interest in the data carried in a payload, other than its size. From the network perspective, the payload is data lacking structure and interpretation. It is up to the sender and recipient to interpret the payload data.

ANALOGY: *A packet is analogous to a single railroad train. The train includes an engine with driver, who maneuvers the train through the railroad system and is analogous to the packet header. The passengers and freight are analogous to a packet payload.*

Another—in some ways better—analogy to the packet header is the envelope for a postal letter. The envelope, like the header, includes sender and recipient identification and address. The recipient discards the envelope to access the enclosed letter.

Packet forwarding makes use of information in the header giving the location of the destination host. As described in "Locating Things" on page 333, there are three ways to locate that host: by name, by address, and by reference. Internally, the network includes the address of the destination host in the packet header. This address is data specifying the destination host location, from which a route (series of communication links) to that host can be inferred by packet switches.

EXAMPLE: *The packet header used by the basic Internet service layer IP includes an IP address, which uniquely identifies the destination host. In the latest version of IP (version 6), the IP address is 128 bits, which is capable of identifying $2^{128} = 3 \times 10^{38}$ hosts (older versions of IP use only a 32-bit address). This very large number—even considering inefficiencies, it represents about 1,500 addresses per square foot of the earth's surface—anticipates a future in which many devices will have Internet access.*

As shown in Figure 18.2, each switch maintains a *routing table* consulted by the switch to determine the appropriate output link for each packet (from among all those connected to the switch). For each packet, the switch follows these steps:

1. While the packet is queued (as in Figure 18.1), the destination address (or more likely some portion of the address) in the packet is noted. That address is used as an index into the routing table.

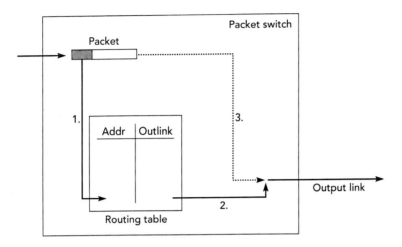

Figure 18.2 Forwarding of a packet requires three steps; routing updates the routing table based on the network topology

2. The appropriate output link is read from the table, and meanwhile the packet is queued until there is an opportunity to transmit the packet on that output link.
3. When the chosen output link is available (no other packet is being forwarded), the packet is transmitted on the chosen link.

This entire process is called packet *forwarding*. The entries in the routing table must be chosen carefully so that packet forwarding brings the packet closer to its destination, depending on the network topology (see the sidebar "Routing").

18.1.3   Name Services

For purposes of packet forwarding, a destination address is included in each packet header (128 bits of data in the latest IP). Users would find it unpleasant to deal with these addresses directly, so to the user and application, hosts are usually identified by name. Since the network internally uses addresses and not names as the basis of packet forwarding, a host name has to be converted to an address before a packet can be sent to that host. This is the function of a name service.

ANALOGY: *Telephone numbers are currently ten to thirteen digits. Users do successfully deal with telephone numbers, but IP addresses would be much larger—the equivalent of thirty-five digits—and would be very difficult for users to remember.*

Routing

The packet forwarding function in a switch consults a routine table to determine the appropriate output link. The updating of this routing table is a critical function called *routing*, and packet switches that implement routing are called *routers*. Each router periodically exchanges network topology information with nearby routers—which over time propagates through the entire network—employing *routing protocols*. In effect, routers collaborate in collectively updating their routing tables.

For scalability, routing is hierarchical. The internetwork is partitioned into *routing domains*. Routing within domains is separated from routing among domains. Routers located at the edge of a routing domain have special responsibilities.

Routing is one of the most difficult technical challenges in networking, with approaches too complex to be described here. Multicast requires more complicated routing.

Simulcast and Multicast

In a broadcast communication service, replicas of the source messages are communicated to multiple recipients. As discussed in "The Broadcast" on page 361, this is useful for multiparty video conferencing, remote learning, and similar applications, and can be accomplished by simulcast or multicast, as shown in Figure 18.3. *Simulcast* requires that the source send replicas independently to each destination, but it has two problems:

- Simulcast is not scalable (see "*Scalability as a Performance Consideration" on page 475). In some applications, the number of destinations may be *very* large. As the number of recipients increases, both the processing requirement and the bit rate of the network access link increase, so eventually both resources are exhausted.
- Simulcast is inefficient. For example, on the network access link, the same data is sent repeatedly—once for each destination—whereas once would suffice.

In the Internet, these problems are mitigated by *IP multicast*, which replicates the data *within* the network for all recipients. To the source, multicast looks essentially the same as unicast, and the network makes replicas as "close" (in terms of network topology) to the recipient as possible to minimize network traffic and congestion. So the source does not know about every recipient, multicast uses a publish-and-subscribe protocol. Each recipient asks the network to subscribe to a particular source.

ANALOGY: *IP multicast is like a radio network. The programs at*

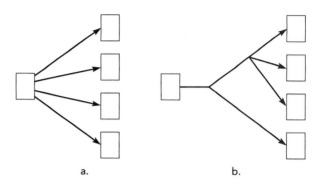

a.   b.

Figure 18.3 (a) Simulcast and (b) multicast allow communication of the same information to multiple hosts

EXAMPLE: *A typical Internet host name is* info.sims.berkeley.edu, *and a typical IP address (older 32-bit variety) is* 128.55.156.273, *where the 32 bits are actually represented by four decimal numbers for the convenience of humans. In the Internet, the name service is the domain name system (DNS). For example, when the user invokes a hyperlink in a Web document, the URL includes the host name where the page can be found. The application then obtains the IP address of the host from the DNS before initiating the HTTP. The DNS is like the telephone white pages: If you know the name of a person or company, the white pages provides the telephone number (the telephone network address).*

Hierarchical Names and Addresses

For the purpose of network scalability, both names and addresses are hierarchical. Addresses—which indicate where the host is connected to the network topology—reflect the "network of networks" structure. The Internet topology has a two-level hierarchy, where the two levels are "network" and "internetwork." An IP address has this hierarchical structure of the form (Network, Host), where Network is a unique identifier for a given network, and Host is a unique identifier for a host topologically connected to that network. (Originally, this breakdown was static, but more recently a refinement called *classless interdomain routing* has created a more dynamic boundary as a way of deriving more efficient use of the addresses.) Telephone numbers have a similar hierarchy, with a country code, city code, and local number uniquely identifying a telephone.

Host names also have a hierarchical structure, where the levels of hierarchy are delimited by a "dot" notation, representing the administrative partitioning of the network.

EXAMPLE: *In* info.sims.berkeley.edu, *"edu" indicates that this host is administered by an educational institution,* "berkeley" *indicates that this educational institution is Berkeley,* "sims" *designates the school within Berkeley, and* "info" *distinguishes this host from others within that school.*

There is no particular relationship between administrative and topological structure, as a given organization may be geographically distributed.

EXAMPLE: *IBM has many offices in cities around the world. All IBM host names include* "ibm.com" *(often with a country mnemonic added) in spite of the fact that these hosts connect topologically in many different geographical locations.*

Host names (and names in general) are not unique, so two or more names may correspond to the *same* host address. Whenever multiple names correspond to the same address, they are called *aliases*.

EXAMPLE: *It happens that* sims.berkeley.edu *and* info.sims.berkeley.edu *are two names locating the same host (and thus the same IP address). Such aliases are convenient tools for network administrators. For example, if a user needs to know the address of* some *host within the* sims.berkeley.edu *organization, this alias allows an administrator to designate an arbitrary (and changeable) host as the default.*

18.1.4   Flow Control

Anytime one entity (a producer) sends a stream of messages to another (a consumer), as illustrated in Figure 18.4, there is the question of whether the consumer can keep up with the producer. For example, the producer might be running on a faster computer, or the processing required to generate messages may be much less than the processing required to consume them. *Flow control* is a protocol coordinating the producer and consumer to prevent the producer from generating data faster than the consumer can accept it. Recall from "Interfaces" on page 163 that a protocol is a specified sequence of actions engaged in by two subsystems to accomplish some higher purpose. In this case, the flow control protocol is engaged in by the producer and consumer to prevent the consumer from being overwhelmed. A typical flow control protocol requires acknowledgment of messages by the consumer, and a policy that the producer must limit the number of unacknowledged messages sent.

EXAMPLE: *Flow control might be executed on a per-packet basis. The producer could keep track of past packets sent and receive acknowledgment from the*

the source are not broadcast directly to the listeners, but rather to a limited set of radio stations. Each listener tunes into the broadcast (analogous to subscribing) without the knowledge of the source.

While efficient and scalable, multicast places special burdens on routers. They must be prepared to replicate—not simply forward—packets within the network, and also to accept subscriptions. Routing is more complicated, since subscriptions must flow from the recipient back toward the source.

The Value of a Domain Name

Internet domain names have serious political and commercial implications. Commercially, companies want to protect their trademarks and not allow others to use those trademarks in domain names. This also has value to consumers, who can often guess a domain name. There are often geopolitical implications as well. Except in the United States, domain names end in a mnemonic for the country. If countries split or unite, should their domain names change accordingly?

In light of this, it is surprising that domain names can be obtained for a very small administrative fee with minimal restriction. Some enterprising folk have speculated on names that might be of value to large companies in the future. So the question arises, should domain names be subject to trademark laws? If a company owns the trademark for "xyz," should that trademark also apply to domain name "xyz.com"? What should be the process for assigning names? So far this issue is not resolved, although the U.S. courts have temporarily suspended the use of some domain names that are also registered trademarks through injunctions. It is also possible to obtain a trademark on a domain name, but only if it serves a dual use as an identifier of the source of goods or services.

The assignment of domain names is also subject to serious conflicts among legitimate interests, particularly in light of the small fields typically used.

EXAMPLE: Domain names in the country of Tuvalu end in ".tv". This domain name is clearly of great economic value to Tuvalu. However, it is also in conflict with those in the United States who might seek a new domain associated with television. Arguably the fair resolution of this conflict would be to stipulate that all domains in the United States end in ".us".

Figure 18.4 With a producer-consumer communication, flow control is required to prevent overflow of intermediate queues

consumer that those packets have been accepted. If the producer insures there are no more than n unacknowledged packets (by refusing to send more), an intermediate queue with a capacity of n packets cannot overflow. This is roughly how the internet transport service TCP implements flow control. UDP, another internet service, does not provide flow control, so this burden is shifted to the application. A message with reply service (such as RMI) has implicit flow control, since the reply from the recipient provides an implicit acknowledgment that it is ready to receive another message. Because the source blocks, there is only a single unacknowledged message at any time.

18.1.5   Network Congestion

Packets arriving too fast (or that are too big) result in an increasing number of packets waiting in queues. This is one manifestation of the congestion problem described in "Congestion" on page 477, and its impact is to increase the time required for each packet to traverse the network from one host to another, because each packet is spending time in queues waiting to be transmitted.

From an application perspective, the performance parameter of interest—called the *message latency*—is the time that elapses between the generation of a message in one host and the receipt of that complete message in another host. (Latency is the time the message is latent, or "hidden" and unavailable to the application.) A message may be fragmented into packets and those packets reassembled to recover the original message at the destination. One component of the message latency is the congestion-induced time that packets sit in queues awaiting transmission on communication links (see Chapter 20 for a discussion of other contributors to message latency). Thus, the application sees increased message latency as a result of network congestion.

EXAMPLE: A remote method invocation (RMI) is constructed from two messages, the first from client to server marshalling the parameters, and the second from server to client marshalling the return values, as was described in "RMI Can Be Layered on Messages" on page 365. The client is blocked until the return, and this blocking time includes two message latencies. Thus, network congestion forces the client object to wait longer before resuming its work.

The storage capacity of queues in a packet switch is finite, so severe congestion can result in a packet arriving at a switch to find the queue full. The packet must then be discarded. Thus, it cannot be guaranteed that packets actually arrive at their destination during periods of congestion, unless additional measures are taken by the network.

Congestion Instability

Network congestion tends to be unstable; that is, moderate congestion causes more severe congestion. To understand why, it is important to distinguish traffic *offered* to a network (the aggregate packets that sending hosts *wish* to communicate) and traffic *carried* by the network (the aggregate packets actually delivered to the destination hosts). The carried traffic cannot exceed network capacity; that is, the utilization of each link in the network cannot exceed 1.0. However, the offered traffic *can* exceed the network capacity. If so, queues within the network must accumulate the excess offered traffic, and eventually become full, causing packet loss. The instability results from senders attempting to get lost packets through by resending them, resulting in an artificial increase in offered traffic, thus making the congestion more severe.

E X A M P L E :   *Some network services (such as TCP) provide reliable delivery of packets. They achieve that reliability by a special protocol that detects lost packets and resends them as many times as necessary until the destination host acknowledges their reception. As a result, every lost packet will result in at least one resending, which increases the offered traffic. This increase in offered traffic will cause a higher percentage of packet losses, making the problem progressively worse.*

Even if the network operates at less than full utilization, congestion instability can push it "over the brink." For example, as described quantitatively in "Modeling Congestion" on page 478, each packet will wait longer in a queue for transmission—and more packets will be waiting—as the link utilization approaches 1.0. In practice this queue has limited space, so as the average wait increases, packets will be more frequently discarded when they arrive to find the queue full. This may create additional offered traffic if senders resend these lost packets, resulting in higher utilization and average waits, which further aggravates the situation by causing even more resent packets.

A qualitative curve illustrating offered versus carried traffic is shown in Figure 18.5. The network "capacity" is the hypothetical carried traffic if every link in the network were running at full utilization and there were no resent packets. Unfortunately, as the offered traffic increases, the carried traffic peaks out at less than full network capacity (reflecting packet loss and resending), and further

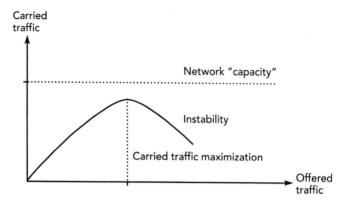

Figure 18.5 Networks often display unstable behavior, and the goal of congestion control is to limit the offered traffic to the point where the carried traffic is maximum

increases in offered traffic cause the carried traffic to actually *decrease* because of the increased number of resent packets.

Clearly, restricting offered traffic to a level that maximizes carried traffic is to the users' collective benefit. *Congestion control* is a protocol and associated policies engaged in by the network and its sources to attempt to maximize the carried traffic. It works by artificially limiting the offered traffic, keeping it within the stable region. Each user participating in congestion control is artificially restricting his or her offered traffic in favor of the common interest.

ANALOGY: *Metering lights at the entrance to a major highway are a form of congestion control. By limiting offered traffic, carried traffic (throughput drivers actually reaching their destinations) is increased. They trade higher throughput for the greater delay experienced by drivers entering the highway.*

Flow control and congestion control are different. Flow control is a protocol implemented between a single source and a single destination with the goal of keeping the destination from being inundated by too many messages. Congestion control is a protocol conducted between the *aggregate* sources of traffic and the network, with the goal of keeping the network operating in the region of maximum carried traffic. Flow control concerns only the sender and receiver and is required regardless of the traffic conditions in the network.

Congestion control must resolve the social issue of how the burden of restricting offered traffic is distributed among users and applications. Representative alternatives include asking each source to generate the same fraction of its

Table 18.1 Alternative approaches to congestion control

Approach	Description	Typical examples
Voluntary policies	Sources voluntarily adhere to policies restricting offered traffic, acting for the collective good. "Bad" citizens ignoring these policies are rewarded by receiving a larger share of the carried traffic and create congestion impacting others.	The widely used Internet TCP de facto standard incorporates congestion control protocols. Hosts can avoid TCP congestion control by using another transport service, such as UDP.
Mandatory policies	Policies are mandated for the allocation of offered traffic.	Metering lights at highway and bridge entrances are mandated, with legal sanctions for violation.
Pricing incentives	The pricing of network services is adjusted to influence offered traffic. Sources shifting offered traffic to less congested times are rewarded by lower prices, and a side benefit is additional revenue to upgrade overloaded facilities.	Telephone companies use time-of-day pricing, generally increasing prices during periods of peak demand. Supply and demand are matched for most goods and services through pricing mechanisms.

Congestion as Network Externalities

Recall that an externality is an impact of one user on another without a compensating payment. Congestion is thus a network externality, but one very different from the type discussed in Chapter 8. There, one added user *increases* the value of a network to its users, because there is one more user to participate in applications. Congestion has the opposite character: One more user *reduces* the value of the network to other users, because of the increased congestion he causes. (The first type is called a "positive consumption externality," and the latter is a "negative consumption externality.") Adding a user to a network is thus a double-edged sword.

desired traffic, placing a maximum offered traffic restriction on all sources, or somehow allocating more offered traffic to "compelling" uses. Choosing the right approach can be a contentious issue.

From a social perspective, there are at least three generic options, which are listed in Table 18.1. All three approaches encourage users and applications to shift their demand from periods of congestion to less busy periods. The incentives approach does this through pricing and the others through restrictions to offered traffic.

Both the voluntary and incentivized approaches have the significant advantage that sources presumably know something about the "importance" of their traffic and can voluntarily allocate the limited network resources during periods of congestion to the most compelling purposes. Mandated policies are inflexible in this regard. However, voluntary approaches are easily circumvented by "bad" citizens, who are rewarded for doing so. Pricing incentives preserve user flexibility without creating "bad" citizens, since users generating more offered traffic during periods of congestion assume a disproportionate share of costs.

Implementation of Congestion Control

How is congestion control realized? From a technical perspective, there are two basic approaches, as listed in Table 18.2. Unlike the network, each source cannot see the global picture. Thus, a source-initiated algorithm must be designed

Table 18.2 Two technical approaches to implementing congestion control

Approach	Description	Analogy
Source initiated	Sources detect network congestion, or are informed by the network (either directly or through pricing adjustments), and limit the offered traffic. This has the advantage that sources can offer the most compelling traffic or shift less compelling traffic to another time.	Customers finding long lines at ATMs and teller windows may voluntarily leave, returning later. Alternatively, the bank may charge lower fees for customers served during light periods, rewarding those customers who choose them.
Network policing	The network enforces limits on the traffic it will accept from each source. The network may engage in flow control with each source, or it may silently drop excess traffic.	Highway metering lights are an involuntary flow control; a restaurant only accepting customers with reservations may stop answering the phone when it becomes fully booked.

in such a way that the sources collectively reduce the offered traffic appropriately, without global knowledge. Similarly, pricing incentives have to be designed to encourage the desired collective behavior.

EXAMPLE: *The Internet TCP incorporates congestion control, which was introduced after the Internet experienced considerable congestion instabilities. Each TCP source estimates congestion by noting the incidence of lost packets and voluntarily reduces offered traffic.*

As described in "The Conversation" on page 356, the session is a bidirectional flow of packets sharing a common context. Where sessions are provided, network policing can take the form of *admission control*, in which session establishment requests are refused if the session would adversely impact existing sessions. Another form of policing discards selected packets. This is indiscriminate—important packets could be discarded as easily as unimportant packets. But this can be redressed by asking the sources to attach a priority to each offered packet, and the network can then discard traffic in order of priority (starting with the lowest, of course).

When offered traffic is mandated, the usual goal is some measure of fairness—but a difficult question is the interpretation of "fairness": Is it fair to *equalize* offered traffic for different sources or give each source a *fraction* of its offered traffic? Different applications have different inherent traffic requirements. Thus, mandating equal offered traffic will, for example, be quite restrictive to some sources and not to others.

Except for pricing incentives, these approaches do not allow sources complete freedom to choose the traffic they offer at times of congestion. A primary advantage of pricing incentives is that users or applications with compelling needs are able to satisfy those needs (with a price penalty). The primary objection to pricing is the cost of the needed monitoring and billing infrastructure (see the sidebar "Cost of Congestion Control").

Discussion

D18.1 Discuss the social issues inherent in deciding who bears the brunt of limitations to offered traffic during times of congestion.

D18.2 As examples of alternative hierarchical naming schemes, discuss street addresses and people's names in different countries.

D18.3 What are some of the implications of the rush to obtain domain names? How should this be addressed by government policies and laws?

18.2   Quality of Service (QoS)

As described in Chapter 17, networked applications are concerned with performance parameters such as task throughput, task time to completion, or interactive delay. The impact of inevitable network impairments (such as message latency and loss) therefore depends on the application.

EXAMPLE: *Applications using distributed objects interacting through RMI will experience greater blocking time—and hence increased task completion time or reduced task throughput—when the packet (and hence message) latency increases. Streaming audio and video will experience greater end-to-end delay as the packet latency increases. Packet loss may have even more serious consequences.*

To the extent the application incorporates interhost communication over the network, its performance parameters are impacted by network *impairments*, including

- *Packet and message latency*: Packet latency is caused by the speed-of-light propagation delay, transmission time, queueing delay, and processing time in the software infrastructure (the first two are discussed in Chapter 20). Message latency is caused by the latency of packets that make up the message.
- *Packet and message loss*: Once a message is fragmented into packets, loss of one or more of those packets causes loss of the message. In practice, if loss is unacceptable, a service like TCP is used to guarantee packet delivery by resending unacknowledged packets. In this case, packet loss results in increased message latency (but not loss).

Cost of Congestion Control

Today's internet protocols emphasize simplicity and low cost, and this is reflected in congestion control. Whether more sophisticated approaches are needed, desirable, or affordable is controversial. Those opposed mention the cost of a pricing infrastructure, including the required metering of source usage and the billing of users. Relating congestion in a particular part of the network back to the sources causing that congestion—and notifying them of a price increase—is also not a simple technical problem.

On the other hand, today's internet protocols—like the standby service on airlines—transfer the risk of congestion to every user. This risk reduces the value of the network service, and thus probably also users' willingness to pay. Thus, the issue is not the absolute cost of a congestion control infrastructure, but rather that cost in relation to the collective benefit to users and providers.

Applications Have a QoS Too

QoS is an issue for processing as well as networking services. Many of the application performance parameters discussed in Chapter 17 may be associated with objectives or guarantees and task completion times or throughput.

EXAMPLE: *An electronic commerce site is likely concerned that a customer who has initiated a purchase transaction be allowed to complete it expeditiously even in the presence of severe processing congestion. This customer may therefore be given priority over other customers who are merely browsing through the offerings.*

The status of processing QoS is similar to network QoS. It is a recognized need not yet reflected in current product offerings (for example, for Web servers), but it will appear soon.

- *Packet corruption:* Communication links can cause bit errors (changing a "0" to a "1" or vice versa). This is more frequent on wireless communication media. If a packet must be delivered with integrity, then a single bit error in a packet is equivalent to the loss of the entire packet.

In summary, the application is concerned with *message* latency, loss, and corruption (or their impact on higher-level communication services like RMI), and in a packet network these concerns are translated into *packet* latency, loss, and corruption. These latter are called *network quality-of-service* (QoS) parameters.

18.2.1   The Internet Transport Services and QoS

The internet UDP, TCP, and RTP services described in Chapter 12 are called transport services, while IP is a network service. The purpose of the transport service is to condition or customize the network service to the needs of the application. One of those conditionings is in QoS.

IP provides a best-effort datagram service. Datagram refers to the fact that packets each stand on their own; they do not share a context (like a session). "Best effort" describes the QoS; that is, IP makes no guarantee that a given datagram is delivered, nor does it guarantee its latency if it is delivered. It simply makes its best effort to deliver the datagram and deliver it as early as possible. The design philosophy of IP is to make it a general and simple service that can be specialized in various ways by transport services.

Recall that the operating system supports multiple processes, as described in Chapter 17. Routing a message to an application requires routing that message to a particular process on the host. UDP does not add much to IP, except some additional addressing to specify the destination process. UDP also promises not to deliver corrupt packets.

Many applications demand *reliable* delivery of messages, meaning they are actually guaranteed to be delivered and to be uncorrupted. This feature is offered by TCP—in the context of a session—by resending packets that are lost or corrupted. The destination acknowledges each received uncorrupted packet (by sending an acknowledgment packet in the reverse direction), and the source resends packets for which it receives no acknowledgment. TCP also incorporates flow and congestion control.

Why not *always* stipulate reliable delivery for all transport services? The reason is a penalty is paid in latency for reliable delivery, because resent packets arrive later. Some applications prefer some unreliability in exchange for lower latency. One example is direct-immediate applications using audio or video media, as discussed next.

18.2.2   Integrated Services

The Internet originated as a data network, but recently its capabilities have begun to overlap the telephone network, providing audio and video incorporated into direct-immediate social applications such as remote conferencing and telephony. In short, the Internet has become an *integrated services* network, defined as one providing the full range of services needed by applications (data, audio, video, and others). The telephone industry developed an alternative integrated services network called *asynchronous transfer mode* (ATM) (see the sidebar "ATM: Another Integrated Services Network").

Of course, the public telephone network (PTN) provides excellent audio and telephony and is also capable of reasonable video conferencing. The interest in Internet audio and video relates to integrated layering in the infrastructure. A *single* integrated services network infrastructure providing many communication services that may be incorporated into each application offers powerful advantages. The Internet (or ATM) is much more promising than the PTN as an integrated services network because of the flexibility of packet switching.

An integrated services network must satisfy a wide range of application needs, which requires a range of transport services. Using layering ideas, a variety of transport services can be layered on a single network service such as IP.

EXAMPLE: *As described in "Internet Streaming Multimedia Protocols" on page 365, the RTP transport service is one response to the particular needs of streaming multimedia services. It supplements TCP, which is more appropriate for applications where delay is less critical and reliability is more critical.*

An issue particular to direct-immediate applications is delay. As illustrated in Figure 18.6 for an audio service, subjective quality is adversely affected by end-to-end delay (the time offset from microphone input to playback at the destination), particularly in a direct-immediate application such as remote conferencing. For example, in a remote conferencing application, this delay interferes with a normal conversation. The audio or video medium is streamed over the network as a sequence of packets, and one component of end-to-end delay is packet latency. In this case, the added latency of reliable delivery is problematic, and more likely a datagram service would be used.

Expanding the capabilities of the Internet—making it an integrated services network that provides good performance and quality for all services—is an ongoing issue (see the sidebar "Evolution of the Internet"). In particular, how are the differentiated QoS requirements of different applications to be satisfied? One approach is an expanded set of *service models*. One of these service models

ATM: Another Integrated Services Network

ATM networking has its origins in the telephone industry, where it was originally conceived as a new foundation for the public telephone network, extending that network to integrated services. The ATM network also uses packet switching, except that its packets (called cells) are *fixed*-length and *small* (48-byte payload and a 5-byte header). A small header is possible because it uses a different form of routing based on unique addressing within each link. ATM is connection oriented, meaning that all host-to-host communications request and are provided a connection (fixed route) through the network. ATM from its beginning has emphasized the active configuration of QoS parameters because of its desire to offer guaranteed-delay voice and video. Thus, ATM was designed with a different philosophy than the internet protocols, although the two are becoming more similar over time, as both address essentially the same set of requirements.

The more interesting story is the design and standardization approach. ATM was originally conceived as a network layer upon which new ATM *native* applications could be built (that is, directly using ATM cells). Like all new networking technologies, however, ATM has had to overcome the strong effects of network externalities. In this regard, ATM is suffering a bit of the same fate as the ISO protocols, and for many of the same reasons. The entire ATM network was designed by a standardization process prior to implementation. As a result, before ATM was even available, the Internet was well established as a commercial entity. While the proponents of ATM still hold to the notion that it may support its own suite of native end-to-end applications, in fact the primary application of ATM thus far has been as a foundation for IP. Externalities represent a serious obstacle to ATM.

At the same time, ATM has some technical strengths for its intended applications, and there have been some interesting efforts to incorporate the best technical features of ATM into IP networks, without modifying the host view of IP itself. These efforts come under the heading *IP switching* and *tag switching*.

Evolution of the Internet

The Internet did not start out trying to be all things to all users. For many years it was designed, prototyped, and operated with a limited best-effort service model and used for a more narrowly defined set of applications. Improvements have been added incrementally as problems arose, such as scalability and congestion. Recently, driven by integrated services (including audio, video, and multicast), the Internet has been retrofitted to meet new needs. It is a testament to the flexibility of the original design that this is possible. On the other hand, it might be better (from the perspective of cost or performance, for example) to design a completely new network around the expanded requirements (called a *greenfield approach*).

The Internet is an interesting test of the relative merits of a process of incremental improvement and expansion versus a greenfield approach. Certainly when compared to the networks that preceded it, the Internet is *itself* a premier example of greenfield

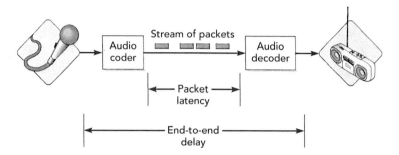

Figure 18.6 Network packet latency is one source of end-to-end delay in a streaming multimedia service

would be the best effort, which remains appropriate for many data purposes, but added would be service models providing QoS guarantees such as delay. These guarantees require the reservation of resources within the network, such as dedicated space in queues, some fraction of a communication link capacity, etc. Expanding the service models of the Internet introduces significant network design complications, but it is needed to provide predictable QoS.

18.2.3   Pricing of Network Services

The pricing of network services is of concern to users and organizations, but critical to the economic viability of service providers. Users collectively finance and utilize a shared network—and the actions of each user affect others—making pricing a complex issue. As in any social context, the concern is the financing, deployment, and operation of the network to maximize the collective benefit to the users, and how costs are divided among those accruing those benefits.

The challenges are similar to the pricing of software, as described in "Selling Content and Software" on page 247. Like software, networks benefit from large economies of scale: In the absence of congestion, new users can be accepted at a very low marginal cost. This is troublesome in a competitive market, because prices are driven toward marginal costs, which are much lower than average costs. Pricing therefore cannot be based strictly on costs, but must take into account the value to the customer. Sophisticated pricing strategies—similar to value pricing and versioning in software—are helpful to network service providers. This can have direct benefits to users as well. A network must allocate limited network resources among users, and pricing can help make this equitable. Users also have a collective interest in the provider having the revenue and incentives to upgrade network capacity as needed.

Economists advocate aligning prices and costs, which induces each user to indirectly consider the consequences of his or her actions on others and make individual decisions contributing to an efficient collective allocation of resources.

Before considering pricing, the first question is the costs:

- *Fixed costs:* Each user requires an access link to the network and also permanently shares in the use of an access switch with a modest number of other users. Relatively fixed costs also include customer support, billing, marketing, etc.
- *Usage-related costs:* It is more difficult to allocate the cost of the backbone network, as it is not dedicated to a single user. The backbone facilities (switches and communication links) must be sized in anticipation of the aggregate traffic, and frequent and heavy users have a greater impact on these costs than light users. Thus, the backbone costs attributable to a given user are reasonably approximated by the traffic generated by that user, measured by total number of bits—which takes into account the number of packets and the size of packets—or a similar measure.
- *QoS-related costs:* When users request QoS guarantees, such as reliable or delay-bounded delivery of packets, there are costs associated with resources reserved for one user and not available to be shared with other users.
- *Congestion costs:* In a packet network, congestion results primarily in increased latencies, which can be considered a "cost" to the collective users—not in monetary terms, but in terms of productivity or aggravation or other indirect measures. Each user offering traffic during congestion impacts other users by increasing the latencies and losses her messages experience.

Each of these costs can potentially be reflected in the pricing, and each has a strong argument in its favor (see Chapter 8):

- A fixed price for Internet access based on the fixed costs is well accepted. No other user will be willing to offset fixed costs directly attributable to another user.
- A component of price based on usage is more controversial. It can be the basis of value pricing—making usage a basis of price discrimination—since heavy users may have a higher willingness to pay.
- QoS predictability offers direct value to the user, but would be futile in the absence of associated pricing mechanisms, since rational users would always choose the highest-quality option. QoS could also form the basis of versioning as a strategy for deriving more revenues from users with a greater willingness to pay.
- Congestion pricing creates a source of revenue for a congested network that can be used to expand capacity. As a form of congestion control by

thinking. On the other hand, for networks, the obstacles of network externalities strongly favor a process of continuous improvement, since this allows new features to be systematically propagated to existing users (see "Network Effects" on page 232).

Today's Internet Pricing

Today, Internet service providers usually price based on the maximum bit rate of the access link. This approximates usage-based pricing, because a user with large maximum bit rate likely generates more traffic. However, this approximation makes an implicit assumption that the access link is heavily utilized; that is, the actual traffic is roughly measured by the access bit rate. New technologies discussed in Chapter 20 will provide much higher bit rates for residential access; these will not be purchased with the intention of high utilization, but rather to allow large messages (such as Web pages) to be transferred with low latency.

EXAMPLE: *If two 10 Mbps access links were provided to a residence and a university campus, the utilization of the latter would probably be much higher. Charging each the same price is unfair to the residence, which is creating less backbone traffic. Arbitrarily charging the university a much higher price might induce the university to purchase the residential service.*

Generally the Internet access service provider and the backbone service provider are not the same company. The pricing scheme described above recovers revenue for the access provider, but who pays the backbone provider? The answer is it basically works the same way between access and backbone provider as it works between customer and access provider. Access providers, wherever they connect to the backbone network, pay for the traffic they pass to the backbone (today based usually on the maximum bit rate). Of course,

influencing user behavior, it gives users freedom of action without creating bad citizens who violate voluntary policies with impunity. Unlike other forms of congestion control, congestion pricing allows users freedom to generate high-priority traffic during periods of congestion if they are willing to pay the price. (Other forms of congestion control dictate to the user what traffic can be generated.) Congestion pricing also rewards users for shifting lower-priority traffic to less congested times.

Ideally, pricing would reflect these four components. A fixed-price component would offset the capital expenditures on access facilities, a usage component would offset capital expenditures and operational costs of the backbone network, a QoS component would offset resources reserved (denied other users) to guarantee that QoS, and a congestion component would not only provide incentive for shifting traffic to less congested periods but also provide a source of revenue to relieve congested facilities.

At present Internet pricing is simple (see the sidebar "Today's Internet Pricing"). In the future, the Internet likely needs more sophisticated pricing strategies, particularly as it provides an increasing number of service models with QoS differentiation. The strongest counterargument is the cost of the monitoring and billing infrastructure supporting pricing, described in "Cost of Congestion Control" on page 505.

Discussion

D18.4 Discuss the QoS differentiation and pricing strategies of the airline industry. How does the cost structure compare to networking? What ideas here might be applicable to networking?

D18.5 Would there likely be customer resistance to any of the four pricing components listed?

18.3   Open Issues

Internet service and the selling of content over the Internet are new businesses, so there are many unresolved issues.

18.3.1   Future of the Internet

The Internet is a research infrastructure that "grew up" to find itself a commercial phenomenon. As a research infrastructure, some capabilities required to make it a viable commercial network were naturally not addressed, and as a result it misses some arguably important capabilities. Foremost among these are the lack of QoS configurability and the lack of an infrastructure to support any but fixed pricing. An unanswered question is whether these capabilities are really needed, and if so how they will be deployed.

Best-effort service is simple, but it transfers risk to the customer, reducing the value of the service. (It is analogous to standby service in airlines, which is priced considerably below reservation service.) The absence of QoS configuration also precludes versioning—quality-differentiating pricing strategies—which can help the provider take advantage of variations in consumer willingness to pay. The absence of congestion pricing eliminates one important mechanism to affect customer behavior, reduce congestion, and pay for network upgrades to relieve congestion.

18.3.2 Multiple Networks

While the provisioning of multimedia services in applications such as remote conferencing is compelling, there is serious talk of the Internet displacing the public telephone network in its traditional role in providing telephony (this is called Voice over IP, or VoIP; see Chapter 20). There is a question as to whether delay QoS can match the telephone network, and whether the cost of an IP telephone can approach existing telephones. Of course, such a development would have to overcome a number of economic obstacles, such as lock-in and stranded investments in the existing telephone infrastructure.

Review

Packet switches allow full communication connectivity among hosts without requiring dedicated host-to-host communication links. A given backbone link is shared among multiple concurrent host-to-host communications, and this statistical multiplexing underlies the favorable economics of networks. Switches forward packets to output links based on the destination address (included in the packet header) and a local routing table. The routing table is updated by routing network protocols, which seek the best available path from source to destination based on network topology and traffic conditions.

Applications typically use host names rather than addresses, with the translation provided by a network name service. Both names and addresses are arranged hierarchically, with assignments delegated to lower-level administrative organs. In the Internet, the domain name system (DNS) provides this service. It is a good example of a scalable networked application. Each host delegates name service to its own local name server, which in turn contacts other name servers to

they are m
portion of
from the customer.

Many users in organizational settings think of the Internet as "free." This is because their organization is paying for access charges. Unlike the public telephone, there is today no usage-based charge and no metering or accounting, so users are not likely to be criticized for using the Internet a lot, as they might be with the telephone.

resolve the name. The local name server also resolves repeated queries locally by caching past queries.

In a broadcast service, replicated data from a single source has to reach many destinations. This is supported by simulcast (the source replicates the data) and multicast (the data is replicated within the network).

Two essential network functions are flow control and congestion control. Flow control allows a destination to control how much data it receives—the source must slow transmission to accommodate this. Congestion control allows the network to regulate the total traffic offered to the network to limit congestion-induced latencies and losses. Congestion control must address the social issue of how limited network resources are allocated among users and hosts, and avoid the undesirable overloaded conditions where the total network through-put is diminished. There are several approaches to congestion control, including mandatory or voluntary policies, network policing, and economic incentives.

A network may provide quality-of-service (QoS) objectives or guarantees. The internet protocol (IP) does not offer QoS, but gives its best effort to deliver packets in timely fashion. Examples of QoS attributes include guaranteed reliable or timely delivery of packets—a network can offer one or the other, but not both (because reliability requires an indeterminate number of retransmissions). In a session, QoS attributes include packet delivery in the same order as sent. The timely delivery of packets requires dedicated resource allocations within the network, reducing the benefits of statistical multiplexing.

An integrated services network can support a variety of applications with differing needs. Typically this implies providing different classes of QoS guarantees tailored to those differing needs—a form of versioning. ATM (asynchronous transfer mode) is an example of a network catering specifically to integrated services, and the Internet is rapidly evolving in that direction.

Service versioning requires coordinated pricing, or otherwise rational users and applications will choose the highest QoS. There are four natural components to pricing based on service provider costs, including fixed (based on the cost of a dedicated access link and switch), usage (based on the cost of shared backbone links and switches), QoS (based on the added cost of dedicated resources), and congestion (based on the cost of upgrading the network to alleviate congestion).

Key Concepts

Packet switching:

- Statistical multiplexing
- Packet forwarding
- Routing

Name service:

- Names versus addresses
- Domain name system

Broadcast:

- Simulcast versus multicast

Flow control

Congestion control:

- Network policing

Quality of service (QoS)

Integrated services

Further Reading

A superior general textbook on network protocols is [Pet96], and [Wal96] is a more advanced book that has a chapter on network pricing. General social issues in the Internet are discussed in [Mck97a, b], and a more complete discussion of pricing issues is given in [Mac95a, b, c]. [Mck97a, b] are good general introductions to social issues in network design.

Exercises

E18.1 Give three examples of sharing in the physical world analogous to statistical multiplexing. For each example, how does it contribute to "efficiency"?

E18.2 For the comparison between statistical and time-division multiplexing in "Advantage of Statistical Multiplexing" on page 495, assume the packet latency in the two cases is equal. Show that statistical multiplexing can achieve a higher utilization and throughput, and quantify the difference.

E18.3 Consider a street address uniquely locating an individual home or business in the United States (which has a population of about 250 million).

    a. If this address was represented as a bit string, estimate how many bits would be required in that address if it was as efficient as possible. Make reasonable assumptions about the number of residences and businesses, and state those assumptions. (Hint: $2^{10} \approx 10^3$.)

    b. Repeat using the actual physical-world addressing, using character strings. Again, make and state reasonable assumptions.

E18.4   Make a list of ten everyday items, other than computers and telephones, that you think might benefit from being connected to the Internet. Explain in a single sentence what that benefit might be.

E18.5   What do the following domain names tell you about the organization or administration of the corresponding host?

   a. research.ibm.com

   b. polysci.ucla.edu

   c. www.lords.parliament.gov.uk

E18.6   Consider astronomical objects (planets, stars, etc.).

   a. Design a hierarchical naming scheme. Since new astronomical objects are being discovered all the time, they are given names once they are discovered.

   b. Design a distributed governance mechanism for assigning the names, so that different organizations will be responsible for assigning different kinds of names, but it will be guaranteed that there will be a single official name for each astronomical object. (Hint: This is analogous to DNS.)

E18.7   How long would phone numbers have to be (how many digits) in order to accommodate as many different numbers as can be identified with the following (Hint: $2^{10} \approx 10^3$):

   a. 32-bit IP V.4 addresses

   b. 128-bit IP V.6 addresses

E18.8   For a multicast service:

   a. Considering only the access communication link, what is the savings in traffic for multicast relative to simulcast?

   b. Qualitatively, how will this traffic savings change on downstream communication links?

E18.9   Why does flow control only have to worry about a producer that produces too much, as opposed to a consumer that consumes too much?

E18.10   You are made "transportation czar" and placed in charge of reducing the congestion on the highways.

   a. Describe at least five ways you might reduce highway congestion.

   b. Which ways will be most politically palatable?

   c. Which will result in the greatest societal economic efficiency?

E18.11 Discuss the network QoS requirements of the following applications:

   a. Video on demand

   b. Remote conferencing

   c. Email

   d. Chatroom

   e. Web

E18.12 Discuss the application and network QoS requirements for each of the following electronic commerce applications, and in particular how they may differ from one another.

   a. Clothing sales

   b. Stock trading

   c. Music playback on demand

E18.13 Discuss in more detail than the chapter how each of the following pricing components might be established. In particular, what specific cost factors might be taken into account?

   a. Fixed

   b. Usage based

   c. Congestion based

   d. QoS based

E18.14 Make a concise argument for each of the following assertions:

   a. If pricing has a congestion component, there is no need for a usage-based component.

   b. It is advantageous to the seller to have both usage-based and congestion pricing components. (It is useful to refer back to "Challenges for Suppliers" on page 242.)

E18.15 Discuss qualitatively the variation in users' willingness to pay for network services in terms of how this might impact pricing strategies for a revenue-maximizing service provider. Repeat this for each of the four components of pricing in Exercise 18.13.

E18.16 Currently Internet service providers (ISPs) typically charge a fixed price per month for voiceband data modem access to the Internet, with unlimited usage.

a. Discuss what perverse incentives this pricing model places on the ISP. Also explain why ISPs find it hard to make a profit on this service (as evidenced by their movement toward advertising revenues).

b. If this is not a good business model for ISPs, speculate as to how this pricing structure might break down to achieve something more economically viable in the long term.

Network Architecture
and Protocols

19

The general functions of the network were discussed from an application perspective in Chapter 12 and from the perspective of its collective users in Chapter 18. This chapter completes the picture by delving into a number of internal design issues for the network. How do hosts find and address one another? How do messages get delivered to particular applications, not just hosts? How does traffic within the network influence application performance and quality metrics, in terms of the reliability and latency of message delivery? What other important functions does the network perform? It is useful to develop a deeper understanding of how a computer network works in order to appreciate these and other issues.

The global Internet has been an important development as the first packet network that connects not only organizations of all sizes, but also individual citizens. This enables, for the first time, the widespread deployment of the electronic commerce and social applications described in Chapter 2 and Chapter 3. For this reason, the Internet is used in this chapter as a concrete example to illustrate many general concepts in network architecture.

If you are less interested in the internal network design issues, this chapter can be skipped without loss of continuity.

19.1 Network Architecture

Like all complex systems, the network has an internal architecture. The decomposition of the network into subsystems can be viewed in two complementary ways:

- The equipment is decomposed into network interface hardware in hosts, communication links, and packet switches.

The ISO Reference Model

The ISO protocols were established by a lengthy de jure international standardization effort. The triumph of the internet protocols (which are emphasized in this book) illustrates positive feedback in network effects combined with the greater speed in defining an open de facto standard. Nevertheless, the reference model defined by ISO is a useful conceptual framework for decomposing the functionality of network protocols. It defines seven layers, each building on the capability of the layer below. Starting at the top, these layers are as follows[Wal91]:

- The *application layer* is the unique functionality of the application.
- The *presentation layer* includes any preprocessing of data presented to the application before it passes through the network. This includes encryption (for confidentiality, as described in Chapter 13) and compression (a way of mitigating communication bottlenecks, as described in Chapter 20).
- The *session layer* creates the common context for an end-to-end conversation, including establishment and disestablishment, as described in Chapter 12.
- The *transport layer* delivers individual messages from a process on one host to a process on another host.
- The *network layer* delivers individual packets from one host to another.
- The *data link layer* delivers packets from one network switch to

- The infrastructure software runs in hosts and switches and has an internal modular decomposition based on layering. This layered architecture allows the distinctively different needs of different applications discussed in Chapter 12 to be realized in a common infrastructure. In particular, the services of a common underlying layer can be specialized and elaborated by placing different layers above it for different purposes.

EXAMPLE: *In the internet architecture shown in Figure 12.10 on page 363, the lowest IP layer is a spanning layer that provides host-to-host communication of packets and hides the heterogeneity of the subnetwork technologies below it. The services provided by the IP layer are, however, too limited to be of direct use to applications. For example, just getting a packet to the right host leaves open the question of what application running on that host is to receive the packet (represented by the operating system process). Also, applications typically require communication services such as messages and sessions that are not provided by IP. Thus, the internet adds a new layer, which can be TCP or UDP or something else, to elaborate and specialize IP. Both TCP and UDP direct packets to the right application, and TCP provides message and session services. Layers can be added on top of TCP or UDP to further elaborate and specialize these services for particular applications. For example, RTP can be layered on UDP to provide the special capabilities needed to transport audio and video through the Internet.*

Although layering is the standard approach to decomposition of computer networks, the internet approach is not the only way this can be done. Another prominent example is the ISO reference model, which is described in the sidebar "The ISO Reference Model."

This section discusses the internal architecture of the network layer in more detail. Specifically, what is the functionality of the layers, and how do they interact to achieve network features such as flow and congestion control? Four fundamental concepts—network protocols, packet encapsulation, packet fragmentation, and protocol layering—underlie these architectural questions. These are discussed now, before moving on to the concrete example of the Internet.

19.1.1   Network Protocols

The first fundamental concept in the network architecture is the network protocols that govern the interaction among network modules. Flow control and congestion control discussed in "Functions of a Network" on page 493 are examples of protocols accomplishing higher-level functions of the network. In fact, almost all functions of a network involve the essential use of protocols to coordinate the actions of entities on different hosts and in switches. The importance of protocols is magnified by bad things that can happen internally to a network, such as the loss of packets caused by the overflow of queues in switches or corruption of data on communication links. Protocols are so important that the design of networks is almost synonymous with the design of the protocol used in the network. Recognizing the importance of protocols, internal network layers are often called *protocol layers*.

EXAMPLE: *The internet layers illustrate this terminology. IP stands for Internet Protocol, and TCP stands for Transmission Control Protocol. These are discussed in more detail later in this chapter.*

19.1.2   Packet Encapsulation

The second key concept in the network architecture is *packet encapsulation*. In the course of transporting packets through the network, a packet must be passed down through the protocol layers on the sending host and back up through protocol layers on the originating host. When one layer receives a packet from the layer above, an oft-used trick it uses to deal with that packet in its own terms is packet encapsulation. That way, it can attach its own packet header for its own purposes, without dealing with or seeing the header passed from the layer above, but at the same time maintaining the integrity of that header.

As illustrated in Figure 19.1, one whole packet (including header and payload) can become the payload of another packet. This is called encapsulation because the header of the original packet becomes just a part of the payload, and it is no longer visible unless and until the encapsulated packet is extracted from the payload.

Packet encapsulation is a form of hierarchical decomposition and assembly of data. A packet is a package of data transported by a network, and encapsulation allows these packages of data to be contained one within another.

One use of packet encapsulation is *tunneling*. One packet network can cause a second packet network to transport its packets by presenting its packets (both header and payload) as messages to the second network. The second network then transports those messages as payloads of its own packets. At the other end, it can extract the original packets from those payloads.

EXAMPLE: *Point-to-Point Protocol (PPP) is a packet protocol widely used on access links. PPP defines its own packet header and payload structure, as well as establishment and disestablishment procedures, for purposes of the access*

another, through a single communication link.

- The *physical layer* corresponds to the functionality of a single link, as described in Chapter 20.

The internet protocols define fewer layers, and decompose functionality in different ways, illustrating that there is never a single "right" architecture.

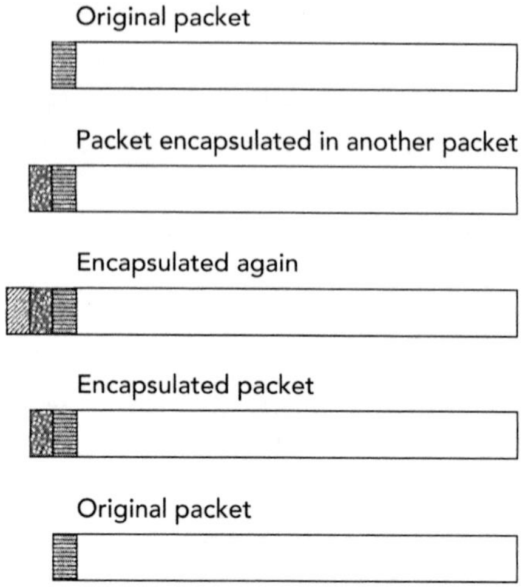

Original packet

Packet encapsulated in another packet

Encapsulated again

Encapsulated packet

Original packet

Figure 19.1 A packet can be encapsulated as the payload of another packet, and later recovered

link only. Other packet networking protocols, such as the Internet or Appletalk (a network used by Macintosh computers), can tunnel through PPP. If you use a modem to access the Internet, chances are you are using PPP, even though it is not specific to the Internet.

19.1.3   Packet Fragmentation and Reassembly

The third key concept in the network architecture is *packet fragmentation* and *reassembly*. The network transports packets, consisting of header and payload. Messages communicated between hosts have to be fragmented into packets, or if small enough, they can be transported in a single packet payload. For reasons of fairness to different senders and recipients utilizing a common link, packet payloads have a maximum size, as described in "Why Networks Use Packets" on page 472. Each subnetwork sets its own policy as to maximum packet size. (In fact, in an ATM subnetwork all packets have a fixed size and are called *cells*.)

Just as a message can be fragmented into packets, as shown in Figure 19.2 a packet (including both header and payload) can be fragmented and then encapsulated into the payloads of two or more packets with smaller payloads. This allows different packet length policies in subnetworks to be accommodated. Each of the smaller packets must have its own header, which is distinct from the header of the original packet. Those new headers must include, in addition to the information required by the network, the information required to reassem-

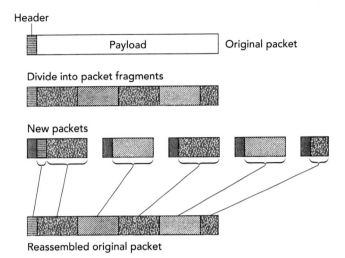

Figure 19.2 A packet, with its own header and body, can be fragmented into smaller packets and later reassembled into the original packet

ble the original packet from the fragments encapsulated in two or more packet payloads.

19.1.4   Protocol Layering

The fourth key concept in network architecture is the particular form of interaction that occurs among protocol layers. This interaction makes use of protocols, packet encapsulation, and fragmentation and reassembly of packets, but it adds particular conventions on how each layer interacts with the layer above and below, and how that interaction is coordinated at both ends of the network. The internet gives a concrete example of protocol layers—the next subsection describes that example—but first it is useful to understand the general schema of protocol layering.

Protocol layering is illustrated in Figure 19.3. The first principle is that each layer defines its own special packet header format for packets that it communicates across the network. At that layer, there are two peers, one at each end of the network. These peers communicate with one another by sending packets bidirectionally. These peers also share a common definition of the format of the packet headers they are using, as well as the protocol they engage in to realize the functionality assigned to that layer (as, for example, the reliable delivery of a payload). In fact, they use the headers in part as small messages from one peer to the other in the course of realizing that protocol.

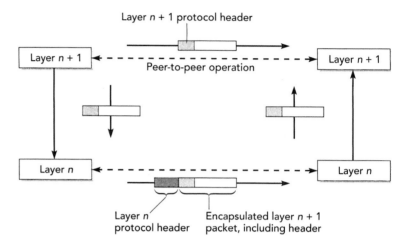

Figure 19.3 The layered architecture of network protocols is based on the encapsulation of layer n + 1 packet in a layer n packet

EXAMPLE: *In the course of delivering a packet payload reliably, the sending peer might have to send that payload to its counterpart multiple times, and the receiving peer may have to inform the sender when the payload has been received correctly. The protocol used includes small messages such as "this is a repetition of the payload I sent you before" and "stop sending replicas of that payload, I have received it correctly." Those small messages are incorporated in the packet header format defined by that layer.*

However, each layer has no way to convey packets *directly* to its peer; rather, it makes use of the services of the layer below (except, of course, the bottom layer). Thus, a packet sent by a layer n + 1 peer destined for another layer n + 1 peer is actually presented to layer n, which delivers that packet to the layer n + 1 peer. Internal to layer n, the layer n + 1 packet is encapsulated as a payload of a layer n packet, with a header added by layer n.

Layer n probably also has a policy on the maximum payload size for its own packets. If the layer n + 1 packet violates that policy, it may have to be fragmented and encapsulated into multiple layer n payloads. If so, there must be some convention (that is part of the horizontal layer interface specification) as to whether layer n + 1 or layer n is responsible for performing that fragmentation and reassembly.

ANALOGY: *Protocol layering is analogous to containerized shipping. A manufacturer sending parts to another manufacturer puts those parts in a container (box) and presents them to an end-to-end shipping company. This container is analogous to the packet payload, and the shipping instructions on the outside (destination address, bill of lading, etc.) are analogous to the packet.*

Protocol layering, like other forms of modularity, separates concerns and contributes to reuse. By partitioning end-to-end protocol functionality into layers, the special capabilities added by that layer can be dealt with independently of distinct capabilities provided by other layers. Each layer doesn't have to implement all the functionality, but can make use of existing services provided by the layer below. Distinct functionality can be achieved by adding new layers without having to start from scratch. Each layer's services can be reused by more than one layer above.

E X A M P L E :   *In the internet protocol layers shown in Figure 12.10 on page 363, the IP layer is the basis of all the layers above, including UDP or TCP. Similarly, RTP specializes the services of UDP rather than implementing them from scratch.*

This example is expanded in the next section, where the internet protocols are discussed. Layering does have its limitations. The shortcomings or assumptions of a lower layer may preclude realizing the desired capabilities of a higher layer. Thus, protocol layering, to be fully effective, requires foresight on the part of the architects, particularly the architects of the lower layers.

E X A M P L E :   *Although unreliable delivery in a lower layer can be overcome by resending lost packets at a higher layer, there is no way a higher layer can make up for very large packet latency at a lower layer. In general, rate-and-delay QoS guarantees at a higher layer depend on complementary guarantees at lower layers.*

Discussion

D19.1 Discuss the network protocol architecture from the perspective of the good qualities of an architecture as described in Chapter 6: modularity, abstraction, and encapsulation.

19.2   *Internet Protocols

The internet suite of protocols illustrate the network protocol architecture, including packet fragmentation and encapsulation and protocol layering. In particular, they illustrate how the overall network functions described earlier (packet forwarding and routing, flow control, and congestion control) and the communication services required by applications (such as reliable message

Some Lessons from the Internet
Architecture

The Internet has been successful for a
number of reasons—such as standardization process, the triumph of
de facto over de jure standards, government funding of research, a culture of experimentation and
refinement—but the foresight of its
architects stands out as an inspiration
for the future.

The key architectural choice in the
internet protocols was to keep the
internal network minimal and simple.
This is reflected in the design of IP,
which is the only protocol layer that
needs to be deployed in switches
within the network. IP conveys packets from one host to another, but that
is all it does. It does not guarantee
delivery, it does not guarantee
latency, and it provides no shared
context of packets to create sessions.
This not only keeps switches simple,
but also, more importantly, makes it
possible to add new capabilities to
the network (by adding protocol layers within hosts) with no change to
the network itself. Anybody administering hosts can define his own
higher-level services without the
compliance or involvement of the
network operators or their equipment suppliers, and without the
economic and logistical obstacles of
making global upgrades. This results
in rapid innovation, experimentation,
and refinement.

In addition, the embrace of multiple
solutions in the layers above IP avoids
the complexities of attempting a
"catch-all" solution in the higher
layers, and has stimulated a process
of incremental improvements, as
opposed to trying to solve all problems at once.

delivery or sessions) can be partitioned among layers. They also give a concrete
illustration of how protocol layers work, including the format of packet headers.

19.2.1   Internet Protocol Architecture

The internet protocol architecture in Figure 19.4 illustrates three views:

- *Logical view:* Each layer consists of peers that send bidirectional messages
  to realize the protocol at that layer. Typically these messages are contained
  in the headers of packets that may or may not have payloads. (Packets without payloads are "pure" protocol messages, and those with payloads are
  protocol messages carrying encapsulated application data.) This peer-to-
  peer relationship is indicated by the dashed lines.
- *Layered view:* Each layer makes use of communication services provided by
  the layer below to actually send packets to its peers.
- *Physical view:* In the horizontal direction, the partitioning of protocol elements onto two hosts and a single intermediate packet switch is shown. In
  practice there may be many more switches, depending on the number of
  communication links.

The top two layers in Figure 19.4 are not internet protocols, but are added layers
supporting networked applications. The Internet Inter-ORB Protocol (IIOP) is a
communication protocol layered on TCP, allowing one object request broker
(ORB) to interoperate with another, as described in "Interoperability among
ORBs: IIOP" on page 454. The ORB middleware layer provides RMI services
based on IIOP, as well as many other functions in distributed object management.

EXAMPLE: *When one object does a remote method invocation, the arguments
are marshalled into a message in the IIOP layer, as described in "RMI Can Be
Layered on Messages" on page 365. TCP is used to convey a series of these
request messages and their replies (marshalled return values) between the two
processes running ORBs on different hosts. TCP in turn builds on the host-to-
host communication service of the IP layer.*

The remaining internet protocol layers perform the following functions:

- The network layer is associated with each subnetwork (typically a LAN or the
  backbone WAN) that is internetworked. This layer sends packets from one
  host or switch to another, using subnetwork capabilities.
- The internetworking layer IP communicates packets from a sending host to a
  recipient host through one or more subnetworks. Figure 19.5 illustrates this
  function of IP. An IP layer peer is resident in each of the hosts *and* in the intermediate switches interconnecting subnetworks. The success of the Internet

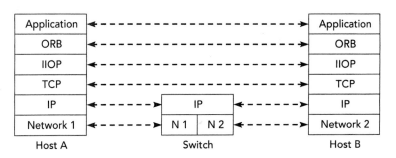

Of course, the internet architects didn't get it right on all counts—it has been necessary to modify IP several times. The original design did not anticipate QoS guarantees, or the special problems imposed by multicast or wireless access. Nevertheless, their achievement is an inspirational beacon in technological history.

Figure 19.4 This internet protocol suite illustrates the horizontal (host, link, switch), layered, and logical (peer-to-peer) structure; also shown is a CORBA ORB middleware layer providing distributed object management services to the application

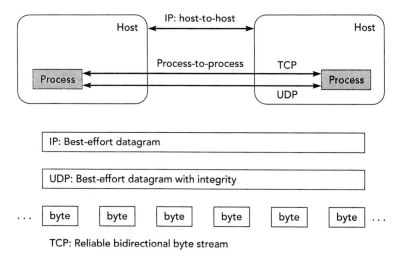

Figure 19.5 The three primary communication services provided by the internet protocols are IP, UDP, and TCP

can be attributed in no small part to the foresight exhibited by the designers of IP (see the sidebar "Some Lessons from the Internet Architecture").

- An application partition runs in a process, and thus to communicate with that partition, it is necessary to have a process-to-process communication service. TCP and UDP are *transport layer* protocols, which communicate from one process to another, as illustrated in Figure 19.5. They make use of IP host-to-host communication and arrange for packets to be presented to the designated process. The transport layer, because it leverages the host-to-host communication of the IP layer, need only be resident in the host operating systems and not in packet switches.

TCP and the PTN

The public telephone network (PTN) provides a communication service superficially similar to TCP, in that it also forms a connection and delivers a bidirectional byte stream. However, the PTN is different in three fundamental ways. First, the PTN delivers bytes at a fixed rate (8,000 bytes per second) using a technique known as *circuit switching;* whereas the TCP byte stream is variable rate (as determined by the two communicating processes). Second, in the PTN the bytes all experience exactly the same latency, whereas in TCP they have a variable latency (generally larger than the PTN). Third, the delivered bytes in the PTN have no guarantee of integrity—they may infrequently be corrupted. The PTN byte-stream service was originally designed primarily to carry voice, although it can be used for other purposes as well.

ANALOGY: *A company mailroom—analogous to the transport layer—takes responsibility for delivering an envelope to a specific location in the company. The mailroom may make use of an outsourced package delivery service to convey envelopes between its locations, analogous to the internetwork layer. The package delivery service may in turn make use of trucking companies or airlines to convey envelopes, analogous to the subnetworks.*

Understanding IP, UDP, and TCP requires dealing not only with their connectivity (where packets are sent and received), but also with other details of the communication service they provide to the application that were described in "Internet Communication Services" on page 362.

ANALOGY: *We can ask a number of other questions about the mailroom and the package delivery company. Do they guarantee that an envelope is delivered? Do they guarantee that the envelope is delivered within a certain time period? Do they acknowledge that the envelope has been delivered? If given two different envelopes at different times, do they guarantee delivery in the same order?*

IP tries to deliver individual packets (called datagrams because they have no shared context) to a destination host. It offers no guarantees as to delivery, order of delivery, packet latency, or the integrity of delivered packets. It simply does the best it can (called best effort). UDP, in addition to directing datagrams to a specific process rather than host, delivers only packets with integrity (no bit errors in the payload, which it insures through a *payload checksum* in the header). TCP provides a bidirectional byte-stream session between two processes, and includes reliable and ordered delivery of the bytes in the byte stream.

How do applications typically use TCP and UDP? UDP is appropriate for sending an isolated message from one process to another. That message can be packaged in a single datagram (if it doesn't violate packet length policies), or it can be fragmented into multiple datagrams and delivered by UDP. However, UDP requires the application to deal with complications, such as datagrams received in a different order than sent or not arriving at all. TCP is especially appropriate for a conversation (series of back-and-forth messages) but can also be used for a single reliable message using one of two approaches:

- *Single message per connection:* A process establishes a new TCP connection, sends a message as a stream of bytes, and when finished disestablishes that connection. This can also be used for a single message with reply. Due to the establishment and disestablishment overhead, this is only appropriate for large messages. For example, the protocol for the Web, HTTP, uses TCP as its transport service, establishing one TCP connection per page request.

- *Multiple messages per session:* The sending and receiving processes can easily establish their own protocol for sending a sequence of messages in a byte stream. They can agree on a way to signal (within the byte stream) the beginning and end of each message. For example, IIOP establishes a single TCP connection between two ORBs to support a series of remote method invocations.

EXAMPLE: *As an example of a message protocol built on TCP, consider the problem of sending ASCII messages via a byte stream. A message could be delimited by the characters < and >. However, what if the characters < or > are inside the message? A convention could be that each character < inside the message is replaced by << at the sender, and every << is assumed not to be a message delimiter and replaced by < at the destination process (similarly for >). This is called the escaping of special characters. Convince yourself that this avoids confusion about the beginning and end of messages.*

19.2.2 Packet Header Formats

There are two aspects to understanding further the design of the internet protocol: not only the sequences of messages included in packet headers, but also the formats (structure and interpretation) of those messages. The formats allow the recipient protocol peer to interpret messages contained in packet headers, and the protocols specify the sequence of messages.

The format of the IP packet header is shown in Figure 19.6 (this header is for IP V.6, the latest version that is not yet widely deployed). Each host has a unique 128-bit address, its IP address. The header includes the SourceAddress and DestinationAddress. The latter is used for packet forwarding in switches, and the former is needed by the destination host to distinguish packets multiplexed from multiple sources (among other purposes).

The other header fields in IP packets support other capabilities:

- PayloadLen specifies the number of bytes in the payload, allowing the payload to be variable length.
- NextHeader specifies optional features to be added in an extension header (which is added only when those optional features are invoked).
- HopLimit prevents some subtle problems with packets circulating in the network indefinitely. This field specifies the number of additional hops (link plus switch) permitted before the packet is discarded, and is decremented at each switch.

Managing Addresses

The assignment of addresses is a major issue in any network. There is a strong tendency to exhaust the address space.

EXAMPLE: *In the public tele-phone network (PTN), the pro-liferation of second and third telephone lines (for computers and facsimile machines) and cellular telephones is rapidly exhausting the ten digits allo-cated to telephone numbers in the United States.*

It is complex to manage the relation-ship of administrative domains to hierarchical addressing schemes. For example, if a telephone area code is assigned to a small region, it may be inefficiently utilized, but if it is assigned to a larger region, the num-bers will be more quickly exhausted.

The designers of IP assume many of these problems will be mitigated by designing a large address space at the expense of a larger header on each IP packet. They have also added autoconfiguration capabilities, so that hosts can automatically be assigned unique addresses.

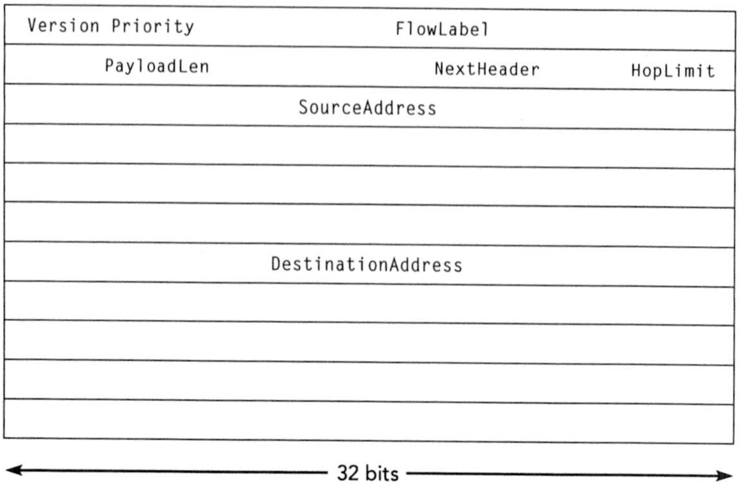

Version Priority	FlowLabel	
PayloadLen	NextHeader	HopLimit
SourceAddress		
DestinationAddress		

←———————————— 32 bits ————————————→

Figure 19.6 The format of the IP packet header for version six (V.6)

Most IP layer functionality resides in its routing subsystem. Packet header for-mats support both packet forwarding and routing.

UDP and TCP are layered on IP, which delivers packets from host to host. For this purpose, a UDP or TCP packet (both header and payload) is encapsulated as an IP payload. To realize their transport level functions, UDP and TCP define their own packet header format to communicate with their peer entity in another host. What is included in those transport headers? One important requirement is additional addressing necessary to forward packets to a particu-lar destination-host process. This is done by the indirect publish-subscribe mechanism illustrated in Figure 19.7. Each transport packet includes a 16-bit *port address*, and a process registers when it wishes to listen to a port or ports. As shown, each transport packet header includes a `SourcePort` and a `DestinationPort`.

How does an application know what port to use when it sets up a TCP connec-tion? Each application is normally assigned a default port.

EXAMPLE: *File transfers default to port 21, and HTTP uses port 80. Also, a URL can optionally include the port number, as in* `http://www.sims.berke-ley.edu:80/`, *which specifies port 80. If there is a process with a Web server running on a host, normally it is "listening" to (waiting to accept client TCP connections on) port 80.*

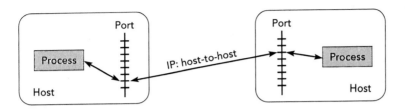

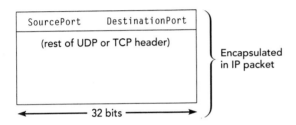

Figure 19.7 UDP and TCP add the port abstraction; each packet header specifies the `SourcePort` and `DestinationPort`, and processes register with the OS as to which ports they use

Additional information is included in the transport packet header as required to implement other aspects of the transport service, such as reliable delivery, flow control, and congestion control.

19.2.3 IP Multicast

From a packet forwarding and routing perspective, multicast is quite different from unicast IP. Like TCP, IP multicast requires the establishment of a type of connection—in this case a multicast tree with branches to each recipient. Each such connection has its own *multicast address*—an idea similar to the TCP/UCP port—and a recipient can join, knowing only the multicast address without knowledge or permission of the source. A source specifies the multicast address without knowing the individual recipients.

19.2.4 Domain Name System

The domain name system (DNS) and Internet routing system described in "Packet Forwarding and Routing" on page 495 are themselves large-scale networked applications. The DNS faces interesting challenges: Although its functionality is simple—it maps names to addresses—it must span many administrative domains and has significant scalability issues. The way DNS addresses these challenges is instructive. In the interest of clarity and brevity, this description will be simplified.

Host names are hierarchical according to administrative domains. At each level, there is an administrative organization—called a zone—that manages names at the next lower level of the hierarchy. This provides a measure of administrative scalability. Rather than a single organization managing names across the entire Internet, there is hierarchical delegation—at each level of hierarchy, the naming may be delegated to zones (administrative entities) at the next level of hierarchy.

EXAMPLE: *An administrative organization within Berkeley manages the host names that end in* berkeley.edu; *these hosts are all in a common zone. This organization accepts requests from system administrators to assign a given host name to an address within that organization and, after checking that there is currently no other host with that same name, grants that request. However, within Berkeley, there is another organization that manages the names that end in* sims.berkeley.edu, *and thus this is defined as its own zone. In effect, the* berkeley.edu *zone has delegated responsibility for this portion of its name space to this self-contained zone.*

A host consulting the DNS to resolve a name into an address sends a query to a database known as a *name server*. The important principle is that each zone administers its own name server; that is, it updates name to address translations therein. As discussed in "Organizational Rationale for Networked Computing" on page 274, with inexpensive computers, it is advantageous to align databases with host administration with administrative organizational boundaries.

EXAMPLE: *This is illustrated in Figure 19.8 for the* sims.berkeley.edu *zone. A "root" name server knows about all names that end in* edu, *a name server administered by the* berkeley.edu *zone that knows names administered within its zone, and a name server administered by zones within* berkeley.edu, *such as* sims.berkeley.edu *and* eecs.berkeley.edu. *Whenever the* berkeley.edu *name server receives a query that ends in* sims.berkeley.edu, *it delegates that query to the* sims.berkeley.edu *name server.*

Alignment of administrative responsibility (assigning names) with the responsibility of managing the name server database simplifies the administrative challenge of updating the name server databases and also contributes to scalability.

An actual query to the DNS is constructed hierarchically. A local host delegates to its local name server the resolution of name to address and thus doesn't deal directly with the DNS complexities. The local name server searches hierarchically through the name servers that command the zones assigned those names.

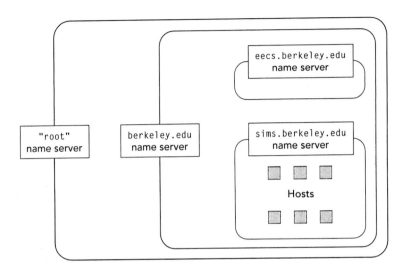

Figure 19.8 Administrative boundaries and associated name servers for
`berkeley.edu`

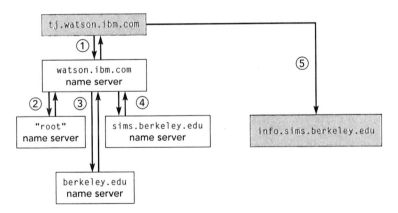

Figure 19.9 Example of the sequence of queries required to obtain the IP
address of `info.sims.berkeley.edu`

EXAMPLE: *A host* `tj.watson.ibm.com` *can find the IP address of host*
`info.sims.berkeley.edu` *in the manner illustrated in Figure 19.9. It consults
the local name server for the* `watson.ibm.com` *zone, which resolves the name
and returns the address. If the* `watson.ibm.com` *name server doesn't find the
relevant information directly in its own database, it consults a* `root` *name
server, which knows about all zones whose names end in* edu. *That* `root` *name
server examines its database for relevant information and returns the address
of the* `berkeley.edu` *name server. The* `watson.ibm.com` *name server then*

consults the `berkeley.edu` *name server, which redirects its query to the* `sims.berkeley.edu` *name server by supplying its address. Finally, the* `watson.ibm.com` *name server is able to get the address of* `info.sims.berkeley.edu` *from that name server and return it to* `tj.watson.ibm.com`.

In actuality, the local name server can store previously resolved name-address pairs. Often applications request the same names repeatedly, and this may avoid many external queries. This refinement is an example of caching, which is discussed in Chapter 20.

19.2.5   Reliable and Ordered Delivery

Many applications require a message service with reliable delivery. Further, a conversation requires ordered delivery of a stream of messages, which is closely related to reliable delivery. Reliable and ordered delivery increase message latency—thus, if latency is critical, it may be better to use a communication service without ordered or reliable delivery. Understanding how reliable and ordered delivery are achieved helps appreciate this trade-off.

TCP—an example of reliable and ordered delivery—uses as a foundation the best-effort datagram service of IP, as shown in Figure 19.10. A group of successive bytes from the byte stream are encapsulated in a single packet payload with a TCP header. At the destination, the original bytes can be extracted from the TCP packet payload. However, there is no guarantee that IP delivers a given TCP packet payload to the destination, and thus TCP must resend the packet (possibly multiple times) if it wasn't received. This is called packet *retransmission*. In addition, IP may deliver those TCP packets in a different order than they were sent (particularly if retransmissions are needed), and thus TCP must *reorder* its packets once they are delivered.

Two cases are illustrated in Figure 19.10. On the left side, a TCP packet is sent to the TCP peer in a destination host (utilizing IP) and is received correctly on the first try. The destination TCP peer sends a TCP *control* packet back to its source TCP peer (again utilizing IP), where this control packet contains an *acknowledgment* message (called an ACK) informing the source peer that the TCP packet was correctly received. However, as illustrated on the right side, IP may not deliver the original TCP packet, or it may have arrived corrupted. The source can detect that failure by the *absence* of an ACK. After waiting in vain for the ACK for a period of time called the *time-out*, the source will retransmit the TCP packet, again using IP. In fact, the source will repeatedly retransmit the TCP packet (each time after waiting for another time-out) until it eventually receives an ACK.

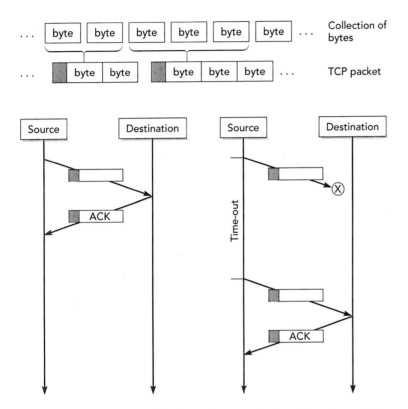

Figure 19.10 At the source, TCP encapsulates a collection of bytes into a TCP packet and utilizes IP to deliver this packet to the destination host

The loss or corruption of a TCP packet results in an increased latency because of the time required to detect that loss (the time-out period) plus the retransmission time. If the packet is not correctly received the second time, even more latency is introduced. This is the essence of the trade-off between reliability and latency: Reliable delivery necessitates occasional retransmission, which adds to packet latency.

IP does not offer *reliable* datagram delivery in part because that would increase latency for every datagram. Applications would not have the option to favor low latency over reliable delivery. Once introduced, latency can never be removed. Reliability, on the other hand, can be regained by retransmission. Thus, it makes good sense to provide low-latency (and simple) unreliable datagram service as a foundation, and for applications desiring reliability to add retransmissions.

Figure 19.11 shows how a sequence of TCP packets can be sent reliably to the destination, as is required to construct a byte stream. Consider the reliable

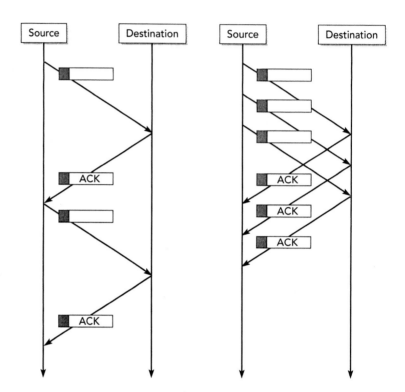

Figure 19.11 TCP could conduct reliable delivery of packets sequentially or concurrently; the latter will result in higher throughput

delivery of a single packet as a single task, including any retransmissions and ACKs. Then those individual tasks can be conducted sequentially (left side) or concurrently (right side). The throughput of those tasks corresponds to the throughput of correctly delivered TCP packets. The sequential throughput would be quite susceptible to IP datagram latencies, for example, due to greater geographic separation of hosts. As those latencies increase, each task time would increase, and the throughput would decrease. For that reason, the concurrent approach is used—new packets can be sent before the reliable delivery of earlier packets is complete. This is an example of parallel concurrent tasks.

One loose end is how TCP keeps track of its concurrent tasks. Each TCP header and ACK message contains a packet SequenceNumber. By monitoring SequenceNumbers, TCP can keep track of which packets have been acknowledged and which have not. TCP can also reorder the packets properly at the destination using the SequenceNumber, should they be received out of order.

19.2.6   Flow Control

Flow control can easily be added to the TCP reliable and sequenced delivery algorithm. The throughput of TCP will be directly related to the number of allowed concurrent packet deliveries (see Figure 19.11). TCP adds a parameter `MaxUnackedPackets` to the sender, where `MaxUnackedPackets` is the maximum number of unacknowledged packets allowed at any time (this equals the number of concurrent packet deliveries currently in progress). As necessary, the source doesn't initiate new packet delivery tasks if this maximum would be exceeded. `MaxUnackedPackets=1` is the sequential case, and `MaxUnackedPackets=0` means the sender cannot initiate *any* new packet transmissions.

The destination includes the parameter `MaxUnackedPackets` in every ACK message. As it finds packets arriving too fast (its queue fills up), it reduces `MaxUnackedPackets` to reduce throughput. Eventually, it may set `MaxUnackedPackets=0`, stopping further transmission altogether. (Obviously, there must be a way to get the transmission started again; see the exercises).

In TCP, congestion control uses a similar source control mechanism as flow control (see the sidebar "TCP Congestion Control").

19.2.7   Integrated Services

Since IP provides a best-effort service, the transport services utilizing IP are not able to provide QoS guarantees, as required by multimedia and integrated services. To fix this problem, IP must be modified. To guarantee QoS attributes to individual sessions, resources (such as bit rate and space in queues) are reserved within the network. QoS thus requires an establishment phase for reserving resources and setting the state of network switches.

Admission control—a protocol that determines whether the network can accommodate a new requested session without violating existing commitments—is included in establishment. A request for a new session may be rejected, which is a draconian form of congestion control, as it limits the offered traffic to the network by rejecting session requests as necessary.

The IETF is in the process of standardizing new service models in the network and modifying the network protocols accordingly. In particular, IP V.6 incorporates some needed modifications. The IETF is also focused on multicast and other new services that complicate these issues (see the sidebar "RSVP: Service Models for Multicast").

TCP Congestion Control

TCP uses a source throttle during periods of congestion. It is policy driven—the congestion algorithm is included in the TCP protocol specification—but compliance is voluntary:

- Applications are not constrained to use TCP as a transport protocol at all. As an alternative, UDP includes neither flow control nor congestion control.
- The flow control algorithm in the sender does not impact functionality or flow control, so there is nothing to prevent "cheating."

TCP detects congestion by observing how many times it has to retransmit packets, making the assumption that congestion is manifested by packet losses or large latencies. It uses the same mechanism to reduce offered traffic as flow control, reducing `MaxUnackedPackets`.

This congestion-detection algorithm does not work well with wireless access links, which are rapidly increasing in popularity (see Chapter 20). Often packets are lost due to noise- and interference-induced corruption, which do not reflect congestion. In the future, TCP will likely have to be modified; fortunately, the IETF has demonstrated in the past the ability to make modifications to meet new requirements.

RSVP: Service Models for Multicast

The ReSerVation Protocol (RSVP) is the IETF response to the need for new internet service models, particularly to support high-quality streaming audio and video. RSVP also supports multicast, which is of particular interest to audio and video broadcast and remote learning. (Unicast can be treated as a simpler special case.) To be source scalable, any multicast protocol must put the burden on the destination hosts for establishment protocols. In RSVP, each destination negotiates independently with the network to receive network QoS and audio or video quality guarantees.

How can different destinations get distinct QoS parameters? Recall that multicast requires a tree topology to be set up in the network, with the source at the root and each destination at one branch. One way to tailor QoS is to differentiate resources on the final branch of the multicast tree to the needs of that branch's destination. With respect to bit rate, RSVP does more than this. It arranges for the bit rate to be reduced as source data passes through the multicast tree by selectively discarding packets. Doing this while achieving the best audio or video subjective quality (consistent with the bit rate actually delivered to the destination) requires a prioritization of the traffic generated by the source and a tolerance for the loss of low-priority packets.

Discussion

D19.2 What are some issues raised when an internetwork is owned by multiple entities (companies and governments)? Operational issues? Pricing issues?

D19.3 What are some lessons about the architecture of networked applications from the design of DNS?

D19.4 The inspired architectural choices discussed in "Some Lessons from the Internet Architecture" on page 524 occurred in the context of government-sponsored research projects. Could a similar result have been obtained in a commercial context? Or would profit motives have pointed in a different (and in retrospect less successful) direction?

Review

The network protocol architecture uses packet fragmentation/reassembly and encapsulation to build layers of protocols—each layer uses the communication services of the layer below. The fundamental internet protocol (IP) provides a best-effort host-to-host datagram service. Layered on this are the UDP and TCP transport protocols, which provide process-to-process communication. TCP establishes a byte-stream session with ordered and reliable delivery, and includes flow and congestion control.

Key Concepts

Protocols:

- Packet fragmentation
- Packet encapsulation
- Protocol layering
- Internet: IP, UDP, TCP, RSVP

Further Reading

A superior general textbook on network protocols is [Pet96], and [Wal97] is a more advanced book that has a chapter on network pricing. A well-written general reference on network security is [Gar96], and specifically for Web server security, see [Gar97]. An encyclopedic reference on security on the Internet is [Atk96].

Exercises

E19.1 Describe at least two transport services (other than UDP and TCP) that you believe might be valuable to applications. What advantages might they offer? (Hint: The abstract communication services of Chapter 12 might be a source of ideas.)

E19.2 Give two real-world analogies to each of the following:

a. Switching

b. Multiplexing for link sharing

c. Concurrent messages by splitting into packets

d. Packet fragmentation and reassembly

e. Packet encapsulation

f. Peer-to-peer operation utilizing the services of a layer below

E19.3 Discuss the following issues in the design of the TCP protocol.

a. What happens if a return acknowledgment is sent but never reaches its destination (the original packet sender)?

b. What can cause TCP packets to be delivered out of order?

c. It seems as if once `MaxUnackedPackets=0`, there is no way to get transmission started again, since there are no acknowledgments available to increase `MaxUnackedPackets`. Describe a modification to the protocol that fixes this flaw.

d. Is there any relationship between `MaxUnackedPackets` and the size of queues in packet switches?

E19.4 Consider the following alternative flow control algorithm for TCP: `MaxUnackedPackets` is kept fixed, rather than controlled by the destination. When the destination wants to slow down the source, it simply delays acknowledging received packets temporarily.

a. Would this behavior on the part of a receiver cause the sender to slow down its send rate; that is, would it work as a flow control algorithm?

b. Does it have any disadvantages relative to the actual TCP protocol?

c. Are there any new problems that could arise as a result of this change in the flow control protocol?

E19.5 Invent an alternative flow and congestion control protocol for TCP. Discuss the relative merits of your approach and the one chosen by the designers of TCP.

E19.6 Discuss the scalability of the DNS. As the number of hosts and zones grows, are there any bottlenecks that might impact the ability of the DNS to handle the load? If so, can you invent a modification that overcomes that problem?

E19.7 In the DNS example of Figure 19.9 on page 531, is there any reason the `root` name server should not complete the job of finding the address, rather than passing the remainder of the task back to the `watson.ibm.com` name server?

E19.8 Consider the impact of finite storage capacity in queues in packet switches.

    a. How does packet loss, and hence the need for retransmission, depend on the size of the queues?

    b. In light of *a*, how does queue size affect network congestion?

    c. How does queue size impact the maximum latency of those packets that are delivered during periods of congestion?

    d. In light of *c*, discuss the relationship of packet latency due to queue waiting time and due to packet retransmission.

E19.9 The packet header is network overhead—nonapplication data that consumes capacity on the communication links.

    a. How does overhead, expressed as a percentage, depend on the size of the packet payload?

    b. In the interest of minimizing network congestion, how should the application implementer keep header overhead in mind?

    c. Discuss how a congestion control algorithm might exploit the opportunity to reduce overhead and hence congestion during periods of congestion. Is this a good idea?

Communications Providers and Links

20

The communications industry provides various communications and network services. Its impact on networked computing is manifested in two principal ways. First, the availability of networking services—especially nomadic and broadband access—depends on the communications industry, which is the primary network service provider. Second, digital communications—the technology underlying the communication links connecting hosts and packet switches—directly impacts network performance and thus application performance. This chapter addresses both issues relevant to the communications industry, as well as technology issues relating to how communication links work and impact networked applications.

20.1 Communications Service Providers

The computer industry emphasizes direct sales of equipment and software to end-users (individuals and organizations). There are systems integrators who develop and deploy new applications, and more recently there is a growing emphasis on outsourcing of operations to specialized firms as well. In contrast, communications has always emphasized a *service provider* that constructs and deploys facilities and leases communication services to end-users and organizations. Thus, the industry has a vertical structure consisting of three levels: equipment and software suppliers, network service providers, and end-users (individuals and organizations). There are several reasons service providers play a prominent role in communications:

- Communications networks require public rights of way for communications facilities that are buried in trenches along highways or railroad tracks, or strung from telephone poles. Given the associated regulatory and logistical problems, end-user organizations are generally precluded from constructing their own communication links between facilities.

- Direct network externalities favor a public network—rather than a proliferation of private networks serving subsets of customers—because such a network can provide greater value to users.
- Sharing facilities among many users is economical, both because of statistical multiplexing (described in Chapter 18) and other economies of scope and scale.

An exception to the service provider model is the local area network, traditionally installed and operated by an internal networking support organization. (This is also changing, with many companies choosing to outsource their internal network operations.) The LAN connects to a wide area service provider at a *point of presence* (POP).

There are an expanding number of communications service providers:

- *Telephone operating companies* have been a government-sanctioned and regulated monopoly for most of the past century. Their business model has emphasized turnkey applications (telephony or video conferencing), although they also lease communications facilities. (A turnkey application is one that is bundled with the complete infrastructure and sold as a unit, simplifying the life of the consumer but possibly precluding reuse of that infrastructure for additional purposes.) Foreign attachments (such as voiceband data modems or facsimile machines) providing nonvoice services over a voiceband channel have been permitted for a couple of decades. The most common Internet access link for residences exploits a foreign attachment— the voiceband data modem. Telephone operating companies also operate the Internet backbone.
- *Cable television* (CATV) *service providers* emphasize video broadcast and video-on-demand applications to residences over coaxial cable facilities paralleling the twisted-wire-pair facilities of the telephone companies. (The twisted pair consists of two wires twisted about one another, and the coaxial cable consists of an inner wire encased in a cylindrical sheath. The latter has considerably greater capacity, as needed for multiple channels of broadcast-quality video.) CATV companies have a local franchise and are subject to regulation. While CATV is available to most residences in the United States, it is not as common in most other countries.
- *Wireless service providers* offer primarily radio-based telephony (the mobile phone or cellular phone), although there are a few wireless Internet providers. There are independent companies as well as major telephone operating company divisions or subsidiaries. Most wireless services require a government license for the radio spectrum they use, although there is a trend toward unlicensed radio spectrum with associated "etiquette" policies (relaxed rules that restrict interference with other users).

- *Internet service providers (ISPs)* offer Internet access to consumers and businesses. These companies lease high bit rate access to the Internet backbone, and lease a number of lower bit rate connections to consumers and companies, aggregating their traffic into the backbone. Increasingly, telephone operating and CATV companies have entered this business.

The core competency of these service providers is customer service and operations, not technology. They rely on equipment and software suppliers (much like end-users depend on computer manufacturers).

20.1.1   Trends in Communications

Today this industry is experiencing chaotic change brought on by the rising importance of data services (including the Internet and networked computing), deregulation and greater competition, and industry globalization. There are numerous divestitures, mergers, and start-ups. Amid all this chaos, a few general trends can be discerned:

- In consonance with the globalization of industry and rise of the multinational corporation, most competitive communications providers can provide businesses with turnkey end-to-end communication services on a global basis. Thus, the industry is reorganizing around a smaller number of service providers, each operating on a global scale.
- The rising importance of data in relation to voice—as a revenue generator and as a fraction of the overall traffic—is shifting the technology from data retrofitted onto voice networks to integrated networks that can handle multimedia applications.
- The greater mobility of users, together with low-cost portable computers and information appliances, is shifting the emphasis from users in fixed locations to providing users with networked and application services seamlessly from any location, even while in motion.

20.1.2   Data Communications

With the exception of the ISPs, these players have been slow to provide data services desired by computer users, creating a major opportunity for internet technologies. There are a number of reasons for this:

- Much attention (and capital) has been drawn to wireless telephony—itself a rapidly growing and profitable market.
- While wireless telephony is a natural extension of telephony, data networking has quite different needs. Telecommunications companies have been slow to understand and appreciate the needs of computer users.

- The Internet, with its separation of application from infrastructure and its horizontal integration architecture, is antithetical to telecommunications suppliers' business model and culture.
- The culture of telecommunications has always been to provide consistent and reliable service with well-established quality-of-service (QoS) attributes. Thus, there has been some skepticism about the willingness of consumers to accept the best-effort service model prevalent in the Internet and especially about companies' ability to make a profit based on such a service model.

Among these trends, most germane to this book is the rise of data networking and the Internet, which have captured the attention of communications companies. The Internet is having a destabilizing impact in many ways analogous to the impact decentralized computing had on the companies that emphasized centralized computing. The computing industry moved from stovepipe applications (supported by vertically integrated companies) toward layering (supported by a fragmented industry), as was described in Chapter 7. Likewise, traditional communications companies—emphasizing vertical integration and turnkey applications such as telephony and video conferencing—are retrenching to provide digital communications and integrated services networks, with applications coming from elsewhere.

20.1.3   Communications Regulation

A striking difference between communications and computing is the role of government. In many countries, the communications infrastructure is government owned—like the postal service and the highways. Where communications providers are privately owned, as in the United States, they have been government regulated. Some reasons for this include the following:

- Communications facilities based on wire and fiber communications media often require a public right of way—like a street or highway—which in turn requires a franchise from the government.
- Like the highways and postal system, communications has been viewed as a *natural monopoly*; that is, society could not afford duplicative communications infrastructures. The companies thus operated as government-sanctioned monopolies, relying on regulation to keep prices and profits in check.
- There is a societal interest in achieving *universal service*, keeping prices of basic communication service very low so that almost everyone can afford it. This has resulted in a system of cross-subsidies (long distance subsidizing local service, and businesses subsidizing residential). Since such subsidies are antithetical to free markets and competition, this also suggests the need for a regulated monopoly.

- Communications is a critical infrastructure for national defense and for dealing with natural disasters, and thus it may be too important to entrust to the vagaries of free market competition. Through regulation, various availability and reliability objectives unjustifiable in a competitive industry have been mandated.

Many industry observers argue that due to technology advances, communications is no longer a natural monopoly. For example, communication services to residences can now be offered by several wireless technologies, satellite, cable television, and telephony facilities. Wireless is particularly propitious to competition, since facility costs are more incremental than for wired approaches.

Since universal service is a reality in developed countries, cross-subsidies may no longer be needed. In addition, there is today much greater faith in the free market and the benefits of competition in increasing efficiency, reducing prices, and speeding the adoption of new technologies. If universal service remains an objective, economic theory prefers a targeted user subsidy (like food stamps) since it does not interfere with the market.

The first deregulation step in the United States was the separation of long-distance and local service providers—called *local-exchange carriers* (LECs)—with a phase-out of cross-subsidies from long distance to local service. More recently, LECs have been encouraged to accept local-access competition, with the right to compete in long distance promised in return. Further, LECs have been allowed to enter cable television and other businesses outside their service territory. Recent laws have mandated that carriers freely connect their network to other networks. While this is clearly in the customer's interest—due to the benefits of network effects—the purpose of the law is to prevent interconnection restrictions from being used as a competitive strategy.

Meantime, the Internet has flowered without regulation. Indeed, this may account in part for its dramatic success and growth. As public policy issues relating to the Internet have arisen, it appears increasingly likely that some activities on the Internet will be government regulated.

Discussion

D20.1 Do you believe Internet service providers of the future will be today's telecommunications providers? Or do you think new dominant service providers emphasizing the integrated services network will arise?

D20.2 What do you think is the future of the public telephone network? Will it disappear someday (if so, when?), or will it coexist with integrated services networks indefinitely?

20.2   Current Developments in Internet Access

Communications has experienced rapid changes in technology and industry structure. Networked computing is impacted by several issues relating to the communications industry, and as a result computer companies have become increasingly active in trying to influence it.

20.2.1   Broadband Network Access for Residences

While the commercially available Internet access is adequate for businesses, many residential users crave higher bit rates than they are able to get. Achieving higher rates, as well as QoS guarantees, is an important enabler for many advanced commercial applications serving the citizenry, such as social applications and multimedia information access or entertainment. The reasons for this demand will be discussed in more detail later in this chapter.

Today the most common vehicle for Internet access is voiceband data modems, offering bit rates up to 33.6 kilobits per second (Kbps). Less widely used is ISDN at 128 Kbps. *Broadband* access—defined as bit rates approximating the 10 megabits per second (Mbps) of Ethernet LANs or higher—is an elusive target. Some computer equipment vendors believe that limited access bit rates may stifle their future business opportunities, since demand for more computing power is increasingly tied to networked applications, and many applications that are the most promising consumers of processing power (such as television-quality video) require higher access bit rates. Limited access bit rates may also stifle opportunities for businesses selling large-volume information (especially in audio and video media) over the network and some social applications needing high bit rates, such as remote conferencing. Some technical implications of bit rate bottlenecks are discussed later in this chapter.

Broadband Internet access has proven a daunting technical, economic, and regulatory challenge. Here are some technical challenges for residential access to the Internet:

- *Broadband:* Increasingly, multimedia applications benefit from higher bit rates than are available with access by voiceband data modems. To reasonably support today's application suite, a few megabits per second should suffice, but high-definition television and other advanced services require tens of megabits per second.
- *Symmetry:* Many service providers assume that broadband is required only in the direction of a residence, in order to support such applications as Web

browsing and video on demand. This assumption is quite limiting, because it ignores the possibility of residential users publishing information, and user-to-user applications like video conferencing require high bit rates in *both* directions. Further, mobile code, mobile agents, and other advanced technologies suggest symmetrical bit rate needs.

- *Internet dialtone:* Consumers should be able to purchase and install their own modem, install the software, and have everything work on the first try. This is analogous to plug-and-play in computer peripherals, and the term internet dialtone is an analogy to telephone dialtone. Often today it is necessary to send a service person to install the service, which is expensive.
- *Confidentiality* and *authentication:* Many broadband access technologies are multiple access, as described later in this chapter, meaning each consumer's equipment sees all the packets destined for many consumers and picks out its own. This technology raises inherent privacy, confidentiality, and authentication issues. They can be addressed with link-level encryption and challenge-response authentication protocols, described in Chapter 13.

There are two basic approaches to residential Internet access:

- Utilize an existing medium—the telephone twisted pair or CATV coaxial cable—and achieve broadband by adding sophisticated digital communication electronics.
- Install new facilities, leveraging advanced fiber optics or wireless media.

The installation of residential access fiber optics is economically difficult to justify. The fiber and its electronics are not necessarily the problem; the cost of digging trenches or stringing wires is staggering. This is accentuated by two adverse economic factors:

- Achieving a reasonable unit cost depends on economies of scale; thus, incremental installations responsive to actual service orders is uneconomic. A substantial sunk investment in facilities to serve an entire neighborhood at once is necessary.
- Only a small fraction of residences (called the *penetration*) would be expected to initially subscribe to broadband access. They must bear the facilities cost for everybody. If there are competitive access offerings, each will achieve an even lower penetration.

Putting these together, the service provider sees a high risk that its investment will not pay off and cannot be recovered (this is called a *stranded* investment). Similar reasoning led the government to conclude decades ago that communications was a natural monopoly and that a high penetration (universal service) required government intervention. It may be that broadband access remains

Wireless Access Protocol (WAP)

Economies of scale in terminal production and user nomadism are motivations to standardize on common protocols and "air interfaces" for wireless data services. WAP is an industry consortium pursuing de facto standards. WAP currently focuses on making the mobile terminal (including cellular telephone) a thin client based on Web de facto standards. The architecture of WAP—typical of similar efforts to define wireless interfaces—is shown in Figure 20.1. WAP defines a *Wireless Markup Language* (WML) that exploits the extensibility of XML (see "Documents and XML" on page 423) to define a markup language specific to wireless terminals with limited display capabilities. XML or HTML can be converted to WML by a filter. To reduce the processing requirements of the portable information appliance, WAP defines a proxy for the wireless device. The proxy performs as many functions as possible on behalf of the portable device and also converts media such as images and video to a form appropriate for the wireless channel. WAP also uses Web technology to define better user interfaces for standard telephony features (such as call forwarding).

**Internet Access with
Incremental Investments**

Three technologies provide a graceful path to higher bit rates for Internet access: fixed wireless networking, satellite, and the retrofitting of existing communications media (twisted pair and coax).

Fixed wireless networking uses wireless radio technology to provide service to fixed locations. The investments are more incremental; that is, a wireless transceiver need only be installed at residences actually subscribing. Direct-broadcast services (such as DirecTV) by satellite are already delivering broadband to residences for television (although they do not provide a link in the reverse direction).

The options for using existing telephone and cable television media include

- The twisted wire pair already installed for the telephone can carry much higher bit rates on the access link than voiceband data modems (which in contrast transmit data through the entire telephone network). The relevant technology is the *digital subscriber loop* (DSL). The capacity is dependent on the distance to the telephone company's central office and interference from other twisted pairs (this is called *crosstalk*—signals on different cables interfere with one another just like radio transmitters interfere with one another). Bit rates of tens of megabits per second are possible for short distances and megabits per second for longer distances.

- The CATV coax can accommodate high bit rates by displacing

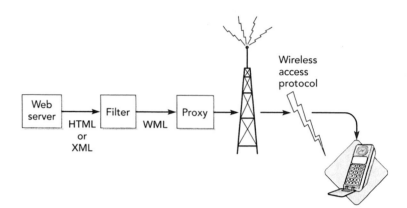

Figure 20.1 The WAP architecture for wireless Internet services to untethered information appliances

today a natural monopoly. Fortunately, several less radical technologies are available that provide considerable increases in bit rate (see the sidebar "Internet Access with Incremental Investments").

Hybrid approaches—combining existing communication media with new facilities in ways that exploit the best characteristics of both—are also promising. Examples include *fiber-to-the-curb* and *hybrid fiber/coax*, both of which exploit modern fiber-optic technologies in the shared portion of the access network (which is economically more feasible) and use existing media for per-residence access.

20.2.2   Nomadic and Untethered Internet Access

Internet access is ideally available to nomadic users, especially business travelers, as described in "Nomadic and Mobile Internet Access"on page 131. In telephony, nomadic users are supported by pay telephones and cellular roaming. Analogous services can be provided for Internet access. Today the dominant nomadic access uses voiceband data modems and the telephone. Alternatives are arising, including

- *Roaming:* This type of Internet access works worldwide using local telephone numbers. The most promising of these approaches uses third-party settlement, so that each service provider doesn't have to construct worldwide facilities (see the sidebar "Internet Roaming").
- *Wireless nomadic and mobile access:* Digital cellular telephony systems are being retrofitted to provide data services, and new wireless networks (both satellite and terrestrial) are being constructed for this purpose.

- *Broadband nomadic access:* This might be achieved using DSL technology, with a service analogous to the public telephone.

EXAMPLE: *Many nomadic users will use an information appliance rather than a complete computer to access the Internet. An example of a wireless information appliance is the Nokia 9000, pictured in Figure 20.3. In addition to standard personal digital assistant functions (calendar, address list, etc.), it includes a cellular telephone, facsimile, and Internet applications (messaging, email).*

20.2.3   IP Telephony

Just as telephony and audio conferencing can be incorporated into networked applications, the standard telephone service—using either standard phones or computer terminals—can be accommodated over the Internet. This is called *IP telephony* or *Voice over IP (VoIP)*. As illustrated in Figure 20.2, there are three cases of VoIP to consider:

- Special Internet phones (that speak IP directly) can realize a telephony application. Alternatively, one or both of these phones could be replaced by a desktop computer or information appliance (similar to the Nokia 9000 in Figure 20.3).
- A special conversion device called an *IP telephony gateway* can connect the public telephone network (PTN) to the Internet. It converts between formats and protocols used in the PTN and those of the Internet, allowing a plain old telephone (POT) to make a call to an IP telephone, that call being completed over the concatenated telephone network and Internet.
- A telephone call can be made between two POTs over the Internet using *two* gateways. This concatenates the PTN at the two endpoints with the Internet in the middle.

IP telephony phones and gateways must be interoperable. Thus, the success of IP telephony hinges on standardization, given the resulting direct network externality.

EXAMPLE: *The standard for VoIP with the greatest momentum is the International Communications Union (ITU) H.323. It is built on RTP as described in "Internet Streaming Multimedia Protocols" on page 365, and it uses bit rates from 56 Kbps down to 5.3 Kbps. RTP uses UDP for low delay, and H.323 can suffer up to 15 percent packet loss with good voice quality.*

Today IP telephony is used by corporations wishing to save on internal long-distance costs. The most effective approach is to integrate IP telephony into a company's PBXs, so that the switch can automatically choose the best option, IP

television channels (roughly 30 Mbps per TV channel). Unlike the telephone twisted pair, CATV broadcasts to a large number of homes over the same coax, so this link is multiplexed (see "Sharing Communication Links: Statistical Multiplexing" on page 494).

Both options bypass a primary disadvantage of the voiceband data modem; namely, the need to suspend access while making telephone calls. Ideally, Internet access should be continuously available.

Internet Roaming

Some ISPs provide worldwide access with a local telephone call by constructing dedicated access points or by contracting with locals to construct and operate them. Another expeditious approach—modeled after roaming in cellular telephony—uses bilateral arrangements among ISPs so each provides access to the other's customers. A third approach is to create a third-party settlement process. A third party forms an association of ISPs that collectively agree to provide service to one another's customers. Roaming customers invoke a settlement (payment from one ISP to another) by way of the association, and they are billed through their home ISP. This works very similarly to credit card settlements (in that case the association is Visa or Mastercard), or to floral delivery services.

EXAMPLE: *iPass is a third-party settlement company. Any ISP joining iPass allows its subscribers to roam worldwide, accessing the Internet with a local phone call to another ISP that is an iPass member.*

The obstacles to such an arrangement are mainly technical: A single software and protocol implementation has to work with all ISPs. IP dialtone is needed, so that no special configuration is needed to call any number of ISPs.

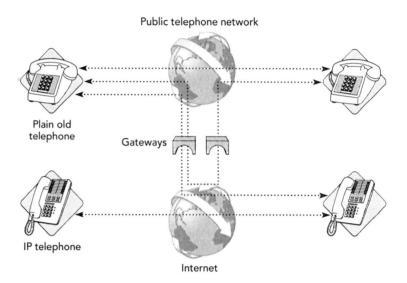

Figure 20.2 IP telephony allows telephone calls over the Internet from either standard phones or special Internet phones

Figure 20.3 The Nokia 9000 is a combination cellular phone and computer terminal in a small package

or PTN. Telephone companies are also likely to offer IP telephony to POTs customers using gateways.

20.2.4   Integrated IP Networks

Digital communication links have traditionally been shared between the Internet, PTN, and other communications networks. Since the data traffic has been a small fraction of the PTN voice traffic, this retrofitting of data on a predominantly voice network makes sense. However, data traffic is growing much faster than voice and by 2001 to 2003 should be bigger. In not too many years—as voice becomes a fraction of the total traffic—it makes more sense to carry voice on the data network. Thus, stand-alone IP data networks also providing multimedia services (including voice telephony) are likely. This should make Internet access even more common—expanding opportunities for consumer electronic commerce—and also achieve higher bit rates, improving performance for social applications such as remote conferencing.

EXAMPLE: *In a 1998 milestone, a new company—Level 3 Communications—planned on investing more than $8 billion in an international fiber-optics backbone and local IP-based network. This is the first large-scale wide area network constructed exclusively for IP.*

Discussion

D20.3 Forgetting cost for a moment, what would be the ideal mix of Internet access services for a residential user? Business user? Next discuss how the cost of such services may limit available options.

D20.4 Discuss what role government regulation might have in encouraging either nomadic or broadband Internet access.

D20.5 What do you believe would be some of the positive or negative implications of broadband access from residences on networked applications and the industry supporting them?

20.3   *Communication Links

Backbone communication links connect packet switches, and access links connect users to an access packet switch. These links carry large amounts of data as a sequence of packets (see Chapter 18). From the perspective of the network, and ultimately the application, the primary impact of a communication link is twofold: It inevitably adds latency to packet and message delivery, and occasionally, it corrupts packets by introducing bit errors. When added to the network protocol (see Chapter 18), these *impairments*—latency and packet loss—result in added message latency and reduced application performance (see Chapter 17).

Communication links deal with data with no structure or interpretation whatsoever. The link simply conveys a continuous stream of bits at a constant bit rate. The link is not even aware of the packet structure, which is both imposed and interpreted by the packet switches at each end of the link. Each bit traverses the link at the speed of light (or a large fraction thereof, depending on the medium). Each bit reaches the other end with a delay (called the *propagation delay*) equal to the distance traveled divided by that speed. This delay is one of the components of message latency, which will be considered in more detail later.

The bit rate on a communication link is *not* determined by the speed each bit traverses the link, but rather is determined by the space each bit takes up on that link. Bit rate is increased by reducing the space occupied by each bit, not increasing its propagation speed.

A N A L O G Y :   *A precise mechanical analogy to a communication link is a conveyor belt, as shown in Figure 20.4. The conveyor belt moves at a constant speed. There are two piles of wooden blocks—one with blocks painted black and representing "0" bits, the other with blocks painted white and representing "1" bits. Blocks (drawn from the appropriate pile to represent each bit) are placed on the belt at a constant rate (the bit rate). At the destination, the bit stream is recovered by noting whether each block is black or white. Since the conveyor belt moves at a constant speed, the bit rate is related to the size of the blocks; that is, the space each one takes up on the belt. The time it takes a single bit to travel the entire belt is the propagation delay, determined by the speed of the belt and its length.*

The bit rate can be increased by reducing the size of each block, but this is not the only method, as illustrated in Figure 20.5. Another is to increase the number of colors of blocks. For example, if blocks are painted four different colors rather than two, two bits are communicated with each block, which has the same impact on bit rate as making blocks half the size.

An optical-fiber communication link works the same way as the conveyor belt, except that the "blocks" in this analogy are replaced by optical pulses. Typically, in fiber optics, a "1" is communicated by transmitting a pulse of light (a white block), and a "0" is communicated by the absence of a pulse (a black block). The speed of propagation, roughly 300,000 kilometers per second, seems quite impressive when compared to the mechanical analogy. However, in relation to the high instruction rates of today's computers, it is a serious limitation, as will be seen.

A communication link has two key parameters: The bit rate B is the rate at which bits are transmitted and received on the link, and the propagation delay τ is the

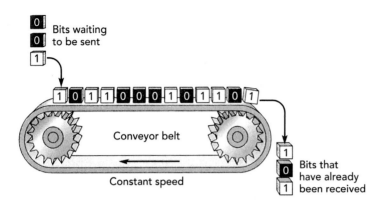

Figure 20.4 Conveyor belt analogy to a communication link

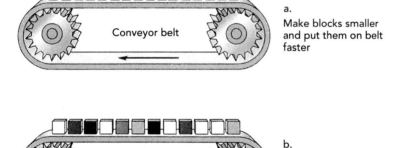

a.
Make blocks smaller and put them on belt faster

b.
Use blocks with more shades of gray (more bits per block)

Figure 20.5 The bit rate can be increased by (a) reducing the size of the blocks or (b) increasing the number of different colors

delay each bit experiences traversing the link. The product of these two parameters—the bit rate–delay product $B\tau$—is actually the most important characteristic of a link from the perspective of the application (see the sidebar "Components of Message Latency").

The bit rates that can be achieved by modern fiber-optics technologies are quite impressive (see the sidebar "Fiber Optics and Optical Networking"). Bit rates are expressed not only in kilobits and megabits per second but also in gigabits per second (Gbps) and terabits per second (Tbps). While voiceband data modems can achieve tens of kilobits per second, fiber optics is today into the tens of gigabits per second range, with commercial systems in the terabits per second range on the way shortly.

Components of Message Latency

The two components of message latency, transmission time and propagation delay, are easily quantified. If a message has m bits, then the time it takes to transmit it is m/B seconds. This equals the propagation delay τ when $m/B = \tau$ or $m = B \times \tau$; that is, the message length equals the bit rate–delay product.

The bit rate–delay product has the interpretation as the number of bits in transit on the link at any time. This follows from the observation that the number of bits transmitted on the link in time t is Bt, and thus the number of bits transmitted during the time it takes the first of those bits to reach the other end is $B \times \tau$.

Fiber Optics and Optical Networking

The premier communications media for new installations are fiber optics and wireless radio. There is also considerable interest in retrofitting legacy facilities for broadband Internet access (see "Broadband Network Access for Residences" on page 544). As in electronics and storage, advances in fiber optics have been remarkable. The capacity of a single fiber is, for all practical purposes, unlimited, but the associated electronics is a limitation that is bypassed by *wavelength division multiplexing* (WDM). Independent bit streams are carried by different wavelengths (colors of light) over the same fiber, thus vastly increasing its total capacity.

A N A L O G Y : *In the conveyor belt analogy of Figure 20.5, WDM is analogous to increasing the bit* rate by having blocks of different colors. For example, suppose there are red blocks and green blocks, and each comes with two intensities. The red blocks are put on the conveyor, and the green blocks are stacked on top of the red blocks. In effect, two independent streams of blocks are conveyed, increasing the aggregate bit rate without reducing the size of the blocks.

The total bit rate of a fiber often exceeds the needs of one packet switch. The fiber can be shared over multiple bit streams not only by WDM but also by *synchronous optical networking* (SONET), in which the bits from different bit streams are time interleaved. All bit rates carried by SONET are multiples of a basic rate, 51.84 Mbps. In SONET terminology, a bit rate of $n \times 51.84$ Mbps is called an OC-n. The highest SONET rate that has been standardized in 1998 is OC-192 (9953.28 Mbps), and commercially available systems that carry 32 OC-48 bit streams for an aggregate capacity of 79.626 Gbps are available. In the laboratory, bit rates greater than 2 Tbps over a single fiber have been demonstrated [Ram98]. This capacity is so great as to be almost inconceivable.

EXAMPLE: *The telephone network uses a bit rate of 64 Kbps to represent speech. At this rate, a 2 Tbps fiber could carry over 31 million simultaneous telephone conversations.*

Until recently, networking used optical communication links in conjunction with electronic multiplexing and switching. The next step is networks—called *optical networks*

For users at fixed locations and with the luxury of fiber-optic access, bit rates are seldom a limitation on application performance. For users in residences and those who are nomadic, bit rates remain a severe limitation.

20.3.1   Message Latency on a Link

Hosts send messages to one another using a communication link, and they care about the message latency—the time elapsing between when a message is sent and when it is received in its entirety. There are a number of contributors to message latency, including processing time in the host software infrastructure and queueing delay in packet switches. The contributor addressed here is the communication link, with two components:

- *Transmission time* is how long it takes to transmit the message on the link (analogous to the time it takes to put all the blocks composing the message on the conveyor belt).
- *Propagation delay* is the time it takes each bit in the message to traverse the link at some fraction of the speed of light (analogous to the time it takes one block to traverse the conveyor belt).

Since the transmission time depends on the size of the message, but the propagation delay doesn't, the relative importance of these two contributors to message latency depends on the message size. The crossover is when the message size equals the bit rate–delay product, where the two contributors are equal (see the sidebar "Components of Message Latency"). Thus, there are two distinct cases, as listed in Table 20.1.

EXAMPLE: *On fiber optics, bit rates of 2.5 Gbps were routinely available in 1998. The propagation delay across the United States is roughly 30 milliseconds, for a delay–bit rate product of 75 Mb. Thus, messages shorter than 75 Mb—which is quite large—are already delay limited.*

There are two important points. First, there are ways of mitigating message latency, discussed later, but distinctively different approaches are appropriate for the bit rate– or delay-limited cases. Second, as fiber-optics (and wireless) technologies advance, available bit rates increase, but propagation delay remains constant. Thus, over time all communication links become delay limited, even for very long messages. This observation has profound implications for networked computing, because as all other technology performance parameters (such as processing speed, storage size and speed, and communications bit rate) advance, speed-of-light propagation delay looms as the ultimate performance limitation.

Table 20.1 Two limitations to message latency on a communication link

Case	Condition	Analogy
Bit rate limited	For large messages (much greater than the bit rate–delay product), the dominant contributor to message latency is transmission time. Increases in bit rates due to technology advances will reduce message latency.	Using the conveyor belt, the blocks are large enough and the message long enough that the entire message does not fit on the belt, as seen in Figure 20.6. The transmission time dominates the message latency.
Propagation delay–limited	For short messages (much smaller than the bit rate–delay product), the dominant contributor to message latency is propagation delay. Further increases in bit rates will have limited impact on message latency. Unfortunately, propagation delay remains fixed, not subject to technological advance.	The blocks are small enough and the message short enough that the entire message fits on a portion of the belt at one time. The propagation delay dominates the message latency.

[Ram98]—that perform more multiplexing and switching functions in the optical domain, bypassing the speed limitations of electronics.

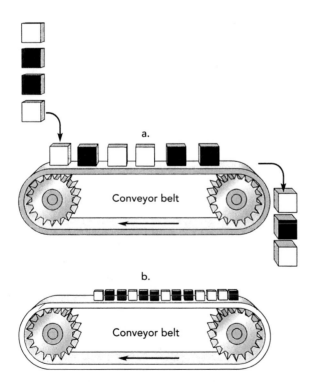

a.

Conveyor belt

b.

Conveyor belt

Figure 20.6 In the (a) bit rate–limited case, the entire message won't fit on the conveyor belt, and in the (b) delay-limited case it does

Processing and Message Latency

The speed of light is an increasingly serious limitation even *within* a computer or a single integrated circuit. For applications distributed over wide geographic areas, it is particularly important for the future.

If the propagation delay is τ, the propagation delay contribution to request/response latency is 2τ. If the processor instruction rate is P, then the number of instructions lost to message latencies is at least $2P\tau$. These are instructions that could, if a task were executing on a single host, be applied to reducing the completion time of a tightly coupled computation.

E X A M P L E :   *We will soon have processors with instruction rates of $P = 10^9$ instructions per second. For a worst-case round-trip propagation delay of 0.3 seconds, the lost instructions would be 300 million. Of course, for hosts geographically closer, the propagation delay is correspondingly smaller, but nevertheless significant.*

The distance such that propagation delay equals one processor instruction time is called the *event horizon*. This is roughly the distance over which processors can engage in really tightly coupled interactions. The distance d corresponding to the event horizon is given by

$$\frac{1}{P} = \frac{d}{c} \text{ or } d = \frac{c}{P}$$

E X A M P L E :   *For $P = 10^9$, the event horizon is about 15*

20.3.2   Impact of Message Latency on Application Performance

Because of message latency, an application should minimize tightly coupled computations, such as those that require repetitive request-response interactions between hosts, especially for geographically separated hosts (see the sidebar "Processing and Message Latency").

As fiber-optics technology continues to advance, the message transmission time decreases. This in turn reduces the time messages await access to a communication link (at fixed utilization), since it is proportional to transmission time, as described in "Modeling Congestion" on page 478. Similarly, advances in electronics technology reduce processing time and also the time waiting for processing (at fixed utilization). Thus, virtually all the performance parameters scale with technology, with one glaring exception—propagation delay, which remains fixed. Thus, the architectural techniques used in networked applications will increasingly be dominated by propagation-delay-induced message latency, rather than congestion-induced latency. Even at bit rates widely available today, the bit rate–delay product can be quite large for global distances—see Table 20.2 for some numerical examples. Some techniques for mitigating message latency where it is significant will be described shortly.

20.3.3   Why Broadband?

The popular demand for higher bit rate access to the Internet was asserted earlier, but more precisely why is this valuable? There are several motivations:

- Some applications of interest require a high sustained bit rate to meet quality objectives. A premier example is video, where achieving a perceptual quality comparable to commercial television requires sustained average bit rates in excess of 1 Mbps, and high-definition television requires bit rates more than ten times higher. A powerful application of the Internet would be higher-quality video, for example, to support remote conferencing and video broadcasting. With such a capability, the Internet might supplant not only the telephone network but also cable television, providing greater flexibility and interactivity.

- Within a given household, there may be more than one concurrent application requiring high sustained bit rates. For example, one family member may want to participate in a remote conferencing session, while another watches broadcast television. The access bit rate then has to exceed the aggregate sustained bit rates required by all these applications.

Table 20.2 Numerical examples of bit rate–delay product (number of bits in transit on a link) for representative distances and bit rates

Distance	Bit rate 28.8 Kbps	Bit rate 1.5 Mbps	Bit rate 622 Mbps
Across chip (1 cm)	$B\tau \ll 1$ bit	$B\tau \ll 1$ bit	$B\tau \ll 1$ bit
One meter	$B\tau \ll 1$ bit	$B\tau \ll 1$ bit	$B\tau = 5$ bits
Across United States	$B\tau = 891$ bits	$B\tau = 4.8$ Kbits	$B\tau = 19$ Mbits
Halfway around world	$B\tau = 4.5$ Kbits	$B\tau = 239$ Kbits	$B\tau = 96$ Mbits

centimeters (6 inches). Another order of magnitude increasing in processing rates, and the event horizon shrinks to roughly the size of a chip.

- A higher bit rate reduces the transmission time and hence message latency, accordingly. For example, the time from clicking on a Web hyperlink until viewing the requested page will be reduced as the bit rate increases. This has the most impact on large messages, for example, accommodating Web pages with high-resolution graphics and animation with fast response time.

The last point is an adequate motivation for broadband Internet access by itself. Interactive applications with rich content and fast response time may be justification enough, even if the link sits idle much of the time. Of course, the value derived by the consumer is an important input to network pricing strategies.

Discussion

D20.6 Discuss the impact on the rate of progress in the advance of human knowledge of immediate communications, such as email and the telephone, as compared to deferred (high-latency) communications (such as the postal letter) in an earlier age. Relate this to concepts in this section.

20.3.4   Mitigating Communications Bottlenecks

Communication links are often a bottleneck, whether it is the low bit rate of a voiceband modem or the substantial propagation delay of long-distance fiber optics. Fortunately, there are techniques that can mitigate these bottlenecks to some extent.

Data Caching

Suppose a client is repeatedly accessing data from a remote server, and there is an unacceptably high message latency. *Data caching* may help. As shown in Figure 20.7, the idea is elegantly simple. Each time the client accesses data, it is stored in local memory or storage (called a *data cache*). If the client accesses the

Caching Is Used in Many Circumstances

Caching is a general technique used in many contexts of computing. The operating system attempts to keep often-used data as high in the hierarchy as possible, as it can be accessed more quickly. When reference data is not in one level of cache (called a *cache miss*), it will be referred to progressively lower levels until the data is found. The performance of the computer system depends not only on the speed of processing but also on the frequency of cache misses, since a miss results in much slower data access.

Unless the hit rate is fairly high, caching can actually be harmful due to the extra time required to check the cache before accessing the data remotely. To model this, assume the fraction of hits is H, the access time for a hit is C, and the access time for a miss is $S + \Delta$, where S is the remote access time and Δ is the extra time required to first rule out the data being in the cache. The average access time is then $HC + (1 - H)(S + \Delta)$. Caching is beneficial—this average is less than the remote access time—only if the hit rate is sufficiently large.

$$H > \frac{1}{1 + \frac{S - C}{\Delta}}$$

For example, if detecting a miss takes as long as a hit, $\Delta = C$, then it is required that $H > C/S$. The closer the local and remote access times, the higher the hit ratio needed to make caching advantageous.

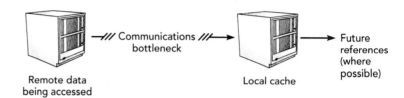

Remote data being accessed — /// Communications /// bottleneck — Local cache — Future references (where possible)

Figure 20.7 Data caching attempts to resolve data references from local storage or memory

data more than once, it can be accessed locally (without a message latency) except for the first access. Of course, in practice the cache is of finite size, so not all past accesses are stored in the cache indefinitely.

EXAMPLE: *Web browsers typically cache recently accessed pages. Not infrequently, the user will request the same page again.*

A variation on this approach uses information push. The server not only returns the particular data requested by the client, but also tries to anticipate future requests and pushes additional data as part of the response. This *predictive caching* algorithm can eliminate message latencies completely for those accesses that can be predicted.

EXAMPLE: *In a Web browser, when the user requests a certain page, it is likely that their next request will be a hyperlinked page. (The other possibility is a URL, either typed in by the user or accessed from a stored bookmark.) Thus, a predictive caching algorithm might return not only the page requested but also all hyperlinked pages. That way, if the user clicks any hyperlink on that page, the result will be available in a local cache.*

ANALOGY: *You search for information first in reference books on your desk, then in your office at work, then in your local library, and as a last resort from remote libraries. Each of these is a cache attempting to supply the information needed most often. A decision to purchase a reference book is predictive caching.*

Predictive caching depends on *data locality*. High locality means that future requests for data tend to be "near" past requests. Of course, what "near" means is open to question, but that is the essence of the design of an effective prediction algorithm.

Recall that when the message latency is bit rate limited, latency is strongly dependent on the *size* of the message. For this case, predictive caching is not as effective, since the essence of the technique is to return a lot of data even when little data is requested, increasing interactive latency. On the other hand, when the message latency is delay limited, a large reply message will not significantly impact message latency, and hence predictive caching is most valuable. In general, the predictive caching algorithm should return the largest message (most data) it can without pushing the response latency into the bit rate–limited regime.

EXAMPLE: *Since the threshold of bit rate limitation is on the order of the bit rate–delay product, ideally a predictive caching algorithm would be cognizant of this parameter. For example, for communication across the United States, the propagation delay is on the order of 25 milliseconds, and if the bit rate is 1 Gbps, the bit rate–delay product is about 26 megabits. Thus, predictive caching would want to keep messages below roughly one megabyte.*

There are several cautions about predictive caching:

- Predictive caching usually causes much more communication than necessary, since the client application may never access much of the data that is cached. This will contribute to network congestion (see Chapter 18).
- Predictive caching, and caching in general, can never improve the worst-case latency, since there will always be data requests that cannot be resolved from the cache. Caching can, however, reduce the average latency (see the sidebar "Caching Is Used in Many Circumstances"). Thus, caching provides average rather than consistent latency improvement.
- As described, a cache can only store data, not objects. Thus, remote object invocations are not subject to caching. However, we will discuss a method of caching objects shortly.

Data Compression

When message latency is bit rate limited—as is often the case today for users accessing the network by a voiceband modem or wireless link—a helpful technique is *data compression*, which reduces the number of bits required to represent the data (and thus the message size and latency). Compression removes *redundancy* from the data, which occurs when not all bit patterns occur with the same relative frequency. The trick is to ensure that the most frequent bit patterns are represented by fewer bits and the least frequent by more bits. To see how this works, see the sidebar "Data Compression Algorithms" for an example.

Lossless data compression allows the exact recovery of the original data. This type of compression is all that is available where information integrity is a foremost consideration. On the other hand, data representing media to be displayed to users—audio, images, graphics, facsimile, video, and animation—

Caching and Copyright Law

A policy issue arising in caching is the fair use of copyrighted material (see "Copyrights" on page 255). Although viewing the information is fair use (why else would the information be made available on the network?), making a permanent copy and distributing it to others would be a copyright violation. Caching is an intermediate case that is without nefarious intentions but may still be a copyright violation. This is another difficult legal question arising in the digital age.

EXAMPLE: *Current copyright law in the United States seems to make caching legal, as it says a work is protected by copyright only when it is "fixed in a tangible medium of expression, when its embodiment. . . is sufficiently permanent or stable to permit it to be perceived, reproduced, or otherwise communicated for a period of more than transitory duration." However, there is currently discussion of not permitting the "transitory fixing" of copyrighted material, which would seem to rule out caching, except with explicit permission.*

Caching creates other problems and issues. Information content suppliers want to monitor the number of accesses to their content, especially if their revenue is from advertising, but the content supplier is not aware of cache hits. It would be technically feasible, of course, to monitor access to cached content and inform the content supplier.

These problems illustrate that good technical solutions sometimes clash with business or policy issues.

Data Compression Algorithms

As an example of data compression, consider a string of ASCII characters representing text in English (or other languages). The relative frequency of the characters is consistently different. For example, the letter e occurs much more often than once in twenty-six characters and the letter z much less frequently. There are a number of ways to exploit this property to reduce the total number of bits, but without losing information.

Assume for simplicity that a string includes only e's and z's, where the former are much more frequent, and use the following encoding: code each "eeee" (sequence of four e's in a row, which are common) by "0," each single e by "10," and each z by "11." Then, for example,

zeeeezeeeeeeeeeeeeeeezz

is coded as
"11,0,11,0,0,0,10,10,11,11",

where the commas separate the characters for our convenience, but they are actually not needed (see the exercises). A straightforward coding with one bit per character requires twenty-two bits, but the code defined requires only seventeen bits. This compression is achieved by associating a short one-bit code for the most common case, which is sequences of e's. In this case, sequences of four e's require only one bit rather than four. The price paid is that all other cases, such as z or three or fewer e's, require an increase in the number of bits, from one to two. However, since these cases occur less frequently, there is a net gain.

Widely used compression algorithms are much more sophisticated than this example, as they can actually adapt to the relative frequencies in

does not have to be reproduced precisely and can suffer *lossy* compression. In this case, while the possibility of recovering the original is foregone, a "reasonable rendition" can be represented by discarding information not subjectively important to the human auditory or visual system. In contrast to lossless compression, which typically reduces the amount of data by a factor of two or three, lossy compression can typically reduce the data by 100 with good quality (see the sidebar "JPEG and MPEG").

Mobile Code

Mobile code, which was described in Chapter 16, is another response to unacceptable message latency, since it can allow computation to be moved closer to needed data (as opposed to the other way around). Alternatively, moving computation to a client improves interactivity by executing application logic locally rather than on the server. Mobile code suffers the initial delay required to transport the mobile code, which is often quite large but will become less serious as communication technology achieves higher bit rates.

Discussion

D20.7 Do you think there should be a copyright exemption for data caching as fair use of information? What are the issues?

D20.8 What do you think the business model (software licensing arrangements, etc.) should be for mobile code? Should there be a copyright exemption for fair use if mobile code is cached and discarded?

20.4   Open Issues

The communications industry is undergoing massive consolidation and change, so there are numerous contentious issues.

20.4.1   Is Communications Regulation Needed?

Traditionally, the reasons for imposing government regulation of communications have been the "natural monopoly" and the need for "universal service." Those arguments are not as compelling as they once were, and at the same time there is greater faith in the marketplace and competition and a desire on the part of both industry and government to increase the velocity of new services and technologies to the customer. Hence there is an international desire to deregulate the industry.

While this has proven successful in the United States, a couple of festering problems remain. For one, competition and universal service are largely incompatible, so providing the most advanced services such as Internet access to all citizens will be difficult, accentuating the division between haves and have-nots. For another, there has been limited success in introducing competition in residential access. It may be that there remains a natural monopoly in this part of the market, based on the large capital investments.

A major question for the future is the appropriate balance between regulation and free markets. This will strongly influence the availability of broadband services to residences and hence the ability of consumers to participate fully in the networked computing revolution. It will impact the availability of an infrastructure for opportunistic nomadic connection to the global network—the networked computer equivalent of the pay telephone. Who is going to develop, capitalize, and deploy both these infrastructures?

20.4.2   Regulation of the Internet

IP telephony raises thorny policy issues. Much of its attraction derives from the lack of regulation of IP networks. But how does a fully competitive market (IP telephony) compete against a regulated one (PTN)? Should similar regulation be extended to all telephony, regardless of the medium? That would "level the playing field" but would also subject one Internet application to regulation, but not others.

Review

Different types of network service providers—including telephone companies, cable television companies, wireless providers, and internet service providers—increasingly vie to provide networking that supports networked computing applications. They seek to provide a diversified mix of services on a global basis and to provide multimedia and wireless services. There is also a global trend toward deregulation, with the regulators focusing on insuring competition and concentrating on issues such as universal service and wireless spectrum allocation.

Major issues for the future of the Internet include broadband residential access, wireless mobile and nomadic access (including broadband), and the relationship to the public telephone network.

Communication links transport a fixed bit rate with a speed-of-light propagation delay. Like electronics, the underlying communications technologies are rapidly advancing. Fiber optics can provide virtually unlimited bit rates, but wireless and cable access provide much lower bit rates. An important parameter of a link—the bit rate–delay product—has the interpretation as the message length that separates the bit rate–limited and delay-limited regimes.

the data, typically reducing the number of bits representing data by a factor of two to three. A common adaptive compression algorithm is Lempel-Ziv. In simplified form, Lempel-Ziv keeps track of the last n bytes of data, and when a particular sequence of bytes (called a "phrase") is encountered that has already been seen, it outputs a pair of values corresponding to the *position* of the phrase in the previously seen data, and the *length* of the phrase. Thus, when certain sequences of bytes occur more commonly, they tend to have been seen previously, and position information is substituted for the actual data.

JPEG and MPEG

Images and video can be substantially compressed. The structure of image data—discussed in "Multimedia Transport" on page 358—consists of a rectangular array of *pixels* (picture elements), each represented by a data value. As in the character string example in the sidebar "Data Compression Algorithms," redundancy in the pixel values can be exploited in compression. For example, the pixels in proximity to one another may typically have similar values. Video is composed of a sequence of images, each called a *frame* (one every 1/10 of a second for video conferencing to 1/30 of a second for broadcast television). The array of pixels in each frame is called the *spatial* dimension, and the progression of the same pixel in successive frames is called the *temporal* dimension. Compression in the spatial dimension is similar to compression of an image. In the temporal dimension, the pixels at the same spatial location in successive frames typically have similar values, allowing further compression.

The Joint Picture Experts Group (JPEG) and Motion Picture Experts Group (MPEG) are both standardization efforts under the auspices of ISO (see "International Organization for Standards (ISO)" on page 218). JPEG is the most commonly used compression algorithm for images, and MPEG is for video. MPEG is not only used in networked computing, but has also become the standard video encoding for digital television in the United States. Both standards can be configured to different compression ratios, which of course affect the quality. MPEG includes many system features as well as compression.

MPEG is an excellent illustration of standardization as a collaborative design process. No single company would possess the range of expertise necessary to set the requirements for or design MPEG. The MPEG standardization committee designed many new algorithms, rather than simply specifying existing algorithms.

All performance factors in computing and communications improve rapidly with technological advance. An exception is the speed-of-light propagation delay, which therefore looms as a major limitation to computing, particularly networked computing. In particular, message latencies become delay limited and thus virtually immutable for all but the shortest distances and largest messages.

Application techniques for mitigating communications-induced message latencies include (in the bit rate–limited regime) compression and historical caching and (in the delay-limited regime) predictive caching. Mobile code can improve interactive delay in the presence of communications bottlenecks. Compression removes data redundancy to reduce the number of bits in a data representation without losing information. For audio or video, compression can also remove perceptually unimportant information, achieving much higher compression ratios.

Key Concepts

Network service providers:

- Broadband residential access
- Nomadic and mobile access
- IP telephony and Voice over IP (VoIP)

Communications media:

- Fiber optics, wireless radio, telephone wire pair, coaxial cable

Communication links:

- Bit rate and propagation delay
- Bit rate–delay product

Message latency:

- Bit rate versus delay limited
- Compression, caching, and mobile code

Further Reading

A general textbook on digital communication is [Lee94]. [Per85] gives a good background on fiber-optics technology, and [Ram98] is a comprehensive textbook on optical networks. [Abe97] gives a thorough treatment of broadband access, including technical, business, and economic aspects. [CST97a] gives a good background of the history, applications, and technology of wireless communications, and [Rap96] and [Pah95] give excellent coverage of the technology of wireless communications.

Exercises

E20.1 Compare the network service provisioning and customer service challenges of the wireline ISP and wireless ISP service providers. What challenges are similar, and what challenges are distinctly different?

E20.2 Discuss the relative importance of high availability for telephony, cable television, and internet service. What challenges in terms of achieving the necessary availability will a service provider in one domain have when moving to a different domain?

E20.3 A problem with voiceband data modem access to the Internet is the preemption of telephone service. Discuss the importance of full-time availability of Internet access. For what types of applications is it important, and not important?

E20.4 Describe how the following two methods of connecting to the Internet work, without getting into much detail. Then compare them: What are the advantages and disadvantages of each?

    a. Using a voiceband data modem to call an internet service provider (ISP).

    b. Using a direct broadband Internet access link provided by your cable television provider.

E20.5 A number of telephone operating companies and cable television companies have held trials of proprietary content information-on-demand systems. The trials have generally not been considered successful. Discuss the pros and cons of the following proposition: Internet access will be a more profitable business than proprietary content information on demand.

E20.6 Discuss the relative merits of wireless and tethered broadband nomadic access to the Internet for traveling businesspersons. Is wireless important?

E20.7 Give three examples from your personal life in which VoIP might offer significant advantages, other than just cost.

E20.8 For the conveyor belt mechanical analogy to a communication link, assume that a block (conveying one bit) is 1 meter long, the speed of the conveyor is a constant 100 kilometers per hour, and the length of the belt is 50 kilometers.

    a. What is the number of blocks per second passing any point along the belt?

b. What is the time spent on the belt by each block?

c. If a message has 50 blocks, what is the time it takes to put the entire message on the conveyor?

d. For a 50-block message, what range of block sizes is the message latency dominated by the transmit time?

E20.9   For a fiber-optics link, the propagation speed is 2×10^8 meters per second, and each bit in transit occupies 3 meters. What is the bit rate?

E20.10   You find that at least some Web pages are taking too long to access and view on your home PC.

a. What things that are under your control (PC, modem, ISP, software, etc.) could be causing problems? For each one, what could you do about it?

b. What possible problems could there be that are essentially outside your control?

c. What experiments could you do to figure out exactly what the problems are?

E20.11   For which of the following situations is the communication link message latency bit rate limited, and for which is it propagation delay limited?

a. Bit rate 28.8 Kbps, delay 40 milliseconds, message size 1,000 bytes

b. Bit rate 28.8 Kbps, delay 40 milliseconds, message size 40 bytes

c. Bit rate 45 Mbps, delay 10 milliseconds, message size 900 kilobytes

d. Same as c, except you are downloading a class (program code) that is 1.4 megabytes in size.

E20.12   A packet size, and hence packet latency, is dependent on the packet header overhead (see Exercise 19.9).

a. What is that dependency between packet header overhead and packet latency?

b. What is the direct dependency between network congestion and packet header overhead? Keep the application data communication requirements fixed.

c. Following from a and b, what is the relationship between network congestion and packet latency? This is not referring to queueing delay, which forms another relationship.

E20.13 Consider a task performed *repetitively* as a cooperation between two hosts, where the *throughput* is the appropriate measure. Consider how the task is split between the two hosts.

   a. Under what conditions on the communications pattern in a task does communication latency significantly reduce the task throughput?

   b. Under what conditions does communication latency have little impact on the task throughput?

E20.14 Considering the efficacy of predictive caching:

   a. Give two examples of applications where this will work effectively.

   b. Give two examples where it will offer little or no advantage.

E20.15 For the compression algorithm illustrated in "Data Compression Algorithms" on page 558:

   a. Code the character string "zezeezeeezeeeezeeeeez."

   b. Why is it possible to decode the characters e and z uniquely without the need for commas as a delimiter between characters?

E20.16 Design a compression algorithm similar to that described in "Data Compression Algorithms" on page 558 for the following situation: There are known to be three characters in the source, e, s, and v, where e's are far more common than s's, which are far more common than v's.

E20.17 Which of the following video sources do you think could be more successfully compressed, and why?

   a. A football game

   b. A surveillance camera in a barber shop

   c. A video conference

E20.18 Java mobile code allows application functionality to run in a Web browser with faster response time. Give three examples of specific applications for which this may prove quite valuable.

E20.19 For an Internet telephony application, describe any implementation or performance issues that would have to be overcome when layering on each of the following protocols, and state the reasons:

   a. TCP/IP

   b. UDP/IP

   c. Which of *a* or *b* would you prefer, and why?

E20.20 The analysis of caching efficiency in "Caching Is Used in Many Circumstances" on page 556 did not take into account the greater message size required for predictive caching. Develop a small model for this phenomenon as follows: Assume that predictive caching increases the average message size m on a communication link with bit rate–delay product $B\tau$ by a factor of k, and as a result the cache hit rate is H. The access time for a cache hit is assumed to be zero, and for a miss it is assumed to be the communications message latency.

    a. What is the average access time, taking into account both cache and remote accesses? Under what conditions is caching beneficial?

    b. In the bit rate–limited regime, what hit rate has to be achieved to make caching beneficial? Interpret this result intuitively.

    c. Repeat b for the delay-limited regime.

E20.21 As described in the chapter, predictive caching put the requested information and the predictive information in the same message for transport to the requester.

    a. Give an alternative strategy that does not change the prediction algorithm, but performs better.

    b. Repeat the modeling of Exercise 20.20 for the alternative strategy in a, and analyze the results.

Glossary

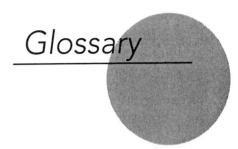

abort One of two possible outcomes of a transaction, the other being a commit. It indicates a failure, and all resources are rolled back to the initial durable state.

abstraction Hiding irrelevant detail at the interface to a subsystem in order to manage system complexity and enhance flexibility.

access control In computer security, a limitation on which users or hosts can access a particular host or application resource.

ACID properties Describes four important properties of a transaction, including atomicity, consistency, isolation, and durability.

action At an interface, a behavior that is promised by a subsystem, customized by parameter data and with returned data. In object-oriented programming, an action is called a method.

address Data representing the physical, geographical, or topological location of something, or from which that location can be inferred. For example, the address of a host is used by the network to forward a packet and is often obtained from a name server.

administration The ownership and operation of an application and associated computing infrastructure.

advertising An information push model in which information about a product or service from a third party is offered by an information or service provider in return for payment. Networked computing allows advertising to be customized to the viewer, thus enhancing its value.

agent A mobile agent with additional properties, including autonomy, interaction, reactivity, and proactivity.

algorithm A specified sequence of steps designed to accomplish a specific task in a finite number of steps.

analog Describes the representation of information by some continuous physical property, such as air pressure for sound or paint in a work of art. As distinct from digital.

antitrust Government-imposed restrictions on business practices deemed anticompetitive, particularly aimed at preventing or mitigating the anticompetitive effects of monopolies.

application Computer software that performs useful capabilities for a user or organization, incorporating the storage, manipulation, and communication of information.

application logic The portion of the application, distinct from the presentation and the shared data, that constitutes the assumptions and operations that define application functionality.

architecture Decomposition of a system into subsystems, including a definition of the functionality of each subsystem and its interaction.

assembly In software development, integrating existing components to compose a system. The opposite of decomposition.

asymmetric encryption An encryption protocol in which two complementary keys are required, one for encryption and the other for decryption. For confidentiality, the encryption key can be made public, but the decryption is secret and known only by the recipient. Also called public key encryption.

asynchronous transfer mode (ATM) A packet networking technology based on fixed-length packets (called cells) and emphasizing QoS guarantees.

atomic Cannot be split into constituent parts and yet retain its utility.

attribute Referring to a software object or component, data representing an observable and changeable property.

authentication In security, obtaining assurance of the identity of a user (or other entity, such as a host). It requires a trusted authority to confirm some credential (such as a secret or physical characteristic) offered by the user.

authority In security, some entity that is trusted and can provide assistance. A digital certificate authority, for example, confirms an association between a user's identity and his public key for asymmetric encryption.

autonomous publisher A publisher that chooses what information is supplied to a user, or when it is provided, or both. The opposite of interactive information access, where the user retains control of content and timing.

availability A metric or reliability specifying the fraction of time an application is running correctly.

awareness	Property of an application that autonomously notifies the user of newly available information or some event of interest. Usually associated with a subscription by the user to that notification.
batch processing	A style of noninteractive processing in which a task is completed in its entirety before any results are made available. Often associated with centralized computing.
best effort	Applied to the completion time of a task, the latency of a message, or the reliability with which a message is delivered, the absence of any guarantees. The infrastructure simply promises to do its best consistent with available resources and fairness to competing demands.
binding	An artificial linkage between two or more entities.
biometrics	In security, authentication based on some physical characteristic of the user, such as fingerprint or pattern of the iris of the eye.
bit	Short for "binary digit," an atomic piece of data assuming the value "0" or "1." It is the basis of computer-mediated information.
bit rate	The rate at which bits are conveyed by a communication link. In networking, sometimes called bandwidth.
bit rate–limited latency	For long messages, the condition in which the message latency is dominated by the transmission time on a communication link.
blocking	A condition of one object that has invoked a method of another object and is awaiting a response (including returns) before it can resume processing.
broadband	The telephone industry name for access links with high bit rate, generally exceeding 1 to 10 Mbps.
broadcast	A communication service in which identical replicas of data are sent to multiple recipients. In social applications, a publication-immediate style in which multiple users are provided the same information—an immediate version of mass publication.
browse	Interactive information access, looking for nonspecific but useful or entertaining information.
business application	An application serving business purposes, including commerce.
business logistics	In electronic commerce, an inter-enterprise application that coordinates material flows, finished goods, services, and workers.

business process   A collection of related activities, including everything from acquiring resources to delivering a product or service to customers. It is repetitive and spans multiple departments, and sometimes also suppliers or customers.

business process reengineering   *See* business transformation.

business transformation   Also called business process reengineering, the systematic design of a business process to include networked applications, workers, and interface between them.

C++   A commonly used object-oriented programming language.

cable television (CATV)   A class of communications service providers originally focused on broadcast video, but more recently diversifying to video on demand, Internet access, and telephony.

caching   The temporary local storage of data so that it can be accessed without network latency.

centralized computing   An early computing model in which a relatively few mainframes run batch programs.

challenge-response   In security, a protocol for authentication in which one entity challenges another entity to prove that it possesses a secret, but without revealing that secret.

citizenry   The totality of users sharing a network and available to participate in social applications.

class   In object-oriented programming, what is in common among a set of objects with identical functionality and implementation, but with distinct attributes. In practice, it includes the interface specification and implementation.

client   An entity that performs its function by making requests of entities called servers. A client initiates requests and need not be available at all times. Applied to desktop computers providing a user interface and also to an object in the process of invoking the method of another object.

client-server   A networked computing equipment architecture in which hosts are specialized to client and server functionality.

collaboration style   Describes social applications allowing users in a group to coordinate their activities or shared resources.

collaborative authoring	A direct style (immediate or deferred) of social application that supports a work group cooperating to author a document.
commercial off-the-shelf (COTS)	A product (equipment or software) purchased and integrated into an application, rather than custom designed and built.
commit	One of two possible outcomes of a transaction, the other being an abort. It indicates a successful completion.
communication link	A communication channel that conveys a string of bits from one geographic location to another (usually in both directions) using radio, fiber, cable, or wires. A physical analogy is the conveyor belt.
communication style	Describes social applications allowing users in a group to share information.
complexity	The property of a system that has many subsystems interacting in complicated ways, such that the system operation is difficult to understand by an individual or small group.
component	A subsystem that is accepted as is and integrated into a system. Often components are purchased from outside vendors.
component-oriented programming (COP)	In software development, a programming methodology based on assembly and integration of software components. COP requires a component supply industry, programming tools, and standardization of component interfaces.
compression	An algorithm that reduces the number of bits required to represent information by throwing away information insignificant to the human visual or aural system, or by exploiting redundancy—the uneven frequency of occurrence of distinct bit patterns. Can mitigate inadequate storage or communication bit rates.
computer	Equipment that executes programs, allowing them to store, manipulate, and communicate information under software program control.
concurrency	When the processing of two or more tasks or communication of two or more messages overlap in time.
confidentiality	A property of communicated or stored data that it is unintelligible to someone viewing it. Typically achieved by encryption.
congestion	Applied to task processing or communications where demands fluctuate with time, temporary oversubscription of the processing or communication resource resulting in an increase in task completion time or message latency.

congestion control   In networking, the avoidance of congestion by artificially reducing total originating traffic.

congestion pricing   For a network service (or other shared resource, such as server capacity), a component of price based on the aggregate usage with the goal of reducing excess demand and paying for a needed expansion of facilities.

connection   A specific and static route through a network topology from one host to another. The Internet does not provide connections, but the telephone network does.

consumer electronic commerce   Electronic commerce involving the citizenry.

content   Specific information that is sold as a good.

convergence   Applied to industries, when two industries that were once independent become, for the first time, strongly complementary or competitive or both.

conversation   A generic communication service that supports the repeated back-and-forth interaction of two entities.

copy   Make a reasonable but not exact rendition of an original work. Information represented in analog media can only be copied, not replicated.

copyright   Government-sanctioned property rights for the expression of ideas in an authored work (such as information or a software program). It does not prevent others from independently creating a similar work based on the same facts or ideas.

CORBA   An industry standard for distributed object management; stands for "common object request broker architecture."

critical mass   For a product or service with network effects, when the number of adopters increases to the point that the value of the product or service exceeds the supplier or service provider cost so that the market size can increase without subsidy.

cyberspace   Within a wide area network, such as the Internet, the public place where the citizenry accesses information and interacts without regard to geographic distance.

data   A collection of bits representing information.

Data Encryption Standard (DES)   A standard for symmetrical encryption and commonly used in commerce.

data mining A type of application that processes massive amounts of data using statistical tools looking for unexpected and useful patterns pointing to commercial opportunity.

data type A description of the structure and interpretation of data specifying the range of values represented and a set of allowable manipulations. Simple examples are `Float` and `Character`.

data warehouse A large nonoperational database aiding decision support, and acquired by consolidating and archiving information from multiple operational databases.

database A file containing data with a specific structure. The relational database structures the data into tables with rows and columns.

database management system (DBMS) A large-grain software component that manages the storage, processing, and retrieval of information from one or more databases. Functions include data integrity, access control, and many others.

datagram Describes a message sharing no context with other messages.

de facto standard A standard that arises from market dominance rather than a formal standards-setting process.

de jure standard A standard that is mandated, as by government policy.

decentralized computing A computing model in which inexpensive personal computers are dedicated to single users, but are not yet networked.

decision support Describes business applications supplying consolidated information about operations and aiding management decisions.

declarative language Describing a programming language that expresses directly the abstractions of an application domain, as distinct from an imperative language.

decomposition The partitioning of a system into cooperating subsystems that interact to realize higher system functionality.

deferred style Describes social applications in which users can interact without having to participate at the same time.

delay-limited latency For short messages, the condition in which the message latency is dominated by the propagation delay. As technology advances, all communication links become delay limited.

departmental application A business application primarily serving one functional department, such as accounting, human resources, or manufacturing.

deployment   Everything required to bring a developed and tested application into operation, including installation and testing of infrastructure, installation of software, training of workers, and import of legacy data.

desktop computer   A personal computer or workstation accessed by a single user and used for running personal productivity applications and for the presentation aspect of networked applications. The client in the client-server architecture.

digital   Describes the representation of information by entities that are discrete and finite, such as data (a given number of bits) or text (a given number of characters). As distinct from analog.

digital cash   Data representing monetary value—functionally similar to cash in a wallet—that can be used to make payments in person or over the network.

digital certificate   In security, a message with integrity and nonrepudiation and provided by a trusted authority that authenticates the association of a user identity and that user's public asymmetrical encryption key. Others can use it to authenticate and communicate confidentially with that user.

digital library   A large well-organized and well-indexed repository of information available for access over the network.

digital signature   In security, data added to a message that assures its integrity and authenticates its source. It is the foundation of nonrepudiation.

direct style   Describes social applications in which users communicate directly with other users whose identity is known to them.

discussion forum   A publication style of social application that supports discussion and brainstorming among members of an interest group. The newsgroup and listserver are deferred versions, and the chatroom is an immediate version.

distributed object management   Middleware that allows objects to interact using remote method invocations across distributed hosts, and provides many other functions.

distributed system   A system that incorporates two or more hosts communicating with one another. A distributed application is synonymous with a networked application.

diversification   The business strategy of a company that accumulates a portfolio of distinct products across industry segments.

document   A form of structured data, typically containing text, images, video, and audio, that is self-contained and suited to capturing or presenting information and knowledge to users.

domain name
A name associated with a particular host that is easy for users to remember and has a hierarchical structure reflecting administrative responsibility.

domain name system (DNS)
A name service provided by an internet that accepts a host domain name and returns an IP address.

electronic commerce
Describes an application supporting the order of and payment for goods and services between suppliers and customers, whether they be enterprises or individual consumers.

electronic data interchange (EDI)
Describes electronic commerce applications allowing businesses to electronically exchange information in standard business documents.

electronic money management
In electronic commerce, reducing transaction costs by making or authorizing payments over the network.

embedded computing
A computing model in which processors are built into everyday products, giving them added software-defined features and sophistication.

emergence
Additional capability and functionality of a system not provided directly by subsystems, but resulting from the interaction of subsystems. Also describes undesirable and unanticipated behavior resulting from the complex interaction of subsystems.

encapsulation
Subsystem implementation details hidden and inaccessible from the interface. Encapsulation enforces abstractions and enables implementation details to be modified without affecting interoperability with other subsystems.

encryption
An algorithm transforming data and an encryption key into a form unintelligible to anyone without a complementary decryption key. The original data can be recovered using a decryption algorithm and decryption key.

enterprise
A unit of economic organization and activity with a common ownership and management, such as a company or a university.

enterprise application
Describes a business application supporting a business process spanning multiple functional departments.

enterprise resource planning (ERP)
A packaged application serving a business process that is reasonably standardized across different organizations, yet configurable and extendable to meet the needs of individual enterprises.

equipment
A component included in the infrastructure that typically incorporates integrated hardware and software. Examples are a computer or packet switch.

event   An external occurrence beyond control. A user or application may subscribe to notification of a specific event.

Extensible Markup Language (XML)   A markup language expected to replace HTML in representing documents on the Web. Unlike HTML, it stresses document structure as well as formatting.

extranet   An extension of an intranet across the public Internet using security tools to insure confidentiality and authentication.

fat client   A partitioning of an application that includes relatively more functionality in a client host. The opposite of a thin client.

fault tolerance   The ability of an application to continue to run correctly even during and after equipment failure.

fiber optics   A communications medium using pulses of light guided through a cylindrical glass strand to represent bits.

file   Data named and stored as a unit for the benefit of some application.

file system   A service of an operating system that stores and manages files stored hierarchically in folders or directories, together with an associated hierarchical file naming convention.

firewall   Equipment imposed on communication links into and out of an intranet and enforcing security policies, thereby creating a protected enclave.

flow control   In networking, control of the rate at which a sender communicates data to match the rate a recipient is able to consume it.

flowchart   A visual representation of an algorithm using interconnected blocks.

format   The manner in which a document is displayed to the user. Also, a specification of the structure and interpretation of data contained in a message.

framework   A reusable architecture for a software application, often accommodating modification and extension.

goods   In economics, items that are bought and sold. Information goods and software goods are emphasized in this book.

granularity   A property of an architecture that defines the number of subsystems and the range of functionality of each. Granularity can range from coarse (few large subsystems) to fine (many small subsystems). Hierarchy supports multiple granularities in the same system.

groupware A collection of social applications that support the activities of work groups.

hardware The electronics and remaining physical embodiment—as distinct from software—that make up a piece of equipment.

hierarchy A decomposition in which subsystems are themselves decomposed into subsystems, enabling a system to be viewed at different granularities. Also describes naming schemes (such as file names and Internet domain names) that locate entities through a series of smaller physical or logical groupings.

host Computer connected to the Internet or other network and having a single address.

hyperlink An association between a document and the address of another document containing related information. In the Web, a hyperlink is indicated by a special formatting, where the user can access the associated document by clicking with a mouse.

Hypertext Markup Language (HTML) The first markup language representing documents on the Web, focused on presentation (formatting and display) rather than document structure.

IIOP Part of the CORBA standard, a protocol layered on the internet protocols supporting interoperability of distributed objects and remote method invocations; stands for "Internet Inter-ORB Protocol."

immediate style Describes social applications in which users must participate at the same time.

imperative language Describes a programming language that expresses direction operations to be performed by the computer, as distinct from declarative language.

implementation The concrete realization of functionality embodied in a hardware and/or software design.

index A list of topics or terms, with associated hyperlinks or references to information or documents pertaining to those topics or terms.

information Applied to people, it is patterns or meaning in data that affect their perspective, understanding, or behavior. In the infrastructure, it is structure and interpretation attached to data, usually added in an infrastructure layer or application.

information appliance A device providing a single packaged application, often small, portable, battery operated, and with wireless network access.

information management	Describes the organized storage, access, and manipulation of large repositories of information.
information systems department	A department within an enterprise with primary responsibility for acquiring, deploying, and operating a networked computing infrastructure and applications.
information technology	Technology is the application of scientific principles to human needs. Information technologies store, communicate, and manipulate information, and include computers, peripherals, storage devices, the network, and software.
infrastructure	Equipment and software provided for the benefit of many applications.
instance	In object-oriented programming, each object belonging to a particular class is an instance of that class. A class can have many instances.
integrated	In an infrastructure layer or network, the property of being able to accommodate all media required to support a variety of applications.
integrated infrastructure	Infrastructure specifically designed to support a variety of media—such as audio, video, and documents—and multimedia applications.
integration	In software development, arranging for modules or components to interoperate once they have been individually implemented and tested.
integrity	In security, it is the assurance that a message or file hasn't been modified since it was created by an authenticated entity. Applied to data, it is the preservation of its completeness and accuracy following communication or processing.
intellectual property	Information or ideas with commercial value for which the government has granted exclusive property rights, including copyright, patent, trademark, and trade secret.
interaction	Cooperative behavior of subsystems to achieve some higher purpose. Usually it takes the form of one subsystem invoking predefined actions of other modules.
interaction diagram	A visual representation of a protocol illustrating the time sequence of messages among interacting entities.
interactive	Describes applications in which the user has frequent opportunities to direct or inform. The opposite of batch processing.
interest group	A group of users sharing a common interest in a discipline, hobby, profession, or political goal.

interface	The external view presented by a subsystem, carefully designed and well documented. It defines how other subsystems can interact with it and informs the implementer of promises made to other subsystems.
interface definition language (IDL)	A language specialized for describing the interfaces of objects.
internet	A network consisting of interconnected subnetworks (in practice, a wide area network interconnecting local area networks). Also refers to a set of de facto standards for both networking protocols and applications. The (uppercase) Internet is a global public internet.
internet protocol (IP)	The lowest-layer protocol in the internet that allows subnetworks to be networked. IP is often synonymous with an internet, as in "IP telephony."
Internet service provider (ISP)	A communications service provider specializing in access to the Internet.
interoperable	Describes two subsystems or modules that successfully interact to achieve some higher purpose.
interpretation	Attaching significance to structured data in some application context.
intranet	A private network constructed for the exclusive use of an enterprise using the internet architecture, standards, equipment, and applications.
invocation	Applied to an action or method at a subsystem interface, causing that action or method to be executed, customized by supplied parameters.
Java	A commonly used object-oriented programming language and middleware environment for mobile code.
JPEG	An internationally standardized data representation for images employing compression to reduce storage and communication requirements.
key	In security, data required to encrypt or decrypt a message.
knowledge	Applied to people, it is concepts, relationships, truth, or principles derived from a large body of information. Applied to networked computing, it describes a large repository of information that is well organized to inform users.
latency	The time elapsed from creation of a message or packet to reception in its entirety. It is an important performance metric of the network.

layering	A specific architecture in which ordered subsystems interact only with their nearest neighbors. Used in the networked computing infrastructure, in which each layer makes use of the services of the layer below, adds elaboration or specialization, and provides services to the layer above.
legacy	Describes an application or infrastructure using obsolete technology but remaining operational.
license	A granting of a right to make, use, or sell products incorporating intellectual property, often in exchange for a fee or royalty.
lifecycle	Referring to networked applications, the stages in their acquisition and operation, including conceptualization, analysis, architecture, implementation, testing and evaluation, deployment, operations, maintenance, and upgrade.
limit pricing	For a product or service with large supply economies of scale, a price low enough to discourage competitive products or services, taking into account a competitor's high creation cost.
link	*See* communication link.
load balancing	Where concurrent tasks are assigned to different hosts, the utilization of each host is approximately equal.
local area network (LAN)	A network connecting hosts within a building or campus.
local-exchange carrier (LEC)	A communications service provider specializing in local telephone service.
lock-in	For a supplier or consumer, the obstacle to adopting or providing new products or services arising from tangible and intangible costs of switching.
mainframe computer	A physically large, high-performance, and expensive computer, used by large organizations to run mission-critical applications requiring reliability and security and managing large amounts of data.
markup language	A language specialized for representing the structure and formatting of documents; especially valuable in exchanging documents among applications and across heterogeneous computing platforms.
mass customization	The tailoring of a product or service to each customer, usually dependent in part on an enterprise application.
mass publication	Describes a publication-deferred style of social application in which identical information is made available to a group of users. An example is the Web. An immediate version is broadcast.

medium or media	In digital information, a reference to a particular type of information, such as a document, numbers, audio, or video. In communications, the physical channel, such as wire pair, coaxial cable, fiber optics, or radio.
message	An atomic unit of information sent from one user to another, or from one module to another, to inform or direct. There is one sender, but there may be more than one (or even an indeterminate set of) recipients. Also describes a generic communication service that allows one module to send a message to another.
message with reply	A generic communication service in which one module sends a message to another and receives an immediate shared-context reply.
message-oriented middleware (MOM)	A middleware category that supports sophisticated messaging services with multiplexing and queueing.
metadata	A description of information content such as a document or image, most often conveying information that is not easily extracted from the data itself (such as human judgement regarding the information).
method	For an object, an action the object is prepared to perform, customized by parameters and with returns.
middleware	A software infrastructure layer that falls between the operating system and application. There are two distinct types, supporting storage and communications. Distinct middleware solutions support different application categories.
mobile	Referring to users who may access the network while in motion, as in a moving vehicle.
mobile code	A program that can be opportunistically transported to a host for immediate execution there. Mobile code must be supported by an appropriate infrastructure.
mobile computing	A computing model in which networked computers can be taken anywhere—including moving vehicles—without losing networking connectivity.
mobile object	Mobile code describing a class, together with object instance data, effectively allowing an object to be mobile. Sometimes used for searching through multiple information repositories.
modeling	Using a system of mathematical postulates, data, and inferences to imitate or emulate a physical or logical entity and predict its behavior. Unlike representation, modeling does not substitute for that entity.
modeling object	In object-oriented programming, an object that models a real-world object, attempting to predict its behavior for purposes of interaction or control.

modularity	A system architecture with desirable properties, such as separation of concerns, interoperability, and reusability. A subsystem in such an architecture is called a module.
MPEG	An internationally standardized data representation for video employing compression to reduce storage and communication requirements.
multicast	In networking, a realization of broadcast services in which the network internally replicates data and forwards it to multiple recipients. An alternative to simulcast.
multimedia	The combination of information from different media (text, images, video, audio, etc.) within the same document, social application, or infrastructure.
multiple access	Two or more hosts communicating by a shared broadcast medium. Examples are Ethernet and wireless access.
multiplexing	A service allowing a recipient to receive messages from multiple senders. Necessarily combined with queueing, since two messages can arrive simultaneously.
multitasking	A feature of modern operating systems that supports concurrent tasks in a single host through time-slicing.
name	A symbolic representation of an entity, such as a user, a host, a module, or an object. A name is normally chosen to be easy for people to remember or guess. Naming conventions are often hierarchical.
name service	A service that provides an address associated with a name. In the network, users and applications use names, but the network requires an address to route packets to a host or application.
navigate	Follow a prescribed route to finding specific information.
network	Collection of equipment that allows one computer to communicate with another, incorporating switches connected by communication links.
network computer (NC)	An ultrathin client host. Often it does not host application programs, but provides only the user interface.
network effect or externality	Applied to products and services, when their value to the consumer depends on the number of other consumers who have adopted the same product or service. The value may increase (as in a social application) or decrease (as in congestion) with more adoptions.
networked application	A computer application that is distributed across two or more hosts communicating over a network.

networked computer	Any computer connected to a network (same as a host).
networked computing	A computing model in which hosts—including possibly mainframes, servers, and desktop computers—are connected to a network and execute networked applications.
nomadic	Refers to users who may access the network from many geographic locations.
nonrepudiation	In security, the ability to prove (in court if necessary) that a message has integrity and was created by an authenticated user.
notification	Describes an application autonomously informing a user about external events.
object	In software, the smallest unit of modularity in a program, consisting of an interface and an implementation.
object database (ODBMS)	A database that adds persistence to objects, supporting complex data structures and avoiding the use of SQL.
object-oriented programming (OOP)	A programming methodology based on decomposition of an application into interacting objects. OOP is supported by OOP languages such as C++ and Java and various development tools.
object-relational database (ORDBMS)	A relational database with extensions allowing it to manage complex data types and objects as table entries, and continuing to use SQL for access.
on-line analytical processing (OLAP)	An application providing—usually for decision support—multidimensional views into a relational database.
on-line transaction processing (OLTP)	A departmental application supporting human agents gathering and disseminating business information.
open standard	A standard that is well documented, unencumbered by intellectual property rights and restrictions, and available for any vendor to implement.
open system	A system that outside vendors are free to enhance and append because it is based on open standards.
operating system (OS)	A layer of software infrastructure between the processing, storage, and communications infrastructure and the application that performs a number of functions, including abstraction of the equipment infrastructure, management of resources, and support for concurrency.
optical networking	A networking technology in which light is switched, avoiding slower electronics.

packet	A unit of data transported across a packet network, including a header (with recipient address and other information used by the network itself) and payload (message or fragment of a message transported on behalf of the application).
packet encapsulation	Carrying one packet (header plus payload) as the payload of another packet. The foundation of layered network protocols.
packet forwarding	In packet switches, the determination of an output link based on each packet header and a stored routing table.
packet fragmentation	Splitting one packet into a set of smaller packets, which can be conveyed by a lower-layer protocol and reassembled. A technique for bypassing packet length policies.
password	A secret string of numbers and characters that a user commits to memory and is available to authenticate him or her.
patent	Government-sanctioned property rights for an invention (an idea that is useful and novel).
path dependence	In economics, the condition in which market forces are constrained by past history or investments and factors such as network effects and lock-in.
peer-to-peer	An architecture in which peers deal directly with one another symmetrically, as equals. Distinct from client-server, where a client initiates and a server responds.
performance	Quantitative measures of operation, such as speed of processing repetitive tasks or the completion time of a single task.
persistence	Describes data that outlives the application that created it. Often, mission-critical business data must persist for decades, and persistence is an important capability of databases.
personal computer	A desktop computer suitable for less computationally intensive tasks.
pipelining	A form of concurrency in which throughput is increased by dividing a task into subtasks called stages and dedicating different hosts to each stage.
platform	A particular computing environment, including a microprocessor instruction set and computer architecture and operating system. Partitioning a networked application across heterogeneous platforms is a major challenge for enterprise and inter-enterprise applications.

policy	In computing, a specification of permitted and prohibited behaviors that is an important enabler of both interoperability and security. Also describes government-mandated limits on action or behavior.
portability	The ability of software or applications to run on platforms from different vendors.
positive feedback	For a product or service with network effects, when the number of adopters exceeds critical mass, the demand breeds more demand, causing adoptions to increase rapidly.
predictive caching	A caching algorithm that predicts what information will be needed so it can be sent in advance, mitigating network message latency.
presentation	The portion of the application concerned with how information is presented to and direction is solicited from the user through the user interface.
privacy	Freedom from unnecessary monitoring of one's activities, habits, communications, or financial affairs by others.
process	Supports a single executing program within the operating system. Multitasking supports concurrent processes.
processing	Manipulation of data by a computer under control of a software program.
processor	A hardware engine that executes computer programs. A host incorporates one or more processors, together with memory, storage, peripherals, and network interface.
procurement	When a company buys materials and supplies for its manufacturing or operations from a supplier.
product	Equipment or infrastructure or application software or development tool that is sold as is. Components are examples of products.
program	A representation of what a computer is instructed to do.
propagation delay	The delay on a communication link due to the finite speed of light.
protocol	A distributed algorithm performed by two or more interacting modules, incorporating messages communicated among them.
proxy object	In object-oriented programming, an object that interacts with a real work object and acts as a surrogate for it within an application. An example is an object acting as a surrogate to a customer.

publication style A style of application in which users communicate indirectly with other users—often not known to them—by making information available in a form and place where it can be accessed by others.

publish-subscribe A protocol used for one module to obtain a series of updates from another, consisting of a subscription message from the first module and response messages from the second, unknown as to number and timing.

pull Applied to either information access or social applications, a style in which the user initiates an interaction or access. Examples include searching, browsing, and navigation.

push Applied to either information access or social applications, a style in which a source or publisher autonomously initiates an interaction with the user. Examples include autonomous publication, messaging, and notification.

quality Refers to measures of merit, such as program correctness and subjective measures of audio or video fidelity that are difficult to quantify.

quality of service (QoS) Control and reproducibility of performance and quality parameters. May be applied to communication (networks) or processing (servers).

queueing A service that stores messages temporarily until the recipient accesses them, allowing messages to be sent to a recipient not prepared to receive them immediately.

recommender system Describes a publication-deferred social application that collects and aggregates advice or judgement from many users to guide others.

redundancy In system reliability, nonoperational equipment that can take over immediately upon a failure. In data, distinct patterns of bits that occur with different frequency and enable compression.

reference An abstract representation of the location of an entity. A client can interact with a reference, that interaction being redirected to the actual server by the infrastructure.

reference model In the standardization process, an architecture assumed as a starting point for defining and standardizing interfaces.

regeneration The process of making an exact replica of digitally represented information, by copying the data representation. Used in storage and communications to preserve information across time and space.

regulation A government-sanctioned process of placing constraints on the actions and behavior of private companies for the public good. Long a reality in telecommunications.

relational database	A database in which the data is structured in row-column tables.
reliable	A property of an infrastructure or application that operates correctly almost all the time.
remote conferencing	A direct-immediate style of social application that attempts to emulate a face-to-face meeting at a distance.
remote learning	Remote conferencing and collaboration applied to education and training.
remote method invocation (RMI)	A communication service allowing an object on one host to invoke the method of an object on another host, and immediately receive the returns.
replication	Make multiple replicas (equivalent to the original in every respect) of digitally represented information by repeated regeneration.
representation	Takes the place of information, from which that information can be recovered. For example, data can represent speech (in the sense that intelligible, accurate, and natural speech can be recovered from it) or a document.
representation object	In object-oriented programming, an object that temporarily replaces a real-world entity within an application. An example is an object representing a bank account.
request-response	A simple protocol used for one module to obtain information or service from another, in which a request from a client is followed by a coupled immediate response from a server.
resource conflict	For concurrent tasks sharing common resources, an inappropriate interaction between the tasks resulting in an incorrect outcome.
reuse	Infrastructure, subsystems, and components that can be assembled and integrated into multiple applications.
roaming	The ability to access communication services from different locations.
routing	A function of packet networks in which routing tables in packet switches are updated, with the goal of forwarded packets reaching their destination while traversing the fewest communication links or encountering minimum congestion.
RSA encryption	A standard for asymmetrical encryption widely used for digital signatures and authentication.
scalable	Describes an architecture with the property that capability can be increased as necessary by adding (but not replacing) equipment. In addition, it usually means the cost increases no faster than capability.

scheduling   Establishing in advance when something will happen. Social applications support the scheduling of group immediate interactions, operating systems schedule processing tasks, and packet switches schedule packet transmission.

scripting language   A language suitable for specifying the assembly of existing components, as distinct from a systems programming language.

search   A style of information access in which the user poses a question (often in terms of keywords), with information returned relevant to that question.

secure electronic transactions (SET)   In electronic commerce, a standard for on-line credit card payments to merchants, with many features to insure privacy, confidentiality, and security.

security   Protection against hostile threats, such as vandalism, theft, or denial of service.

send-receive   A simple protocol used for one module to inform or direct another, in which a message is sent by the first module and received by the second.

server   A module that does not initiate an interaction, but is available at all times to satisfy requests from other modules. The term is applied to a host existing primarily to satisfy external requests, and to an object whose method is invoked.

service   An action or capability that is provided or sold, often by a service provider or a special host called a server.

service provider   A company leasing or selling services—such as networking or applications—to other companies or users.

session   A generic communication service that conveys a sequence of messages with a shared context and guaranteed to be delivered in the same order as sent. Often a session is bidirectional and incorporates establishment and disestablishment phases.

simulcast   In networking, an implementation of a broadcast service in which the source rather than the network replicates data and sends it to separate recipients. An alternative is multicast.

social application   An application serving a group of users in some shared activity.

software   That portion of the information technology not established at the time of manufacture, as distinct from hardware.

software component   A software module that can be purchased and assembled with other components.

software program	Represents an algorithm by a series of specific instructions to the computer, determining the functionality of an application.
spanning layer	An infrastructure layer that both hides any heterogeneity in the layers below it, and is also nearly ubiquitous. It effectively separates the infrastructure into two pieces that can evolve independently.
standard	A specification of an architecture (reference model and interfaces) that is generally agreed upon, precisely defined, and well documented.
standardization body	An industry organization dedicated to defining and promulgating standards, usually with the assistance of many companies.
state	A collection of data that represents the past history of an entity and, together with future interactions, can be used to predict future behavior.
statistical multiplexing	Sharing a communication link among packets from different sources and destinations, resulting in more efficient use.
storage	That portion of the equipment infrastructure devoted to safekeeping of data from the time it is created until it is used.
stovepipe	An architecture and associated business model in which separate infrastructures are built for different services or applications.
streaming multimedia	The network transport of multimedia information by a sequence of messages while it is viewed by the recipient. In the internet, supported by the RTSP protocol.
structure	Applied to data, a pattern and organization that is specified and adhered to.
structured query language (SQL)	A standardized and widely used language for applications to manage data in a relational or object-relational database.
subscription	A request from a user to receive specific autonomously published information on a specific topic. Also applies to a request for notification of an event.
subsystem	A portion of a system that realizes some defined self-contained purpose, and is itself a system.
supply-chain management	An enterprise resource planning application that monitors and coordinates the flow of materials, goods, services, and payments between suppliers and customers.
switch	Within a network, equipment that routes packets from one communication link to another reaching closer to its destination.

symmetric encryption   An encryption protocol in which replicas of a key are used for both encryption and decryption. For confidentiality, the key must be kept secret. Sometimes called private key encryption.

system   Something with a defined higher-order purpose that is not atomic, but is created by the decomposition into subsystems.

system integration   The phase of system implementation in which subsystems are made to interoperate.

system programming language   A language suitable for writing programs from scratch, as distinct from a scripting language.

task   For either a user group or a computer application, some grouping of operations that must be accomplished together and with a short-term goal and outcome.

task group   A group of users giving their undivided attention to completing a short-term goal.

TCP   The internet transport service most widely used; stands for "Transmission Control Protocol." It provides a bidirectional reliable byte stream.

telephony   An audio conferencing service, equivalent to the familiar service provided by the public telephone network (PTN).

terminal   From the era of time-shared computing, an information appliance that provides the user interface, offering only textual display and keyboard input.

testing   Trying out a system in a realistic operational context to gauge whether it works correctly and reliably.

thin client   A partitioning of an application that places relatively little application functionality in a client host. The opposite of a fat client.

threading   In operating systems, similar to multitasking, but with less isolation of tasks and less overhead. Also called a lightweight process.

three-tier client-server   A client-server architecture in which there are two specialized types of server, one providing application logic and the other managing shared data.

time-sharing   An obsolete computing model in which terminals connected directly to a centralized computer allow a group of users to share the use of that computer.

topology   Applied to networks, the pattern of interconnection of packet switches by communication links.

transaction	A set of resource management actions that are atomic, consistent, isolated from other transactions, and durable. Transaction processing is middleware that supports transactions and thereby simplifies application development.
transport protocol	In the network infrastructure software, a layer immediately above the network layer (such as IP) that elaborates and specializes the communication service to application needs. In the internet, two widely used examples are UDP and TCP.
trustworthy	Term applied to a system or application when it works correctly, almost all the time, and is secure against internal and external threats.
two-phase commit	A protocol used for transaction processing, in which a set of resources vote on whether a transaction has successfully completed, and only if the vote is unanimous does the transaction commit.
two-tier client-server	A client-server architecture with only one kind of server, as distinct from three-tier.
ubiquitous computing	An emerging computing model in which networked computers are unobtrusively sprinkled throughout the physical environment.
usage pricing	For a software application or network service, a component of price based on monitoring of how much the product or service is used.
user	A person who benefits from a networked computing application.
user interface	The interface between a desktop computer and a single user, incorporating information output (graphics, audio, video) and input (keyboard, pointing device, microphone, camera). The presentation portion of the application manages the user interface.
utilization	For a host or a communication link, the fraction of the maximum capacity actually consumed.
value pricing	The price of a product or service based on the consumer's willingness to pay, rather than costs.
versioning	For a product or service, supplying distinct flavors that differ as to functionality, features, quality, or performance.
vertical integration	A business strategy in which a company chooses to make rather than buy all subsystems for its products.
virus	In security, a program that attaches itself to a program (or other executable file) and surreptitiously runs, replicating itself by attaching to other programs and possibly causing harm, whenever that program executes.

Voice over IP (VoIP)	Provision of a standard telephony service using an internet in whole or in combination with the public telephone network.
Web	A deferred or immediate publication-style application based on a document model, in which a Web client is used to browse or navigate through information made available by a Web server. The information is provided in pages, which typically contain hyperlinks to other pages.
wide area network (WAN)	A network that interconnects local area networks over a wide geographic area. The Internet is a WAN.
wireless	In communications, links not requiring wire, coaxial, or fiber media.
wireless access protocol (WAP)	An emerging standard for providing Web services on information appliances such as cellular telephones.
work group	A group of users collaborating to complete a longer-term project (such as a design, proposal, etc.).
workflow	Describes an application that controls the flow of repetitive work tasks among human workers, including multiplexing and queueing.
workstation	An especially powerful (in terms of processing speed) desktop computer, often used for computationally intensive tasks.

References

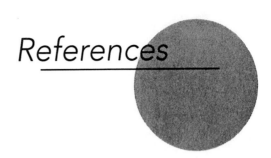

[Abe97]   G. Abe, *Residential Broadband*. New York: MacMillan, 1997.

[Abr92]   N. Abramson, *Multiple Access Communications: Foundations for Emerging Technologies*. Los Alamitos, Calif.: IEEE Press, 1992.

[Arn96]   K. Arnold and J. Gosling, *The Java Programming Language*. Reading, Mass.: Addison Wesley Longman, 1996.

[Atk96]   D. Atkins et al., *Internet Security: Professional Reference*. Indianapolis, Ind.: New Riders Publishing, 1996.

[Bak97]   S. Baker, *CORBA Distributed Objects Using Orbix*. Essex, UK: Addison Wesley Longman, 1997.

[BCK98]   L. Bass, P. Clements, and R. Kazman, *Software Architecture in Practice*. Reading, Mass.: Addison Wesley Longman, 1998.

[Bee99]   G. Beekman, *Computer Confluence: Exploring Tomorrow's Technology*. Reading, Mass.: Addison Wesley Longman, 1999.

[Ben98]   W. Bennis and P. Ward Biederman, "None of Us Is as Smart as All of Us." *IEEE Computer*, March 1998.

[Ber97]   P. Bernstein and E. Newcomer, *Principles of Transaction Processing for the System Professional*. San Francisco: Morgan Kaufmann, 1997.

[Bie97]   A. Biermann, *Great Ideas in Computer Science: A Gentle Introduction*, 2d ed. Cambridge, Mass.: MIT Press, 1997.

[Bir96]   K. Birman and R. van Renesse, "Software for Reliable Networks." *Scientific American*, May 1996.

[Bol96]   W. Bolton, *Mechatronics: Electronic Control Systems in Mechanical Engineering*, 2d ed. Reading, Mass.: Addison Wesley Longman, 1999.

[Boo94]   G. Booch, *Object-Oriented Analysis and Design with Applications*, 2d ed. Redwood City, Calif.: Benjamin/Cummings, 1994.

[Bry98]   E. Brynjolfsson and L. Hitt, "Beyond the Productivity Paradox." *Communications of the ACM*, August 1998.

[Buc91]   M. Buckland, *Information and Information Systems*. Westport, Conn.: Greenwood Press, 1991.

[Cai97]   F. Cairncross, *The Death of Distance: How the Communications Revolution Will Change Our Lives.* Boston: Harvard Business School Press, 1997.

[Cat97]   R.Cattell et al., *The Object Database Standard : ODMG 2.0.* San Francisco: Morgan Kaufmann, 1997.

[CDK94]   G. Coulouris, J. Dollimore, and T. Kindberg, *Distributed Systems: Concept and Design.* Harlow, UK: Addison Wesley Longman, 1994.

[Cha91]   D. Chaum, "Numbers Can Be a Better Form of Cash than Paper," pages 151–156 in *Smart Card 2000*, D. Chaum ed., Amsterdam: North Holland, 1991.

[Cla97]   D. Clark, "Interoperation, Open Interfaces, and Protocol Architecture," in *White Papers from the Unpredictable Certainty*, Computer Science and Telecommunications Board, National Research Council. Washington, D.C.: National Academies Press, 1997.

[Con98]   T. Connolly and C. Begg, *Database Systems: A Practical Approach to Design, Implementation, and Management.* Reading, Mass.: Addison Wesley Longman, 1998.

[CST94]   Computer Science and Telecommunications Board, National Research Council. *Realizing the Information Future: The Internet and Beyond.* Washington, D.C., National Academies Press, 1994.

[CST95]   Computer Science and Telecommunications Board, National Research Council. *Evolving the High-Performance Computing and Communications Initiative to Support the Nation's Infrastructure.* Washington, D.C.: National Academies Press, 1995.

[CST96a]   Computer Science and Telecommunications Board, National Research Council. *Cryptography's Role in Securing the Information Society.* Washington, D.C.: National Academies Press, 1996.

[CST96b]   Computer Science and Telecommunications Board, National Research Council. *The Unpredictable Certainty: Information Infrastructure through 2000.* Washington, D.C.: National Academies Press, 1996.

[CST97a]   Computer Science and Telecommunications Board, National Research Council. *The Evolution of Untethered Communications.* D. J. Goodman, Chair. Washington, D.C.: National Academies Press, 1997.

[CST97b]   Computer Science and Telecommunications Board, National Research Council. *White Papers from the Unpredictable Certainty: Information Infrastructure through 2000.* Washington, D.C.: National Academies Press, 1997.

[CST98a]   Computer Science and Telecommunications Board, National Research Council. *Trust in Cyberspace.* F. B. Schneider, Chair. Washington, D.C.: National Academies Press, 1998.

[CST98b]   Computer Science and Telecommunications Board, National Research Council. *Funding a Revolution: Government Support for Computing Research.* T. Hughes, Chair. Washington, D.C.: National Academies Press, 1998.

[Dav93]   T. Davenport, *Process Innovation: Reengineering Worth through Information Technology.* Boston: Harvard Business School Press, 1993.

[Dif97]   W. Diffie and S. Landau, *Privacy on the Line: The Politics of Wiretapping and Encryption*. Cambridge, Mass.: MIT Press, 1997.

[DLM96]   A. Dahl, L. Lesnick, and L. Morgan, *Internet Commerce*. Indianapolis, Ind.: New Riders Publishing, 1996.

[Dre99]   G. N. Drew, *Using SET for Secure Electronic Commerce*. Englewood Cliffs, N.J.: Prentice Hall, 1999.

[Eco96]   N. Economides, "The Economics of Networks," *International Journal of Industrial Organization*, 14(6):673–699 (October 1996).

[Fan97]   C. Fancher, "Smart Cards." *Scientific American*, August 1996.

[Far88]   J. Farrell and C. Shapiro, "Dynamic Competition with Switching Costs." *Rand Journal of Economics*, 19(1):123–137 (Spring 1988).

[Fei73]   H. Feistel, "Cryptography and Computer Privacy." *Scientific American*, May 1973.

[Fla96]   D. Flanagan, *Java in a Nutshell*. Sebastopol, Calif.: O'Reilly, 1996.

[Gam95]   E. Gamma, R. Helm, R. Johnson, and J. Vlissides, *Design Patterns: Elements of Reusable Object-Oriented Software*. Reading, Mass.: Addison-Wesley, 1995.

[Gar89]   B. Garson, *The Electronic Sweatshop: How Computers Are Transforming the Office of the Future into the Factory of the Past*. New York: Penguin Books, 1989.

[Gar96]   S. Garfinkel and G. Spafford, *Practical Unix and Internet Security*. Sebastopol, Calif.: O'Reilly, 1996.

[Gar97]   S. Garfinkel and G. Spafford, *Web Security & Commerce*. Sebastopol, Calif.: O'Reilly, 1997.

[Gils97]   P. Gilster, *Digital Literacy*. New York: Wiley, 1997.

[Gra93]   J. Gray and A. Reuter, *Transaction Processing: Concepts and Techniques*. San Francisco: Morgan Kaufmann, 1993.

[Gre96]   R.Grenier and G. Metes. *Going Virtual: Moving Your Organization into the 21st Century*. Englewood Cliffs, N.J.: Prentice Hall, 1996.

[Gut95]   M. Guttman and J. Matthews, *The Object Technology Revolution*. New York: Wiley, 1995.

[Haf95]   K. Hafner and J. Markoff, *Cyberpunk: Outlaws and Hackers on the Computer Frontier*. New York: Touchstone Books, 1995.

[Har97]   P. Harmon and M. Watson, *Understanding UML: The Developer's Guide*. San Francisco: Morgan Kaufmann, 1997.

[Haw96]   G. E. Hawisher and C. L. Selfe, eds., *Literacy, Technology, and Society: Confronting the Issues*. Englewood Cliffs, N.J.: Prentice Hall, 1996.

[How85]   Denis Howe, ed., "The Free On-Line Dictionary of Computing." *http://wombat.doc.ic.ac.uk/*.

[Hwa98] K. Hwang and Z. Xu, *Scalable Parallel Computing: Technology, Architecture, Programming*. New York: WCB/McGraw-Hill, 1998.

[Ing98] D. E. Ingber, "The Architecture of Life." *Scientific American*, January 1998.

[JGJ97] I. Jacobson, M. Griss, and P. Jonsson, *Software Reuse: Architecture Process and Organization for Business Success*. Reading, Mass.: Addison Wesley Longman, 1997.

[Jon97] K. Jones, "Auto Net To Pave E-Commerce Way." *Inter@active Week*, September 15, 1997.

[Kah97] B. Kahle, "Preserving the Internet." *Scientific American*, March 1997.

[Kat92] M. Katz and C. Shapiro, "Product Introduction with Network Externalities." *Journal of Industrial Economics*, 40(1):55–83 (March 1992).

[Kee97] P. Keen and C. Ballance, *On-Line Profits: A Manager's Guide to Electronic Commerce*. Boston: Harvard Business School Press, 1997.

[Kep97] J. Kephart, G. Sorkin, D. Chess, and S. White, "Fighting Computer Viruses." *Scientific American*, November 1997.

[KFN93] C. Kaner, J. Falk, and H. Nguyen, *Testing Computer Software*. Scottsdale, Ariz.: The Coriolis Group, 1993.

[Kri98] D. Krieger and R. Adler, "The Emergence of Distributed Component Platforms." *IEEE Computer*, March 1998.

[Lau98] S. St. Laurent, *XML: A Primer*. Foster City, Calif.: IDG Books Worldwide, 1998.

[Lau99] K. Laudon and J. Laudon, *Essentials of Management Information Systems: Transforming Business and Management*, 3d ed. Englewood Cliffs, N.J.: Prentice Hall, 1999.

[Lee94] E. Lee and D. Messerschmitt, *Digital Communication*, 2d ed. Boston: Kluwer Academic Press, 1994.

[Les97a] M. Lesk, "Going Digital." *Scientific American*, March 1997.

[Les97b] M. Lesk, *Practical Digital Libraries: Books, Bytes, and Bucks*. San Francisco: Morgan Kaufmann, 1997.

[Lyn95] D. C. Lynch and L. Lundquist, *Digital Money: The New Era of Internet Commerce*. New York: Wiley, 1995.

[Lyn97] C. Lynch, "Searching the Internet." *Scientific American*, March 1997.

[Mac95a] J. MacKie-Mason and H. Varian, "Pricing the Internet," in *Public Access to the Internet*, B. Kahin and J. Keller, eds. Cambridge, Mass.: MIT Press, 1995.

[Mac95b] J. MacKie-Mason and H. Varian, "Pricing Congestible Network Resources." *IEEE Journal on Selected Areas in Communications*, 13(7) (September 1995).

[Mac95c]   J. MacKie-Mason and H. Varian, "Some FAQs about Usage-Based Pricing." *Computer Networks & ISDN Systems*, December 1995.

[Mah97]   D. O'Mahony, *Electronic Payment Systems*. Norwood, Mass.: Artech House, 1997.

[Mar95]   J. Martin and J. Leben, *Client/Server Databases: Enterprise Computing*. Englewood Cliffs, N.J.: Prentice Hall, 1995.

[MBD99]   E. Martin, C. Brown, D. DeHayes, J. Hoffer, and W. Perkins, *Managing Information Technology: What Managers Need to Know*, 3d ed. Upper Saddle River, N.J.: Prentice Hall, 1999.

[McC95]   S. McCanne and V. Jacobson, "vic: A Flexible Framework for Packet Video." *Proceedings of the Third International Conference on Multimedia '95*, pp. 511–522.

[McC97]   S. McConnell, *Software Project Survival Guide*. Redmond, Wash.: Microsoft Press, 1997.

[Mck97a]   L. McKnight and J. Bailey, "Internet Economics: When Constituencies Collide in Cyberspace," *IEEE Internet Computing*, December 1997.

[Mck97b]   L. McKnight and J. Bailey, *Internet Economics*. Cambridge, Mass.: MIT Press, 1997.

[Mes96a]   D. Messerschmitt, "The Convergence of Telecommunications and Computing: What Are the Implications Today?" *IEEE Proceedings*, August 1996.

[Mes96b]   D. Messerschmitt, "Convergence of Telecommunications with Computing," invited paper in special issue "Impact of Information Technology," *Technology in Society*, 18(3).

[Mit96]   W. Mitchell, *City of Bits: Space, Place, and the Infobahn*. Cambridge, Mass.: MIT Press, 1996.

[Mok97]   P. Mokhtarian, "Now That Travel Can Be Virtual, Will Congestion Virtually Disappear?" *Scientific American*, October 1997.

[Neg96]   N. Negroponte and M. Asher, eds., *Being Digital*. New York: Vintage Books, 1996.

[Neu95]   P. Neumann, *Computer Related Risks*. Reading, Mass.: Addison-Wesley, 1995.

[Oak96]   R. Oakman, *The Computer Triangle: Hardware, Software, People*. New York: Wiley, 1996.

[OHE96a]   R. Orfali, D. Harkey, and J. Edwards, *The Essential Client/Server Survival Guide*, 2d ed. New York: Wiley, 1996.

[OHE96b]   R. Orfali, D. Harkey, and J. Edwards, *The Essential Distributed Objects Survival Guide*. New York: Wiley, 1996.

[Oke96]   A. Okerson, "Who Owns Digital Works?" *Scientific American*, July 1996.

[Ole98]   D. O'Leary, "Enterprise Knowledge Management." *IEEE Computer Magazine*, March 1998.

[OPR96]   R. Otte, P. Patrick, and M. Roy, *Understanding CORBA, The Common Object Request Broker Architecture*. Englewood Cliffs, N.J.: Prentice Hall, 1996.

[OST97]   Office of the President, Office of Science and Technology Policy, "Cybernation: The American Infra-structure in the Information Age," April 1997.

[Oud97]   B. Oudet, "Multilingualism on the Internet." *Scientific American*, March 1997.

[Ous98]   J. Ousterhout, "Scripting: Higher-Level Programming for the 21st Century." *IEEE Computer*, March 1998.

[Pah95]   K. Pahlavan and A. Levesque, *Wireless Information Networks*. New York: Wiley, 1995.

[Pan98]   A. Pang, "General Motors' New Intranet Sets the Pace." *Internet Computing*, March 2, 1998.

[Pen96]   A. Pentland, "Smart Rooms." *Scientific American*, April 1996.

[Per85]   S. Personick, *Fiber Optics: Technology and Applications*. New York: Plenum, 1985.

[Pet96]   L. Peterson and B. S. Davie, *Computer Networks: A Systems Approach*. San Francisco: Morgan Kaufmann, 1996.

[Pre96]   R. Pressman, *Software Engineering, A Practitioner's Approach*. New York: McGraw-Hill, 1996.

[Rad89]   L. Rade and B. Westergren, *Beta Methematics Handbook*. Boca Raton, Fla.: CRC Press, 1989.

[Ram98]   R. Ramaswami and K. Sivarajan, *Optical Networks: A Practical Perspective*. San Francisco: Morgan Kaufmann, 1998.

[Ran95]   J. Ranade, *CORBA: A Guide to Common Request Broker Architecture*. New York: McGraw-Hill, 1995.

[Rap96]   T. Rappaport, *Wireless Communications: Principles and Practice*. Englewood Cliffs, N.J.: Prentice Hall, 1996.

[Res97a]   P. Resnick and H. Varian, eds., "Special Section: Recommender Systems." *Communications of the ACM*, March 1997.

[Res97b]   P. Resnick, "Filtering Information on the Internet." *Scientific American*, pp. 106–108, March 1997.

[Ros97]   R. Rosenberg, *The Social Impact of Computers*, 2d ed. San Diego, Calif.: Academic Press, 1997.

[Row92]   L. Rowe and B. Smith, "A Continuous Media Player," *Proceedings of the Third International Work-shop on Network and Operating System Support for Digital Audio and Video*, San Diego, Calif., November 1992.

[RSA78]   R. Rivest, A. Shamir, and L. Adleman, "A Method for Obtaining Digital Signatures and Public-Key Cryptosystems." *Communications of the ACM*, February 1978.

[RSA96]   "Answers to Frequently Asked Questions about Today's Cryptography," RSA Laboratories, Version 3.0, 1996. *http://www.rsa.com/rsalabs/newfaq/*.

[Sam90]   P. Samuelson, "Should Program Algorithms Be Patented?" *Communications of the ACM*, 33(8) (August 1990).

[SAP97]   "An Integrated Vision for High Performance Supply Chain Management," white paper by SAP AG, 1997.

[Sch90]   M. Schroeder, *Number Theory in Science and Communication*, 2d ed. Berlin: Springer-Verlag, 1990.

[Sch95]   B. Schatz, "Information Analysis in the Net: The Interspace of the Twenty-First Century," white paper for *America in the Age of Information: A Forum on Federal Information and Communications R & D*, July 1995, National Library of Medicine.

[Sch96]   B. Schneier, *Applied Cryptography*. New York: Wiley, 1996.

[SDK94]   P. Samuelson, K. Davis, M. Kapor and J. Reichman, "A Manifesto Concerning the Legal Protection of Computer Programs." *Columbia Law Review*, December 1994.

[Set98]   V. Sethi and W. King, *Organizational Transformation through Business Process Reengineering*. Englewood Cliffs, N.J.: Prentice Hall, 1998.

[Sha98]   C. Shapiro and H. Varian, *Information Rules: A Strategic Guide to the Network Economy*. Boston: Harvard Business School Press, 1999.

[Sie96]   J. Siegel, *CORBA: Fundamentals and Programming*. New York: Wiley, 1996.

[Sil97]   A. Silberschatz and P. P. Galvin, *Operating System Concepts*. Reading, Mass.: Addison-Wesley, 1997.

[Smo97]   L. Smolin, *The Life of the Cosmos*. New York: Oxford University Press, 1997.

[Sta99]   W. Stallings, *Cryptography and Network Security: Principles and Practice*, 2d ed. Englewood Cliffs, N.J.: Prentice Hall, 1999.

[Ste97]   M. Stefik, "Trusted Systems." *Scientific American*, March 1997.

[Szy98]   C. Szyperski, *Component Software: Beyond Object-Oriented Programming*. Reading, Mass.: Addison Wesley Longman, 1998.

[Tag95]   J. Tague-Sutcliffe, *Measuring Information: An Information Services Perspective*. Boston, Mass.: Academic Press, 1995.

[TWW97]   A. Tanenbaum and A. Woodhull, *Operating Systems: Design and Implementation*. Englewood Cliffs, N.J.: Prentice Hall, 1997.

[Tyg96]   J. Tygar, "Atomicity in Electronic Commerce," in *Proceedings of ACM Symposium on Principles of Distributed Computing*, Philadelphia, Pa., May 1996.

[Var87]   H. Varian, *Intermediate Microeconomics*. New York: W. W. Norton, 1987.

[Var95]   H. Varian, "Pricing Information Goods," *Research Libraries Group Symposium on Scholarship of the New Information Environment Proceedings*, Harvard Law School, May 1995.

[Var97a]   H. Varian, "Versioning Information Goods," unpublished paper available at *http://www.sims.berkeley.edu/~hal/Papers/version.pdf*.

[VLB98]   T. P. Vartanian, R. H. Ledig, and L. Bruneau, *21st Century Money, Banking & Commerce*. New York: Fried, Frank, Harris, Shriver & Jacobson, 1998.

[Wal89]   R. Walton, *Up and Running: Integrating Technology and the Organization*. Boston: Harvard Business School Press, 1989.

[Wal91]   J. Walrand, *Communication Networks: A First Course*. New York: Irwin McGraw-Hill, 1991.

[Wal96]   J. Walrand and P. Varaiya, *High-Performance Communication Networks*. San Francisco: Morgan Kaufmann, 1996.

[War99]   D. R. Warwick, *Ending Cash: The Public Benefits of Federal Electronic Currency*. Westport, Conn.: Quorum Books, 1999.

[Wat95]   K. Watterson, *Client/Server Technology for Managers*. Reading, Mass.: Addison-Wesley, 1995.

[Way97]   P. Wayner, *Digital Cash: Commerce on the Net*. Boston: AP Professional, 1997.

[Wei93]   M. Weiser, "Ubiquitous Computing." *Computer*, October 1993.

[WGH98]   J. Ware, J. Gebauer, A. Hartman, and M. Roldan, *The Search for Digital Excellence*. New York: McGraw-Hill, 1998.

[Woo94]   M. Wooldridge and N. Jennings, eds., *Intelligent Agents, Proceedings of ECAI-94 Workshop on Agent Theories, Architectures, and Languages*. Amsterdam: Springer-Verlag, August 1994.

[You97]   E. Yourdon and P. Becker, *Death March: The Complete Software Developer's Guide to Surviving "Mission Impossible" Projects*. Englewood Cliffs, N.J.: Prentice Hall, 1997.

Index

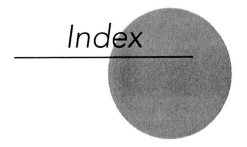

About the Author

David G. Messerschmitt is the Roger A. Strauch Chaired Professor of Electrical Engineering and Computer Sciences at the University of California at Berkeley. From 1993–96 he served as chair of EECS, and prior to 1977 he was with AT&T Bell Laboratories. He received a Ph.D. from the University of Michigan, is a fellow of the Institute of Electrical and Electronic Engineers, a member of the National Academy of Engineering, and a recipient of the IEEE Alexander Graham Bell Medal recognizing "exceptional contributions to the advancement of communication sciences and engineering."

For the past few years, Messerschmitt has been active in curriculum development that brings highly relevant social science concepts to engineering students and that teaches information technology to a broader cross section of students. He initiated both undergraduate and graduate courses in networked applications and computing aimed at social science and business students, and *Understanding Networked Applications: A First Course* is an outgrowth of this effort. With Hal R. Varian, he also initiated a graduate course in the nontechnical factors that contribute strongly to the success or failure of new high-technology products. *Understanding Networked Applications* is also used for a portion of this course, which is taught to a mixture of engineering, information science, and business students.

Messerschmitt's current research focuses is on the interaction of technology, industry structure, economics, and policy in the wireless networking industry, as well as the application of e-commerce to the networking industry in general. In the past, he has been published extensively in the areas of network management (especially the application of advanced software technologies to service configuration), wireless networking, signal processing, and communications.

Messerschmitt is a cofounder and director of TCSI Corporation and a director of Coastcom Inc. He is on the advisory boards of the Fisher Center for Management & Information Technology in the Haas School of Business, the Kawasaki Berkeley Concepts Research Center, and the Directorate for Computer and Information Sciences and Engineering at the National Science Foundation. From 1992–98 he was a member of the Computer Sciences and Telecommunications Board (CSTB) of the National Research Council (NRC), and he currently cochairs an NRC study on the future of information technology research in a competitive environment.